Fundamentals of Integrated Design for Sustainable Building

Fundamentals of Integrated Design for Sustainable Building

Marian Keeler
Bill Burke

WILEY

John Wiley & Sons, Inc.

Published by John Wiley & Sons, Inc., Hoboken, New Jersey
Published simultaneously in Canada

For general information about our other products and services, please contact our Customer Care
Department within the United States at (800) 762-2974, outside the United States at (317) 572-3993 or fax
(317) 572-4002.

Wiley also publishes its books in a variety of electronic formats. Some content that appears in print
may not be available in electronic books. For more information about Wiley products, visit our web site at
www.wiley.com.

Library of Congress Cataloging-in-Publication Data:

Keeler, Marian.
    Fundamentals of integrated design for sustainable building / Marian Keeler, Bill Burke.
        p.   cm.
    Includes bibliographical references and index.
    ISBN 978-0-470-15293-5 (cloth)
        1. Sustainable architecture. 2. Architecture—Environmental aspects. I. Title.
    NA2542.36.K44   2009
    720'.47—dc22
                                                    2008047064
Printed in the United States of America
10 9 8 7 6 5 4 3 2 1

To the memory of my father,
Harry Keeler,
my environmentalist mentor,
and to my son,
Joseph Samper Finberg,
who shares the future with so many

Contents

Foreword

The construction and operation of buildings are the major sources of demand for energy and materials that produce by-product greenhouse gases. To successfully slow, and then reverse, global warming and world resource depletion, it is imperative that ecological literacy become a central tenet of design education and practice. Architecture 2030, through the 2010 Imperative, has called for all architecture design studio problems to include a requirement that student work engage the environment in a way that dramatically reduces or eliminates the need for fossil fuel. *Fundamentals of Integrated Design for Sustainable Building* offers students an introduction to green building concepts as well as design approaches that reduce and can eventually eliminate the need for fossil fuel use in buildings while also conserving materials, maximizing their efficiency, protecting the indoor air from chemical intrusion, and reducing the introduction of toxic materials into the environment. This is the first textbook to respond to the 2010 Imperative's call for integration of sustainable building design in the curricula of design schools. It represents a necessary road map to future designers, builders, and planners of a post-carbon world.

The issues and principles addressed in this book must be central to the education of this generation of architectural educators and design students. By making our homes, public buildings, and infrastructure less toxic and much more energy efficient, we can prevent catastrophic climate change, create healthy environments for humans and other species, and rebuild a more equitable society that considers the needs of all members.

—Ed Mazria

Preface

[C]hange comes like a little wind that ruffles the curtains at dawn, and it comes like the stealthy perfume of wildflowers hidden in the grass.
—John Steinbeck, *Sweet Thursday* (1954)

The schools, then, have the potential to institute changes in the profession so profound that we can begin to speak about a new direction in architecture. It thrusts architecture into a pivotal role in solving a critical global dilemma, and in doing so it serves the highest creative purpose.[1]
—Ed Mazria, *It's the Architecture, Stupid!*

When I am president, any governor who's willing to promote clean energy will have a partner in the White House. Any company that's willing to invest in clean energy will have an ally in Washington. And any nation that's willing to join the cause of combating climate change will have an ally in the United States of America.
—*then President-elect Barack Obama, addressing a Los Angeles climate change conference, November 18, 2008*

In April 2008 Canadian scientists announced a study that tracked the infestation of mountain pine beetles in their western pine forests.[2,3] The beetle, well-known to scientists, was proliferating at an alarming rate and had the capability to destroy these forests on an unprecedented scale. In the years modeled for the study, 2000–2020, the beetle infestation's impact is projected to destroy 374,000 square kilometers of forest, fully one order of magnitude greater than previous infestations. While it is always a tragedy when trees die through human activity such as clear-cutting or through natural cycles of fire and fertility, the damage caused by this beetle is troubling in many ways, and its genesis and future impact is disquieting. Apparently, record warming in the study region of Canada encouraged the evolutionary success of this insect and its fungus passenger. Typically, in a matter of months, areas of forest are wiped out, leaving decaying vegetation to emit the atmospheric carbon dioxide (CO_2) they have stored over their life cycles. Laudable Canadian goals to reduce carbon dioxide emissions will be negated. Not only will this effort be counteracted, but the large Canadian forest reserves relied upon by many nations to balance and combat carbon dioxide production, instead of becoming a carbon dioxide–storing organism, will become a *contributor* to carbon emissions, projected by the study to be 270 megatonnes, which is coincidentally the amount of carbon that Canada had pledged to offset. The culprit at the root of this self-feeding life-cycle chain? Climate change.

Where is the connection? What does the mountain pine beetle have to do with making green buildings? The answers to these questions form the core of this book: Every activity we take on has impact—sometimes immediate, other times latent—on nature's exquisitely linked balance. Choosing to recycle a plastic container rather than pitching it into the landfill

[1] E. Mazria, "It's the Architecture, Stupid!" *Solar Today* May-June (2003): 48–51; http://www.mazria.com/publications.
[2] W. A. Kurz, C. C. Dymond, G. Stinson, G. J. Rampley, E. T. Neilson, A. L. Carroll, T. Ebata, and L. Safranyik, "Mountain Pine Beetle and Forest Carbon Feedback to Climate Change," *Nature* 452 (24 April 2008): 987–990.
[3] John Nielsen, "Beetle Infestation Compounds Effects of Warming," *Morning Edition*, April 24, 2008.

has impact; replacing incandescent lamps with fluorescents has impact; finding clean alternatives to coal-fired plants has impact. Building environmentally sound structures has impact.

When we first embarked on this journey to provide a learning guide for building greener buildings, we believed that the act of spreading the knowledge would no doubt benefit the environment and biodiversity of species through waste reduction, cradle-to-cradle resource management, energy conservation, and better indoor air quality. Since that time, we have seen burgeoning attention paid to the far-reaching and cyclical impacts of global warming and climate change. Fortunately, we have also witnessed the mushrooming of all things green: lower-impact lifestyles, efforts to reduce toxic materials in our environment, a slow-food movement, fair-trade products, alternative fuel vehicles, green insurance, clean technology, eco-travel, and more recently—and perhaps most importantly—goals calling for zero energy, zero carbon, and zero waste.

There is no question that we have the capacity to create solutions to climate change and to reduce the level of toxic materials in the human-built environment. Through technological innovation and a return to sound design principles, we can address these issues. This effort would stimulate the economy, provide jobs, and bridge political divisions. But it requires collective resolve—like that of the military mobilization of World War II or the Apollo moon missions. We must first decide where we want to be, and then go there.

We need vision and a large-scale framework through which to address these issues of climate change and toxics. Whatever your career path, whether in one of the design professions, engineering, land-use planning, resource and waste management, or government, understanding the fundamentals of integrated building design is essential to helping create that framework.

Even in the absence of government action and legislation, institutions and individuals need to begin to take action. The information in this book provides ways to begin doing so, by learning approaches to planning, designing, and building structures that mitigate, or even reverse, the impacts of buildings on the environment.

As you continue your studies, bolster your knowledge of green building by keeping current with new developments. Understand the source of the information, and evaluate it critically. Do not let the abundance overwhelm you. There is always more to know and more research to be done. But accomplishing more research is not necessary to realize the fundamental issues that need to be addressed. Focus on the concerns you find most compelling, whether deep reductions in energy use or the elimination of persistent bioaccumulative toxins in the environment. Filter the data, and look for meaningful applications that make buildings more energy and resource efficient and less toxic for all life on the planet.

On January 20, 2009, U.S. president Barack Obama entered office on the wave of a grassroots movement. President Obama's "Organizing for America" is a continuation of this movement whose goal is to address and propose solutions to the pressing issues of the country. Online surveys revealed active support of the president's sustainability agenda: renewable energy technology, creation of five million clean tech jobs, enhanced energy independence, and scrutiny of the drivers of climate change, among others. Building sustainably will contribute to the president's plan for reduction of carbon emissions—a targeted 80 percent reduction by 2050. With an expected $150 billion investment in energy technology, it is certain that green building is a necessary companion along the road to energy use reduction.

In December 2009, the United Nations will convene the fifteenth Conference of the Parties (COP15) under the United Nations' Climate Change Convention in Copenhagen, Denmark. A renewed and expanded commitment by world delegates to carbon emissions reduction is expected during that conference.

We hope this book will help start and guide the careers of those charged with transforming the way buildings are planned, designed, and constructed.

Contributors

Leon Alevantis, MS, PE, LEED AP, is a senior mechanical engineer with the California Department of Public Health (CDPH) and was formerly the deputy chief of the Indoor Air Quality Section at the California Department of Health Services where he coordinated the state's numerous pioneering efforts to conceive, specify, design, and implement indoor air quality and other sustainable measures in California state buildings. Leon was a key individual in the development and implementation of California Section 01350, an internationally recognized health-based specification for testing and selecting building materials. Among his research projects was the largest study of emissions from building materials with recycled content. Leon is an active committee member of the American Society of Heating, Refrigerating and Air-Conditioning Engineers's ASHRAE Standard 62.1 (Ventilation for Acceptable Indoor Air Quality) and contributing author of ASHRAE's *IAQ Design Guide*.

Kevin Conger is a landscape architect, educator (University of California, Berkeley; Rhode Island School of Design; and Boston Architectural Center), and founding partner of Conger Moss Guillard Landscape Architecture, a firm based in San Francisco that focuses on vibrant civic public space and sustainable environmental design. His projects include the Crissy Field, a waterfront park in the Presidio National Park, the Treasure Island Master Plan, and the San Francisco Museum of Modern Art (MOMA) Sculpture Garden.

Eva Craig received a master's degree in architecture and urban design, with a sustainable design concentration, from Harvard University. Her practice of architecture has evolved into consulting services for the design of healthful green living spaces, offering expertise focused on the health impacts of chemicals in residential environments and specializing in issues facing families with children. She practices in the San Francisco Bay area.

Jamie Phillips is a landscape architect at Conger Moss Guillard Landscape Architecture with specific expertise in storm-water systems and the design of large-scale storm-water treatment projects that interconnect public open space, habitat, and natural systems. Her projects include the Butterfly House and Supershed at the Auburn Rural Studio and the Treasure Island Master Plan and Storm-water Management Plan.

Sarah Pulleyblank Patrick is a senior planner at Raimi+Associates, Berkeley, California, with expertise in planning for public health, district and corridor restructuring strategies, and form-based coding. Her project work includes comprehensive plans for South Gate, Santa Monica, and Tracy (California), the Public Health Element for the City of South Gate (California), the Downtown Revitalization and Code Update for Bothell (Washington), and the LEED-ND Public Health Criteria Study for the U.S. Green Building Council.

Matt Raimi, AICP, is the founding principal of Raimi+Associates. He has led or participated in numerous planning efforts, including comprehensive plans for the cities of Santa Monica, South Gate, and Tracy (California) and the Eden area of Alameda County (California), and area plans for California's Oakland Army Base, Hunters Point Shipyard (in San Francisco), and downtown El Paso, Texas. He has spoken extensively on applying new urbanism to planning and has written several books, including *Understanding the Relationship between Public Health and the Built Environment* (Washington, DC: U.S. Green Building Council, 2006) and *Once There Were Greenfields* (New York: Natural Resources Defense Council, 1999).

Aaron Welch is a planner at Raimi+Associates, an urban planning firm that specializes in comprehensive planning, sustainable neighborhoods, and achieving public health through planning. Aaron's expertise is in sustainable neighborhoods, and his project work includes project review for the Leadership in Energy and Environmental Design (LEED) for Neighborhood Development (ND) pilot (U.S. Green Building Council), the Syracuse (New York) Near Westside sustainable neighborhood initiative, a Redwood City (California) sustainability assessment, and comprehensive plans for the cities of Santa Monica and South Gate (California).

Bill Worthen, AIA, is an architect, LEED AP, and green building consultant with Simon & Associates Inc. in San Francisco, a nationally recognized green building consulting firm. Bill focuses on the practical application of sustainable design and construction strategies. He has presented at American Institute of Architects (AIA) national conventions on green building and the LEED certification process, and he serves on the AIA Committee on the Environment (COTE) advocacy subcommittee. Bill also serves on the advocacy committee of the U.S. Green Building Council's Northern California Chapter and the San Francisco Mayor's Green Building Task Force.

Graham Grilli is a native Rhode Islander and an active environmentalist from an early age. After achieving a bachelor's degree in environmental science and spending several years gaining on-site building experience, he is now pursuing a master's of architecture degree at the Illinois Institute of Technology. Graham hopes that smart design and innovative thinking will soon revolutionize the way we live on this planet.

Acknowledgments

People often speak of writing as parallel to the birth process—book birthing as an implied rite of passage, or as a long, creative journey, perhaps alternately joyful and painful, but certainly requiring the guidance of many. This project was inspired and conceived by the work of practitioners, theorists, philosophers, and visionaries in green building design, and it could not have been delivered without an equally numerous and dedicated group of people I have met along the path to sustainability and with whom I am fortunate enough to collaborate.

I would like to thank our editor at John Wiley & Sons, Paul Drougas, for his support of our project and his commitment to energy-efficiency topics and sustainable building. His guidance was invaluable at every stage of writing and book production.

We were fortunate to have an excellent book-birthing development team: author and playwright Peter Vincent of *The 60's Diary*, who conducted essential style and copyediting, and who gave us the benefit of his extensive experience in publishing; Graham Grilli, who sourced many images for the book; and Killer Banshee Studios, skilled artists and technologists, researchers, copyright experts, and image sorcerers, who logged early-morning hours and delivered resources, images, and permissions at astonishing speed and with prescient accuracy. The book would not have been fully clothed had it not been for their considerable efforts.

MARIAN KEELER WOULD LIKE TO THANK:
Journeys are always enhanced by the company of fellow travelers, in this case, by my colleague Bill Burke, who helped sketch a road map and offered navigation tools and technical skill. Bill's generous nature and humility accompany a deep and authoritative knowledge of highly technical energy-related issues. Bill is an inspiring mentor dedicated to enlightening green builders and designers. His skill, wit, and friendship are sincerely valued and appreciated.

I am fortunate to be acquainted with many of the crafters of sustainable building practice, those who are "on the ground" in a change-making capacity: contributors Eva Craig of Imogen Home (friend and human/environmental health crusader); Kevin Conger and Jamie Philips of CMG; Leon Alevantis of the California Department of Public Health (one of my first IAQ mentors); Bill Worthen of Simon & Associates, Inc. (respected colleague); and Matt Raimi, Sarah Pulleyblank Patrick, and Aaron Welch of Raimi+Asscoiates.

Family is both the soil and fruit of the creative process and I thank mine: Chris Keeler, Cathy Keeler Presher, Tony Keeler, and my parents Natalie Keeler and Harry Keeler. Harry was the first person to take the time to read and offer insightful commentary on every chapter of the manuscript, and it is his memory I acknowledge with this work. My son, Joe Finberg, would frequently check in: "So how's the book, Mom?"

Many thanks to Lynn Simon, for her friendship, patience, and support as the book came into being, as well to colleagues at Simon & Associates: Dani Levine, Jennifer Nicholson, Raphael Sperry, and Billy Worthen.

I also thank the following people for their insight, activism, and encouragement: Cassandra Adams, Steve Berg, Brian Campbell, Diane Campbell, Julie Cox, Peter Coyle, Sean Culman, Anne Esmonde, Eric Corey Freed, Chris Hammer, Kathryn Hyde, Louise Louie, Karen Lovdahl, Heather Newbold, Carrie Strahan, esteemed colleague Michael Bernard of Virtual Practice, and everyone at the Allegro Ballroom in Emeryville, California, for the salsa magic.

Thanks also to valued clients and colleagues: Shelley Ratay, Jeff Oberdorfer, and Marty Keller at First Community Housing; Paula Lewis of the St. Anthony Foundation; Dennis Okamura of HKIT; Tom Lent, Bill Walsh, and Julie Silas of Healthy Building Network; Marc Richmond of Practica Consulting; Kirsten Ritchie of Gensler; Penny Bonda; Dr. Andrew Persily, engineer with NIST's Building and Fire Research Laboratory; Wagdy Anis, architect with Wiss, Janney, Elstner Associates; Jim Chapell, president of SPUR; Richard Parker and David Bushnell of 450 Architects; author Jennifer Roberts; Erik Kolderup of Kolderup Consulting; Jane Bare of the U.S. EPA; Darrel DeBoer of DeBoer Architects; artist and photographer Diego Samper; Marlene Samper; Jeorg Stamm; Alice Philips; and Anthony Bernheim, for his past friendship and mentorship.

BILL BURKE WOULD LIKE TO THANK:
Marian Keeler, Karen Buse, Killer Banshee Studios, Peter Vincent, James Bae, Nick Rajkovich, Anna LaRue, Alison Kwok, Valeriy Boreyko, Bob Theis, Dan Varvais, Joel Loveland, and Chris Meek.

Fundamentals of
Integrated Design for
Sustainable Building

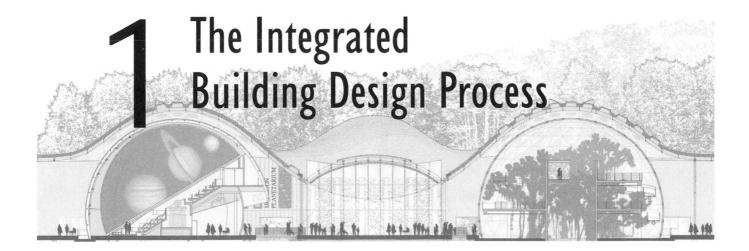

1 The Integrated Building Design Process

The good news is we know what to do. The good news is we have everything we need now to respond to the challenge of global warming. We have all the technologies we need; more are being developed. And as they become available and become more affordable when produced in scale, they will make it easier to respond. But we should not wait, we cannot wait, we must not wait.

—Al Gore, former vice president of the United States, addressing the National Sierra Club Convention, 9 September 2005

What Is the Process of Integrated Building Design?

Integrated building design is the practice of designing sustainably. *Green design* and *integrated building design* should be thought of as equivalent terms.

Not so long ago, the term "green design" was seen only in quotation marks, causing the meaning to seem infirm and of questionalble viability. Today, green, or sustainable, design is a well-established design-and-build model with a proven history—and integrated design is its natural evolutionary form. An integrated building is a green building.

Integrated design is the overarching theme that governs energy, resources, and environmental quality decisions. These decisions and strategies will be outlined in this chapter and given in-depth treatment in the chapters that follow.

With integrated design, it is necessary to consider design variables as a unified whole and use them as problem-solving tools. As architecture and design students, you are learning to be problem solvers, which should prompt you to imagine and anticipate the potential implications of even the most benign design decision. Learning integrated design will solidify these skills and improve a proficiency every architectural student should have—being a productive and efficient team member.

More than mainstream design, the integrated design process requires intense balance—and a path of priorities—to produce a successful green building. The process works because there is communication among team members, and because each team designer has a thorough understanding of each teammate's design challenges and responsibilities.

Because every design decision produces a cascade of multiple effects, rather than an isolated impact, successful integrated design requires a necessary understanding of the interrelationship of each material, system, and spatial element (Figure 1-1). It requires all players to think holistically about the project rather than focus solely on an individual part.

The Process

The process of working collaboratively in studio as a team member on a student design project of any stripe mimics the reality of professional practice. It can be applied to a graphic design problem, such as a branding exercise, the development of a master plan, and even the creation of land-use policy or neighborhood development.

Because of this, it is beneficial to learn the process of integrated design from the beginning of one's architectural education. There is no script for the perfect integrated design process, but there are several levels of decision making that must take place at the start of conceptual design, while the design is being refined, during design development, and during construction. At the completion of a project, during critique, it is a valuable lesson to evaluate the effectiveness of the integrated design process for each team.

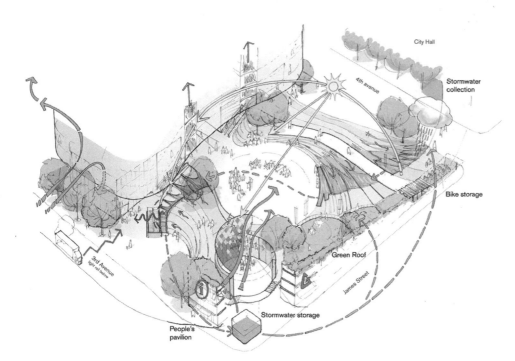

Figure 1-1 Sketch showing site conditions and green site technologies in the Civic Square project, Seattle, Washington. Foster + Partners. The square provides a series of linked permeable urban rooms.

In this chapter we will see how the practice of integrated design plays out in professional practice.

Understand the Scope of the Project

It is helpful to develop a schedule of team meetings around project milestones or class deadlines, the first of which should be a discussion that encompasses the following questions:

- What is the project type?
- What is the size and scale of the project? Is the project a large commercial high-rise tower; a sustainable neighborhood development; or a small, private school on five acres?
- Is the project an urban infill or an open space development?
- Is there a master plan governing new construction for the site that describes the project scope and construction phasing?
- Are there legislated guidelines for envelope design?
- Are there municipal, regional, state, or federal regulations governing sustainable design?
- What are the geographical and project site constraints?
- What are the population densities and land-use regulations of the project site?
- Where is the money coming from to fund the project? Is the source of funding a government agency or municipality, or is it a private developer or homeowner?
- How will the involvement of each team player and *stakeholder*[1] affect the integrated design process?

Answers to these questions will help integrated design teams map out their process.

---
[1] A stakeholder is a person, entity, or agency that has some investment—either as an owner, funder, occupant, or designer—in the design, construction, and ultimate outcome of the building project.

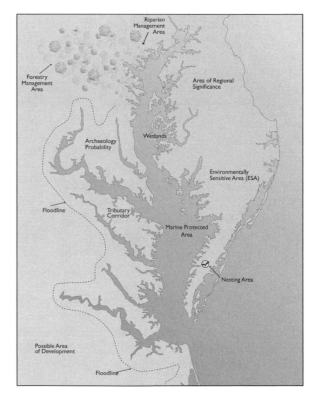

Figure 1-2 An example of a resource map.

What Environmental Impacts of Your Project Will the Team Consider?

Before you can design responsibly, you need to understand the potential vulnerabilities of the site and community. Figure 1-2 is an example of a resource map, the kind of graphic exercise that would help discover environmental impacts on the site. Many issues can be mapped, from demographics to noise levels. For the integrated green building design process, your team will devote considerable time to scrutinizing the details of the site. Some questions to consider include the following:

- Will endangered species or wildlife be affected?
- Are there wetlands nearby?
- Should the project restore wetlands or green fields, if it has an impact on these?
- Is there a riparian corridor on the site?
- How will potable water quality be affected?
- What is the current pattern of storm water runoff?
- Does storm water percolate and drain into the water table or a body of water nearby?
- Are there impervious surfaces on the undeveloped site?
- How will impervious surfaces affect the loss of water through the sewer system or through the evaporation process?
- Will construction cause soil erosion or soil loss due to wind?

Understand Team Responsibilities and Define Roles

Which team members should be responsible for researching, presenting, and advocating for the issues identified in the questions above?

Ideally, each member of the project team in integrated design will have a clearly defined role and area of expertise for which he or she will be responsible and from which he or she will inform the project design. Adopting these roles can create advocacy for certain design solutions. Again, this exercise mimics the practice of integrated design in real life.

In integrated design practice, the range of stakeholders includes the owner, the various designers and engineers (structural; civil; heating, ventilation, air-conditioning, and refrigeration [HVAC&R]; plumbing; electrical; and energy engineers), the builder and contractor, specialty consultants (daylighting, energy, sustainable design, and commissioning consultants), building users and operators (Figure 1-3).

Additional team members will be responsible for more focused issues, such as green roofs, on-site wind-generation, or site wastewater treatment. It may be that manufacturers of high-efficiency systems, such as building-integrated black-water treatment technology and photovoltaic systems, are present at least on some phases of the project.

In a studio project, each team member should be assigned to traditional and basic roles, and each member should be responsible for documenting strategies and decisions.

Consider How Your Team's Design Project Will Address the Issues of the Site and Community

View the solutions to the project site, materials, energy, and air quality challenges as potential design elements, and set specific measurable goals.

For example, a flat roof on a longitudinally oriented building, with its longer facade facing south and whose

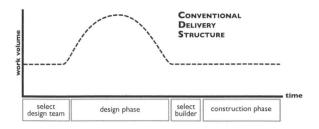

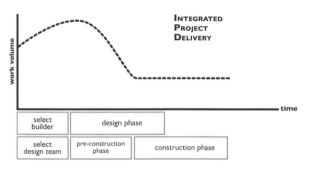

Figure 1-3 Integrated project delivery requires involving the builder early and front-loading design work.

Figure 1-4 Porous paving allows rainwater to percolate rather than run off.

floor is a thick concrete surface, will have the potential for heat gain and retention, while a building in a hot climate with deep overhangs will protect occupants from glare and unwanted heat gain.

A project with an asphalt parking lot will shed water to the storm sewer that could be captured for other uses, while a project with a pervious paved surface handles recharge to the water table and contributes to the overall water-cycle efficiency. Figure 1-4 shows a porous surface area that functions as a durable hardscape, but it also allows water to percolate through.

Because sustainable design involves social justice, designing for community is considered a part of the integrated design process and thus takes on a deeper nuance. In terms of community, any project has the potential to enhance or displace existing communities. The team for an integrated project will examine the history of the site

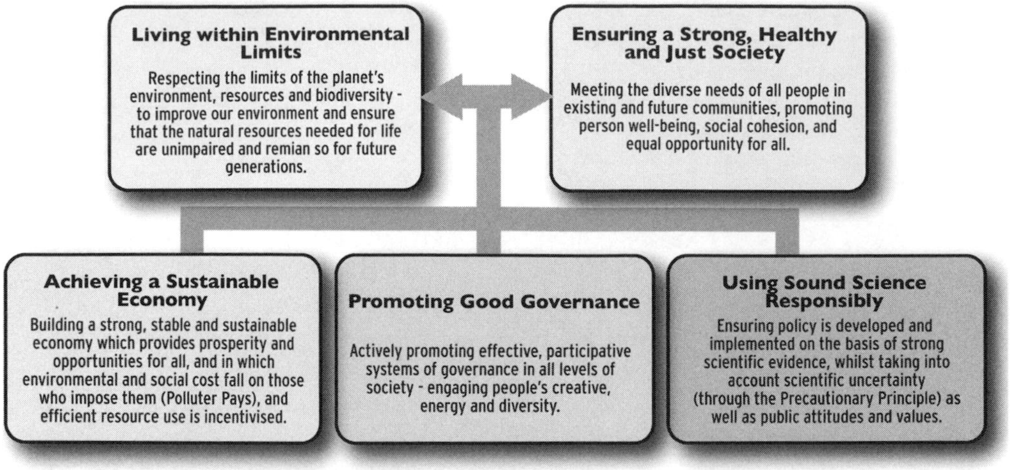

Figure 1-5 Three of five key points in the British sustainability plan concern social issues.

and its ethnographies and determine optimal solutions for enhancing quality of life for existing communities.

At the same time, a project has the potential for *creating* community, a concept that is part of a complete and traditional architectural education. Using integrated design, creating community takes on a new dimension.

For example, a team must consider future tenants in a multifamily housing project as more than simply an element of programming. The team must also ensure that social structure is preserved and must provide opportunities for inhabitants to engage or retreat from their environment and to participate in the planning of their living environment and its future incarnations. The United Kingdom's most recent sustainability plan, "Securing the Future—UK Government Sustainable Development Strategy,"[2] highlights social justice and inclusion as one of several key sustainable development themes (Figure 1-5).

The integrated project will educate inhabitants on their green building, as well as on the relationship of their building to the surrounding community and landscape. Though seemingly mundane, teaching future inhabitants about the unique maintenance and cleaning practices necessitated by a green building is part of the integrated design process.

Weigh Interrelated Impacts of Proposed Solutions

At this particular point in the process, it is typical for the various team members to contribute their expertise and offer for discussion the relative merits and downsides of the solutions identified. Team members should communicate and interact.

For example, the team member responsible for energy analysis can point out that a building with daylight efficiency and harvesting technology, such as light shelves, could also have the potential for unwanted glare or heat gain.

The interior designer will recommend interior finishes, and this work will have a major impact on the quality of the indoor air. The designer may propose that a particular floor surfacing material with 100-percent-recycled rubber be considered; however, though the material uses resources wisely, it presents a stronger odor for several months after installation, unlike rubber flooring manufactured from virgin rubber.

The project client may argue that some sustainable strategies carry with them a higher cost impact than others. A traditional design approach, which usually treats green design as an add-on, leads to higher costs. The integrated design approach typically requires higher design fees, but it can also lead to lower first costs and reduced operating costs. In professional practice, a life-cycle-costing analysis or pricing exercise may be conducted to weigh these strategies and assess their long- and short-term economic viability. Figure 1-6 compares building-life costs across building alternatives, illustrating that a sustainably constructed building that generates its own power provides the best cost-to life relationship.

The client may say that unproven technology is not a risk they wish to pursue because of liability and the potentially unpredictable nature of innovative systems. What are the effects on design aesthetic? The green designer will argue that high-technology systems can lead to good design, but the views of the owner occupants and the community as to what constitutes good design need to be included as part of the integrated design process.

Establish Priorities

A troubling reality about the integrated design process is that there are no perfect solutions and that no project can achieve complete greenness, as we are defining the term in this book. But we can come close by weighing the merits and complementary effects identified above and testing their solutions and impacts.

---

[2] Available at the United Kingdom Department for Environment, Food, and Rural Affairs, http://www.defra.gov.uk/environment/sustainable.

For each project, there are frequently several optimal design solutions that are uniquely connected to project constraints. Team leadership becomes crucial during the discussion and winnowing process, because, ultimately, to be efficient, the team must commit to a certain approach and direction, such as those identified earlier.

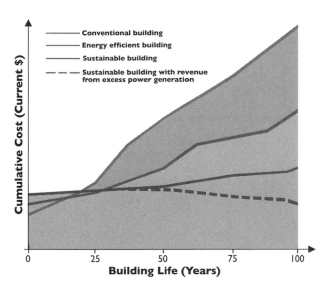

Figure 1-6 A life-cycle cost comparison of four building types: a conventional building, an energy-efficient building, a sustainable building, and a sustainable building with revenue from excess power generation. Cumulative costs of a building with energy-efficiency strategies and energy revenue are significantly lower, while a conventional building's costs rise steeply over time.

This is another area where team roles and the integrated design process come into play. Needless to say, at the end of all this, a final decision must be made. It is in this area that project design can fully benefit from an integrated design process and can reap the benefits of the various team members' shared expertise.

Take a Step Beyond

In professional practice, the integrated design process does not end with construction. Operators, occupants, tenants, lessors, and facilities managers need training to understand how every interrelated green decision should behave. Tenant and operator manuals amplify this understanding and improve the likelihood of a successful integrated green building. Commissioning, a process defined and outlined below, is assurance of a healthy and functioning building and is the mechanism to confirm that design intent is met.

Integrated Building Design: Energy, Resources, and Air

Methodology and Tools of the Integrated Design Process for Energy

As discussed earlier in the chapter, integrated design is a process that recognizes the relationships among the many decisions made when designing a building. Early design decisions regarding the site and building orientation, building plan and section, and size and location of windows have a great effect on building aesthetics (Figure 1-7).

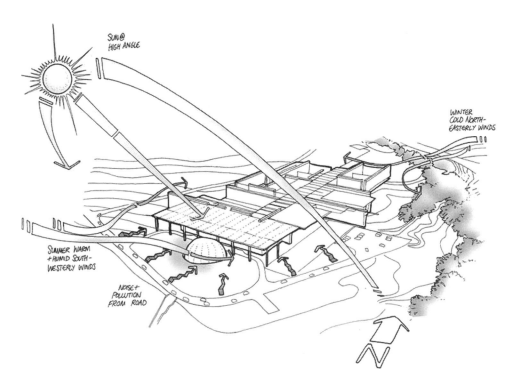

Figure 1-7 A sketch of the Istanbul Science Centre helps designers understand the site's wind patterns and the sun's path, which will then inform design decisions.

In many cases, the interrelationships of design decisions also determine how much energy a building will require to operate. In the integrated design process, a designer is conscious of a more complete set of impacts, including aesthetics, energy, environment, and occupant experience.

In the real world of architecture and design, integrated practice usually requires additional design time in the schematic phase. This is so that the architect, mechanical and electrical engineers, and other members of the team can ask questions, discuss options and their impacts, and model the energy and cost implications of the choices under consideration. (See Figure 1-3.)

Fundamental sustainability goals should be established early in design to set meaningful targets against which to assess options and level of achievement. The goals should specify a measurable and easily understood target for building performance rather than prescribe specific solutions.

As a student considering energy performance, you might establish a goal of reducing building energy use by 50 percent compared to the average energy use for buildings of that type in your region. Demonstrating achievement of your goal could vary from a simple list of low-energy design strategies you have incorporated to a simple energy model of your design made with easy-to-use software, such as Energy-10 or eQUEST (Figures 1-8A, B, and C). Getting some experience with computer tools that assess building energy performance prior to graduating should be a goal of all architecture and engineering students.

At the professional level, setting performance targets and assessing your design must be a more rigorous process. Many professional societies in the design professions have established standards for recommended practice.

The American Society of Heating, Refrigerating, and Air-Conditioning Engineers (ASHRAE) has created an energy use standard known as ASHRAE 90.1, which is updated periodically; the most recent update is from 2007.

The State of California's *Title 24 Building Energy Standards*[3] set requirements for new construction and renovation projects in the state. Both ASHRAE 90.1 and California Title 24 requirements vary by region. Overall energy goals should reference such existing standards, for example, calling for energy performance 50 percent better than ASHRAE 90.1-2005 or California Title 24-2008.

At the professional level, it is important to model the options for informed decision making. This makes it possible to better understand interactions between building systems and between the other elements of sustainable design, such as material resource use and indoor air quality.

Whether student or professional, the goal should be to maximize efficiency of building systems, looking for complementary interactions that reduce waste—for example, using waste heat from one system to preheat inputs for another. At the professional level, this involves using high-efficiency equipment, sizing systems properly, and incorporating renewable energy once other systems have been optimized.

(a)

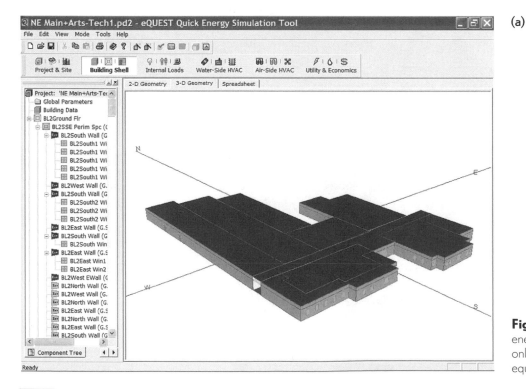

Figure 1-8 a–c Screenshots of the energy software eQUEST, available online at http://www.doe2.com/equest/.

[3] California Energy Commission, *2008 Building Energy Efficiency Standards for Residential and Nonresidential Buildings,* CEC-400-2008-001-CMF (Sacramento, CA: California Energy Commission, December 2008).

(b)

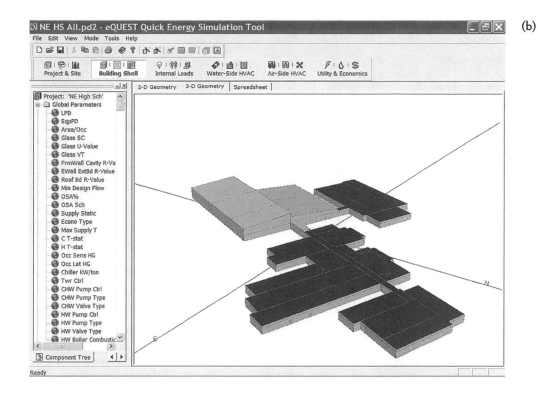

(c)

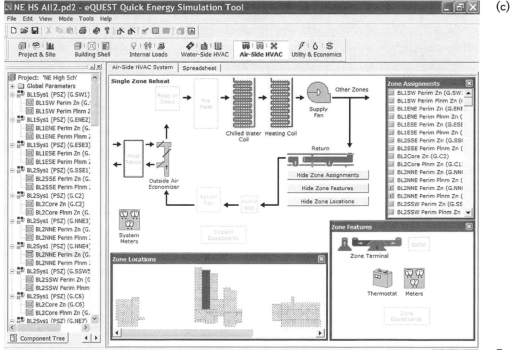

Figure 1-8 a–c *Cont'd*

Resources: Water and Raw Building Materials

As with all green decisions, an early start to thinking about resource management is essential to meaningful design. The building industry accounts for 40 percent of all raw material use in the United States (3 billion tons annually).[4] So conscientious use of water and soils, as well as mined and harvested resources, is critical.

[4] N. Lenssen and D. M. Roodman, "Paper 124: A Building Revolution: How Ecology and Health Concerns are Transforming Construction," *Worldwatch* (1995), Worldwatch Institute.

Two keys to wise resource management require that you maximize their potential to increase effectiveness and efficiency and to reduce or entirely to "eliminate the concept of waste," as William McDonough and Michael Braungart proposed in *The Hannover Principles*.[5] Just as some cultures use the entire animal—nose to tail, beak to claw—for both sustenance and warmth, we must do the same with trees, granite, threatened and overharvested resources, judiciously using their full potential.

The flip side of resource management is to understand natural balance and to avoid damaging interventions while extracting these resources. This is the moment that the troubling reality of integrated design becomes the opportunity to determine priorities, balance, and options. Figures 1-9 and 1-10 show the results of sustainable versus nonsustainable forestry practices.

Resources, materials, products, and systems, including their life cycles, need to be examined to implement integrated design thoroughly. We are confronting a crisis in climate change and the linked impacts of solar dimming and water depletion. The effort to balance energy, emissions, and water flows is the monumental planetary task we face.

On the local scale, as architects and designers, we can address these issues with a much smaller order of magnitude by designing sustainable buildings; this task is not only manageable but also meaningful in its cumulative effect.

Water
Buildings use 12.2 percent of all potable water, or 15 trillion gallons per year.[6]

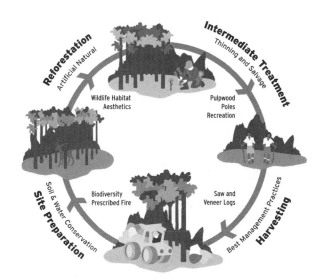

Figure 1-9 Responsible resource extraction techniques.

[5]William McDonough and Michael Braungart, *The Hannover Principles, Design for Sustainability*, 10th Anniversary Edition, commissioned as the official design guide for the EXPO 2000 World's Fair, William McDonough + Partners, McDonough Braungart Design Chemistry, 2003.
[6]United States Geological Service data (1995).

Figure 1-10 Destructive resource extraction techniques.

In the chapters that follow we will discuss specific strategies to reduce consumption of water during construction and occupancy and to use nonpotable and harvested water for uses other than human consumption. Harvested rainwater needs to be managed, as described in Figure 1-11.

As architects and designers, our job is to think of built solutions, such as water storage systems, both natural and human made, and treatment solutions on the site and in the building. For purposes of integrated design, water conservation strategies revolve around *sewage conveyance*, *landscape concerns*, and *water sources*.

Sewage Conveyance. A green building can affect integrated design around water issues in a major way by reducing the potable water needed to manage human waste. Recycling gray water and black water are two potable water-conserving strategies (Figure 1-12).

Plumbing design, according to occupant demand, is another way to reduce potable water use. The approach involves calculating several factors by using a baseline or standard design scenario and proposing a design case with which to compare it. This is a modeling exercise and, therefore, can be used as a design tool. Factors to consider when modeling for a reduction in potable water use in sewage conveyance include the following:

- Occupancy, or the number of people using the building and times of day they are present
- Frequency of use
- Types of plumbing fixtures

Landscape Concerns. Design teams have the opportunity to design meaningful water use reductions in the outdoor landscape in concert with potable water use reductions inside the building. Again, a simple scenario comparison modeled using consistent assumptions about climate and landscape area is a recommended way to approach irrigation efficiency. Some factors to consider when modeling landscape concerns include the following:

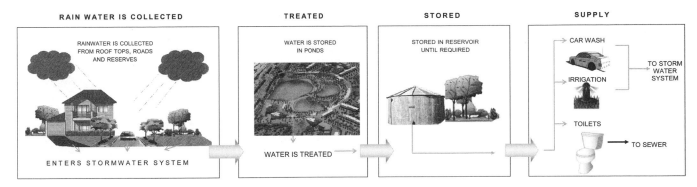

Figure 1-11 Rainwater collection system at the community level in New Zealand.

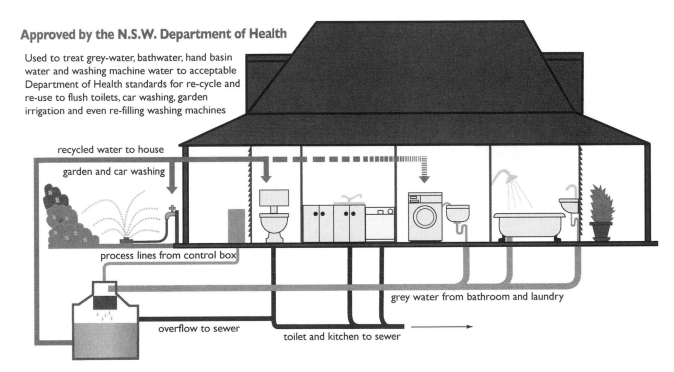

Figure 1-12 Gray water captured from bathtubs, showers, sinks, and laundering can be treated and reused to flush toilets and irrigate landscape.

- Planting types (climate adaptive, native species, xeriscape, monoculture avoidance)
- Irrigation systems
- Erosion control
- Storm-water management

Water Sources.   Controlling water consumption, of course, is only one aspect of maximizing water effectiveness; others are wise management of water sources and even the potential to produce usable water, through treatment technologies or desalinization. Water control methods in use include the following.

- Rainwater harvesting and storage
- Black-water treatment, on-site and integrated into buildings
- Municipal gray water use

- Future technologies include desalinization and water recycling for potable use

Other opportunities to protect and manage water resources exist in developing water conservation education programs for building occupants. Historical methods of managing water supply, community water, and diversion will need to be reimagined.

Raw Building Materials
In the chapters that follow, we will discuss examples of resources. There are many types of resources, for example *living and nonliving,* such as metals, minerals, oil, and timber; *flow (or energy) resources,* such as tide, wind, and solar; as well as *other renewable and nonrenewable resources.*

Raw materials for building are most directly addressed by the living and nonliving category of resources, but flow resources figure into their life cycles.

Building material specification is an absolutely critical element of green building design. Asking questions about a product's life cycle is a good way to educate yourself as to the materials' variability, utility, and contribution to environmental degradation. (Materials selection will be discussed in a later chapter.)

As part of the integrated design process, architects and designers must gather data on the materials and products they wish to specify in order to design a resource-efficient building that uses mined and harvested materials wisely. Among other considerations, the designer should know about product:

- packaging;
- embodied energy;
- recycled content;
- recyclability, reuse, and salvageability;
- waste production;
- closed-loop manufacturing process;
- durability and lifespan; and
- renewable or nonrenewable resource composition.

A materials assessment database and system like Pharos (Figure 1-13), which will be discussed in the green materials chapter, makes the job of researching the best environmental choices much easier.

Indoor Air and Environmental Quality

Indoor environmental quality refers to an abundance of issues relating to occupant comfort and quality of work or living space: temperature, humidity, glare, acoustics, access to daylight, the efficiency of air movement through occupied spaces, and the quality of the indoor air itself. Building occupants themselves can address many of these concerns, provided that building systems are creative enough to give people an opportunity to control their own environment.

Indoor air quality (IAQ) should be the foremost concern for designers of integrated buildings, as indoor air correlates directly to long-term occupant health. Bad IAQ is a problem on many levels, as described in Figure 1-14. Achieving good IAQ involves reducing the building occupants' exposure to chemicals of concern (e.g., carcinogens, reproductive toxicants, and other potentially harmful chemicals) by considering the following four elements of good IAQ design throughout the project:

- *Source control* through wise selection of building materials, finishes, and furnishings, while screening them for their volatile organic compounds (VOCs) emissions and not simply content.
- *Ventilation control* through carefully designed systems that adequately filter outside air and circulate it such that guideline rates of air exchanges are surpassed.
- *Building and IAQ commissioning*, by which engineers and builders determine if a building's systems are functioning as designed.
- *Building maintenance* involves the introduction of new chemicals that often create synergistic effects and generate new chemicals of concern. Using benign cleaning and maintenance products—and establishing a green janitorial program—are other ways of attempting to ensure ongoing improved air quality.

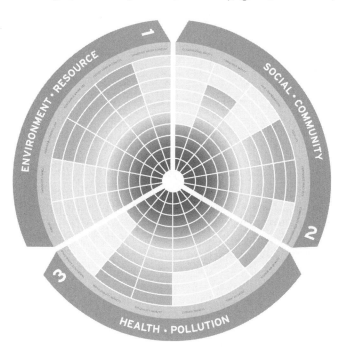

Figure 1-13 The Pharos "wheel" or "lens" illustrates three cores of sustainability: environment and resources; social and community; and health and pollution. It ranks materials along a visual scale within the lens.

SYMPTOMS RELATED TO INDOOR AIR POLLUTANTS

	Particles			Bioaerosols				Gases		
	Dust, Soil, Ash	Tobacco Smoke	Pollen	Molds, Mildew, Fungus	Bacteria, Virus	Pet Dander	Dust Mites	Carbon Monoxide	Formaldehyde	VOCs
Headaches		✓	✓					✓	✓	✓
Dizziness	✓			✓		✓	✓			
Fatigue			✓						✓	✓
Nausea								✓	✓	
Vomiting									✓	
Skin Rash						✓				✓
Eye Irritation	✓	✓	✓	✓	✓				✓	✓
Nose Irritation	✓	✓	✓	✓	✓	✓	✓		✓	✓
Throat Irritation	✓	✓							✓	
Respiratory Irritation		✓		✓	✓			✓		✓
Cough	✓	✓		✓	✓	✓	✓			✓
Chest Tightness		✓		✓		✓	✓			
Respiratory Infections	✓			✓	✓		✓			
Asthma (exacerbation of)	✓	✓	✓	✓		✓	✓			
Allergic Reactions	✓		✓	✓		✓	✓			
Lung Cancer		✓								

Figure 1-14 Poor indoor air quality can have a number of negative effects.

After reading this chapter, you may come away with the feeling that integrated building design is all work and no play. But if you approach this unique design process as an innovative yet grounded way to solve design challenges, in concert with injecting sustainable thinking, both your practice and the results of your efforts will benefit. This book is intended to guide students "toward a new sustainable architecture," an architecture that designs and produces efficient and healthful built environments.

EXERCISES

1. Memorize three key statistics identified in the chapter that illustrate the resource depletion effects of mainstream construction.

2. Create an environmental resources map for a hypothetical building project and determine which location would have the least environmental impact on surrounding resources.

3. Create a simple energy model with Energy-10, using a short list of energy-use assumptions.

4. Plan an integrated design studio charrette. How would team roles be divided? At what level and phases of design would each team member be involved?

5. How would the integrated design process differ for a high-rise tower and a private elementary school? What consultants would be involved for each?

6. Develop a schedule of regular team meetings around project milestones for your current studio project.

2 A History of the Environmental Movements

Meanwhile, at social Industry's command,

How quick, how vast an increase! From the germ

Of some poor hamlet, rapidly produced

Here a huge town, continuous and compact,

Hiding the face of earth for leagues—and there,

Where not a habitation stood before,

Abodes of men irregularly massed

Like trees in forests,—spread through spacious tracts,

O'er which the smoke of unremitting fires

Hangs permanent, and plentiful as wreaths

Of vapour glittering in the morning sun.
            —William Wordsworth, "The Excursion"

I believe in the forest, and in the meadow, and in the night in which the corn grows.
            —Henry David Thoreau, "Walking"

To do justice to the timeline and development of the environmental movement and the emergence of green building is an almost impossible task. We are dealing with a linear timeline overlain by a knotted progression of tracks and trends. The challenge of unraveling them often seems like pulling apart a tangle of yarn. It is easy to trace some threads but difficult to spot others, and it is almost impossible to locate the beginning threads.

To explain the interdependence of the environmental movement and the green building movement, we must consider a number of overlapping factors:

- The tenacity and dedication of key international leaders in pushing global legislation, craft treaties, and action plans on behalf of environmental protections
- The history of the environmental movement as global rather than provincial

- The need to create identifying names and markers for key trends
- Identifying comprehensive, concise pathways to the present, in which we narrow our focus to the pathways that have had the most impact on the development of green buildings
- Understanding the subject thematically rather than chronologically

To that end, this chapter addresses the following themes:

- Roots: converging themes
- Grassroots: early leaders
- The two chief catalysts: the Industrial Revolution and the modern chemical revolution
- The prelude to the conservation and preservation movements
- Companion tracks of the environmental movement: conservation versus preservation and Emerson and Thoreau
- The ecology movement
- Modern international environmentalism
- The emergence of green buildings

Environmental history is a vast branch of study, a complex movement whose sources are social, political, and scientific. Because this chapter is intended as an overview, it provides only an outline of the most prevalent overlapping and interlinked environmental themes. Students are encouraged to continue with additional readings from the list provided at the end of the chapter.

Roots

The origins of the green building movement cannot be traced to a single event but, rather, to the cumulative effects of converging milestones whose beginnings mirror those of

Figure 2-1 Anasazi Palace, built under the natural eave of the cliffs.

humankind. To trace the path of its development, we need to look first at how environmental awareness began.

Our early ancestors were indeed cleaved to their environment, because their survival depended on it. They used the resources available to them to create shelter, to hunt, and later to farm and travel.

Although means were crude and the patterns of daily life basic, resources were abundant relative to population size and density. It is tempting to simplify and romanticize early humans as living in comfortable balance with the earth, but as much as the tradition of living in a small area is part of our early history of sustainability, so is the decimation of our environment. Early peoples were no exception.

We learned early on to deplete the abundant resources available to us, a behavior that has snaked its way through human history, often with cultural casualties. In his book, *Collapse: How Societies Choose to Fail or Succeed* (2005), Jared M. Diamond cites a five-pronged path to the disintegration of certain societies, one of which is the degradation of the environment. Resource depletion was one of the factors that led to the failure of several early societies. As Diamond discusses in his book, the demise of early cultures can be traced to five interrelated causes: environmental damage, climate change, hostile neighbors, friendly trading partners, and human responses to these events. The Easter Islanders, the Anasazi (Figure 2-1), and the Maya are examples of the early cultural casualties studied by Diamond.[1]

Scholars understand that, throughout history, natural disasters and other forms of environmental destruction of various scales, along with extreme weather events and their aftermath, have shaped societies and the environment.

Climate change scientist Nick Brooks names gradual climate change as partially responsible for the creation of adaptive civilizations and cultures; but he adds that sudden environmental disasters did not allow time for some cultures to adapt to their changing environment, also known as their "adaptive capacity."[2]

A failure to engineer and adapt to the effect of climate change on biosystems, food supply, and weather patterns is due to the ineffectual human response Diamond describes in *Collapse*. Environmental destruction is the result of this failure.

Clearly, just as environmental destruction was a primary factor in the failure of early cultures, it continues to pose a threat to contemporary life. We can point to countless examples of such deterioration in our time: species extinction, rain forest destruction, food-crop shortages and soil depletion, irresponsible fishing and forestry practices, and wetland and river damage due to industrial pollution (Figure 2-2). Climate change is one of the most far-reaching expressions of these threats to environmental and human health, as it is not only a result of human intervention but also a contributor to the environmental destruction described above. It is also the most challenging to confront because of heightened controversy surrounding its cause and the reaction to proposed methods to address this destruction.

Although scientists have been studying variations in climate for decades, today, with emerging public consciousness. we are seeing renewed vigor and interest in the subject. The burgeoning environmental movement is beginning to address this global emergency, and it remains to be seen if, as a global culture, we have the adaptive capacity to survive. (The subject of climate change will be discussed in a later chapter.)

Grassroots Movements

"If the backbone of the hills breaks, the plains below will be submerged."

—Slogan of the Chipko Movement

One of the visionary and often quoted writers for those in the environmental movement is Paul Hawken. His book *Natural Capitalism: Creating the Next Industrial Revolution* (1970),[3] coauthored with Amory Lovins and L. Hunter Lovins, is a treatise on an innovative model of a new

[1]Diamond, *Collapse*, 11.

[2]W. Neil Adger and Nick Brooks, "Does Global Environmental Change Cause Vulnerability to Disaster?" in *Natural Disaster and Development in a Globalizing World,* ed. Mark Pelling (London and New York: Routledge, 2003)
[3]Hawken, Lovins, and Lovins, *Natural Capitalism*.

Figure 2-2 A landscape transformed by large-scale industrial activities.

economy in which environmental carrying capacity is nearing its limits. It is a landmark work and required reading in high schools and colleges across many disciplines.

In Paul Hawken's *Blessed Unrest: How the Largest Movement in the World Came into Being and Why No One Saw It Coming* (2007),[4] the author chronicles how the environmental movement started. He describes a movement that began on the twin paths of social and environmental justice, which are now converging into a collective path. That environmental sustainability and social justice cannot be separated is one of Hawken's perceptive conclusions.

The philosophy of building sustainably is an important component of this converging movement. To understand the current movement and the evolution of green building, it is first necessary to trace the beginnings of environmental thinking.

Contrary to general belief, the environmental movement was not born exclusively in the Victorian world; though activism—e.g., the Luddites' loom sabotage in England in 1811 as a response to loss of employment through the advent of the modern loom—was unknown until then (Figure 2-3). Early pollution laws were enacted in Rome and China, while Peru and India were aware of the need for soil preservation.[5] The United Kingdom established a pollution control agency through the Alkali

THE LEADER OF THE LUDDITES

Figure 2-3 The term Luddite is frequently misapplied to those who do not support mechanized modern industry and technology. In reality, the Luddite movement was about economic sustainability that was threatened by the advent of the Industrial Revolution.

---

[4]Hawken, *Blessed Unrest*.
[5]"Environmentalism?—A History of the Environmental Movement," Lorraine Elliott, *Encyclopedia Britannica*, 2007, in *Encyclopedia Britannica Online*, http://www.britannica.com/eb/article-224631 (accessed July 11, 2007).

Act in 1863 to urge controls on hydrogen chloride gas emissions by the alkali industry.

One of most moving expressions of these early conservation efforts came in India in the 1730s, when a group led by Amrita Devi, a matriarch of the Bishnoi, a Hindu sect from the Rajasthan region in northwest India known for its fierce dedication to protecting the environment and belief in the sacred nature of trees, thwarted the maharaja of Jodhpur's efforts to harvest trees from the region for construction purposes. Although accounts vary, it is clear that, one by one, villagers went to their deaths as they encircled the trees in the face of the maharaja's tree-felling crew. Amrita Devi is said to have uttered: "If a tree is saved even at the cost of one's head, it's worth it," as she was cut down (Figure 2-4). Before the effort was called off, 362 people of all ages lost their lives. As a response to the tragedy, trees were subsequently protected by royal decree.[6]

This early Hindu protest formed the origins of India's Chipko Movement of the 1970s and gave rise to the term *tree hugger*. As with the Bishnoi, the Chipko Movement was spearheaded by women who were against logging for corporate interests and who, again, encircled trees with their bodies to protect them. Accompanying the resistance to the government's logging practices, members of the movement also protested against the limitations on tree harvesting that had earlier been placed on their own pattern of living and sustenance.

The environmental action continued for several years and was a progenitor of the ecofeminist branch of environmentalism.[7]

In the Chipko Movement, we see a parallel with Mohandas K. Gandhi's nonviolent protest methods. Here, twin issues—feminism and environmentalism—correspond in spirit, and both are expressions of the twin paths Hawken describes, namely, the merging of social and ecological themes.

Ecofeminist luminaries include such notable women as Wangari Maathai (Figure 2-5), who received the Nobel Peace Prize in 2004 for implementing both a Kenyan and international Green Belt Movement, a widespread tree-planting effort to prevent erosion and restore forests. Again, this movement was propelled and implemented by women, whose patterns of work and life were intri-

Figure 2-4 People of the Chipko Movement embrace a tree, hence the term tree hugger.

Figure 2-5 Dr. Wangari Maathai, founder of the Green Belt Movement and winner of the 2004 Nobel Peace Prize.

[6]"India's Original Green Brigade," *Times of India*, April 11, 2006.

[7]Ramachandra Guha, *The Unquiet Woods: Ecological Change and Peasant Resistance in the Himalaya* (Berkeley and Los Angeles: University of California Press, 2000).

cately bound with the larger health of their environment and revolved around symbols of life and protection, including the tree.[8]

Many such indigenous grassroots environmental actions took place internationally. But notice that these early activists were members of small communities whose work was defined by challenges posed by their regional geography and heavy-handed politics. Yet in today's narrow chronicles of environmental history, the stories of these indigenous peoples are conspicuously absent.

In North America, as in countries across the world, many indigenous peoples were defined by their respect for nature and sacred esteem for natural elements that formed their surroundings. They understood the need to balance the interrelationship between their community's need for sustenance and the responsibility to honor their spiritual practices as embodied in nature. They viewed themselves as a part of the integrated cycle of nature and life, acknowledging the fusion of their ancestors with elements of the natural world.

Because of the diverse forms of sustenance and patterns of living, in these cultures, even these early approaches toward the environment varied. Some societies exploited their environment, though never more than the European population once it gained a foothold in the New World.[9]

One of the winners of the Goldman Environmental Prize in 2007 was Sophia Rabliauskas, member of the Poplar River First Nation in Canada, who became an activist in the preservation through sustainable forestry of the boreal forest in her region, a successful example of environmental activism on a social justice scale.[10]

The Industrial Revolution

One might say that the infrastructure created by the Industrial Revolution of the nineteenth century resembles such a steamship [The Titanic]. It is powered by fossil fuels, nuclear reactors, and chemicals. It is pouring waste into the water and smoke into the sky. It is attempting to work by its own rules, contrary to those of the natural world. And although it may seem invincible, its fundamental design flaws presage disaster.

–"The Next Industrial Revolution," William McDonough and Michael Braungart, *Atlantic*, October 1998

Any discussion of environmental consciousness begins with the variously dated Industrial Revolution, in all its phases and regional incarnations.[11] At its core, the Industrial Revolution caused the international transition from an agricultural, land-based society that encapsulated small-scale rural community and self-sustenance to an industrial-based, fast-paced society. This was a largely faceless and impoverished urban community in which women and children formed a key element of the workforce. Living and working conditions during this time of transition were appalling, as were the environmental effects of this huge change. With the advantage of hindsight, it is possible to understand both the historical costs and benefits of the revolution's contribution to the growth of modern cities; new technologies for commerce, trade, and manufacturing; and eventually improved public health.

With the Industrial Revolution the stage was set for emergent social conflicts that were inextricably linked to a parallel environmental impact across many continents and for an extended period of time. The Romantic Era poets and novelists were noteworthy for their firsthand observations of the revolution and its social and environmental implications.

As a reaction to the Industrial Revolution, Mary Wollstonecraft Shelley (1797–1851) wrote of the perils of science and machinery in *Frankenstein: Or, The Modern Prometheus* (1818), whose subtitle refers to the mythical figure who brought fire to humankind and who symbolizes human creativity and daring (Figure 2-6). In the end, both Prometheus and Dr. Frankenstein were punished for unleashing an undefined and modern terror. Frankenstein's monster was both the result of modern science and its victim.

The reaction from poet William Blake (1757–1827) was no less vigorous. He wrote of "England's green and pleasant land" in contrast to the Industrial Revolution's "dark satanic mills."[12] George Orwell, whose fertile writing period is often linked to the end of the second industrial revolution in England, described in much of his work the social and political ills of the Industrial Revolution's progress, bemoaning the advent of machinery and its toll on people's understanding of their own humanity. Orwell's *The Road to Wigan Pier* (1937) was the result of his firsthand experience of the impoverished and unemployed in a northern English coal-mining town. "From his perspective, Wigan was the historical terminus

---

[8] For information about the Green Belt movement: http://greenbelt-movement.org (accessed July 22, 2007).

[9] Kline, *First Along the River,* 14.

[10] For information about Sophia Rabliauskas and the Goldman prize: http://www.goldmanprize.org (accessed July 22, 2007).

[11] Peter N. Stearns, *The Industrial Revolution in World History* (Boulder, CO: Westview Press, 1998).

[12] William Blake, *Jerusalem, The Emanation of the Giant Albion* (1804–1820?). *Jerusalem* appears in many collections. Blake printed four copies himself, one of them in color, which was reproduced in a recent publication: *Jerusalem: The Emanation of the Giant Albion, The Illuminated Books of William Blake,* vol. 1, ed. Morton D. Paley (Princeton, NJ: William Blake Trust and Princeton University Press, 1997; orig. 1991).

Figure 2-6 In Mary Shelley's *Frankenstein*, the monster was a metaphor for modernism.

Figure 2-7 Rachel Carson, whose *Silent Spring* (1962) was a touchstone of the environmental and health movements.

of the industrial revolution, the unfortunate precipitate of 'progress.' [Orwell] used Wigan to speculate on the fate of the human subject within a settled, mature and bleak machine age."[13]

During this period, nature itself was objectified and viewed as an agricultural and economic commodity. One of the early economists to study the Industrial Revolution, land economist Richard T. Ely noted that the early economic concept of "land" was devoid of its association with nature; it was thought of primarily in terms of property or possession, separate from nature.[14]

It was not until the twentieth century that subbranches of economic theory evolved into thinking of land in terms of environment and resource economics, disciplines that are founded on preserving the limited yield of land based on conservation of land and nature.

As Bill McDonough reminds us, we are still living with the infrastructure created by the Industrial Revolution. Further, in the late nineteenth and early twentieth centuries,

toward the end of the second industrial revolution, the advent of modern chemistry and warfare spawned another transformation, the development of synthetic chemicals.

The Modern Chemical Revolution

The DuPont motto of the 1930s—"better things for better living through chemistry"—became a victim of cultural skepticism during the years of protest in the 1960s in the United States, and society has become increasingly more wary and suspicious of such corporate slogans.

This skepticism largely resulted from the efforts of the young biologist Rachel Carson (Figure 2-7) and her seminal book, *Silent Spring* (1962), which brought to light the large-scale proliferation of harmful insecticides, pesticides, and herbicides and their impact on the biosphere, food chain, water cycle, and ultimately humans. Perhaps no one more than Carson has provided a springboard for the discussion of modern industry's impact on environmental and human health. Carson's main observation was that lipid-soluble insecticidal chemicals find ideal residence in the fat tissues and organs of humans and other mammals.[15] The concept of a long-term chemical storage and body burden was not something that the general public understood until her book was serialized in the *New Yorker*. Her book prompted discussion and controversy,

[13] Hamza Walker, "Darren Almond, May 06–June 20, 1999," The Renaissance Society at the University of Chicago, n.d., http://www. renaissancesociety.org/site/Exhibitions/Essay.40.0.0.0.0.html (accessed December 23, 2008).

[14] Herman E. Daly and John B. Cobb Jr., *For the Common Good: Redirecting the Economy toward Community, the Environment, and a Sustainable Future* (Boston: Beacon Press, 1994).

[15] Carson, *Silent Spring*. Carson cites two classes of insecticides: chlorinated hydrocarbons and organic phosphates, which act on the nervous system and vital organs.

Figure 2-8 Cleanup efforts after the Exxon Valdez oil spill, Prince William Sound, Alaska, in 1989.

which eventually gave rise to the establishment of governmental oversight agencies, such as the U.S. Environmental Protection Agency (EPA), in spite of the chemical industry's efforts to discredit and vilify Carson.

In 1972 DDT (dichloro-diphenyl-trichloroethane), the pesticidal chemical, was banned, and many other insecticides (or, to use Carson's term, "biocides") were withdrawn from the U.S. market. But manufacture and shipment of banned and restricted pesticides to other parts of the world continues with an internationally mandated notification mechanism in place.[16]

Since the mid-twentieth century, chemical releases and industrial accidents, such as the 1984 Union Carbide methyl isocyanate gas release in Bhopal, India, the surfacing of Hooker Chemical and Plastics Corporation's[17] decades-long chemical dumping in the Love Canal community of Niagara Falls, New York, and toxic releases to the environment, such as the Exxon Valdez spill in 1989 in Prince William Sound, Alaska (Figure 2-8), have underscored the need for regulatory oversight of the chemical and manufacturing industries.

Nuclear industrial accidents—such as the 1957 fire in a Windscale, England, nuclear plant (Figure 2-9); the 1979 Three Mile Island nuclear accident near Harrisburg,

Pennsylvania; and the Chernobyl reactor meltdown in 1986 in northern Ukraine—have created an air of suspicion regarding government. The distrust permeating these times sparked the antinuclear protests of the late 1970s. A new brand of environmental activism emerged, largely driven by passion, that tended to draw skepticism from the mainstream public because of its activist edge. Yet the reality of environmental disasters, coupled with this social activism, triggered what became known as New Environmentalism. In spite of the passionate tenor, there was a clear call for developing public policy on environmental issues, in the United States and on a global scale.

Prelude to the Conservation and Preservation Movements

The earliest Western environmentalists were exclusively men: naturalists who honored wildlife and habitat through science, philosophy, art, and literature. Others were leaders who promoted public health and disease-prevention strategies, such as new sanitation and modern sewage-conveyance infrastructure.

But before considering the conservationists and preservationists, we will briefly present the relevant environmental health issues: pollution control and public health. Along with many social welfare proponents, Benjamin Franklin, in eighteenth-century Pennsylvania, headed protests calling for regulation of water-polluting slaughterhouses, tanneries, and skinner lime pits. He also developed such civic innovations as firefighting "clubs" and the Pennsylvania Hospital, which was devoted to the

---

[16] For more information on the internationally mandated notification mechanism for manufacture and shipment of banned and restricted pesticides to other parts of the world, see the Environmental Protection Agency's Web site: http://www.epa.gov/oppfead1/international/trade-issues.htm (accessed July 28, 2007).

[17] Hooker Chemical and Plastics Corporation is a subsidiary of Occidental Petroleum.

Figure 2-9 Creamery workers dumping milk after the Windscale nuclear plant fire in 1957 in the United Kingdom.

care of the underserved poor and mentally ill.[18] Another such leader was civil engineer Sir Joseph Bazalgette, who was charged with modernizing sewage systems in response to the Great Stink of 1858, the result of massive, ongoing pollution originating from London's open sewers, which drained into the Thames River, a condition Charles Dickens described as "obscene."

Interest in public health rose at this time, and measures were taken to engineer new systems and shape policy regarding legal protection of health and quality of life. Again, we see two converging branches of environmentalism and social responsibility.

Emerson and Thoreau as Key Figures

The West of which I speak is but another name for the Wild; and what I have been preparing to say is, that in Wildness is the preservation of the World. Every tree sends its fibres forth in search of the Wild. The cities import it at any price. Men plow and sail for it. From the forest and wilderness come the tonics and barks which brace mankind. Our ancestors were savages. The story of Romulus and Remus being suckled by a

wolf is not a meaningless fable. The founders of every State which has risen to eminence have drawn their nourishment and vigor from a similar wild source.[19]

—Henry David Thoreau, "Walking"

In good health, the air is a cordial of incredible virtue. Crossing a bare common, in snow puddles, at twilight, under a clouded sky, without having in my thoughts any occurrence of special good fortune, I have enjoyed a perfect exhilaration. I am glad to the brink of fear.

—Ralph Waldo Emerson, "Nature"

To see the origins of conservationist-preservationist philosophy, we need to pick up a particular strand of modern, Western environmentalism—romantic transcendentalism—which can be traced from the English poet William Wordsworth (1770–1850) to Ralph Waldo Emerson (1803–1882), the Unitarian minister turned philosopher, writer, and poet.

Wordsworth and Emerson met in 1833 during a pivotal period in Emerson's European travels in which his

---

[18]"Benjamin Franklin: An Extraordinary Life, An Electric Mind" (Public Broadcasting Service documentary), aired November 19 and 20, 2002, http://www.pbs.org/benfranklin/ (accessed on July 28, 2007).

[19]Henry David Thoreau, "Walking," *Atlantic Monthly* 9, no. 56 (1862): 657–674.

Figure 2-10
Founder of the Hudson River School, painter Thomas Cole was captivated by the majesty of the American landscape.

exposure to contemporary scientific thought and new discoveries in the natural world soon caused him to conclude that "nature was the embodiment of divine mind. Through knowledge of nature the human mind embodied itself, until at last body and spirit were not the sundered halves of Creation but one great whole."[20] Emerson's contact with Wordsworth and the other English Romantics deepened his interest in the spirituality of the natural world.

These interests took shape in Emerson's essay "Nature" (published in 1836). This work captured Emerson's philosophy that nature is the "universal spirit" that exists in the service of humanity. It was Emerson, through his essay and the formation of the transcendentalist movement (which held that true spirituality is not a construct of organized religion), who provided a formative framework for essayist, naturalist, protester, and philosopher Henry David Thoreau (1817–1862).

It was in Emerson's woods that Thoreau observed the rhythm of nature, recorded his coexistence with the natural world, and articulated a belief that without the wilderness, humanity could not exist. Among his writings, *Walden, or, Life in the Woods* (1854), as well as his essays on nature and nonviolent civil disobedience, embody key tenets of environmental thinking and activism.

Emerson was a preservationist who frequently remarked on the power of nature and humanity's attempt to subdue and conquer it. To him, civilized society,

industry, and the growth of cities intervened in the landscape, while farmers, whose sustenance necessitated a careful coexistence with nature, seemed to wisely nurture and depend on it. Thoreau is widely acknowledged to be the father of environmentalism, in part because of his enormous influence on future leaders of the movement, including John Muir, environmental preservationist and founder of the Sierra Club in 1892; David Brower, founder of the Earth Island Institute and Friends of the Earth; and others. Because of his own acts of nonviolent, civil disobedience and because he was one of the only environmentalists of his time to study the marginalized Native Americans of New England, his social justice message was carried even further, to twentieth-century leaders such as Mohandas Gandhi and Martin Luther King, Jr.

In North America, artists and writers of the day were influenced directly by the lineage of Wordsworth, Emerson, and Thoreau.[21] The father of the Hudson River School of landscape painters, Thomas Cole (1801–1848) promoted a Romantic view of nature, capturing the majesty and immensity of the mountains (Figure 2-10) in a way similar to that of Chinese landscape scroll painters who portrayed their own human insignificance in contrast to the enormity of nature. But Cole did this with a twist. Though romanticizing nature was a central theme for him, Cole also remarked in his work, through allegory, on the steady pace of human intervention on the savage

[20]Laura Dassow Wells, *Emerson's Life in Science: The Culture of Truth* (Ithaca, NY: Cornell University Press, 2003), 4.

[21]Barbara Novak, *American Painting of the Nineteenth Century: Realism, Idealism, and the American Experience* (Boulder, CO: Icon Editions, 1979), 61.

landscape as a response to what he observed firsthand in Europe's industrial revolution.

■ Companion Tracks of the Environmental Movement: The Separation of the Conservation Movement from the Preservation Movement[22]

Another influential writer of the Thoreau lineage was George Perkins Marsh, whose book, *Man and Nature; or, Physical Geography as Modified by Human Action* (1864), was pronounced by Lewis Mumford to be the "fountainhead of the conservation movement."[23]

Though a lover of nature, in contrast to Thoreau, Marsh believed that the wilderness was there to be tamed but protected by good stewardship. Unlike his contemporaries, however, Marsh did not believe that natural phenomena were drivers of physical geography, and therefore they were not shapers of humans. He believed that the intensity and extent of human intervention, such as irresponsible forestry practices, would cause damage to the environment.[24]

Of today's two dominant American political parties, one can make the case that the word "conservative" stemmed from the first truly environmentally conservative U.S. president, Theodore Roosevelt (1858–1919). One of his presidential mandates was the protection of natural resources, and his administration (1901–1909) oversaw legislative contributions, such as forest protection, public land management, and wilderness preservation.

Roosevelt's establishment of the U.S. Forest Service added millions of acres of national parks (the first of which was Yellowstone National Park) and placed wildlife refuges under the protection of the government. He was also the first U.S. president to convene an international conference, the North American Conservation Congress, held on February 18, 1909; representatives from Canada, Mexico, and Newfoundland attended. The most significant principle to emerge from this conference was the intention to convene a future international conference to address the theme of conservation. Roosevelt clearly saw the need for a global solution: "It is evident that natural resources are not limited by the boundary lines which separate nations, and that the need for conserving them upon this continent is as wide as the area upon which they exist."[25]

A lifelong hunter, Roosevelt is often cited by current hunting enthusiasts who believe that resources should be conserved for such recreational activities. This period gave birth to what is known as the *resource conservation ethic*, which corresponded with the Progressive Era reform agenda. Proponents of both agendas were wary of the motives of private business and corporate farming and thought both needed to be placed under government regulation in order to be wisely managed and to control their profligate use of natural resources.

These progressive conservationists believed that resources could only be effectively managed by the government, thereby ensuring not only a natural bounty but also economic vigor.[26] Roosevelt, along with chairman of the National Conservation Commission, Gifford Pinchot, also the first chief of the U.S. Forest Service, believed that natural reserves should be "conserved" for the economic betterment of humans. His view did not negate the rights of private enterprise to utilize natural resources; rather, the goal of resource management was to provide direction and management of feedstock, harvest, and manufacturing waste disposal.

Pinchot, educated in German forest management principles, which encouraged maximum yield, is credited with dividing conservationists and preservationists. While Roosevelt and other traditional conservationists believed that nature needed to be managed wisely for use by humans, preservationists like John Muir sought to protect the wilderness as a place of study, reflection, and enjoyment.

Roosevelt encountered firsthand the preservationist viewpoint in 1903, when he was invited to tour Yosemite Valley with John Muir (Figure 2-11).[27] During their three-day camping trip, the activist Muir lobbied Roosevelt for protection of wilderness areas, and he was successful in inspiring Roosevelt to usher protections of the Yosemite Valley through Congress. In 1892 John Muir founded the Sierra Club, an organization whose vitality continues to prompt protection legislation to the present day. Today, we see an abundance of such private organizations that advocate for the preservation of wilderness areas.[28]

[22] John McCormick, *Reclaiming Paradise: The Global Environment Movement* (Bloomington: Indiana University Press, 1989).

[23] Lewis Mumford, *Brown Decades: A Study of the Arts in America, 1865–1885* (Mineola, NY: Dover Press, 1972), 78. See also Mumford, *Condition of Man*, Houghton Miflin, 1973, and Peter Smith, *Technics and Civilization*, 1984.

[24] Daniel W. Gade, "Review of '*George Perkins Marsh: Prophet of Conservation* by David Lowenthal,'" *The Geographical Review* 92, no. 3 (2002): 460–462; David Lowenthal, *George Perkins Marsh: Versatile Vermonter* (New York: Columbia University Press, 1958), 248.

[25] "Roosevelt Invites Canada and Mexico; Calls a North American Conference on Conservation of Resources for Feb. 18. Pinchot to Take Letters Will Journey First to Canada and then to Mexico to Discuss the Proposed Meeting," *New York Times*, December 28, 1908.

[26] Kline, *First Along the River*, 54.

[27] Theodore Roosevelt, "John Muir: An Appreciation," *Outlook* 109 (January 15, 1915): 27–28, http://www.sierraclub.org/John_Muir_Exhibit/life/appreciation_by_roosevelt.html (accessed July 29, 2007).

[28] Hawken's *Blessed Unrest* and his Web site, Wiser Earth, contain a compendium of such organizations: WiserEarth: Community Tools for Creating a Just and Sustainable World: http://www.wiserearth.org/

Figure 2-11 Theodore Roosevelt and John Muir on Glacier Point, Yosemite Valley, California, in 1906.

The Ecology Movement

Another emerging practice of the twentieth century was the ecology movement, which bears special relevance to integrated green building. This new branch of science—ecology—existed in human consciousness earlier in the century and postulated that the environment is a set of interrelated organisms. Ecology was given further currency by another luminary, Aldo Leopold (1887–1948). Much like Thoreau, Leopold had his "back to the woods" period, in which he lived in a "shack" on his Wisconsin Sand County farm. Leopold's resulting work, *A Sand County Almanac* (1949), was his *Walden*.

Leopold began as a wildlife manager—in fact, as a forester, like Gifford Pinchot—yet viewed his work in a broader context than Pinchot. He wanted to influence how scientists explained environmentalism in terms of the new ecology. He was disenchanted with scientists, because they did not consider the ecosystem as a whole. Leopold preferred to look at ecology in an integrated way, by examining the balance of ecosystems and their interrelationships.

Leopold believed there were two kinds of conservationists:

• Those who looked at land as soil capable of yielding economic value by growing trees for wood or sowing pastures for cows *(economic land-use conservationists)*.

• Those who viewed land as a biota, a collection of interrelated species, that, when damaged in one aspect, shows repercussions for a set of accompanying issues *(ecologists–land ethicists)*.

This concept of land ethics is probably Leopold's greatest contribution to environmental philosophy; his reading of history and his milieu led him to believe that an ethical treatment of the "land" did not exist. Leopold's land ethic, summarized in the final chapter of *A Sand County Almanac,* actually urges humans to consider their obligations and relationships to the land, emphasizing that these obligations should extend to environmental conservation, even if "conservation" does not provide economic gain to humans.

As an extension of classic philosophy, land ethics incorporate the "biotic community." About his land ethic, Leopold said, "in short, a land ethic changes the role of *homo sapiens* from conqueror of the land-community to plain member and citizen of it. It implies respect for his fellow members, and also respect for the community as such."[29]

Later in the twentieth century, James Lovelock's "Gaia hypothesis" drew from the philosophy of ecology and supported the concept of integrated green building. Lovelock was a National Aeronautics and Space Administration (NASA) scientist and therefore a credible source for mainstream audiences, even though his theory drew derision from his colleagues.

Lovelock's original philosophy (first published in The Gaia hypothesis in 1979) held that the earth is a "superorganism," a sum of interrelated parts that keep the environment in balance—in essence, regulating itself.[30] Lovelock later reframed his thinking on self-regulation, which is interesting to reflect upon today, as we face the results of human action on an abundant planet.

EXERCISES

1. In the poems "Jerusalem" (William Blake) and "The Excursion" (William Wordsworth), nature is anthropomorphized and extolled in the terms the poets use to definite it. How would you describe the resolutions or directives that each poet gives to his reader?

2. What contemporary figure in the public eye can be likened to John Muir in terms of his or her capacity to encourage change, motivate participation in the environmental movement, and create awareness of the issues? What do these individuals share in common?

---

[29] Leopold, *Sand County Almanac*, 204.
[30] Lovelock, *Gaia*, 144.

■ Resources

Diamond, Jared M. 2005. *Collapse: How Societies Choose to Fail or Succeed.* New York: Viking Press, 2005.

Hawken, Paul, Amory Lovins, and L. Hunter Lovins. 2008. *Natural Capitalism: Creating the Next Industrial Revolution.* Snowmass, CO: Rocky Mountain Institute.

Hawken, Paul. 2007. *Blessed Unrest: How the Largest Movement in the World Came into Being and Why No One Saw It Coming.* New York: Viking Press.

Kline, Benjamin. 2000. *First Along the River: A Brief History of the U.S. Environmental Movement.* San Francisco: Acada Books.

Carson, Rachel. 1962. *Silent Spring.* Boston and Cambridge, MA: Houghton Mifflin and Riverside Press.

McCormick, John. 1989. *Reclaiming Paradise: The Global Environment Movement.* Bloomington: Indiana University Press.

Thoreau, Henry David. 1899 (orig. 1854). *Walden, or, Life in the Woods.* New York: T. Y. Crowell & Company.

Emerson, Ralph Waldo. 2003. *Nature and Selected Essays.* New York: Penguin Classics.

Leopold, Aldo. 1949. *Sand County Almanac and Sketches from Here and There.* New York: Oxford University Press.

Lovelock, James. 1982 (orig. 1979). *Gaia: A New Look at Life on Earth.* Oxford and New York: Oxford University Press.

3 Modern International Conferences and Treaties

The history of environmental activism, discussed in Chapter 2, draws out how New Environmentalism emerged from the various social, cultural, and environmental movements to spur international activism within the framework of public policy. In this transitional period, chroniclers of the new environmentalism shifted from artists and writers to legislators and politicians.

As the great quipper, Unknown, said: "Any sufficiently advanced bureaucracy is indistinguishable from molasses." Like the movement itself, international treaties have been created by competing institutions, which, while well intentioned, have slowed the implementation process. Thankfully, though, with the valuable participation of nongovernmental organizations (NGOs), environmental policy reached some consensus on many issues.

To thoroughly understand the history of these new environmental directives, conferences, and treaties, comprehensive accounts of the emerging conventions that spawned the green building movement, including some of the far-reaching environmental protections, can be found in *Reclaiming Paradise* (1989) by John McCormick and *Environmentalism, A Global History* (2000) by Ramachandra Guha.

Internationally, environmental thinking, aided by eventual intergovernmental accords, emerged from a political thicket quite different from today's. The early conferences focused on the protection of wildlife species through exchange of scientific research. Congresses for scientific inquiry were convened regularly, though at first without a goal toward regulation.

The first international environmental organization, the 1913 Consultative Commission for the International Protection of Nature, was established to protect migratory birds. In a similar vein, in 1900, in Africa, the Convention for the Preservation of Animals, Birds and Fish in Africa convened to control trade of game animal parts, such as ivory, though many lesser species were not

Figure 3-1 Franklin Delano Roosevelt.

issued protections, serving as an early example of the limitations of international protections.

In the 1930s, President Franklin Roosevelt's New Deal (Figure 3-1) sought, among other things, to protect and manage environmental resources. Roosevelt also established the National Resources Board by executive order in 1934, whose purpose was to report on "physical, social, governmental, and economic aspects of public policies for the development and use of land, water,

Figure 3-2 Harry S. Truman.

and other national resources, and such related subjects as may from time to time be referred to it by the President."[1]

Mid-twentieth century developments after World War II saw Gifford Pinchot and others continuing to fight for congresses, conferences, and organizations for conservation and wildlife protection on an international level.

Ushering in further progress, President Harry Truman (Figure 3-2) established the President's Materials Policy Commission (the Paley Commission), an important energy and resources policy study directed at strengthening national security in the face of the "Communist threat" and crafting the mechanisms to cope with potential energy shortages and rising costs. *The Paley Commission Report* (1952) urged conservation and alternative energy strategies to propel economic growth. It looked to private enterprise with governmental oversight to engineer new technology such as solar hot water and solar energy technology.[2]

After World War II and United Nations (UN) environmental advancements, the global environmental movement flourished. There were rapid and far-reaching developments in U.S. environmental regulations and federally enacted protections through government oversight. Refer to the sidebar for a summary of these issues and impacts.

---

[1] Franklin Delano Roosevelt, Executive Order no. 6777 (establishing the National Resources Board), June 30th, 1934, http://www.presidency.ucsb.edu/ws/print.php?pid=14715 (accessed August 16, 2007).
[2] Frank N. Laird, *Solar Energy, Technology Policy and Institutional Values* (Cambridge and New York: Cambridge University Press, 2001).

ADDITIONAL POST–WORLD WAR II ENVIRONMENTAL MILESTONES

1948: The United Nations Educational, Scientific, and Cultural Organization (UNESCO) established the International Union for the Preservation of Nature (IUPN), Switzerland/Belgium.

1949: The IUPN convened a UN Scientific Conference on the Conservation and Utilization of Resources in New York.

1956: The IUPN became the International Union for the Conservation of Nature (ICUN) and Natural Resources because scientists and ecologists got involved.

1960: The World Wildlife Fund (WWF) became the fund-raising branch of ICUN.

On the international political landscape of the 1970s and 1980s, environmental consciousness bore the activist tone of new environmentalism and carried it to the political arena. The birth of "greens" and their assimilation into mainstream politics as the Green Party was a further coup for environmentalists (Figure 3-3). The Green Party developed in Germany in 1979, and though their platform was largely environmental, their members also opposed nuclear power and supported the peace movement and feminist ideals.

Other green parties flourished between 1978 and 1984 in Switzerland, Belgium, West Germany, Luxembourg, Austria, Finland, Italy, Sweden, Ireland, and the Netherlands. Since then, green parties have formed in Canada, Mexico, Peru, Australia, New Zealand, North Korea, and numerous other countries in Europe, Eastern Europe, and Asia. Alternative environmental parties such as the British Ecology Party and the Mouvement d'Ecologie Politique in France were established in 1973 and 1980, respectively.

Figure 3-3 Green parties, which follow the values of the original German Green Party, flourish internationally.

U.S. ENVIRONMENTAL LEGISLATION
1970–2000s

1970s

- 1969: National Environmental Policy Act.
- U.S. Environmental Protection Agency (EPA) and the Council on Environmental Quality established.
- 1970: Clean Air Act.
- 1972: Clean Water Act.
- Protections for marine mammals, and endangered species.
- Regulations on ocean dumping, pesticide and water quality controls, radiation programs, toxic substances.
- 1975: Fuel-efficiency standards set.
- 1976: Resource Conservation and Recovery Act (control of hazardous waste disposal).
- 1977: Department of Energy (DOE) established.
- 1979: Solar thermal panels were installed on the White House (Carter Administration).

1980s

- 1980: Superfund Act.
- Emphasis on energy conservation and efficiency.
- 1980: Solar thermal panels on White House were removed (Reagan Administration).
- 1981: *The Global 2000 Report to the President* (commissioned by President Carter) released by the Council on Environmental Quality.[3]
- 1986: Safe Drinking Water Act.
- Deregulation of many environmental regulations.
- Congress reinforced existing environmental laws.

1990s

- Pollution Prevention Act.
- Tighter amendments to Clean Air Act.
- Energy Policy Act of 1992: Revised energy codes, provided support for alternative energy sources.

- Issues: Clean technology, environmental outreach to minorities, global warming, ozone layer depletion.
- California Desert Protection Act.
- Rio treaties signed.
- Regulations: pollution emissions controls.
- Congressional cutbacks on existing federal environmental programs.

2000s

- EPA Energy Star budget cuts.
- EPA weakens plans for testing pesticides and reporting standards for chemical industry.
- Protections on wildlife areas and forests are eased.
- Threefold increase in oil and gas drilling permits.
- Energy Policy Act of 2005: Increased coal energy and ethanol production; provided energy companies with tax incentives and loan guarantees for energy technology. Oil drilling in the Arctic National Wildlife Refuge removed from final bill.
- No support for Kyoto protocol ratification.
- Carbon dioxide (CO_2) deemed not a pollutant under the Clean Air Act.
- Administration and auto industry in lawsuit to overturn California's zero emissions vehicle rule.
- U.S. Forest Service approves roads and logging in some national forests; no permit under the Clean Water Act would be required for some projected roads near wetlands.
- Energy Independence and Security Act of 2007: grants for ethanol, coal, landfills, and biomass and waste incineration; loosens definition of "renewable energy"; incandescent bulbs phased out; new fuel economy standards; relaxed laws that cite polluters of "isolated water bodies."

The Conferences

In the late 1970s political leaders began to notice that environmental crises cut across all regions of the planet, affecting both less developed countries and industrialized nations, with large and small populations alike.

Countries such as Kenya and India saw burgeoning grassroots environmental and wildlife nongovernmental organizations (NGOs).[4] Issues such as wetlands'

[3] Gerald O. Barney, *The Global 2000 Report to the President, A Report Prepared by the Council of Environmental Quality and the Department of State* (Charlottesville, VA: Blue Angel, 1981), 1. Researchers used computer modeling to predict future environmental and demographic trends. One of the report's conclusions stated: "If present trends continue, the world in 2000 will be more crowded, and more vulnerable to disruption than the world we live in now. Serious stresses involving population, resources, and environment are clearly visible ahead. Despite greater material output, the world's people will be poorer in many ways than they are today."

[4] John McCormick, *Reclaiming Paradise: The Global Environment Movement* (Bloomington: Indiana University Press, 1989).

pollution and acid rain crossed political and geographic boundaries. Of course, developing nations face enormous challenges in providing education and health care to (and supporting gender equity for) their populations. It has been difficult to focus on issues such as renewable energy, if the goal is perceived to be at the expense of job creation and economic self-sufficiency in Africa or improving living conditions in the favelas of Rio de Janeiro, Brazil, for example.

In addition, many developing countries lack the environmental policy to use as a tool for implementing new international accords. Their monumental social burdens may trump traditionally defined environmental issues and delay environmental, or "green," policies. Often a distinction is drawn between sustainability for developing and developed countries, a "brown" sustainability as opposed to "green." This tradeoff is discussed in *Agenda 21 for Sustainable Construction in Developing Countries*:

> In general, the Green Agenda, which focuses on the problems of affluence and over-consumption, is more pressing in affluent countries. The Brown Agenda, which focuses on the problems of poverty and underdevelopment, emphasizes the need to reduce the environmental threats to health that arise from poor sanitary conditions, crowding, inadequate water provision, hazardous air and water pollution, and local accumulations of solid waste.[5]

Figure 3-4 Emblem of the United Nations.

Figure 3-5 Emblem of the United Nations Environmental Programme.

The environmental movement at least attempted to achieve global unity, beginning with the first UN Conference on the Human Environment in 1972 in Stockholm, Sweden. Other international conferences followed, with varying results as to buy-in, action plans, and future goals. Most prompted the founding of environmental protection agencies within various countries. They also ignited international treaties on the environment. For our purposes, we will focus on the series of such conferences with most bearing on green building.

1972 Stockholm Conference

New environmentalism assumed a political tone in 1972 during the Stockholm Conference, the UN Conference on the Human Environment, which is considered to be a watershed event because of the cascade of UN conferences that followed. The goal of the conference was to draft strategies to correct global environmental problems.

One of the outcomes was the UN Environment Programme (UNEP), which was charged with enacting the twenty-six principles of the resulting Stockholm Declaration.[6] Additionally, an action plan was devised that covered issues of natural resources, human rights, sustainable development, and environmental standards for each country. The consciousness-raising of the conferences spurred Western environmentalists to understand concern for the environment on a global level.[7]

1984 Brundtland Commission

Another bellwether UN conference was convened in Geneva in 1984. A highlight of the conference was the World Commission on the Environment and Development (WCED) charge to its chair, Gro Harlem Brundtland, to produce a report, which was published in 1987 and is known as *Our Common Future*.

The Brundtland Commission report focused on issues of population, food security, species and ecosystem health, energy, industry, and a variety of urban challenges. It concluded that social ills and environmental health are parallel concerns and interlinked issues. In other words, the degree of environmental degradation corresponds to the level of poverty within the developing countries. Chrisna du Plessis notes that "while the developing world consumes far fewer resources, and releases far less greenhouse gasses than the developed world, the environmental degradation experienced has a more direct and visible impact and presents a more immediate threat to the survival of the poor."[8] Sustainable development was one of the common concerns emerging from

[5] *Agenda 21 for Sustainable Construction in Developing Countries, A discussion document,* The International Council for Research and Innovation in Building and Construction and the United Nations Environment Programme, International Environmental Technology Centre (UNEP-IETC), Chrisna du Plessis, CSIR Building and Construction Technology, Pretoria South Africa, 2002, paragraph 2.2.1, page 9.

[6] Stockholm Declaration (June 1972), http://www.unep.org/Documents.Multilingual/Default.asp?DocumentID=97&ArticleID=1503.
[7] McCormick, *Reclaiming Paradise*, 99.
[8] *Agenda 21 for Sustainable Construction in Developing Countries,* op. cit. paragraph 3.1, page 22.

the WCED. Emerging from the Geneva conference was a definition of sustainable development that has been embraced by the green building movement. Sustainable development was determined to be "development that meets the needs of the present without compromising the ability of future generations to meet their own needs."[9]

1987 Montreal Protocol

The ratification of the treaty known as the Montreal Protocol on Substances that Deplete the Ozone Layer in 1987 is worth mentioning because it has led to improvements in building practices and operations, specifically those relating to refrigerants used in mechanical systems, fire retardants, and cleaning materials.

The protocol called for phasing out chlorofluorocarbon (CFC), a halogenated hydrocarbon with ozone-depleting potential, by 1999. Alternatives to CFCs—e.g., hydrofluorocarbons (HFCs) and hydrochlorofluorocarbons (HCFCs)—unfortunately, have significant global warming potential. The Leadership in Energy and Environmental Design (LEED) Rating System awards points for the elimination of CFCs and HCFCs.

Currently, HCFCs are expected to be phased out by 2030.[10] Verifiable results indicate that the ozone layer is responding to actions suggested by the treaty. The treaty, which had been signed by 191 countries as of August 2007, is an example of a successful international accord.

1992 Rio de Janeiro Earth Summit (Eco '92)

In 1992, 179 governments attended the UN Conference on Environment and Development in Rio de Janeiro, Brazil.[11]

The initial follow-up to the 1972 Stockholm Conference took place in Kenya in 1982, but it did not result in meaningful progress. In addition to several key issues, among them alternative energy, production of toxins, public transit, water shortages, and the rights of indigenous people, the issue of economic and sustainable development was again discussed, with an emphasis on the needs of the urban and rural poor.[12]

The Rio summit was another landmark event, because it "influenced all subsequent UN conferences, which have examined the relationship between human rights,

population, social development, women and human settlements—and the need for environmentally sustainable development."[13] The five reports resulting from Rio were:

- *The Rio Declaration*, containing twenty-seven principles ranging from transport of toxins across borders to implementing the precautionary principle to sustainable development: http://habitat.igc.org/agenda21/rio-dec.htm.
- *Agenda 21*, which set forth detailed objectives, action plans, and implementation strategies for environmental and developmental sustainability: http://habitat.igc.org/agenda21/.
- *Statement of Forest Principles*, a nonbinding agreement, which was the first such agreement on international sustainable forestry practices: http://www.iisd.org/rio+5/agenda/principles.htm.
- *Convention on Biological Diversity*, one of the two legally binding conventions dealing with species preservation: http://www.cbd.int/default.shtml.
- *Framework Convention on Climate Change*, the second legally binding agreement resulting from the conference that became the basis for the Kyoto Protocol: http://unfccc.int/not_assigned/b/items/1417.php.

1997 Kyoto Protocol

The Kyoto Protocol, a treaty crafted by the United Nations Framework Convention on Climate Change (UNFCCC) in 1997, was the result of one of the action items from the 1992 Rio Earth Summit. The Kyoto Protocol calls for countries to commit to the reduction of greenhouse gases, including carbon dioxide (CO_2), or trade their emissions where necessary (Figure 3-6).[14]

The U.S. target was a 7 percent reduction of 1990 levels by the year 2012.[15] The Kyoto Protocol bears particular relevance to the study of green buildings, because buildings are responsible for 43 percent of U.S. carbon dioxide emissions as a by-product of construction, refrigerant management, and energy-system operations. This statistic was produced by the Pew Center on Global Climate Change and calculates the contributions of industrial buildings at 5 percent, commercial buildings at 17 percent, and residential buildings at 21 percent.[16]

By February 2005, the effective date of the implementation of the Protocol, 141 countries had ratified the

[9] Brundtland Commission Report, http://www.un-documents.net/wced-ocf.htm.

[10] Ozone Secretariat and the United Nations Environment Programme, *Handbook for the Montreal Protocol on Substances that Deplete the Ozone Layer*, 7th ed. (Nairobi, Kenya: Secretariat of the Vienna Convention for the Protection of the Ozone Layer and the Montreal Protocol on Substances that Deplete the Ozone Layer, United Nations Environment Programme, 2006, http://ozone.unep.org/Publications/MP_Handbook/index.shtml (accessed January 4, 2009).

[11] Information on the Rio Earth Summit: http://www.un.org/geninfo/bp/enviro.html.

[12] Rio Declaration (1992), http://www.un.org/documents/ga/conf151/aconf15126-1annex1.htm.

[13] UN Conference on Environment and Development, http://www.un.org/geninfo/bp/enviro.html.

[14] Kyoto Protocol Reference Manual on Accounting of Emissions and Assigned Amounts, United Nations Framework Convention on Climate Change (UNFCCC) Secretariat, February 2007, http://unfccc.int/kyoto_protocol/items/2830.php. For real-time streaming and updating on carbon dioxide (CO_2) emissions, see: http://breathingearth.net/.

[15] Kyoto Protocol Reference Manual, http://unfccc.int/kyoto_protocol/items/2830.php.

[16] The Pew Center on Global Climate Change, http://www.pewclimate.org.

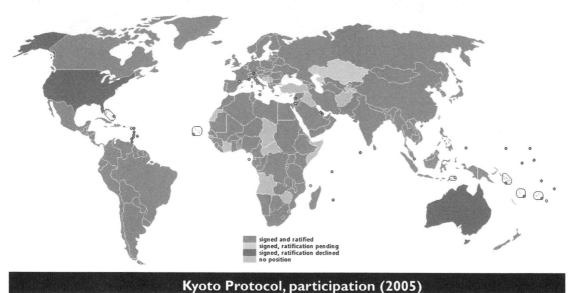

Kyoto Protocol, participation (2005)

signed and ratified
signed, ratification pending
signed, ratification declined
no position

Figure 3-6 The UN Convention on Climate Change in Kyoto, Japan.

protocol and signed on to reduce their greenhouse gas emissions. As of July 2008, 182 countries had ratified and accepted the protocol.[17] The treaty expires in 2012.

Although the United States has not agreed to accept or ratify the Kyoto Protocol, over 600 U.S. cities have agreed to participate in the U.S. Mayors Climate Change Agreement, a mirror of the Kyoto Protocol, that asks civic leaders to develop policies from a menu of twelve action strategies, such as limiting sprawl; funding clean technology and alternative energy; investing in alternative transportation; revising energy-efficiency codes for buildings;

increasing fuel-efficiency standards for municipal fleets; implementing LEED or similar green building rating system; improving recycling efforts; and performing outreach and mentorship to schools, industry, and business.[18]

2002 Johannesburg Earth Summit (Rio +10)

The fourth conference that sprouted from the 1972 Stockholm Conference took place in Johannesburg, South Africa (Figure 3-7). The UN World Summit on Sustainable Development resulted in the Johannesburg

---

[17]For an up-to-date list of Kyoto Protocol ratifying countries, see: http://unfccc.int/kyoto_protocol/background/status_of_ratification/items/2613.php.

[18]The U.S. Conference of Mayors, Mayors Climate Protection Center, http://usmayors.org/climateprotection/ClimateChange.asp and http://usmayors.org/climateprotection/documents/mcpAgreement.pdf.

Plan of Implementation. The plan focused on social issues such as the eradication of poverty, improvement of health conditions, and promotion of economic vigor in developing nations.

The summit recognized the three prongs of sustainability established in 1992 in Rio de Janeiro: economic development, social development, and environmental protection. Specifically, the delegates agreed "to focus

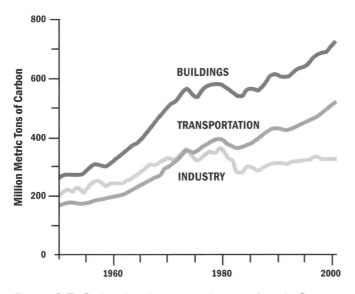

Figure 3-7 Carbon dioxide emissions by sector from the Pew Center.

the world's attention and direct action toward meeting difficult challenges, including improving people's lives and conserving our natural resources in a world that is growing in population, with ever-increasing demands for food, water, shelter, sanitation, energy, health services and economic security."[19]

The United States did not send a delegation to this important conference, but the tenets and commitment to Rio's Agenda 21 were pledged by representatives of many other countries, along with leaders of industry, business, and NGOs.

But one of the most valuable things to emerge from the conference was the importance of sustainable development and green building in less-developed nations.

The UNEP commissioned South African architect, researcher, and activist Chrisna du Plessis to produce *Agenda 21 for Sustainable Construction in Developing Countries* as a contribution to the Johannesburg Earth Summit, which focused on the particular sustainability needs of developing nations.[20]

In brief, *Agenda 21* addressed the need for improving the construction process in developing nations, formulating new construction technologies that conserve resources, energy-efficient operations, water conservation, and responsible waste management practices. In addition, the problems of sustainable housing and the problems of rural and urban social justice were addressed. All were lessons for international best practices in green building.

Figure 3-8 Delegates to the Johannesburg, South Africa, UN World Summit on Sustainable Development in 2002.

[19]Johannesburg World Summit on Sustainable Development, 2002, http://www.un.org/jsummit/html/basic_info/basicinfo.html.
[20]*Agenda 21 for Sustainable Construction in Developing Countries*, op cit.

After Kyoto

Because the Kyoto Protocol expires in 2012, preparations are underway for a successor to the treaty. Talks began in February 2007, through the G8+5 (eight industrialized nations plus Brazil, China, India, Mexico, and South Africa) Climate Change Dialogue, and these talks are expected to continue for several years.

A significant signal of support for Kyoto's goals came in June 2007, when these eight industrialized nations agreed to the Heiligendamm Process, which is intended to involve and assist emerging countries in energy-efficiency efforts and pledges to cut global carbon dioxide emissions by 50 percent by the year 2050.[21] Again, this resolve has relevance to green building technology.

2007 UN Framework Convention on Climate Change, Bali

In Bali, participants of the Kyoto meeting of 1997, representatives from about 180 countries, and observers from intergovernmental and nongovernmental organizations met to discuss a proposed international agreement to reduce carbon emissions according to Kyoto's mandate. This is known as the "Bali roadmap," because it did not delineate actual reductions; rather it paved the way for future discussions before the 2009 target date.[22]

■ Key Trends

This chapter calls attention to key international environmental milestones broadly. The chapters that follow describe how green building emerged from this background.

EXERCISES

1. International environmental summits have addressed themes ranging from ozone protection, pollutant reduction, and carbon dioxide (CO_2) emissions. What criticisms have been leveled at the results of these conferences? To what extent is it possible to achieve global accord on environmental matters? What can be done to ensure future successes of such conferences?

2. Famously, Kyoto's Protocol recommended CO_2 emissions reductions, which 41 countries had ratified by 2005. What were the reasons given by the countries that signed but did not ratify?

■ Resources

Rio Declaration on Environment and Development (1992) http://habitat.igc.org/agenda21/rio-dec.htm

Agenda 21 for Sustainable Construction in Developing Countries, A Discussion Document, http://habitat.igc.org/agenda21/

United Nations Conference on the Human Environment (Stockholm, Sweden), 1997, http://www.unep.org/Documents.Multilingual/Default.asp?DocumentID=97.

Brundtland Commission Report (World Commission on the Environment and Development, Geneva, Switzerland, 1984), June 1987, http://www.un-documents.net/wced-ocf.htm.

Johannesburg (South Africa) World Summit on Sustainable Development, 2002, http://www.un.org/jsummit/html/brochure/brochure12.pdf.

The Pew Center on Global Climate Change, http://www.pew-climate.org.

United Nations Framework Convention on Climate Change, 2007, http://unfccc.int/meetings/cop_13/items/4049.php.

Intergovernmental Panel on Climate Change, http://www.ipcc.ch.

Montreal Protocol on Substances that Deplete the Ozone Layer, Sept. 16, 1987 26 ILM 1541.

Cartagena Protocol on Biosafety, www.biodiv.org/ (2000).

Second World Climate Conference 1YB *International Environmental Law* 473, 475 (1990).

Stockholm Convention on Persistent Organic Pollutants, www.pops.int (2000).

---

[21] G8 Summit 2007 Heiligendamm, "Breakthrough on Climate Protection," http://www.g-8.de/nn_92160/Content/EN/Artikel/__g8-summit/2007-06-07-g8-klimaschutz__en.html.

[22] United Nations Framework Convention on Climate Change (2007), http://unfccc.int/meetings/cop_13/items/4049.php.

4 The Emergence of Green Building and Green Building Legislation

Defining Green Building

The concept of building green grows naturally from the fertile history of environmentalism. As recently as ten years ago, however, the phrase "green building" brought to mind a bold yet unrefined philosophy whose proponents desired to live independently and disconnected from society. Words associated with green building in the U.S. of the 1960s and 1970s included "earth-sheltered," "self-sufficient," and "ecological" (Figure 4-1). Today, we more often hear words such as "integrated," "efficient," "high-performing," "elegant," and "restorative" applied to green buildings (Figure 4-2).

The integrated whole building approach, which considers life cycle at all levels, is essential to our contemporary definition of green building.

Formal definition of contemporary green building abound, but all converge on at least one of several

Figure 4-2 The elegant and green Lotus House, designed by Michelle Kaufmann Designs, in front of San Francisco's City Hall during the West Coast Green Conference in 2007.

critical components, and most practitioners agree that a green building must solve more than one environmental challenge (e.g., natural resource depletion, landfill overflow, carbon emissions). Although it cannot provide solutions for all of the challenges, a green building must:

- Tackle site-demolition issues and construction-and-packaging-waste issues, as well as waste generated by users of the building.
- Strive for efficiency in a broad area of resource use.
  - Minimize the impact of mining and harvesting for materials production and provide measures for replenishing natural resources.
  - Reduce soil, water, and energy use during materials manufacture, building construction, and occupant use.
  - Plan for low embodied energy during shipment.
  - Proceed logically, as the chain of materials production is traced.
- Conserve and design for the efficiency of energy consumed by powering mechanical systems for heating

Figure 4-1 The iconic Earthship, made from used tires and occasionally beer cans, uses passive heating and cooling strategies and ingeniously channels waste products away from the waste stream.

Figure 4-3 Malian earthen architecture. Three billion people worldwide live or work in earthen structures. Twenty percent of buildings on the World Heritage List are earthen buildings.

Figure 4-4 The oil embargo led to gasoline rationing in the 1970s.

and cooling, lighting, and plug loads. Because building construction is a tremendous emitter of carbon dioxide (CO_2), planning for the reduction of carbon emissions is a great challenge and will soon become a nonnegotiable social and political mandate.

• Provide a "healthy" indoor environment:
  • Avoid building and cleaning materials that emit volatile organic compounds (VOCs) and their synergistic interactions.
  • Avoid equipment without controls or appropriate filters for particulate entry or production.
  • Control entry of outdoor pollutants through proper air filtration, ventilation, and walk-off mats, as well as occupant-borne contaminants, such as personal care products.
  • Design a connection to the exterior providing natural ventilation, daylight, and views.

Until the U.S. Green Building Council's Leadership in Energy and Environmental Design (LEED) rating system or other sustainable guidelines become a mandated national standard, accepted by bodies such as the American Society for Testing Materials (ASTM) or the American Society of Heating, Refrigerating and Air-Conditioning Engineers (ASHRAE), there is no national, legally enforceable definition of green building. Although municipalities and government agencies have adopted LEED and sustainable building programs individually, sadly, a rock-solid directive will not emerge until the decision to build green is no longer a choice but a necessity. However, as one can see from the descriptions above, a common theme surfaces—green building equals good design.

Green buildings have a robust design legacy. One can point to countless buildings (Figure 4-3) that could be considered well-designed, because their design adapted to regional climates; made efficient use of readily available construction materials and tested techniques; ensured

a level of comfort through heat storage (via thermal mass); or reaped the benefits of the environment by storing water.

Pockets of countercultural forces were inspired by the intelligence and efficiency of such building strategies.

The Roots of Green Building[1]

The roots of the modern green building movement in North America are lodged in economic and environmental landmarks. The tradition of building intelligently was significantly redefined after the fossil-fueled economies of North America ignored the essence of good design and instead designed tighter buildings to mitigate the political impacts of oil availability rather than adapt to its effects. Response to the mid-1970s oil embargo by OPEC (the Organization of Petroleum Exporting Countries), with some exceptions, led to design of tightly sealed buildings to reduce heating and cooling costs. This practice was the predominant response to restrictions on oil importation. Ironically, this trend toward tighter buildings became a touchstone of the green building movement, in terms of energy conservation and indoor air quality, which will be addressed in a separate chapter.[2] (Figure 4-4 illustrates the impact of gas rationing, due to the oil embargo, on the daily lives of North Americans.)

Yet, the oil crisis bore unexpected benefits, because it made personal the need for conserving household energy, developing alternatives for energy delivery, and rationing gasoline for fuel conservation. This interest in energy efficiency led to the establishment of federal agencies with missions propelled by the environmental movement.

---

[1]Portions of this chapter first appeared in connection with a California Public Employees' Retirement System (CalPERS) LEED application.
[2]Tighter buildings also were the basis for other negative consequences: e.g., bad indoor air quality, sick building syndrome, and building-related illness.

The early 1970s were witness to the birth of the U.S. Environmental Protection Agency (EPA) and the Department of Energy (DOE). The building industry followed suit with the development of the American Institute of Architects (AIA) Committee on Energy, which evolved into today's AIA Committee on the Environment (COTE). Green building emerged from these groups, and it was seen as a multibranched discipline, encompassing a concern for the life cycle and waste generation of building materials, soil and water conservation, indoor air and indoor environmental quality, and, as well, the original linchpin, energy reduction.

In the 1990s, the Clinton administration issued several executive orders related to the environment, establishing a case study through the Greening of the White House project. Later, President Bill Clinton established the President's Council on Sustainable Development. The federal government seized upon the benefits of the sustainable building movement to enact green benchmarks for many government branches, including the military, national parks, and numerous agency buildings.

Environmental Toll

When governments and municipalities begin legislating green building measures, it indicates that an economic basis exists that supports change in how we make buildings. Streamlined operating costs, improved worker efficiency, and durable buildings mean money saved in the long run.

But it also pays to be mindful of the extensive environmental damage that is avoided when constructing sustainable buildings. According to the U.S. Green Building Council (USGBC), "the building industry is one of the most energy and water intensive industries on the planet."[3]

Buildings account for 48 percent of total energy use[4] and 73.1 percent of electricity consumption in the United States (Figure 4-5).[5] They are also responsible for 30 percent of U.S. greenhouse gas emissions, and expend 30 percent of raw materials. Close to 136 million tons of waste are produced on an annual basis from buildings and their construction.[6] As well, the building industry soaks up 12 percent of our fresh drinking water.

---

[3]The U.S. Green Building Council, http//:www.usgbc.org.
[4]U.S. Energy Information Administration data as presented by Architecture 2030, http://www.architecture2030.org/current_situation/building_sector.html. The percentage varies according to the reporting agency. For example, percentage of energy consumed by buildings is often listed as 39 percent by the USGBC and DOE. USGBC statistics appear on http://www.usgbc.org/DisplayPage.aspx?cmspageID=1718.
[5]U.S. Department of Energy, *Buildings Energy Data Book* (Washington, DC: U.S. Department of Energy, 2008, available for download at http://buildingsdatabook.eren.doe.gov/Default.aspx).
[6]U.S. Environmental Protection Agency (EPA) Municipal and Industrial Solid Waste Division, "Characterization of Construction and Demolition Debris in the United States," prepared by Franklin Associates, Prairie Village, Kansas, June 1998.

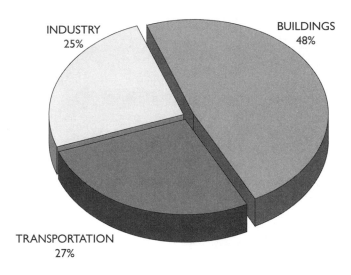

US ENERGY CONSUMPTION

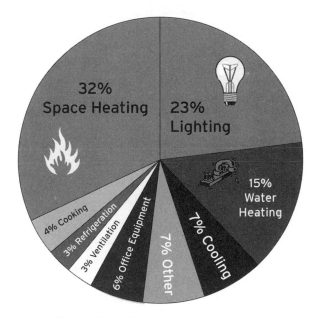

Figures 4-5 a, b Three illustrations show energy-consumption figures from Architecture 2030, the U.S. Energy Information Administration, and the 2003 Commercial Buildings Energy Consumption Survey.

Buildings are clearly responsible for an enormous environmental burden. The response to this environmental degradation has been, since the OPEC oil embargo of the 1970s, the green building movement.

The oil price increases of the 1970s spurred significant research activity to improve energy efficiency and find renewable energy sources. This, combined with the environmental movement of the 1960s and 1970s, led to the earliest experiments with contemporary green building. In 2008, rising fuel costs, once again, spurred heightened research and development, but this time in clean and renewable energy technology.

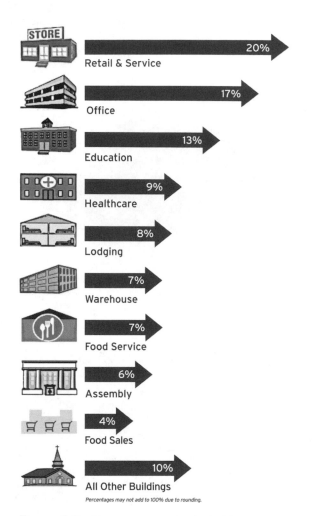

Figure 4-5c Energy consumption by building type.

Figure 4-6 The modern aesthetic of this Corona-brand solar-powered outdoor light-emitting diode (LED) lamp speaks to the elegance in green technology. Photovoltaic cells transform sunlight into energy during the day, and its LEDs automatically start to glow when the sun sets. It uses no glues or fasteners, making it simple to disassemble for recycling or salvage.

Green Building Today

Green building has emerged from its rustic genesis and association with an alternative-lifestyles culture and a belt-tightening philosophy. It is no longer emblematic of a countercultural sociopolitical movement; rather, green buildings of the twenty-first century make sense as machines, appliances, and industrial design; they are high-performance inventions (Figure 4-6).

Just as there are high-performance audiovisual components, appliances, and automobiles, there are also high-performance buildings in terms of their energy utilization, indoor air quality, and resource expenditure (or natural capital consumption). The benefits of these high-performance buildings are quantifiable and authentic to owners, occupants, designers, and builders.[7]

At a very basic level, integrated building design can be associated with the Gaia concept proposed by James Lovelock—namely, a building can be seen as an organism comprised of interacting and interrelated systems (Figure 4-7). In the world of metrics and results, however, integrated sustainable design's benefits speak directly to the triple bottom line (Figure 4-8), supplemented by its goals to keep people healthy, reduce waste, save energy, and lower operating costs.

To the *owner and developer*, the fruits of green building mean a rapid return on investment and a swift sale or lease that reduces carrying costs.

To the *facilities manager*, long-lasting and low-maintenance materials, products, and systems spell less frequent replacement costs and a reduced maintenance schedule.

To the *employee*, comparing the prospect of working in a green building's comfortable and controllable indoor environment with a mainstream office environment can be a deciding factor in choosing one job over another.

To the *homeowner*, a green home can provide a healthful indoor environment, durable materials and systems, and lower energy costs.

Although the economic, health, social, and environmental benefits are wide-ranging, they can be understood and assessed in an integrated way. In a later chapter, we will examine the methods commonly used to analyze and set goals for green building design through the use of a number of national and international rating systems.[8]

---

[7]See Matthiessen and Morris, "The Cost of Green Revisited."

[8]"Making the Case for Green Building," *Environmental Building News* 14, No. 4 (April 2005).

Figure 4-7 Paolo Soleri's Arcosanti embodies the concept of *arcology*, the interaction of living systems with architecture.

Figure 4-8 The triple bottom line links economic, environmental, and social sustainability.

Green Policy, Permitting, and Politics in the United States

William J. Worthen, AIA, LEED AP

If Mother Nature were a credit card company, then climate change might be her way of reminding us that we have been carrying a very large and growing balance for all those natural resources and fossil fuels consumed since we started using machine-based manufacturing, steam power, internal combustion engines, and electrical power generation. She is giving us notice to begin making arrangements for a payment plan, and soon; if not, she will have no choice but to cancel our account and refer us to her collections agency.

Measured in climate change currency (atmospheric tons of carbon dioxide), since the Industrial Revolution the natural resources we burn and consume have allowed us to build our society and mass produce most of the things we use and consume inexpensively; but as we now understand, these things have not come cheaply. Despite all of humanity's accomplishments, we have been living on Mother Nature's tab, which is about to come due. There is no free lunch.

Green building policies, permit requirements, and building codes are ways to bring sustainable design from the realm of voluntary initiatives to mandated public policy. These methods provide a way for the design and construction of new buildings to become part of the solution as well as the payment plan to Mother Nature (before that balloon payment comes due). Implementing effective green policies in today's building codes, along with the required transitions and changes to our socio-economic structure and to the "way things are done" in modern capitalist societies, will continue to play an increasing role in the politics of this century.

Function of Modern Building Codes

Modern *model building codes* are an integrated set of building regulations adopted by a local government with or without modification of the body of law pertaining to all aspects of a building construction. Codes typically use nationally accepted safety, materials, and testing standards; they are designed to protect building occupants and to set minimum standards acceptable for all building types as well as allowable methods for construction and building systems.

Many of today's built environment are products of code-minimum design; that is, most building projects use the least-bad allowable by the applicable building code to recieve the necessary permits and be granted a certificate of occupancy by local code officials. Design decisions are typically governed by simple first-cost economics and project schedules.

Green building codes represent a fundamental paradigm shift from code-minimum design and lowest-common-denominator construction standards. Green building policies are distinct. Instead of code-minimum design, green building codes foster—and in many cases mandate—specific high-performance materials and energy performance. The way we measure the viability and economic implications of such policies is by looking at perhaps the best precedent for the future green building ordinances—in San Francisco, California.

San Francisco Ordinance

On August 4, 2008, the mayor of San Francisco, Gavin Newsom, signed what was arguably the most comprehensive green building ordinance (Ord. No. 180-08) adopted by any government in the nation.[9] The legislation is comprehensive and aggressive, defining quantifiable green building goals for construction, with phased-in, incremental requirements over time, and the ordinance applies to all permitted new commercial, new residential, and major new commercial renovations. The green building ordinance represents the collaborative efforts of the city's planning and building inspection departments

SAN FRANCISCO'S GREEN BUILDING ORDINANCE

San Francisco's Green Building policy requires all newly constructed commercial office buildings over 5,000 gross square feet and major building alterations over 25,000 gross square feet to achieve base-level LEED Certification from the USGBC, and then steadily increase the level of required certification to LEED Gold level certification by 2012. This policy will also apply to all sizes and types of residential construction, but smaller projects will not be required to use LEED. Rather, an alternative, residentially based system known as GreenPoint Rated[10] will be required. The GreenPoint Rated system is designed for smaller-scale and single- and multi-family design, construction, and renovation and is based primarily on field verifications and documentation better suited to this type of construction.

and the mayor's office with a coalition of design, construction, and real estate industry leaders.

San Francisco may be the first U.S. city to take this step, but it will by no means be the last. Green building policies and ordinances, priority permitting plans, carbon-reduction pledges, and zero-waste efforts are being adopted by city councils across the country (Figure 4-9). To understand this movement toward green building, it is necessary to examine it through the lens of the development of federal energy policy over the last half century and to review the events leading to today's U.S. Department of Energy and its research and efficiency standards agencies. In the process, we will see how the phrase *green buildings* came to imply a better-than-industry-standard conventional building in both design and construction. It is also worth noting that green building ordinances will be most successful when the municipalities' planning principles encourage infill with high density, walkable communities and transit-oriented oriented design instead of low-density suburban sprawl.

Where We Are Today

The Energy Policy Act of 2005 is the first U.S. policy that includes high-performance buildings as a way to reduce the country's energy consumption. The act also acknowledges global climate change as fact and as something that needs to be addressed in U.S. energy policy. The Energy Independence and Security Act of 2007 includes the reduction of building-related energy with the need to reduce our foreign dependence on fossil fuels. These two federal Acts combined with Executive Order 13423, Strengthening Federal Environmental, Energy and Transportation Management, signed by President George W. Bush and the 2007 Federal Leadership in High Performance and Sustainable Buildings Memorandum of Understanding (Guiding Principles MOU), 2006 are key components defining green priorities in federal policy and funding.

The current climate change crisis is fundamentally about the characteristics of energy technologies and energy conservation, and, much in the same vein as the energy crisis of the 1970s, has triggered a movement toward green. Today that same desire to conserve and maximize the efficiency of our energy supply as well as to seek new and cleaner energy technologies is encouraging builders to rediscover time-tested natural, passive, and elegant solutions to energy-efficient building design. The impetus, however, is slightly different than the green building movement of the 1970s. As discussed in the beginning of this chapter, early experiments in green living were considered a countercultural ideal. By contrast, modern green buildings in the United States germinated primarily from a single motivator—financial incentives.

The State of New York in 2000 enacted a Green Building Tax Credit Program to provide incentives of up to $2 million per building, which can be applied to corporate or personal insurance or to banking corporate

---

[9]San Francisco Green Building Ordinance (Ord. No. 180-08, added September 4, 2008). Available for download at http://www.sfenvironment.org/downloads/library/sf_green_building_ordinance_2008.pdf
[10]"Introducing GreenPoint Rated: Your Assurance of a Better Place to Live," http://www.builditgreen.org/greenpoint-rated.

NATIONAL GREEN BUILDING ORDINANCE COMPARISON
COMMERCIAL AND RESIDENTIAL REQUIREMENTS (partial listing)

CITY	Commercial	Residential	Alteration
San Francisco	YES 25, 000 sf*	YES ALL**	YES
Austin	NO Utility Incentives	NO	NO
Boston	YES 50,000 sf LEED Cert-2007	NO	NO
Chicago	NO	NO	NO
New York	NO Tax Incentives	NO	NO
Pasadena	YES 25, 000 sf Non-LEED Cert	YES 4+ stories Non-LEED Cert	NO
Pleasanton	YES 20,000 sf Non-LEED Cert	YES 2,000+ sf Alameda County	NO
Portland	NO State Tax Credits	NO	NO
Seattle	NO Zoning Bonuses	NO	NO
Washington DC	YES 50,000 sf LEED Cert 2012	NO	NO

All cities on this list have City and/or Municiple LEED requirements
The information reflects Private commercial and residential requirements and standards

* Stepped LEED requirement: Cert-2008 thru Gold 2012
** Stepped Green Points Rating Score: 25 2009 thru GPR-75 2012

Figure 4-9 Summary of commercial and residential requirements of various U.S. cities, as of June 2007 (partial listing). Many municipalities across the United States and Canada have adopted green building regulations or incentives in some form.

Figure 4-10 Federal support for energy-related innovation can be seen in educational events such as the Solar Decathlon. Technische Universität Darmstadt was one of seven teams to score a perfect 100 points in the Energy Balance contest as part of the 2007 Solar Decathlon sponsored by the U.S. Department of Energy. Energy balance refers to a balance between energy inputs and energy outputs, or net zero energy.

The American Recovery and Reinvestment Act of 2009

The economic stimulus package then President-elect Barack Obama requested of the 111th Congress on December 6, 2008, in its House of Representatives draft form (at date of this publication) allocates approximately $850 billion to three basic stimulus categories: middle-class tax and higher education tuition relief; medical expense relief; and direct aid to states for infrastructure, energy efficiency, and green collar jobs training. Referencing many program federal bills and policies, including the Energy Independence and Security Act of 2007 and the Energy Policy Act of 2005, specific program funding appropriations are proposed including: $18.5 billion for 'Energy Efficiency and Renewable Energy'; $6.2 billion for 'Weatherization Assistance' and $3.4 billion for 'State Energy Programs.'

Federally Funded Areas of Research
Source: US Department of Energy

Source Energy	Energy Efficiency	Biological Sciences
Bioenergy	Buildings	Carbon Sequestration
Coal	ENERGY STAR	Chemical Science
Electric Power	Financing	Climate Change
Fossil Fuels	Homes	Computing
Fusion	Industry	Energy Sciences
Geothermal	Power Utilities	Environmental Science
Hydrogen	State Activities	Fusion Energy
Hydropower	Transportation	Genome Research
Natural Gas	Weatherization	Geoscience
Nuclear		Grants & Contracts
Oil		High Energy Physics
Renewables		Information Resources
Solar		Life Sciences
Wind		Materials Sciences
		Nanotechnology
		National Labs
		Nuclear Medicine
		Nuclear Physics
		National Science Bowl®
		Teaching & Education
		Workforce Development

Figure 4-11 A partial listing of federally funded areas of energy research.

taxes. The law required building owners and tenants to work through design and construction with the project design team to ensure the effectiveness of increased energy efficiency and indoor air quality and to reduce the various environmental impacts of commercial and residential buildings in the state. The Green Building Tax Credit Program offers owners and/or tenants six possible program components, from whole building and tenant build-outs to fuel cells and photovoltaic systems, with an original fund allocation of $25 Million In its original legislative form the law allowed applicants to apply a credit-component certificate in 2001–2004 and to claim the credits over five years.[11]

For the first time in the United States, green building design had a tangible financial benefit to offer large-scale commercial construction. Savvy developers seeking tax breaks promptly seized upon incentives. They soon learned that the added costs and design fees of green building were far outweighed by the incentives offered, and as well, along the way, green building itself added value to a project. The developer and design teams of the Hearst Tower and The Solaire, both in New York City, used tax breaks to pay for the buildings' green features (see Appendix A for summaries of these building projects). High-performance design made green a

financial deal, perhaps not as noble as the earnest green trend of the 1970s, but, nevertheless, a clever move demonstrating that major commercial developers had not only a use but a desire for green building rating systems that would quantify their commitment.

The History of U.S. Energy Policy

Not surprisingly, energy, in all its forms and political ramifications, has been on the minds of our political leaders and part of government since the race to develop nuclear weaponry during World War II. This is the provenance of today's United States Department of Energy (Figures 4-10 and 4-11). The question of our nation's energy security, since September 11, 2001, has risen to the forefront of federal policy. How energy is generated, consumed, protected, used as a weapon and method of control, cannot be overlooked under the lens of national security. Additionally, is an important key to the success of today's green building movement. After World War II, there was debate as to whether a civilian or military agency should control atomic energy technology, which had previously centered on the vast and largely mysterious Manhattan Project infrastructure, its research labs, and a payroll of world-renowned leaders doing atomic research.

The U.S. National Laboratory system was launched from the infrastructure of the Manhattan Project, and the Atomic Energy Commission was placed under civilian rather than military administration. In 1974 the Atomic Energy Commission was reorganized; atomic energy regulation fell to the Nuclear Regulatory Commission, while research and development in energy fell to a newly created Department of Energy.

[11] New York State Green Building Tax Credit Legislation Overview, http://www.dec.ny.gov/energy/1540.html

Energy Star: Energy and Buildings

Energy Star is a joint program of the U.S. Environmental Protection Agency and the U.S. Department of Energy . . . [to] protect the environment through energy efficient products and practices. . . . Americans, with the help of Energy Star, saved enough energy in 2007 alone to avoid greenhouse gas emissions equivalent to those from 27 million cars—all while saving $16 billion on . . . utility bills.

—Energy Star website, http://www.energystar.gov/index.cfm?c=about.ab_index

Energy Star is probably the most widely recognized energy-performance tool in the United States. Consumer value is provided by Energy Star purchasing guides for appliances and other electrical equipment. Building owners, developers, and other industry professionals value the name recognition as well as the energy-performance-management, goal setting, monitoring, savings reporting, and assessment tools that the U.S. EPA provides. The EPA's outreach materials illustrate the innovative energy-performance rating system that businesses have used for over 62,000 U.S. buildings. The EPA also recognizes top-performing buildings with the Energy Star rating. To lend further credence to both programs, Energy Star is the energy-performance standard used by LEED through its "one portfolio manager system" to benchmark and rate the energy performance of existing buildings on a comparative percentile-performance rating.

Energy Conservation in Existing Buildings Act of 1976

As a reaction to the energy crisis, the U.S. Congress encouraged states to develop energy-conservation plans for their existing buildings.

The *Energy Policy Act of 1992* set national green standards, such as those defining allowable limits for low-flow and low-flush plumbing fixtures, including toilets, dual-flush toilets, lavatories (faucets), kitchen sinks, and showerheads. This enabled the plumbing fixture industry to have uniform, clear, and measurable performance requirements for allowable water use. Similarly, the influence of the private sector on the high-performance standards agency, the National Institute of Building Sciences (NIBS), was to promote consensus and encourage freedom from bureaucracy. As a result, the early green building rating systems were developed largely, free from lobbying by major stakeholders in the building industry interested in maintaining the status quo.

Executive Order 13123, Greening the Government Through Efficient Energy Management

A new era in the development of energy policy occurred with executive order EO13123. Signed by President Bill Clinton in June, 1999, this legislation required the greening of the federal government in many areas: promoting energy efficiency through leadership, greenhouse gas reduction goals, energy efficiency improvement goals, and renewable energy, among others.

National Energy Policy 2001

The 2001 National Energy Policy[12] briefly mentions Energy Star, showcases a net-zero home, and includes an image of an integrated photovoltaic (PV) installation on the Condé Nast Building at Four Times Square, New York City. It also discusses renewable energy features that can be used on buildings and urges whole-building design as a way to attain energy conservation and efficiency.

The *Energy Policy Act of 2005*,[13] in addition to climate action reporting by the U.S. government, is the first U.S. policy that suggests high-performance buildings as a way to reduce the country's energy consumption. The act also acknowledges global climate change as fact and as something that needs to be addressed in U.S. energy policy. The Energy Independence and Security Act of 2007 includes the reduction of building-related energy with the need to reduce our dependence on foreign fossil fuels. The 2005 Energy Policy Act also defined the term "high-performance building" and created a high-performance buildings program with the National Institute of Building Sciences, which is a policy- and standards-review agency.

The National Institute of Building Sciences was created by the U.S. Congress via the Housing and Community Development Act of 1974. The Institute's original mission was to "improve the building regulatory environment; facilitate the introduction of new and existing products and technology into the building process; and disseminate nationally recognized technical and regulatory information."[14]

Today's U.S. Department of Energy

The Department of Energy did not spring full grown from Zeus' head like Athena. Instead, the DOE developed from a series of agencies (with differing names; see sidebar) that were responsible for overseeing energy interests and had control over various energy-related functions. The DOE today is "committed to reducing America's dependence on foreign oil and developing energy efficient

---

[12]For more information on the 2001 National Energy Policy, refer to the following summary: http://www.whitehouse.gov/energy/Overview.pdf.
[13]For more information on EPACT 2005, refer to the U.S. Department of Energy Summary, http://www.energy.gov/about/EPAct.htm
[14]National Institute of Building Sciences, mission statement, http://www.nibs.org/aboutnibs.html

KEY DATES IN ENERGY POLICY DEVELOPMENT

1973: Energy Policy Office and Federal Energy Office (Nixon Administration)

1974: Federal Energy Administration

1974: Atomic Energy Commission (AEC) is abolished and the Energy Research and Development Administration, Nuclear Regulatory Commission, and Energy Resources Council are established.

1975: The Energy Research and Development Administration is established, and the AEC is placed under its aegis.

1977: The Federal Energy Administration and Energy Research and Development Administration are abolished, and the Department of Energy is established.

technologies for buildings, homes, transportation, power systems and industry."[15]

One of the offices under the DOE is the Office of Energy Efficiency and Renewable Energy (EERE), whose mission is "to strengthen America's energy security, environmental quality, and economic vitality in public-private partnerships that: enhance energy efficiency and productivity; bring clean, reliable and affordable energy technologies to the marketplace; and make a difference in the everyday lives of Americans by enhancing their energy choices and their quality of life."[16] The U.S. Office of Energy Efficiency and Renewable Energy has direct benefits for and clear support to green buildings with its brace of green research programs: Biomass, Building Technologies, Federal Energy Management Program, Geothermal Technologies, Hydrogen, Fuel Cells and Infrastructure Technologies, Solar Energy Technologies, and Intergovernmental Wind and Hydropower Technologies offices, among others. With this level of governmental commitment and an anticipated shift toward aggressive and strengthened energy policies, we can begin to look at the movements toward integrated building design and construction.

The Road to Sustainable Design

The days of making the business case for sustainable design or even explaining what LEED means and why it is important have passed. Today's green building challenges have moved to more complicated areas of policy—permitting and politics—and the motivating sense of competition to be "the greenest."

Green building requirements are rippling through local municipalities across the country and the globe. Such requirements take many forms, including planning incentives that allow greater density, and bonus incentives for green building practices. In the United States, a few local governments are amending local codes adopting comprehensive green building ordinances or LEED requirements for all commercial and residential construction. State-level commitment can be seen in the recent adoption by the California Energy Commission and the California Public Utilities Commission of the goals of the 2030 Challenge.[17]

A first round of various state assembly bills were put forth: California's AB 2030 and AB 2119, which propose that all new commercial and residential construction in California be designed as net-zero-energy buildings by year 2030. Future architects, designers, and builders, while leading clients and project teams through the new complexities and conflicts that will emerge as we witness such shifts toward building green, need to understand these bills and their progeny as components of design.

The USGBC states that there are currently over 1,200 LEED-certified buildings around the world (and another 8,500 in the process of achieving certification) (Figure 4-12).

The Leadership in Energy and Environmental Design Green Building Rating system in its current form as a family of green building rating systems breaks down the green building technologies into five basic, quantifiable categories of credits, and for each achieved credit a project team can get a point toward making a building more green. (See Chapter 18, for more information on rating systems.) These green improvements effectively make a building "less bad" from an environmental perspective than a comparable non-LEED building or what would otherwise be a code-compliant project, typically known as a least-first-cost project.

The transformation of the green building market began to take hold in late 2006, with new construction from major developers on both coasts, including Tishman Speyer, Beacon Capitol, AMB, and Shorenstein. These developers were motivated by tax incentives like those offered by the State of New York[18] or San Francisco's Priority Gold Permitting Process.[19] Tangible indoor air quality and operations-cost benefits are a requirement for maintaining a marketing advantage, because in 2008 major tenants started to ask if a project would have a LEED rating. These buildings are much more effective at conserving resources and increasing efficiencies and thereby reducing their overall environmental footprint—but they

---

[15]U.S. Department of Energy, http://www.energy.gov/energyefficiency/index.htm

[16]U.S. Department of Energy, Energy Efficiency and Renewable Energy, http://www.eere.energy.gov/

[17]Architecture 2030, http://www.architecture2030.com.

[18]New York State Department of Environmental Conservation, New York State Green Building Tax Credit Legislation Overview, http://www.dec.ny.gov/energy/1540.html

[19]San Francisco Planning Department, Revisions to Director's Bulletin 2006-02, regarding the Planning Department's priority of processing applications, from John Rahaim, Planning Director to the Members, San Francisco Planning Commission, October 30, 2008.

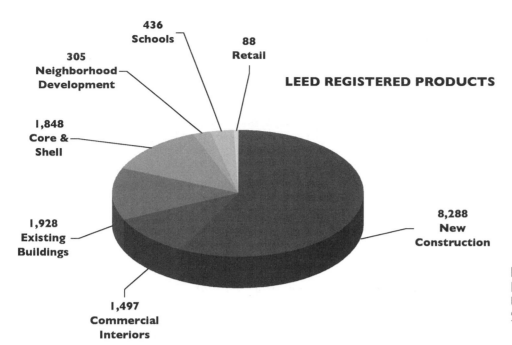

436
Schools

88
Retail

305
Neighborhood
Development

LEED REGISTERED PRODUCTS

1,848
Core &
Shell

1,928
Existing
Buildings

8,288
New
Construction

1,497
Commercial
Interiors

Figure 4-12 An illustration of the LEED-registered buildings in the United States as of June 2008. Source: U.S. Green Building Council.

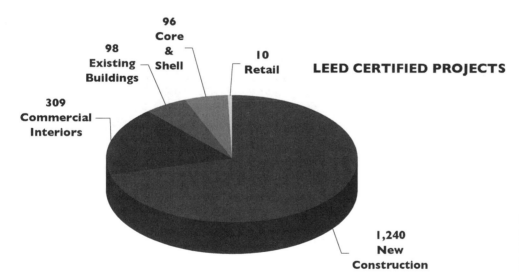

96
Core
&
Shell

98
Existing
Buildings

10
Retail

LEED CERTIFIED PROJECTS

309
Commercial
Interiors

1,240
New
Construction

Figure 4-13 An illustration of the LEED-certified buildings in the United States as of June 2008. Source: U.S. Green Building Council.

still have a footprint. Even when the higher-level Gold or Platinum LEED certification is achieved, many practitioners, such as Bill McDonough, believe that such buildings remain in the realm of the "less bad." Less bad is much better than maintaining the status quo of typical code-compliant construction, and all those who own, operate, lease space in, or work in a LEED-certified building have bragging rights. But technologies that are considered current and of the moment, worthy of accolades today, generally trend toward the mainstream very quickly and become easily attainable earlier.

The LEED building rating system could potentially be headed in a similar direction, toward mainstream

acceptance and use. Today green building consultants across the United States are fielding requests for assistance from developers, land-use attorneys, building owners, and brokers about getting their projects and portfolio buildings LEED certified (Figure 4-13).

However, industry adoption of new technologies is sometimes hampered by the success of these new technologies. For example, the State of California's Building Code and Energy Code (Title 24) are updated on a standard three-year cycle. This means that, on a regular cycle, what constitutes a "least-bad" building in terms of the state's minimum codes for permittable building in construction and energy performance is enhanced. So the State of California continues to raise the requirements on acceptable building efficiencies, while green building developments driven by the commercial real estate market's desire to always "out-build" your competition, far outpace the legal engagement of such green building codes and mandated construction practices. In early 2008, the State of California Energy Commission, significantly influenced by the passage of Assembly Bill 32 (California Global Warming Solutions Act of 2006), issued the 2007 Integrated Energy Policy Report (IEPR) that advanced policies enabling the state to meet its energy needs in a carbon-constrained world[20] and embracing many of the goals of Architecture 2030. In fall 2007, the state also issued its first set of proposed green building amendments to the state building code.[21] In July 2008 California became the first state in the nation to adopt green building standards as part of its building code.[22] In December 2008 the California legislature passed the Climate Change Proposed Scoping Plan, defining strategies California will use to reduce greenhouse gases (GHG) emissions that cause climate change. As state code and energy policy move toward the goal of green building, the definitions of green building and as well permittable building will coalesce, and it will not be possible to build a nongreen code-minimum building. The concept of green building being "less bad" will transform into the second concept and be defined as "sustainable design and construction." Simply put, if green building is about making buildings less bad, then the goal behind sustainable design is about making "good" buildings. The resulting trend will push sustainable design past the simple cost-benefit metrics of building components toward a broader definition of the built environment, integrating the principles of economic, social, and ecological sustainability.

Sustainable design and construction (restorative and living buildings) promotes and uses systems with minimal to zero environmental footprints. These systems can clean the water they use and generate power, as well as a host of other integrated design concepts. In addition, sustainable design and construction is a fundamental shift in thinking based on the idea that traditional technologies often work naturally; it fundamentally changes the ground rules about how to build a building through today's design-build, low bid, and bid-build process in favor of integrated design and project delivery.[23] Sustainable design takes buildings beyond a rating system scorecard and makes integrated design a fundamental

requirement. Collaboration of the most effective systems with less impact together with regenerative building systems, like building-integrated solar- and vertical-access wind turbines, start to make sense in the light of regional climatic differences.

In effect, current green building is raising the standard of care and performance; but with very few exceptions, green building has yet to evolve to a state of true sustainability. The goal is to convert buildings and operations into carbon-neutral architecture, to develop the capacity to produce at minimum as much energy as they use, to clean and produce as much potable water as they consume, and to provide healthy, safe, and nontoxic environments for their occupants, all while making the energy used in their design and operations a sum net-zero gain.

What Is Carbon Neutral?
The term "carbon neutral" is the nirvana of sustainability. It is a complete cradle-to-cradle analysis of all embodied energy in the making of an object (or building, if you will), the use and recycling of that product so it can be used again instead of becoming waste. To date, the nature of its methodology is a point of major discussion among the green building and scientific community.

Zero-Energy Buildings
The first major step toward carbon neutrality is something called a zero-energy building (ZEB), and if California's proposed legislation is approved, the state will require all new residential construction to be zero-energy buildings by the year 2020 and all commercial construction by 2030. This is the first bill that attempts to align the joint energy policy goals of the California Public Utilities Commission and the California Energy Commission with legislation.[24]

Simply put, a net zero-energy building is a residential or commercial building with a greatly reduced energy need through efficiency gains such that the balance of energy needs can be supplied with renewable technologies.[25] The National Renewable Energy Laboratory (NREL) has published four definitions of how to calculate a net-zero building; however, California's proposed legislation—as currently written—uses the California Energy Commission's definition: "a building that implements a combination of building energy efficiency design features and on-site clean distributed generation that result in no net purchases from the electricity or gas

[20]California Energy Commission, 2007 Integrated Energy Policy Report? (Adopted December 5, 2007), http://www.energy.ca.gov/2007_energypolicy/index.html.
[21]California Building Standards Commission, Green Building Standards, adopted by the California Building Standards Commission on July 17, 2008, as amended for publication in the 2007 California Green Building Standards Code, CCR, Title 24, Part 11, http://www.bsc.ca.gov/prpsd_stds/default.htm.
[22]Final code was issued on July 17, 2008.
[23]American Institute of Architects and Associated General Contractors of America, Primer on Project Delivery, October 15, 2004.

[24]State of California Public Utilities Commission and California Energy Commission, 2008 Update Energy Action Plan, February 2008, available for download at http://www.cpuc.ca.gov/NR/rdonlyres/58ADCD6A-7FE6-4B32-8C70-7C85CB31EBE7/0/2008_EAP_UPDATE.PDF.
[25]"Zero Energy Buildings: A Critical Look at the Definition," P. Torcelli, S. PLess and M. Deru, National Renewable Energy Laboratory, D. Crawley, U.S. Department of Energy preprint conference paper NREL/CP-550-39833, presented August 14–18, 2006, Pacific Grove, California. http://www.nrel.gov/docs/fy06osti/39833.pdf.

Figure 4-14 The CADE Winery Solar Array. 168 Sunpower Corporation solar panels generate approximately 53,750 kilowatt-hours annually. The array was sized to meet 100 percent of the winery's estimated annual power consumption ($0 utility bill over one year) making it an example of a net ZEB "site" building.

grid." Effectively, every building would have to generate on its own site all the power that it needs to operate.

The California Energy Commission's definition is the strictest and purest definition of a ZEB. If the goal of any carbon-neutral legislation is to reduce carbon emissions coming from nonrenewable sources and to encourage the highest level of energy conservation in design and construction of all new buildings, then a better definition would be one that does not restrict renewable power generation to a location on-site, because most urban projects would not be able to locate—at any cost—enough renewable wind or solar generation on-site.

All parties involved in power generation, conservation, and energy-efficient materials production would be encouraged to work together to achieve carbon-neutral design goals only if several conditions are met:

(1) if the source energy generated from renewable sources by utilities are included in calculations;

(2) if buildings are allowed to locate renewable technologies off-site, where more cost-effective renewable systems can be located; and

(3) if utilities and owners are allowed to count fossil-fueled power generation only when they use carbon dioxide–emissions sequestration or bioremediation technologies.

It is critical, if carbon-neutral building legislation is adopted, that the legislation define the term "net-zero energy" in a broader manner, or it will face opposition.

As noted above, the National Renewable Energy Laboratory[26] has published four definitions of zero-energy buildings[27] (Figure 4-15). The differences in the definitions address the physical location and calculation methodology used for determining the net-zero energy,

including site, source, cost, and emissions. The intent of these definitions is to ensure that any building (after implementing highly efficient strategies and energy systems) be able to meet all its energy requirements from locally available, nonpolluting renewable resources. Very few net-zero-energy buildings exist today, and most are not of notable scale. (Figure 4-14 illustrates a building that has attempted zero energy in a number of ways.)

■ Conclusion

In 2007 the California Public Utilities Commission unanimously approved an agreement with twenty-two parties and governmental agencies that effectively reduces electricity rates by 9 percent for large commercial office buildings. This will allow building owners to submeter their tenants for their actual, individual energy consumption. It is anticipated that end users, when they have to pay for each kilowatt of power they use, will be encouraged to consider the direct impact to their bottom line through energy conservation and advanced energy and lighting controls.

In late 2008 the San Francisco mayor planned to ask voters to approve a carbon tax on businesses. If approved, the City of San Francisco would increase its commercial utilities tax by 5 percent to encourage businesses, hotels, and all nonresidential buildings to implement energy-saving measures. In return, businesses would get a reduction of 1.5 percent in the payroll tax.[28]

Perhaps the most counterintuitive obstacle to green building is not based on cost, risk, technical knowledge, or even availability of materials but, rather, on when the

[26][National Renewable Energy Laboratory, http://www.nrel.gov.
[27]"Zero Energy Buildings," op. cit.

[28]Building Owners and Managers Association of California, "CPUC Approves Historic Reduction in Energy Rates for Commercial Buildings and Embraces Use of Energy Saving Commercial Submetering," http://www.bomacal.org/documents/PG&E%20GRC%202007%20Summary.pdf.

Definition	Positives	Negatives	Other Issues
Site ZEB	• Easy to implement • Verifiable through on-site measurements • Conservative approach to achieving ZEB • No externalities affect performance, can track success over time • Easy for the building community to understand and communicate • Encourages energy-efficient building designs	• Requires more PV export to offset natural gas • Does not consider all utility costs (can have a low load factor) • Not able to equate fuel types • Does not account for nonenergy differences between fuel types (supply, availability, pollution)	
Source ZEB	• Able to equate energy value of fuel types used at the site • Better model for impact on national energy system • Easier ZEB to reach	• Does not account for nonenergy differences between fuel types (supply availability, pollution) • Source calculations too broad (do not account for regional or daily variations in electricity generation heat rates • Source energy use accounting and fuel switching can have a larger impact than efficiency technologies • Does not consider all energy costs (can have a low load factor)	• Need to develop site-to-source conversion factors, which require significant amounts of information to define
Cost ZEB	• Easy to implement and measure • Market forces result in a good balance between fuel types • Allows for demand-responsive control • Verifiable from utility bills	• May not reflect impact to national grid for demand, as extra PV generation can be more valuable for reducing demand with on-site storage than exporting to the grid • Requires net-metering agreements such that exported electricity can offset energy and nonenergy charges • Highly volatile energy rates make for difficult tracking over time	• Offsetting monthly service and infrastructure charges require going beyond ZEB • Net metering is not well established, often with capacity limits and at buyback rates lower than retail rates
Emissions ZEB	• Better model for green power • Accounts for nonenergy differences between fuel types (pollution, greenhouse gases • Easier ZEB to reach		• Need appropriate emission factors

Figure 4-15 The zero-energy definition affects how buildings are designed to achieve the goal. It can emphasize energy efficiency, supply-side strategies, purchased energy sources, utility rate structures, or whether fuel-switching and conversion accounting can help meet the goal. The table highlights key characteristics of each definition. A source ZEB definition can emphasize gas end uses over the electric counterparts to take advantage of fuel switching and source accounting to reach a source ZEB goal. Conversely, a site ZEB can emphasize electric heat pumps for heating end uses over the gas counterpart. For a cost ZEB, demand management and on-site energy storage are important design considerations, as is selecting a favorable utility rate structure with net metering. An emissions ZEB is highly dependent on the utility electric generation source. Off-site ZEBs can be reached just by purchasing off-site renewable energy—no demand or energy savings are needed. Consistent ZEB definitions are needed for those who research, fund, design, and evaluate ZEBs. (Source: NREL.)

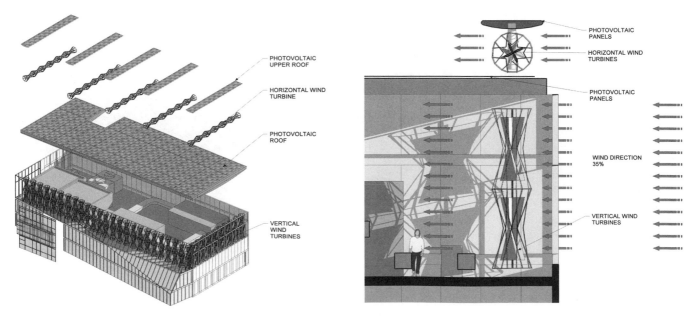

Figure 4-16 Proposed San Francisco Public Utilities Commission headquarters, currently the best example of an urban mid-rise commercial office building to truly embrace integrated design with solar and wind turbines, innovative structure, and passive ventilation. Perhaps the greenest building in the nation.

system or materials selected adversely affect a stakeholder's generation of revenue.

An example of this comes from a desert community complex, an 800-unit, mid-rise luxury condo. This project's team made a decision early in design to incorporate an on-site black water–treatment facility sized to meet 100 percent of the project's irrigation and cooling tower needs and to provide all the water needed to run an on-site car wash for residents. The owner made the decision to proceed, because building a luxury condo development that reuses its water from sinks, showers, and toilets would make it a first in the region and demonstrate the owner's commitment to sustainable design. As the project broke ground, the owner became aware of a hold on the plumbing permit. The department of water reclamation placed the hold, requiring proper permitting of the treatment facility prior to any subgrade utility work would be allowed.

As discovered, there is no approval process in place that any agency could use to allow a private developer to install this type of facility. It was clearly expressed that this department's fee structure is based on the volume of water discharged into its system by each ratepayer. A black water–treatment system of this scale would reduce this project's sewer discharge by millions of gallons a year. Delays caused by this obstacle ultimately eliminated the black water facility, a crime in a desert climate where water supply is at a minimum. Establishing permitting processes that allow these types of decentralized green infrastructure systems requires a fundamental paradigm shift in the way we manage our resources.

Emerging architects, designers, and builders need to compare the technologies presented in this book with the long-practiced ways the industry has made buildings up to this moment. We must be more concerned about the where, how, and why of the materials we select and the sustainable potential of a site. We must reap the knowledge of all project team members, the values used to measure work, and the way the collaborative team understands the costs of buildings and their operations.

EXERCISES

1. Sim Van der Ryn, architect and coauthor of *Ecological Design* (2007), says: "We can learn a great deal by moving beyond abstract statements of policy toward the particulars of design. It's here, at the level of actual farms, buildings or manufacturing processes, that relationships of culture and nature are thrown in sharp relief. It's here that the contours of a sustainable world become definable."[29] Compare Van der Ryn's statement on the factors that combine to form sustainability with James Lovelock's Gaia philosophy or Paolo Soleri's concept of arcology.

2. What steps can you take on a local level to enact green building legislation or guidelines in your municipality or campus setting?

3. Where do you predict federal-level green building legislation will be in the year 2015? What are the bases for your prediction?

▪ Resources

Van der Ryn, Sim. 2005. *Design for Life: The Architecture of Sim Van der Ryn*. Salt Lake City, UT: Gibbs Smith.

Matthiessen, Lisa Fay, and Peter Morris. 2007. "The Cost of Green Revisited: Re-examining the Feasibility and Cost Impact of Sustainable Design in the Light of Increased Market Adoption," http://www.davislangdon.com/USA/Research/ResearchFinder/2007-The-Cost-of-Green-Revisited/ (accessed December 29, 2008).

McDonough, William, and Michael Braungart. 2002. *Cradle to Cradle, Remaking the Way We Make Things*. New York: North Point Press.

California Building Standards Commission. 2008. *2007 California Green Building Standards Code, CCR, Title 24, Part 11*. Sacramento, CA: State of California.

Mazria, Ed. 1979. *The Passive Solar Energy Book: A Complete Guide to Passive Solar Home, Greenhouse, and Building Design*. Emmaus, PA: Rodale Press.

Brand, Stewart. 2005. 1999. *Clock of the Long Now: Time and Responsibility: The Ideas Behind the World's Slowest Computer*. New York: Basic Books.

Lima, Antonietta Iolanda. 2003. *Soleri: Architecture as Human Ecology*. New York: Monacelli.

Soleri, Paolo. 1987. *Arcosanti: An Urban Laboratory?* 2nd ed. Santa Monica, CA: VTI Press.

National Green Building Standard ICC/NAHB/ANSI. Draft number two was submitted to ANSI for review on November 24, 2008. Notifications are available at http//:www.nahbrc.org/GBStandard.

GBI Proposed American National Standard 01-200XP: Green Building Assessment Protocol for Commercial Buildings. Second public comment period ended December 8, 2008. Release of the standard is expected in the first quarter of 2009. For notifications refer to http://www.thegbi.org/.

---

[29]Sim Van der Ryn and Stuart Cowan, *Ecological Design* (Washington, DC: Island Press, 2007).

5 Sources of Chemicals in the Environment

Introduction

You may wonder what chapters on chemistry, chemicals, and their health effects are doing in a textbook for sustainable building design. In the same way that the requirements for architects have evolved over time to include computer-aided design (CAD) and design in an age of high security, architects need to keep pace with the demands of their profession. The practice of architecture is now more complex because we need to know so much more: ever-shifting building codes, accessibility requirements, and regulations regarding specialized areas of practice like schools and hospitals. Even the concept and practice of sustainability, a soon-to-be required practice for architects, is multipronged. One of the prongs involves architects thinking critically about how to evaluate products, materials, and systems based on their capacity to affect the environment and human health. The goal of these chapters is to introduce concepts that will raise questions about the components in various building systems. Just as we have learned to read nutrition labels on packaged foods, we will need to apply the same technique and critical thinking skills to the way we select building materials.

For a clear explanation of the human health effects of chemicals in the environment, refer to Appendix C, "The State of Our Health in Buildings," as it provides a comprehensive explanation of why it is critical to have an understanding of how chemicals affect living systems. Methods for reducing our exposure to these chemicals are quickly becoming part of the mainstream consciousness. In relation to green building, this knowledge prepares us to achieve integrated design with an eye to creating a healthier environment.

First, we will try to understand a little background on how pollutants and human-made chemicals end up in our bodies.

Figure 5-1 Controls on manufacturing or energy-producing plants should be reassessed to limit emission, transmission, and deposition.

Emission, Transmission, Deposition, and Immission

Pollutants and chemicals begin their journey to our bodies through the act of being released (*emission*) (Figure 5-1). They travel (*transmission*) over distance and time, where they end up (*deposition*) in the air, water, soil, and food we consume. From there, they travel up the food chain to become a source of exposure (*immission*, a medical term). Transmission distance and speed of dispersal depends on climatic conditions such as wind velocity, turbulence, heat, cloud cover, wet weather, and geographical characteristics such as desert and mountain topography. Transboundary pollutant migration is the result of industry and agriculture, and it is the term

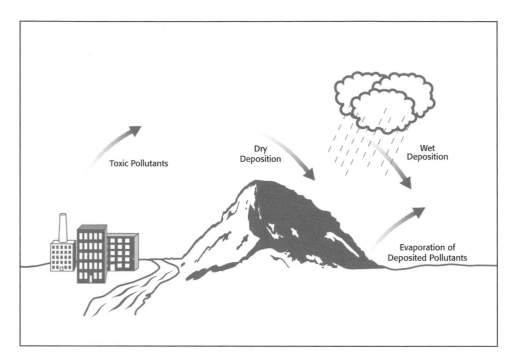

Figure 5-2 Toxin transport occurs through repeated cycles of precipitation, deposition, and evaporation.

used to describe the propensity of pollutants to travel indiscriminately over human-defined boundaries. Long-range transport is the ability of a chemical to reach remote areas. A study conducted using remotely located Inuit populations in the Arctic revealed double the concentrations of dioxin in their bodies than in those of non-Inuit Canadians living closer to the chemical sources (Figure 5-2).[1] Other factors contribute to chemical and pollutant migration, among them, climate change, severe weather, volcanic activity, natural disasters, bioterrorism, and overuse of antibacterials and antibiotics.

Overview of Chemical and Pollutant Sources

Although we can appreciate the fact that modern chemistry has made possible huge technical and medical advances in the last two centuries, at the same time, we are now more aware that engineered chemicals continue to find their way, by design, into the processing of everyday products such as cosmetics, electronics, processed foods, and building materials as well as being used in agriculture (Figure 5-3). This consciousness first dawned, prompted by Rachel Carson's *Silent Spring* (1962) and a series of widely publicized chemical releases to the environment, in the mid-twentieth century. Up until that time, many of these engineered chemicals—polychlorinated biphenyls (PCBs), for example—were unknown.[2]

Of the more than 80,000 chemicals registered with the U.S. Environmental Protection Agency (EPA), roughly 15,000 are on the market, and only a small percentage of these have been tested for human toxicity, and an even smaller percentage tested specifically for their effects on children.[3,4] This statistic is an important consideration when we examine the history of how a significant number of these chemicals were developed. Some products used today for a variety of seemingly benign and outwardly beneficial purposes originated from petroleum and plastics industries, weapons development, pesticide

[1] Barry Commoner, Paul Woods Bartlett, Holger Eisl, and Kimberly Couchot, Center for the Biology of Natural Systems (CBNS), *Long-Range Air Transport of Dioxin from North American Sources to Ecologically Vulnerable Receptors in Nunavut, Arctic Canada* (New York: Queens College, City University of New York). The report concludes: "In sum, the results of this project confirm that the atmospheric and ecological processes that carry airborne dioxin from its numerous sources, through terrestrial and marine food chains, to human beings, is a problem of continental, if not global, dimensions." Available electronically on the NACEC web site <http://www.cec.org>.

[2] Roberta C. Barbalace, "The Chemistry of Polychlorinated Biphenyls, PCB, the Manmade Chemicals That Won't Go Away," http://environmentalchemistry.com/yogi/chemistry/pcb.html.

[3] Moyers and Jones, *Trade Secrets: A Bill Moyers Report,* Dr. Philip Landrigan (chairman, Preventive Medicine, Mt. Sinai School of Medicine, New York) comments: "There are 80,000 different [human]-made chemicals that have been registered with the EPA for possible use in commerce. Of those 80,000, there are about 15,000 that are actually produced each year in major quantities, and of those 15,000, only about 43 percent have ever been properly tested to see whether or not they can cause injury to humans."

[4] Environmental Working Group, "Body Burden—The Pollution in Newborns."

DDT...FOR CONTROL OF HOUSEHOLD PESTS

Figure 5-3 The benefits of DDT (dichloro-diphenyl-trichloroethane), were perceived as universally healthy.

Figure 5-4 Petroleum processing and its resulting products are major sources of chemicals in the environment.

production, manufacturing, and health-care waste. We shall now examine these sources in a little more detail.

By-Products of the Petroleum Industry

Synthetic petroleum products from coal and coke were originally developed during World Wars I and II to help fuel equipment and machinery, and they were a great boon to powerful nations whose interests hinged on maintaining their defense technology. Today, petroleum is widely used in commercially available solvents, fuels, lubricants, adhesives, asphalt, synthetic fibers, plastics, paint, detergents, pharmaceuticals, and fertilizers (Figure 5-4). A particularly extreme example of a product with military purposes that has become a widely used commercial product is seen as we trace the development of synthetic petroleum and how research into the product led to the development of methane. Methane occurs naturally and is often associated with biogas and natural gas. Nevertheless, methane is a greenhouse gas, and it can be explosive in certain mixtures. Methane derivatives, in turn, led to the production of tetryl, which was used as an explosives component during both world wars. Although no longer manufactured, tetryl is found in many hazardous waste sites in the United States.

Figure 5-5 Children playing in a playground near an industrial site in Texas City, Texas.

Petroleum is problematic because the products that result from it are difficult to dispose of, contribute to greenhouse gas emissions, and are hard to capture and contain effectively; consequently, petroleum by-products are released into the environment (Figure 5-5).

Parallel to the intrusion of chemicals into the design of everyday products, herbicides and pesticides are being introduced directly into our food supply through genetically modified organisms. The advent of genetically modified

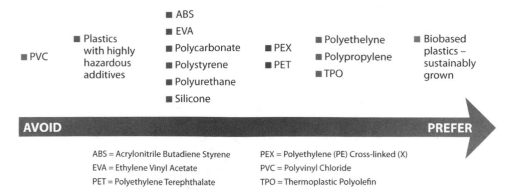

ABS = Acrylonitrile Butadiene Styrene
EVA = Ethylene Vinyl Acetate
PET = Polyethylene Terephthalate

PEX = Polyethylene (PE) Cross-linked (X)
PVC = Polyvinyl Chloride
TPO = Thermoplastic Polyolefin

Rossi, Mark & Tom Lent, "Creating Safe and Healthy Spaces: Selecting Materials that Support Healing" in *Designing the 21st Century Hospital*, Center for Health Design & Health Care Without Harm, 2006, page 66 (http://www.healthybuilding.net/healthcare/HCWH-CHD-Designing_the_21st_Century_Hospital.pdf)

Figure 5-6 The Environmental Preference Spectrum of plastics from Health Care Without Harm.

crop seed in the 1990s created a delivery system for these chemicals.[5] Even manufacturers of building-material components have diversified to engineer chemicals for food. Here we see the dovetailing not only of industries and the chemicals they create but also the creation of synthetic chemicals across a wide variety of applications.

Plastics—The "Miracle Material"

Mr. McGuire: I want to say one word to you. Just one word.
Benjamin: Yes, sir.
Mr. McGuire: Are you listening?
Benjamin: Yes, I am.
Mr. McGuire: Plastics.
Benjamin: Just how do you mean that, sir?
Mr. McGuire: There's a great future in plastics. Think about it. Will you think about it?

—*The Graduate*[6]

As in these famous lines from the movie *The Graduate*, plastics were the miracle materials of the post–World War II years, even though their development began as far back as the eighteenth century. Milestones in the history

of plastics include the development of rubber in 1839, polystyrene in 1839, phenol formaldehyde resin in 1907, polyurethane in 1937, nylon in 1939, and high-density polyethylene (HDPE) and polypropylene in 1951. In the 1950s focused polymer research led to the development of numerous plastics, including polyvinyl chloride (PVC).[7]

The term *plastics* encompasses organic materials with the elements *carbon* (C), *hydrogen* (H), *nitrogen* (N), *chlorine* (Cl), and *sulfur* (S), which have properties similar to those found naturally in inorganic materials such as wood, horn, and rosin (Figure 5-6). "Organic materials are based on polymers, which are produced by the conversion of natural products or by synthesis from primary chemicals that come from oil, natural gas, or coal."[8]

Plastics can be considered thermoset and thermoplastic, with a variety of products resulting from each. Plastic is an extremely versatile material that can be molded, extruded, and—depending on the types of additives and plasticizers involved—used for a wide array of applications, such as impact-resistant car bumpers, adhesives, helicopter blades, mattresses, floor and wall coverings, and carpet fibers.

Plastics also result in problematic poisons during manufacture and use. Many of plastic's precursors and additives are considered harmful and pose a threat to human health. *Phthalates* are an excellent example of a plastics additive that has been found to impact health. Phthalates can be added, for example, to the PVC production process, because it makes the material softer and pliable. Yet studies conducted in 2005 determined that phthalates found in household dust caused abnormal

---

[5]In a 2005 German study on rats fed on Mon 863, a corn variety engineered by Monsanto, the rats developed an array of health problems, including anemia, cancer, and kidney and liver lesions. See Stephen Lendman, "Potential Health Hazards of Genetically Engineered Foods," *Global Research*, February 22, 2008. http://www.globalresearch.ca/index.php?context=va&aid=8148.
[6]*The Graduate,* film, Mike Nichols, director (1967).

[7]For more information on polymer research in the 1950s, see http://www.plasticsresource.com and http://PlasticsResource.com, (accessed October 27, 2007).
[8]"Plastic waste recycling in progress: watch out for the bags, Help save the environment." Rosanne Koelmeyer Anderson, *Sunday Observer*, July 15, 2007.

genital and reproductive development in rats.[9] Phthalates can be found in personal care products, such as fragrance and nail polish, as well as in building materials, including vinyl wall coverings and resilient flooring.

Another chemical found in polycarbonate plastic is *bisphenol A* (BPA), which leaches from the plastic when heated. Though BPA's effects have been controversial, studies show that it mimics the estrogen hormone, and in nonhuman test subjects it causes harm to developing fetuses and poses potential transgenerational reproductive harm.[10]

Human exposure to plastics and their by-products occurs through many consumer products, such as baby bottles and the coating on the insides of canned food containers, as well as through building materials, but another route to environmental exposure is through the disposal of plastics. Plastics are properly disposed of, according to the plastics division of the American Chemistry Council, at a landfill, where prevention of degradation is achieved by constructing the landfill using sheets of EPA-mandated plastic liners. This is a problem, though, because plastic does not decompose, and human behavior regarding proper disposal needs to be addressed. Organochlorines such as dioxin and furans are released when plastics are disposed of through incineration.[11] Through transmission routes that include storm sewers, solid waste, and littering, plastics contribute to environmental litter, with the most impact on the marine surface and the sea floor. A large portion of marine debris can be attributed to improper disposal of plastic grocery bags, for example. Ocean biomes are affected by entanglement in and ingestion of plastic debris by sea life.

An extreme example of the ubiquitous presence of plastics in the environment, the result of improper plastics disposal, is the ominous "Great Pacific Garbage Patch," a vast collection of floating debris between California and Hawaii, 80 percent of which is plastic. Communities from Coles Bay, Tasmania, to San Francisco have instituted bans on plastic bags and Styrofoam in an effort to address this kind of environmental problem.

Communities whose waste-management goals include zero waste are actively exploring new ways to collect and recycle a wide variety of plastics, with an eye toward forcing industry to reduce production to begin with. Recycling rate statistics are encouraging. The HDPE recycling rate went up to 27.1 percent in 2005. Still, there is room for

more robust recycling. In 2004, U.S. consumers threw out three times as many billion pounds of plastic as they recycled. That means it either ended up in a landfill or as litter.[12] As we will see in later discussion, waste streams pose another chemical route to the environment.

Fortunately, there are many end products made from recycled plastics, which create a market and new industry growth for plastics recycling. Today, recycled plastic is used to manufacture building products such as plastic lumber, parking bumpers, resilient flooring, wall and window coverings, and surfacing materials. As builders and designers, we can appreciate the flexible and moldable properties of plastic, their array of design possibilities. Yet as holistic thinkers, we should attempt to limit exposure of building occupants to plastic-containing building materials by asking about durability, disposal, and recycling options for these materials at the end of their useful lives.

PVC: The Controversy Summarized for Architects[13]

Let's first understand the distinction between the useful catch phrase "vinyl" and PVC. Not all "vinyls" are PVC. Pure PVC is almost 60 percent chlorine, and from this chlorine molecule springs the root of the difficulty. The Healthy Building Network cites certain other vinyls similar to PVC but without the chlorine. They are all petrochemically based, but they are as yet unstudied to the same depth as PVC and possibly

(continued)

Figure 5-7 A playground set made from recycled plastic materials.

[9]Shanna H. Swan, et al., "Decrease in Anogenital Distance among Male Infants with Prenatal Phthalate Exposure," *Environmental Health Perspective* 113, no. 8 (August 2005): 1056–1061. See also: Julia R. Barrett, "Phthalates and Baby Boys: Potential Disruption of Human Genital Development," *Environmental Health Perspective* 113, No. 8 (August 2005): A542.

[10]'Plastic Chemical Safety Weighed,' "Miranda Hitti, Web MD," August 8, 2007, http://www.ewg.org/node/22367 (accessed December 17, 2007).

[11]"Some chemicals like dioxins and furans are created unintentionally by industrial processes using chlorine and from the manufacture and incineration of certain plastics," Coming Clean, Body Burden, http://www.chemicalbodyburden.org/whatisbb.htm.

[12]An interesting side note: Much of U.S. plastic debris is sent overseas for recycling.

[13]This excerpt was first published as "PVC: The Controversy Summarized for Architects," *arcCA, Architecture California, the Journal of the American Institute of Architects California Council* 05 no. 4 (Fall 2005).

more environmentally benign: for example, ethylene vinyl acetate (EVA); polyethylene vinyl acetate (PEVA), which is a copolymer of polyethylene and EVA; polyvinyl acetate (PVA); and polyvinyl butyral (PVB), used in safety-glass films. Many of these are being substituted for PVC in various materials.[14]

PVC's Structure

PVC's molecular structure consists of strings of *vinyl chloride monomers* (VCM), each made up of three hydrogen atoms, one chlorine atom, and two carbon atoms. The source materials for this monomer are oil and salt. Through electrolysis of the *sodium chloride*, a chlorine molecule is produced. By combining the chlorine with ethylene, produced from oil, the result is *ethylene dichloride*. This element is heated at high temperatures to create VCM; with the addition of heat stabilizers and fillers such as lead and plasticizers, or phthalates, it attains its workable form—either rigid or flexible—for such materials as resilient flooring, carpet backing, wall covering, wall guards, window frames, siding, furnishings, cable and wiring sheaths, piping, shower curtains, raincoats, car interiors, medical devices, drug delivery systems, food packaging, and children's toys. You will even find vinyl in hip, modernist home-furnishing stores—in those cool tote bags, welcome mats, and placemats. Cheap, lightweight, and workable, PVC has been hailed as the miracle plastic since its invention in 1872 as a source for directing chlorine waste from the acetylene gas-lamp industry.[15] Taking pigment well, with a degree of saturation that designers like, it is literally the "fabric of our lives."

Human Health

The fabric of our lives, however, is really the web of our food chain, water cycle, and our physical environment. When we add to that web a burden of bioaccumulative toxic by-products like dioxin, lead, various phthalates or plasticizers, and heavy metal stabilizers, we begin to toy with environmental balance and to affect human health. Throughout the life cycles of the versatile PVC products we use, their by-products, additives, and precursors can lead to serious health impacts, among them, cancer, endocrine disruption, endometriosis, neurological damage, birth defects, impaired child development, and reproductive and immune system damage.[16] The additives used to make PVC a viable product flake, off-gas, or leach out over time and can cause cancer, asthma, and lead poisoning.[17]

By-Products of Weapons Development

Would it surprise you to learn that certain plastic products of today were derived from chemicals used for military purposes? The mid-twentieth century saw the development of numerous chemicals that were used in large-scale war efforts, both for moving equipment and people and for weaponry. Chemical warfare agents (CWA) are classified into groups according to which system they target: nerve agents, blister agents, and choking agents. An example of such a chemical is *phosgene*, which is a poisonous gas at room temperature and was made into a chemical weapon first used in 1915 as a choking agent. Among the chemicals used in the war, phosgene was responsible for the large majority of deaths. (80 percent).[18] Phosgene today is used for plastics like polyurethane (used for insulation and carpet cushion) and polycarbonate (used to make compact discs) and pesticides.

Chlorine perhaps best exemplifies the transformation from military use to mainstream use. Chlorine was the basis for mustard gas weaponry, whose deadly effects were seen in 1917 in Ypres, West Flanders, during World War I. Today, chlorine and its components are used for plastics, coatings, and adhesives; all are relevant to the manufacture of building materials.

Ammonia was one of the first chemicals developed during the world wars; its derivatives nitric acid and nitrates were used in explosives. Today, ammonia is a component used in fertilizer and refrigerant.

World War II saw the development of further nerve gases, and during the Cold War and the Vietnam War, insecticides, herbicides, and fungicides were used. One

---

[14] Healthy Building Network, "Sorting Out the Vinyls—When is Vinyl not PVC?" http://www.healthybuilding.net.

[15] Mary Bellis, "History of Vinyl, Waldo Semon Invented Useful Polyvinyl Chloride aka PVC or Vinyl," http://inventors.about.com/library/inventors/blpvc.

[16] Healthy Building Network, "PVC Facts, " http://www.healthybuilding.net/pvc/facts.html

[17] Ibid.

[18] "Facts about Phosgene," CDC Fact Sheet (Centers for Disease Control), Department of Health and Human Services, 2/7/05, http://www.bt.cdc.gov/agent/phosgene/basics/pdf/phosgene-facts.pdf.

Figure 5-8 The herbicide and defoliant Agent Orange being sprayed during the Vietnam War.

Figure 5-9 The ladybug's pest-eating prowess forms the basis of nonchemical pest-control strategies.

of the most notorious of these is Agent Orange; which, when degraded, produces dioxin (Figure 5-8). Agent Orange is estimated to have caused birth defects in upwards of 500,000 Vietnamese children.[19] This research built upon earlier pesticides development and led to the manufacture of commonly used modern pesticides, fungicides, herbicides, and fertilizers.

One of the biggest legacies of CWA development was the introduction of pesticides into the agricultural web. Investigation and development of synthetic organic insecticides began by the 1930s. Swiss chemist Paul Hermann Müller won the 1948 Nobel Prize for Physiology or Medicine for the development of DDT, largely responsible for all but eradicating malaria in certain parts of the world. But because synthetic pesticides were so popular, research and development for less toxic botanically based insecticides was effectively slowed. Following the publication of Rachel Carson's *Silent Spring* (see Chapter 2 on the history of environmental movements), DDT was finally banned— but not until 1972. It is a testament to the insecticide's tenacity, as we will see later under the discussion of body burden, that we still carry the legacy of DDT in our bodies. Thanks to the Food Quality Act of 1996, the EPA was charged with analyzing pesticide tolerances and changing its pesticide regulations. One of the triumphs of this legislation was the removal of diazinon from the market.[20]

Unsurprisingly, before pesticides came along in the 1930s, pests were controlled through a combination of mechanical methods; petroleum oils; traditional, culturally based inorganic materials such as arsenic and sulfur; and botanically based methods. These techniques led to the concept of integrated pest management (IPM), beginning in the 1970s. Current research on pest control is focused on types of baits, targeted less-toxic controls, biopesticides, pheromones, and insect growth regulators (IGR). Today, in the effort to green buildings holistically, IPM is frequently used as an innovation credit in the LEED rating system (Figure 5-9).

Chemicals from the Waste Stream

Chemicals in the environment are also generated by waste streams: construction and demolition, mining, quarrying, manufacturing, and municipal solid waste. Before regulations were enacted in the United States (see Chapter 4 on the history of environmental regulations), the natural environment was the disposal ground for manufacturing and industrial waste by-products, specifically through incineration. An amendment to the Clean Air Act, the Solid Waste Disposal Act of 1965, restricted this disposal method. Controls for waste and the chemicals in the waste stream have been developed as a result of this legislation.

Landfill disposal, even with the regulation of industrial and hazardous wastes, presents a continued source of chemical transmission to the environment, despite containment practices and improved landfill construction. Landfills are still the predominant disposal method for municipal solid waste streams (Figure 5-10). Certain types of landfill space can be topped with poured concrete slabs and subsequently reused for building projects. Although opinions vary as to the rate and extent of landfill development, landfill-reuse strategy is still a problem,

[19] Geoffrey York and Mick Hayley, "'Last Ghost' of the Vietnam War," *Globe and Mail*, July 12, 2008.
[20] EcoSMART Technologies, "History of Pesticides: A Brief Overview," http://www.ecosmart.com/commercial/about/history.asp.

Figure 5-10 A large landfill site.

because landfill space is by definition limited and, ironically, could be considered a finite resource. Landfill-disposal impacts, as they relate to building construction and demolition waste, will be discussed in more detail in the later chapters on waste management.

Other types of waste include industrial and hazardous wastes. Industrial waste is defined as the nonhazardous waste generated by the production of goods. The United States produces, according to EPA estimates, 7.6 billion tons of industrial solid waste per year.[21] Hazardous waste is defined by Congress, and its control is regulated by the EPA. There are many types of hazardous wastes that fall into the categories of ignitability, corrosivity, reactivity, and toxicity. These waste materials are not reclaimable or recyclable and must be disposed of through restricted, controlled methods. Some sources of hazardous waste are produced by industries whose wastes include solvents generated by petroleum refining or pesticide manufacturing. Another hazardous waste source is the treatment industry's waste sludge and wastewater. In fact, discarded chemicals used to make other chemicals are themselves a hazardous waste source.

Significant progress in *right-to-know laws* have raised public awareness to the chemical disposal and waste-management activities of industry and government agencies. The Emergency Planning and Community Right-to-Know Act (EPCRA) was enacted in 1986, followed by the Pollution Prevention Act in 1990. The EPA developed the Toxics Release Inventory (TRI) in 1988, a public database of up to 650 chemicals that collects information on chemical releases. According to the EPA, "[t]he goal of TRI is to empower citizens, through information, to hold companies and local governments accountable in terms of how toxic chemicals are managed."[22]

Designers and builders should respond to this increased transparency by becoming aware of which building materials and associated manufacturing processes have a relationship to such EPA regulated chemicals. Tools for thoughtful materials selection will be covered in much more detail in a later chapter, but a few examples of such regulated materials include the following:

Arsenic occurs naturally in copper ores and through smelting. It is transformed from solid to gas, and it is emitted into the air through smokestacks and then deposited into soils. Copper is commonly used for decorative finishes and paneling as well as in electrical wiring.

Barium is a naturally occurring metal that is used in petroleum drilling, fluorescent lamp manufacturing, welding, rubber production, reflective "luster of glass" production, spark plugs, and vacuum tubes. Barium dissolves in water and is found in soils, lakes, rivers, and streams. It is carried long distances by aquatic life, as well.

Selenium-79 is a nuclear waste by-product that is present in soil. Its presence in the environment results from radioactive fallout. Naturally occurring selenium is a nonmetallic mineral, but it can also be created from the electrolytic copper-refining process. Of most relevance to the building sector is its use in the manufacture of photovoltaic systems.

Benzene is an organic chemical compound, a petroleum-derived liquid; formerly a gasoline additive, benzene is used in the manufacture of drugs, plastic, synthetic rubber, and dyes. It is deposited in soil and groundwater. Both rubber and plastics are used frequently as building components.

Vinyl chloride is the monomer used to make PVC, and it is widely used in many building materials. (See "PVC: The Controversy Summarized for Architects")

Hospital Waste

Hospital waste streams pose considerable problems because of the breadth of waste types and because of the ongoing development of waste-procedure regulations. Health-care waste (HCW) is typically disposed of in landfills or most commonly, through incineration, where it can release dioxin and mercury through air and ash (Figure 5-11). We have seen that the biosphere is not protected by these disposal methods. The World Health Organization (WHO) notes that 10 to 25 percent

[21]Environmental Protection Agency (EPA), Office of Solid Waste, National Environmental Performance Track, Waste Management, Conversion and Contextual Factors for Waste Management, http://www.epa.gov/perftrac/tools/wasteman.htm

[22]EPA, "What is the Toxics Release Inventory (TRI) Program," http://www.epa.gov/tri/whatis.htm (accessed February 19, 2008). Data access tools for TRI, see http://www.epa.gov/triexplorer/, http://www.epa.gov/enviro/, http://www.scorecard.org, and http://www.rtk.net.

Figure 5-11 A pyrolytic medical waste incinerator.

CHEMICALS OF CONCERN[26]

- Persistent organic pollutants (POPs) and other persistent bioaccumulative toxic chemicals (PBTs)
- Carcinogens
- Neurotoxins
- Reproductive toxicants
- Developmental toxicants
- Endocrine disruptors
- Mutagens
- All halogenated chemicals, including brominated or other halogenated flame retardants
- Other acute or chronic toxicants

Source: Sustainable Biomaterials Collaborative and Healthy Building Network, "Sustainable Bioplastic Guidelines," Version 7 (6/25/2007), http://www.healthybuilding.net/bioplastic/SustBioplasticGuide.pdf (accessed December 31, 2008).

of HCW is hazardous infectious waste, referred to as health-care risk waste.[23]

Health-care risk waste can include pharmaceuticals, infectious agents, and genotoxins, but, mirroring the building industry, it can also include heavy metals and certain chemical agents.[24]

Green purchasing policies in the health-care industry are aimed at preventing environmental damage from HCW. By understanding the life cycle and technology of health-care materials and by adopting the precautionary principle, health-care practitioners are implementing more responsible treatment and disposal procedures for HCW.

Armed with even these basic concepts, building designers of the future will be better informed and able to address this chemical waste issue directly, through responsible hospital building design. This is a perfect example of holistic thinking in green building design. For a continued discussion of hospital waste–management issues, see Chapter 21 on waste management.

In summary, powerful EPA-regulated chemicals, whether during active use in industrial processes or at the end of their life cycles, as waste, are found in commonly used compounds in plastics, pesticides, herbicides, fertilizers, petroleum products, and solvents, where they enter the air, water, and soil and where, over time and distance, they become part of our biosphere's chain of interdependent life.[25]

EXERCISES

1. To what extent is it possible for architects and designers to create an indoor environment that actively contributes to good health? On what factors would this depend?

2. What were the benefits of DDT? After Rachel Carson's *Silent Spring* (1962), which prompted the pesticides controversy, what events served to propel a move toward a DDT ban?

▬ Resources

Health Care Without Harm, http://www.noharm.org.

Green Guide for Health Care, http://www.gghc.org.

Kaiser Permanente, http://www.kaiserpermanente.org.

Healthy Building Network, list of scientific data on PVC and "Must Reads," http://www.healthybuilding.net/pvc/must_reads.html and http://www.healthybuilding.net/pvc/resources.html.

[23]World Health Organization (WHO), "Healthcare Waste Management, Some Basic Information on Healthcare Waste," http://www.healthcare-waste.org/en/123_hcw_general.html (accessed February 19, 2008).

[24]Ibid.

[25]Clean Production Action is currently developing "The Green Screen for Safer Chemicals," http://www.cleanproduction.org, which will rate chemicals on their potential persistence, bioaccumulation, and toxicity and their level of safety testing.

[26]For further information on high-hazard additives to avoid, refer to Rossi and Lent, "Creating Safe and Healthy Spaces: Selecting Materials that Support Healing" in *Designing the 21st Century Hospital Environmental Leadership for Healthier Patients and Facilities*, http://www.healthybuilding.net/healthcare/HCWH-CHD-Designing_the_21st_Century_Hospital.

Joe Thornton, "Environmental Impacts of Polyvinyl Chloride (PVC) Building Materials," a briefing paper for the Healthy Building Network, 2002, http://www.healthybuilding.net.

Blue Vinyl, Judith Helfand and Dan Gold, Sundance Film Festival Award-winning documentary on the PVC life cycle, produced 2002, http://www.bluevinyl.org.

"Body Burden—The Pollution in Newborns, A benchmark investigation of industrial chemicals, pollutants and pesticides in umbilical cord blood," July 14, 2005, Report, Environmental Working Group, http://archive.ewg.org/reports/bodyburden2/execsumm.php

Trade Secrets: A Bill Moyers Report. 2001. Written by Bill Moyers and Sherry Jones. Produced by Sherry Jones. New York: A Production of Public Affairs Television, Inc., in association with Washington Media Associates, Inc., A Presentation of Thirteen / WNET New York. http://www.pbs.org/tradesecrets/.

6 Environmental Chemicals in Humans and Buildings

Pathways of Transmission

We have looked at the materials and their chemical components—truly "poisons without passports"[1]—that are deposited in the environment from human activity; now we will examine the pathways of transmission, or routes of exposure, to the human body as well as to other living organisms whose existence is entwined with ours in the food web (Figure 6-1). Other factors to be considered in understanding transmission pathways include: amount of exposure to certain chemicals, the length of exposure (acute, short term, chronic, or continuous and repeated over time), and sensitivity. Many populations are more vulnerable to chemical exposure because of illness, or because they are immunocompromised, pregnant, poorly nourished, alcoholic, or drug abusers.[2]

According to researchers in Australia, the world production of organic (carbon-based) chemicals has increased from about 1 million tonnes/year in the 1930s to 250 million tonnes/year in 1985. They estimate that the annual production of organic chemicals will double every seven or eight years. Because human targets were involved in the development of chemical weapons, pathways of chemical transmission came to be understood. Absorption through inhalation is a common transmission pathway. Breathing the chemical emissions of certain interior finishes, such as wood sealer or paint, can have an impact on the lungs and can cause long-term effects on other systems in the body. Another method of transmission is direct or indirect contact through mucous membranes and skin; this can occur between humans and between animals and humans. In buildings, this kind of contact can occur via common household and industrial cleaners. Ingestion through food or water is another transmission pathway. The effluent of industries or manufacturing plants also can contaminate drinking water. There are other exposure routes, which are not the subject of this book, that can be attributed to human activity, the most salient of which is exposure to radiation.

Damage from chemicals can be classified into four major categories: *carcinogens* (causing cancer), *teratogens* (causing birth defects), *developmental and reproductive toxicants* (causing abnormal fetal development or harm to the reproductive system), and *endocrine disrupters* (interfering with normal hormone function).

Impacts to Humans

In 2001 a journalist with early, key roles in both the Kennedy and Johnson administrations, Bill Moyers (Figure 6-2), brought the concept of a "chemical body burden" to mainstream audiences in his televised investigative report, *Trade Secrets*.[3] The concept of chemical body burden is defined as "the total amount of a substance in

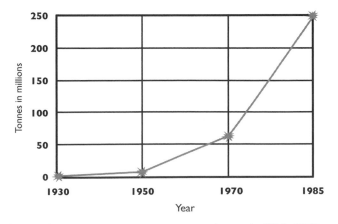

Figure 6-1 World production of organic chemicals, 1930–1985.

---

[1] National Toxics Network, http://www.oztoxics.org/ntn/lobby.html.
[2] New York State Department of Health, http://www.health.state.ny.us.
[3] *Trade Secrets*, Moyers and Jones, http://www.pbs.org/tradesecrets/ (accessed January 1, 2009).

Figure 6-2 Journalist Bill Moyers.

the body."[4] Some substances build up in the body because they are stored in fat or bone and thus leave the body very slowly. The amount of a particular chemical stored in the body at a particular time, especially a potentially toxic chemical, is a result of exposure. Body burdens can be the result of long- or short-term storage, for example, "the amount of a metal in bone, the amount of a lipophilic (fat-loving) substance such as PCB in adipose tissue, or the amount of carbon monoxide in the blood."[5]

With the airing of Bill Moyers' report, the general public became aware of the chemical body burden concept, although it had been known among toxicologists before that. For about thirty years, the National Center for Environmental Health at the Centers for Disease Control (CDC) and Prevention has been biomonitoring human subjects to understand human exposure to toxic substances in the environment. Biomonitoring involves measuring substances in blood, urine, breast milk, hair, organs, and tissues. The kinds of chemicals that show up as a body burden are PCBs (polychlorinated biphenyls, a chlorinated compound used as coolant in electrical equipment), DDT (dichloro-diphenyl-trichloroethane, a pesticide banned in the 1970s), PBDE (polybrominated diphenylethers, a fire-retardant treatment for building materials), dioxins (used in the manufacture of polyvinyl chloride [PVC] and other plastics and released during their incineration), phthalates (a plasticizing component of PVC and used in cosmetics as well), triclosan (a common antibacterial agent), furans, metals, organochlorine, and organophosphate insecticides. Many of these chemicals could contribute to syndromes

---

[4] Green Facts: Facts on Health and the Environment (a Belgian nonprofit organization founded in 2001), Glossary, http://www.greenfacts.org/glossary/abc/body-burden.htm
[5] Green Facts: Facts on Health and the Environment (a Belgian nonprofit organization founded in 2001), http://www.greenfacts.org; EPA healthcare glossary, http://www.epa.gov/ttn/atw/hlthef/hapsec1.html; for a list of chemicals and their effects: Human Toxome Project, Environmental Working Group, http://www.bodyburden.org.

EIGHT THINGS ARCHITECTURE AND DESIGN STUDENTS SHOULD KNOW ABOUT POISONS WITHOUT PASSPORTS

Bill Walsh, founder and national coordinator of Healthy Building Network, and Julie Silas, lawyer and researcher, director of Health Care Projects, Healthy Building Network

Bill

Think about the whole material and the impact of unintended uses of the materials, components, waste by-products, and manufacturing process. Employ life-cycle thinking.

Consider not only user exposure but that of manufacturer, installer, and cleaning personnel.

Study the best corporate stewards, companies that set targets to eliminate chemicals and materials of concern from their product or manufacturing process. Students should identify which companies pay lip service to sustainable change and which companies are good stewards.

Use the precautionary principle when deciding between two materials.

Julie

Graduating architects should understand the power of the materials library in architecture firms. These are the marketplaces where product manufacturers place their goods. The materials librarian is the last line of defense. They have the ability to vet materials before they are admitted and thus guide what designers specify. This is a good lesson in using life-cycle thinking.

Ask questions of product manufacturers! This will lead to consciousness-raising on many levels. Find out what chemicals are not listed on a material safety data sheet (MSDS). Often these are not disclosed under the claim of proprietary formulas.

Designers should become familiar with green chemistry, and young chemists should build green expertise.

Learn about the health effects of nanotechnology or nanomaterials, their presence in all consumer products, the lack of safety testing and public information.[6]

---

[6] "Nanotechnology's Invisible Threat," Sass.

such as autistic spectrum disorder, autoimmune disease, and learning differences, which are currently considered beneath the lens of environmentally contributing factors. More quantifiable and "visible" health effects are seen in the increased rates of allergies, asthma, and cancer and the results of endocrine disruption by chemicals known as reproductive toxicants.

Recommendations

Several environmental and public health organizations and nonprofit research groups have helped make the issue of chemicals in the environment more visible and accessible to the public. In concert with medical researchers, several of them have made recommendations for revised legislation.

The Environmental Working Group (EWG) is a nonprofit team of engineers, scientists, and policy experts whose mission is to expand the public's right to know when chemical trespass and environmental impacts occur. One of its funded studies demonstrated that 287 of 413 targeted chemicals appeared in the umbilical cord blood of newborns. Of the chemicals found, 180 cause cancer in humans or animals, 217 are toxic to the brain and nervous system, and 208 cause developmental problems.[7] The EWG has recommended revamping the Toxic Substances Control Act of 1976 into a "true public health and environmental law" that would require more stringent testing of chemicals, demand that manufacturers demonstrate the safety of their chemicals, remove from the market all chemicals that have not undergone safety testing, grant the U.S. Environmental Protection Agency (EPA) clear authority to demand safety studies as a requirement for chemical sales, and provide incentives to the development of green alternatives to these mainstream consumer and industrial chemicals.[8]

The Community Monitoring Working Group (CMWG) of Australia's National Toxics Network makes several recommendations specifically geared toward chemical exposure in children. Their recommendations are compiled in the "Body Burden Community Monitoring Handbook," an initiative of the International POPs Elimination Network. CMWG assists in the realization of the Stockholm Convention on Persistent Organic Pollutants (POPs) 2001 by "facilitating and supporting community monitoring of POPs and other persistent toxic substances."[9] Among their recommendations are to assess chemical body burdens, conduct research on these body burdens, strengthen existing laws governing chemical risk analysis before these chemicals become available on the market, and promote greener chemistry and greener alternatives.[10]

These recommendations feed directly into the *precautionary principle*, adopted by the European Union (EU) in 1992. The precautionary principle statement was issued at the culmination of a landmark conference of scientists, philosophers, lawyers, and environmental activists to develop an "anticipatory approach" with regard to environmental and public health decision making. Their "Wingspread Consensus Statement on the Precautionary Principle" (January 1998), named after the location of the meeting, resulted in the following imperative:

> When an activity raises threats of harm to human health or the environment, precautionary measures should be taken even if some cause and effect relationships are not fully established scientifically. In this context, the proponent of an activity, rather than the public, should bear the burden of proof. The process of applying the precautionary principle must be open, informed and democratic and must include potentially affected parties. It must also involve an examination of the full range of alternatives, including no action.[11]

An excellent example of the precautionary principle on a global scale was the Stockholm Convention on Persistent Organic Pollutants (POPs), which was convened in 2001 and resulted in a treaty that spurred an

[7] "Detailed findings," *Body Burden: The Pollution in Newborns*, Environmental Working Group (EWG) Study (Washington, DC: EWG, 2005), http://archive.ewg.org/reports/bodyburden2/part8.php (accessed January 1, 2009).
[8] Ibid., http://archive.ewg.org/reports/bodyburden2/part4.php.
[9] Community Monitoring Working Group, Introduction to the Body Burden Community Monitoring Handbook, 2005: http://www.oztoxics.org/cmwg/bb_introduction.html
[10] Marianne Lloyd-Smith, Coordinator, National Toxics Network, Community Monitoring Working Group, http://www.oztoxics.org.

[11] Science and Environmental Health Network, "Wingspread Statement on the Precautionary Principle," January 1998, http://www.sehn.org. The Wingspread Conference on the Precautionary Principle was convened by the Science and Environmental Health Network, an organization that links science with the public interest, and by the Johnson Foundation, the W. Alton Jones Foundation, the C. S. Fund, and the Lowell Center for Sustainable Production at the University of Massachusetts-Lowell. The complete statement:

The Wingspread Consensus Statement on the Precautionary Principle: The release and use of toxic substances, the exploitation of resources, and physical alterations of the environment have had substantial unintended consequences affecting human health and the environment. Some of these concerns are high rates of learning deficiencies, asthma, cancer, birth defects and species extinctions; along with global climate change, stratospheric ozone depletion and worldwide contamination with toxic substances and nuclear materials.

We believe existing environmental regulations and other decisions, particularly those based on risk assessment, have failed to protect adequately human health and the environment—the larger system of which humans are but a part.

We believe there is compelling evidence that damage to humans and the worldwide environment is of such magnitude and seriousness that new principles for conducting human activities are necessary.

While we realize that human activities may involve hazards, people must proceed more carefully than has been the case in recent history. Corporations, government entities, organizations, communities, scientists and other individuals must adopt a precautionary approach to all human endeavors.

Therefore, it is necessary to implement the Precautionary Principle: When an activity raises threats of harm to human health or the environment, precautionary measures should be taken even if some cause and effect relationships are not fully established scientifically.

In this context the proponent of an activity, rather than the public, should bear the burden of proof. The process of applying the Precautionary Principle must be open, informed and democratic and must include potentially affected parties. It must also involve an examination of the full range of alternatives, including no action.

international effort "to phase out harmful chemicals that persist in the environment and that can be transported around the world. The initial list of 12 chemicals targeted by the treaty includes nine organochlorine pesticides, all of which have already been banned in the U.S."[12]

In June 2003 San Francisco became the first city in the United States to use the precautionary principle as a foundation for its environmental policy. Since then many other municipalities and U.S. agencies have adopted the principle in whole or in part, despite the fact that many industry and chemical trade associations continue to oppose it (Figure 6-3).

Chemicals and Pollutants from the Construction Industry

The sources, transmission routes, and human health and body burden impacts of chemicals in the environment are well-known. Many of these sources are building materials whose indoor chemical emissions cause a variety

Figure 6-3 The precautionary principle is invoked.

of health effects. Because we spend most of our time (approximately 90 percent) indoors,[13] the presence of these chemicals in our indoor environment is of special concern. Modern buildings are often tightly sealed for acoustical and energy-conservation purposes. This tightly sealed condition, in addition to emissions from building materials, can contribute to a building's overall chemical load through the introduction of several chemicals, many of which show up in our chemical body burden and fall under the classification of volatile organic compounds (VOCs) or hazardous airborne pollutants (HAPs)[14] (Figure 6-4).

VOCs evaporate quickly, and their presence in the air diminishes with time. Benzene and toluene are examples of VOCs. Semivolatile organic compounds (SVOCs)—unlike VOCs, whose emissions are rapid—emit slowly and over a longer time period. Examples of SVOCs are phthalates, softeners used in PVC manufacture, and halogenated flame retardants (HFRs). These are of special concern, because they interact with particulates and dust to create an efficient delivery system. VOCs are often precursors to other chemicals whose presence is not part of the manufacturing process of the building material.

In addition to VOCs and SVOCs, and among the eighty (as of May 2008) chemicals of concern, building industry professionals should know about the following classifications:

ASTHMA, ALLERGY, AND CANCER STATISTICS

- Asthma accounts for approximately 24.5 million missed workdays for adults annually. Approximately 20 million Americans have asthma.[i]

- Asthma rates in children under the age of five have increased more than 160 percent from 1980–1994.[ii]

- Asthma and allergies strike 1 out of 4 Americans.[iii]

- The National Cancer Institute (NCI) estimates that the incidence of cancer could be reduced by as much as 80 to 90 percent if environmental causes such as diet, tobacco, and alcohol, as well as radiation, infectious agents, and substances in the air, water, and soil were addressed.[iv]

---

[i] American Lung Association, Epidemiology and Statistics Unit, Research and Program Services, *Trends in Asthma Morbidity and Mortality* (Washington, DC: American Lung Association, May 2005).

[ii] David M. Mannino, David M. Homa, Carol A. Pertowski, Annette Ashizawa, Leah L. Nixon, et al., "Surveillance for Asthma—United States, 1960–1995," *Morbidity and Mortality Weekly Report* 47(SS-1) (1998): 1–28.

[iii] Centers for Disease Control, *CDC Fast Facts A–Z. Vital Health Statistics* (Atlanta, GA: CDC, 2003).

[iv] National Cancer Institute (NCI): http://www.cancer.gov.

---

[12] For more information on the chemical body burden concept, see http://www.chemicalbodyburden.org/cs_organochl.htm. For the full list of chemicals and countries that have signed and ratified the convention, see: http://www.pops.int/.

---

[13] U.S. Environmental Protection Agency Green Building Workgroup, "Buildings and the Environment: A Statistical Summary (December 20, 2004)" (Washington, DC: U.S. EPA, 2004), http://www.epa.gov/greenbuilding/pubs/gbstats.pdf (accessed January 4, 2009).

[14] The term—hazardous airborne pollutants (HAPs)—is increasingly preferred to volatile organic compounds (VOCs), which can encompass a number of chemicals that are not strictly toxic.

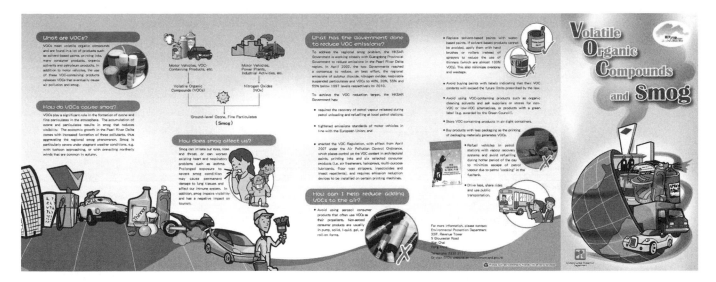

Figure 6-4 An educational pamphlet, from Hong Kong's Environmental Protection Department, outlining the relationship between VOCs and smog.

- Persistent bioaccumulative toxins (PBTs): Some PBTs are chemicals that fall into a category of toxins known by the acronym CMRTNEs, for carcinogens, mutagens, reproductive toxicants, developmental toxicants or teratogens, neurotoxicants, and endocrine disruptors. Heavy metals, including lead and mercury, and organotins are examples of PBTs.
- Persistent organic pollutants (POPs) are a subset of PBTs and include furans, dioxins, and PCBs.

As future green building professionals, we need to be aware of specific PBTs and POPs found in building materials, including the following:

- By-products and precursors of such materials as PVC and other plastics—for example, phthalates in flooring, rubber, and other pliable materials;
- Brominated fire retardants (BFR) and PBDEs in furniture;
- Metal, lead, and chromium compounds in paints, coatings, inks, and plastics;
- Bisphenol A (this is also found in the linings of cans used for food) in paints and coatings;[15]
- Halogenated flame retardants, especially chlorine and certain bromine halogens, used in wiring and upholstery fabric;
- Perfluorocarbons (PFCs) used as a refrigerant or coolant; and
- Arsenic, now banned from preservative treated wood.

Human-health impacts of bad indoor air quality (IAQ) created by the chemicals in building materials may not

Figure 6-5 Mold growth in buildings is the cause of some illnesses and requires professional remediation.

be manifested for long periods; others surface comparatively quickly. Three conditions commonly associated with buildings are sick building syndrome (SBS), building-related illness (BRI), and multiple chemical sensitivity (MCS) (Figure 6-5).

SBS exists when symptoms of runny nose—irritation of mucous membranes—occur in an indoor environment but abate when the affected individual is no longer in the building. BRI is when permanent health impacts can be directly linked to exposure to chemicals in the indoor environment. The definition, and even the existence, of MCS is under debate. Generally, MCS is caused by a number of chemicals in our environment that come from building materials, pesticides, and petroleum products ranging from gas to cosmetics, solvents, and office

---

[15] Extremely small quantities of BPA can cause harm. It was found that products made from polycarbonates leach higher amounts of BPA with each washing in a dishwasher than they did when new.

equipment. MCS affects more than one organ system and can occur at low levels of chemical exposure. (A later chapter will discuss IAQ issues in more detail.)

■ Building Systems: Let's Fix Them

How can we help create healthful places to live, work, and play without the ability to adjust processes or raw materials at the manufacturing source? The answer is another example of how sustainability has taken on the mantle of social activism. As architects, we are charged with designing to prescribed standards of life safety and reasonable care. Our responsibility does not end with the design of the seismic structure or planning for the appropriate number of emergency exits. Under the life-safety standard of care, our responsibility broadens to include the indoor environment quality (IEQ) and, by extension, the health of those who inhabit our buildings. This provides an excellent opportunity to incorporate the precautionary principle into our practice of architecture. The list includes the areas where we have the potential to enhance environmental and public health by responsible design and product specification and installation. (Interior finish materials are addressed in more detail in subsequent chapters.)

Building Systems: Enablers or Guardians?

Some of the purposes of building systems are to provide thermal comfort through control of humidity, heat, and cold. Energy efficiency has been addressed in more significant ways over the past few decades than the human-health impacts of heating, ventilating, and air-conditioning (HVAC) systems. Because the focus of this chapter is chemicals in the environment, we will examine this additional layer in addition to building systems. Often to blame for indoor pollutant entry and circulation through buildings, building systems may also be "enablers" of these conditions. Accordingly, whatever pollutants or particulates enter the building—through any route—should be dealt with and either mitigated or prevented from access to building systems. Think of the consequences of poor air circulation during airline travel as an example of trapped and repeatedly exhaled air, along with exposure to passengers' fragrances and personal care products, airline cleaning materials, and by-products of jet fuel combustion.

There are several ways in which mechanical systems can affect the quality of indoor air.

- *Ventilation*: Natural, passive, or mechanical system–based ventilation is a vital topic with many variables. Consider the following: quality of exterior air; location of polluting sources—vehicle traffic, local industry, manufacturing, or processing; placement of intakes and exhausts (Figure 6-6); climatic conditions; and air exchanges necessary for comfort and health. Air exchanges by code can be low; but for clean environments, such as hospitals and laboratories, the air-exchange rate should be higher. Some ventilation strategies include the use of high-efficiency filters to effectively screen particulates in outside air. Areas of chemical storage or garages should be isolated from occupied areas of a building by means of separate ventilation systems.
- *Heating systems:* These systems are most effective when the building envelope is tightly sealed and insulated;

Figure 6-6 Air-supply intakes should not be located close to sources of airborne pollutants.

Focus Areas for Designers:

A. Nonfinish materials of the building envelope:
- Skin, glazing, vapor barriers, insulation, framing

B. Interior finishes:
- Carpet
- Paints and coatings
- Adhesives and sealants
- Sources of formaldehyde: ceiling tile, composite wood
- Upholstery fabric and other furniture
- PVC-containing materials such as resilient flooring and wall coverings

C. Maintenance products and cleaners

Figure 6-7
Potential sources
of pollutants
affecting water
quality.

however, this is how indoor air quality (IAQ) was compromised after the energy crisis of the 1970s. Temperature and humidity of delivered heat, when incorrectly calibrated, can lead to growth of mold spores, for example. It is important to enlist mechanical engineers to balance, test, and commission building heating systems.

- *Cooling and refrigeration:* Refrigerants in mechanical systems have been the subject of much regulation over the years. Once commonly used chlorofluorocarbons (CFCs), which affected the ozone layer, are now outlawed. As well, hydrochlorofluorocarbons (HCFCs) are now beginning to be phased out. Alternative refrigerants are on the market, and manufacturers of HVAC systems will increasingly accommodate them. As with heating and humidity systems, mold development from moisture during cooling is a concern.

Plumbing: Water Delivery, Treatment, and Filtration

Buildings have many water demands that vary according to location and building type, including drinking, bathing, cleaning (personal, household, or structure itself), landscaping, irrigation, and process water for plumbing fixtures. Each of these demands has the potential to affect human health, and each calls for scrutiny on two levels: *mitigating the chemicals* in our water supply and *introducing cleaner water* into our buildings (Figure 6-7).

These demands should be thought of in an integrated way. The following are among the various holistic considerations surrounding water use in buildings:

- *Delivery:* Delivering water from municipal or on-site rural sources and circulating it with appropriate piping systems is the main concern. The Safe Drinking Water Act (SDWA, enacted in 1974) mandates that the EPA establish regulations to protect human health from contaminants present in drinking water. Under the authority of the SDWA, the EPA developed national drinking water standards and created a joint federal and state system to ensure compliance with these standards. The EPA also regulates underground injection of liquid wastes, under the SDWA, to protect underground sources of drinking water.[16]

- *Quality:* Drinking-water quality is affected by the need to remove particulates, bacteria, and pollutants from our water supply. Chemicals such as chlorine have been introduced to act on these bacteria, creating another set of problems. Sources of water and methods used to treat water vary among municipalities. Remote locations often rely on well water, which—as we have seen—can be the final point on the transmigration of a number of environmental chemicals.

- *Treatment:* Treating water for reuse through on-site technology or natural systems is another supply-and -return issue with significant effects on health. The concept of on-site water treatment is not new. The French designed septic tanks in the late nineteenth century. In addition to septic tanks, treatment can be done naturally (bioswales) or mechanically (building integrated or larger scale

---

[16]U.S. EPA, Office of Ground Water and Drinking Water (OGWDW), "Ground Water and Drinking Water," http://www.epa.gov/ogwdw.

black water—a term referring to domestic wastewater from toilets—treatment systems) whether the result is used as process water, for irrigation, or returned to the sewer system and from there to a municipal water-treatment facility. Constructed wetlands or rock-filter systems are other means of water treatment. There are two types of treatment, for black and gray water—the latter a term referring to domestic wastewater from laundry, dishwashing, or bathing activities. As yet, neither type of on-site water treatment yields potable water.

What are the potential human-health impacts of treating water on-site? Treatment tanks, absorption or leach fields, stabilization ponds or lagoons, and pit privies and composting toilets should not be too close to drinking water sources, or they risk exposure to rodents or other pests that could transmit pathogens. Enteric diseases are waterborne.

There is no doubt that wastewater will be a future source of drinking water. An important consideration with regard to current wastewater treatment on the infrastructure level is that wastewater-treatment techniques were not designed to remove some of the more than 126 chemicals originating from our use of an average of ten personal hygiene products per day.[17] Bisphenol A, phthalates, and triclosan (found in antibacterial soaps) are three endocrine disruptors found in wastewater discharged to the San Francisco Bay in a 2007 study of chemicals. Among those are galaxolide, a synthetic masking fragrance (or "musk"), that bioaccumulates in tissue and breast milk and that has been found to cause endocrine disruption in test animals.[18] The green building designer should be aware of this water quality and treatment concern when considering chemicals in the environment.

- *Filtration:* Filter water at points of use. Regardless of the source water to buildings, it needs to be conveyed responsibly and delivered with health issues in mind. Considerations include piping, treatment (if necessary), and in-faucet filtration. Piping materials are a source of controversy. Should copper piping, made using an energy-and-water intensive process, be encouraged? Should piping for drinking water be made of PVC? Filtration at the faucet can occur through many types of technology or any type of commercially available filter, although these are not without controversy.

Again, the focus of this book is not an in-depth examination of building systems but, rather, an overview. Familiarity with concepts and understanding that all building systems need to be considered holistically is valuable. In the case of water delivery, circulation, treatment, and management, such understanding will require, at the very least, that the designer program space with integrated building systems in mind. In all building systems, it is critical to design for chemical mitigation at points of delivery, circulation, and use. As with most systems technologies, it is wise to engage mechanical, electrical, plumbing engineers, and landscape architects who specialize in integrated systems thinking.

Green Chemistry and Building Materials

The mandate to develop greener alternatives to industrial chemicals is at the top of the list of recommendations by such research groups as the Environmental Working Group and the Healthy Building Network, among others. The "green chemistry" field is gaining currency in response to such recommendations. This has meaning for many players in the green building world, as well as for those in the mainstream building industry. Given healthier indoor materials made from green chemistry processes, for example, designers and builders will have a tool with which they can design healthy indoor spaces.

Though green chemistry is only now being integrated into university curricula, the concept of green chemistry originated in the late 1990s, assisted by the publication of a groundbreaking book by Paul T. Anastas and John C. Warner, *Green Chemistry: Theory and Practice.*[19] *Green chemistry* is officially defined as "[t]he design of chemical products and processes that reduce or eliminate the use and generation of hazardous substances."[20] The mission of green chemistry is to "direct enterprises to the ethics and science of precaution."[21] Again, the ideal of the precautionary principle comes into play. As with the task of addressing climate change, the incentives to speed up innovation and technology in this relatively new field could spur large-scale mobilization and, as well, create new jobs.

Greener and less health-compromising alternatives to toxin-containing building materials are guided by green chemistry principles (summarized in the sidebar). Of

[17] "Down the Drain: Sources of Hormone-Disrupting Chemicals in San Francisco Bay," Rebecca Sutton, PhD (EWG), and Jennifer Jackson (EBMUD), Environmental Working Group, July 11, 2007, http://www.ewg.org.
[18] Naidenko, Olga, "Not a Drop to Drink—Part 1: Down the Drain," *EWG Toxics Newsletter* (25 Feb 2008), http://www.enviroblog.org/2008/02/not-a-drop-to-drink-down-the-drain.html.
[19] Paul T. Anastas and John C. Warner, *Green Chemistry: Theory and Practice* (Oxford and New York: Oxford University Press, 1998).
[20] Warner Babcock Institute for Green Chemistry, "The Twelve Principles of Green Chemistry" (Woburn, MA: Beyond Benign, a Warner Babcock Foundation, n.d.), http://www.beyondbenign.org/pdf/gengc12p.pdf (January 3, 2009).
[21] San Francisco Department of the Environment, White Paper, The Precautionary Principle and the City and County of San Francisco, March 2003.

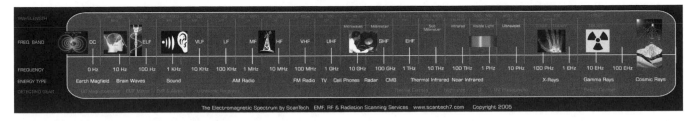

Figure 6-8 The electromagnetic fields (EMF) spectrum.

PRINCIPLES OF GREEN CHEMISTRY

1. Prevent waste instead of treating it or cleaning it up.

2. Maximize atom economy to avoid wasted atoms.

3. Design less hazardous chemical syntheses.

4. Design safer yet functionally performing chemicals and products.

5. Use safer solvents and reaction conditions.

6. Increase energy efficiency, using ambient temperature and pressure.

7. Use renewable, not depleting, feedstock (use agricultural waste rather than feedstock from fossil fuels).

8. Avoid chemical derivatives, which use additional reagents and generate waste.

9. Use catalysts, not stoichiometric reagents, to minimize waste.

10. Design chemicals and products to degrade after use.

11. Analyze in real time to prevent pollution and by-products.

12. Minimize the potential for accidents: Design chemicals and their forms (solid, liquid, or gas) to minimize the potential for chemical accidents, including explosions, fires, and releases to the environment.[22]

relevance to students are the references to "design" of chemicals and processes, but it should also be noted that the final principle calls for prevention of accidents and potential releases of chemicals to the environment.

Many practitioners agree that the future of healthy-building design lies in the design of health-care facilities.

Design of health-care facilities is setting the trend for innovative and integrated green building design. Design teams for health-care projects may even have a heightened awareness of the effects of the tools of their trade—building materials. A frequently stated opinion of health-care designers is that people who enter hospitals seeking relief from illness or disease should not be exposed to building materials that have the ability to cause harm.

A recent paper produced by Healthy Building Network and Health Care Without Harm, "The Future of Fabric—Health Care," is a rich, scientific resource that illustrates the wide-ranging effects of chemicals in fabrics for interior furnishings.[23] Sadly or not, depending on your viewpoint, this report applies to chemicals of concern in many building products. If the student reads no other document cited in these chapters but this report, he or she will be provided with a comprehensive exploration of chemicals in building materials and their effects.

By now, you have probably surmised that designers of the green era have been charged with a large task. Not only do we need to know about the structural integrity of buildings, the mechanical systems, appropriate ventilation rates, writing contracts, building schedules and fees, but we need to have an awareness of the presence of chemicals in the environment and how we can intelligently specify materials and be confident that the spaces we create are not adding significantly to the chemical body burden. Clearly, petrochemicals and synthetic chemicals are ubiquitous in our daily lives.

In truth, *chemical* should not necessarily have a negative connotation. No one doubts that technological advances wielded by innovative chemistry are critical to sustaining a competitive edge in a tight marketplace and to improving security, standards of living, and protection from disease, especially in developing countries. But more efficient chemical testing, more robust controls, and increased transparency are necessary to educate a largely trusting population about the substances in

---

[22] Anastas and Warner, *Green Chemistry*, 29–54.

[23] Julie Silas, Jean Hansen, and Tom Lent, "The Future of Fabric—Health Care," Healthy Building Network in conjunction with Health Care Without Harm's Research Collaborative, October 2007, http://www.noharm.org/us.

their building materials, products, and finishes, in addition to food, water, and air. Until then, and in tandem, building designers who emerge from school with an interest in green buildings need to look closely at the materials they are designing into buildings. It is our duty to do so because of architectural practice and the standard of care.

In a later chapter, we will look at ways to cut through the greenwashing exercised by manufacturers and to ask relevant questions to assist in this process.

EXERCISES

1. The *precautionary principle* begins with a statement of beliefs, including this one: "We believe there is compelling evidence that damage to humans and the worldwide environment is of such magnitude and seriousness that new principles for conducting human activities are necessary" (from the "Wingspread Statement on the Precautionary Principle"). It is likely that, coupled with the need to regulate carbon emissions, the theme of chemicals in building materials will become the future of green building technology. Research manufacturers of three diverse building products (insulation, paint, and wood cabinets, for example), and determine which, if any, have built the precautionary principle into their corporate policies.

2. Much attention, controversy, and contradiction has been given in recent years to electromagnetic fields (EMFs) (Figure 6-8). An early study found an association between incidences of childhood leukemia and the proximity to high-voltage power lines.[24] Is it possible to design EMF protection or avoidance into a green building? To what extent can one consider such design efforts as true design technology?

■ Resources

Chemical Trespass: A Toxic Legacy. 1999. Gwynne Lyons. Surrey, UK: World Wildlife Fund-UK.1999.

Our Stolen Future: Are We Threatening Our Fertility, Intelligence, and Survival?—A Scientific Detective Story. 1977. Theo Colborn, Dianne Dumanoski, and John Peterson Myers. New York: Penguin Group.

Trade Secrets: A Bill Moyers Report. 2001. Bill Moyers and Sherry Jones. Produced by Sherry Jones. New York: Public Affairs Television, Inc., in association with Washington Media Associates, Inc., A Presentation of Thirteen / WNET New York. http://www.pbs.org/tradesecrets/.

Centers for Disease Control (CDC) and Prevention. 2005. Third National Report on Human Exposure to Environmental Chemicals. Atlanta, GA: CDC.

"Nanotechnology's Invisible Threat: Small Science, Big Consequences." 2007. Jennifer Sass. NRDC Issue Paper. New York: Natural Resources Defense Council, Inc. http://www.nrdc.org/health/science/nano/nano.pdf.

Healthcare Without Harm, a global coalition of 473 organizations in more than fifty countries that is working to protect health by reducing pollution in the health-care sector, http://www.noharm.org.

Healthy Building Network, http://www.healthybuilding.net.

Guenther, Robin, and Gail Vittori. 2007. Sustainable Healthcare Architecture. Hoboken, NJ: John Wiley & Sons.

Cartagena Protocol on Biosafety, www.biodiv.org/ (2000).

Maastricht Treaty on the European Union, Sept. 21, 1994, 31 ILM 247, 285-86.

Ministerial Declaration Calling for Reduction of Pollution, Nov. 25, 1987, 27 ILM 835.

Montreal Protocol on Substances that Deplete the Ozone Layer, Sept. 16, 1987 26 ILM 1541.

Stockholm Convention on Persistent Organic Pollutants, www.pops.int (2000).

---

[24] N. Wertheimer and E. Leeper, "Electrical Wiring Configurations and Childhood Cancer," *American Journal of Epidemiology* 109, no. 3 (1979): 273–284.

7 Indoor Air Quality Technologies—Green Design for Long-Term Occupant Health

Leon Alevantis, MS, PE, LEED AP

Why Is Good IAQ Important?

Indoor air quality (IAQ) affects worker productivity, health, and comfort. In the case of schools, good IAQ, coupled with good lighting, has been shown to enhance learning.[1,2] Sick building syndrome (SBS) includes a range of health symptoms, such as ear and nose irritation, increased allergies, and asthmatic symptoms, as well as increased colds and infectious diseases (Figure 7-1). In the past, IAQ was overlooked by employers and building owners, primarily because its economic impacts had not been clearly defined. However, recent studies have documented these impacts.

The direct impacts of IAQ include increased health-care costs, lost productivity, worker's compensation claims, undesirable real estate, and, in more extreme cases, expensive legal-settlement costs. In the United States, the potential reductions in health care costs and improvements in work performance, from providing better IAQ, are estimated at an annual value ranging from tens of billions of dollars to more than $100 billion.[3]

Detailed analyses of the existing literature indicate that increases in ventilation rates and better control of temperatures can improve office and school work performance

Figure 7-1 Allergens can affect air quality.

(Figure 7-2).[4] Buildings with demonstrated measures to enhance IAQ and sustainability are more desirable to work in, have higher employee retention, and in most cases attract a premium rent. Some insurance companies offer discounts for enhanced IAQ and sustainability.[5] Designers and employers need to be aware that employees have a right to healthy indoor air as advocated by the World Health Organization (WHO).[6]

[1]Mendell, M; and Heath, G. 2005. "Do Indoor Pollutants and Thermal Conditions in Schools Influence Student Performance? A Critical Review of the Literature". *Indoor Air Journal*, vol. 15, pp. 27–32. Also available at http://eetd.lbl.gov/ied/sfrb/pdfs/performance-2.pdf

[2]*California Energy Commission. 2003.* Windows and Classrooms: A Study of Student Performance and the Indoor Environment. *Report P500-03-082-A-7. Available at:* http://www.h-m-g.com/

[3]Fisk, W.J. 2000. "Health and productivity gains from better indoor environments and their relationship with building energy efficiency". *Annual Review of Energy and the Environment* 25(1): 537–566

[4]Fisk W.J. and Seppanen O. 2007. "Providing Better Indoor Environmental Quality Brings Economic Benefits". *Proceedings of Clima 2007 Well Being Indoors,* June 10–14, 2007. Helsinki. Paper A01. Published by FINVAC, Helsinki. Available at: http://eetd.lbl.gov/ied/sfrb/sfrb.html

[5]Fireman's Fund Insurance Company. http://www.firemansfund.com/

[6]World Health Organization. 2000. *The Right to Health Indoor Air.* Available at: http://www.euro.who.int/document/e69828.pdf

Figure 7-2 As ventilation rates increase, so do productivity and performance.

Figures 7-3 Location and siting of a building are variables that affect indoor air quality.

Contributors to IAQ

Volatile organic compounds (VOCs). The quality of indoor air is dependent on numerous contaminants generated from indoor sources, as well as contaminants transported from outdoors via ventilation and infiltration. Most building construction materials and office furniture emit VOCs after manufacturing (dry products) or after installation (wet products). With few exceptions, such as products containing formaldehyde, the emissions of building materials decay considerably within the first few months after manufacture or installation. Afterward, VOCs associated with cleaning products and occupants and their activities, such as personal care products, copiers, and printers, typically dominate the indoor environment[7](Figure 7.5).

Ventilation. The purpose of dilution ventilation in buildings is to dilute and to remove contaminants. Sometimes the ventilation system itself becomes a source of contamination—for example, when mold grows in and around cooling coils and drain pans that do not drain properly, or when ducts are loaded with dust due to lack of proper filter maintenance.

Designing and maintaining a watertight building envelope and eliminating plumbing leaks are important elements in preventing water intrusion and mold formation.

Location and siting of a building are variables that affect indoor air quality and should be addressed very

Figure 7-4 Planners should consider proximity to industrial activities when designing communities.

early in the design of a building (Figures 7-3 and 7-4). Intrusion of naturally occurring radon gas in the soil, or other gases emitted from contaminated soil, can be avoided by providing active soil depressurization and sealing vapor intrusion routes. Positioning buildings away from strong electromagnetic fields (EMFs)[8] and positioning building intakes away and upwind from pollution sources, such as highways, are important considerations in avoiding SBS (Figure 7-7).

[7]Alevantis, L. 2006. *Long-Term Building Air Measurements For Volatile Organic Compounds (VOCs) Including Aldehydes At A California Five-Building Sustainable Office Complex.* California Department of Health Services (renamed California Department of Public Health). Available at: http://www.cal-iaq.org/VOC/East_End_Study_2006-09.htm

[8]California Electric and Magnetic Fields Program Website, http://www.ehib.org/emf/

Figure 7-5 Indoor air quality in our world: ETS, fuel emissions and "air."

■ Types of Indoor Pollutants

There are literally hundreds of chemicals in the indoor environment. Most building products emit VOCs, resulting in indoor concentrations that are few to several times higher than those found outdoors. Although a lot of emphasis has been given to volatile organic compounds, as new analytical techniques are developed and our understanding of indoor air chemistry improves, other compounds—such as semivolatiles (semivolatile organic compounds, or SVOCs), including phthalates, pesticides, and flame retardants, and chemicals formed from reactions with other indoor chemicals—are becoming increasingly important factors when evaluating the indoor environment (Figure 7-6).

Our understanding of the health and odor effects of most of these compounds, individually and collectively, at concentrations typically measured in the indoor environment is very limited. When assessing the impact of specific indoor chemicals to building occupants, it is important to realize that most of the existing health guidelines for chemicals are applicable to industrial settings for healthy adult workers, and it is inappropriate to apply these same guidelines to nonindustrial settings, which include a wide range of occupant types, such as children and the elderly.

Besides controlling chemicals in the indoor air, it is equally important to control microbial growth inside buildings. Mold insurance claims skyrocketed a few years ago, leading numerous insurance companies to explicitly exclude this type of coverage from their policies. Leaks from the building enclosure, condensation inside buildings, and plumbing leaks are some of the causes of mold. Limiting the growth of *Legionella pneumophila* in cooling towers and service water systems is important to minimizing the potential for Legionnaires' disease.

Other important indoor pollutants include particulate matter, carbon monoxide, and ozone. Their health effects are well-known, and the U.S. Environmental Protection

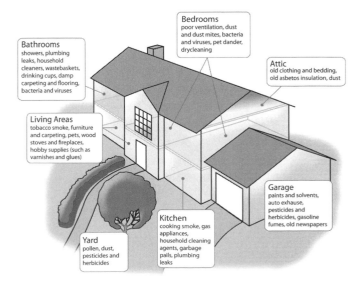

Figure 7-6 Hazardous airborne pollutants can be both emitted and stored in buildings. Sources of emissions range from the flame retardants in fabrics and upholstery to polyvinyl chloride (PVC) in shower curtains to the formaldehyde in pressed-wood products.

Figure 7-7 A smog emergency.

Agency (EPA) has established maximum allowable outdoor concentrations for these pollutants.[9]

Integrated Building Design for Good IAQ

Integrated building design (IBD) is a process by which multiple disciplines are integrated in a single team with the goal of achieving a high-performance building at a competitive overall cost. IBD for IAQ requires, at a minimum, the participation of architects, as well as mechanical, plumbing, civil, structural, and electrical engineers and interior and landscape designers, from the earliest phases of the project.

Indoor air quality goals should be set early in the conceptual and schematic phases, and the person from each design team responsible for their implementation should be identified. A single overall IAQ coordinator should be selected and regular meetings with the design teams should be scheduled to ensure that IAQ goals continue to be met during construction. The IAQ coordinator will have the additional responsibility of ensuring that IAQ goals are met on a day-to-day basis during construction.

Some of the initial goals may include the following:

- Building siting, orientation, location of building openings such as entrances and air intakes.
- Establishment of interior light and noise criteria.
- Selection of a heating, ventilating, and air-conditioning (HVAC) system (including filtration and air cleaning)

appropriate for the climate, location, and type of building occupancy.
- Selection of the ventilation rates and method for ensuring that adequate ventilation is provided to all occupants under all operating conditions. If the selected ventilation rates are higher than required by the local energy code, the building's overall energy budget should be reduced by implementing additional energy-conservation measures to compensate for the energy required for the increased ventilation. In most cases, it is advisable to reduce emissions from indoor sources rather than increase ventilation rates to achieve good IAQ.
- Determination of the building's thermal requirements.
- Design of all HVAC systems and components for ease of service.
- Establishment of a commissioning program that includes all mechanical, plumbing, energy management, and life-safety systems.
- Selection criteria of low-emitting building and finish materials. Selection should take into account the durability of these materials as well as cleaning and maintenance requirements.
- Sequence of installation of finish material (porous materials, such as carpet, should be installed last).
- Design of building enclosure to minimize water intrusion, condensation, and infiltration.
- Establishment of a flush-out schedule.
- Continuous review of construction schedule to ensure that the IAQ goals are not compromised.
- Review of all change orders and submittals to ensure compliance with IAQ goals.

Material Emissions Testing

Source control—the selection and installation of low-emitting building materials—is the most cost-effective method of reducing the contribution of building materials to the indoor air quality of buildings when compared to increased ventilation or possible material replacement after occupancy due to high emissions.

In the 1980s researchers investigated the effectiveness of "bake out," an alternative method to source control. 'Bake-out' is a process in which the temperature of a building is elevated to its maximum setting for a few days before occupancy to reduce chemicals associated with building materials. The results of this research indicated that the effectiveness of this practice was very limited in reducing indoor VOCs and therefore IAQ professionals no longer advise it.

There are several emissions-testing protocols and product-certification programs. Although all these protocols and certification programs have a common goal of reducing the number and strength of chemicals emitted from building materials, they are considerably different in their approach, and caution should be exercised when interpreting or comparing their results.

The U.S. EPA funded a study to analyze all available product-testing programs, and the published report is the best available resource for the architect today.[10]

It should be pointed out that some testing programs, such as those for cleaning products, are based on a weight percentage of VOCs compared to the total product weight. Such programs require modeling with several assumptions to calculate indoor air concentrations. Other programs are based on small chamber–emissions testing, while others are based on mid- to large-scale chamber emissions testing. For these chamber-based programs, "emission factors," based on a certain sample size, ventilation rate, temperature and relative humidity, "loading ratio" (area of the sample and volume of test chamber), and sampling duration are obtained for each target chemical and then converted to indoor concentrations based on a number of assumptions.

Laboratory testing conditions as well as the list of target compounds and their concentrations can vary considerably from program to program. Pass-fail criteria for some programs are based on exposures of healthy workers in industrial environments; some are based on more specific to nonindustrial environments, taking into consideration "sensitive populations," such as asthmatics, children, and the elderly; and other (primarily a few European) programs are based also on comfort (including irritation).

In almost all certification programs, only a pass-fail report is issued, and the emissions-test data and calculated concentrations are not disclosed. Since the experimental protocols, and therefore test conditions, vary from program to program, it is almost impossible to compare the results of one program against another.

In the United States, efforts to harmonize all these protocols and programs have been unsuccessful due to strong commercial interests. In addition, in the United States, independent third-party certification bodies do not exist for laboratories evaluating the indoor air quality of nonindustrial workplaces, as they do for other types of laboratories (such as those for industrial-workplace exposures). It is important for the architect to ask the representatives of certification programs for their testing protocol (experimental conditions, duration of testing), list of target compounds and their concentrations, as well as the parameters used to convert laboratory emission rates to indoor concentrations.

Evaluation of products should be made on individual VOCs and not on total volatile organic compounds (TVOCs), which is a poor indicator of potential health and odor effects. In addition, since very limited data exist on SVOCs, product comparison on this basis is more difficult.

It is important to realize that emissions from some products are initially very high, followed by rapid decay (e.g., paints), while emissions from other products may be moderate initially, but may decay very slowly (such as formaldehyde-containing pressed-wood products). When selecting low-emitting building materials, it is important to consider for each product:

• Durability
• Cleaning requirements
• Emissions from required cleaning products

Figure 7-8 lists some examples of building materials with IAQ implications, considerations that need to be made prior to their selection, and relevant U.S.-based testing and certifications programs.

■ Pushing the Envelope for IAQ Design

Building design professionals need to perform their due diligence on matters related to IAQ during design. Today there is more practical information on IAQ than ever before. Professional organizations such as the American Institute of Architects[11] and the American Society of Heating, Refrigerating and Air-Conditioning Engineers (ASHRAE)[12] have publications for the practicing professional on this and related topics.

In addition, government agencies such as the EPA[13] and the State of California[14] have numerous IAQ publications on their Web sites. Independent, third-party organizations[15,16,17] also have useful publications. It is important for the architect to stay informed on IAQ developments and be cautious with industry claims, unless these claims are supported by independent third-party organizations.

The area of IAQ emissions testing is still evolving, and as our understanding of this issue improves, so does the available information. It is important for the architect to realize that evaluating materials based on their emissions requires careful consideration of the available information and that decisions are based on a multitude of factors specific to each project (such as client's requirements, type of building occupants, building location, and material availability in the local market).

[10]Tichenor, B. 2006. "Criteria for Evaluating Programs that Assess Materials/Products to Determine Impacts on Indoor Air Quality". Final Report Submitted to the United States Environmental Protection Agency under EPA Order No. EP 05WO00995. Available at: http://www.epa.gov/iaq/pdfs/tichenor_report.pdf

[11]American Institute of Architects: Sustainability Resource Center at: http://www.aia.org/susn_rc_default
[12]American Society of Heating Refrigerating and Air-Conditioning Engineers. 2009. *Indoor Air Quality Guide: Best Practices for Design, Construction, and Commissioning.* Available at http://www.ashrae.org
[13]United States Environmental Protection Agency: Indoor Air Quality Website at: http://www.epa.gov/iaq/
[14]California Indoor Air Quality Program, IAQ Information: Volatile Organic Compounds, (VOCs) Website at: http://www.cal-iaq.org/VOC/
[15]Collaborative for High Performance Schools, Low Emitting Materials Table. Available at http://www.chps.net/manual/lem_table.htm
[16]Scientific Certifications Systems, Indoor Air Quality Website at http://www.scscertified.com/ecoproducts/indoorairquality/index.html
[17]Greenguard Environmental Institute Website at: http://www.greenguard.org/

Building Material Category	Examples of Building Materials In Material Category	Emissions-Related Considerations	Testing Programs In the United States				
			CHPS [a]	Green Guard [b]	Green Seal	SCAQMD	Other
			Based on emissions testing – does not address short term emissions – limited list of compounds. CHPS includes additional health-based criteria		Based on total VOC contents and "reactive" VOCs		
Architectural Coatings	Sealers, primers, paints, enamels, lacquers, varnishes, stains	• Use water-based products where possible • Zero-or low VOC paints may contain numerous "reactive" VOCs exempt from the USEPA definition of VOCs (any compound of carbon which participates in atmospheric photochemical reactions to form ozone[c]) under the Clean Air Act • Emissions depend on substrate • Consider durability. A moderately emitting paint requiring re-coating once every few years may be preferable to a low-emitting paint requiring frequent re-coating. • Consider sequence of construction (complete painting before installing "fleecy materials" such as carpet and ceiling tiles)	X	X	GS-11[d]	Rule 113[e]	
Caulks, Sealants and Adhesives		• Use water-based or low-VOC products • Large variations in reported emissions due to type of substrates	X	X	Aerosol Adhesives: GS-36[f]	Rule 1168[g]	
Ceiling Tiles		• Formaldehyde and SVOC emissions • Large surface area of installed panels (both sides exposed) may result in: (a) considerable indoor concentrations of an otherwise low-emitting product; and (b) sink effects	X	X			
Composite Wood Products	Particleboards, oriented strand board, fiberboard	• Specify urea formaldehyde-free products or encapsulate surfaces	X	X			• Composite Panel Association: Environmentally Preferable Product Specification CPA 2-06 [h] (industry standard: not very stringent formaldehyde requirements)
Flooring Materials	Resilient tile, laminate, hardwood, linoleum, carpet	• Consider emissions from adhesives. Test as assembly. Substrates also vey important – most testing programs based on standardized substrate (such as stainless steel) • Consider cleaning products	X	X			• CRI Green Label Plus[i] • Resilient Floor Covering Institute, FloorScore Program[j] • California Gold Sustainable Carpet Standard[k]
Insulation Materials		• Consider urea formaldehyde-free based binder in fiberglass and mineral fiber	X	X			
Office furniture systems	Workstations	• Specify low emitting products • Airing out in lieu of specifying low-emitting products is not very practical and marginally effective for some chemicals (urea formaldehyde) • Install office furniture systems last followed by building flush-out • Consider low-emitting cleaning materials					• BIFMA[l] • California Modular Office Furniture Specification[m]

[a] http://www.chps.net/manual/lem_table.htm
[b] http://www.greenguard.org/uploads/TechDocs/GGTM.P066.R6_04-29-08_FINAL.pdf
[c] http://www.epa.gov/EPA-AIR/2004/November/Day-29/a26070.htm
[d] http://www.greenseal.org/certification/standards/paints_and_coatings.pdf
[e] http://www.aqmd.gov/rules/reg11/r1113.pdf
[f] http://www.greenseal.org/certification/standards/commercial_adhesives_GS_36.cfm
[g] http://www.aqmd.gov/rules/reg11/r1168.pdf
[h] http://www.pbmdf.com/
[i] http://www.carpet-rug.org/
[j] http://www.rfci.com/int_FloorScore.htm
[k] http://www.documents.dgs.ca.gov/green/epp/standards.pdf
[l] http://www.bifma.com/standards/FES/FES.html
[m] http://www.ciwmb.ca.gov/GreenBuilding/Specs/Furniture/default.htm

Figure 7-8 Examples of building materials with IAQ implications and related emissions considerations.

A criticism associated with green building programs is that they tend to oversimplify important environmental issues such as indoor air quality. Although this argument has some merit, it is important to realize that green programs, such as the Leadership in Energy and Environmental Design (LEED), have brought increased awareness of building environmental matters to building professionals and to building occupants. It is important for building professionals to realize that existing green building programs should be viewed only as minimum requirements, much like building codes, and that designers should continue to strive for better performing buildings.

8 Indoor Environmental Quality Issues

What Is IEQ?

Architecture is the study of shelter, the design of its spatial environment, and the human relationship to it. Architecture considers scale, proportion, order, mass, texture, function, context, and social conditions; it reflects culture, climate, region, and economy; it is a machine and a sculpture; and it is a blend of technology and design.

Of all the myriad, connected themes and functions that buildings possess, probably none is as quickly perceived and responded to as the quality of indoor space. Aesthetics, comfort, and function are the primary descriptors of the quality of the interior environment. In a way, this is what students learn throughout design school: how to design an environment that is *beautiful*, *comfortable*, and *functional*. Sometimes known as building ecology, indoor environmental quality (IEQ) refers to how efficiently and comfortably people inhabit their indoor spaces as interpreted by the sum of their psychological and physiological reactions to architectural design factors.

IEQ requires integrating many functions and systems within a building, just as we have been studying throughout this book. Successful IEQ requires integrated design. The designer can contribute a certain level of indoor comfort through the use of green design principles, but the building user also needs flexible and effective tools to further refine his or her environment—fine-tune it—and to control its temperature, humidity, ventilation, and lighting, at a minimum.

In fact, the ability to control one's environment (sometimes referred to as personal or individual control) is a primary consideration in successful IEQ design. Increasingly, a worker's right to a comfortable workplace is gaining attention. The optimal green design solution for an office environment would be to design individual controls for task lighting, temperature, and air, at a minimum (Figure 8-1).

Components of IEQ

Our nervous system and all our senses define the components of our indoor environment: olfactory, auditory,

(a)

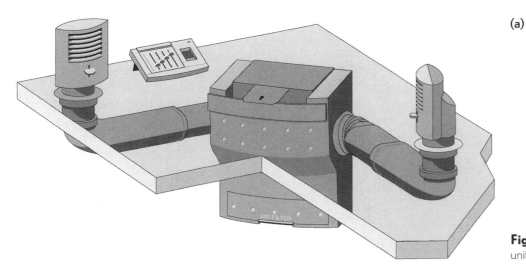

Figures 8-1 a, b Personal controls units for the office environment.

(b)

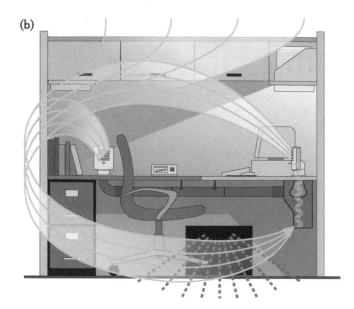

Figure 8-1b

visual, and emotional. The components of IEQ are acoustics, daylight, visual comfort, connection to the outdoors, and thermal comfort.

IAQ and Olfactory Issues

There are many indoor environments: vehicles, buildings, submarines, ships, trains, and airplanes, each with different occupant densities, ventilation rates, and access to sensory input. Indoor air quality (IAQ), a predominant theme in this book, is a critical and variable subset of IEQ. With IAQ, we are concerned with a variety of contaminants, inorganic and organic (pesticides, semi-volatile organic compounds, or SVOCs), and combustion by-products (environmental tobacco smoke [ETS] and by-products from candles, incense, cooking appliances, heating systems, and fireplaces, all with a range of fuel sources). Human illness, bacteria, pets, and dust mites are just a few of the other contributors to IAQ. Especially in high-density, overcrowded situations—such as aircraft cabins, where ventilation is not optimal—everyday substances, such as personal care products, dry cleaning, and computers are sources of chemical emissions.

As we saw in Chapters 5, 6, and 7 on chemicals and IAQ, there are four major factors to consider when designing for optimal air quality:

- *Source control:* Potential areas of contaminants— e.g., kitchens, janitorial closets, labs where chemical processing occurs, copy rooms (where equipment can be a source of ground-level ozone), and smoking rooms—should be isolated from regularly occupied spaces. They should be designed with an appropriate pressure differential, so contaminants within these rooms do not bleed into occupied zones. Outdoor contaminants, such as pesticides and particulates, should

be trapped by entryway systems that capture dirt from peoples' shoes as they enter a building. Volatile organic compounds (VOCs) from building materials such as paint and composite wood are another source of contaminants, previously discussed in Chapter 7, and these should be carefully considered by the green building designer, as source control is the most cost-effective way to build good IAQ. Other contaminant sources are emissions from nearby industry or roads and the building's occupants themselves.

- *Ventilation:* Bad ventilation is most immediately noticeable when we detect odors through our olfactory system or feel a room is stuffy (oppressive to breathing). Some plastic materials, when exposed to heat, can emit very strong odors and alert inhabitants of a building to a problem. Carbon dioxide (CO_2) sensors are frequently used in sustainable building design practice because a triggered alarm indicates insufficient ventilation rates. Substandard ventilation rates can cause an array of sensory and health impacts, while good ventilation can enhance productivity and wellness. As architects, one of the more direct ways of supplying access to good ventilation is through the design of operable windows. These provide natural ventilation, and they are easily controlled by occupants of a building. Natural ventilation has its pros and cons, especially on building sites near busy roads, heavy industry, and noise problems. Sustainable guidelines for health and human comfort often suggest exceeding code-required ventilation rates for various occupancy types. Again, as in most integrated building design, designing for good ventilation is a question of balancing priorities and site concerns. In mechanically ventilated buildings, an array of technologies can be used to ensure adequate ventilation.

- An excellent solution is an underfloor air-distribution system (a mixed ventilation system) or a displacement ventilation system, both of which use a physics principle known as the stack effect, where the differences in temperature and moisture (density) between inside and outside air cause the warmer air to rise and cooler air to be drawn into a building. Heated air is supplied at the floor level via diffusers in raised floor panels (Figure 8-2) that can be angled or sealed to regulate the flow of air, a system known as an underfloor air-distribution system. The air gains heat as it rises due to the presence of equipment and people; then it is exhausted at the ceiling level. Raised-floor technology allows for flexible space planning, but it also introduces better quality air and provides improved thermal comfort over conventional ceiling-supplied mixed ventilation. Its added benefit is the occupant's ability to control the thermal environment.

- *Building commissioning:* Commissioning is the process of ensuring that the building's systems operate as its design intends. A commissioning agent will review the building owner's project requirements, and the mechanical engineer will produce a basis of design

Figure 8-2 Underfloor air-distribution system and raised floor.

for the mechanical system. In parallel, the commissioning agent will write a commissioning plan, verify equipment function at various stages of design and installation, ensure the proper functioning of certain building systems, and produce a final commissioning report. Principally, the mechanical systems that introduce, filter, condition, and deliver air to occupied spaces, as well as domestic hot water systems, lighting and daylighting controls, renewable energy systems, and refrigeration equipment, will be commissioned. Even though the process is directed at energy-using systems, commissioning is also key to ensuring the good indoor air quality. Components such as fans are tested in the factory, and a full testing and balancing process is conducted in the field, as well when the systems are installed and sometimes after the building has been occupied. Equipment failure can thus be minimized, and training of facility personnel can occur during this time. Operations and maintenance policies can be incorporated into the standard warranty file that is handed over to the owner upon construction completion.

• *Building maintenance and flush out:* Formerly known as a *bake out* or purge, a *flush out* is the process of supplying a large volume of outside air continuously over a prescribed period of time after construction and touch-ups are complete but typically before furniture and occupants have moved in. This process aids in the removal of VOCs, particulates, and other contaminants before the building is occupied.

No matter how thoughtfully designed the system or how efficient the filter, any mechanical or energy-using equipment needs regular maintenance, cleaning, and filter changes. The cleaning policy of the building as a whole should be addressed carefully. Many experts believe that cleaning materials for a typical floor are responsible for many more times the VOC emissions than the actual flooring material. Repeated cleanings essentially deliver continuous long-term exposure to harmful substances. Green cleaning, the practice of using environmentally benign products, is gaining currency and acceptance.

"According to various studies (reported by carpet manufacturer Milliken & Company), 70–80 percent of the dirt in a commercial building arrives on the shoes of building occupants. During dry weather, 1,000 people in a large office building will track in a quarter-pound (113 g) of dirt per day; in wet weather that increases to three pounds (1,360 g)."

Source: "Keeping Pollutants Out: Entryway Design for Green Buildings," *Environmental Building News* 10, no. 10 (October 2001).[1]

[1]Wilson, Alex, "Keeping Pollutants Out: Entryway Design for Green Buildings," *Environmental Building News* 10, no. 10 (October 2001), http://www.buildinggreen.com/auth/article.cfm/2001/10/1/Keeping-Pollutants-Out-Entryway-Design-for-Green-Buildings/.

Many industrial hygienists and other air quality scientists are beginning to recommend air quality testing within occupied spaces. Because of the potential risk to public health, indoor air quality testing should occur regularly in the same way that municipal water supplies and outdoor air quality are regularly tested and analyzed. This is ever more important as the Science Advisory Board of the U.S. Environmental Protection Agency (EPA) has identified indoor air quality as one of the top five environmental impacts to public health.[2] Another startling statistic is that in 1998 the Occupational Safety and Health Administration (OSHA) estimated that 30 percent of Americans who work in nonindustrial buildings are exposed to indoor air pollution.

A good way to check progress in the IEQ design is to conduct a post occupancy evaluation (POE) or survey. According to the founders of Post Occupancy Evaluation (http://postoccupancyevaluation.com), an architectural practice specializing in this field: "Post Occupancy Evaluation involves a systematic evaluation of opinion about occupied buildings from the perspective of the building users. It assesses how well buildings match users' needs, and identifies ways to improve building design, performance and fitness."[3] Some of the factors addressed in such a survey are functionality, productivity, sustainability, and safety.[4]

In Melbourne, Australia's Council House 2 (CH2), POE surveys showed an increase in worker productivity of 10.9 percent, among many positive ratings on its other IEQ factors.[5] The images in Figures 8-3 and 8-4 show airflow design and cooling schemes, both using cutting-edge technology. (Council House 2 is explored as a case study in Chapter 17.)

Acoustics

Acoustics and privacy design techniques have been important architectural design considerations for several decades. Interestingly, the word *noise* has roots in the Latin word for seasickness—*nausea*. Noise is ubiquitous in both public and private areas of contemporary society, and it is increasingly viewed as a major public health concern (see the sidebar below for a list of noise-related health impacts). Just as there is a health concern regarding second-hand smoke, there is a corresponding concern for second-hand noise as both a public health and a privacy issue.

Sources of noise include proximity to airports and outdoor equipment (from jet skis to leaf blowers), as well as

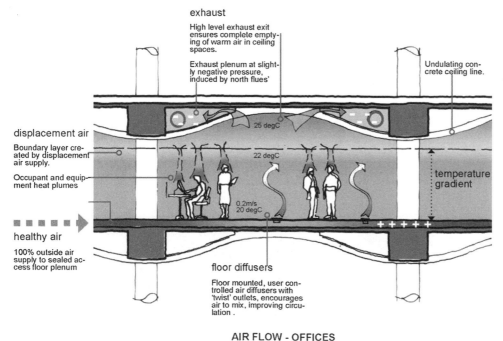

exhaust

High level exhaust exit ensures complete emptying of warm air in ceiling spaces.

Exhaust plenum at slightly negative pressure, induced by north flues'

Undulating concrete ceiling line.

displacement air

Boundary layer created by displacement air supply.

Occupant and equipment heat plumes

25 degC

22 degC

temperature gradient

0.2m/s
20 degC

healthy air

100% outside air supply to sealed access floor plenum

floor diffusers

Floor mounted, user controlled air diffusers with 'twist' outlets, encourages air to mix, improving circulation .

AIR FLOW - OFFICES

Figures 8-3 Melbourne, Australia's Council House 2: personal controls for airflow.

[2]U.S. Environmental Protection Agency (EPA), "Indoor Air Quality," http://www.epa.gov/iaq.

[3]"Defining Post Occupancy Evaluation," http://postoccupancyevaluation.com (accessed January 4, 2009).

[4]"Facility Performance Evaluation (FPE)," Craig Zimring, Mahbub Rashid, and Kevin Kampschroer, last updated: 05-22-2008, Whole Building Design Guide, www.wbdg.org/resources/fpe.php.

[5]Philip Paevere and Stephen Brown, "Indoor Environment Quality and Occupant Productivity in the CH2 Building, Post-Occupancy Summary," March 2008, http://www.melbourne.vic.gov.au/rsrc/PDFs/CH2/CH2PostOccupancySummary.pdf.

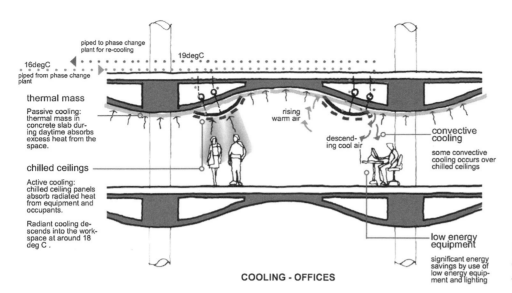

COOLING - OFFICES

Figures 8-4 Melbourne, Australia's Council House 2: personal controls for cooling.

the noise of crowded restaurants, concerts, car alarms, industry, and occupational machinery. Lobbying by communities near airports to change flight paths and landing pattern changes is an example of noise control efforts. Airport and aviation noise monitors are ubiquitous these days, with some airports housing as many as thirty monitors and sophisticated monitoring and measurement data-collection systems. Such abatement efforts make clear that noise is intrusive and does not respect boundaries.

Noise levels can cause significant hearing loss, which affects 10 million Americans, the Harvard School of Public Health estimates, with approximately 30 million workers exposed to noise daily in the United States.[6] According to the EPA, an estimated 15 million American workers are exposed to noise levels of 75 decibels or above, which may be hazardous to their hearing.

Noise adds to stress levels and reduces productivity. Studies on schoolchildren whose classrooms were located near an elevated train line revealed that they were a year behind in their reading ability compared to their contemporaries whose classrooms were in another part of the school building. After sound deadening design strategies were incorporated in the classrooms and on the train track, these students' reading ability improved, to be in line with expected grade-level milestones.[7]

Noise causes pollution when it occurs in the "commons," which is defined as a public good and a resource, like a national park, but it is the air in which sound travels.[8] In the same way that we protect a national park or wildlife preserve, we need to be good stewards of this shared resource.

Techniques for mitigating noise include the use of a sound-masking system or active noise control. The latter uses sound at the same amplitude and the opposite polarity to cancel the existing noise, after computer analysis of the noises sources. Sound masking is the technique of using loudspeakers in the plenum space of dropped ceilings, with careful tuning and adjustment. Outdoor sound-masking systems can take the shape of landscape design elements to mask roadway noise, using a waterfall, for example.

A green designer practicing an integrated approach to building design should consider the effects of noise on the indoor environment. One way to prepare for the design is by conducting a noise survey of the project site, noting the sources of noise impacts and proposing possible mitigation measures. As is typical with other aspects of integrated building design, one must first look at siting and building orientation and layout. Locate openings with consideration to noise sources, and use building materials such as high-performance insulation for acoustical performance between walls, ducts, plenums, and other sources of noise infiltration.

ILLNESSES THAT CAN BE ATTRIBUTED TO NOISE POLLUTION[9]

- Neuropsychological disturbances
- Headaches
- Fatigue
- Stress
- Insomnia and disturbed sleep patterns
- Mood effects: irritability and neurosis

(continued)

[6] Harvard School of Public Health, http://www.hsph.harvard.edu/ccpe/programs/ACNE.html.
[7] Arline L. Bronzaft, "A Quieter School: An Enriched Learning Environment," http://www.quietclassrooms.org/library/bronzaft2.htm.
[8] Noise Pollution Clearinghouse, http://www.nonoise.org.
[9] Green Building Briefing Paper, Leonardo-Energy, January 2007, "Green Buildings: What Is the Impact of Construction with High Environmental Quality?"

Daylight

Human exposure to green space and daylight and their relationship to health is well understood. A 1984 study showed that patients who recovered from abdominal surgery in rooms with views recovered faster and with less need for pain medications than patients whose view was a brick wall.[10] It is also known that light is used to treat people who suffer from seasonal affective disorder (SAD). The artificial light approximates daylight, which is an influencing factor on the circadian rhythms (the daily cycles of life) that regulate the biochemistry, physiology, and behavior of all living things.

In all spaces that humans inhabit, certain tasks benefit from daylight, while others do not. Learning and visually oriented tasks, such as reading, fine needlework, and drawing, benefit from daylight. Other activities, such as theater performances, would be hampered by daylight.

A study on test scores and daylit classrooms by the Heschong Mahone Group revealed some interesting though controversial findings. In one classroom setting, researchers found that skylights with no controls, which caused glare and thermal discomfort, resulted in a 21 percent decrease in reading test scores. The study also found that there was a "7 percent improvement in test scores in those classrooms with the most daylighting, and a 14 to 18 percent improvement for those students in the classrooms with the largest window areas."[11]

This particular IEQ component—daylight—also provides a remarkable opportunity to couple and balance dual benefits, because daylighting techniques are also an opportunity for energy reduction. For example, it is possible to design significant energy savings through reduction of artificial lighting–electrical loads by using skylights with daylight sensors that trigger artificial lighting when daylight levels decrease by a certain amount. Another design strategy is to install sensors on the lighting fixtures nearest the sources of daylight, causing them to shut off when light levels reach a designated intensity (Figure 8-5). The efficacy of a commissioned and well-designed daylighting system is maximized and the building's energy use expanded through this benefit balance. This is yet another example of integrated thinking.

Techniques for good daylight design occur during site, envelope, interior, and material elements design. Consultants working together on these issues should help to avoid much of the need for the postconstruction forensic analysis of daylighting imbalance that has occurred in many high-profile green buildings. Such fixes are costly and often produce contradictory aesthetic values, ultimately revealing a lack of integrated design.

Good daylighting strategies involve architectural building-site design decisions. If nothing else, the green designer should remember to design a building footprint along the east-west axis, with sources of daylight from more than one side, and thin (rather than wide) floorplate plan configurations, thus maximizing light and

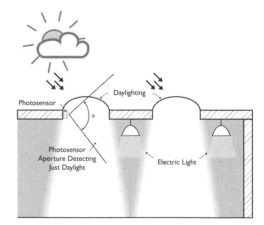

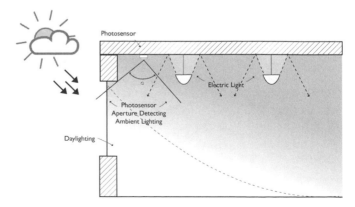

Figure 8-5 Daylight sensors and lighting controls integrate and balance light sources and contribute to reduced energy loads from lighting.

---

[10] R. S. Ulrich, "View through a Window May Influence Recovery from Surgery," *Science* 224, no. 4647 (27 April 1984): 420–421.

[11] Lisa Heschong, Roger L. Wright, and Stacia Okura, "Daylighting Impacts on Human Performance in School," *Journal of the Illuminating Engineering Society* (Summer 2002): 101–114.

minimizing heat gain. Window dimensions should be sized in proportion to the depth of the particular room in question. A narrow, deep room will not only have poor lighting uniformity, but it will be difficult to reap the benefits of daylight from a single, small window.

Openings, in balance with building siting, must be carefully designed. Le Corbusier's Chapel of Notre Dame du Haut in Ronchamp, France, is entirely a study in daylighting design (Figure 8-6). A variety of openings can be used to enhance, diffuse, and control the effects of light (Figure 8-7). Designing sawtooth skylights that reflect light from a rooftop, or admitting light through a clerestory, are two building-design methods that can admit light without the unwanted effects of solar heat

gain. Using interior light shelves can project light deeper into a space (Figure 8-8). Transoms connecting rooms with access to daylight can direct light into adjoining spaces. Generally, admitting light from higher in the room space is desirable in terms of uniformity and effectiveness.

Wherever openings are designed, consider not only how daylight will enter the opening but also how direct solar light will be blocked. Shading devices can be designed into the building envelope, both interior and exterior, or shading can be incorporated into the interior. There are interior shades on the market that have controls that allow in various levels of light. Even more sophisticated shading systems incorporate controls that automatically dim electric light levels. Taking advantage of site features, such as trees as shading devices, is a passive lighting-control strategy.

Louvers can provide dynamic control, and even track sun angles, based on time of day and season. Accurate readings of solar path charts during both the low-angle winter months and the steeper angles of the summer months should be studied by the astute green designer.

Designers must also think about numbers and locations of daylighting controls to design an efficient system that

Figure 8-6 Le Corbusier's Notre Dame du Haut, Ronchamp, France, expresses the profound effects of light.

Figure 8-8 Light shelves.

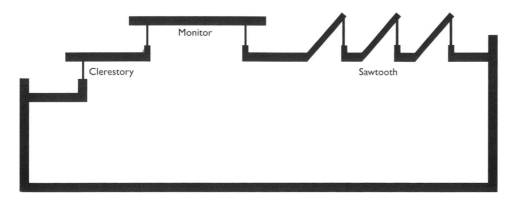

Figure 8-7 Building section showing a variety of openings designed for daylighting.

maximizes the use of daylight. These decisions are based on occupant density, type of construction, and the various functions and visual tasks that are performed in the spaces.

Combining daylighting controls with artificial lighting controls is also key. Dimming technologies can be used that range from simple manual dimming, to automatic stepped dimming, ranging from 100 to 50 percent, to continuous dimming over the full range of percentage by using sensors, or guided by a preset schedule. Other techniques include automatic shutoffs, or more sophisticated shutoffs, with photocell sensors.

Even the decisions that go into designing interior surfaces, such as upholstery, carpet, and other finishes and furnishings, should be considered in terms of their power to reflect or absorb light and heat. Generally, light-colored surfaces are more reflective than dark. Interior space planning considerations, such as orienting computer monitors perpendicular to sources of daylight rather than facing them, also come into play. Visual tasks should benefit from closer proximity to windows.

A simple way to test your design decisions in studio is by building a physical model and then taking it outside and orienting it according to the site geography. Observe the angle of light access into the various spaces. For more accurate measurements, designers will often employ a lighting consultant to perform daylight-modeling techniques to inform their design. Using daylight-simulation modeling software is another way of predicting successful daylight design. A device known as a *heliodon,* or sun simulator, can program the accurate sun declination, site latitude, and the earth's rotation so that you can use a physical model to determine optimal siting conditions for shade, energy, and daylighting design issues. In addition to these passive design strategies, there is a range of high-performance glazing on the market that functions to admit light (visible light transmittance) and shade, and then spectrally select or reflect light and heat.

Visual Comfort

In the last few decades, the field of physical ergonomics—the correct and comfortable relationship between body and task, body placement, the use of tools, and correct positioning for tasks—has become a major topic and a field of scientific study. A component of physical ergonomics is visual ergonomics, where the design of the indoor environment has the potential to create the correct fit of light to task. Effects that can inhibit visual comfort and efficiency include glare, incorrect artificial lighting, and the color, texture, contrast, and brightness of the surrounding interior.

With the benefits of daylighting discussed above, come the inherent downsides; the major issue is glare. The simple rule of thumb with regard to avoiding glare is to diffuse the light rather than admit it directly into a space. Shading devices can control glare, but it is easier to address the potential for glare early in the design phases

of a building by designing windows and openings with accommodation for fluctuating sun angles and by considering the materials of the surroundings. It is important to reiterate that proper building orientation is a major consideration in green buildings, especially those that aim to benefit from passive daylighting and visual comfort.

When designing a lighting plan and selecting fixtures, remember that fluorescent flicker, a common culprit of bad visual ergonomics in the workplace, occurs in magnetic fluorescent lamps. Noise from conventional ballasts also contributes to discomfort.[12] Design with high-frequency electronic ballasts instead. Energy-efficient fluorescent bulbs operate at a higher frequency than conventional fluorescents and have been associated with improved visual performance.

Color is a characteristic of light; therefore, it is energy. Color has the power to affect mood and alter comfort levels. Some even claim that color has the power to heal various conditions, ranging from migraines and allergies to skin disorders and memory problems. *Color therapy,* or *chromatherapy,* has been used in alternative medicine practice and in the ancient cultures of Egypt and China, where each organ has a corresponding color associated with it. In ayurvedic medicine, different colors correspond to distinct chakras.

When it comes to designing a visually ergonomic indoor environment, it is preferable to create a visually dynamic space rather than a uniform and dull space that is unrelieved by pattern and texture. At the same time, overly bright interior design color schemes, using combinations of complementary colors (red and green, orange and blue, yellow and violet), cause visual discomfort. A certain level of brightness and contrast is desirable from a design and visual ergonomics perspective; such a scheme can actually heighten visual acuity.

Adaptation is the ability of the eye to shift from one light level to another, as in the experience of driving out of an underground tunnel into a brightly lit exterior. If the shift from shadow to brightness is too extreme, or if the introduction of shadow is too abrupt, adaptation will be difficult and this will become a source of visual discomfort, causing the eye to transition too rapidly from a dark surface to a lighter one. Thus, it poses an interesting challenge to design a visually comfortable environment with appropriate levels of shadow and with adjoining surfaces that transition from light to dark without sudden swings. Daylighting and artificial lighting both must be factored into the design.

Connection to the Outdoors

In fields as diverse as architecture and biotechnology, we frequently take our most innovative design cues from the natural world, a concept known as *biomimicry.* The need

---

[12] J. A. Veitch, and S. L. McColl, "Modulation of Fluorescent Light: Flicker Rate and Light Source Effects on Visual Performance and Visual Comfort." *Lighting Research and Technology* 27 (1995): 243–256.

for humans to form a connection to the outdoor environment is a fundamental one. Proximity to green space, visual access to the sky, and the sense of outside air movement on the skin is pleasurable and innately soothing.

Unfortunately, the way we live and work in industrialized settings severely limits our ability to regularly connect with nature in these ways. Many architectural icons have embraced this relationship as the center of their design values. An integrated building not only has the power of such precedents but a meaningful sustainable design directive to address the lack of this connection with nature. The desirable and salubrious effects of biophilic design, as the concept is known, must also come into play as a component of good IEQ, as well as responding to an architectural edict of sorts.

There are several design approaches, both interior and architectural, that can facilitate or mimic this connection to the outdoors. As part of concept design, rough window placement and openings can be designed with consideration to what functions the spaces serve and what number and types of people will inhabit these spaces. Will the occupants be office workers who sit in cubicles throughout most of the day? If so, they would benefit from visual access to higher levels with a view of the sky and a slice of green space—tops of trees or other surroundings.

Another option would be to bring green plantings indoors, which has a number of benefits. In addition to the psychological benefits that an element of green can provide, indoor plantings are said to help purify air—although the soil of poorly maintained plants can be a source of mold and allergens.[13] (Figure 8-9 shows the Bel-Air Mini Mobile Greenhouse, an innovative VOC-cleaning design object, based on findings by the National Aeronautics and Space Administration [NASA] and designed by Mathieu Lehanneur in conjunction with Harvard University–based scientists.)

A recent study was done to gauge the ability of plants to cleanse indoor air of contaminants. Using seven plant species in the study site, researchers concluded that benzene (a powerful VOC) was removed to varying degrees from the indoor air of the site. Researchers discovered that both the potting soil and the plants and their interactions were responsible for removing 12–27 ppm d^{-1} (the designation d refers to diamagnetic, or the inability to produce a magnetic field) of benzene within 24 hours.[14]

It is also known that plants increase well-being. Studies conducted among people being treated for dementia found that the presence of plants not only improved the quality of the indoor air but also increased patients'

Figure 8-9 Mathieu Lehanneur, the designer of the Bel-Air Mini Mobile Greenhouse says: "Upon the return of the first space flights and many analyses, NASA discovered a high level of toxic volatile organic compounds in the astronauts' body tissues. The American spacecraft, mostly constructed of plastic, fiberglass, insulating materials and fire retardants, gradually poisoned the astronauts. The same effect is experienced in our living spaces. Each manufactured product gives off or—more precisely—emits, even several years after having been manufactured."

responsiveness and overall well-being.[15] Yet another study concluded that plants indoors help attention levels, increase productivity, and lower blood pressure.[16]

A particularly appealing green building strategy, encapsulating the concept of improved well-being through interior landscape design, is the idea of living walls—large-scale greenscape elements that can stand alone or become part of a building's vertical plane (Figure 8-10). In addition, they provide active air-quality benefits. Some living-wall technologies incorporate the air-handling system within the wall, making it an integrated filtering system. Forced air through a living wall is designed to degrade compounds like formaldehyde and benzene in the indoor environment. In addition to providing a sense of well-being, the living wall can improve air quality and energy efficiency.

[13]B. C. Wolverton, *How to Grow Fresh Air: 50 House Plants that Purify Your Home or Office* (New York: Penguin, 1997).

[14]Ralph L. Orwell, Ronald L. Wood, Jane Tarran, Fraser Torpy, and Margaret D. Burchett, "Removal of Benzene by the Indoor Plant/Substrate Microcosm and Implications for Air Quality," *Water, Air, & Soil Pollution* 157, nos. 1–4 (September 2004): 193–207.

[15]E. Rappe and L. Lindén, "Plants In Health Care Environments: Experiences of the Nursing Personnel in Homes for People With Dementia," *ISHS Acta Horticulturae 639: XXVI International Horticultural Congress: Expanding Roles for Horticulture in Improving Human Well-Being and Life Quality,* convened June 2004, Toronto, Canada, proceedings published June 30, 2004, D. Relf, editor, ISHS Acta Horticulturae 639.

[16]Virginia I. Lohr, Caroline H. Pearson-Mims, and Georgia K. Goodwin, "Interior Plants May Improve Worker Productivity and Reduce Stress in a Windowless Environment," *Journal of Environmental Horticulture,* 14, no. 2: 97–100.

Figure 8-10 A living wall (*mur végétal*) by botanist-artist Patrick Blanc.

Thermal Comfort

We will explore the notion of thermal comfort as a component of IEQ, because it is one of the most immediately palpable and recognized indoor characteristics, especially if designed incorrectly. Entire books and conferences have been written and staged around the topic. Our codes and mechanical system design are centered on this variable of IEQ. In fact, the work of one of the first scientists to understand thermal comfort concepts became the basis for an ISO standard.

P. Ole Fanger, a Danish scientist and university professor, developed a complex equation to arrive at a mathematical definition of thermal comfort.[17] The equation has six variables that are integral to human thermal comfort. Ambient temperature, radiant temperature, humidity, and air velocity are the four environmental variables, while clothing insulation and activity level are the two metabolic variables in the model.

Often, other less quantifiable variables are discussed as pertinent to thermal comfort. The mood of those inhabiting the spaces, workers' motivation levels, the simple patterns of everyday life, and other behaviors

are contributors to perceptions of thermal comfort. It is the interaction of these parameters that creates the difference between human awareness of an unpleasant indoor space and its antithesis: a comfortable indoor environment.[18]

How can we design for thermal comfort? Clearly, Fanger's equation, with its multiple mathematical values, implies a corresponding complexity in terms of design. For this area we turn to engineers of indoor environments, whose disciplines range from mechanical engineering to organizational psychology. As green design professionals, it is important to understand these variables and be able to collaborate with the disciplines. In the end, it comes down to the synergies of architectural design and mechanical system design, whose combined work involves balancing the appropriate amount of ventilation and temperature for the occupant density, the activities of the space, the patterns of use, and ultimately the individual control, or at least the perception of control, of these factors.

Other IEQ Issues

Much of good IEQ design hinges on the concept of *biophilia*, an innovative design approach that "emphasizes the necessity of maintaining, enhancing, and restoring the beneficial experience of nature in the built environment."[19] The components of IEQ embody these fundamental links between humans and nature and, if well designed, will also deliver a space that addresses these links. Additional components of IEQ that the prescient green building designer will integrate involve the several components described below, as well as many others.

- The variations of climate affect interior levels of noise, temperature, air quality, and human activity level. Wind, for example, can contribute changes in perceived comfort, as well as subtle shifts in mood and social interaction.
- By-products of the site—such as asbestos, radon, lead, and other inorganic contaminants—can cause harmful effects to health.
- Counted among the by-products of the site that receive current media attention are mold and electromagnetic frequencies (EMFs), which have been associated with illnesses ranging from leukemia to memory impacts.[20]

---

[17]P. Ole Fanger's work shows that poor air quality in homes can cause asthma in children and that poor air quality in workplaces decreases productivity.

[18]Kenneth C. Parsons, *Human Thermal Environments: The Effects of Hot, Moderate, and Cold* (London: CRC Press, 2003); P. O. Fanger, *Thermal Comfort: Analysis and Applications in Environmental Engineering* (Copenhagen: Danish Technical Press, 1970; New York: McGraw-Hill: 1970).
[19]Stephen R. Kellert, Judith H. Heerwagen, and Martin L. Malor, eds., *Biophilic Design* (Hoboken, NJ: John Wiley & Sons, 2008).
[20]WBDG Sustainable Committee, "Enhance Indoor Environmental Quality (IEQ)," *The Whole Building Design Guide* (Washington, DC: National Institute of Building Sciences, October 14, 2008), http://www.wbdg.org/design/ieq.php (accessed January 5, 2009).

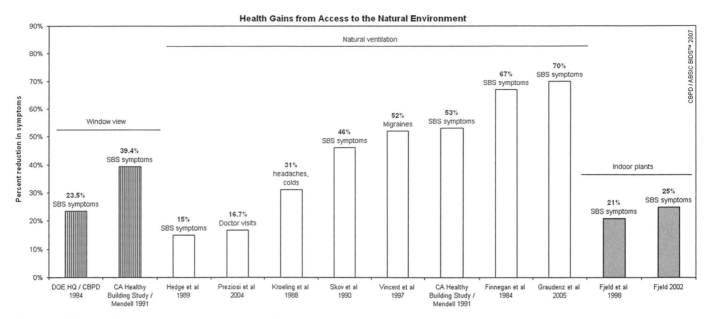

Figures 8-11 Health gains from access to the natural environment.

• Building type and function may create special concerns. Hospitals have the ability to harbor bacteria and illnesses that affect both patients and health-care workers, and their indoor environment must be carefully monitored. Surgical spaces are often kept at extremely low temperatures to stave off growth of harmful organisms. Industrial manufacturing facilities may involve the creation or use of synthetic chemicals and hazardous materials. In such situations, the experience of those inhabiting indoor spaces is reduced to personal protection mechanisms.

• The quality of drinking water is also considered a driver of indoor environmental quality. Drinking water should be tested regularly, along with air quality.

• Finally, how comfortable can an indoor environment be when it is not properly maintained or cleaned? Regular cleaning schedules are optimal, but so is the use of appropriate, environmentally benign, green cleaning products. In addition to diverting waste from landfill, regularly scheduled collection of compost, recycling materials, and other waste is necessary for indoor olfactory comfort and air quality.

Benefits of Good IEQ

No doubt you have realized that the indoor environmental quality factors reviewed in this chapter supply several converging benefits, all closely associated with common themes. Studies have argued that human wellness, task-related productivity, and quality of performance in test scores can be attributed to a physical or perceived tie to nature, one of the biophilic goals of effective IEQ.

In 2002 M. J. Mendell compiled a summary of then-current productivity-research studies and concluded that many factors can negatively affect a child's performance in school, among them poor ventilation controls as well as indoor microbiological and chemical pollutants. In addition, newer buildings and the presence of carpets have had a negative effect on certain tasks and on mental performance, while daylight and personal controls have had a positive effect on academic testing.[21]

There is an entire body of research by psychologist Judith H. Heerwagen and many others on green building and productivity relationships that conclude that improved focus, effectiveness, and reduced absenteeism can be encouraged by the interior built environment.

Some claim that the results are mixed and health and productivity studies are still controversial, but as we see in Figures 8-11 and 8-12, representing the results of Carnegie Mellon University's Center for Building Performance and Diagnostics research into the existing literature, health and productivity benefits are clearly associated with access to the natural environment.

In our review of IEQ factors, we've seen that the interior space is a part that represents the whole. An indoor space must be an integrated, functional organism within the larger, integrated, functional building, both embodying and defining the notion of holistic building design. Although it's possibly a tidy conceit, note that we again return to the concept of integrated design, the salient lesson of sustainable building design.

---

[21]G. A. Heath and M. J. Mendell, "Do Indoor Environments in Schools Influence Student Performance? A Review of the Literature," IV-20–IV-26.

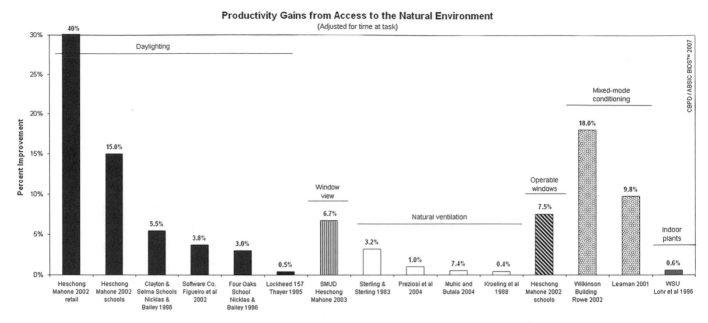

Figures 8-12 Productivity gains from access to the natural environment.

EXERCISES

1. Conduct a noise survey of the project site from one of your studio assignments, noting at least six sources of noise impacts, and discuss possible mitigation measures. Use various architectural, envelope, and siting solutions, as well as advanced technologies in conceptual design sketches.

2. What additional components of indoor environmental quality could be addressed by a designer of integrated green buildings?

■ Resources

Godish, Thad. 2000. *Indoor Environmental Quality.* Boca Raton, FL: CRC Press.

Heath, G. A., and M. J. Mendell. 2002. "Do Indoor Environments in Schools Influence Student Performance?

A Review of the Literature." In *A Compilation of Papers for the Indoor Air 2002 Conference, Monterey, California,* IV-20–IV-26. Berkeley, CA: Indoor Environment Department, Lawrence Berkeley National Laboratory.

Kellert, Stephen R., Judith H. Heerwagen, and Martin L. Malor, eds. 2008. *Biophilic Design.* Hoboken, NJ: John Wiley & Sons.

May, Jeffrey C. 2006. *My Office Is Killing Me! The Sick Building Survival Guide.* Baltimore, MD: Johns Hopkins University Press.

Green Cleaning Web Sites

Green Seal: http://www.greenseal.org

Healthy House Institute: http://www.healthyhouseinstitute.com

Green Clean Certified: http://www.greencleancertified.com

The Ashkin Group, Green Cleaning Experts: http://www.AshkinGroup.com

Healthy Schools Campaign: http://www.healthyschoolscampaign.org

9 Introduction to Energy Issues: Use and Standards

Architectural Design and Changing Technologies

Occupants have come to expect a building to foster comfort by mitigating the negative impacts of climate. Present-day building occupants expect a high level of comfort, even under extreme weather conditions. From antiquity until quite recently, the provision of thermal and visual comfort for building occupants was chief among the architect's responsibilities. Until the turn of the twentieth century, the architect typically served as "master builder," overseeing and integrating design and construction. New technologies that appeared in the nineteenth century and came to fruition in the twentieth century changed the way we build, along with the role and self-image of the architect. New structural materials such as iron, steel, and reinforced concrete made it possible to build tall buildings and freed walls from the structural role they had played for centuries. A framework of columns, beams, and a reinforced concrete floor slab could carry structural loads. Walls could be made of thin, lightweight materials, such as aluminum, and in some cases could be reduced to little more than glass.

By the second half of the twentieth century, new developments in cooling and lighting, specifically air-conditioning and fluorescent lighting, resulted in even more dramatic changes in building design. By the 1950s, traditional design methods used to provide thermal comfort and good lighting conditions were ignored by many architects, who substituted lightweight materials for thermally massive masonry and mechanical cooling and electric lighting for natural ventilation and daylight. Heat-absorbing glass was specified in lieu of sunshades. An unquestioning faith in technological solutions, widespread at the time, led many to believe an unchanging, "optimal" indoor environment was preferable to one that varied with diurnal and seasonal variation. While, with hindsight, it is easy to see this mindset as naive, environmental awareness at the time was low, and few were concerned about energy use in buildings. Utilities at this time promised nuclear power would result in electricity so cheap it would not be metered. While discussion and research on energy-efficient, climate-responsive design never completely disappeared, the historic American vision of a resource-rich landscape, ripe for mining and development, was not widely questioned.

Fragmentation of Design Process

In the post–World War II period, architects ceded responsibility for comfort to mechanical and electrical engineers, believing that comfort was best provided by equipment rather than architectural design. Architects grew dependent upon outside consultants, each of whom had a defined area of technical expertise and responsibility. The implications of a given design approach on energy use and occupant comfort were difficult to understand, or they could be ignored because of new technologies—or so it seemed at the time. Integrated, climate-responsive design was difficult to achieve in this increasingly fragmented process. A business model that paid engineering consultants based on overall cost gave little incentive to the design team to reduce the use of energy-intensive technical solutions. Because these changes are so significant, it is important to remember how recently in the history of architecture they actually occurred.

The Development of Air-Conditioning

The invention of what we now call air-conditioning is credited to Willis Carrier, who built upon earlier cooling technologies developed in the nineteenth century. Adding the ability to not only cool air but control humidity,

Carrier received a patent for this new technology in 1906. In the 1920s his company installed air-conditioning in theaters, department stores, and the chambers of the U.S. Senate and House of Representatives. Small, residential air-conditioning units were developed by Carrier Corporation in 1928, but the Great Depression limited their spread. It was not until the late 1930s that Carrier developed an air-conditioning system small enough for use in high-rise buildings. Because of U.S. involvement in World War II in 1941, it was not until the late 1940s and early 1950s that air-conditioning became commonplace in high-rise buildings. And it was not until the 1960s and 1970s that residential air-conditioning became widespread. Currently, more than 90 percent of new homes are built with central air-conditioning.

Prior to the advent of air-conditioning, hot conditions were ameliorated by shading, air movement, and—in dry, western climates—thermal mass. If humidity is not extreme, shading and air movement can effectively provide comfort if air temperatures are less than 85 degrees Fahrenheit (F) or about 30 degrees Celsius (C). Awnings were often added seasonally to windows to provide shading. To permit ventilation, windows were operable and distributed across different building elevations. Window and ceiling fans were used to create air movement when cross-ventilation, induced by wind, was not available. When both air temperature and humidity were high, it was possible to temper the indoor environment, but providing conditions expected by present-day building occupants was not possible. Building occupants understood that thermal conditions would vary with the seasons and dressed accordingly. Learning to provide shade and opportunities for air movement were part of an architect's education.

The Impact of Fluorescent Lighting

Fluorescent lighting uses less energy and produces less heat to achieve a given light output than incandescent lighting. It was first commercially available in 1938, even later than air-conditioning. World War II hastened its spread. Factory production boomed to support the war effort, and fluorescent lighting was frequently used in industrial facilities. By the early 1950s, it was commonplace in commercial buildings.

The combination of air-conditioning and fluorescent lighting had a dramatic effect on building form. A tall building in the first half of the twentieth century was designed with a narrow floor plan, typically no wider than 50 feet, and tall ceilings. This made it possible to light the building during most operating hours with daylight and to cool the building much of the year with cross-ventilation through operable windows. Larger, wider buildings requiring incandescent lights in areas

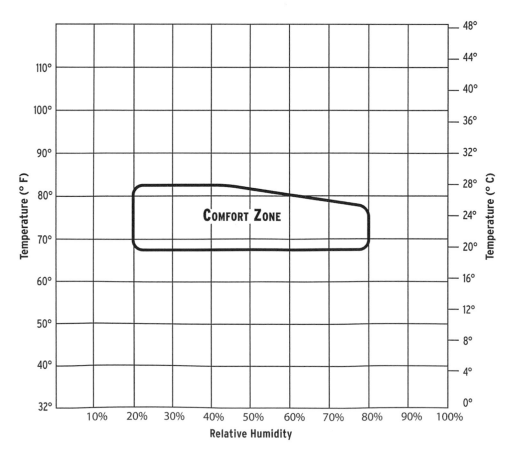

Figure 9-1 The comfort zone: Shading the sun, air movement, humidification, and the use of thermal mass can extend the limits of the human comfort zone.

(a)

(b)

Figure 9-2 a, b High-rise design: High-rise buildings in the first half of the twentieth century were designed to use daylight as the primary lighting system and operable windows for ventilation and cooling.

that did not receive daylight would have been uninhabitable much of the year due to heat from the lighting equipment and correspondingly greater difficulty in providing cross-ventilation. With fluorescent lights and air-conditioning, bigger buildings were possible, but they required energy to operate and reduced the connection between occupants and the exterior world.

Examining Your Environment

Take a few moments during your daily activities to identify and observe buildings constructed before 1950. Determine for yourself how they differ from more recent buildings. Compare the size, ceiling height, and window area with newer buildings. Can the windows be opened? Do you see skylights or evidence that there once were skylights? In older residential buildings, do you see roof overhangs that shade windows? Whether residential or commercial, look for differences between older and newer buildings in the way they admit, block, or filter sun, wind, and light.

Resource limitations, geopolitics, and recognition of the environmental impacts of energy use have generated interest in significantly reducing energy use in buildings. At the same time, there has been renewed interest in providing building occupants with a connection to daylight and a sense of personal control over their immediate environment. Study of the benefits and limitations of traditional building designs, coupled with an understanding of appropriate application of modern technologies, addresses both of these concerns.

Energy Efficiency, Resource Limitations, and Global Warming

Why be concerned with the energy used to operate the buildings in which we live, work, and play? Four reasons are foremost. First, the fuels we currently use to generate power are largely nonrenewable, and supplies will not last indefinitely. Second, deposits of natural gas, the "cleanest" fossil fuel currently in widespread use, are limited and mainly located in geopolitical hot spots. Third, demand for fuel on global markets continues to rise, and production levels—especially as some current fuel exporters develop economically and become net importers—may not remain high and may lead to price increases. Fourth, coal, the resource domestically available and burned to generate much of our electricity, releases gases into the atmosphere that are dramatically changing the Earth's climate.

For these reasons, it is important to understand the central role building design and operations play in shaping our energy future. In North America, building operations directly account for more than one-third of all energy use and over 60 percent of the consumption of electricity. At the turn of the twenty-first century, buildings located in the United States accounted for almost 10 percent of global energy use. If we include industrial activity that provides resources to the building sector, the impact of buildings on energy use is considerable.

The link between the energy used in building construction and operations and global environmental problems is indisputable. Carbon dioxide and other greenhouse gasses create an insulating layer around the earth, trapping

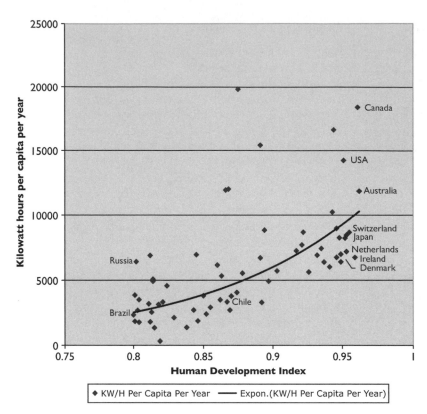

Figure 9-3 Human Development Index and electricity use: The United Nations Human Development Index, which combines statistics on longevity, educational attainment, and standard of living per capita, suggests that North American electricity use could be reduced with few negative impacts.

heat from the sun. Increasing levels of these gases in the atmosphere change both global and regional climates.

The Intergovernmental Panel on Climate Change (IPCC), organized by the United Nations' World Meteorological Organization (WMO) and the United Nations Environmental Programme (UNEP), stated in February 2007 that "[t]he primary source of the increased atmospheric concentration of carbon dioxide since the pre-industrial period results from fossil fuel use, with land use change providing another significant but smaller contribution."[1] While a full discussion of global warming is beyond the scope of this book, there is scientific consensus that global warming's impacts for life on Earth are profound and could lead to the extinction of half of living species. Our economy also faces significant risks from climate change affecting water resources, agriculture, forests, and the natural habitats of a number of indigenous plants and animals. Rises in sea level, resulting from unrestrained emission of greenhouse gases, will cause flooding and refugee crises in many coastal areas.

The depletion of ozone in the stratosphere, and the resulting *ozone hole* that has led to increased ultraviolet radiation at the surface of the Earth, is directly attributable to refrigerants used in air-conditioning systems. At a local level, the demand for more power, and the accompanying need for new power plants, large-scale dams, natural gas and oil exploration, and mining sites,

contributes to habitat destruction, deforestation, and degradation of air and water quality.

Addressing global warming and ecological sustainability will require more than just changes in the way we build. There is no such thing as a sustainable building, only sustainable societies. However, designing buildings that use much less energy is an essential step in meeting these environmental challenges.

When designing to greatly reduce building energy use, what standards can guide our efforts?

◼ STANDARDS FOR ENERGY-EFFICIENT BUILDINGS

Energy Use in North America

In designing a home or commercial building, the first question is, What level of performance is achievable, and at what cost? How low can we go in terms of energy consumption? How difficult will it be to do so? What impact will it have on our standard of living? The United Nations calculates a Human Development Index (HDI), which combines statistics on longevity, educational attainment, and standard of living per capita.[2]

[1] Intergovernmental Panel on Climate Change, Fourth Assessment Report, available at http://www.ipcc.ch/ipccreports/ar4-syr.htm

[2] United Nations Development Program, Human Development Report 2007/2008, available athttp://hdr.undp.org/en/reports/global/hdr2007-2008/

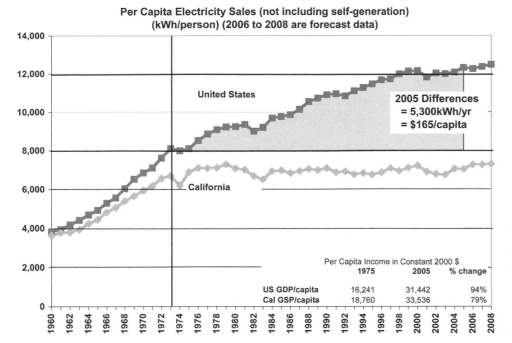

Figure 9-4 The impact of energy-efficiency standards in California: California instituted energy standards for buildings and appliances more than thirty years ago. Since 1973, per capita electricity use in California has remained almost constant while rising by approximately 50 percent in the rest of the United States.

The human development indices for the United States and Canada are no higher than those of the Netherlands, Germany, and France, yet energy use is much higher. In fact, U.S. and Canadian energy use and greenhouse gas emissions on a per capita basis are among the highest in the world. Regional and local conditions have a major effect on energy consumption. However, the data suggest that energy consumption could be lowered in the United States and Canada without altering the level of human development. We would simply need to employ design and building practices already in common use in other developed countries.

The California Experience

Within the United States, per capita energy use varies greatly between states. Energy use in a number of states, in particular California, is significantly lower than in others. This has not always been the case. Since 1973 per capita electricity use in California has remained almost constant, while in the nation as a whole per capita use has risen by approximately 50 percent. In the 1970s California initiated standards for building and appliance energy use, standards that have grown more stringent with development of new technologies and methods. Californians are not known for maintaining a spartan lifestyle, yet they use electricity at levels closer to those of France and Japan than to other parts of the United States. This is further proof that strategies already in use in states such as California can serve as models for significant reductions in energy use in buildings throughout the United States and Canada, without negative impact on living standards.

For practicing professionals, a standard or benchmark makes it possible to assess success in designing a building that meets minimum standards of energy efficiency. As mentioned, California has had building energy-efficiency standards since the 1970s. These are officially Title 24, Part 6, of the *California Code of Regulations, Energy Standards for Residential and Non-Residential Buildings,* but they are more commonly referred to as the Title 24 Energy Standards. The Standards are updated on a regular cycle and are available from the California Energy Commission's Web site.[3] Compliance with the Title 24 Energy Standards is required before a building permit is issued and construction can begin. However, because the Title 24 Energy Standards are written for specific California climate zones, their use in other parts of the country is limited.

National Energy Standards

The American Society of Heating, Refrigerating and Air-Conditioning Engineers (ASHRAE) publishes Standard 90.1 (for nonresidential and high-rise residential buildings), which is applicable for locations in the United States and Canada. The ASHRAE standards published in 2007 create eight climate zones with varying requirements. The International Code Council (ICC) develops

---

[3] Title 24, Part 6, *California Code of Regulations, Energy Standards for Residential and Non-Residential Buildings,* CEC-400-2008-001-CMF (Sacramento: California Energy Commission, December 2008). The California energy standards are updated regularly and are available from the California Energy Commission's Web site, http://www.energy.ca.gov/title24/ (accessed January 5, 2009).

the International Energy Conservation Code (IECC), first released in 1998, supplanting the earlier Model Energy Code (MEC). The latest version of the IECC was released in 2006.

Energy Standards and Computer Simulation

The ASHRAE, ICC, and California standards are similar in that they establish minimum prescriptive requirements for the building envelope, mechanical systems, and electric lighting. Variations from the prescriptive norms are possible through an energy simulation of the building performed with approved software. The simulation must demonstrate the proposed scheme taken as a whole is equal to a similar design that complies with all of the prescriptive requirements. It is important to understand what these computer simulations do and do not indicate. These simulations are *not* predictions of building-energy performance but, rather, documentation of compliance with a given standard. In addition to compliance documentation, computer energy simulation is an excellent tool for evaluating and choosing among competing design alternatives. It is rarely intended as a precise prediction of energy performance once a building is occupied. Energy-simulation tools are discussed further later in this chapter.

It is important to remember that these energy standards are for design. Good design is a necessary step but does not guarantee energy savings. Building operation is equally important. Have we seen real energy savings from advanced design requirements? Because of the different ways in which buildings are used once occupied, and the varying quality of building operations and maintenance, the answer is sometimes but not always.

Toward National Energy Standards

In the 1992 Energy Policy Act (EPAct), the U.S. Congress mandated that all states must review and consider adopting ASHRAE Standard 90.1 for commercial buildings and the Model Energy Code, now the IECC, for residential construction. Congress requires that the U.S. Department of Energy (DOE) review new versions of ASHRAE Standard 90.1 and the IECC as they are published to determine whether the new version would improve energy efficiency in commercial and residential buildings. For commercial buildings, if the DOE makes a positive determination, states are required to update their code to meet or exceed the new version. For low-rise residential construction of less than four stories, if the DOE makes a positive determination, states are required to *consider* adopting a code that meets or exceeds the new version. At the moment, the Department of Energy's latest published determinations are for Standard 90.1-1999 and the 2000 IECC. The DOE determinations on more recent versions of these standards are forthcoming.

The complete determination process and all available results to date may be found at http://www.energycodes.gov/implement/determinations.stm. The DOE's maps and databases on state adoption may be found at http://www.energycodes.gov/implement/state_codes/index.stm.

Achieving Deep Reductions in Energy Use

Implementation of the latest energy standards across the United States would slow the need for new electrical generation facilities and reduce on-site use of natural gas for space and water heating and cooking. However, to meet the challenge of global warming, we must rapidly achieve major reductions in building energy use, while greatly increasing the supply of renewable energy for remaining power requirements. Thus, energy efficiency and renewable energy go hand in hand. By greatly reducing demand, renewable energy sources can provide a larger percentage of our energy needs.

Architecture 2030, an independent nonprofit organization, has been at the forefront in calling for drastic improvements to building performance to combat global warming. Established in 2002, Architecture 2030 wants to rapidly transform the U.S. and global building sector from their status as the major contributor of greenhouse gas emissions to becoming a central part of the solution to the global-warming crisis by changing the way buildings and developments are planned, designed, and constructed. Architecture 2030 issued *The 2030 Challenge*,[4] asking the global architecture and building community to design all new buildings, developments, and major renovations to reduce consumption of greenhouse gas–emitting energy and fossil fuels to 50 percent of the regional average for a given building type. The fossil fuel reduction standard would become more stringent every five years—60 percent in 2010, 70 percent in 2015, 80 percent in 2020, 90 percent in 2025—with carbon neutrality, using no fossil-fueled, greenhouse gas–emitting energy for building operations targeted for the year 2030.

A number of national organizations, including the American Institute of Architects (AIA), Royal Architecture Institute of Canada (RAIC), American Society of Heating, Refrigerating, and Air-Conditioning Engineers, and U.S. Green Building Council (USGBC), have endorsed the 2030 Challenge.

Recognition of the critical nature of the goals promulgated by Architecture 2030 is beginning to have an impact. The U.S. Green Building Council's Leadership in Energy and Environmental Design (LEED) Rating System promotes environmental-building practices that address energy efficiency and other environmental building practices. To meet the 2030 requirement for 50 percent

[4]Architecture 2030, the 2030 Challenge, available at: http://www.architecture2030.org/2030_challenge/index.html

energy reduction compared to the regional average energy consumption by building type, the USGBC now mandates that LEED projects exceed ASHRAE Standard 90.1-2004. The USGBC's LEED for New Construction (LEED-NC 2.2) sets a minimum design level of 14 percent beyond the latest ASHRAE standard for non-residential projects.

New Developments in California

Even more important, recent goals announced by two State of California agencies, the California Energy Commission (CEC) and the California Public Utilities Commission (CPUC), mirror the 2030 Challenge targets, calling for zero-net energy residential buildings by 2020 and nonresidential buildings by 2030. Questions remain as to the precise definition of zero-net energy and associated building performance metrics. However, the direction is clear. The State of California will require steep reductions in energy use in buildings in response to global warming and uncertainties about the supply of fossil fuels.

The State of California, ASHRAE, IECC, and LEED requirements are influencing professional practice. However, because of the high degree of specificity of all of these standards, applicability to student work is limited. How can students learn to design buildings that use much less energy? An understanding of basic principles of climate, heat transfer, and solar geometry is a good place to begin. This should be coupled with knowledge of how these principles affect the energy performance of common building materials. Passive design strategies that reduce the need for mechanical cooling and electric lighting should be studied. We will delve into these topics in the following sections.

Standards and Computer Modeling

Computer energy models are used to demonstrate compliance with building standards such as ASHRAE 90.1 and California Title 24. To create a level playing field, compliance models make a number of assumptions about hours of operation and patterns of use. Compliance models do not necessarily reflect how the building is used and operated when occupied. Strategies such as elimination of mechanical cooling through passive design are not recognized in compliance models. In a design that eliminates the need for mechanical cooling, the compliance modeling software assumes a cooling system that meets minimum requirements of the standard. Thus a design that eliminates the need for mechanical cooling entirely may exceed the overall standard by a smaller margin than a building that has an energy-efficient air conditioner.

Modeling software used for compliance can typically be used in a noncompliance mode, permitting inputs to more closely reflect anticipated operating conditions. Such a model can be an excellent analytical tool for evaluating and choosing among competing design alternatives. However, computer-based energy modeling software is rarely intended as a precise prediction of energy performance once a building is occupied and should not be perceived as such.

10 Basic Energy Principles

Heat as Energy

Heating, cooling, and lighting a building involves the addition or subtraction of heat. Thus a basic understanding of physical principles of energy transfer and storage is indispensable for low- or zero-net energy building design.

Heat is a form of energy that is particularly relevant to building designers. Its unit of measurement in the United States is the British thermal unit (Btu) and in all other countries, the joule (J). The British thermal unit is by definition the amount of heat needed to raise one pound of water by one degree Fahrenheit. Heat flows directionally from hot to cold. The only exception occurs when mechanical energy is used to "pump" heat in the opposite direction. Without a temperature differential, there can be no transfer of energy.

Heat energy can be *sensible* or *latent*, while heat transfer occurs through conduction, convection, radiation, and change of phase. What do these terms mean?

Figure 10-1 Direction of heat transfer: Without the introduction of mechanical energy, heat moves only from hot to cold.

Sensible and Latent Heat

Sensible heat is dry heat. It is the result of molecular vibration in a substance. Temperature is a measure of the average intensity of the molecular vibration in that substance and is calculated in degrees using one of three scales, typically Fahrenheit (F) in the United States and Celsius (C) or kelvin (K) in the rest of the world.

All materials on earth above absolute zero ($-459.69°F$, $-273.15°C$, or $0°K$) have some molecular vibration and thus hold some heat. As molecular vibration speeds up, the measured temperature rises, meaning hotter objects have greater intensity of molecular vibration.

The amount of heat contained in an object is not indicated by temperature alone. Heat is a function of temperature and mass, the amount of matter in an object. Two blocks at a temperature of 50°F, each 1-foot long in all three dimensions, could contain different amounts of heat depending upon the density and thus the mass of the object. A block of stone has more mass than an equally sized block made of corrugated cardboard or Styrofoam.

Latent heat is heat released or absorbed by a substance during a change of phase, for example, from solid to liquid, liquid to gas, or vice versa. As previously stated, 1 Btu is the amount of heat required to raise the temperature of a pound of water by 1°F. If we add 50 Btu to a pound of water at 100°F, the temperature will increase by 50°F. There is a clear and direct relationship between the temperature of water and its heat content. This is true in all instances, except at the point of a change of phase.

Breaking the molecular bonds and transforming a water molecule from liquid to gas requires a large amount of energy. When water reaches its boiling point at 212°F, adding heat does not raise the temperature until 970 Btu have been absorbed. Only then has the water completely evaporated into steam. As the water evaporates and is transformed to vapor, air temperature drops while the moisture content of the air increases. The total amount of heat remains the same, but the 970 Btu of heat that were previously *sensible* in the air temperature are now *latent* in the water vapor. The *latent heat of evaporation* for water is thus 970 Btu.

Similarly, if we cool the 100°F water, it will lose 1°F for every British thermal unit removed, until it reaches 32°F. At that point, we must remove 144 Btu in order to completely change the pound of water into ice. Thus, the *latent heat of fusion* for water is 144 Btu.

If water vapor condenses back into a liquid, the latent energy absorbed from the air during evaporation is released as sensible heat. Evaporation and condensation of liquids, be they water or some other form of refrigerant, makes it possible to move heat from one location to another. The release or absorption of latent energy during change of phase is what makes possible steam heat and refrigeration systems. Absorption of sensible heat from the air through the introduction of moisture is the principle behind evaporative cooling, which will be discussed later in this chapter. Removal of latent heat through humidity control is central to air conditioning.

Heat Transfer

There are four primary methods of heat transfer in a building: *conduction*, *convection*, *evaporation*, and *radiation*.

Conduction

If two objects of different temperature are in direct physical contact, heat will be transferred by *conduction*. The high-speed vibrating molecules of the warmer object collide with the slower moving molecules of the cooler object. The high-speed molecules slow down as a result of the collision, and the warm object cools, while the low-speed molecules speed up, and the cool object becomes warmer.

For conduction to be effective, the molecules must be close to one another. For practical purposes, conduction occurs between objects that are touching one another. Because molecules in gases are rarely dense, air is not a good conductor of heat.

A measure of the rate at which heat is transferred through a material by conduction is the U-value (or U-factor). In the United States, the U-value is expressed in British thermal units per hour per square foot per degree Fahrenheit (Btu/h ft^2 F). In the metric system, it is expressed as watts per square meter per degree kelvin (W/m^2 K).

If our goal is to design a building in order to limit heat transfer between inside and outside, a lower U-value is better because it indicates a lower rate of transfer. The insulating value of a material, or the measure of its ability to *resist* heat transfer, is the inverse of the U-value and is indicated by the R-value. The higher the R-value, the greater the material's resistance to heat flow and the better its insulating value.

Convection

Convection is another form of heat transfer. Fluids, which—for architectural purposes—mean liquids and gases, expand as they absorb and contract as they lose heat by conduction. Upon expansion, a substance becomes less dense and less subject to gravitational forces. The substance naturally rises, creating convective currents within the fluid and transferring heat.

Thus, natural convection moves heat from lower to higher locations within an enclosed space. Forced convection occurs when air is moved by a fan or wind or when liquid is moved by a pump.

Radiation

The third form of heat transfer is *radiation*. Radiant heat moves through a vacuum or air. All objects above absolute zero emit and absorb electromagnetic energy by means of radiation.

The frequency of the wavelength at which an object radiates is directly related to that object's temperature.

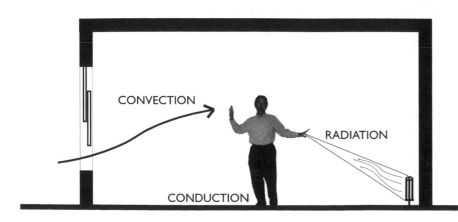

Figure 10-2 Mechanisms of heat transfer: The three primary mechanisms of heat transfer are *conduction*, *convection*, *radiation*. Conduction requires direct physical contact. Convection requires a movement of a fluid such as air or water. Radiation occurs between surfaces.

The hotter the object, the shorter the wavelength will be. The sun, being quite hot, emits radiation in relatively short wavelengths: the ultraviolet, visible, and near infra-red. Terrestrial objects, being cooler, radiate energy in the far-infrared wavelengths.

Ultraviolet (UV) radiation from the sun has a wave-length shorter than that of visible light but longer than X-rays. Solar UV waves vary in length from 200 nanome-ters (nm, or one billionth of a meter) to 400 nanometers. Most UV radiation is filtered by the Earth's atmosphere before reaching ground level. Radiation in the UV spec-trum has both beneficial and damaging impacts upon human health.

The human eye is sensitive to solar radiation between 400 nm and 700 nm in length. Human sight occurs when radiation in these wavelengths is reflected by an object and strikes our eyes. The eye and the brain's visual sys-tem process the reflected radiation into different shades and hues that we then assemble into a perception. Solar energy in the wavelengths visible to humans brings light and heat.

The near-infrared solar wavelengths bring heat but do not create light visible to humans and range between 700–2,500 nm. Far- or thermal-infrared wavelengths, at which most earthly objects radiate, ranges from 8,000 nm to 15,000 nm. Radiation is not affected by gravity. It travels in all directions, up and down, from its source.

Radiated electromagnetic energy of a given wave-length interacts with a material in three ways. It is *trans-mitted, absorbed,* or *reflected.*

Radiation may be transmitted through the material. An example of this is electromagnetic energy in the vis-ible spectrum. These wavelengths, which we humans perceive as light, are largely transmitted through glass. Electromagnetic energy that is not transmitted is either absorbed by the material or reflected away.

The interaction between radiant energy and material is affected both by the material and the wavelength of radiation. While solar radiation in the visible wavelengths is largely transmitted through glass, the far-infrared radia-tion from terrestrial objects is not transmitted. It is mostly absorbed, warming up the glass. The warm glass then reradiates the energy, some to the interior and some to the exterior.

Emittance

The ability of an object, such as glass, to radiate elec-tromagnetic energy is affected by its emittance. In order to emit heat, a material's surface must face an air gap or vacuum. Thus, emittance is a property of the surface of a material.

Without air or a vacuum, heat is transferred by conduction, until it reaches a surface where radiation can occur. Because emittance is a surface property, it can vary if the same material is given different surface treat-ments. The emittance of two panels manufactured from the same metal will vary if the surface of one is polished while the other is not.

Similarly, coatings applied to glass can produce great variation in the emittance from two sides of the same piece of glass. High emittance indicates that a surface can freely radiate heat energy, while low emittance indi-cates the ability to radiate heat is limited.

Polished metals typically have high reflectance but low emissivity. For example, a polished metal wrench left in the sun will get quite hot to the touch. While the pol-ished surface reflects most solar radiation, the radiation that is absorbed is not freely emitted. If the wrench were painted white, its surface properties would change. White surfaces typically have high reflectance *as well as* high emittance. Thus, the wrench would stay cooler because the solar energy it absorbed would be freely emitted.

Neither high nor low emissivity is inherently prefer-able. Low-emittance glass saves energy by reducing win-ter heat loss through windows. Roofing materials with

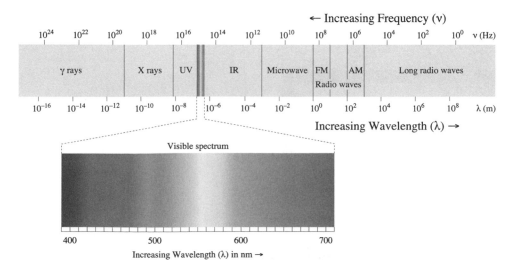

Figure 10-3 Electromagnetic spectrum: The electromagnetic spectrum represents the full range of possible forms of radiation. The *ultraviolet, visible,* and *infrared* are the wavelengths of greatest concern for general building.

high reflectance and high emittance reduce the need for cooling by reflecting solar radiation and reradiating the solar energy that was absorbed rather than reflected.

Mean Radiant Temperature

Whether an object becomes warmer or cooler due to radiant exchange is affected by mean radiant temperature. The rate of exchange of radiant energy between two objects results from the temperature difference between them and their angular relationship.

Imagine an individual standing in the middle of a square room with a very large window on one wall and a small window on the opposite wall. When it is cold outside, the individual's radiant relationship to the two walls will be markedly different.

The window glass will be colder than the adjacent opaque walls, both of which will be colder than the skin temperature of the person's face. The angle of view from face to large window will be greater than to the small one. The angles to the opaque walls will be just the opposite. As a result, the individual will have greater net-radiant loss to the wall with the large window than to the small one.

Climate and the Sun

Climate

Human comfort is affected by outdoor climate, given the way we occupy the buildings we design, and the nature of the activities we conduct inside those buildings. A characterization of outdoor climate includes data on temperature, relative humidity, wind speed and direction, sky conditions, and precipitation. A more complete climate picture includes a look at diurnal temperature swings and seasonal precipitation patterns.

A term commonly used in describing climatic regions is "heating degree day." Heating degree day (HDD) is a measure derived from daily temperature data. The number of heating degrees in a day is defined as the difference between a reference value, typically 65°F (18°C) and the average outside temperature for that day.

Sixty-five degrees Fahrenheit is used because in most residential buildings heating is not required at outside temperatures above that level. If the average temperature for a day in a given location were 35°F, there would be 30 heating degree days, using a 65°F reference point. Making this calculation for every day of the year and summing the results is one method of approximating heating requirements for a location.

Depending upon the criteria, we could define many different climate zones in North America. The struggle lies in balancing specificity against complexity. The U.S. Department of Energy divides North America into five categories, a simple yet still useful categorization. Significant variations exist within each of these categories. Always consider local conditions. The five categories are:

- *Cold or very cold:* A region with approximately 5,400 heating degree days or greater. If there are more than 9,000 heating degree days, the region is considered very cold. Saint Paul, Minnesota, is an example of a cold climate. Calgary, Alberta, is an example of a very cold climate.
- *Hot and humid:* A region that receives more than 20 inches of annual precipitation and where, during the six warmest consecutive months of the year, a 67°F or higher wet-bulb temperature is achieved for 3,000 or more hours or a 73°F or higher wet-bulb temperature is achieved for 1,500 or more hours. Wet-bulb temperature is the minimum temperature that can be achieved solely by evaporative cooling. High wet-bulb temperatures indicate the air is moisture laden, and there is limited opportunity for evaporative cooling. New Orleans, Louisiana, is an example of a hot and humid climate.
- *Hot dry and mixed dry:* Both hot dry and mixed dry regions receive less than 20 inches of annual precipitation. A location where the monthly average outdoor temperature remains above 45°F throughout the year is considered hot dry. Tucson, Arizona, is an example of a hot dry climate. A location that has less than 5,400

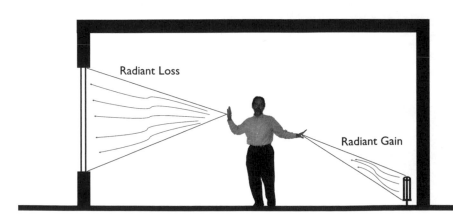

Figure 10-4 On a winter day we receive radiation from hot surfaces and transmit radiation to cool surfaces.

heating degree days and where the monthly average outdoor temperature drops below 45°F during the winter months is a mixed dry climate. Albuquerque, New Mexico, is an example of a mixed dry climate.

- *Mixed humid:* A region that receives more than 20 inches of annual precipitation, has less than 5,400 heating degree days, and where the monthly average outdoor temperature drops below 45°F during the winter months. Nashville, Tennessee, is an example of a mixed humid climate.
- *Marine Mediterranean:* A region where the mean temperature of the coldest month is between 27°F and 65°F; the mean temperature of the warmest month is less than 72°F; at least four months have mean temperatures over 50°F; there is a dry season in summer; and where the month with the heaviest precipitation in the cold season has at least three times as much precipitation as the month with the least precipitation during the rest of the year. The marine Mediterranean climate covers the Pacific Coast from Seattle, Washington, in the north to Santa Barbara, California, in the south. In some areas it extends little more than 10 to 15 miles inland.

Climate zones can be greatly refined beyond these fundamental categories. Climate zones for use with the International Energy Conservation Code and ASHRAE 90.1 are available online from the U.S. Department of Energy. Detailed climate data for a host of locations is available online from the National Oceanic and Atmospheric Administration's (NOAA), part of the U.S. Department of Commerce. Data is also available online from regional climate centers, which are joint programs among university, state, and/or federal government agencies.

The Sun

The Earth rotates once on its polar axis every 24 hours. At any moment, half of the Earth is in sunlight, while the other half is in darkness. Because the Earth's surface moves with axial rotation, the boundary of light and dark is always changing, and the sun appears to move across the sky. The location on the horizon where the sun rises and sets, the path it takes across the sky, and the number of hours it is above the horizon varies, depending upon the observer's distance from the equator, or latitude, and the time of year or season.

The Earth's distance from the sun varies slightly, depending on where the planet is in its yearly orbit. However, this is not the cause of seasonal climatic variation. Seasonal variation results because the Earth's polar axis is not perpendicular to the plane of the planet's orbit around the sun. Because of this the amount of solar radiation that reaches a given location on the surface of the Earth varies throughout the year.

The polar axis is tilted 23.5 degrees from a line vertical to the plane of Earth's orbit. The tilt of the axis remains constant during the year it takes for the planet to orbit the sun. This results in seasonal changes in solar declination, which is a measure of the angular relationship of the sun to the Earth when viewed from the equator.

From that location, the equator, on approximately March 21 and September 21, the sun appears directly overhead at midday. These dates represent the vernal and autumnal equinoxes, which occur at the beginning of spring and fall. As the Earth's position in its orbit changes, so does declination, with maximum variations on June 21 and December 21. On June 21, at midday, at the equator the sun is due north and 23.5 degrees below the vertical, or 66.5 degrees above the horizon. Similarly, on December 21, at midday, at the equator the sun is due south and 23.5 degrees below the vertical, or 66.5 degrees above the horizon. By convention, declination is said to be positive when the sun is north and negative when south.

As the Earth orbits the sun, declination varies from plus 23.5 degrees on June 21 to minus 23.5 degrees on

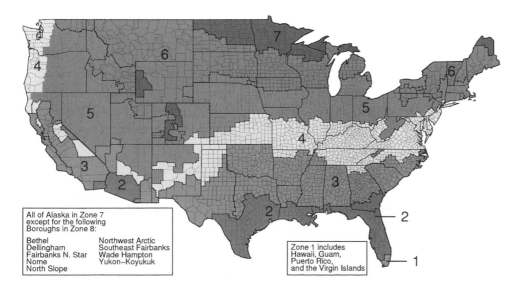

Figure 10-5 ASHRAE climate zones: ASHRAE divides the United States into eight climate zones. Energy-efficiency requirements for new buildings vary by zone.

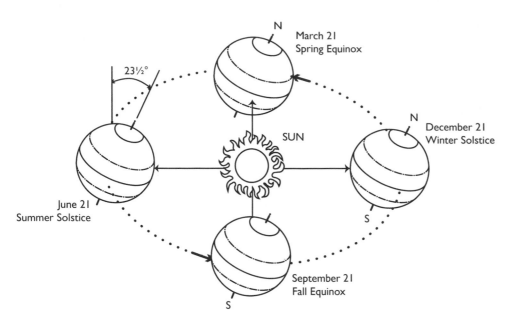

Figure 10-6 Declination and season: The Earth's axis is tilted at an angle of 23.5 degrees in relation to the plane of the planet's orbit around the sun. This tilt results in seasonal weather changes on the earth's surface.

December 21, with declination of zero on September 21 and March 21. The Tropics of Cancer and Capricorn mark the maximum declination of the sun in the northern and southern hemispheres, respectively.

If the axis of the Earth were at a right angle to the plane of orbit, for a given location, the sun would take the same path across the sky every day of the year, rising due east and setting due west, and spending twelve hours above the horizon. There would be no seasonal variation, because the amount of daily solar radiation reaching a given location on Earth would vary only slightly over the course of the year.

It is the tilt of the Earth's axis that causes seasonal change. As a result of the tilt, the location of the sun in the sky and with it the amount of solar radiation that reaches the surface of the Earth at a given location. When the sun is directly overhead, it travels the shortest possible distance through our atmosphere. When the sun is low in the sky, it travels a longer distance through the atmosphere in the same way that the hypotenuse of a triangle is always longer than the opposite leg. As the sun's radiation travels through our atmosphere, some of it is reflected back into space, some is absorbed by elements in the atmosphere, some is diffused by gas molecules, and some is transmitted through the atmosphere and absorbed by the surface of the Earth.

For a given distance above sea level, the Earth becomes warmer as we move, from both poles, toward the equator. At the equator, the Earth receives more solar radiation than in any other location, because the midday height of the sun is consistently high in the sky, varying between 66.5 degrees above the horizon and directly overhead. By comparison, in Washington, D.C., the height of the sun varies between 28 degrees above the horizon at midday on December 21 (approximately)

Figure 10-7 Regional design for a cold climate: The form of the New England saltbox house directed wind away while conserving heat from a central fireplace.

and 75 degrees above the horizon on June 21 (approximately). The sun is never directly overhead.

Traditional Design Responses to Climate

Without electricity or mechanical cooling, historic vernacular building was strongly shaped by response to climate. Early settlers in New England developed the saltbox form with a steep roof to redirect winter winds and a central chimney to maximize conservation of heat within the living space.

In Virginia, fireplaces moved from interior to exterior walls, with a central corridor to allow air movement between rooms. Farther south, in Mississippi and Alabama, the main floor was raised off the ground to increase ventilation. The house was surrounded by a deep veranda, providing outdoor living space in summer while shading the interior.

The hot and dry desert climate of the American Southwest, with high daytime temperatures and cold nights, resulted in earth-sheltered pit houses and adobe pueblos with thick walls and small windows. The thermal mass of adobe brick absorbed heat during the hot days. This heat was then conducted through the thick wall, reaching the interior by evening and warming occupants as temperatures dropped.

Figure 10-8 Regional design for a hot and humid climate: The form of buildings in the American south allowed air to circulate while providing shade from the summer sun.

Much can be learned from the study of traditional, climate-responsive building forms. Shading and sheltering living space from the sun remains central to design in hot climates and hot periods in more temperate climates. However, not all traditional approaches directly translate to modern building techniques. In particular, this is the case with the use and placement of thermal mass, which plays a somewhat different role in contemporary building than it did in the historic vernacular. In addition, some contemporary building types simply did not exist a hundred years ago.

Low-Energy Buildings: Balance Point and Building Type

The building balance-point temperature is the outdoor air temperature required for the indoor temperature to be comfortable without the use of any mechanical heating or cooling. At the balance-point temperature, heat gains due to lighting and equipment, occupants, and solar radiation match heat losses throughout the building envelope driven by temperature differences between interior and exterior.

In most residences, the amount of heat generated internally is relatively small. Such buildings are referred to as skin-load dominated, meaning the exterior climatic forces acting upon the building enclosure are the largest factors determining the need for heating or cooling. When exterior conditions are cold, the building should admit and trap heat. When exterior conditions are hot, the building should reject additional heat from the sun.

Orientation of windows, design of the building enclosure, and selection of interior building materials shape the amount of energy used to maintain comfort. A house

Figure 10-9 Regional design for a hot and dry climate: The form of buildings in the American Southwest blocked the sun from the interior. The thermally massive materials absorbed the sun's heat and transmitted it to the interior in the evening, when temperatures dropped.

without adequate insulation, and with single-pane, aluminum windows, may need to start the heating system when the outside temperature drops below 60°F. A well-designed residence with a high-performance skin, meaning good insulation, high-performance windows, sealed to prevent air infiltration, and detailed to eliminate thermal bridging, could receive and store enough solar radiation that outside air temperature will fall below 30°F before the interior temperature drops below the 68°F set point for start-up of the heating system. Through the incorporation of well-designed summer shading and operable windows, the building enclosure can vary with the season. This variability, coupled with the use of thermally massive materials at the interior, as well as other low-energy strategies, can enable the same building to maintain comfort when exterior conditions rise above 75°F.

In large buildings, whether they contain offices, retail, industrial, or any other occupancy type, the electric lighting, equipment, and high number of people per square foot generate heat. For these building types, the ratio of the area of the building skin to the interior volume ratio limits outward heat flow. As a result, the exterior temperature at which mechanical heating is needed to maintain a 68°F temperature inside might be as low as 20°F. Such buildings are referred to as internal-load dominated, meaning the internal thermal loads are the largest factors determining the need for heating or cooling.

The design of the building envelope is still important in internal-load-dominated buildings. However, requirements for the building envelope may run counter to expectations for exterior conditions. In a building with high internal-heat gains, the best building envelope design may be one that rejects solar heat at windows, even in midwinter. Understanding balance point clarifies how thermal energy moves differently in large and small buildings. A common mistake in architectural design is the application of solutions intended for small buildings to large ones, and vice versa.

11 Energy-Efficient Building Design: Residential and Small Commercial Buildings

■ Introduction

Energy as an issue for building design is wide and deep in scope. Here we provide an introductory overview to equip the reader for more in-depth investigations of the subject as a whole or particular topics.

■ Predesign: Site Selection, Building Size, and Transportation Options

Decisions made prior to the start of design, site selection, and building size, in particular, can be major determinants of energy use and environmental impact in residential buildings. Site selection shapes transportation energy use. Occupants of an efficient building on an exurban site are more dependent on the automobile, with limited choices for other transportation options. As a result exurban dwellers are likely to use more energy on an annual per capita basis than occupants of a less-efficient building located in a denser setting.

A building site where many or most daily tasks can be accomplished without the automobile starts off with an energy advantage. Reduced expenditures for transportation, including a possible reduction in the number of vehicles per household, translates into an economic advantage as well, making housing more affordable. Site selection is often beyond the control of the building designer. However, the designer can educate clients on the implications for transportation energy associated with a given site. (For more information, see "Smart Growth and New Urbanism" in Chapter 16.)

Building size correlates with energy use; therefore, bigger buildings typically use more energy and require more resources to construct. An efficient 4,000-square-foot building will often require more operational energy than a somewhat less efficient design of 2,500 square feet or less. While establishing the size of a project is often beyond the scope of the building designer, an analysis of the client's spatial needs is not. Help the client define the building volume needed to provide utility, convenience, and beauty. Consider space needs that may arise in the future, but do not routinely oversize buildings.

Occupant Behavior and Lifestyle

While building size typically correlates to demand for power, lifestyle choices and the plug loads associated with them greatly affect energy consumption. A plug load is any electrical device plugged into a wall outlet. Examples include a computer, television or home theater system, refrigerator, washing machine, DVD player, cordless phone, battery charger, video game console, and a host of other near-essential appliances and discretionary gadgets. Not only do these devices use electricity, many of them continue to use it even after being turned off. As the energy associated with heating, cooling, and lighting is reduced through design, the importance of plug loads increases.

The energy use of two identical homes with the same number of occupants may vary considerably as a result of behavioral differences. Where possible, educate clients on the energy use and financial cost of unrestrained plug loads. Use U.S. Environmental Protection Agency (EPA) Energy Star guidelines where applicable for selection of consumer products.

Design of Low-Energy-Use Residential Buildings

To reduce energy use and environmental impacts to very low levels in residential building design, there are several objectives that apply across the board. A designer must properly site the building, use forms appropriate for the climate, thermally separate interior and exterior, provide fresh air, select properly sized energy-efficient equipment, and then use these elements to incorporate renewable energy.

Simply put, energy goals in residential design rest on five elements:

- Use of climate-responsive design incorporating passive techniques to reduce the energy use associated with space heating, cooling, and water heating.
- Use of building envelope design that creates a good thermal boundary between interior and exterior through air sealing, insulation, elimination of thermal bridging, selection of exterior finish materials, and location and use of appropriate high-performance windows and glass.
- Provision of controlled ventilation.
- Use of properly sized equipment for heating and cooling and selection of energy-efficient equipment and appliances.
- Maximum use of renewable energy to meet the remaining demands for power.

Response to Climate and Passive Design

The first step in climate-responsive design is to identify the regional climate type associated with a given site. Use the maps or zip code climate-zone data available online for use with the International Energy Efficiency Code (IEEC) and ASHRAE 90.1.[1] The Building America Web site also provides regional climate maps that are useful for this purpose.[2] Because there is considerable variation within regional climate zones, acquire a historic climate summary for a location as close as possible to the actual building site. The Regional Climate Centers provide a great deal of climate information online at no charge.[3] Compare the historic data against the norms for regional climate to determine where the site climate falls in the continuum of the regional climate zones.

Passive designing techniques reflect knowledge of climate, site conditions, solar geometry, and building form and materials to utilize or reject the natural energies at a site affecting a building. Passive techniques need to be combined with thoughtful selection of building materials and detailing to control heat flow between the interior and exterior. Integrating passive techniques can provide comfort while lowering the need for heating and cooling. The

comfort zone for building occupants is widely agreed to include consideration of air temperature, humidity, mean radiant temperature, the presence or lack of direct solar radiation, and air velocity within the space, along with the personal factors of clothing insulation and activity level. Comfort is typically assumed for 80 to 90 percent of building occupants when temperature is between 68°F and 82°F (20°C –27.75°C) and relative humidity is between 20 to 50 percent. As humidity rises from 50 to 80 percent, the acceptable upper temperature range declines from 82°F to 75°F (27.75°C to slightly under 24°C).

Beyond these factors, there is much debate as to what results in perceived comfort for building occupants. Degree of control over one's personal environment, for example, has been shown to increase occupant satisfaction under given thermal conditions. For more information on this topic, see ASHRAE *Standard 55—Thermal Environmental Conditions for Human Occupancy*, as well as the thermal comfort research at the University of California, Berkeley, Center for the Built Environment.[4] Also useful is the work of P. Ole Fanger, developer of the thermal-comfort-calculation method, as well as the work of Richard De Dear, Gail Brager, Alison Kwok, Michael Humphreys, and Fergus Nicol on adaptive comfort models and cultural expectations for thermal comfort.

A basic tool used by engineers in design of mechanical systems is the psychrometric chart.[5] For architects and designers, a simplified bioclimatic chart that defines a comfort zone based on temperature and relative humidity is more useful. The bioclimatic chart shows how the comfort range can be expanded, using five passive, or very low-energy, strategies.[6] These are passive solar heating, natural ventilation, thermal mass, night ventilation of thermal mass, and evaporative cooling.

Passive solar heating is effective in residential design when temperatures drop below 68°F (20°C). Radiation from the sun, admitted to the interior of the building, warms individuals and objects. This provides immediate warmth. If thermally massive materials, such as a concrete floor slab, brick wall, or containers of water, are placed so that they receive the sunlight, these objects will store the heat. In the evening, these materials will reradiate the heat, warming occupants and the interior of the house, even as outside temperatures fall.

Natural ventilation can increase the upper limit of the comfort zone by nearly 10°F (5°C) when relative humidity is between 20 and 50 percent. As humidity increases to 80 percent, natural ventilation continues to expand the upper

---

[1]For climate-zone data, see: U.S. Department of Energy, Pacific Northwest Lab: http://resourcecenter.pnl.gov/cocoon/morf/ResourceCenter/article/1420.
[2]For regional climate maps, see: U.S. Department of Energy, Building Technologies Program, Building America, http://www.eere.energy.gov/buildings/building_america/climate_zones.html.
[3]Regional Climate Centers: http://www.wrcc.dri.edu/rcc.html.

[4]University of California, Berkeley, Center for the Built Environment: http://www.cbe.berkeley.edu/research/research_envelope.htm.
[5]2005 ASHRAE Handbook of Fundamentals, American Society of Heating, Refrigerating and Air-Conditioning Engineers, Inc, 1791 Tullie Circle, N.E., Atlanta, GA 30321, Chapter 6.
[6]G.Z. Brown and Mark DeKay, *Sun, Wind, & Light*, 2nd edition (Hoboken, NJ: John Wiley & Sons, 2001).

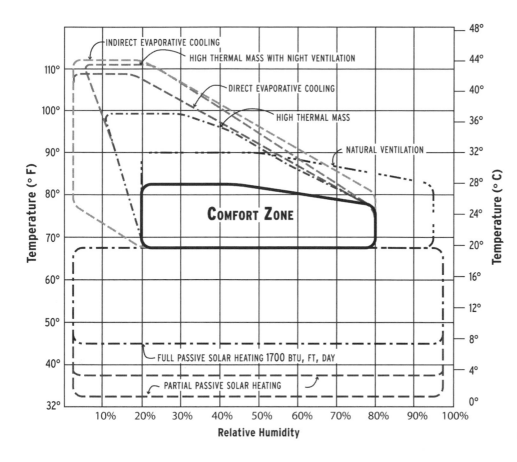

Figure 11-1 The comfort zone and passive design: Shading the sun, air movement, humidification, and the use of thermal mass can extend the limits of the human comfort zone.

temperature range of the comfort zone. As relative humidity increases above 80 percent, the upper limit of comfort without air movement, natural ventilation can maintain comfort when temperatures are between 68°F–82°F. Natural ventilation depends solely on air movement to cool occupants. Inlets and outlets in the form of windows or louvers are required on opposite sides of the building, and they must be open. Because the availability of wind speeds sufficient to assure comfort cannot be predicted, stacks and fans are often used. A stack has openings at top and bottom and must be tall enough to create a temperature differential within the stack that will induce upward air movement. Fans may also be employed to create air movement. While this is not a passive technique, it requires far less energy than air-conditioning. At air temperatures above 90°F (32.2°C), ventilation alone cannot maintain comfort.

When shielded from direct sunlight, exposed thermally massive materials in the building can absorb heat as it accumulates over the day. If there is a sufficient drop in outside temperature, the mass releases heat at night and the pattern can be repeated the next day. The capacity of the mass to absorb heat can be increased with night ventilation. There must be a significant diurnal temperature swing if night ventilation of thermal mass is to be effective. Cool outside air is drawn over the exposed mass, either by natural or fan-induced ventilation. The mass is precooled and has increased capacity to absorb

Figure 11-2 Thermal mass in contemporary buildings: If shaded, thermal mass absorbs internal heat, improving comfort conditions and reducing the need for cooling.

heat the next day. Thermal mass and night-ventilated thermal mass are effective passive strategies in hot-dry climates. Thermal mass cannot provide passive cooling under hot and humid conditions.

Evaporative cooling is another strategy effective in hot and dry climates. By adding moisture to hot and dry air and raising its relative humidity, evaporative cooling reduces the sensible temperature, converting heat to its latent state.

Site Response

Site factors—such as topography, landscape elements, adjacent buildings, and microclimates—will affect passive design strategies for low-rise residential buildings. A site on the south side of a hill may have excellent opportunities to use solar energy for space heating, water heating, and electricity generation. A site on the north side of a hill may have limited access to sun during the winter, the season when it is most needed for space heating. Neighboring buildings can block the sun with both negative and positive results. An adjacent building may shade a solar electric array and reduce power generation in one case, while effectively blocking unwanted, low-angle sun from entering through west windows in another.

Similarly, the variety and density of trees and other vegetation on and near a site offer opportunities and obstacles for a designer. The characteristics of a specific site will promote or limit opportunities for passive heating and cooling. Targets such as zero-net energy may not be achievable at individual building scale in every location. Such a goal is possible at neighborhood or community scale if buildings with good solar access produce an energy surplus for use by those with reduced solar capabilities. Site limitations only strengthen the case for thoughtful orientation of the building form and window openings as key to low-energy building design.

Building Envelope Design

Response to the Sun

Central to every project is response to the sun. In skin-load dominated buildings, such as residences, direct sunlight should be admitted when exterior climate is cold and rejected when hot. The precise time periods when each should occur varies with climate. Controlled admission and rejection of solar heat shapes building orientation, massing of forms, and the location of windows and skylights. Response to sun also influences the orientation of roofs and placement of chimneys, vents, and equipment, as these decisions affect the performance of systems for solar water heating and electricity generation.

Orientation

Before air-conditioning was common in residences, greater care was devoted to building orientation. The widespread inclusion of air-conditioning in new homes assumes energy to run the equipment will be available at a relatively low cost. Increased global demand for energy has led to price increases for oil and natural gas and construction of new coal-burning power plants in many parts of the world. Economic, geopolitical, and environmental concerns suggest we have little to lose and much to gain by reducing the need for cooling with good building orientation and envelope design.

From an energy-performance perspective, in all climates of North America it is preferable to elongate residential and small commercial buildings on an east-west axis. This increases the percentage of building walls that face north and south, providing access to the sun when desired for heating. As noted in the previous chapter, the sun is high in the southern sky during hot months and lower in the southern sky during cold ones. Roof overhangs, shading devices, and trellises are more easily designed to block sunlight during hot months while admitting it when the sun is lower during cold months, if the windows face south. Elongating the building along an east-west axis also makes it easier to create balanced interior illumination through admission of diffuse light from the north.

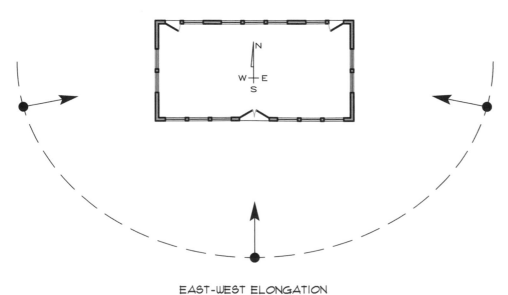

EAST-WEST ELONGATION

Figure 11-3 Building orientation for solar control: The sun is higher in the southern sky than in the east or west. Elongating a building on an east-west axis, with more windows facing south and north, makes it easier to include solar control in designs.

Climate conditions across the continent vary widely, as do the length of the heating and cooling seasons in different regions. The depth and width of roof overhangs and shading devices must be designed to match specific climatic requirements. Deep, wide overhangs that severely limit interior solar gain fit the hot and humid climate of North America's Gulf Coast. Narrower, shorter overhangs fit the predominantly cold climate of the Rocky Mountain states, the northern United States, and Canada. A number of books discuss design of solar shading in great detail.[7] In terms of solar heat, west-and east-facing windows are problematic in almost all locations. Between approximately September 21 and March 21, the sun sets south of west. West-facing windows cannot admit nearly as much heat as southern windows during the winter. However, in summer, the sun drops lower in the sky as it reaches the west and northwest. At the hottest hours, when interior spaces have accumulated heat over the course of the day, the sun is difficult to shade. Unlike windows with a southern orientation, west windows do not provide a good source of heat during the winter, but they do bring heat to the interior in summer, the exact opposite of what conditions require. From an energy perspective, west windows are best minimized.

East windows parallel west windows in that the sun rises south of east in the winter and is difficult to shade in the summer. Where east windows perform differently is in the hot and dry climates found in parts of the North American West. In such climates, there is a large diurnal temperature swing, a significant difference between daytime high temperatures and nighttime lows. Because of the cool mornings, a limited amount of solar heat in the morning may be desirable. The key is not to oversize the area of east windows.

Energy performance is critical but not the sole factor in shaping architectural form. Views, functional needs, urban setting, and aesthetic considerations all influence how project design goals are established and balanced. A west-facing residence on a north-south street must engage the public sphere while limiting summer heat gain. A good designer will maximize energy performance, sheltering and/or limiting the size of west windows, while recognizing overall project needs.

Air Barriers

A tight building envelope that creates a continuous thermal barrier from the foundation, up through opaque wall surfaces, around doors and windows, to the peak of the roof, will greatly reduce uncontrolled movement of air between interior and exterior. This increases the effectiveness of passive-design strategies and reduces energy needed to supplement passive approaches.

An air barrier is an important component in creating a tight building envelope. Any material that is relatively air impermeable and long-lasting can be used as an air barrier. The challenge is to design an air-barrier system, made from materials and assemblies, that is continuous from foundation to roof. Once designed, proper installation is essential. Air barriers represent an area of overlap between energy efficiency, design for durability, and healthy interiors. Reducing air infiltration will aid all three areas.

An air barrier also reduces the possibility of back drafting of combustion gases from furnaces and water heaters into occupied space. Back drafting can occur when combustion devices are not well separated from living quarters. Significant air infiltration, or use of devices such as kitchen exhaust fans, can create uncontrolled pressure differentials at openings to the exterior, including flues intended for venting of combustion gases. Thus, gases that would otherwise vent to the exterior can be drawn back into occupied space, with serious negative health effects.

By limiting the ability of air to move through a building assembly, an air barrier will reduce convective loss or gain of heat. An air barrier will also reduce moisture carried by uncontrolled air infiltration into building assemblies. Cool surfaces within the wall assembly may be at or below the dew-point temperature of the moist air. When this happens, the moisture condenses on these surfaces within the wall assembly. During heating season, condensation can occur on a cold surface toward the outside of the wall as warm air moves from the inside. The reverse is likely during cooling season, as hot air from the exterior condenses when it reaches cooler interior surfaces. If the condensate cannot dry out or drain to the exterior, it can cause mold, structural damage, and indoor air quality problems.

An air barrier differs from a vapor barrier in that the former is somewhat permeable to moisture, whereas the latter, by definition, is not. Keeping water out of buildings and reducing condensation in building

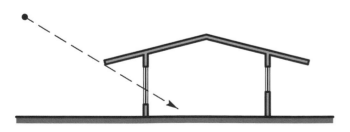

WEST FACING GLASS

Figure 11-4 Liabilities of west windows: Because the sun is low in the western sky, controlling solar gain through west-facing windows during hot times of day and year is difficult.

---

[7]Benjamin Stein, John S. Reynolds, Walter T. Grondzik, and Alison Kwok, *Mechanical and Electrical Equipment for Buildings,* 10th ed. (Hoboken, NJ: John Wiley & Sons, 2006).

assemblies has always been one of the top priorities for designers. However, even in the best designs, some moisture enters the wall. Good design limits the ability of moisture to enter a wall assembly, while creating a path for the moisture that does enter to escape. A well-sealed, moisture-permeable air barrier can be paired with a properly detailed drainage plane to achieve this goal.

The drainage plane, located directly behind the exterior cladding, promotes movement of water to the outside of the building. Commercial drainage-plane products are available or can be built up from other materials. Specific moisture strategies will vary with climate. See the regional climate best-practice guides from the U.S. Department of Energy's Building America Web site for more information and additional resources.[8]

Insulation

Insulation limits the transfer of heat across wall and ceiling assemblies, below raised floors, in crawl spaces, and at the structural slab, basements, and foundations. Insulation is made from a number of different materials and comes in a variety of forms, most typically as batts, loose fill, and low-density foam, either foamed in place or premanufactured as boards. The performance of insulation is measured by its ability to resist the flow of heat and is indicated by the R-value (or R-factor) of the material. The R-value is typically listed per inch of material or for the total thickness of the cavity in which insulation is placed.

Batt insulation typically comes in rolls and is made from fiberglass or other mineral fibers. It is available in widths based on standard wall, floor, and attic framing dimensions. Blown-in, loose-fill insulation includes mineral fibers or recycled paper in the form of cellulose. As the name implies, it can be blown into building cavities or attics. Foamed-in-place insulations are viscous materials that can also be sprayed into building cavities. One of the side benefits of foam is that, when properly installed, it also provides an air seal. However, it can be difficult to achieve an effective air seal in existing buildings where it is not possible to see the inside of the wall.

Rigid insulation is made from fibrous materials or plastic foams that are pressed or extruded into sheets or boards. Rigid insulation may be used in combination with other insulation types, for example, on the exterior of walls filled with cellulose or fiberglass insulation. Rigid insulation at the exterior is common when steel studs are used. The rigid insulation stops thermal bridging across the stud. Rigid insulation is also used in foundation walls.

Whatever the form, most insulation works by creating a multitude of dead air spaces that limit air movement within the insulation material. This eliminates heat loss by convection and greatly reduces it by conduction. It is important to understand that insulation only stops air movement within the material itself. Insulation works with an air barrier rather than serving as a substitute for one. Insulation must completely fill a cavity and fit tightly to be most effective. The quality of installation of insulation greatly affects its performance.

Reflective insulation products, often referred to as radiant barriers, work by reducing radiant-heat transfer. They are typically made from shiny metals having low-emissivity (low-e) surface properties. Emissivity is a measure of the ability of a surface to radiate heat. Because radiation occurs between two surfaces separated by an air space, reflective insulation products are only effective when one side of the product faces into an air space. If the surface opposite the reflective insulation is warmer, the insulation reflects the radiant energy back to that surface. If the reflective insulation is warmer, the low-e quality of the shiny metal surface limits the ability of the material to radiate heat across the air space.

Thus, regardless of which surface is hotter, reflective insulation keeps heat on the side of the air space that is already warmer. It is important to understand that reflective-insulation products do little to reduce conductive and convective losses. Thus, they should not be considered a replacement for other forms of insulation. There are many sources for climate-specific recommendations on placement and detailing of insulation. As a starting point, see the regional climate best-practice guides from the U.S. Department of Energy's "Building America" Web site and the Oak Ridge National Laboratory's insulation fact sheet.[9]

How much insulation is enough? That depends upon the goal. The International Energy Efficiency Code requires cost-effective insulation levels based on assumptions about current and future energy costs. The Energy Star program Web site contains Builder Option Packages (BOPs) that recommend insulation levels, on a county-by-county basis, necessary to achieve the Energy Star–home qualification.[10] If the goal is a zero-net energy home, insulation levels will be higher. Insulation levels must also take into consideration the wall or ceiling assembly required to contain the insulation.

Thermal Bridging

Heat flows from hot to cold. Across a building assembly, heat will seek the path of least resistance. This path will be through elements that are more conductive than

---

[8]U.S. Department of Energy, Building Technologies Program, Building America, http://www.eere.energy.gov/buildings/building_america/.

[9]U.S. Department of Energy, Building Technologies Program, Building America, http://www.eere.energy.gov/buildings/building_america/. Oak Ridge National Laboratory: http://www.ornl.gov/sci/roofs+walls/insulation/ins_01.html.

[10]Energy Star Builder Option Packages: http://www.energystar.gov/index.cfm?c=bop.pt_bop_index_.

surrounding materials. If a thermally conductive path is provided across a building assembly, rapid heat transfer can occur. Lower temperatures along the path can also result in condensation on the surface of the conductive material. Such a path is described as a *thermal bridge*.

Among standard building materials, aluminum is the most conductive. Steel also has high conductivity. However, any material, or series of materials in physical contact, that creates a path across a building assembly and is significantly more conductive than surrounding materials represents a thermal bridge. The bridge reduces the overall thermal resistance of a building assembly such as an insulated wall. Studs, plates, and rafters, the structural members of a traditionally framed wall, are thermal bridges. As a result, the effective R-value for a wood-framed wall with R-11 insulation is closer to R-8. A nonthermally broken aluminum-frame window in a well-insulated wall serves as a major thermal bridge.

Metals used in a wall assembly present excellent opportunities for thermal bridging. Carefully consider details to eliminate thermal pathways through highly conductive materials. If steel studs are used on exterior walls, board insulation must be placed over the studs and attached with nonmetallic fasteners. Thermal bridges are also common at the sill, corners, and roof-wall junctions of traditional wood-framed buildings. Wood framing around doors and windows reduces insulation material and presents a thermal bridge. Details at these locations need special attention to reduce bridging. Increasing the spacing of structural members will increase the insulated wall area. Other things being equal, a wall with studs 24 inches on center will have a higher effective R-value than one framed at 16 inches on center.

Windows and Glass

Window and glass technology has improved dramatically over the past thirty years. Double-pane windows with insulated glazing units have become the norm. While not common, triple-pane units are available. Double-pane units that incorporate one or more polyester films are also available. These units can match or exceed the performance of triple-pane windows without the added weight of additional panes of glass.

New window-frame materials with good thermal performance and low-maintenance requirements have appeared. Low-emissivity coatings for glass are common. However, not all low-e products are the same. It is important to select the right product for both the climate and architectural design to achieve the best building-energy performance. Using a product intended for a hot climate in a cold one, or vice versa, can result in poorer energy performance than otherwise possible.

The three most important metrics when selecting windows and glass are U-value (or U-factor), solar heat gain coefficient (SHGC), and visible transmittance. When evaluating these metrics, the value must represent the performance of the entire window assembly, meaning the frame and the glass in combination. The National Fenestration Rating Council (NFRC) is a nonprofit organization created by the window, door, and skylight industry. The NFRC has developed an energy rating system for the entire product assembly, using test procedures developed by Lawrence Berkeley National Laboratory. The NFRC-tested window, door, and skylight products carry a label showing the key energy metrics for the product. For the designer or home owner, the NFRC label provides the only reliable way to understand window energy performance and to compare products.

The U-value (or U-factor, per NFRC usage) is most important in relation to winter heat loss from the building interior; the U-value represents the rate of heat loss through a window assembly. A low U-value indicates a low rate of heat loss and better insulating value. Low U-value is recommended for all climates. Even in hot climates, a U-value below 0.40 is advised. A very low U-value grows increasingly important as climate conditions grow colder and winter heating predominates over summer cooling. In cold climates, a U-value of less than 0.30, and lower if possible, is recommended.

Solar heat gain coefficient is important in relation to heat gain, largely from direct solar radiation passing through the window assembly to the building interior. Solar radiation striking a window is transmitted to the interior, reflected back to the exterior, or absorbed by the window assembly and subsequently radiated to the interior and exterior. The SHGC is the ratio of solar radiation admitted through a window assembly to the amount of radiation incident on the assembly. SHGC is a number between 0 and 1. An SHGC of 0.50 indicates one-half of the incident radiation is admitted to the interior. The lower a window's solar heat gain coefficient, the less solar heat it transmits. Low SHGC is important where windows are not shaded and climate conditions are hot, with summer cooling predominating over winter heating. Where these conditions prevail, SHGC of 0.30 or lower is recommended.

Visible transmittance (VT) indicates the percentage of visible light striking the window assembly that is transmitted to the interior. As tested using NFRC procedures, VT includes the impact of the frame, which does not transmit any visible light. The VT for a wall opening where no window has been inserted would be 1.0. For commercially available windows, VT varies between 0.3 and 0.8. The higher the VT, the more light is transmitted. The window frame material and aspects of frame construction greatly affect U-value. Available frame materials include aluminum, wood, vinyl, cladding, hybrid-composite, and fiberglass.

Aluminum window frames are light, strong, and durable, but they have high thermal conductance. The U-value of aluminum windows is higher than for

World's Best
Window Co.
Millennium 2000+
Vinyl-Clad Wood Frame
Double Glazing • Argon Fill • Low E
Product Type: **Vertical Slider**

ENERGY PERFORMANCE RATINGS

U-Factor (U.S./I-P)	Solar Heat Gain Coefficient
0.35	**0.32**

ADDITIONAL PERFORMANCE RATINGS

Visible Transmittance	Air Leakage (U.S./I-P)
0.51	**0.2**

Manufacturer stipulates that these ratings conform to applicable NFRC procedures for determining whole product performance. NFRC ratings are determined for a fixed set of environmental conditions and a specific product size. NFRC does not recommend any product and does not warrant the suitability of any product for any specific use. Consult manufacturer's literature for other product performance information.
www.nfrc.org

Figure 11-5 NFRC label: The NFRC label provides the only reliable way to understand window energy performance and to compare products. It provides information on the energy performance of the entire window assembly, both frame and glass.

windows using other frame materials. By dividing the frame into interior and exterior components, joined by a less conductive material, a window manufacturer can introduce a thermal break. This reduces the conductance of the window assembly, but even thermally broken aluminum-frame windows cannot achieve the low U-value levels available with other frame types. Aluminum windows may be appropriate in some hot climates, but they should be avoided in residential construction in regions with more than minimal heating requirements. Where aluminum frames are used in small commercial storefronts, incorporate a thermal break.

Wood has been used for window frames for centuries. Wood frames perform well thermally. They require more maintenance than other materials, but well-built and well-maintained wood windows can last a very long time. To reduce maintenance, the exterior of wood frames are sometimes clad with a more weather-resistant surface such as vinyl or aluminum.

The thermal performance of vinyl window frames is comparable to wood windows. These frames are virtually maintenance free. However, they are less dimensionally stable than other materials, undergoing greater expansion and contraction with temperature variation. Vinyl frames are typically hollow. The thermal performance of vinyl frames can be improved to exceed that of wood by filling the hollow cavity with insulation. While vinyl windows perform well thermally, the environmental impacts associated with the production of the material—health impacts upon workers in the vinyl industry, end-of-product-life questions regarding difficulty of reuse or recycling, and concerns about toxic gases released from the finished product in case of fire—have led many to avoid specifying vinyl as a window frame material.

Fiberglass window frames are available with excellent thermal performance. These frames have the benefits associated with vinyl frames, such as very low maintenance, and few of the drawbacks. They are dimensionally stable, strong, and—like vinyl—available with air cavities or filled with insulation. Insulation-filled fiberglass units exceed the performance of wood frames.

Hybrid frames that reduce initial cost and maintenance requirements while improving thermal performance are increasingly common. Some new designs pair a fiberglass exterior with a wood interior. Wood-polymer composite frames are another new development. Very dimensionally stable, they are as strong or stronger than conventional wood and offer more resistance to moisture and rot. Similar to other engineered wood products, they reuse recycled sawdust and scrap wood. However, like many composite products, their recyclability at end of life may be compromised.

Budget and maintenance requirements will affect window and frame selection, as will environmental concerns such as durability, toxicity, recycled content, and recyclability at end of life. However, the only reliable indicator of thermal performance is the NFRC label. Low-e coatings can lower both U-value and SHGC. Not all low-e coatings affect performance in the same way. Some low-e coatings reduce U-value but have little effect on SHGC. Other low-e coatings reduce U-value and greatly lower SHGC. High solar gain, low-e coatings are ideal for northern climates. They also work well in residential or small commercial buildings designed in accordance with passive solar principles in almost any climate in North America. Effective passive solar design requires that windows be located and shaded with an understanding of the varying position of the sun over the day and year. If a window is shaded, solar gain is prevented from entering through the glass, and there is no need for a low-SHGC coating.

Coatings that reduce SHGC do so year round. Coating performance characteristics do not change with season. A low solar gain coating prevents heat from the sun from entering a building in summer, reducing the need for cooling. It also reduces heat from the sun in winter, potentially increasing the need for heating. With conventional building practice in warm and hot climates, where windows are not well shaded, the reduction in cooling energy more than offsets the increase in heating energy. However, in temperate and cold climates, or in homes with no air-conditioning, the cooling savings may not offset the increase in energy for heating.

As mentioned in the previous chapter, solar energy in the form of electromagnetic radiation varies in wavelength from ultraviolet (UV) at 200 nanometers (nm, or one billionth of a meter) to near infrared at 2,500 nm. The human eye is sensitive to solar radiation between 400 nm and 700 nm in length. Forty-six percent of radiation from the sun is within this range. Solar energy in the wavelengths visible to humans brings light and heat. The near-infrared solar wavelengths bring heat but do not create light visible to humans and range between 700–2,500 nm. Fifty-one percent of solar radiation is within this range. The remaining three percent is UV radiation.

Far- or thermal-infrared, the wavelengths at which most terrestrial objects radiate, ranges from 8,000 nm to 15,000 nm. Whether solar or terrestrial, when radiation strikes glass it is transmitted through to the other side, reflected away, or absorbed. If absorbed, the heat energy is reradiated. The rate of radiant heat transfer is

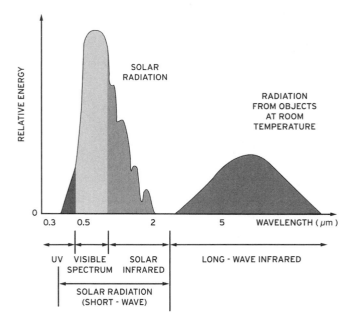

Figure 11-6 Spectral distribution of solar radiation: Solar radiation varies in wavelength from ultraviolet at 200 nm to near infrared at 2,500 nm. The human eye is sensitive to solar radiation between 400 nm and 700 nm in length. Visible light makes up slightly less than half of all solar radiation.

shaped by the difference in temperature between the two glass surfaces and surfaces within view of the glass on either side. Thus, more heat is radiated to the cooler side. In summer this is typically the interior, while in winter it is the exterior.

The percent of radiation that is transmitted, reflected, and absorbed varies with wavelength. Clear glass is highly transmissive to the solar wavelengths but absorbs rather than transmits or reflects terrestrial radiation in the far infrared. This results in what is often called the greenhouse effect. Solar radiation is transmitted through glass, where it is absorbed by and warms interior objects. Those objects radiate heat energy that cannot be transmitted through the glass. However, a greenhouse still loses much of the heat radiated by interior objects.

Far-infrared radiation from warm interior objects is not transmitted through glass but is absorbed. This heat conducts through the glass and radiates from the outer surface to cold exterior objects. The process works in a similar fashion with double-pane windows. In a double-pane window there are four glass surfaces. By convention, these are numbered one through four—surface one is the exterior surface of the outer pane, two the surface of the outer pane facing into the air space, three the surface of the inner pane facing into the air space, and four the interior surface of the inner pane. Heat from the room is absorbed by surface four and conducts through the glass, where it radiates across the air space from surface three to two. Again, the heat conducts through the glass and radiates from surface four to a colder exterior surface.

Radiant Energy

When radiant energy strikes glass it is:

- Reflected (R)
- Absorbed (A)
- Transmitted (T)

R + A + T = 100%

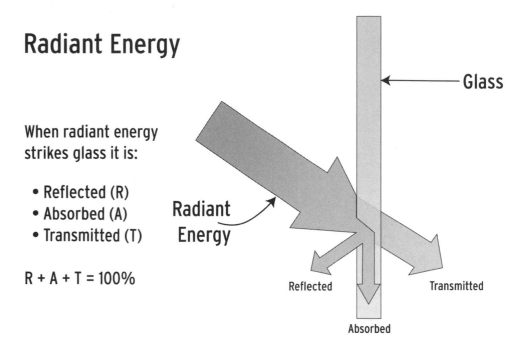

Figure 11-7 Solar radiation and glass: Solar radiation that strikes a window is either transmitted through to the building interior, reflected away, or absorbed by the glass. Absorbed solar radiation warms the glass, which reradiates the energy to both interior and exterior surfaces.

Radiant Losses

Uncoated glass allows for greater heat losses

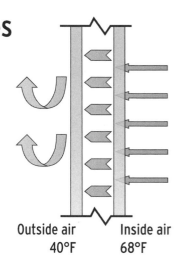

Outside air 40°F Inside air 68°F

In uncoated glass, heat is absorbed and radiated across the air space where it is absorbed and conducted across the glass and convected to the exterior

Figure 11-8 Heat loss through window glass: In an insulated glazing unit, the surfaces of the glass are numbered one through four, starting from the exterior surface and moving inward. Warm interior objects radiate heat as long-wave infrared energy. Glass is opaque to these wavelengths, which are absorbed by surface four rather than transmitted. The absorbed heat conducts through the glass and then is freely emitted by surface three to the outer pane of glass.

Clear glass, like many building materials, has high emissivity. Emissivity is a dimensionless quantity between zero and one. High emittance indicates a surface can freely radiate heat, while low emittance indicates the ability to radiate heat is limited. Highly polished metals have very low emissivity. Applying a microscopically thin, shiny metallic coating to the surface of a pane of clear glass dramatically changes the emissivity of that surface, lowering it from 0.9 to 0.2 or lower.

The first low-e glass products on the market were intended to reduce the need for winter heating and did little to reduce summer heat gain. Lowering the emissivity of one glass surface in a double-pane window has the effect of reducing heat loss to the exterior when outside conditions are cold. Warm objects in the room radiate to the glass, which absorbs the far-infrared radiation at surface four. The heat conducts through the glass, but because the emissivity of surface three, facing into the air space, has been lowered by the metallic coating, the heat cannot be radiated across the air space to surface two. As a result, the inner pane of glass stays warmer, slowing the rate of radiant heat exchange between objects in the room and the glass.

This type of low-e coating has little effect on the shorter wavelength solar radiation transmitted through the glass into a room. The coating lowers U-value but has a very small effect on SHGC. Thus, it reduces heat loss but does not limit the ability to heat the room with solar radiation. A second generation of low-e coatings intended for solar control appeared on the market a few years later. These coatings are better described as *spectrally selective* low-e coatings. They transmit most of the

Reducing Radiant Losses

Low-emissivity coatings reduce radiant heat losses

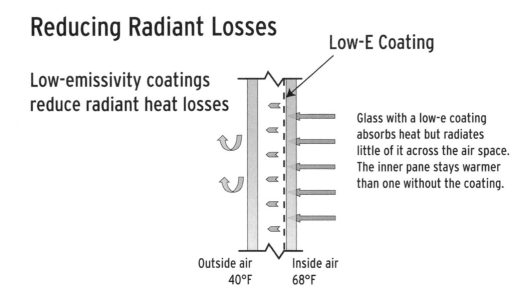

Low-E Coating

Glass with a low-e coating absorbs heat but radiates little of it across the air space. The inner pane stays warmer than one without the coating.

Outside air 40°F   Inside air 68°F

Figure 11-9 How high-gain, low-e glass slows winter heat loss: Low-e coatings reduce the emissivity of the surface to which they are applied. Long-wave infrared heat is absorbed by the glass and conducts through to the other side. The low-e coating on surface three limits the ability of that surface to radiate heat across the air space. The interior pane of glass stays warmer.

Solar Transmission in Spectrally Selective Glass

Glazing responds differently to visible & infrared wavelengths

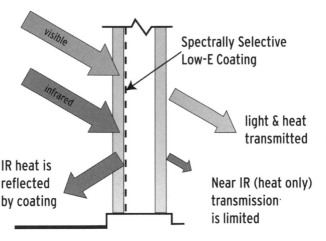

visible

infrared

Spectrally Selective Low-E Coating

light & heat transmitted

IR heat is reflected by coating

Near IR (heat only) transmission is limited

Figure 11-10 Spectral selectivity in glass: Spectrally selective low-e glass responds differently to the various wavelengths of solar radiation. It is typically transmissive to the solar wavelengths humans perceive as light, while being reflective to a large percent of the near-infrared wavelengths that bring heat but no light. As a result, the glass can admit a large amount of daylight while rejecting much of the heat striking the glass.

visible wavelengths of solar radiation, while reflecting the near-infrared wavelengths not visible to the human eye. Mirrored glass, which does not differentiate between the visible and near-infrared wavelengths, limits heat gain but at the expense of blocking daylight. Spectrally selective low-e coatings reflect 40 to 70 percent of the heat that would otherwise be transmitted through the window, but they also transmit a high percentage of the daylight.

Spectrally selective low-e coatings lower U-value and SHGC while maintaining high visible transmittance. Where windows are not shaded during hot times of year, or in larger commercial buildings, low-e coatings can greatly reduce the need for cooling. However, using spectrally selective low-e glass in a residential building designed according to passive solar principles will short circuit the performance of the building.

The thermal performance of windows that contain two or more panes of sealed glass, or glass and polyester films, can be improved by replacing the air in the gap with a gas fill. Filling the gap with a less-conductive gas such as argon or krypton reduces the transfer of heat across the space, lowering the U-value. Argon is most commonly used, because it is inexpensive. Krypton has better thermal performance, but it is more expensive to produce. These gases are nontoxic, clear, and odorless.

Single-pane windows and conductive frames led to unwanted heat gain and loss at daylight openings with resultant energy use for heating and cooling. Passive designs of the past sometimes included awkward movable insulation systems at windows to reduce nighttime heat loss. The combination of double- or triple-pane, insulated glazing units, gas fills, and low-e coatings make possible windows that admit winter sun and retain the heat. High-performance windows are a key part of the design of very low-energy residential and small commercial buildings.

Ventilation

Houses and small commercial buildings need to breathe. A low-energy-use building, with a tight thermal boundary, requires a ventilation system designed to assure that energy efficiency does not compromise indoor air quality. If air is drawn into a house without adequate means of exhaust, the building is pressurized. Pressurization pushes interior air into wall and ceiling openings. When air is exhausted from a house without sufficient air inlets, for example from a range hood, the building is depressurized. Depressurization pulls air through openings in the building envelope, potentially causing back drafting.

Back drafting means air is flowing against its intended direction, often through a flue. Back drafting pulls contaminants intended to be exhausted back into the house. In the worst case scenario, this could cause death from carbon monoxide poisoning. Uncontrolled ventilation through infiltration leaks not only wastes energy but could have serious health impacts. Because indoor air grows more polluted from contaminants in a house, fresh air must be regularly supplied. But first, sources of indoor air pollution should be controlled. Contaminants in construction materials should be eliminated from the construction process to the fullest possible extent. Low–volatile organic compound (VOC) paints and finishes, low-toxicity carpet and carpet pad, and boards without toxic binders and no-added formaldehyde in furniture and cabinetry are examples of source reduction. Materials that contain contaminants should be isolated from living quarters. In spaces such as kitchens, laundries, utility rooms, and bathrooms, contaminants should be exhausted. However, whole-house ventilation is still required.

Good whole-house ventilation brings in fresh air and exhausts indoor air in balance to avoid pressurization or depressurization, and conserves energy. A heat-recovery ventilator (HRV) uses the heat and humidity in exhaust air to temper incoming air. Heat-recovery ventilators heat, cool, or dehumidify incoming fresh air. They save up to four-fifths of the heat energy that would otherwise be lost. Intended for use in hot, humid climates, HRVs dry incoming air, reducing the need for air-conditioning. Heat-recovery systems require regular maintenance, such as filter replacement. Otherwise, the system itself becomes a source of poor indoor air quality. ASHRAE 62.2 is a recent ventilation standard intended for new and existing homes. It represents a minimal level of performance for residential ventilation.

Lowering the Energy of Residential Heating

Climate-appropriate design strategies reduce the need for energy used for comfort conditioning in residential buildings. Architectural detailing that provides high levels of insulation, an air barrier between conditioned spaces and the exterior, appropriate windows, and adequate controlled ventilation are part of climate-responsive design. An efficient building envelope often allows for downsizing of heating and air-conditioning units, reducing their initial cost.

Mechanical systems that supplement climate-responsive approaches work in several ways. For heating, one of the most common approaches is to warm air and deliver it to occupied spaces through ducts. Other approaches heat water, which circulates through radiators that warm air, creating convective air loops in a room. The radiator also warms occupants through direct radiation, when there is a direct line of sight between the two. Water can also be circulated through the floor slab or under the finish floor to provide radiant heat across the entire space. Electric-resistance heat is a third approach to heating.

A gas-fired furnace mixes fuel with air and burns it in a combustion chamber. A heat exchanger transfers heat from the combustion chamber to the air or water used to deliver the heat to occupied areas. Combustion gases are vented out of the building through a flue.

In open combustion, the combustion chamber, heat exchanger, and flue are open to the surrounding air. In sealed combustion they are not. This means all air for combustion is provided through a dedicated, sealed passage from the outside to the sealed combustion chamber within the furnace. Conversely, all products of combustion are vented to the outside through a separate, dedicated, sealed vent. Sealed combustion is safer and, in many cases, more efficient. For these reasons, new heating equipment should operate using sealed combustion. This reduces possible contamination of indoor air quality and lessens the possibility of sickness or death from carbon monoxide poisoning.

The furnace should be properly sized and chosen for efficient performance. All combustion furnaces and boilers for water heating must be labeled to show annual fuel utilization efficiency (AFUE). The AFUE figure represents the energy in the fuel that is transferred to the heating distribution system. It does not include distribution losses resulting from duct leaks or running poorly insulated ducts through unconditioned spaces. Look for Energy Star–rated furnaces with an AFUE of 90 or above.

A heating system should be properly sized to minimize equipment cost and maximize efficiency. This means the system's rate of heat production should be slightly larger than the building's rate of heat loss under extreme weather conditions that can reasonably be anticipated for the climate. Rules of thumb for equipment sizing should not be used. Residential heating and air-conditioning units are routinely oversized. An oversized unit that cycles on and off will not operate as efficiently as a properly sized unit that runs for a longer period of time to meet the demand for heating or cooling.

In air-delivery systems, reducing duct losses is very important. Forced-air systems are very popular, because heating, cooling, and ventilation air can all share the ducting system. However, they have drawbacks in that they are more difficult to divide into separately controlled zones than water-delivery systems and are susceptible to efficiency losses in the distribution system.

Losses of conditioned air through leaks in ducts can make a tremendous difference in overall system efficiency. Leaking ducts in an unconditioned attic or crawl space can introduce humid or particulate-laden air into the living quarters. Sealed ducts also reduce differential pressure that can result in back drafting of combustion appliances or create air movement through the building envelope.

Air-delivery ducts should be placed in conditioned space whenever possible. Unconditioned spaces can be quite hot or cold. A large temperature differential between air inside the duct and the surrounding space will severely compromise performance. If ducts must be run through unconditioned spaces, they must be well sealed and well insulated.

Regular maintenance, including changing of air filters, is important to keep air systems operating at peak efficiency.

Hydronic, or water-based, heating systems are increasingly common and provide great occupant comfort. Water systems typically include a boiler. As with air systems, it is important that the boiler be properly sized to achieve system efficiency. It is also possible to preheat water using a solar water-heating system, meeting part of the demand for heat with renewable energy.

Hydronic systems distribute hot water through pipes to heat emitters in occupied space. These can be radiators, baseboard convectors, fan coils, or building floors or ceilings. In a fan coil, hot water is used to transfer heat to air. A fan blows air across tubes of hot water, warming the air and delivering it to the space. Fan coil units are placed in individual rooms or zones.

Radiant floor systems use the floor itself as a relatively uniform emitter of heat. Flexible tubing made of cross-linked polyethylene runs through a concrete floor slab. The slab—or, in some cases, a thermally separated topping slab—heats up and radiates long-wave infrared radiation to building occupants, warming them. Slab systems typically have slow response times, meaning they are less effective where heat is required intermittently. Quicker response times can be achieved by placing the tubing in slots in a subfloor or through metal heat-transfer plates fastened to the finish wood floor.

Floor coverings, such as rugs and carpets, reduce the effectiveness of radiant systems by insulating the floor from the building occupants. These must be taken into account if the system is to be properly designed and sized.

Electric furnaces heat air by moving air over electric-resistance heating elements. They are the most expensive method of heating a home and have become quite rare as a result. Electric radiant systems, with heating cables embedded in a topping slab, gypsum board, or in overhead panels, have fallen into disuse for the same reason.

Electric, air-sourced heat pumps are effective for heating in mild climates where temperatures do not drop below freezing. Using the refrigeration cycle, they move heat from one location and "pump" it to another. They can reverse the cycle to provide cooling.

Ground-sourced, or geothermal, heat pumps are more efficient. In a ground-sourced system, coolant is pumped through tubing that is placed underground, either in vertical "wells" or horizontally. Because the earth stays at a constant temperature of about 55°F (12.75°C) year round, the heat pump never encounters extreme temperatures and works efficiently in both heating and cooling modes. The drilling or excavation required to place the tubing is expensive. The initial cost of geothermal systems is typically higher than other alternatives, although their life-cycle cost may be lower.

Thermostats are the common interface for heating systems. They enable occupants to establish when heating equipment turns on or off in response to changing room temperatures. Programmable thermostats incorporate a clock and temperature sensor. They permit occupants to adjust thermostat settings by both temperature and time and can save a lot of energy. To save energy occupants must program thermostats to lower the temperature setting during the day when occupants are at work and school or at night after going to bed. Studies have shown many occupants never program a programmable thermostat.

Lowering the Energy of Residential Cooling

As with heating, first use building design to reduce the need for cooling. Size overhangs to shade windows during hot times of year, while admitting sun in winter. Also, use landscaping to shade the building.

While solar angles are symmetrical around June 21, temperature and humidity are not. The earth's thermal mass stores solar radiation and releases it over hot months. Thus, while the sun is highest in the sky in North America on June 21, temperatures typically peak about six weeks later in early August. While solar angles are identical on March 21 and September 21, in many climates solar heat is desired on the first date and not desired on the second. Trees and plants respond more to temperature than sun angles. Size an overhang for conditions on March 21, but incorporate deciduous trees in the landscape design for shade in September. Similarly, trellises planted with vines and leafy plants will admit a significant proportion of sunlight in winter but reject it when it is least desirable at the building interior.

During summer, solar heat loads are greatest at the roof and at windows. A well-insulated roof with "cool" roofing materials reduces heat gain, as does window shading and spectrally selective glass.

For cooling, ventilation, even if induced by fans, is always cheaper than air-conditioning. Where temperature is below 85°F (29.5°C) and humidity is not extreme, ventilation alone can provide comfort. Evening and night ventilation can also reduce the need for air-conditioning in hot climates without extreme humidity, where night-time temperatures typically drop significantly. When evening temperatures drop, windows can be opened and a whole-house fan will quickly replace the air inside a house with cooler outside air. With adequate thermal mass, a whole-house fan can be used to precool the building at night. This delays the hour of day when air-conditioning is first required, reducing the overall run time of the air conditioner.

In hot and dry climates, evaporative cooling can provide comfort with considerably less energy than air-conditioning. With evaporative cooling, moisture is added to dry air, reducing the sensible air temperature while increasing the relative humidity. Vents or windows high in occupied spaces must be open to permit the existing hot air to be discharged as cooler air drops into a space. In a two-stage evaporative cooler, the cooler, moister air is run through a heat exchanger. While this reduces the overall efficiency of the system, it means the air in the conditioned space can be cooled without an increase in humidity.

For hot and humid climates, ventilation can be an effective cooling method up to a point. However, high temperatures and high humidity are the climate where passive cooling techniques are most limited. When night-time air temperatures remain high, thermal mass is not effective in reducing the need for cooling, as the mass itself never cools down. In such climates, air-conditioning is common. Recommendations that apply to air-based heating systems also apply to air-conditioning. Make sure the system is properly sized. Do not use rules of thumb to size an air-conditioning unit. Seal and run ducts through conditioned space or insulate them very well if this is not possible. Once you have made sure that the system is properly sized, look for the most efficient air-conditioning unit possible. One measure of air-conditioning efficiency is the SEER (seasonal energy efficiency ratio) rating. At minimum, use SEER-14 air-conditioning equipment; also, SEER-20 equipment is now available.

An air-conditioner designed for a hot and dry climate could operate more efficiently, because it need not address the latent heat load of a hot and humid climate. The ability of an air conditioner to remove moisture is measured by sensible heat factors (SHFs), a number between 0.5 and 1.0. The lower the SHF, the greater is the ability of the unit to remove moisture. In a hot and dry or moderate climate, there is less latent load associated with moisture. The State of California has sponsored research on highly efficient air conditioners for hot and dry climates. Such models are likely to appear on the market in the next decade.

Residential Daylighting

The size of residential buildings is such that most rooms should receive adequate illumination through windows and have little or no need for electric light during daylight hours. Thus, properly sized single-family residences offer few opportunities for energy savings from daylighting.

Proper placement of windows and skylights to high-light building form has a long history as an architectural art. Daylight can certainly be introduced in ways that are aesthetically pleasing and produce a good visual environment for building occupants. But residential daylighting should not be considered an energy-efficiency measure.

In residential buildings, the introduction of daylight more often than not leads to greater energy consumption rather than savings. When windows and skylights are oversized, a building can overheat in summer and lose heat in winter. Daylighting as an energy-efficiency measure is best thought of as a commercial building strategy. In residential buildings, the design priority should be to avoid oversized windows and skylights. If a house is larger than can be adequately daylit through windows, most likely it is larger than it should be when measured against a host of environmental criteria.

Residential Lighting

Lighting efficiency results from selecting the right fixture, using the right lamp, and controlling the time when lights are on. The efficiency of a lamp is known as lighting efficacy. Light output is measured in lumens. Efficacy is a measure of light output per input of power, or lumens per watt.

Illumination is measured in density of light output per a given area. One lumen distributed over one square foot is one foot-candle. Illumination is relatively easy to measure and thus is commonly used in lighting recommendations. However, humans perceive light largely through luminance rather than illuminance. Luminance is a measure of light *exitance* from a surface. Given the same measured illuminance in a room, a white wall has much higher exitance than the same wall if it were painted black. Human perception of light, rather than measured illuminance, is what matters in a well-designed space. Design of the entire room, not just the lighting system, will determine how bright and balanced light levels appear, or do not appear, in a room.

Correlated color temperature (CCT) is an indication of whether a lamp is perceived as cool or warm. Color temperature is a theoretical concept and does not indicate heat production. The values for CCT are counterintuitive in that lamps rich in reds and yellows have low CCT, yet are considered warm. Those producing white and blue light have high CCT and are cool. For most residential applications, lights with a correlated color temperature of between 2,700 and 3,000 K are preferable. Incandescent lamps are only available in warm color temperatures. Fluorescent lamps are available across a much broader range, so it is important to know the CCT of the lamp.

The color rendering index (CRI) number is a measure of the ability of a lamp to accurately depict different colors. These two measuring tools—CRI and CCT—are independent of one another. Cool fluorescent lamps can have high color rendering analogous to colors rendered through a north-facing skylight admitting daylight.

In residential applications, select compact fluorescent lamps (CFLs) with a color temperature in the 2,700 to 3,000 K range and with a high color rendering index of 80 or above.

Lighting energy use is a factor of power consumption and run time. Using high-efficacy bulbs in lamps or fixtures that distribute light where it is needed or desired, without lighting peripheral areas, reduces power consumption. Lowering light levels by dimming a lamp also reduces power consumption. Turning off a lamp when it is not needed reduces run time. Three energy-efficient lighting technologies that improve efficacy, reduce light levels, and reduce run time will result in high-quality indoor lighting environments with low energy use.

High-efficacy luminaires are designed to operate using energy-efficient light sources, such as fluorescent T8 or T5 lamps, compact fluorescent lamps, high-intensity discharge (HID) lamps, and in some instances light-emitting diodes (LEDs). Dimmers enable occupants to lower light levels and associated power use. Occupancy sensors, vacancy sensors, motion sensors, and daylight sensors automatically turn off lights in response to conditions.

Where dimming or focused spot lighting is not required, incandescent lights can be replaced with high-efficacy, compact fluorescents. A compact fluorescent using between one-third and one-quarter the power of a traditional incandescent lamp will produce about the same amount of light. It will also last much, much longer before burning out.

Light bulbs come in a variety of types. Incandescent bulbs that distribute light over a broad area are available for general lighting and are commonly referred to as A-type lamps. Reflector lamps incorporate a reflective-metal surface, used to direct the light in a particular direction, and are referred to as R (reflector) or PAR (parabolic aluminized reflector) lamps. When replacing an incandescent lamp with a CFL it is crucial to understand the type of lamp originally intended for the fixture. A spiral CFL intended for general lighting will work well when replacing an A-type lamp, but it is not intended as a replacement for a reflector lamp.

Where dimming is desired use incandescent lights. In kitchens, use nondimming fluorescent lights under cabinets, above cabinets, and in wall sconces. Use dimming, if desired, for pendant and ceiling-mounted downlights.

Occupancy sensors that automatically turn off lights when no one is in a room reduce the run time of lights. For residential use, sensors that require lights to be turned on manually and permit them to be turned off manually are recommended.

Outdoor lighting should only use high-efficacy sources and should include daylight and motion sensors.

Figure 11-11 Lamp types: An A-type incandescent with visible filament, A-type incandescent, a spiral compact fluorescent with screw-base, a linear compact fluorescent with pin-base, and a linear compact fluorescent with screw-base.

Water Heating

Heating water with the sun, also referred to as solar thermal, is very cost-effective and significantly reduces the use of fuel. It is one of the best opportunities in residential buildings to reduce the use of natural gas. Where gas service is not available, or in existing buildings where water is heated with electricity or propane, solar thermal offers an even better opportunity to reduce energy use. To reduce energy used to heat water, designers should think beyond the water heater. When selecting showerheads, toilets, faucets, and appliances such as washing machines and dishwashers, choose high-quality, water-efficient models that exceed code requirements as much as possible. The simplest and cheapest way to reduce energy associated with heating water is to reduce demand for hot water. Reducing demand for hot water also means the solar thermal system can potentially be downsized, reducing first cost. Determine the hot water set point needed. Many water heaters are set at 140°F (60°C) or higher. Lowering the set-point temperature to 120°F (48.9°C) may be possible or even preferable.

Once cost-effective hot water demand–reduction techniques have been implemented, consider the water-heating system itself. In most solar thermal systems, there is a gas or electric backup water heater. The heater raises the water temperature to the required level when the solar thermal system cannot provide all of the needed heat. The solar thermal system uses the sun to preheat water, which then runs to the backup water heater. Since water typically enters the solar system at about 55°F (12.75°C), any boost in temperature provided by the sun reduces energy use at the heater. Even on a cold, cloudy day, a solar system will usually raise water temperature a few degrees above entry temperature. In North America, it is very rare that the solar system replaces the water heater rather than supplements it.

Various approaches exist for solar water heating. The first distinction to understand is the difference between

Figure 11-12 Solar thermal installation: A solar thermal installation at a small National Park Service building.

passive and active systems. Active systems use pumps, while passive systems rely only on thermodynamics to circulate water through the collector and storage tank. A second distinction is that between direct and indirect systems: in a *direct system*, the water used by building occupants first runs through the solar collector where it is heated. In an *indirect system*, an antifreeze mixture, typically propylene glycol, runs through the solar collector. The warm mixture then passes through a heat exchanger and transfers its heat to the water used by building occupants. Propylene glycol, unlike ethylene glycol used in automobiles, is nontoxic.

Open-loop systems have two complicating factors. First, they are subject to corrosion from oxygen. Potable water for use by residents runs through the collector, bringing with it fresh oxygen that will eventually corrode cast iron, steel, and other parts. As a result, you must use materials that are resistant to corrosion, such as copper, bronze, brass, stainless steel, plastic, and glass-lined hot water tanks. Closed systems are filled with fluid when the system is installed, and the fluid is not replaced. Heat is transferred through a heat exchanger. Because new oxygen is not introduced, corrosion is not a problem.

A second consideration for an open-loop system is whether the water supplied is hard. Calcium deposits from hard water will clog the collectors. Deposits can be removed with regularly scheduled descalings of the system. However, this maintenance is critical, and without it the system will eventually be destroyed. As a result, a closed-loop system should be used where the water supply is hard.

The simplest passive-direct system is the batch heater. Thermosiphon systems are also passive. However, direct and indirect thermosiphon systems are possible. In both batch and thermosiphon systems, the collector and storage

tank are typically placed on the roof. This adds significant weight to the roof and may affect structural requirements. Of solar thermal systems, the batch heater is among the cheapest and requires the least maintenance. It is also among the least efficient, but it can work very well in a warm climate.

In a batch heater, the storage tank also serves as the collector. As a result, heat is gained during the day but lost at night. To limit losses, the storage tank is placed inside an insulated box. The insulated box is placed in a location to maximize solar access, typically the roof of the building. One side of the box is covered with glass and properly oriented to the sun for the latitude of the site. The sun enters through the glass and warms the water in the tank.

Water enters through an inlet low in the tank and leaves through an outlet high in the tank. When hot water is used, system pressure causes cold water to flow through the inlet of the batch heater. Because the water in the solar storage tank is stratified by temperature, warmer water is driven through the higher outlet and piped to the bottom of the water heater. If additional heating is required, gas or electricity is used to provide it. If the sun has raised the water temperature to the level of the domestic hot water set point, no fuel is needed. If the sun has warmed the water to above the set point, cold water is added through a tempering valve to prevent scalding water.

Batch heaters work best for modest-sized households in warm climates. They cannot be used where below-freezing temperatures are possible. Even in warm climates, the temperature of the water in the insulated tank will drop overnight, meaning they are less well suited to a situation where there is a high demand for hot water early in the day.

A thermosiphon system resembles a batch heater, but it separates the storage tank and collector. While there are a number of types of collectors for solar thermal systems, flat-plate collectors are the simplest and most common. In a flat-plate collector, copper pipes wind back and forth inside a box, painted black to absorb heat, and covered with glass to reduce heat loss. Separating the collector from the storage tank means the surface area of the collector can be increased. If the collector area is increased for a given amount of water being heated, the water temperature will rise more quickly.

In thermosiphon systems, fluid flows between the collector and tank entirely by stratification, so the tank must be located at least one foot above the collector. However, the tank can be highly insulated, thereby reducing nighttime losses. Passive-direct thermosiphon systems are limited to climates where temperatures overnight do not drop below freezing. However, passive-*indirect* thermosiphon systems, where propylene glycol is substituted for water and passed through a heat exchanger at the water heater, work in climates where temperatures only drop below freezing occasionally.

Active-direct systems work well in climates where freezing temperatures never occur. These systems allow the storage tank to be located below the collector and inside the basement or utility room. However, lengthy pipe runs should be avoided, as they reduce efficiency. An electric pump moves hot water from the collector to the storage tank. Sensors measure water temperature at the inlet and outlet of the collector. When a significant temperature difference exists, a controller turns on the pump. When the difference is small, the controller turns off the pump.

Active-direct systems that relied on controllers, pumps, and/or valves to provide freeze protection were once common, but now they are rare. In warm climates, where temperatures only rarely dropped below freezing, sensors at the collector also checked for possible freezing conditions. When cold conditions were measured, a controller turned on the pump, circulating hot water from the storage tank through the collector. The assumption was that this would only be needed occasionally and wasted energy would be minimal.

In climates where freezing temperatures commonly occur, a similar but more complicated open-loop system, known as a drain-down system, was common. When conditions were warm, differential temperatures measured at the collector inlet and outlet triggered a controller to turn on the pump, moving water from the tank through the collectors, just as in a nonfreezing climate. With possible freezing conditions measured by the sensors, the controller triggered valves that isolated the collector inlet and outlet from the tank, while simultaneously opening a valve that allowed water in the collector to drain down to the tank.

Neither of these freeze-protection systems is commonly used today, due to failures from power outages, sensor or controller malfunction, and valve breakdown, among others.

Closed-loop antifreeze systems provide the most reliable protection from freezing. These systems run food-grade glycol antifreeze through the collectors and a heat exchanger. Their weak point is that when no additional heat is needed at the hot water heater, the pump stops—antifreeze stops circulating, and temperatures in the fluid can get high. Additional components are needed to address this problem and make these systems more complex. Despite this drawback, closed-loop antifreeze systems are very reliable.

A variation on closed-loop antifreeze systems, known as a drain-back system, eliminates the drawback of high fluid temperatures. Not to be confused with drain-down systems, the drain-back system empties the collector whenever the pump is not in operation. Although water can be used, antifreeze is more common to guarantee freeze protection in the event that any part of the system malfunctions.

Similar to active open-loop systems, a pump operates in response to sensor readings at the inlet and outlet of the collector. When the collector outlet is significantly warmer than the inlet, liquid is pumped from a small reservoir tank, through the collector, and back to the tank. A heat exchanger in the reservoir tank transfers heat to the hot water heater. When weather conditions change, and no more heat can be collected, the pump is turned off, and all the fluid drains back to the reservoir tank. While the closed-loop drain-back system is less efficient, because it uses a heat exchanger and requires a larger pump, it is very reliable in cold climates and in any climate where supply water is hard.

When selecting the solar thermal system most appropriate for a given project, consider water supply, climate, and size of demand. Where water supplied is hard, use a closed-loop system, whatever the climate.

Where soft water is supplied, more options exist. In a freeze-free climate, a simple batch heater or thermosiphon unit can meet the demands of a small family. An active open-loop system, circulating water from storage tank to flat-plate collector, will meet larger demands. Where freeze protection is required, use a closed-loop system with antifreeze and a heat exchanger.

Solar Electric

On a regional scale, the sun's energy can be used to generate electricity at a community, neighborhood, or individual building scale.

Large-scale solar thermal electric plans make use of focusing mirrors to heat water until it becomes steam. The steam turns a turbine that produces electricity. This type of plant is regional in scale and produces power for thousands of homes. The electricity is fed into the transmission grid in the same way as power produced at any other generation station.

Figure 11-13 Solar electric installation: A solar electric system installed on a south-facing roof in San Francisco.

Electricity can also be generated from the sun using photovoltaic (PV) cells. Photovoltaic solar cells are made from conductive materials such as silicon. When solar radiation within certain wavelengths strikes a solar cell, electrons are released from the silicon and generate electricity. This means photovoltaic cells convert light energy into electrical energy.

Individual PV cells are grouped together to form a PV module. Modules are grouped together in an array. The array is part of a PV system, which includes components such as mounting hardware, the various electrical connections, an inverter, and in some cases batteries for energy storage.

Mounting hardware can be used to improve the orientation of the panel to the sun, as it secures the panel to the building or supporting structure. Electrical connections are needed to link the components of a system. In most cases, an inverter is used to convert the direct current (DC) produced by the modules into the alternating current (AC) commonly used in buildings. Disconnect switches are required to provide safety during maintenance. For grid-tied systems, a disconnect switch isolates the individual solar system from the electrical grid. This is needed to eliminate the possibility of electrocution in the case of repair personnel working on the grid in the event of grid failure.

Increasingly, solar arrays are connected to the utility grid. This eliminates the requirement for battery storage, as the building can draw power from the grid when the sun is not shining. If the solar system produces more power than is needed by the house during times of peak sunshine, the utility may purchase the excess power and provide a credit to the homeowner. The credit can be used to offset the cost of grid-supplied electricity used at night or during winter months when a surplus of power is not generated. However, without some form of battery backup, if the grid should fail, the PV system cannot

provide power to the residence because of the required disconnect switch at the inverter.

Grid-tied systems also have the potential to improve stability of the grid and reduce the need for construction of new electrical power plants. The production of electricity from PV systems occurs during some of the peak periods of demand on the power grid. Surplus production fed into the grid can help utilities meet this demand. However, utility peak-demand periods typically continue through late afternoon in response to the use of air-conditioning. From an individual building perspective, orientation of a PV array due south will usually maximize production of electricity. This can vary depending upon climate and microclimate. From a utility perspective, a more western orientation is best. Power produced at 3 P.M. is more valuable to a utility than the same amount of power produced at 9 A.M., because the overall demand for electricity is higher in the afternoon than in the morning. The financial incentives offered by some states and utilities for installation of PV systems reflect time-usage needs.

Off-grid PV systems make sense when the cost of the system is less than the cost of extending the distribution line from the local utility. At present, two forms of PV modules are most common: crystalline and thin film, also known as amorphous silicon. Crystalline silicon solar cells have been in use since the 1950s. Amorphous silicon is a more recent technology, although it has been in use for nearly two decades.

Crystalline silicon modules are the more efficient of the two in converting light to electricity. However, focusing solely upon efficiency is misguided. Power output of amorphous silicon is less affected by shading of the module. Amorphous silicon can also be used in ways that crystalline silicone modules cannot. And while crystalline modules are more efficient, their cost is higher. In terms of cost per power generated, both types are about equal. Neither form of PV is inherently superior to the other. In an urban situation, where space is limited, crystalline may be the best choice. On a rural building, such as a barn, where roof space is not an issue, amorphous silicon might be preferable. Many factors will affect selection.

Other materials are now used to manufacture thin-film solar cells. New technologies for depositing the conductive material on a substrate, similar to inkjet printing, have also been developed. These materials hold great promise for lowering the price and increasing the applications of solar electric generation. Building integrated photovoltaics, where the PV material serves double duty by replacing building materials such as roofing shingles or skylight glazing, are likely to become much more widespread. However, it would be a mistake to hold off on the use of currently available solar electric technologies out of a belief that revolutionary new products are just over the horizon. Changes in price and application are likely to be evolutionary rather than revolutionary.

Regardless of the technology employed, solar electric systems work best when they encounter no obstructions to sunlight. Partial shading of an array can result in a large percentage drop in power production. Careful analysis of the time period, and extent of area of solar access, are key to the success of solar electric installation.

Compared to the first cost of many other methods of generating electricity, PV systems remain expensive. However, as a result of concerns about global warming and resource depletion, the long-term benefits of converting to low environmental impact generation systems are increasingly recognized. Many state-sponsored financial incentive programs for solar installations exist, as do state and federal tax credits.

Energy Efficiency and Renewable Energy

Passive-design techniques increase the effectiveness of renewable energy in reducing the environmental impact of a building. As mentioned above, on-site renewable energy, such as solar electric, remains relatively expensive. Building design measures that improve energy efficiency are, up to a point, much cheaper than providing on-site power generation. Good site orientation, air sealing, high-performance windows, high levels of well-installed insulation, efficient appliances, and other such "low-hanging fruit" are cost-effective in reducing the need for energy.

Very low-energy buildings will incorporate renewable energy, but as part of an overall strategy to reduce building energy use. It is important to first design an extremely energy-efficient building, or retrofit efficiency improvements into an existing one, before powering the remaining building loads with building-integrated or grid-supplied renewable energy. By design, the building should be worthy of the investment in on-site generation of renewable energy.

Use of solar energy also influences the orientation of roofs and placement of chimneys, vents, and equipment. These must be carefully located to permit successful integration of solar thermal water heating and generation of electricity using photovoltaics.

12 Energy-Efficient Building Design: Nonresidential Buildings

Energy Efficiency: The Commonalities among Building Types

Many of the approaches to energy-efficient design discussed in previous chapters are appropriate whatever the building type. In some cases, however, larger nonresidential buildings require different design strategies. In this chapter we will discuss some of the major differences between residential and nonresidential buildings in regard to energy-efficient design.

Predesign: Site Selection and Transportation Options

As with residential buildings, site selection has a major impact on transportation energy use associated with nonresidential buildings. When building operation- and transportation-energy usage costs are added up, an energy-efficient office building in an exurban or suburban site may result in more daily energy use than a less-efficient building located in a more densely developed area or an area with a developed network of transportation options. With the steep rise in the cost of gasoline, locating a commercial building where good transportation options exist will make it more attractive to potential tenants and increase its value to the owner.

Internal-Load Dominated Buildings

Nonresidential buildings have higher occupant densities than residential buildings. People generate heat, adding to the sensible cooling load of a building. One need only think how quickly a crowded room can overheat to understand this. People also sweat, releasing moisture into the air, raising humidity levels, and adding to the latent heat energy in indoor air.

Nonresidential buildings contain equipment and appliances used in the work environment. These include computers, copy machines, printers, and a host of additional devices, all using electricity. These devices release heat, adding to sensible cooling load, and in some cases release moisture, adding to the latent load.

In most buildings designed since 1950, electric light is the main source of illumination. Buildings built prior to 1950, which in most cases were designed to operate with daylight as the primary source of illumination, often run electric lights throughout the day. Many of these buildings have been renovated and/or incorporate furnishings in ways that block daylight. Lighting systems have been renovated as well, in many cases without incorporation of controls that would permit some percentage of fixtures to be switched off in response to daylight. Because they are much more efficient than incandescent lights, fluorescent or discharge lamps have been incorporated in building renovations. However, these lights still generate a considerable amount of heat that adds significantly to cooling loads.

The internally generated heat from high occupant density, equipment, and electric lights results in a situation where, even when outside temperatures are low, cooling rather than heating is required in much or all of the building. To reduce operational energy use in large buildings, designers should limit external heat gain, reduce internal heat gain, use low-energy cooling approaches and equipment to offset the remaining load, and use building-integrated renewable energy to meet as much of the remaining load as possible.

The single biggest source of heat gain at the building envelope is solar radiation through glass. To achieve excellent energy performance, designers of large nonresidential buildings must focus upon control of heat gain from the sun year-round, rather than rejecting heat in summer and admitting it in winter.

Daylighting is the easiest means of achieving major reductions in both operational energy use and internal

Figure 12-1 Internal- and skin-load dominated buildings: The need for cooling or heating in large buildings is driven by the internal loads from lights, people, and equipment. Heating and cooling requirements in residential and small commercial buildings is usually dominated by conditions at the building skin. Heat is needed when it is cold at the exterior of the skin, and cooling is needed when it is hot.

heat gains. It should be pursued to the fullest extent in all projects, especially one- or two-story nonresidential buildings where even light levels can be achieved using toplighting. Efficient lighting can fill in the gaps in daylit areas and provide night lighting. Efficient equipment, with controls to limit run time, will also reduce operational-energy consumption.

When internal loads are reduced through daylighting and controls on plug loads, passive- and low-energy design strategies can further reduce energy demand. Low-energy approaches include natural ventilation, mixed-mode ventilation, night ventilation with thermal mass, radiant cooling, displacement ventilation, and other strategies. Load shifting through methods such as thermal storage can also reduce the environmental impact of energy use.

In large buildings, complete elimination of mechanical systems for heating and cooling is rare. Selection of the most energy-efficient and properly sized mechanical systems also plays a role. Self-generation, in the form of solar electric, wind electric, solar thermal, or combined

heat and power systems, will further reduce building energy consumption.

To fully reduce building operational energy to net zero, meaning the building draws no more power from the electrical grid than it puts into it, may require an investment in off-site renewable energy.

The implications of the above upon design decision making are discussed below.

Reducing External Heat Gain: Response to Climate

As with residential building, climate-responsive design, the first step is to identify the site climate. Use the maps or zip code climate zone data available online for use with American Society of Heating, Refrigerating and Air-Conditioning Engineers (ASHRAE) Standard 90.1.[1] Acquire an historic climate summary for a location as close as possible to the actual building site. The

---

[1] U.S. Department of Energy, Pacific Northwest Lab, http://resource-center.pnl.gov/cocoon/morf/ResourceCenter/article/1420.

Regional Climate Centers provide a great deal of climate information online at no charge.[2] Compare the historic data against the norms for regional climate to determine where the site climate falls on the continuum of the regional climate zones.

Climate summaries reflect historic data, and in some cases do not include data from the previous decade. Because global warming is changing the climate, summaries do not necessarily reflect current conditions, and they may not accurately predict future ones. As we move into the twenty-first century, cooling loads are likely to increase while heating loads fall. Given the long life span of buildings, climate may change noticeably during that period. Designers need to keep abreast of scientific reports on changing climate to create a building that meets current needs yet can adapt as climates grow warmer.

Building Envelope

Daylighting

In nonresidential buildings, daylighting is often one of the simplest and most effective methods to reduce the use of electricity. Buildings have operated with daylight as the primary means of illumination for thousands of years. Before looking for new daylighting technologies, designers should first relearn techniques that fell into disuse in the era of abundant and inexpensive energy.

A large percentage of nonresidential new construction consists of one- or two-story buildings. The simplest, cheapest, and most effective method to facilitate daylighting of these buildings is to use skylights. Properly sized, diffusing or prismatic skylights provide uniform

Figure 12-2 Diffusing skylights: Skylights that diffuse sunlight and distribute the light evenly throughout the space.

---

[2]Regional Climate Centers, http://www.wrcc.dri.edu/rcc.html.

lighting for commercial or industrial buildings without excessive heat gain or loss. Skylights in standard sizes, often referred to as unit skylights, are widely available. They can be creatively incorporated to provide daylight in almost any building.

Custom-designed skylights, atria, and other more complex approaches to toplighting can also reduce the need for electric lighting. These toplighting elements often play a major role in shaping building aesthetics. Because of their complexity, a number of iterative design studies are usually required to assure the provision of good-quality illumination without glare. We encourage effective use of these types of toplighting systems, but their design is beyond the scope of this book. Here we will focus on relatively simple systems that can be widely used.

Skylights bring daylight into a building, making it possible to dim or switch off some, or all, of the electric lights. Skylights do result in heat gain from the sun. However, for a given illumination level, daylight adds less heat to a room than would result from using the most efficient electric lights. Less heat means reduced cooling loads. Skylights can also potentially increase heating loads by allowing more heat to escape through the roof.

The key to skylighting is to balance light levels and energy savings against heat gain and loss. An undersized skylighting system will not save enough energy to justify the cost of electric lighting controls, nor will it provide adequate illumination levels. An oversized skylighting system will provide too much light, admit too much heat from the sun, and lose too much heat when it is cold outside. The optimum balance will be a function of building design, building operation, and local climate conditions.

The sources of light for skylights are the sun, the blue sky, and overcast or cloudy skies. Each has different characteristics. The most important differences include intensity or brightness, direct or diffuse light, and color.

Sunlight is bright and direct. It is similar in effect to an electric spotlight. Light from an overcast or blue sky is diffuse. It is similar in effect to a fluorescent light, where the lamp is shielded from the eye and directed to reflect off a white wall.

Sunlight varies considerably in intensity and color over the course of the day. It is brightest at midday, when it is high in the sky. In color, it is reddish and yellow early and late in the day and neutral or slightly cool in quality at midday. Daylight from overcast and blue skies is much less intense than direct sun and tends to be cooler in color at all times.

In some instances, direct sun—because it is extremely bright and creates high contrast—can enliven a space. Examples include lobbies, entries, and circulation spaces. However, where a skylight is intended to provide ambient light for general illumination, direct sun from the skylight is problematic. In a classroom or office, direct sun can create glare that makes it nearly impossible to see a teaching surface or computer screen. In most applications, skylights should completely diffuse direct sun, scattering it as it passes through the glazing material in the skylight.

Glass and plastic glazing materials, including acrylics, polycarbonates, and fiberglass, are common in skylights. As with residential windows, visible transmittance, U-value (sometimes termed U-factor), and solar heat gain coefficient (SHGC) affect performance. The purpose of the skylight is to admit light, so a fairly high visible transmittance is essential, at least 50 percent. To limit heat loss, select a skylight with U-value and SHGC as low as your budget will permit.

With skylights, the degree of diffusion of incoming light is an additional factor that needs consideration. Except for special applications where direct sun is desired, choose skylights with a haze factor of 90 percent or more. Haze factor does not affect the total amount of light coming through the skylight. It is possible, even desirable, to select a skylight with a high visible transmittance and high haze factor. High numbers for both metrics means a lot of light is admitted, but the light is broadly diffused even when direct sun strikes the glazing material.

The number, size, and location of skylights determine the way in which daylight is distributed across a room. To achieve even distribution, the rule of thumb is to space the skylights 1.0 to 1.5 times the ceiling height, measured from center to center of each skylight in both directions. As with all rules of thumb, this is a starting point and does not apply in every situation.

Human perception of light intensity is largely shaped through reflection of light. With the same measured illumination level, a room with light-colored vertical surfaces that reflect daylight will appear brighter than a

similar space where the walls are dark. Adding skylights close to vertical surfaces to increase their brightness can make a big difference in how bright a room appears to occupants.

Because of reduced installation costs, installing a few large, widely spaced skylights is certainly cheaper than installing a greater number of small, narrowly spaced skylights. However, wide spacing of large skylights can result in uneven distribution and glare. It can also reduce energy savings, as the uneven light distribution affects the ability to switch or dim lights. Using smaller skylights and spacing them more closely results in better uniformity and presents more opportunities for energy savings but will mean increased installation costs. As with many design decisions, a good solution must balance cost against the desired level of performance.

Adequate light levels and visual comfort are essential parts of good lighting design, whether the source is electric light or daylight. Addressing glare is key. Both ceiling-mounted electric lights and skylights can cause visual discomfort because of excessive brightness within the field of view of building occupants and/or from reflections on room surfaces.

Diffusing skylights can be very bright when sunlight falls upon them. If the skylight is in the field of vision of a building occupant, it will cause visual discomfort. Discomfort results because the eye has difficulty adjusting between the bright skylight and the darker ceiling and wall surfaces that surround it. Room proportions play a role in whether or not this becomes a problem.

Rooms with tall ceilings are less problematic, because skylights tend to be out of the field of view. In very large spaces, such as a gymnasium or warehouse, skylights are less prominent when in the distance and above the field of view as occupants move in their direction. In this case, no glare-control device is needed.

If a room has a very low ceiling, it is more likely that a skylight will be within an occupant's field of view. Where there is a finished ceiling, a light well will serve as a glare-control device and improve light distribution. *Cut-off angle*, a term used in electric lighting design, applies equally well to skylights. The cut-off angle is the viewing angle that prevents an occupant from seeing the bright surface of the skylight. Wherever computers are used, a cut-off angle of 55 degrees or higher is preferred. In buildings with low ceilings but less critical tasks, such as a supermarket, a cut-off angle for the skylight of 45 to 50 degrees is likely to work well.

Reducing the cut-off angle widens distribution of light but increases the possibility of glare from the skylight. A deep light well with a narrow cut-off angle eliminates glare but reduces distribution, concentrating the daylight in a small area. A light well that has straight walls at the top and splayed walls at the bottom can combine the best of both. A splayed light well can improve visual comfort by providing an intermediary surface, one not as

Figure 12-3 Direct sunlight: Without diffusion, patches of direct sun cause uneven light levels and visual discomfort.

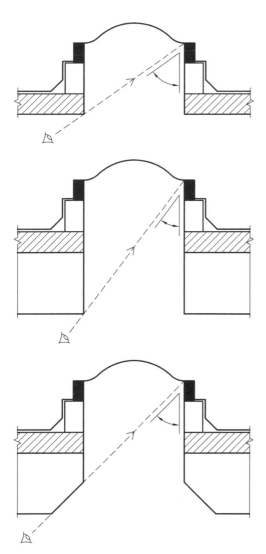

Figure 12-4 Cut-off angle for light wells: The depth and splay of the light well affects light distribution and the potential for glare. A shallow light well with a wide cut-off angle permits a view of the bright skylight. A deep light well with narrow cut-off angle prevents glare but limits light distribution. A moderate depth with splayed walls can be a good compromise.

Figure 12-5 Sidelighting: Daylight through windows has historically been the main source of interior illumination.

bright as the light well wall but brighter than the ceiling plane. The splay at the bottom of the well also permits the daylight to spread across a broader area as it enters the occupied space.

Sidelighting with windows can be combined with skylighting in low-rise buildings or serve as the primary method of daylighting in multistory buildings. Prior to the advent of fluorescent lighting and small air conditioning units, around 1940, all multistory buildings were designed to operate with daylight as the primary source of illumination.

Design for daylighting will require analysis and coordination among members of the design team. Performance goals should be established with the owner, and achieving these goals must remain a priority. All members of the team need to understand the goals and the level of analysis required to achieve them. As with so many other aspects of building design, schedule and cost must be balanced against the desired level of performance. It makes no sense to establish lofty goals without the resources to achieve them.

In some cases, daylighting may not be appropriate to a building type. For example, some museums may need to limit daylight in certain areas. While this is the exception rather than the rule, determine whether daylighting fits the building program. Also, some building types or sites may permit daylighting some parts of a building but not others. Take advantage of the opportunities that do arise, even if the entire building cannot take advantage of daylighting.

Successful sidelighting requires that windows see the sky to admit daylight but that they also incorporate some form of shading to reduce glare. As with skylighting, direct sunlight is usually not a good source of daylight in work areas. Incoming light needs to be diffused off building surfaces. Unlike with skylights, diffusing glazing is rarely an option because windows are in the direct line of sight of occupants. Diffusing glass at view windows creates excessive glare.

In designing the building form and skin, increase exposure to daylight but in a way that permits shading of windows. Long and narrow floor plans, elongated on the east-west axis, usually work better than square floor plans. Placing more windows on south and north exposures rather than east or west makes it easier to shade these windows at latitudes common in North America. Designing a facade with some depth also can improve sidelighting. Deep or splayed window reveals and exterior fins reflect daylight and modulate glare.

With sidelighting, the depth to which daylight can penetrate is limited. A look at tall daylit buildings indicates that they are narrower than very large buildings lit primarily with electric light. The depth of the daylighted zone is driven by the height of the window. The higher the window, the deeper will be the daylighted zone. Low glass, especially below desk height, provides little in the way of daylight or view. It does add to the solar heat load on a building. As a rule of thumb, the daylighted zone is limited to 1.5 times the window head height. With a well-designed light shelf, the zone can be as deep as 2.5 times the head height.

Prior to the use of fluorescent lights for ambient lighting, building occupants were forced to adjust window blinds over the course of the day to admit daylight while controlling glare. With incorporation of fluorescent lights into commercial and institutional buildings, the blinds often are adjusted to a closed position and electric lights remain in use throughout the day. To lessen the likelihood of this happening, use separate apertures for view and daylight.

Locate a view window with a head height of 7 feet (2.13 meters) and a second daylight window above that to admit daylight. Ideally, incorporate an exterior shading device and interior light shelf between the two windows. Use high-transmission, clearer glazing in clerestory windows and lower-transmission glazing in view windows to control glare. Even when occupants close the blind at the view window, glare-controlled daylight can enter through the high window. The light will be reflected by the light shelf onto the ceiling, providing ambient light that can be supplemented as needed with task lights.

Large windows require more control. Buildings with floor-to-ceiling glass require complex controls to manage glare and heat gain. The larger the glass area in the view zone below 7 feet, the lower should be the required visible transmittance and SHGC of the glass. A strategy to consider is creation of a ribbon of daylight glazing above 7 feet to provide continuous, even illumination. A more limited area of windows can then be added below to provide occupants with views, to animate the space, and to reflect additional light onto vertical sidewalls.

Effective sidelighting through windows works best with exterior shading devices, be they projecting

Figure 12-6 Interior shades: Interior shades provide occupant control but do little to block solar heat. If shades are closed, daylight cannot reach the interior of the building.

Figure 12-7 View and daylighting glazing: Separate glazed areas for view and daylight increase the likelihood that daylight will offset the use of electric light.

elements, louver screens, or other mechanism. Shading devices block heat gain. They also are key in creation of a comfortable visual environment by limiting direct sun and balancing daylighting levels across the daylighted zone by sharply reducing illumination levels next to the window. Solar control glass with a low SHGC only performs part of this function and cannot serve as a substitute for all of the roles played by shading devices.

Whether daylighting is through skylights or windows, interior finishes greatly affect light distribution. On ceilings and walls select white or very light colors to reflect as much light as possible. Use more saturated colors on secondary surfaces where light distribution is not as important, or as design highlights. Avoid specular surfaces, such as mirrors or reflective glazed tile.

It is essential that light colors also be used when selecting interior furnishings. The height and layout of furnishings also affects light distribution. Tall, dark-colored workstations inserted into the best daylight design will have a severe adverse effect upon performance.

Integration with Electric Lights

Because daylight is not always available, a full electric lighting system must be provided in daylit buildings. Several considerations must be addressed.

Depending upon the building type, electric lighting systems should be designed to supplement light from skylights during daytime hours. Specific electric light fixtures can provide additional task light, as needed, while daylight provides general ambient light. Electric light can also be used to illuminate select vertical surfaces. Careful use of this technique can greatly increase perceived brightness of a space with very limited energy use. The electric lights must also be adequate to light the space at night or when daylight is insufficient.

The electric lights must dim or switch in response to signals from daylighting controls. If use of the electric lights is not reduced, no energy will be saved. In fact, the opposite will be the case, as cooling loads increase with the introduction of solar heat without a reduction in heat produced by electric lights.

Whether to switch or dim electric lights is an important question in any daylighting design. Dimming systems are more expensive, because they require dimming ballasts for fluorescent and discharge lamps. However, dimming is much less noticeable to building occupants. In general, dimming is used in locations where occupants have a sense of ownership of the space or remain in a given location over extended periods of time. An office building is a good example. Switching results in more abrupt and noticeable changes in light levels. It works well where occupants are more transitory or move through the space: for example, a high school gymnasium, big box retail store, or warehouse.

Control over the electric lighting can be automatic or manual, although ASHRAE 90.1 and California Title 24 require controls in certain daylit areas. Some degree of manual control is usually desirable for occupant satisfaction, but only an automatic system can bring about guaranteed, sustained energy savings. Automatic control can be regulated by an astronomical time clock, but it more typically involves a photosensor that measures light levels.

Open-loop systems measure daylight levels at a skylight well or near a window and adjust electric lights in response to given measured values. Closed-loop systems are more complex and measure combined daylight and electric light contributions within the occupied space. The number of sensors and complexity of the control system varies with the gradient of daylight created by the building design. Buildings with skylights and very even levels of daylight across a space can sometimes use a single sensor. Sidelighted buildings require more complex systems. Determining the best location for the photosensor can be difficult, but new software tools can assist with this process.

Control systems must be commissioned before a building is occupied to assure the electric lights respond as intended. There are many documented cases where lighting controls have been installed but wired incorrectly or not calibrated to dim or switch lights when adequate daylight is present. Without commissioning, both energy performance and occupant satisfaction with the building are likely to be severely compromised.

Specifying an appropriate circuit design that reflects the control zones for the electric lights is essential. If one lighting circuit crosses areas of significantly different levels of daylight, the ability to dim or switch off electric lights in response to daylight will be compromised. Lights must be organized in circuits that match the relative daylight levels, or gradient of daylight, in the space. This will permit the electric lights within a given daylight zone to respond in unison.

As with electric lighting, heating, ventilating, and air-conditioning (HVAC) systems must be integrated with skylighting and/or daylighting design requirements and components. Sizing of the HVAC system should accurately reflect cooling-load reductions achieved with good daylighting.

Duct runs can block the distribution of daylight from skylights and high windows or conflict with vertical skylight wells in buildings with finished ceilings. Requirements for roof-mounted mechanical equipment may conflict with skylight layout. These are just a few examples of possible conflicts at the component level. Coordination is required.

Windows, Glass, and Curtain Walls

The discussion of the properties of glass in the previous chapter on residential design, in particular visible transmittance, U-value, and solar heat gain coefficient,

Figure 12-8 Site-built fenestration: A site-built fenestration system being assembled.

applies equally well to nonresidential buildings. Several fundamental differences between residential and nonresidential window openings are discussed below.

Most windows used in residential buildings are premanufactured units. These windows arrive on-site fully assembled and ready to be framed into a wall. While premanufactured windows are not uncommon in nonresidential buildings, in many cases site-built systems are used. Small, commercial, building-wall systems, commonly referred to as "storefronts," and curtain-wall systems in high-rise construction are examples of site-built systems.

As the name implies, site-built window systems are assembled at the job site from separate framing components, typically metal and glass or insulated glazing units (IGU). An IGU is made from two or more sheets of glass or from two sheets of glass and suspended plastic films. The sheets of glass are separated by a spacer and sealed to form a single glazed unit with an air space between each sheet. Insulated glazing units have greatly improved thermal performance over single-pane glass. Their use should be standard in all projects except in the mildest of climates.

The thermal performance of site-built fenestration is dependent upon several variables. A high-performance storefront or curtain-wall system should incorporate a thermal break to prevent heat transfer from one side of the wall to the other via conduction through the frame material. Systems with a thermal break separate

frame components into interior and exterior pieces and use a less conductive material to join them. This is important, because commercial framing systems are almost universally made from metals, which are highly conductive.

The frame must be properly detailed and installed to prevent thermal bridging. The performance of a thermally broken frame can be short circuited if it is attached to other building components in a way that creates a thermal bridge.

The performance of the IGU is another major influence on system performance. Tinted glass is common in nonresidential buildings, but it is a mistake to assume that dark tints reject more solar heat than lighter ones. Solar heat gain coefficient is the metric for evaluating and comparing heat gain through glass. Because of their internal loads, large nonresidential buildings are likely to require low-SHGC glass, although this will depend upon the specifics of use and climate.

After years of research, a switchable glass that can change the degree of both visible and solar transmittance in response to sunlight is now available. While promising, it remains expensive and applications have been limited. While this may change with time, the goal should always be good, climate-responsive design that provides visual comfort for occupants. Switchable glass should be integrated into well-designed buildings rather than thought of as a technological fix for poor design.

Buildings incorporating double-skin facades, in which two layers of glass are separated by a significant amount of air space, have appeared in recent years. Double skins offer a number of ways to incorporate elements that lower building energy use. One such strategy is the addition of adjustable shading devices between the two skins. In such an interstitial space they are protected from the elements and can be more easily maintained. Double-skin facades also have been used to reduce energy used to heat, cool, and ventilate buildings. Their use in North America has been limited by first cost and to some extent by fire codes.

High-performance facades, including double skin, do have higher initial cost. However, in a truly integrated design process, their higher first cost will be weighed against other considerations, such as their impact on the need for perimeter heating or their role in garnering savings from daylighting. As previously stated, most office buildings need cooling more often than heating. With a standard facade, a separate perimeter heating system is required to add warmth to areas adjacent to windows. This is because of thermal losses across the facade when exterior temperatures are cool.

High-performance facades can eliminate the need for a perimeter heating system. The cost savings from elimination of this system may offset much of the cost of the facade upgrades. Additional savings from daylighting may mean the cost of the facade pays for itself over a number of years. These financial considerations will depend upon climate and specific use of the building but should be included when evaluating the cost of different design options.

Cool Roofs

When the sun is high in the sky between late March and mid-September, building roofs receive a large amount of solar radiation. Many commercial buildings have dark roofs. Dark roofs absorb solar radiation and get much hotter than the ambient air temperature. The heat absorbed by the roof is conducted through the roof assembly, warming the interior and adding to the cooling load of the building.

A roof will stay cooler if it can reflect this radiation rather than absorb it, and it can readily reradiate the heat it absorbs. Roof materials with both high reflectivity and emissivity will lower the temperature of the roof and reduce heat transmission to the interior. Solar reflectance indicates the fraction of solar energy reflected by the roof. Thermal emittance indicates the fraction of the heat absorbed that is radiated away by the roof. Both properties are represented as a number between zero and one. The higher the value, the greater the reflectance or emissivity, and, therefore, the cooler the material will be.

There are numerous benefits to a cool roof. The need for cooling and associated energy use is reduced. Because cooler roof temperatures reduce thermal stress on materials, the life of the roof is increased. With load reductions, it may be possible to downsize the mechanical system. Occupant comfort may be increased.

Because of the lack of vegetation and the large surface area of absorptive materials in urban areas, the air temperature is typically higher in cities than in surrounding locations. This is known as the urban heat island effect. Cool roofing products can help lessen this effect.

Figure 12-9 Cool roof: Light-colored roofing materials or applied coatings will reflect solar heat and reduce the need for cooling.

Cool roofs are beneficial, even in cold climates. Because the sun is lower in the sky and above the horizon for fewer hours during winter months than in summer, the roof absorbs much less heat. While a cool roof will reduce winter heat gain, the reduction is much lower in winter than summer. Savings from reduced cooling will more than offset increased heating costs in most North American climates. Even if a building is not air-conditioned, a cool roof can be a cost-effective, passive measure to keep summer interior conditions for occupants in the comfort zone.

Cool roofs are not a substitute for insulation, but they are an additional means of improving the performance of the building envelope. It is essential to remember that the design of the entire roof assembly shapes the thermal performance of the roof.

The California Title 24 Energy Standards have included cool roofs as a prescriptive requirement for low-slope roofs since 2005. A low-slope roof is defined as one having a rise of less than 2 inch per run of 12 inches. Under Title 24, low-slope roofing materials must have a solar reflectance of at least 0.70 and thermal emittance of at least 0.75. The U.S. Green Building Council (USGBC) Leadership in Energy and Environmental Design (LEED) standard also includes a cool roof credit for materials meeting a similar level of performance.

Ratings for roofing products must be from tests sanctioned by the Cool Roof Rating Council (CRRC), rather than from individual manufacturers. The CRRC defines test procedures for establishing the reflectivity and emittance of roofing materials. The council lists these properties for commercially available roofing products on their Web site at http://www.coolroofs.org. However, it is important to understand that not all products listed on the CRRC Web site meet California Title 24 Energy Standards and the LEED standard for a cool roof product.

Low-slope roofing products with high reflectivity and emittance are widely available. With low-slope roofs, it is possible to specify a white, or near white, roofing product or coating. The costs of these roofs are low and typically have a short economic payback period.

Fewer high-slope materials are available. Because they are usually colored rather than white, high-slope materials rarely achieve the level of performance of low-slope products. However, research into new aggregates, pigments, and spectrally selective coatings that reflect nonvisible wavelengths of solar radiation have made it possible for colored, high-slope products to have significantly improved thermal performance over standard high-slope products. The 2008 California Title 24 Energy Standards for residential buildings incorporate prescriptive requirements for *cool* high-slope roof products. This is likely to increase the number of products available, not only in California but across North America.

Vegetated roofs, or green roofs, are another form of cool roof. They have the additional benefits of retaining storm water and providing habitat support for birds and small wildlife. Prior to the recent past, earthen roofs were often more than a foot in depth over a membrane roof and planted with conventional landscaping. Newer green roof systems are lighter and can be incorporated into almost any building.

Electric Lighting

Some of the best opportunities for cost-effective energy savings are found in lighting systems in nonresidential buildings. High-performance lighting systems not only save energy, but they can improve the quality of the visual environment.

As mentioned above, to reduce the need for electric lighting, design daylit buildings to the fullest extent possible. There is no more effective method of saving energy than turning equipment off. Diffuse the incoming daylight. Avoid direct sunlight, and install controls for the electric lights.

Design lighting systems to provide the right amount of light for the task while preventing glare. Use the recommended illumination levels in the most recent edition of the Illuminating Engineering Society's lighting handbook, or lighting power allowances in the most current version of ASHRAE 90.1 or California Title 24 Nonresidential Energy Standards as a minimum level of performance. By incorporating daylighting, you can reduce the use of electric light and greatly exceed these minimum performance levels.

As mentioned in the previous chapter, correlated color temperature (CCT) refers to the kelvin (K) temperature at which a theoretical blackbody radiator would emit light of a color similar to the fluorescent source. The values for CCT are counterintuitive in that lamps rich in reds and yellows have low CCT, yet are considered warm. Those lamps producing white and blue light have high CCT and are cool. Incandescent lamps have a color temperature of about 2,700 K. Because the CCT of a fluorescent lamp results from the phosphor coating on the inside of the glass tube, a range of color temperatures is available, generally from 3,000 K to about 5,000 K, although 2,700 K and 6,500 K are also available.

Color rendering index (CRI) indicates the accuracy of a light source in rendering eight standard colors relative to a reference source. A CRI of 100 means the source renders the eight standard colors in exactly the same way that the reference light source renders the colors. Warm sources and cool sources are measured separately against different reference sources. For this reason, comparing the CRI of a warm source to that of a cool source is not meaningful. For warm sources, incandescent light is by definition the reference source and by default has a CRI of 100. For cool sources, daylight is the reference source.

Light Sources

When comparing light sources, designers must weigh a number of factors including: light output in lumens;

Figure 12-10 Light sources: Fluorescent and discharge lamps are the primary sources of ambient light in nonresidential buildings. Incandescent lamps provide focal lighting.

power draw in watts; efficacy, or lumens produced per watt drawn; lamp life in hours; lumen maintenance, or variation in light output over the life of the lamp; correlated color temperature; color rendering index; ability to be dimmed; ability to operate with controls; and temperature considerations.

Incandescent lights work by heating a tungsten filament to the temperature of incandescence. That is the temperature at which the filament radiates electromagnetic energy in the visible wavelengths. However, along with the visible light, a great deal of infrared heat is also produced.

Incandescent sources are popular because of their good color rendition, low first cost, ease of dimming, and immediate "on." Their drawbacks include poor efficacy, short lamp life, high operating and long-term costs, and high heat production. The efficacy of incandescent sources is typically 10–20 lumens/watt (lm/W). Their lamp life is short, typically 700–1,000 hours. Incandescent sources are limited to warm color temperatures, typically about 2,700 K.

Tungsten halogen is a premium incandescent source. In a halogen lamp, the tungsten filament is sealed in a small chamber filled with an inert gas, plus a small amount of halogen. The halogen redeposits evaporating tungsten back onto the filament, increasing the life of the lamp to 2,000 hours. Halogen lamps operate at a higher temperature, resulting in 10 to 30 percent greater efficacy and higher color temperature of up to 3,500 K compared to regular incandescents. Because of the small size of the sealed chamber, halogen reflector lamps are commonly used for focal lighting.

Fluorescent is a high-efficacy source. In a fluorescent lamp, the glass tube is sealed with a small amount of mercury inside. An electrode is located at each end

Figure 12-11 Fluorescent lighting: Fluorescent lamps strike an arc between two electrodes. The white coating on the interior of the lamp absorbs the radiant energy from the arc and emits it as visible light. This demonstration lamp shows the coating and an electrode.

Figure 12-12 High-intensity discharge (HID) lamps: These lamps are efficacious and provide good quality light in high-bay spaces. Because of their high light output, HID lamps can cause glare and discomfort if in the field of view.

of the tube. The inside of the tube is lined with a phosphor coating. Electrical energy is used to strike a mercury vapor arc stream from electrode to electrode. The ultraviolet electromagnetic energy released from the stream is absorbed by the phosphor coating and reemitted as visible light.

A ballast is needed to strike the arc and then regulate voltage. A special dimming ballast is required to dim fluorescent lamps. Fluorescent lamps have high efficacy, long lamp life, and low operational and long-term costs, and they produce moderate amounts of heat. The efficacy of fluorescent sources is as high as 100 lm/W. Lamp life is long, up to 30,000 hours. The color temperature and color rendering index of the lamp is determined by the phosphor coating. Fluorescent sources are available with CCT from 2,700 K to 7,500 K and CRI from the mid-50s to as high as 95, with most now being in the high 70s to 80s.

Fluorescent lamps are linear, not a point source of light like a sealed halogen incandescent. They are best at creating a uniform wash of light across an architectural surface rather than focusing light in a small area. Their performance is also temperature sensitive.

Compact fluorescent lamps (CFLs) are similar to regular fluorescent lamps. Their efficacy is not quite as high as regular fluorescent tubes at 60 lm/W, but still three to four times that of regular incandescent sources. Lamp life is typically 10,000–12,000 hours. They are available with a pin or screw base, with the latter intended as a replacement for incandescent lamps in screw-in fixtures. They can be dimmed, but their range of dimming is more limited than for an incandescent lamp.

A high-intensity discharge (HID) lamp also produces light by means of an electric arc struck between electrodes. However, the electrodes are placed in a small, transparent quartz or ceramic arc tube, filled with both gas and metal salts. The arc heats and evaporates the salts, forming plasma and increasing pressure in the arc tube. The plasma increases the intensity of light produced by the arc. Discharge lamps take several minutes to come to full brightness. If turned off, the arc will not restrike until temperatures in the arc tube have cooled down. For this reason they cannot be used with occupancy sensors.

Discharge lamps include high-pressure sodium, metal halide, and ceramic metal halide. High-pressure sodium (HPS) lamps have very high efficacy, long lamp life, and low operational and long-term costs. They get hot; but given the overall light output, the total amount of heat produced is moderate. The efficacy of HPS is as high as 120 lm/W. Lamp life is long, up to 24,000 hours. The color temperature of these lamps is very low, about 2,100 K. Because the light emitted from HPS lamps is concentrated in the yellow-orange band of the visible spectrum, color rendering is extremely poor.

These lamps should be avoided except for very special applications. Although very efficacious, their poor color rendering results in a low-quality visual environment. An alternate, light source, even a less efficacious one producing lower light levels but with better color rendering, can produce a better visual environment in an energy-efficient manner.

Metal halide lamps have high efficacy, long life, and low operational costs. Over the course of the lamp's life, there may be color shift, with resulting inconsistency in the space. Also, lumen maintenance varies from 60 to 85 percent, meaning light output will drop significantly over the life of the lamp. The efficacy of metal halide lamps can be as high as 100 lm/W. Lamp life is as high as 20,000 hours. The CRI varies from a low of 65 to 95 for ceramic metal halide. Because of the size of the arc tube, metal halide is a point source.

Metal halide lamps are best in situations that require a powerful point source. This can include outdoor and indoor applications where color is important. Ceramic metal halide is excellent for color-critical focal and accent lighting where neither dimming nor occupancy controls are required.

A light-emitting diode (LED) is a very small electrical device that produces light through the semiconducting properties of its metal alloys. Many white LED products for general lighting are now available. While LEDs have the promise of high efficacy, most currently available products are only slightly more efficient than incandescent sources. The best white LEDs available today can produce about 45–50 lm/W, but most consumer products are less efficient.

For most illumination applications, white LEDs cannot yet compete with traditional light sources on the basis of performance or cost. Because they are a directional source, even though total light output is lower than other sources, LEDs can provide enough light on the task for some applications. High-quality LED office task lights have been among the first products suitable for commercial applications. Colored LEDs are often cost-effective and offer energy efficiency and durability for traffic signals, exit signs, and commercial signage.

Light-emitting diode lighting products are quite different from previously available sources, and current standards may not adequately describe their performance. Nonetheless, it is best to compare how much total light the LED product provides against other light sources under consideration. While some LED products have very low energy use, their light output is also low.

Claims have been made for LED life up to 100,000 hours. However, a clear definition of LED-lamp life has not yet been established. Light-emitting diodes simply grow dimmer over time, rather than failing completely. A definition of end of lamp life used by manufacturers of high-quality LED products is the point at which light output has decreased to 70 percent of initial output. Using that definition, high-quality LEDs last 35,000 hours.

The lifetime of LEDs is greatly affected by operating temperature and effective heat mitigation. Poor heat management has led to premature failure in some LED products.

The U.S. Department of Energy and U.S. Environmental Protection Agency's Energy Star program are leading efforts to produce standards for LED lighting. Once clear standards have been established, it will be easier to evaluate the many claims currently made about LED products.

Lighting Recommendations and Quality

The best source of information for determining the level of illumination for a space is the Illuminating Engineering Society of North America (IESNA) *Lighting Handbook*.[3] The Handbook's "Lighting Design Guide" provides recommended illuminances for seven general application categories. It is important to remember that illumination alone is not an indication of lighting quality. The handbook discusses twenty-two other criteria, foremost of which is glare control, that shape lighting quality and influence the required level of illumination.

As mentioned above, the energy efficiency of an individual lamp is indicated by efficacy, or number of lumens emitted per watt of electricity supplied as input. Lamp life is indicated in hours. Incandescent lamps have an efficacy of 11–18 lm/W and lamp life of 700 hours. The efficacy of a compact fluorescent lamp ranges from about 40–60 lm/W. Its lamp life varies from about 6,000–10,000 hours. A T8 fluorescent lamp has an efficacy of about 90 lm/W and lamp life of up to 28,000 hours. For this reason, the T8 should be considered the workhorse lamp for nonresidential buildings.

The color rendering of fluorescent sources has improved greatly over the past fifty years. Current high-performance T8 and T5 fluorescent lamps have CRIs in the 80s and 90s, while standard T8 lamps have CRIs in the 70s. For most purposes, a CRI of 80 or above is considered excellent color rendering.

Figure 12-13 Light-emitting diodes (LED): LEDs hold much promise, but they do not yet reach levels of efficacy found in fluorescent lighting. They can, however, be the best choice for special applications such as task lights and traffic signals.

---

[3]IESNA Lighting Handbook - 9thEdition, Editor: Mark Stanley Rea, Illuminating Engineering Society of North America, 2000.

A T8 lamp, meaning a lamp 1 inch in diameter, with a CRI in the 80s and paired with an electronic ballast, should be the designer's starting point for most applications. The correlated color temperature selected will depend upon building use, hours of operation, and the owner's preference. Currently, the most commonly specified lamp for commercial buildings is 3,500 CCT, but cooler lamps have grown increasingly common. Lamps with CCT of 5,000 are a better match for daylight, but can appear overly cool during nondaylight hours. A CCT of 4,100 is a reasonable compromise.

Use high-efficiency, high-color-rendering fluorescent systems as the primary electric light source. Add compact fluorescent and incandescent sources for supplementary lighting and to provide visual interest. Ceramic metal-halide systems are very efficient for spot lighting in applications where color quality is very important and occupancy controls are not typically employed, such as retail stores. Consider fluorescent systems for high-bay lighting applications because of their ability to accept a greater range of controls than high-intensity discharge (HID) systems. Use pulse-start metal halide as the first choice for outdoor lighting. Use the outdoor lighting allowances in the latest version of California Title 24 Nonresidential Energy Standards as a minimum. Also, follow the recommendations of the Dark Sky Association[4] to limit light pollution.

Lighting quality must be a part of lighting efficiency. It is pointless to design a very efficient lighting system where building occupants experience visual discomfort. To improve lighting quality, designers need at minimum to take into account luminance, luminance ratios, color rendering, light quantity, and interior finishes and furnishings, which are discussed below.

Humans perceive light through luminance, the amount of light emitted from a surface through reflection. Humans do not see foot-candles, meaning lumens of light output per square foot. However, foot-candles are measured more easily and by a less expensive measuring device. This partly explains the widespread use of the illuminance rather than luminance in lighting recommendations.

Luminance ratio is a measure of the relative brightness of different surfaces in the field of view. Surfaces with a ratio of 3:1 or less are typically perceived to be of equivalent brightness. Ratios higher than 10:1 create more powerful contrasts. Ratios significantly greater than 10:1 can cause glare. In an office or school environment, low luminance ratios are preferable, as they create the perception of even light levels and allow the eye to relax.

Higher luminance ratios create a sense of drama. If not excessive to the point of glare, they lead the eye to focus upon the area of high luminance. For this reason, it is common to see high luminance ratios in retail stores,

theaters, and restaurants. Luminance ratios above 40:1 in a room can cause glare.

Luminance ratio is a useful guideline, but it is important to remember that almost every rule has an exception. It is important to distinguish between glare and sparkle. Decorative lights, such as those on a Christmas tree, often exceed the 40:1 ratio. Knowing when a design will cause glare and when it will cause sparkle comes with experience.

An effective method of reducing luminance ratios and improving lighting quality is to light vertical room surfaces and the ceiling, while keeping the light source hidden. Examples include cove lighting or direct-indirect pendant fixtures. Using matte finishes and avoiding placing very dark materials adjacent to very light materials will also lessen contrast ratio.

Additional focal lighting can be added to highlight artwork and/or decorative elements, alleviating visual boredom.

Four-foot-long lamps are recommended for general applications, because they are the cheapest and most widely available lamps. They can be easily incorporated into coves and are commonly used in indirect or direct-indirect pendant fixtures and in downlights used in suspended ceilings. Two-foot-long lamps are also readily available. Electronic ballasts, which start the lamp and regulate voltage thereafter, should be employed. If the design calls for dimming, dimming ballasts are required.

For maintenance reasons, standardizing the design on a limited number of lamp types of similar CRI and CCT is strongly recommended. Not all maintenance personnel have been trained in the differences in lamp types. If numerous lamps are used in a design, as lamps burn out, the correct replacement lamp may not be inserted in the fixture.

Compact fluorescent lamps should replace incandescent lamps in many applications, including downlights, sconces, task lights, and wall washers. Except where a narrow-focus spot lamp or dimming is required, CFLs are much more efficient and cost-effective than incandescent lamps.

Compact fluorescent lamps may be self-ballasted or pin-based with a separate ballast. Self-ballasted CFLs are designed for use in existing incandescent lamp fixtures. Self-ballasted lamps work well as a retrofit, but there is no guarantee that an incandescent lamp may not be used again in the future. Pin-based CFLs should be used in new construction and significant renovations.

Lighting Controls

Lighting controls reduce energy use and the cost of operating a building. Energy use is the product of power, or the rate of consumption of electricity, and time, the period of consumption. By reducing either power or time, energy use is reduced. Turning devices off, effectively reducing power consumption to zero or near zero, is a very effective method of saving energy.

[4]International Dark Sky Association, http://www.darksky.org/mc/page.do. Practical guides for lighting practice can be found at http://www.darksky.org/mc/page.do?sitePageId=58823&orgId=idsa

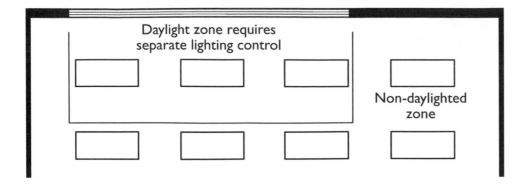

Figure 12-14 Zoning electric lights for daylighting: Electric lights must be grouped in response to daylight-distribution patterns. Electric lights adjacent to windows or below skylights must be controlled separately from lights in nondaylighted zones.

Manual controls can result in energy savings, as occupant behavior is a major determinant of building performance. Designing lighting systems to provide occupants with good options will result in greater savings. A lighting system that can be partially switched off in response to power alerts when demand for electricity reaches critical levels, yet still provide uniform light levels, is more likely to be used than one that produces very low light levels in certain areas. Appropriate zoning of the electric lights to the controls is a part of good design.

Occupancy sensors reduce the time when lighting systems are in use. Similarly, building-level controls that switch off general lighting between specified hours reduce the running time of lighting systems. As mentioned previously, controls that dim or switch lamps in response to daylight can produce large savings of energy.

All controls require commissioning. Commissioning is an ongoing process of review during design and construction. During design, review is required to insure the appropriate controls are specified and coordination occurs between disciplines. During construction, it is essential that controls be properly located and installed and that conflicts between trades are resolved. Locating an occupant or light-level sensor behind an HVAC duct will assure that the controls do not operate as intended. When installed, controls must be properly wired. Finally, controls must be calibrated to produce the desired effect.

Controls need periodic maintenance to assure they continue to work as intended. Changes such as new workstation layouts or changes in store displays can significantly affect the operation of lighting controls. Yearly maintenance checks to inspect lighting controls and verify proper operation are recommended as a standard part of building operations.

Both ASHRAE 90.1 and California's Title 24 Energy Standards have a number of requirements for lighting controls and can serve as a starting point for design.

Mechanical Systems in Nonresidential Buildings

Zoning

Most contemporary large commercial buildings have a central-core zone that never requires heating. In the

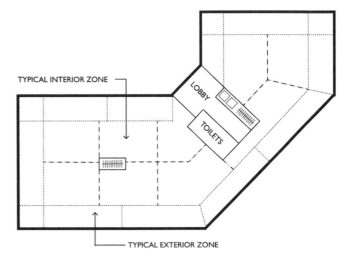

HVAC ZONING

Figure 12-15 HVAC zoning diagram: Most large buildings have at minimum an interior zone and four perimeter zones. Improvements to the building envelope can eliminate the need for separate perimeter zones and systems.

central zone, occupants and equipment generate heat, but there is limited opportunity for heat loss through the building envelope. With standard envelope construction, each side of the building perimeter is typically another zone, resulting in a minimum of five zones. This is because outside conditions are likely to affect occupant comfort at the building edge. Sun may warm the east side of the building in the morning, while the west side may require cooling. The opposite may be the case in the afternoon.

Smaller commercial buildings are likely to have multiple zones as well; sales areas will have one requirement for cooling, a storeroom another, and offices a third. Different uses and occupant loads call for separate zoning. Institutional buildings such as schools and libraries will have different needs for heating and cooling in classrooms, large and small conference rooms, offices, and other room occupancies. A large classroom will require more cooling than surrounding areas when it is full of students. Kitchens, lavatories, and computer server rooms are other examples of spaces likely to be zoned separately from the rest of a building.

If thermal conditions vary between two areas within a building, they should be zoned separately to improve occupant comfort. The more finely zones are subdivided, the more likely occupants will be satisfied with thermal conditions. However, adding zones adds cost for equipment and controls. For this reason, the number of zones is usually limited.

Building form will affect zoning. A long, narrow plan places all of the occupied spaces close to the building perimeter. Multistory daylighted buildings will usually follow this pattern. Large office buildings designed over the past fifty years have tended toward a more blocklike form, which can create quite different core and perimeter zones.

A high-performance-building envelope can reduce the impact of outside conditions on perimeter zones. This can eliminate the need to zone them separately from the central core. In an integrated design approach, the cost of improvements to the building envelope would be considered against the savings from reduced first costs for the mechanical system as well as reduced operational costs.

Ventilation

Aside from the need for cooling and heating, ventilation air is required to remove air pollutants, odors, and water vapor from a building. In small or large but narrow buildings, ventilation air can be provided through operable windows. In new buildings or renovated older buildings with a more airtight building envelope that limits infiltration, a dedicated system will do a better job of providing ventilation. In large office buildings, where fire codes often limit the use of operable windows, ventilation air can be supplied as part of the air used for cooling and heating. It can also be supplied independent of heating and cooling requirements.

The *minimum* standard for ventilation should be the most recent version of ASHRAE 62.1. The U.S. Green Building Council LEED rating system encourages higher ventilation rates. The trade-offs between ventilation rate and energy use are complex. They vary with building occupancy, climate, and system type. A given of building design and construction is that ventilation rates should not be reduced below the minimum standard to save energy.

Heat exchangers make it possible to transfer much of the heat contained in exhaust air to incoming ventilation air. Various types of heat exchangers exist. Some capture only sensible heat. Others capture both sensible and the latent heat contained in humid air. Passive solar collectors can also be used to preheat incoming ventilation air in winter.

Cooling and Heating

Because occupants, electric lights, and equipment generate so much heat in nonresidential buildings, the need for cooling rather than heating usually predominates.

In some cases, cooling can be provided passively with shading, operable windows, stack ventilation, and/or downdraft cooling towers. In other cases, low-energy systems, such as fan-driven ventilation, evaporative cooling, or night ventilation of thermal mass, can meet comfort needs.

Prior to the development of modern air-conditioning in the twentieth century, passive and low-energy techniques were the only methods available to cool buildings. The expectations of building occupants regarding acceptable comfort conditions varied with the season and were reflected in their choice of clothing. Comfort, as currently defined, could not be achieved year round, especially in hot, humid climates.

In contemporary commercial building, especially high-rise buildings, where current fire codes discourage operable windows, air-conditioning is used to create interior conditions that remain within relatively narrow confines of temperature and humidity. Air-conditioning is based upon the refrigeration cycle, an inherently energy-intensive process, because it usually requires an electrically powered compressor.

A low-energy building must begin with design for load reduction. Designs that can provide occupant comfort with noncompressor-based cooling use much less energy than air-conditioned buildings. A high-performance building envelope—one that limits solar heat gain, admits controlled daylight, limits infiltration, incorporates very good window systems, and incorporates a cool or green roof—reduces the need for cooling.

Thermal mass placed inside the building envelope will absorb heat over the course of the day. Where temperatures drop below 70°F (21.1°C) at night, nighttime ventilation of the building with cool outside air will reduce the temperature of the interior thermal mass. This requires adequate area for air intake and exhaust, and uses energy to run fans. The cooled mass absorbs heat from people and equipment over the following day, maintaining comfort and reducing the need for air-conditioning or other forms of mechanical cooling.

In hot and dry and mixed and dry climates, load reduction can make it possible to provide comfort with evaporative cooling. An evaporative cooler adds moisture to air, raising its humidity while lowering its sensible heat. Two-stage, indirect, evaporative coolers can provide cooling without raising humidity of the supply air. They add moisture to a stream of air, reducing sensible heat and lowering the air temperature. Using a heat exchanger, they draw heat from the supply air without raising its humidity.

In mixed-mode buildings, thermal mass, night ventilation, and operable windows provide comfort and occupant control during fall and spring, with air-conditioning used only during the hottest months. Such designs not only use less energy, but they offer occupants greater control.

Whatever the climate, load reduction must come first. Understand the impact of decisions about the building envelope and how they affect the need for electric lighting and cooling. Reduce the need for cooling, then select equipment, and assemble components to design an energy-efficient system to cool and heat air.

The compressive-refrigeration cycle uses a fluid, called a refrigerant, to move heat from one place to another. In the compressive-refrigeration cycle, a refrigerant passes back and forth between liquid and gaseous states, evaporating and condensing as it absorbs and releases heat. In an air conditioner, the cycle flows in one direction only, moving heat from inside to outside the building. In a heat pump, the flow is reversible, making it possible to move heat from outside the building to the interior, providing winter heating and summer air-conditioning in one unit.

For the cycle to operate effectively, the refrigerant must change from a liquid to gas at a relatively low temperature. Refrigerants used in air conditioners typically boil between 40°F–50°F as compared to water's boiling point of 212°F. A compressor, running on electricity, is necessary to induce these changes in phase.

In its liquid state, the refrigerant passes through the evaporator coil, located inside the building. Warm, humid indoor air is drawn over the evaporator. The air transfers heat to the refrigerant and releases moisture through condensation onto the outside of the evaporator coil. The liquid refrigerant in the coil absorbs the heat. Because the refrigerant has a low boiling point, this added heat induces a change in phase in the refrigerant from liquid to gas rather than increasing its temperature. The room air, now cooler and less humid than when it entered the evaporator, is recirculated into the space to be cooled.

The refrigerant gas then moves into the compressor. The compressor is a pump that raises the pressure of the refrigerant. The increased pressure from the compressor causes the temperature of the refrigerant to rise. As it leaves the compressor, the refrigerant is about 140°F.

Refrigerant flows into the condenser where it gives up heat to the outside air. The outside air, while hot, is still cooler than the pressurized refrigerant. As the refrigerant leaves the condenser, it has released the heat it carried from the interior, but it is still under pressure from the compressor. It then reaches an expansion valve on its way back to the evaporator. The expansion valve releases the pressurized refrigerant. As it passes through the valve, the pressure is reduced, and the refrigerant cools back down. The cool, liquid refrigerant reenters the evaporator where it once again picks up room heat.

In a heat pump, the flow is reversed in winter, with the indoor coil operating as the condenser and the outdoor coil as the evaporator. Air-sourced heat pumps can provide cooling and heating in mild climates. However, as the air gets colder, their heating efficiency decreases. Heat pumps that use the earth or a large pond or lake as a heat source or sink are more efficient because ground and water temperatures are less extreme than air temperatures. Vertical or horizontals loops buried in the ground or run through a lake carry refrigerant. In summer, ground- or water-sourced heat pumps move heat from inside a building and use ground or water as a heat sink. In winter, they move heat from the ground or water to the conditioned interior spaces.

Until 1987 almost all refrigerants were chlorofluorocarbons (CFCs), which were damaging to the ozone layer in the high atmosphere. While a pollutant low in the atmosphere, in the high atmosphere the ozone layer filters out ultraviolet radiation that is damaging to many forms of life on earth. Under an international agreement known as the Montreal Protocol, CFCs were phased out and are no longer used in new units. Refrigerants made

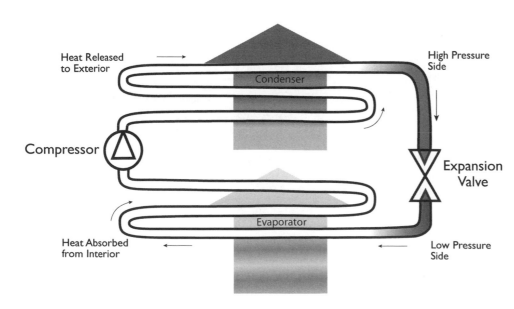

Figure 12-16 Refrigeration cycle: Air conditioners use mechanical energy to compress gases moving in a refrigerant loop and, in the process, move heat from one location to another.

of hydrochlorofluorocarbons (HCFCs) were substituted, because they are much less damaging to the ozone layer. However, they are significant greenhouse gases that contribute to global warming when they are released from refrigeration units, and they will be banned in 2030.

Unfortunately, there are no substitutes for CFCs or HCFCs that combine all their desirable properties while avoiding their undesirable ones. Hydrofluorocarbons (HFCs) have fewer negative qualities than either CFCs or HCFCs. Their ozone depletion potential is next to zero. However, they are a greenhouse gas and are somewhat less thermodynamically efficient than their predecessors. Carbon dioxide can also be used as a refrigerant, but it requires higher pressurization. While a greenhouse gas, it is a less powerful one than other options. In existing buildings, with older air-conditioning systems that contain CFCs and HCFCs, maintenance to reduce refrigerant loss into the atmosphere is essential.

The absorptive, rather than compressive, refrigeration cycle also moves heat from one location to another. The absorptive refrigeration cycle is much less efficient than the compressive cycle and has largely been supplanted by it. The absorptive cycle requires a source of heat, rather than mechanical power in the form of an electrically run compressor, to keep the cycle running. For that reason, there are some instances where waste heat from another process on-site is available and can be used to power an absorption-refrigeration cycle for air-conditioning. In such situations, the inefficiency of absorption chillers is more than offset by the availability of waste heat as a fuel source, as it provides low-cost cooling with little additional environmental impact.

Air-conditioning systems vary in the way heat is transferred to the refrigeration unit and cooling is returned to the interior. The transfer media include air, water, or air and water in tandem.

In an all-air system, incoming air passes over the evaporator coil and is ducted to occupied space. The air in an all-air system provides cooling, dehumidification, air filtration, and ventilation. All-air systems affect building architecture because of the size and height of ducts and the space required for duct runs to both supply and return treated air.

An all-air system can also provide heating. In heating mode, air bypasses the refrigeration unit and is heated by an electric heater, or a gas-fired furnace, and then delivered to occupied space. A hot water run paired with a heat exchanger can also be used for air heating.

In all-water systems, water is chilled at the evaporator and pumped to individual spaces. Fan-coil units in each space use the water to cool air, which is distributed in the space. A fan coil is exactly what the name implies. The water loop is coiled to increase the exposed surface area. A fan moves air over the coil. This limits the ability of the system to provide dehumidification, air filtration, and ventilation.

A water system can also provide heat. In heating mode, the water loop bypasses the refrigeration system and is heated by a boiler. Heated water is then supplied to the fan coil in the occupied space.

In a combination system, water and fan coils provide most of the cooling and heating, while ventilation and dehumidification are provided by ducted air. Duct sizes can be significantly reduced, because the air delivered does not provide cooling.

Refrigeration systems that cool water for use in air-conditioning are known as *chillers* and typically are placed on the roof of the building. In refrigeration systems of all sizes, the condenser rejects heat to the building exterior. In large systems, evaporative cooling is added at the condenser to increase the heat-rejection capacity. With the addition of evaporative cooling, the heat-rejection component is known as a *cooling tower,* which is also typically located on the roof of the building or on the ground immediately adjacent to it. When placed on the roof, the location of chillers and cooling towers must be coordinated with skylights for daylighting and solar electric or solar thermal systems, including systems that may be added in the future.

The number of zones and the size of the load shape the capacity and complexity of the cooling and heating system. Each zone typically has a separate thermostat, so cooling or heating can be supplied separately from the requirements of other zones. The smallest system would be a window unit or through-the-wall heat pump intended to serve one room.

Not all buildings require both heating and cooling. A commercial building, such as a warehouse, may consist of a single zone and require heating only. In such a case, an electric or gas *unit heater* may be employed. If the space is tall and contains a large volume of air, or opens directly to the exterior, a radiant heating system may be the most efficient choice. Radiant heaters warm objects in the space, including occupants, rather than heating air. An electric radiant heater that warms occupants may be a better choice than a nominally more efficient gas heater that warms the large volume of air.

A *package unit* provides heating, cooling, air filtration, ventilation, and moisture control to a small building or single zone, all in a factory-assembled unit. Off-site assembly improves the quality of workmanship and reduces costs. The unit is delivered to the site where required duct runs and plumbing lines are added. Medium-sized buildings can be served by multiple package units.

Package units are commonly located on a concrete pad adjacent to a building or on the roof of a building if ground space is at a premium. As with chillers and cooling towers, if placed on the roof, their location must be coordinated with skylights and solar electric or solar thermal systems.

In a *split system*, the compressor and condenser are moved outside of the building. The air handler—containing the evaporator for cooling and a gas furnace, electric-resistance heater, or heat pump for heating—is placed in an interior space or mechanical room. A split system reduces the acoustic impact of the compressor, which tends to be noisy, on building occupants. The split is limited to about 60 feet, as greater distances will compromise the performance of the condenser.

In large, tall buildings, key components of the air-conditioning system are usually located in the basement, on the roof, or in a combination of these two locations. All-air systems require large vertical duct runs and use considerable energy to move air from the central air handler to each floor.

Common all-air systems include variable-air-volume (VAV), constant-air-volume with terminal reheat, and double-duct systems. In a VAV system, which is the most common system now used in buildings, one duct serves all zones. Within each zone there is a variable-air-volume control box with a damper. The damper opens and closes in response to the thermostat in that zone, regulating the amount of cool air delivered. The VAV systems only supply cooling. Separate heating systems are added at the perimeter zones. Terminal reheat boxes can be added to VAV systems. The box uses electricity to reheat the centrally cooled air when one zone requires cooling while another calls for heat.

While damper-controlled VAV systems are economically attractive, because they save energy, they have the potential to create air-quality problems, as they may not always meet minimum ventilation requirements.

Constant-air-volume (CAV) systems with terminal reheat provide excellent control. In this system air is supplied at the same rate to all zones. Air is cooled to the temperature required for the zone with the greatest cooling requirement. In all other zones, reheat boxes raise the temperature of the air being supplied by the system as needed.

Constant-air-volume systems meet ventilation requirements and enable fine-tuning of air temperature for each zone. However, they waste energy. For most areas of the building, the CAV system first cools air below the temperature needed then reheats the air to the desired temperature. Recent versions of ASHRAE 90.1 and California Title 24 strongly discourage use of these systems.

Dual-duct systems with constant air volume circulate warm and cool air to all parts of the building. Mixing boxes in each zone determine the mix of warm and cool air delivered to each space. Dual-duct systems provide adequate ventilation air and a high degree of control. However, they require more ducts than VAV or CAV systems. Also, because the cool air must be at the temperature required in the zone with the greatest cooling need, these systems are not efficient.

Air systems typically include an outside-air economizer. When the temperature of outside air is close to that of air supplied for cooling and/or ventilation, it can be used directly, bypassing the refrigeration system. Almost all climates have some period of time when the "economizer" cycle can supply air. The marine climates of the coastal regions of California and the Pacific Northwest offer extended time periods when use of an economizer can greatly reduce the need for mechanical cooling of air.

Underfloor air-supply systems and displacement ventilation systems offer advantages over traditional air systems. Traditional systems supply air at the ceiling. To cool occupants at work level, the air must be delivered at a low temperature and at a high volume to promote mixing with warm air in the space. Underfloor air, in theory, can be supplied at higher temperatures and lower rates. Air stratifies, with cool air in the occupied space and warmer air higher in the room where it enters the air-return system.

Displacement air systems deliver large volumes of air at low rates low in the space, but not from below the floor. Again, air can be supplied at higher temperatures, because it is delivered to the occupied zone.

With air-water systems, air is used to meet all building-ventilation requirements and to provide cooling in the central zone. Water and fan-coil units are used to provide cooling and heating at perimeter zones.

Air-water systems also include radiant cooling with separate ventilation air. In mild climates, where demand for cooling is relatively low, water can be run through a concrete floor slab. Because moist air will condense on the floor if it is cooled below a certain point, the cooling capacity of radiant floor systems is limited. Radiant ceiling panels are more common and offer advantages,

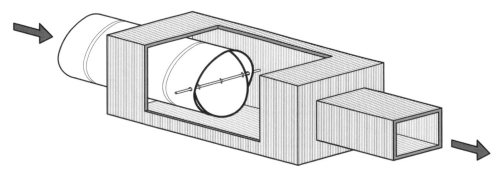

Figure 12-17 Variable-air-volume (VAV) box with damper: The variable-air-volume system is the method of distributing cooled air most commonly found in contemporary building. This photo shows a damper box found in VAV systems.

Figure 12-18 Underfloor air distribution: Underfloor air systems permit delivery of higher temperature air for cooling. The finished floor is raised above the structural slab and air is delivered through the floor.

because they are within the field of view of occupants and unobstructed by furniture and other objects in the space. The air supplied is dehumidified to prevent condensation on the ceiling panels.

Thermal Storage

Storage of thermal energy can reduce the need for energy or reduce the environmental impact of energy use while also reducing cost. The use of thermal mass is a form of energy storage. In passive heating, mass collects solar heat during the day and reradiates that heat at night. Shaded thermal mass also serves as a form of passive cooling by absorbing heat during the day and releasing it at night. Ventilation of thermal mass using nighttime fan energy and cool outside air draws even more heat from the mass, increasing its cooling capacity during the hot hours of the day.

Most electric utilities have a surplus of power during nighttime hours and offer lower rates for power use at that time. Air-conditioning and heating systems can use inexpensive energy at night to cool or heat water. The chilled or hot water can then be used the next day to provide cooling or heating.

Storing thermal energy involves losses over time. In spite of this, it can have environmental benefits. Base-load energy provided by utilities comes from their most efficient energy generation facilities. As the demand for power rises over the course of the day, less efficient and more polluting generation facilities are brought on line.

Because the stored thermal resource is generated at night and drawn down over the next day, heating or cooling is provided with the most efficient sources of grid-supplied power. Also, refrigeration units run more efficiently during lower nighttime temperatures. The total amount of energy required to store and then use the thermal resource may be slightly greater than if the energy were used when heating or cooling was actually needed. However, the environmental impact is likely to be lower.

Shifting the cooling load to off-peak hours reduces the cost of energy to the building owner. It also lessens pressure on, and possible failure of, the power grid on hot days when demand for energy for cooling is greatest. Because utility generating capacity must be sized to meet peak demand, thermal storage and load shifting also reduce the need for construction of new power plants and the environmental impacts of that construction.

Combined Heat and Power Systems

Combined heat and power (CHP) systems match two processes to one fuel source. For the system to work efficiently, the second process must have use for the waste heat of the first. For example, an on-site microturbine, burning natural gas, can generate electricity for a large facility such as a college campus. Waste heat from the microturbine can heat air or water.

A constant, year-round load, such as water heating for the campus swimming pool, is the best match. Essentially, the water is heated with no economic and very little environmental cost. If the waste heat can only be matched to a seasonal load such as winter heating, the overall cost-effectiveness of the system is reduced. Combined heat and power make sense wherever a large load that can utilize the waste heat exists.

Self-Generation and Renewable Energy

Solar electric and thermal systems were covered in the previous chapter on residential and small commercial buildings. Refer to Chapter 11 for more information. Solar systems scale up in size without major changes. Commercial and residential systems operate on the same principles. Commercial systems are very similar, only larger.

Commercial facilities are billed for electricity based on time of use and peak demand, which is typically calculated as the largest amount of electrical power used continuously over a fifteen- or thirty-minute period in a year. Solar electric systems generate power when time-of-use rates are high. Their power generation often occurs during a facility's period of peak demand. By reducing

Figure 12-19 Commercial solar thermal: Solar thermal systems scale up well and can supply hot water for commercial applications such as car washes, laundries, and other facilities.

Figure 12-20 Commercial solar electric: Commercial solar electric systems are fundamentally similar to residential systems. If roof space is available, there are few limits to size. Large arrays require additional inverters.

that peak demand, solar electric systems will lower the associated demand charge.

In addition, large, low-rise buildings and building complexes are excellent candidates for a power purchase agreement. A power purchase agreement (PPA) is a long-term agreement to buy power. In a solar PPA, a building owner contracts with a third party that uses its own funds to install a solar electric system on the roof of the building and maintains and operates the system for a specified time, typically 15 years or longer. The building owner purchases the energy at a predetermined rate over the life of the agreement. The PPA provides the owner with the benefits of solar energy at a fixed cost, while eliminating his or her need to make a capital investment in the solar system.

Solar developers offering PPAs to building owners typically require a large roof area with good solar access.

13 Resource Efficiency and Resource Use in Buildings

Currently, globally we are overshooting the planet's capacity to regenerate natural resources by 23 percent. "In other words, it now takes more than one year and two months for the Earth to regenerate what we use in a single year."[1]

What Are Natural Resources?

A natural resource is a form of wealth drawn from nature, for example, water sources (oceans, freshwater, rainfall), soils, minerals, biomes, agricultural lands, forests, biodiversity of species, and if you think creatively, even landfill acreage.

As E. F. Schumaker has described in his thought-provoking books *Small Is Beautiful*, natural resources are a source of capital and should not be considered as a source of income to be spent.[2] We must manage resources as we would monetary assets, not by liquidating but by using what we need to sustain ourselves and live well.

The process involves taking stock of existing resources (accounting for them), assessing their value to the human and natural environment, and developing a plan to maximize their yield. In sum, we should make the most of the resources at our disposal and maximize their benefits, hence the terms, *resource effectiveness or efficiency*.

Natural Capitalism

The landmark theory that embodies these concepts is put forth in *Natural Capitalism: Creating the Next Industrial Revolution*,[3] a 1994 manifesto by the environmentalist and author Paul Hawken (Figure 13-1), scientist-environmentalist Amory Lovins, and author-educator-lawyer L. Hunter Lovins.

The writers use the language of asset management, generation of capital, and income to put forward the notion that resources must be restored while making the transition from human productivity to resource productivity.

Figure 13-1 Environmentalist and writer Paul Hawken.

---

[1] "Ecological Footprint Overview," Global Footprint Network, http://www.footprintnetwork.org/gfn_sub.php?content=footprint_overview (accessed January 22, 2008).

[2] E. F. Schumacher, *Small Is Beautiful: A Study of Economics as if People Mattered* (London: Blond and Briggs, 1973). The author wrote a series of books with the title *Small Is Beautiful*.

[3] Paul Hawken, Amory Lovins, L. Hunter Lovins, *Natural Capitalism: Creating the Next Industrial Revolution* (Snowmass, CO: Rocky Mountain Institute, 1970).

Value must be assigned to both human and natural capital, and its management should become generally accepted business practice.[4] Furthermore, incorporating management techniques will help capitalism flourish and spur economic growth.

The Ecological Footprint and Environmental Accounting

Where do we take the principles of asset management and resource productivity and find ways to assist us in our understanding of green building? Just as financial asset

Figure 13-2 The Global Footprint Network's mission is to "support a sustainable economy by advancing the Ecological Footprint, a measurement and management tool that makes the reality of planetary limits relevant to decision-makers throughout the world." Source: Global Footprint Network.

management requires assessment, so does resource asset management.

Environmental accounting is a developing field that incorporates environmental and economic data to assess resource use and environmental impact. Instead of financial units, however, physical units are used, such as tons of waste generated by a construction site or acres of forest consumed for building materials.

One of the data tools we can use to arrive at resource management strategies was developed by the Global Footprint Network, based on original research by William Rees and further developed by sustainability advocate Mathis Wackernagel (Figure 13-2). *Ecological footprint* refers to the amount of biologically productive land and water area it takes to produce resources for human consumption and to absorb the waste generated by this consumption. It is a historical indicator of resource use and a measurement tool we can use to wisely manage biological assets in the future. Diverging lifestyles in different countries will yield different environmental impacts. For example, the living patterns and resource consumption by an individual in India compared to the urbanized lifestyle of an inhabitant of London will yield dramatically different footprints (Figure 13-3).[5]

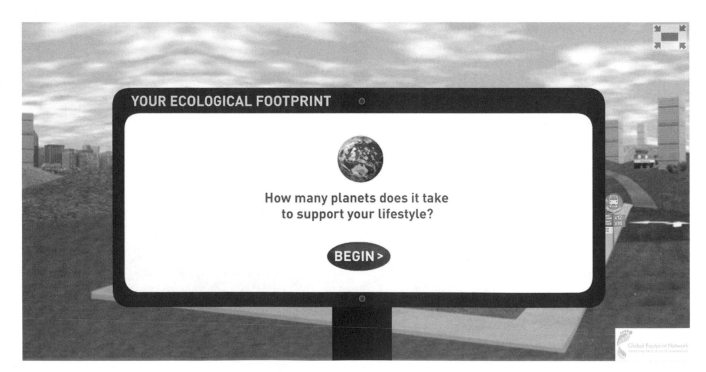

Figure 13-3 a, b The Global Footprint Calculator is a way to understand how our patterns of living affect the earth's resources.

---

[4]The United Kingdom's Forum for the Future developed the "five capitals" model for sustainable development: natural capital, social capital, human capital, manufactured capital, and financial capital. They define *natural capital* as "any stock or flow of energy and material that produces goods and services," including sinks that absorb, recycle, or neutralize waste and processes to regulate and balance, such as the case with carbon dioxide (CO_2) reduction goals. "The Five Capitals Model," http://www.forumforthefuture.org.uk/our-approach/tools-and-methodologies/5capitals (accessed February 28, 2008).

[5]According to the Ecological Footprint and Biocapacity, 2006 edition based on 2003 data in The Global Footprint, Gabon has an ecological reserve of 17.8 global hectares per person, while the United Kingdom has an ecological deficit of 4 global hectares per person. India's ecological footprint is 0.8 global hectares per person, while the United States' ecological footprint is 4.9 global hectares per person. The ecological reserve or deficit is calculated by subtracting the footprint data from the region's biocapacity.

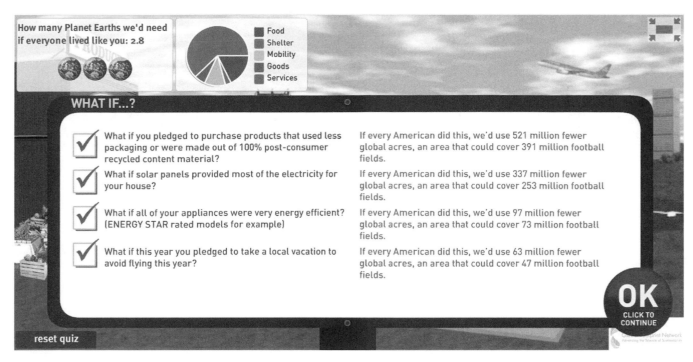

Figure 13-3 a, b *Cont'd*

Trends and assessments are conducted through ecological footprint accounting methodology, a technique adapted from traditional accounting principles.[6] The Global Footprint Network compiles the most current metrics on the quantity consumed per country of cropland; grazing land; forest lands for timber, pulp, paper, and fuel; fishing grounds; carbon and nuclear footprints; and built-up land.

The ecological reserve or deficit is the result of the difference in the biocapacity, or carrying capacity, of each region's resources, including their ecological holdings of water, soils, biodiversity (diversity of both species and ecosystems), and raw materials (minerals, fossil fuels, metals, water).

This data may be used to present a mapped "biological area," which is the geographic land area available to support a population, versus the area consumed by human activity, its footprint (Figure 13-4). Resulting statistics reveal the magnitude of this global resource management challenge.[7]

Both Mathis Wackernagel and Jared Diamond, in his book *Collapse*,[8] believe that resource depletion challenges have the potential to cause social conflicts within, and between, developing and small industrialized nations and nations that are more industrialized but without major renewable resources. In fact, Diamond believes that future geographic boundaries will be drawn on an ecopolitical basis: the owners of resources will become powerful nations, while those with an ecological deficit will struggle.

Biocapacity and footprint data, as well as other trends, can help inform environmental work of many stripes: government policy makers, public health practitioners, corporate sustainability programs, nongovernmental organizations (NGOs), manufacturing industries, and municipal infrastructure providers, including those involved in the design and construction of green buildings.

Resource Effectiveness and the Building Industry

Resource effectiveness can refer to several concepts: consumption, displacement of species and humans, environmental degradation, and the strategies to address these. On the scale of a single building, there are many design techniques that alleviate the strain on natural resources, either through built features like vegetated roofs or through material selection. Vegetated or living roofs function on several levels to preserve resources (Figure 13-5). The roof's surface can have a soil depth of 2 to 4 inches, known as an extensive roof, or 8 to 24 inches for an intensive roof, and functions much in the way a natural landscape would, by diverting rainwater from the storm drain and allowing it to reenter the natural water cycle through evaporation. To local flora and fauna, a vegetated roof can provide a slice of native

---

[6]The Global Footprint Network's Web site explains their methodology, in "Data Methods":http://www.footprintnetwork.org/gfn_sub.php?content=datamethods (accessed March 14, 2008).

[7]The Global Footprint Network, http://www.footprintnetwork.org (accessed March 14, 2008).

[8]Jared M. Diamond, *Collapse: How Societies Choose to Fail or Succeed* (New York: Viking Penguin, 2005).

(a)

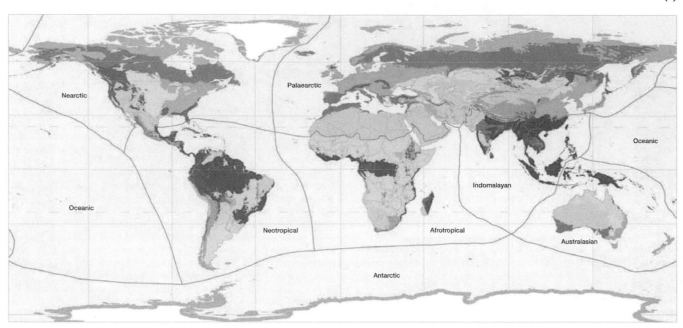

Map 1: TERRESTRIAL BIOGEOGRAPHIC REALMS AND BIOMES

- Tropical and subtropical moist broadleaf forests
- Tropical and subtropical dry broadleaf forests
- Tropical and subtropical coniferous forests
- Temperate broadleaf and mixed forests
- Temperate coniferous forests
- Boreal forests/taiga
- Tropical and subtropical grasslands, savannahs, and shrublands
- Temperate grasslands, savannahs, and shrublands

- Flooded grasslands and savannahs
- Montane grasslands and shrublands
- Tundra
- Mediterranean forests, woodlands, and scrub
- Deserts and xeric shrublands
- Mangroves
- Water bodies
- Rock and ice

(b)

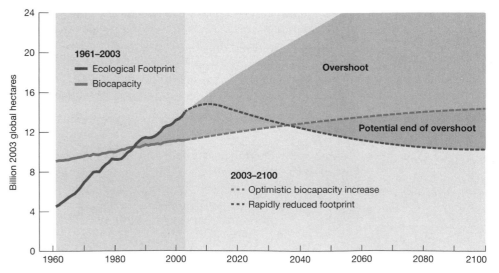

Figure 13-4 a, b The world's biologically productive areas.

habitat, compensating somewhat for the intervention created by the building footprint.

On the scale of a city, principles of *industrial ecology*—grouping small industries in proximity so that they share heat and cooling through each other's waste streams and

heat losses—provides multiple benefits with a single strategy.

At a smaller scale is *service substitution*, a method that involves moving from personal ownership of products to a model based on sharing of resources with similar

Figure 13-5 Vegetated roofs provide habitat and absorb certain quantities of rainwater.

INDUSTRIAL ECOLOGY: In this Danish Industrial Park, Nothing Goes to Waste[9]

If there's anything that sums up the hopes of industrial ecology, it's a tiny pipeline-laced town in eastern Denmark called Kalundborg, where companies have been swapping byproducts like gypsum and waste water for up to 25 years. This "industrial symbiosis" is drawing keen interest from policy-makers in the United States, although opinions vary on its odds of success.

The idea behind "ecoparks" is that one company's sludge is another's manna. As five firms that sprang up at Kalundborg over the years encountered new environmental regulations, they forged exchanges. For instance, flare gas from an oil refinery heats other factories; a power plant sends gypsum—produced by scrubbing sulfur dioxide from flue gas—to a drywall factory; and a biotech's fermentation waste gets shipped to farmers for fertilizing fields. Cooling water from the refinery is used by the power plant as boiler water, while the power plant's excess steam heats Kalundborg's 4300 homes. "There basically is no waste generation, and the energy efficiency is quite

high," says John Ehrenfeld, an industrial ecologist at the Massachusetts Institute of Technology.

In the United States, the ecopark idea has been pumped by an advisory body called the President's Council on Sustainable Development, which points to at least 15 examples on the drawing board in places like Cape Charles, Virginia, and Londonderry, New Hampshire. The approaches range from making "green" products, like photovoltaic panels, to featuring energy-efficient lighting and nature walks. Few of these projects, however, will exchange waste materials, which some experts say is crucial to making a major dent in resource consumption.

Easier to achieve, and common in the United States and elsewhere, is "green twinning" exchanges between two companies, like a steel mill in Midlothian, Texas, that sends waste slag from its furnaces to a nearby cement plant. Another idea is to set up "virtual" ecoparks, in which far-flung companies can exchange materials. The U.S. Environmental Protection Agency has set up databases and developed software tools to help industries find out what each other is throwing away.

Some experts are skeptical that anything like Kalundborg will ever exist in the United States. "The key difference," says Ehrenfeld, "is that Kalundborg is an open culture. They don't have this notion of the corporation as secretive." Yale industrial ecologist Marian Chertow, however, sees an opportunity in the recent push to deregulate the electric industry. More-efficient power plants are expected to spring up from fiercer competition, and these plants would be ideal anchors for ecoparks, she says. "What we're seeing now is the kernels of their evolution."

Source: Jocelyn Kaiser, "In This Danish Industrial Park, Nothing Goes to Waste," *Science* 285, no. 5428 (30 July 1999): 686. [DOI: 10.1126/science.285.5428.686]

purpose. A good example of service substitution is the strategy of using a car-sharing program rather than a privately owned vehicle, thus using a single resource to address multiple needs.[10]

[9]Jocelyn Kaiser, "In This Danish Industrial Park, Nothing Goes to Waste," *Science* 285, no. 5428 (30 July 1999): 686. [DOI: 10.1126/science.285.5428.686]

[10]Chris Ryan, "Dematerializing Consumption through Service Substitution is a Design Challenge," *Journal of Industrial Ecology* 4 no. 1 (2006).

Another resource efficiency concept is *appropriate technology*, essentially the opposite of high technology. It is relevant to green buildings in the environment, because the rural communities and developing countries that employ this level of technology rely on labor rather than material resources to make infrastructure and buildings. The results are durable, low-maintenance structures, using regionally appropriate materials and technology such as adobe or rammed earth. The nonprofit Architecture for Humanity employs the principles of appropriate technology in its mission to serve poor and disaster-affected populations.

Because buildings highly impact the environment, using 40 percent of raw materials globally (3 billion tons annually), designing with *resource effectiveness* in mind has a significant benefit.[11] Resource efficiency goals for integrated buildings refer to many techniques involving both materials and construction methods. Among these goals are:

- To reduce the amount of raw material used for building materials, products, and systems. An example is to design a concrete wall or floor, the interior surface of which is essentially the interior finished surface, as in a stained concrete floor, for example, thereby conserving resources.
- To use products that minimize the impacts of new construction and renovation.
- To design for flexibility or adaptability using reusable components.
- To design for deconstruction, thus reducing the impact of demolition (Figure 13-6).
- To design with prefabricated components, such as tilt-up precast concrete panels. Building in this way will reduce the impact of construction on the site and reduce overall construction waste.
- To select products, materials, and systems based on the following attributes, a method that is sometimes referred to as "precycling," a concept that is covered in Chapters 20 and 21 on construction waste.

In addition, resource effectiveness also requires attention to the following:

- *Durability.* Understanding a product or material's durability involves looking into expected life and assessing it against the length of its warranty and making specification decisions based on this research. An example of designing to extend durability is to protect a structure's large wood members from direct exposure to the elements as much as possible by incorporating overhangs and flashing.[12]

Figure 13-6 A roof is removed or "deconstructed."

- *Packaging.* Manufacturers should reduce the amount of packaging when materials are transported to the construction site. Reusable wood pallets with biobased and compostable plastic film are preferred to nonrecyclable containers.
- *Waste.* Evaluate how much waste is produced during manufacture of a material. Is it a closed-loop process? (See Figure 13-7.)
- *Recycled content.* A little research into the amount of recycled content a material or product has can highlight waste management practices and the level of the manufacturer's cradle-to-cradle commitment. High percentages of recycled content components are desirable, especially postconsumer recycled content, which means that the component has undergone a cycle of production and use. Postconsumer is preferable to preconsumer (formerly, postindustrial) recycled content, but these are still beneficial, because the component becomes part of the manufacturing stream again rather than the waste stream (Figure 13-8).
- *Location.* Determine the location of a material's manufacturing plant in relation to the construction site. Sourcing materials locally may not be feasible in many parts of the world because of proximity to industrial regions, but it is often possible to select the material with the least distance impact.
- *Water.* Just as a product or material has an embodied energy picture (how much energy is used in its mining, harvest, manufacture, transportation, installation, use, and disposal), the same picture can be drawn for how much water is used during these same milestones for a specific material. Periods of heavy water use come during materials harvest, manufacture, and use (Figure 13-9). Mining, for example, is water intensive. Both embodied energy and embodied water are ways of thinking of a material's efficiency and sustainable attributes. Essentially, the questions one asks

[11]David M. Roodman and Nicholas Lenssen, *Worldwatch Paper 124: A Building Revolution: How Ecology and Health Concerns are Transforming Construction* (Washington, DC: Worldwatch Institute 1995).

[12]Ann Edminster and Sami Yass, *Efficient Wood Use in Residential Construction: A Practical Guide to Saving Wood, Money, and Forests,* NRDC Handbook (New York: Natural Resources Defense Council, 1998).

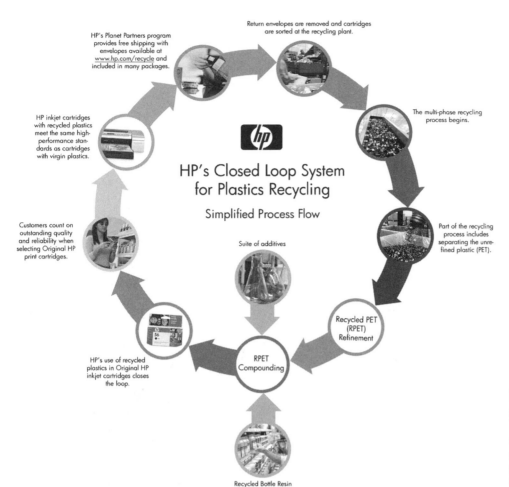

HP's Planet Partners program provides free shipping with envelopes available at www.hp.com/recycle and included in many packages.

Return envelopes are removed and cartridges are sorted at the recycling plant.

HP inkjet cartridges with recycled plastics meet the same high-performance standards as cartridges with virgin plastics.

The multi-phase recycling process begins.

HP's Closed Loop System for Plastics Recycling
Simplified Process Flow

Customers count on outstanding quality and reliability when selecting Original HP print cartridges.

Suite of additives

Part of the recycling process includes separating the unrefined plastic (PET).

HP's use of recycled plastics in Original HP inkjet cartridges closes the loop.

RPET Compounding

Recycled PET (RPET) Refinement

Recycled Bottle Resin

Figure 13-7 The closed loop of a plastics manufacturing process. The technique of designing for deconstruction is gaining currency in such architectural design practices as that of EHDD, a firm that pioneered the concept.

I used to be...
a car tyre

Recycled into something Remarkable

Figure 13-8 Everyday products with recycled content will soon become less of a novelty.

Figure 13-9 It is time to consider the concept of embodied water.

throughout integrated building design elicit information about water and energy use impacts, so this type of thinking is embedded. The U.S. Environmental Protection Agency (EPA) has begun to rate water-using appliances to provide the same consumer awareness for water consumption as it currently does with Energy Star ratings for many types of products, from appliances to roofing materials.

- *Natural resources.* Virgin and nonrenewable materials are best to avoid. Use composite stone instead of marble or granite. In addition, keep in mind that mining, and some harvesting, impacts are damaging to the environment. Salvaged or recovered content takes place when a material is salvaged or recovered and used for another purpose; it is often referred to as *downcycled*. Rubber tires can be made into other products, not necessarily another generation of tires. Salvaged materials can be incorporated into the same use, or they can be retooled for a different application. Old barns, for example, can be salvaged, and their wood members used for similar purposes, or salvaged barn wood can be remilled and made into wide-plank flooring.
- *Reuse.* At times, salvaged materials can include entire components of buildings that can be reused. A marble floor from a public library can be reused as a formal entry lobby for a new office building. Systems furniture can be sourced for reuse. (Figure 13-11)
- *Sustainable forestry.* Use harvested wood from forests that are sustainably managed and cut and that incorporate plans for ongoing growth and health of forests and surrounding communities. Certified ustainably harvested wood products are preferable to wood products from logging practices that disregard these methods.
- *Renewability.* Natural resources can be used judiciously if we consciously make an effort to restore what we harvest. This means that resources that renew rapidly or regenerate within a short time frame are highly efficient and desirable, and they preserve a footprint balance. Bamboo and cork for flooring and paneling are two excellent examples of rapidly renewable material.
- *Biobased materials.* Agrifiber, especially that made from agricultural waste rather than food stock, are usable biobased building materials. For example, these products include wheatboard and soy-based plasters and insulation (Figure 13-10).
- *Low-maintenance materials and cleaning products.* Low-maintenance materials or products that are easily cleaned with zero- or low-emitting cleaning products, including cleaning products that are considered environmentally benign.
- *Maintenance.* Low or infrequent maintenance speaks to a product's durability and reduced costs over the life of the material. Linoleum flooring material does not need the same type or frequency of maintenance that rubber floors do.
- *Materials efficiency.* Using less of a material to accomplish the same goal is called material efficiency; the most frequently seen example of this is the concept of efficient wood framing, spacing studs at slightly wider spacing, 16 inches rather than 14 inches on center. Systems that can be assembled with fewer materials are also desirable.
- *Disassembly.* Related to deconstruction, this refers to smaller components that can be disassembled, also known as DfD.

(a)

(b)

(c)

Figure 13-10 a–f Agricultural waste made into materials: flax into linoleum (a and b), sorghum into an agrifiber board, Kirei (c and d), and cotton blue jeans into insulation (e and f).

(d)

(e)

(f)

Figure 13-10 a–f *Cont'd*

(a)

(b)

Figure 13-11 a, b Salvaged barn wood can have new architectural purpose as a wood floor.

Informed building design and product selection should be based on resource-efficient characteristics in concert with other sustainable design considerations, including energy use and the effect of materials on indoor air.

The governing theory of integrated green building is not as simplistic as buying recycled materials; rather, we should incorporate concepts that promote building to a smaller footprint, designing for long-term durability, sourcing locally produced materials, and ensuring cost-efficiency over the life of the building. Product selection should be made holistically and in consideration of the life cycle of both materials and the building as a whole.

Life-cycle thinking accounts for many factors, such as energy used during manufacture, transportation cost and distance, and impact on indoor air. This comprehensive approach, one of the many components of life-cycle thinking, will be presented in Chapter 19. For the time being, we will focus on resource efficiency during the design and construction processes.

Resource Use in Buildings

A logical way to present resource use is to do so by mirroring the stages of demolition and construction and materials selection. Demolition practices can waste resources, but salvaged materials often contain unusable materials, such as lead paint, and materials impregnated with biocides, halogens, chlorine compounds, halide compounds, chromated copper arsenate (CCA), or arsenic. Nevertheless, there are markets for the less-compromised demolition materials. Salvage yards and materials exchanges, much like a financial trading model, exist for the exchange and purchase of reusable building components. Many waste management companies specialize in collecting and processing demolition and construction waste, a topic that will be covered in a separate chapter.

Examples of Reusable Demolition Materials

These materials are also discussed in the chapters on waste management.

- Concrete and concrete masonry units or brick
- Windows, plumbing fixtures, doors, and hardware
- Glass
- Copper wire and other metals
- Plant materials from land clearing or from clean wood
- Clean wood materials
- Asphalt paving materials
- Gypsum board
- Carpet
- Stone

Examples of Reusable Materials Resulting from Excavation Activities

- Soil
- Planting materials
- Water

Conserve Resources by Controlling the Development Footprint

Limit the size and footprint of the construction staging area, where the builder lays out materials and equipment. Temporary access roads and work areas can significantly reduce the impact on adjoining green spaces and existing landscaping and habitat, wetlands, riparian corridors, and other sensitive habitats.

Heavy machinery used in construction can compact soil, affecting the top layer especially, and impeding the soil's ability to absorb storm water. Contractors have the ability to control the boundaries of the site and limit the number of people with access to it. Construction fences define the limits of the contractor's work but also limit access and further disruption to the site.

Controlling erosion is an important sustainability concept relating to conserving soils and maintaining their integrity. Controlling water runoff helps mitigate erosion and retains water on site.

Erosion and runoff are issues to be grappled with throughout the phases of the construction process, and they continue after completion of a building. Not only must builders engineer ways to mitigate storm-water effects, but they must also account for the impact of water used during construction, for mixing materials, site and equipment cleaning, and dust control.

Pervious paving is often installed as a temporary infiltration measure that allows water to percolate rather than run off. Another method of erosion control is soil stabilization through seeding; trees, grasses, and mulch knit the soil together. Plastic components are used in storm-water and soil control—liners, trenches, piping and gaskets, pervious pavers, and filters.

The building footprint can be manipulated by efficient space planning in the design stage. By stacking functions and cores, sharing walls, and providing flexible open spaces, the designer can maximize efficiency and benefit. Multilevel structures are thus more efficient and leave less impact. Naturally, urban high-density sites are desirable from this aspect as well as in consideration of the movement toward smart growth.

It is also wise to plan for future construction and the design of future communities by giving thought to the types, quality, and layouts for necessary future infrastructure and utilities. Infrastructure should be carefully planned and flexible enough to allow for master planning at a large scale.

Resource Efficient Materials and Methods During Construction[13]

The Construction Specifications Institute (CSI) developed a sequence of fifty divisions describing materials and methods that project teams incorporate as part of the contract documents for a given building project. The specifications are meant to guide the construction process using a language common to the contractor and the rest of the design and construction team. *Specifications* are often referred to as a *project manual,* and they follow a consistent format known as the CSI Master Format.

The specifications fall within divisions ranging from macro scale (exterior of building) to micro scale (interior). As green building enters the mainstream, standard specifications will increasingly incorporate the requirements of integrated building design. The CSI is developing a

---

[13]Culled from various sources: Greenspec Directory; Specifying LEED Requirements, 2nd edition, Christopher Bushnell, ed.; MasterSpec® and SpecWare® by ARCOM, (http://www.csinet.org/s_csi/sec.asp?TRACKID=&CID=129&DID=6026, acessed January 15, 2009); the Collaborative for High Performance Schools (CHPS) Special Environmental Specifications Section 1350, (http://www.ciwmb.ca.gov/greenbuilding/Specs/Section01350/, accessed January 15, 2009).

life-cycle database called "GreenFormat: A Reporting Guide for Sustainable Criteria of Products" intended to provide information on green construction materials for those who specify green building materials.

There are many green model specifications available today; among them are Arcom's Masterspec; Green Spec and California Specification 1350, Special Environmental Requirements; the Whole Building Design Guide and Federal Specifications Guidelines.[14] The information that follows is also captured in many of these sources.

The CSI classification of materials and methods below helps us to understand how to design resource-efficient green buildings.

Following, in CSI order, are characteristics to assess when reviewing materials for both their resource-efficient attributes and negative impacts. Suggestions for recycling, downcycling, salvage, and reuse accompany this section.

CSI TABLE OF CONTENTS

00 00 00	Procurement and Contracting Requirements
01 00 00	General Requirements
02 00 00	Existing Conditions
03 00 00	Concrete
04 00 00	Masonry
05 00 00	Metals
06 00 00	Wood, Plastics, and Composites
07 00 00	Thermal and Moisture Protection
08 00 00	Openings
09 00 00	Finishes
10 00 00	Specialties
11 00 00	Equipment
12 00 00	Furnishings
13 00 00	Special Construction
14 00 00	Conveying Equipment
21 00 00	Fire Suppression
22 00 00	Plumbing
23 00 00	Heating, Ventilating, and Air-Conditioning (HVAC)
25 00 00	Integrated Automation
26 00 00	Electrical
27 00 00	Communications
28 00 00	Electronic Safety and Security
31 00 00	Earthwork
32 00 00	Exterior Improvements
33 00 00	Utilities
34 00 00	Transportation
35 00 00	Waterway and Marine Construction
40 00 00	Process Integration
41 00 00	Material Processing and Handling Equipment
42 00 00	Process Heating, Cooling, and Drying Equipment
43 00 00	Process Gas and Liquid Handling, Purification, and Storage Equipment
44 00 00	Pollution Control Equipment
45 00 00	Industry-Specific Manufacturing Equipment
48 00 00	Electrical Power Generation

Source: The Construction Specification Institute (CSI)

Landscaping (Exterior Improvements)

- Plants bring shade, conduct transpiration (the absorption of water by plants that prevents water loss and assists in remediating contaminated ground water[15]), reduce heat, prevent erosion of topsoil, reduce water loss due to evaporation, and provide habitat.
- Use drought-tolerant native plants to design appropriate planting based on the spoil depth of the soil.
- Design a dry landscape or a xeriscape.
- Avoid monocultures, the cultivation of one type of crop or planting material. Green roofs and living walls provide habitat and absorb storm runoff.
- Water conservation is very important in a landscape. Conserve by controlling how much is used and how much is wasted through runoff into the storm-sewer system. Weather-based irrigation systems that receive weather data and have integrated sensors are a step more sophisticated than systems on a timer. Drip irrigation is preferred to spray hoses or sprinkler systems. Subsurface irrigation is also preferable.
- Tree grates with recycled content or Forest Stewardship Council (FSC) wood.

---

[14]Whole Building Design Guide, http://www.wbdg.org/design/greenspec.php.

[15]Source: U.S. Geological Survey, Toxic Substances Hydrology Program, http://toxics.usgs.gov/definitions/transpiration.html, accessed January 15, 2009.

- Recycled plastics or lightweight materials for planters.
- Mulching also retains moisture in soil, which means less frequent watering. Landscape additives can be chipped plant materials or cellulose in the form of recycled newspaper.

Porous Paving (Exterior Improvements)

- Permeable paving materials help recharge the water table through percolation of water runoff.
- Examples of permeable materials are concrete (to which fly ash and recycled aggregate may be added), stone pavers, loose gravel and gravel pavers, recycled rubber, and plastics with recycled content.
- Install storm systems with permeable paving and layers of aggregate, which can be made from reused crushed materials, and serve to detain water (as in detention ponds). Some systems use detention ponds that can also leave a larger footprint than an engineered fill system.
- Some permeable pavers are built to stand up to traffic, thus reducing soil compaction and retaining the soil's ability to effectively control runoff.
- Using porous pavers that incorporate grass is another good way to provide water control and conservation, provide shade, and reduce ambient temperature.

Site Furnishings (Exterior Improvements)

- In addition to pavement, sidewalk, and parking lot hardscape, you will also need to think of where people sit and where cars park in the landscape. Examples of these are parking bumpers, bollards, and speed bumps.
- Decks; outdoor seating and tables; recycling, composting, and trash containers; bicycle-storage systems; and playground equipment (avoid preservative- or pesticide-treated wood) can be made with recycled plastic content, or plastic "lumber," as well as composite, lumber, which is a mixture of wood fibers and recycled plastic. Look also for FSC-certified wood furnishings, and avoid endangered tropical wood species.
- Some plastic lumber constructions have steel reinforcement in them, thus making use of another highly recycled and recyclable material.
- Using metal furnishings with recycled content is another way to reduce resource use.

Foundations (Structural Elements)

- Foam-based leave-in-place formwork with insulation value, made of polystyrene, is better than using wood formwork that will end up in a landfill.
- If using plywood, use FSC-certified wood, and reuse it.
- Other formwork panels are made with wood fibers mixed with concrete.

- It may be possible on certain types of buildings, such as smaller buildings and residences, to use earth-based formwork, bypassing wood formwork entirely.
- Using less concrete in formwork will not only make it lightweight but also conserve resources and relieve carbon dioxide emissions from production.

Concrete and Concrete Masonry Units
Note: Many concrete curing and slip foams for formwork are now manufactured using biobased ingredients such as soy.

- Use recycled aggregate and fly ash in concrete, because mining for aggregate and manufacture of portland cement is energy intensive and contributes to carbon dioxide production. Other concrete additives and aggregates include rice hull and other agricultural waste ash, plastic and metal aggregates, and recycled glass to replace sand. Note: Recycled aggregates are not suitable for high-performance concrete applications. Plastic-fiber admixtures can improve the reinforcement capability of concrete.
- Concrete can be reused for road base and landscaping materials. Concrete masonry units or brick can be used or crushed for the same purposes as concrete.
- Make concrete lighter: by using lighter aggregates and additives, concrete can weigh significantly less and use less material. Some methods of achieving this involve using plastic-based aggregates or aerating the concrete.
- Coal fly ash is a byproduct of combustion extracted from the inside smokestacks of coal-fired power plants. Because it is a waste material, some argue that demand for fly ash should not grow, because it would provide financial incentive to coal-fired plants and hence contribute to carbon dioxide production. Recently there has been controversy as to the inherently toxic nature of coal ash.

Metal Structural Members, Decking, and Roofing

- The high percentage of recycled content in steel is a major attribute of this metal. It can be recycled or downcycled at the end of its life but remain a durable material. Mining for metals impacts habitat, as well as releasing water and air pollutants. Salvage steel members when possible from other building demo sites. Design structure should be as lightweight as possible for performance and life safety.

Wood-Based Materials
In the category of wood-based materials, we find structural wood framing, casework, cabinets and countertops, plywood, millwork, wood panels, siding and shingles, veneers, substrates, doors, veneers and cores, windows, flooring, and wood blocking.

- Although wood is a renewable resource, it is not rapidly renewable. Source FSC-certified sustainable harvested wood. Typically, lesser known tropical woods, or nonthreatened species, are available. Avoid wood species that affect old-growth forests.
- For finished wood construction, do not seek unblemished or premium-grade wood. Production of these "clear" grades requires mature trees and involves a good deal of waste.
- Use engineered wood, which can reduce waste created from milling, and use composite woods and various grades of plywood as components.
- Optimum-value engineering: Use the smallest size structural member possible for performance and life safety.
- Wide-spaced framing is an option; move from 16 inches on center to 24 inches on center.
- Minimize use of solid lumber for spans where a built-up member is possible.
- Precut openings at factory for more efficiency of construction and waste reduction.
- Design by using trusses instead of solid wood structural members for spans.
- Source premilled and cut wood members, reducing waste on-site.
- Use scrap wood for other construction purposes.
- Salvage wood from other demo sites or use reclaimed material exchanges. Repurpose these members for flooring or smaller units.
- Certain woods are naturally pest and rot resistant, especially marine grade wood, also, redwood and ironwood species.
- Last, in consideration of reducing pollutant emissions to air, soil, and water, use methods for fire- and pest-treating wood that are not as toxic. Also use mechanical fasteners where possible. Adhesives, binders, and sealers contribute to indoor pollution, as well as during the manufacturing process.

Alternatives to Wood-Based Materials

- Prefabricated wall assemblies: These are efficient and can create longer spans, resulting in less material use. Examples are structurally insulated panels (SIPs), which are easy to assemble, and modular construction techniques.
- Composite wood and agrifiber sheathing, substrate, and paneling: e.g., formaldehyde-free particleboard, medium-density fiberboard (MDF), and oriented strand board (OSB).
- Bamboo or cork flooring and underlayments.
- Alternative countertop and solid surfacing materials made from paper, concrete with recycled glass, lava rock, along with other options.
- Plastic lumber for outdoor seating, decks, fencing, and roofing. This material is rot and graffiti resistant, very durable, and can have high recycled content.

- Use salvaged or locally quarried and fabricated stone countertops or counters cast with cementitious mixes with glass or other recycled aggregate, along with paper composite sheets for countertops. Another countertop wood alternative is recycled plastic made from postconsumer products such as milk jugs and yogurt containers.

Insulation

- Insulation concerns revolve around the use of foams and fiberglass and their binders. Energy issues also come into play, demanding high performance and efficient insulation properties. From a resource-efficiency perspective, it is good to focus on materials that make use of postconsumer or preconsumer content, for example, cellulose (from postconsumer paper) and cotton (recycled denim). Be wary of pest and fire-retardant treatments. As with other building materials, minimize on-site waste.
- Vegetated roofs and living walls minimize reflection and heat island effects and reduce storm-water runoff. Plants renew and insulate the interior.
- Reflective, cool roofs with emissivity of less than 0.9 or roofing materials rated as such: Energy Star/Cool Roofs
- Avoid applying mainstream fluid, membrane and bituminous roof systems. They use asphaltic, plastic, and other petroleum products, and they need frequent maintenance and repair.
- Plastic and metal shingles are durable and are rot and pest resistant as well. Asphalt shingles commonly become landfill.
- Alternative roof tile: clay, adobe, mud, and salvaged stone materials.

Siding

- Fiber-cement siding is durable and resistant to fire and pests. It also has wood fibers sourced from post-industrial (preconsumer) manufacturing processes.
- Rain screens extend life of siding materials and prevent rot.
- Exterior wall assemblies have a core, sheathing, and surface suitable for on-site finishing.

Interior Finishes

- *Plaster and stucco:* Preferable are lime- and soy-based clay. Reduce portland cement in some plasters by using fly ash. Acrylic plasters use petroleum products for elastic properties.
- *Gypsum board:* Gypsum board's ecological value used to be based on the recycled content of the facing papers, which amounts to roughly 6 percent of the weight of a single sheet. Now recycled gypsum and synthetic gypsum are being used as core materials. Recycled gypsum comes from clean construction waste and industrial manufacturing scraps. Synthetic

gypsum is a waste product of coal-fueled plant combustion. Again, the larger question arises as to whether
it is wise to provide a market for a product of a polluting process. All this points to the frequent balancing of
one environmental attribute over another.

- *Tile:* The limits of tile selection are nearly boundless and
largely related to mined versus composite and alternative materials. Glass is one of the most frequently
recycled materials; its market has been established for
several decades now. Crushed postconsumer recycled
glass, salvaged and ground quartz, marble and other
stone, all can be used to create composite tiles for many
applications. Recycled glass can form the entire body of
the tile for light flooring applications, as well as decorative wall accents. Many by-products of the manufacturing process can also be incorporated into the final tile
product: dust and sand are two examples. Terrazzo tile
set in a cementitious, rather than an epoxy binder, is
another end use for glass, both window and bottle glass.
- *Ceiling tiles:* There is a wide variety of mixes for office
ceiling lay-in tiles, including cellulose, mineral fiber,
metal, fiberglass, and even wood pulp. Metal, waste
paper from industrial processes, and wood fiber can
be sources of recycled content to varying degrees.
Performance factors such as light reflectance and
sound insulation are other variables to consider in
assessing recycled content ceiling tiles.
- *Resilient flooring:* Many resilient flooring materials—
rubber, a variety of plastics, natural linoleum, and
cork—are excellent alternatives to standard materials
containing polyvinyl chloride (PVC), which bear far-
reaching environmental and human-health impacts.[16]
Cork is a renewable, though overharvested resource.
Linoleum is made with renewable and biobased ingredients, such as linseed oil, flax, and jute, though these
"natural" components do not automatically endow
materials with environmentally benign or "healthful"
status. Rubber and plastics can contain very high levels of recycled content for consumer products, such
as tires and plastic containers, but the odor associated
with rubber is not without impact.[17]
- *Carpet:* carpet, carpet tile, and padding provide
opportunities for recycled-content materials and alternatives. Both fiber and backing can contain a range of
recycled nylon and plastics. Again, PVC or latex are
often included as backing materials, both with their
own air-quality impacts. Face fiber alternatives to
standard yarns are plastic based and include as well
wools untreated by antimicrobials or pest-resistant

ingredients. Several manufacturers are experimenting
with biobased agricultural fibers as alternatives to synthetic fibers. Backing and padding can also be made
with these alternative materials.
- *Stone flooring:* Stone is a natural resource that is finite
and certainly not renewable in any human lifespan context. The main issue with regard to stone is the embodied energy it takes to mine, fabricate, and transport the
finished product to the job site. Much high-end stone
flooring and paneling is quarried in such countries as
Italy and China. Fabrication may even take place overseas as well, even if the stone is quarried regionally or
domestically. Mining is an intensely disruptive activity
in terms of habitat and air pollution. From a resource
efficiency perspective, this is the perfect material for
which the designer should seek alternatives, such as
cast stone, composite stone, and synthetic stone.
- *Paints and associated coatings:* As with many recycled-
content products, paint represents more of a health
concern than its resource-efficient attributes. Milk-
based paints and recycled paints are on the market,
but all of these products are wet-applied and should be
scrutinized for air-quality impacts above all other concerns. Unused paint can be reprocessed by adding
pigments and by mixing it with standard, "new" paint.
That way special disposal methods are not necessary.
- *Paper and alternative wall coverings:* Wall coverings
provide design opportunities through the use of plant
materials, postconsumer paper of all stripes, as well as
plastics such as polyethylene, as both design materials
and alternatives to PVC.

In other chapters, we will consider energy and air-quality
issues, together with the resource-efficiency attributes and
the impact of these products. As you can discern, there is
no perfectly ideal green building material. But understanding the resource-efficiency attributes of building materials,
as well as employing life-cycle thinking, will go a long
way toward arriving at the most optimal design solutions.

EXERCISES

1. Draw a resource map for your current studio project
that shows wetlands, tree stands, and other natural
and built features, such as historic buildings. Address
issues of site, but also consider solar access and wind
patterns. Do an overlay if necessary. Include sources
of noise in the area as described in Chapter 8, Indoor
Environmental Quality Issues.

2. Conduct a resource assessment, either graphically or
in narrative format, of two similar building products to
compare their resource effectiveness and the degree
to which they make optimal use of the raw materials
used in their manufacture. Consider embodied-energy
impacts as well as impacts inherent in activities such
as mining and harvesting.

[16]Joe Thornton, *Environmental Impacts of Polyvinyl Chloride Building Materials*, A Healthy building Report, Healthy Building Network, 2002, www.healthybuilding.net/pvc/Thornton_Enviro_Impacts_of_PVC.pdf accessed January 15, 2009.
[17]*Building Emissions Study* (Sacramento: State of California, California Integrated Waste Management Board, 2003).

Resources

Worldwatch Institute www.worldwatch.org

Global Footprint Network: http://www.footprintnetwork.org

Pharos: http://www.pharosproject.net

Green Home Guide: http://www.greenhomeguide.com

The California Integrated Waste Management Board (CIWMB): http://www.ciwmb.ca.gov/rcp

Green Building Pages: http://www.greenbuildingpages.com

Ecolect Online Material Community: http://www.ecolect.net

Oikos: http:// www.oikos.com

Healthy Building Network: http://www.healthybuilding.net/pvc/alternatives.html

Build It Green Access Green Directory: http://accessgreen.builditgreen.org

Minnesota Building Materials Database: http://www.building-materials.umn.edu

State of California's Environmentaly Preferable Products Database and the U.S. General Services Administration's database: http://www.eppbuildingproducts.org

14 Materials Selection and Product Certification

Why It Is Important to Have a Healthy Dose of Skepticism

Material selection in building design is one of the most frequently performed tasks that students will carry out as they transition to practicing professionals. It is also one of the areas on which most green building professionals base their knowledge and training. The reason for this is that material selection represents the kernel of green building, a metaphor for the entire discipline, and contains its essence: life-cycle thinking. As we have seen, life-cycle thinking considers both environmental impacts and attributes. Using that lens, we can either accept the marketing claims of those trying to sell their products— or we can gather the information ourselves, assess the results, and then balance our materials choices, based on our findings.

It is important to be adept at asking the questions that will lead to basic information: is there added formaldehyde in a certain ceiling tile, or is it labeled formaldehyde free? What is the nature of the recycled glass content in the bathroom wall tile? The manufacturer claims it is 100-percent recycled content but does not mention that the recycled components are recovered from the manufacturing process. A resilient floor manufacturer claims that his product is "nontoxic" and made from "natural" ingredients, implying that the material is benign if not downright good for you. A manufacturer of luminous resin surfacing material claims that it is recyclable through a "take-back program," when, in fact, there is no existing infrastructure for that: no transportation cost coverage, no such recycling facility equipped to "unzip" the film from the plastic, and no technically informed person to explain these roadblocks to sustainability.

This is called *greenwashing* (Figure 14-1), a term that many green building professionals like to think they coined. It refers to a marketing effort to gloss over the

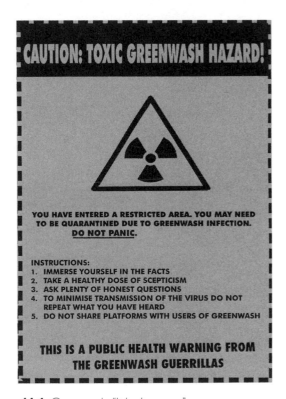

Figure 14-1 Greenwash: "It *looks* green."

negative environmental implications of a material in favor of maximizing even the smallest environmental attribute. *Greenwash* is to the environment what *whitewash* is to politics and history: revisionist, misleading, and sometimes blatantly dishonest. Research, knowledge, and experience are our best defense.

Building Impact

We have known for some time that buildings have impact—advantageous, benign, or detrimental—on our lives and our environment. The currents that carry green thinking are the same ones that bear the need to address building impacts. Materials, literally the building blocks of construction, must necessarily be addressed as a first step to addressing the whole building.

Materials Have Multiple Impacts

The knowledge that building materials have multiple impacts is what helps green building professionals understand the broader implications of a particular material. It helps to seek information on the related cascading impacts of a given material, product, or system. Throughout this book, we refer to the three-pronged understanding of sustainable impacts and attributes:

- resource effectiveness and conservation,
- energy efficiency and conservation, and
- indoor air and environmental quality.

Virtually every environmental and health aspect of a raw material—from its manufacturing process to the finished product, from micro to macro scale—can be understood via these three paths. In this chapter, you will notice many of the themes introduced in earlier chapters on environmentally preferable material attributes. Revisiting these attributes under the lens of these three major categories will underscore their relevance and currency (Figure 14-2).

Basis for Materials Selection

Materials and products all carry the potential to affect resources (such as air and water), to consume certain levels of energy during their life cycles, and to affect the quality of indoor air at the various stages of manufacturing,

Figure 14-2 The interrelatedness of energy, resources, and indoor air quality (IAQ).

installation, maintenance, use, and disposal. Assessing the comprehensive footprint left by the industry presents a challenge not only to identify what material product or system to use for a particular project, but to determine how to balance the benefits and deficits of the material as well.

Resource Efficiency

In an earlier chapter on *resource efficiency,* we described the sustainable attributes of resource-effective materials selection. Resources are essentially the raw materials for everything we consume, and the impacts are broad, multifaceted, and interrelated. The following attributes are beneficial because they have *positive value,* while many other attributes are beneficial owing to the *absence of a detrimental component,* as in the case of polyvinyl chloride (PVC) avoidance in resilient flooring. The entire material, product, and its components should have the following qualities:

- Durability
- Minimal packaging (Figure 14-3)
- Minimal processing with no hazardous by-products
- Minimal waste produced throughout entire life cycle
- High percentage of recycled content, either preconsumer (formerly known as postindustrial) but preferably postconsumer
- Minimal natural resources used and if used, used with its maximum potential
- High levels of salvaged, reused, or recovered content
- Made of renewable materials
- Made of biobased materials
- Easily or minimally cleaned and maintained
- Can be disassembled into separate components
- Made with components that can be reused with existing and planned end products
- Made with components that can be recycled or downcycled
- Low or zero impacts to atmosphere, water, soil, and air—during all phases of life cycle

Energy

As we have mentioned before, integrated design and the life cycle of buildings and their components are closely linked. We have also noted the complexity of creating and understanding a complete environmental picture for a particular product, material, or system. Energy impacts are particularly complex characteristics of materials, because they breach boundaries. As we have seen throughout, embodied-energy studies are extremely involved, complicated by the fact that embodied-energy loads often include features that impact natural resources as well.

All human-engineered materials, products, and systems "carry" embodied energy (Figure 14-4). All products of manufacturing either use or produce energy.

(a)

(b)

Firgure 14-3 a, b Packaging can have positive or negative resource-efficiency attributes.

Figure 14-4 Car manufacture carries embodied energy from the assembly line to consumer use.

If we were concerned only with the energy used by a building product—an electric dishwasher, for example—we would study data, if it were available, on the appliance's energy use during a normal wash-and-dry cycle. Instead of conducting our own research, however, we could look for a product certification, such as the U.S.

Environmental Protection Agency's (EPA's) Energy Star, that would quantify and rate the dishwasher's energy use.

If we wanted to get an idea of how much energy the dishwasher uses along the "conveyor belt" of its manufacture (life cycle), we would examine the production of its components—its aluminum components, for example. Aluminum processing is very energy intensive; consequently, the embodied energy picture is not ideal for products using this element.

To simplify the process, one could break down the materials analysis into two parts:

1. energy produced while in use in the building, as described in the dishwasher example above; or

2. energy expended during manufacturing, transportation, and assembly or installation on-site.

With the materials used for creating building components, systems, or appliances, such as the dishwasher, some understanding of embodied energy is needed, even if it is on a simplified scale. Following are some issues to explore:

- Locations of material harvesting, manufacturing, and distribution centers. Stone is frequently quarried in North America but fabricated overseas. More frequently now, we see stone products being mined and fabricated overseas. Which scenario, then, paints the most desirable environmental picture?
- Means by which materials and products are transported to the job site. Oddly, shipping, which by implication means a material comes from many miles away, is not an optimal sustainable feature, but it has less impact on the environment when compared to trucking or rail transport.
- Fuel type, if any, used in the processing of the material.
- Energy used to install the product or material. Erecting wood framing, for example, requires energy for the power tools, while pouring concrete requires an operating truck to mix concrete during the pour, a boom pump to move the concrete to the site, and at times ride-on compacting machines. In some installations, energy is expended to create a temperature- and humidity-controlled environment for the concrete to cure.
- Ascertain whether an energy-using machine is necessary for cleaning purposes; if it is, determine how frequently it is required.
- Demolition or disassembly technique. Does the material require a hydraulic hammer or a screwdriver?
- Disposal or recycling? It requires a lot less energy to transport a material to a nearby landfill than to transport it to a recycling facility, separate its components in preparation for recycling, then process it into recycled feedstock for the same product's manufacturing line or another downcycled product.

Indoor Air Quality

Unlike the other two categories we have studied, indoor environmental and air quality is strictly health related. The health impacts can occur anywhere along the life cycle of a product's manufacture, affecting the workers and communities surrounding, for example, an adhesives manufacturing facility, workers whose job it is to apply adhesives to a surfacing-material substrate, those who install glue-down carpet on a job site, and those who work, live, and go to school in the spaces where these materials are installed.

A few things are important to understand with respect to indoor air quality (IAQ). The first is that long-term repeated exposure to certain chemical-emitting materials is often more harmful than sudden acute exposure. Children, with

their developing systems, are more vulnerable to long-term and acute exposure. Like adults, they can store chemicals in their bodies, and their systems are less able to break down toxins, or process everything they ingest or are exposed to. They are more susceptible to the higher chemical exposure limits that are established for adults. Several agencies, including the State of California, have responded by generating reference exposure levels (RELs) for chemicals as to how they affect children (Figure 14-5).

As we saw in the chapters on IAQ and chemicals in the environment, the role played by processed synthetic materials in the interior of a building is enormous. In this regard, the role of the green building professional is almost that of a gatekeeper: the green building professional must screen materials based on allowing the least impact to the indoor environment of a green building.

How does a gatekeeper do an effective job with this screening exercise? The subject is complex, and our research often yields technical data that requires experience in the fields of chemistry in order to interpret it. For us, as green builders, it is necessary to be familiar with some of the more general themes and terminology. The task becomes how to unravel, understand, and communicate the information your research is likely to produce.

For the green building professional, the sequence of IAQ research into a material is as follows:

1. Contact the manufacturer's technical department and request all technical data sheets and material safety data sheets (MSDS) relevant to the product's indoor air impacts.
2. Ask if the product has been emissions tested by an independent third party and ask for the report.
3. Check to see if the report reveals any chemicals that are persistent bioaccumulative toxins (PBTs), carcinogens, reproductive toxicants, or endocrine disruptors.[1]
4. Research green building materials reviews to gather user feedback and expert interpretation as to indoor air quality and health impacts.

Making Contact with Technical Staff

People often begin design research by obtaining samples and product literature from the regional product representative. It is important to realize that these exercises are meant to be a marketing tool and source of sales. You may be taken to lunch or hosted at a variety of informational gatherings. Realize that this scenario often

---

[1]Refer to the following comprehensive lists of chemical compounds of concern: State of California's Office of Environmental Health Hazard Assessment's (OEHHA) Chronic Reference Exposure Limits (CREL) Database, http://www.oehha.ca.gov/air/chronic_rels/index.html. The same office offers a Proposition 65 List at http://www.oehha.ca.gov/prop65/prop65_list/Newlist.html. The State of California Environmental Protection Agency's Air Resources Board (ARB), Toxic Air Contaminants list is also available online, http://www.arb.ca.gov/toxics/id/taclist.htm.

Substance (CAS #)	Listed in CAPCOA (1993)	Chronic Inhalation REL ($\mu g/m^3$)	Hazard Index Target(s)	Human Data
1 Acetaldehyde* (75-07-0)	☑	9	Respiratory system	
2 Acrolein (107-02-8)	☑	0.06	Respiratory system; eyes	
3 Acrylonitrile (107-13-1)	☑	5	Respiratory system	
4 Ammonia (7664-41-7)	☑	200	Respiratory system	☑
5 Arsenic (7440-38-2) & arsenic compounds	☑	0.03	Development; Cardiovascular system; Nervous system	
6 Benzene (71-43-2)	☑	60	Hematopoietic system; development; nervous system	☑
7 Beryllium (7440-41-7) and beryllium compounds	☑	0.007	Respiratory system; immune system	☑
8 Butadiene (106-99-0)		20	Reproductive system	
9 Cadmium (7440-43-9) & cadmium compounds	☑	0.02	Kidney; respiratory system	☑
10 Carbon tetrachloride (56-23-5)	☑	40	Alimentary system; development; nervous system	
11 Carbon disulfide (75-15-0)		800	Nervous system; reproductive system	☑
12 Chlorinated dioxins (1746-01-6) & dibenzofurans (5120-73-19)	☑	0.00004	Alimentary system (liver); reproductive system; development; endocrine system; respiratory system; hematopoietic system	
13 Chlorine (7782-50-5)	☑	0.2	Respiratory system	
14 Chlorine dioxide (10049-04-4)		0.6	Respiratory system	
15 Chlorobenzene (108-90-7)	☑	1000	Alimentary system; kidney; reproductive system	
16 Chloroform (67-66-3)	☑	300	Alimentary system; kidney; development	
17 Chloropicrin (76-06-2)	☑	0.4	Respiratory system	
18 Chromium hexavalent: soluble except chromic trioxide	☑	0.2	Respiratory system	
19 Chromic trioxide (as chromic acid mist)	☑	0.002	Respiratory system	☑
20 Cresol mixtures (1319-77-3)	☑	600	Nervous system	
21 Dichlorobenzene (1,4-) (106-46-7)	☑	800	Nervous system; respiratory system; alimentary system; kidney	
22 Dichloroethylene (1,1) (75-35-4)	☑	70	Alimentary system	

Figure 14-5 A partial list of chronic reference exposure levels (RELs) for airborne toxicants.

provides the perfect canvas for greenwashing. Savvy product representatives will indicate a willingness to provide answers to the questions they cannot answer, and they will provide you with appropriate sources of technical information and other resources.

Most often, the technical department of the manufacturer is the first and best source for a product's science-based information. Material safety data sheets and technical data sheets are typically available from the product Web site, and both of these sources will have the technical department's contact information. With these in hand, your research tasks will have a good foundation. Although completely acceptable for purposes of documenting green building rating system credit points—such as Leadership in Energy and Environmental Design (LEED)—MSDS and other data sheets do not paint the entire picture. For one

thing, they calculate volatile organic compounds (VOCs, sometimes termed *volatile organic pollutants*) in terms of their total, not individual, VOCs. Second, they almost always characterize the product's VOC levels in terms of content (grams per liter), rather than airborne emissions from the product (micrograms per cubic meter).

Emissions Testing

Materials emissions testing in a small chamber is the only way of knowing what chemicals are coming off a particular building material or piece of furniture. Reading the side of a paint can will tell you what is in the paint and how much there is of it, but it will not tell you what chemicals are being emitted into the indoor space (and to what degree) before, during, and after the product is applied.

Nor will the content describe the rate and duration of materials off-gassing, on clarify any unknown chemical synergies with the chemical content. Practitioners like to say "content does not equal emissions." A clear lesson to take away from this chapter is that a label, just like so much else in life, does not tell the whole story.

Fortunately, many manufacturers are making the results of their emissions testing public; so it is worth asking the technical department of a paint manufacturer, for example, for a product's emissions-testing report. Manufacturers have been conducting their own emissions testing because of regulations. Now that more and more designers, green building professionals, and consumers are asking for this testing information, manufacturers are aware that the market demand for their product will be in part driven by transparency and information sharing.

What Is an Emissions Chamber Test?

An *emissions chamber test*, using an extremely simplified definition, is a test in which a material is placed in an apparatus about the size of a microwave oven through which air is then passed and collected on the exhaust side. Materials can be tested alone or in an assembly, for example, a carpet adhered to a substrate. The resulting air is analyzed via a gas chromatograph and/or the use of mass spectrometer software. The report issued by the lab (preferably a third-party lab) describes the protocol used and lists the ten most commonly occurring compounds in the product, as well as any and all chemical compounds from a number of chemical lists: the Proposition 65 list, the Chronic Reference Exposure List (CREL), and the Air Resources Board (ARB) Toxic Air Contaminants lists.[2] The resulting emissions data is converted to an emissions rate and then modeled for the specific or default volume of space where the material is to be installed.

There are at least two main protocols or lab-testing procedures that are currently used: one is based on the sequence described in an IAQ emissions specification known as California 01350,[3] and the other is based on a set of laboratory practice guidelines developed by the GreenGuard Environmental Institute[4] (Figures 14-6 and 14-7).

It is optimal for the green building professional to be aware of materials testing processes and how

SECTION 01350 - SPECIAL ENVIRONMENTAL REQUIREMENTS

PART 1 - GENERAL

1.1   SUMMARY

  A. Section Includes Special Environmental Requirements: Work includes special environmental "Green" building practices related to energy efficiency, indoor air quality, and resource efficiency, including the following:

    1. Special Requirements:

      a. Require practices to ensure healthy indoor air quality in final Project.

      b. Maximize use of durable products.

      c. Maximize use of products easy to maintain, repair, and that can be cleaned using non-toxic substances.

      d. Maximize recycled content in materials, products, and systems.

      e. Require use of wood from certified sustainably harvested sources.

      f. Maximize use of reusable and recyclable packaging.

      g. Maximize use of products with low embodied energy (production, manufacturing, and transportation).

    2. Construction team is required to comply with "green" building practices during construction and when considering materials for substitutions. Refer to Article 1.2 – Design Requirements.

  B. Related Requirements:
Refer to Specification sections for special environmental requirements for specific products.

    1. Section 01565: Site Waste Management Program.

    2. Section 01600: Product Requirements.

    3. Section 01810: Building Commissioning.

    4. Section 01820: System Demonstration.

Figure 14-6 The State of California's Section 01350, Special Environmental Requirements, was the first health-based environmental specification section.

[2] The State of California Environmental Protection Agency's Air Resources Board (ARB) Toxic Air Contaminants list is also available online, http://www.arb.ca.gov/toxics/id/taclist.htm.
[3] Section 01350, Special Environmental Requirements, http://www.ciwmb.ca.gov/greenbuilding/Specs/Section01350/.
[4] GreenGuard Environmental Institute, http://www.greenguard.org.

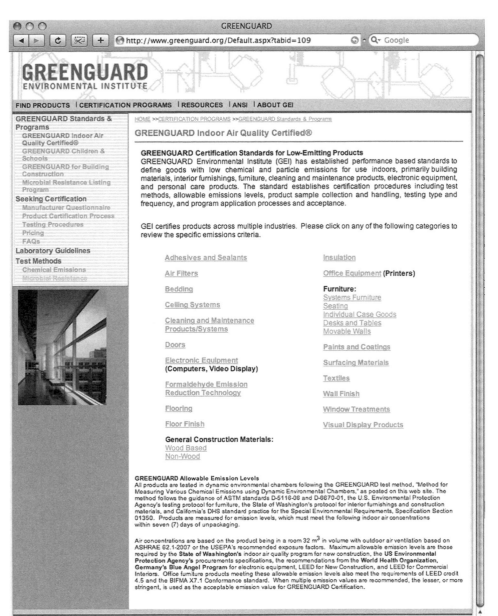

Figure 14-7 GreenGuard Environmental Institute has been successful in moving materials manufacturing industries toward health-based product design and production.

THE HUMAN TOXOME PROJECT

"What is the HTP? Through the Human Toxome Project at the Environmental Working Group, scientists, engineers, and medical doctors use cutting edge biomonitoring techniques to test blood, urine, breast milk and other human tissues for industrial chemicals that enter the human body as pollution via food, air, and water, or from exposures to ingredients in everyday consumer products."

Source: Human Toxome Project (HTP), http://www.bodyburden.org; the data on the HTP Web site is searchable by state or country and health concern.

to understand the results at a general level, because it creates credibility and raises the standard by which product and material manufacturers will be measured. Failing that knowledge, however, there are other ways to obtain a degree of understanding of IAQ impacts as well as impacts to the whole building. The first way is to use product certifications, ratings, and labels.

Product Certification, Rating, or Label

We are creatures of taxonomy—we love sorting and cataloging, gathering things of a type together. We are sometimes driven to collect things of a kind, like collecting comic books or Limoges boxes. It is sometimes tempting to view ecolabels that way. There are many ways to sort the labels. But perhaps the way to make sense of ecolabels is in balance with our comments earlier in the chapter about understanding what *impact* materials can have. By circling from the other direction, looking at product characteristics first, then, we should be able to understand the *virtues* of a product through familiarity with the ratings. Much as one would judge the greenness of a green building by judging the rating system by which it was analyzed, we can do the same with materials. Using this type of questioning, we can determine how appropriately labeled a product is and the degree to which it is a truly sustainable product. By connecting these two approaches, our understanding will be more robust, and we will become flexible thinkers who have confidence in our decisions.

ECOLABELS AND THEIR RELATED ATTRIBUTES

IAQ / Health→ Indoor Advantage / Indoor Advantage Gold, GreenGuard, CRI Green Label Plus, Floorscore

Resources / Waste→ FSC, SCS Recycled Content, SCS Biodegradable, EPA's WaterSense, USDA Organic

Energy / Climate→ EPA's Energy Star, Cool Roof Rating Council, Green-e (geared toward renewable energy and greenhouse gas mitigation products), Climate Neutral

Multiple Attributes→ Green Seal, Eco Logo, SCS Sustainable Choice, SCS Environmentally Preferable Products, Cradle to Cradle (C2C), SMaRT (by MTS), EPEAT

Think about impacts we have studied, for example, indoor air quality. Think about what types of building products could have an IAQ impact: Solid materials, such as resilient flooring, ceiling tile, carpet, upholstery fabric, furniture, wall coverings, and composite wood and wet products such as paints, stains, varnishes, and adhesives. Assessing impacts, as we have done periodically throughout the book, leads to managing the risks. One way to do this is through product certification.

By understanding and assessing the material's impacts, we can understand what type of certification will be meaningful (see sidebar). If a particular product carries no certification, this fact would provide a basis to eliminate that product from consideration, thus managing the risk. We must know about the standards and criteria on which certifications are based, understand who operates and guides the mission (transparency) of the certification bodies, assess the comprehensiveness of the standard and

resultant rating (robust or not?), and assess the reliability and integrity (credibility) of the rating and what it means.

Who Rates?

A *certification*, *rating*, or *label* is literally a seal of approval. Many use these terms interchangeably, but they should really be considered distinct from each other. A certification is different from a label in that it has been verified by an independent third party, while labels often are not supported by such trustworthy bodies. Some certifications have sprung from green building rating systems, like the Building Research Establishment (BRE, and its BRE Environmental Profile),[5] but most are produced by separate bodies. These entities should ideally be accredited (or, in turn, approved) by an outside accrediting organization to ensure that they uphold the guidelines and criteria set by the certification system. A good example is the Forest Stewardship Council (FSC), which accredits the Scientific Certification Systems (SCS) and Rainforest Alliance's SmartWood, two of the numerous international organizations that verify that a forest and its wood products are in compliance with FSC standards and criteria and who are not associated with special interests of the forestry or manufacturing industries.

Bodies that conduct ratings include government agencies such as the U.S. EPA, which issues guidance that in turn evolves into mainstream labels. Energy Star is an example of such a program. Although product approval by a government agency or laboratory carries weight, in the United States as well as in the general global economy, the preference is for product-approval mechanisms that are based on voluntary, consensus-derived standards.

Leadership organizations with a hand in crafting such standards include American Society for Testing Materials (ASTM), NSF International, and International Organization for Standardization (ISO). In the United States, American National Standards Institute (ANSI) is the anointed body responsible for accrediting potential developers of standards as well as certification bodies. Recently, both the Green Building Initiative (GBI) and the Institute for Market Transformation to Sustainability (MTS) were accredited as ANSI standards developers. GBI has the goal of transforming the Green Globes green building rating system and MTS the Sustainable Materials Rating Technology (SMaRT), respectively, into internationally recognized American National Standards (ANS). The Sustainable Materials Rating Technology has produced several standards relating to flooring and textiles and building products in general.[6] Still other organizations are independent third-party certifiers, like Scientific Certification Systems.

---

[5]BRE Environmental Profile, http://www.bre.co.uk/envprofiles.
[6]Institute for Market Transformation into Sustainability (MTS), http://mts.sustainableproducts.com/.

What Gets Rated?

An array of products and processes are rated according to their ability to comply with standards. Materials, entire buildings, energy-using appliances, and building systems, like roofing and irrigation controls, can receive ratings.

For What Attributes and Criteria?

Materials and products have z that are rated and judged using a set of criteria, standards, or protocols. There are ratings that assess both multiple and single attributes, examples of which include energy use, the manufacturing process (polluting vs. closed loop), recycled content levels, VOC emissions, chemical or harmful substances avoidance, "clean" technology, and overall low environmental impact.

Standards are the tools used to assess attributes and grant certifications. An example of compliance with a standard is the California Section 01350 protocol, which provides the basis for many robust certifications, including Indoor Advantage Gold, CRI Green Label Plus, and GreenGuard for Children and Schools. The Sustainable Carpet Assessment Standard of NSF/ANSI 140-2007 is another example of a standard adopted to define and set levels for multiple sustainable attributes using the three environmental factors—environment, economy, and social justice, the first such standard in the United States. Another recent set of criteria is provided by Cradle to Cradle, a product certification program developed by McDonough Braungart Design Chemistry, which has requirements for "product/material transparency and human/environmental health characteristics of materials, product/material reutilization, production energy, water use at manufacturing facility, and social fairness/corporate ethics" in its scope[7] (Figure 14-8).

With What Results?

Certifications can provide scaled ratings, such as stars or four levels—bronze, silver, gold, or platinum—of many certifications. Scaled ratings often assess multiple attributes and employ life-cycle thinking at their core, meaning that a more complete environmental snapshot is obtained. Other certifications have binary scales corresponding to the product's passing or failing the criteria by which it is rated. Although handy for gauging the degree of robustness of the product or material being rated, a "thumbs-up or thumbs-down" rating does not necessarily give any assurances of a product's environmental performance or impact. For the green building professional—in fact, for anyone researching green viability—the most important consideration, in addition to understanding the transparency of the certifying body,

the rigor of its requirements, its scientific basis, and its peer-reviewed coherence, is to know what level of party certification the rating provides.

First-party certification is essentially self-certification, akin to an advertisement or manufacturing claim by a manufacturer, and it is achieved with no peer or outside independent review. These are often called de facto claims. For example, an advertisement states that a product is "environmentally friendly," "natural," or "nontoxic."

Second-party certification occurs when a consultant or industry, trade, or manufacturing group issues the certification. Although the second party may actually produce the standards, the certification is subsequently verified by an outside organization, which sometimes has ties to the product or manufacturer.

A good example of a single-attribute, second-party certification is the Composite Panel Association's Formaldehyde Grademark Program, which tests to an emissions chamber testing protocol, defined by ASTM. Second-party certification may or may not include manufacturing audits, but they do require supporting documentation.

Third-party certification is when an independent group issues the certification. No one associated with this independent organization has ties to the product, manufacturer, or membership in its board or policies.

An example of a third-party certification is Australia's Water Efficiency Labelling and Standards (WELS) Scheme (Figure 14-9), which uses tests that reflect the Australian government's water-efficiency standard for water use via fixtures and appliances. A WELS regulator from the Department of the Environment and Heritage performs the testing, auditing, and oversight and grants the certification. The water-supply issue has become so critical in Australia that WELS compliance is mandatory for all water-using equipment sold after 2006.[8]

Another rigorous Australian third-party certification is the "greenhouse-gas neutral" rating (Figure 14-10) for products and their manufacturing processes. Greenhouse Friendly is administered by the Australian Greenhouse Office, using comprehensive ISO Life Cycle Assessment (LCA) protocol.[9] An emissions abatement study is prepared that quantifies the carbon emissions in the production of the material or product in question. The Panel of Independent Verifiers conducts outside-party verification, made even more rigorous by mandatory recertification. The rating represents offsets through specific abatement activities using preapproved strategies: energy-efficiency measures, waste reduction, and carbon sequestration techniques.

---

[7]MBDC, Cradle to Cradle Certification Program, as of December 2007 is available for download at http://www.c2ccertified.com.

[8]Water Efficiency Labeling and Standards (WELS), http://www.waterrating.gov.au.
[9]Australian Government Department of Climate Change, Greenhouse Friendly, http://www.greenhouse.gov.au/greenhousefriendly/.

▲MBDC

MBDC Cradle to Cradle℠ Certification
www.c2ccertified.com

CRADLE TO CRADLE℠ CERTIFICATION CRITERIA	Basic	Silver	Gold	Platinum
1.0 Materials				
All material ingredients identified (down to the 100 ppm level)	●	●	●	●
Defined as biological or technical nutrient	●	●	●	●
All materials assessed based on their intended use and impact on Human/Environmental Health according to the following criteria: **Human Health:** Carcinogenicity, Endocrine Disruption, Mutagenicity, Reproductive Toxicity, Teratogenicity, Acute Toxicity, Chronic Toxicity, Irritation, Sensitization. **Environmental Health:** Fish Toxicity, Algae Toxicity, Daphnia Toxicity, Persistence/Biodegradation, Bioaccumulation, Ozone Depletion/Climatic Relevance. **Material Class Criteria:** Content of Organohalogens, Content of Heavy Metals	●	●	●	●
Strategy developed to optimize all remaining problematic ingredients/materials	●	●		
Product formulation optimized (i.e., all problematic inputs replaced/phased out)			●	●
No wood sourced from endangered forests			●	●
Meets Cradle to Cradle emission standards			●	●
All wood is FSC certified				●
Contains at least 25% GREEN assessed components				●
2.0 Material Reutilization/Design for Environment				
Defined the appropriate cycle (i.e., Technical or Biological) for the product and developing a plan for product recovery and reutilization	●	●	●	●
Well defined plan (including scope and budget) for developing the logistics and recovery systems for this class of product			●	●
Recovering, remanufacturing or recycling the product into new product of equal or higher value				●
Product has been designed/manufactured for the technical or biological cycle and has a nutrient (re)utilization score >= 50		●	●	●
Product has been designed/manufactured for the technical or biological cycle and has a nutrient (re)utilization score >= 65			●	●
Product has been designed/manufactured for the technical or biological cycle and has a nutrient (re)utilization score >= 80				●
3.0 Energy				
Characterized energy use and source(s) for product manufacture/assembly	●	●	●	●
Developed strategy for using current solar income for product manufacture/assembly		●	●	●
Using 50% current solar income for product final manufacture/assembly			●	●
Using 50% current solar income for entire product				●
4.0 Water				
Created or adopted water stewardship principles/guidelines		●	●	●
Characterized water flows associated with product manufacture			●	●
Implemented water conservation measures				●
Implemented innovative measures to improve quality of water discharges				●
5.0 Social Responsibility				
Publicly available corporate ethics and fair labor statement(s), adopted across entire company		●	●	●
Identified third party assessment system and begun to collect data for that system			●	●
Acceptable third party social responsibility assessment, accreditation, or certification				●

Cradle to Cradle℠ is a service mark of MBDC.

Figure 14-8 MDBC's Cradle to Cradle certification criteria matrix.

ISO Label Types

The International Organization for Standardization (ISO) was founded as a nongovernmental organization (NGO) in 1947, and the organization is known as ISO in spite of the fact that it is not an acronym; rather, the name originates from the Greek *isos,* meaning "equal."[10] The ISO's founding goal was to create international standards of quality, consumer reliance, and safety for goods and services. Among its other goals is the protection of consumers by ensuring standard levels of quality over many activities, including sustainable fishing, children's toys, medical devices, and environmental management. A future standard for social responsibility, ISO 26000, is in development. Since its founding, the ISO has worked to develop, vet, and publish over 16,000 standards, creating a common technical language.

Three of the standards under the ISO 14000 category of Environmental Management govern the types of assertions or claims that manufacturers make regarding their products. The ISO provides conforming standards for organizations that help them to "minimize harmful effects on the environment caused by its activities, and to achieve continual improvement of its environmental performance."[11] The labels under these three standards mirror the first-, second-, and third-party claims discussed above. They are not ratings or certifications, because the ISO is not a certifying body.

[10] International Organization of Standardization, http://www.iso.org.

[11] "Environmental Management," International Organization of Standardization, http://www.iso.org/iso/iso_cafe_environmental_management.htm (accessed January 12, 2009).

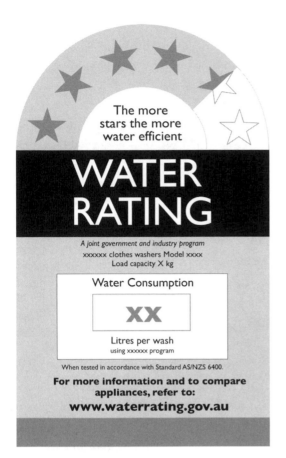

Figure 14-9 Australia's water-consumption rating label.

Figure 14-10 Australia's Greenhouse Friendly program.

ISO Type I (14024) is multiattribute third-party label of comprehensive environmental impact (selective).

ISO Type II (14021) is a self-declared claim by a manufacturer, or any entity with an interest or tie to the product or manufacturer, made without third-party verification. These claims typically use words such as "recycled content," "energy efficient," "water efficient," "recyclable," or "biodegradable." The standards state that the claim must be accurate and verifiable, not vague or misleading.

ISO Type III (14025) is a third-party claim used to verify and report LCA findings in sixteen preset categories or indicators.

An environmentally preferable product often has an ecolabel, the name given to products based on their degree of "greenness." The problem with ecolabels is that the term is vague and not adequately defined.

In a confusing flurry of certifications, ratings, and verifications, the thing to remember is that an environmentally preferable products (EPP) label indicates that some level of research has been done on the material, often reflecting life-cycle assessment. In order to be designated an EPP, a product needs to meet a certain set of standards, so we are again faced with the challenge of assessing how comprehensive and rigorous is the standard and how independent is the testing and verification process. Some ecolabels do bear a pedigree under a set of standards, however, and one example is SCS Sustainable Choice, which certifies furniture that has met the Business and Institutional Furniture Manufacturer's Association (BIFMA) sustainability standards, as well as having earned certification under SCS Indoor Advantage, an indoor air certification referred to in the Glossary.

EPPs influence the purchasing policies for many municipalities, including New York, San Francisco, and King County, Washington. Green procurement (also known as Environmentally Preferable Purchasing) policies exist in California, Georgia, New York, Massachusetts, and many other states, as well as internationally (see sidebar). In California, the Golden Seal Program was established in 2000 as a method for greening operations and maintenance of state buildings. As part of that program, EPPs were vetted by the Department of General Services. Today, environmentally preferable purchasing is required by law in California, as well as by certain federal agencies, including the Department of Defense, Department of HS, Department of the Interior, Department of Energy, GSA, and the EPA. Large institutions, such as health-care centers and universities, find there is an economic benefit to buying green.

ENVIRONMENTALLY PREFERABLE PURCHASING INITIATIVES INTERNATIONALLY

European Union (EU): Green Public Procurement (GPP)

Japan: Promotion of Procurement of Eco-Friendly Goods and Services

Malaysia: Green Purchasing Network Malaysia

Sweden: MSR—Guidance for Sustainable Procurement

United Kingdom (UK): Sustainable Procurement Programme

Vienna, Austria: OkoKauf Wien (EcoBuy Vienna)

The types of green products driven by these policies include carpet, electronics, cleaning products, office supplies, and often more targeted materials. Life-cycle-cost (LCC) analysis (as distinct from LCA) is sometimes conducted on such products to guide the development of an EPP program and the implementation of its policy. Life-cycle costing compares the total cost of one material against another, over its entire life cycle, through operations and maintenance.

An example of a comprehensive green purchasing policy is Alameda County Waste Management Authority's Environmentally Preferable Purchasing Model Policy 2006. It is a valuable resource for organizations interested in formulating a preferable purchasing policy. The model policy covers the areas of source reduction, recycled-content products, energy, water, green building practices, toxics and pollution, and forest conservation. It also lists the steps for creating and maintaining a functioning policy with priorities, goals, implementation plans, and evaluation requirements. [12]

PRODUCT RATING PROGRAMS IN OTHER COUNTRIES

Canada

Environmental Choice Program: Products and services certified by the Environmental Choice Program are proven to have less of an impact on the environment because of how they are manufactured, consumed, or disposed. Certification of products and services is based on compliance with stringent environmental criteria that are established in consultation with industry, environmental groups, and independent experts, and they are based on research into the life-cycle impacts of a product or service.

EcoLogo: A third-party certification and labeling program based on Life Cycle Assessment (LCA), which examines multiple attributes: e.g., energy, toxics, and other environmental impacts.

Australia

Greenstar: A nonprofit that administers the Greenstar Product Certification and Labeling Program. Its purpose is to "promote the production and use of

products that maximize sustainability, protect the environment, and protect human health."

European Union

Eco-Label Programme: In an effort to contribute to sustainable development, the European Union Eco-Label Programme is a Europe-wide program that awards ecolabels to products with a reduced environmental impact (Figure 14-11).

Germany

Blue Angel Program: The Blue Angel Program is a voluntary labeling program. For two decades, the Blue Angel label has signified products with positive environmental features.

Japan

Eco Mark. The Japan Environment Association develops environmental standards, which permits products to bear the Eco Mark symbol.

Green Purchasing Network: The network was established in 1996 to promote green purchasing among consumers, companies, and governmental organizations in Japan.

Norway, Sweden, Denmark, Finland, and Iceland

Nordic Swan Program: The Nordic environmental label is a neutral, independent label, that guarantees

Figure 14-11 The European Union's Eco-Label Programme.

[12]Environmentally Preferable Purchasing Model Policy, StopWaste.org, http://www.stopwaste.org/home/index.asp?page=439.

a certain environmental standard. Only products that satisfy strict environmental requirements on the basis of objective assessments are allowed to display the environmental product label.

Sweden

TCO Development: This program provides certification and environmental labeling of office equipment designed to improve the work environment and the external environment.

Source: U.S. EPA: Programs in other countries

Tools: Putting It Together

We can use several tools as filters in the materials selection process. Starting at the level with the least amount of independent research, we can screen products, materials, and systems using an entire range of certifications and ecolabels. For independent research, databases of sustainable materials, product reviews by green building professionals, and EPP databases belonging to some of the agencies described in this chapter can be useful starting points.

In professional practice, we conduct research and address issues such as those outlined at the beginning of this chapter. To record our research, we want to use a questionnaire that captures the main themes of life-cycle thinking. An excellent example of a product research template is HOK's Materials Evaluation questionnaire, outlined in the second edition of *The HOK Guidebook to Sustainable Design.* (New York: John Wiley & Sons, 2005.) It succeeds because of its detailed approach and its contribution to educating materials suppliers as to the new demands of designers whose focus is shifting to sustainability. Many other architectural firms and consultants have developed their own tools for conducting materials research and sharing their process rather than using it as a competitive advantage.

Specifications

In an earlier chapter we were introduced to specifications that have particular relevance to resource-efficiency attributes and impacts. In this chapter, discussion of specifications will focus on energy and indoor air quality.

Specifications (specs) provide another useful filter to ferret out greenwash. In professional practice, formal specifications become part of a project's contract documents, along with the drawings. Specs guide the bidding and construction process, direct the builder, and become a legally binding document. A typical specification has three parts: a general summary, product data, and execution requirements, which describe workmanship expectations (without telling the contractor exactly how to accomplish the directives in the specifications).

For purposes of materials research, most attention should be focused on the product data section of each specification section. This will record the expectations of environmental attributes for the particular product, be it recycled-content minimums, VOC emission maximum levels, or the expected energy performance of an appliance.

The Special Environmental Requirements Specification Section 01350, developed for the State of California for a state office building (completed in 2001), has undergone many permutations over the years. In its first manifestation, it was adopted as a testing protocol focused on IAQ; it has now become the basis for product certification under several labels, becoming part of a standard in green building guidelines such as the Collaborative for High Performance Schools (CHPS).

California Section 01350 was born out of an interest in human health in the indoor built environment. Its authors believed that human-health issues should be the guiding criteria over a product's sustainable profile. It is considered the first health-based materials specification.

Recent iterations of Section 01350 bring into balance the three components of (a) resource effectiveness and conservation, (b) energy efficiency and conservation, and (c) indoor environment and air quality of sustainable building design. Other versions guide the LEED process only, a very time-consuming "project within the project," where it is often necessary to state explicitly what is required in terms of supporting documentation for LEED credits.

As mentioned earlier, specifications reviews accompany drawing reviews in professional practice. In tandem, these two exercises can act as barriers to greenwash, like a good filter.

Specifying Good IAQ

Similar to Chapter 13's exercise in specifying resource efficiency, we will now review selected materials and their impacts on IAQ in Construction Specifications Institute (CSI) order. Because IAQ-based research is concerned with the interior of a building, the necessary materials reviews will fall under "CSI Division 9, Finishes." A few materials will be captured under other division numbers. Casework, countertops, and cabinetry fall under "Division 6, Wood and Plastic." Insulation and sealants are covered in "Division 7, Thermal and Moisture Protection." Composite wood door cores come under "Division 8, Doors and Windows." In addition to the chemicals of concern mentioned here, keep in mind that many other building components contain additives that affect IAQ, including antifreeze, biocides, fungicides, preservatives, petroleum and plastic materials, and mold (which can grow on nutrient sources such as cellulose paper and fire retardants such as PBDE).

Wood-Based Materials

Most casework, built-in furniture, and countertops use some type of composite wood as a base. Particleboard and medium-density fiberboard (MDF) are examples of composite wood. Moldings, door cores, baseboards, flooring, drawer fronts, tabletops, and wall panels can contain composite wood fibers, plywood and oriented-strand board are made from wood scrap. Adhesive binders used in these wood-based materials, and several cellulose-derived products, are usually based in formaldehyde, a known carcinogen according to California's Proposition 65 and the World Health Organization, which identified it as a toxic air pollutant in 1992. In 2007, the California Air Resources Board set regulations adopting controls over formaldehyde products by lowering their allowable-emissions thresholds to parallel those of Japan and the European Union by 2009 and to even lower levels by 2012 (Figure 14-12).[13]

Formaldehyde is naturally occurring in wood, as well as present in outdoor air. There are two types of formaldehyde encountered in building materials or products: urea (UF) has higher emissions rates than phenol formaldehyde (PF), the lesser of two evils. Its emissions rates are lower due to faster curing time during manufacture; it thus

Figure 14-12 Composite wood products typically contain formaldehyde as the binding agent.

affects workers more than end users. Both types would be avoided in an ideal world, as there is no safe level of exposure; nevertheless, some rating systems call for no added urea formaldehyde in these materials.

Other nonwood-based sources of formaldehyde in buildings include: environmental tobacco smoke, upholstery and draperies, fabric treatments, glues, paints, coatings, fiberglass insulation, household and personal care products, nonvented gas stoves or kerosene space heaters, and other fuel-burning appliances.[14]

Examples of formaldehyde alternatives include soy-based resins or resins made with methylene diphenyl isocyanate (which uses a cyanide-based compound and therefore is not ideal) and polyvinyl acetate (PVA) with no chlorine molecule, which poses the hazards of PVC. Another technology currently in development is a resin made from phenol formaldehyde and sugar compounds, which would replace a certain amount of the phenol.

Batt Insulation

Most fiberglass batt insulation uses formaldehyde resins as a binder. Alternatives include cotton batt insulation, wool, spray-foam insulation (not those with a cyanurate component, but those using soybean and other biobased components), or insulation fabricated without formaldehyde binders.

Joint Sealants, Compounds, and Firestopping

Joint compounds can be either dry mix or mixed in the factory. Premixed compounds may contain vinyl adhesives and other additives that emit slowly. Alternatives are available that are advertised as low VOC and that contain biobased binders.

Tile-Setting Materials

Installation of tile involves a quantity of wet-applied materials: adhesives, mortar (either cement or latex based), grout, and grout sealants. In each case, low- or zero-VOC and water-based products can be used as alternatives.

Acoustical Ceiling Tiles

Standard ceiling tiles made from recycled paper, also known as mineral fiber because of their clay and other mineral additives, contain a certain level of formaldehyde but a high level of recycled content. The formaldehyde may originate from sources of recycled feedstock. Alternatives to these include no-added-formaldehyde ceiling tiles, many of which are mainstream products. Other choices would be metal ceiling panels (some made with formaldehyde containing fiberglass), wood-fiber ceilings, and low-formaldehyde-emitting fiberglass tiles.

[13]California Environmental Protection Agency (Cal/EPA), "Air Board Sets Strict Limits on Toxic Formaldehyde Emissions from Composite Wood Products," news release, April 27, 2007: "Formaldehyde was identified as a toxic air contaminant (TAC) by ARB in 1992 with no safe level of exposure. Once a TAC is identified, ARB is legally required to limit public exposure to the maximum feasible extent through the adoption of one or more Air Toxic Control Measures. As part of that process, statewide formaldehyde exposure was reevaluated by ARB in 2005. That evaluation found that emissions near composite woods were too high and required additional controls."

[14]"Formaldehyde and Wood: Sources of Formaldehyde in Buildings," Healthy Building Network, www.healthybuilding.net/formaldehyde.

Resilient Flooring

Resilient flooring materials have many benefits: They are softer underfoot, deaden sound, and are pliable as well as high in recycled, recyclable, or renewable content. Ironically, it is sometimes these properties that cause IAQ problems. Resilient flooring presents a major impact to indoor air quality. Immediately noticeable is the strong odor, such as that emitted by rubber materials, which tends to cause a perceived sense of compromised IAQ. The odor can linger in an indoor environment for long periods of time, extended further by absorptive, porous materials such as upholstery and drapes.

Cork is rapidly renewable, but it needs several coats of sealer to achieve durability and a surface that will tolerate regular cleaning.

Virgin rubber flooring has less of an odor than rubber flooring made from recycled tires, another example of green material trade-offs.

Linoleum is derived from biobased materials such as linseed oil and flax, but it produces aldehyde emissions that some manufacturers have addressed through an added treatment of the top layer.

Alternative plastics with high recycled content, or with biobased ingredients, such as corn, may have a bright future in the flooring industry, but these materials make a case for asking questions about the emissions testing on any emerging product.

Carpet Products

Carpets can trap dirt, odors, particulates, and pesticides from the outdoors and may contribute to mold growth. Because of the porous "sink" that soft materials such as carpet provide, these contaminants can continue to emit over long periods of time. High-performance fibers for carpet are made from various types of polymers and petroleum products. Carpet backing can be made from any number of plastics, typically PVC or latex. Backing materials also need to be considered for their IAQ impacts. Better backing alternatives that are less environmentally significant plastics include polyethylene and polyolefins such as polypropylene. Biobased plastics are currently in research and development for many applications, carpet backing included. Along with composite-wood products, carpet poses considerable IAQ impact because of the sheer volume present in an indoor space. The Carpet Research Institute (CRI) Green Label Plus is a high standard of carpet certification and an excellent guide to selecting carpet with less impact on the indoor environment.

Wall Coverings, Window Treatments, and Upholstery Fabrics

Wall surfacing, window shades, and certain fabrics frequently contain PVC. Alternatives include using plant-based fiber paper or synthetics (preferred plastics or woven glass) without biocide, fire retardant, or antimicrobial treatments.

Painting

Paints can contain many substances that cause harm to human health: benzene, toluene, lead, mercury, phthalates, and formaldehyde are some of them. Lead was used in the manufacture of paint until the 1940s in Europe, and in the United States until the 1970s. Because paint is essentially a protective film that also needs to have aesthetic benefits, it has various additives for its performance requirements: gloss finish, pigment, binder, antifouling agents (formaldehyde), fungicides, drying agents and others. It is a difficult material to understand because of its chemistry, so this is another instance of a certification coming in handy. Green Seal's voluntary labeling program and the standards of California's Air Quality Management Districts (South Coast and Bay Area) are guides to VOC-content limits for coatings and paints, while California Section 01350 provides VOC-emissions-testing protocols, as previously discussed. Alternatives to petrochemical-based synthetic paints include milk paint, water-based paint, recycled paint (a poor choice because of quality control issues), and boiled linseed oil paint, though none are entirely free of IAQ impacts.

Seating and Office Systems

In an office space, furniture and equipment are large contributors to the quality of indoor air. Increasingly, we see seating and office systems achieving indoor air quality certification. Because these systems have many components, to isolate each and apply IAQ-focused lifecycle thinking would be time consuming. However, IAQ certifications using large-chamber emissions testing are helpful. Many of these systems have the ability to be deconstructed and their components reused or recycled, another environmental benefit. The IAQ-related components are wood-based materials, such as MDF for desktop substrates, panel and seating fabrics, plastic parts, and finishes and sealers. Novel new high-performance office systems are on the market with environmental benefits, such as biobased, salvaged, and recycled materials.

HVAC Systems

Careful material selection is key to healthful indoor air, but so is the thoughtful design of heating, ventilating, and air-conditioning (HVAC) systems. An efficient ventilation (mechanical or heat-recovery) system with high-performance filters and high exchange rates to replace old air, and efficiently sized fans to exhaust and supply air, can contribute to good IAQ. Examples of such design strategies include avoiding wood-burning fireplaces or retrofitting them with an EPA-certified insert. Other systems to consider are sealed-combustion furnaces and water heaters, as well as fans controlled by timers or temperature and humidity sensors that vent range hoods and bathroom fans to the outside.

General Information about Wet-Applied Interior Products

A note about wet-applied products, such as paints, coatings, carpet adhesives, wall-covering adhesives, countertop and stone adhesives, as well as tile-setting materials, such as grouts, joint sealants, caulks, and others: these materials' salient quality is their ability to negatively affect the indoor air quality and human health. The movement toward substituting more benign products to reduce VOC emissions contributes to the health of both the worker and occupant. Again, this is a reminder that materials selection must be an integrated process.

General rules of thumb:

- Look for water-based or low-VOC products.
- Find out if the adhesive or coating is applied in the factory in a controlled environment.
- Precondition (allow building materials to acclimate to thermal conditions similar to those of the installation site) the product off-site and unwrapped, so that it off-gasses.
- Look for alternative products such as floor finish and wax alternatives made from beeswax or biobased oils, for example.

Cleaning products contribute in a major way to VOC loads and other pollutant emissions in a regular, long-term pattern, often contributing much more chemical load than the material itself. New trends in environmentally benign cleaning products and equipment are entering the marketplace, and they are available to consumers and businesses, as well as for industrial janitorial applications.[15]

Question Everything!

Whether it is entering from outside, or already inside and emitting, a chemical compound or other contaminant can produce long-term chronic emissions. Remember that materials can have multiple attributes as well as negative impacts. Our goal is to tease out the green-washed negative impacts and gather the essence of a material's sustainable attributes. The reason this chapter goes into detail about materials research is that, in spite of all the ecolabeling and professional oversight, nothing pays more dividends than forging your own knowledge base. Accustom yourself to independently researching materials for their relevant impacts, because doing so will reinforce your skills and knowledge and have the benefit of educating materials manufacturers about future demands. This type of questioning can transform

---

[15]Green Cleaning Network, http://www.greencleaningnetwork.org; One Source Green Sweep, http://www.greencleaningnetwork.org; and Green Cleaning Certified, http://www.greencleancertified.com.

(a)

(b)

(c)

Figure 14-13 a–c Designers often look to labels and certifications such as FSC, C2C, and SCS to inform their materials selection.

the marketplace (Figure 14-13). The green movement may be perceived as a trend in the world at large, but as green building professionals, we must view this direction as an imperative.

EXERCISES

1. Think of three materials used in the buildings you inhabit daily that have drawbacks because of their distant manufacturing location. Of those, which have the potential to be locally sourced? What are some alternative materials that could have been used instead?

2. Select two interior glossy paints by two different manufacturers, one a zero- or low-VOC example and one a mainstream version. Compare labels for VOC content, Green Seal ratings, South Coast Air Quality Management District (SCAQMD, one of the standards cited by LEED) certification, and emissions compliance with California Section 01350. How easy was it to obtain emissions testing information? How knowledgeable were the product representatives? What were the performance ratings or expectations of each? Try the same with batt insulation, carpet, and linoleum versus mainstream resilient flooring. Present your findings to the class.

3. Create a materials questionnaire that incorporates life-cycle thinking and contact a materials manufacturer

to obtain data for your matrix. What would be the top five environmental attributes you would ask about for the particular product you chose?

◼ Resources

Bonda, Penny, and Katie Sosnowchik. 2006. *Sustainable Commercial Interiors*. Hoboken, NJ: John Wiley & Sons.

"Building Materials: What Makes a Product Green?" *Environmental Building News,* January 2000 (updated February 1, 2006), http://www.buildinggreen.com/ebn/sample/reprints.cfm.

Chemical Database Sites

Environmental Working Group Chemical Index, http://www.ewg.org/chemindex.

Scorecard, http://www.scorecard.org.

U.S. Environmental Protection Agency (EPA), Source Ranking Database, http://www.epa.gov/oppt/exposure/pubs/srd.htm.

U.S. National Library of Medicine Toxicology Data Network, TOXNET, http://toxnet.nlm.nih.gov.

CAS (Chemical Abstracts Services) lists the various names for chemical compounds and assigns them a number, http://www.cas.org/expertise/cascontent.

Kirsten Ritchie, "Sustainable Product Standards: Simplifying the Process of Specifying Green," "Part1: The Role of Voluntary Consensus Standards," August 2007; and "Part 2: The Role of Certification, Labeling, and Branding," September 2007, Greener Facilities, Stamats Business Media.

U.S. Environmental Protection Agency, Comprehensive Procurement Guidelines (CPG), http://www.epa.gov/cpg/.

International Council for Local Environmental Initiatives (ICLEI), EcoProcura Link Database, http://www.iclei.org/europe/economy/links.htm.

Energy Star, http://www.energystar.gov.

International Organization for Standardization (ISO), http://www.iso.org.

Green Materials Databases and Information Sources

Building Green's GreenSpec Directory, *Environmental Building News Product Directory*, 7th edition, Environmental Building News, 2007, is by far the most comprehensive green building product database, arranged in CSI order and providing model specification sections.

Another excellent source is the online City of Austin's (Texas) *Sourcebook for Green and Sustainable Building*, part of its Green Builder Program, originally, the Austin Green Building Program's (GBP) Sourcebook, Sustainable Sources, http://www.greenbuilder.com/sourcebook.

Other databases: Oikos Green Building Source (www.oikos.com), Healthy Building Network's Pharos Project Wiki (www.pharosproject.net/wiki), CIWMB Recycled Content Product Directory (http://www.ciwmb.ca.gov/rcp) (California Integrated Waste Management Board), Access Green by Build It Green (http://accessgreen.builditgreen.org), Green Home Guide (http://www.greenhomeguide.com), The Minnesota Building Materials Database (http://www.buildingmaterials.umn.edu), Ecolect (http://www.ecolect.net), Green Sage (http://www.greensage.com), Green Building Resource Guide (http://www.greenguide.com).

Scientific Certification Systems (SCS), with the Resilient Floor Covering Institute (RFCI), developed FloorScore, which tests hard-surface flooring and adhesives to meet California Section 01350 requirements, thus incorporating by reference the Chronic Reference Exposure Level (CREL) thresholds established by the OEHHA (Office of Environmental Health Hazard Assessment) described under the heading "What Is an Emissions Chamber Test?" Because this certification assumes that there will be other VOC-emitting products within an indoor space, the FloorScore emissions thresholds are half those of the referenced standard.

SCS *Indoor Advantage GOLD* is an IAQ certification for building products that meet the emission requirements of California Section 01350, in addition to BIFMA requirements (M7.1-2006-VOCs and X7.1-2006-formaldehyde) and the California DGS Indoor Air Quality Specifications for Open Panel Office Furniture.[16]

SCS *Indoor Advantage* is a certification for IAQ emissions for office furniture and seating that meet the requirements of ANSI BIFMA X7.1-2006.[17] Both SCS *Indoor Advantage* and SCS *Indoor Advantage Gold* can be applied to any product generally used within an enclosed indoor environment, such as furniture systems seating and components, hard-surface flooring, paint, wall coverings, casework, and insulation.

CRI *Green Label Plus* assesses IAQ emissions based on California's Section 01350 emissions-testing protocol.

Sustainable Carpet Assessment Standard, ANSI-certified NSF 140-2007, available for download at http://www.nsf.org/business/newsroom/pdf/Sustainability2.pdf.

GreenGuard Environmental Institute's GreenGuard for building materials, products, and systems assesses IAQ emissions based on two laboratory emissions-testing protocol, one of which is the CHPS/01350-based Kids and Schools.

Forest Stewardship Council (FSC) Certification assesses sustainable forestry practices from social and environmental perspectives. The FSC accredits certifiers such as SCS, SmartWood, Rainforest Alliance, and others, who in turn provide the certifications.

Green Seal is a voluntary, multiattribute certification for wet-applied products, but it also studies windows, fluorescent lamps, chillers, and occupancy sensors.

SCS *Sustainable Choice* is a transparent, multiattribute certification that includes both social and environmental factors.

MBDC's *Cradle to Cradle* (C2C) is a certification program using five categories to evaluate products based on the

---

[16]Scientific Certification Systems (SCS), Environmental Certification Program, Indoor Air Quality Performance, SCS–EC10.2–2007, http://www.scscertified.com/ecoproducts/PDFS/SCS-EC10.2-2007.pdf.
[17]Ibid.

"cradle-to-cradle" manufacturing philosophy of McDonough and Braungart.

Market Transformation to Sustainability (MTS), *Sustainable Materials Rating Technology* (SMaRT) poses Consensus Sustainable Product Standards to examine building products, fabric, apparel, textiles, and flooring, using an environmental, social, and economic lens.

GreenBlue is a "clean" certification and member of *CleanGredients,* which helps companies find less impactful chemicals for their green formulations. The chemicals themselves have been third-party verified.

Business and Institutional Furniture Manufacturer's Association *(BIFMA) Sustainability Standard* studies materials, energy and atmosphere, human and ecosystem health, and social responsibility under three certification levels: silver, gold, and platinum.

The *Global Eco-Labeling Network* (GEN) is an international nonprofit organization of third-party environmental-performance labeling organizations that promotes the credibility of ecolabeling programs and publicizes their functions.

15 Water Quality and Water Conservation
Kevin Conger and Jamie Phillips, CMG Landscape Architecture

■ Natural Systems and the Shift to Urban Environments

Before our cities developed into thriving metropolises, this continent consisted of a diverse range of habitats, including hardwood forests, native grasslands, riparian corridors, wetlands, and bogs. Streams and lakes conveyed rainwater. Wetlands lined the ocean edge and functioned as natural filtering systems and as buffers from major storms. Rainwater infiltrated into the soil, replenishing groundwater supplies and contributing to stream-base flow.

The Urban Watershed: Watershed Function

Urban areas throughout the country developed in similar ways, progressing from transportation hubs and agricultural hamlets to thriving metropolises. Little by little, throughout this time of development, natural water systems were slowly shifted and rerouted to create developable land. Eventually, urban areas were covered by impervious surfaces such as buildings, streets, and parking lots, preventing rainfall infiltration. Wetlands were diked and filled for farmland and building sites. Streams were diverted or confined within levees to irrigate farms and eventually buried in pipes. The pipes carried storm-water runoff from urban neighborhoods directly into streams or oceans. Instead of percolating into soils, storm-water runoff traveled over impervious surfaces, mobilized pollutants like oil and debris, and washed them into the sewer system and natural water bodies—streams, lakes, bays, and the oceans (Figure 15-2).

Impervious surfaces changed the time and intensity of stream flows during rain events, and a chain of unanticipated consequences were triggered. These consequences

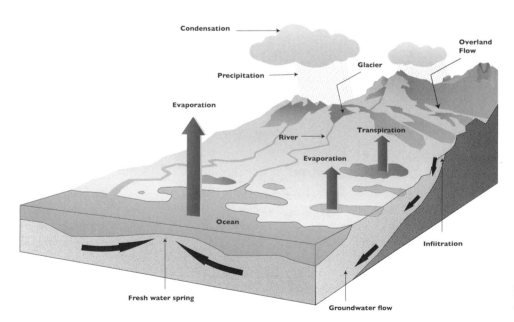

Figure 15-1 A water- or hydrologic-cycle diagram.

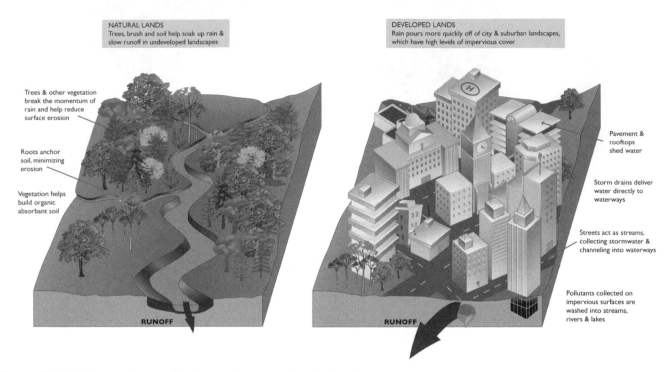

NATURAL LANDS
Trees, brush and soil help soak up rain &
slow runoff in undeveloped landscapes

Trees & other vegetation
break the momentum of
rain and help reduce
surface erosion

Roots anchor
soil, minimizing
erosion

Vegetation helps
build organic
absorbant soil

RUNOFF

DEVELOPED LANDS
Rain pours more quickly off of city & suburban landscapes,
which have high levels of impervious cover

Pavement &
rooftops
shed water

Storm drains deliver
water directly to
waterways

Streets act as streams,
collecting stormwater &
channeling into waterways

Pollutants collected on
impervious surfaces are
washed into streams,
rivers & lakes

RUNOFF

Figure 15-2 A diagram showing development from natural to developed state.

include more frequent and localized flooding, destabilized stream banks, loss of stream-side trees and vegetation, the continued destruction of water-dependent habitat, and the degradation of water quality in the oceans. Of utmost importance, the decrease in infiltration resulting from paved surfaces depletes groundwater recharge.

Once altered, the natural water systems and their habitats and particular ecosystems cannot be fully restored. However, these adverse effects can be reversed through strategies that promote the use of ecological and natural systems for the management of storm-water quality and volume. With every site plan contributing incremental changes, designers can work toward restoring natural hydrologic function in the urban watersheds. While this is an enormous, long-term effort, and managing runoff from a single development site may seem inconsequential, by changing the way most sites are developed we will be able to protect water quality and preserve natural ecosystems in our urban and urbanizing areas.

National Water Policy

In 1972 Congress passed the Clean Water Act (CWA) to regulate the discharge of pollutants to receiving waters such as oceans, bays, rivers, lakes, and streams. The CWA establishes the foundation for storm-water regulation across the country. State, regional, and municipal laws and policies under the CWA help to ensure that storm-water requirements are appropriate to a city's geography, climate, and development patterns.

Storm-water runoff, now recognized by the U.S. Environmental Protection Agency (EPA) as a leading contributor to water quality degradation in the United States, was unregulated until 1987, when section 402(p) was added to the CWA. Section 402(p) established a two-phase plan to regulate polluted storm-water runoff under the National Pollution Discharge Elimination System (NPDES).

Since the 1987 amendment, designers are required to minimize the amount of sediment and other pollutants that enter site runoff during construction, to design projects that minimize new impervious areas, and to incorporate into their plans facilities that detain, retain, or treat storm-water runoff for the life of the project.

As technology and design innovation improve, low-impact design (LID) and storm-water treatment best management practices (BMPs) become more effective and are used more consistently throughout site planning and design projects.

Pollutants of Concern

As mentioned above, when storm water travels across impervious surfaces, it mobilizes the pollutants resting there, carrying those pollutants in concentrated levels to natural water systems, which causes severe degradation in natural water systems and wildlife habitat.

To that end, it is important to understand the types of pollutants found in storm water, their general sources, and ways to remove them from storm water before they

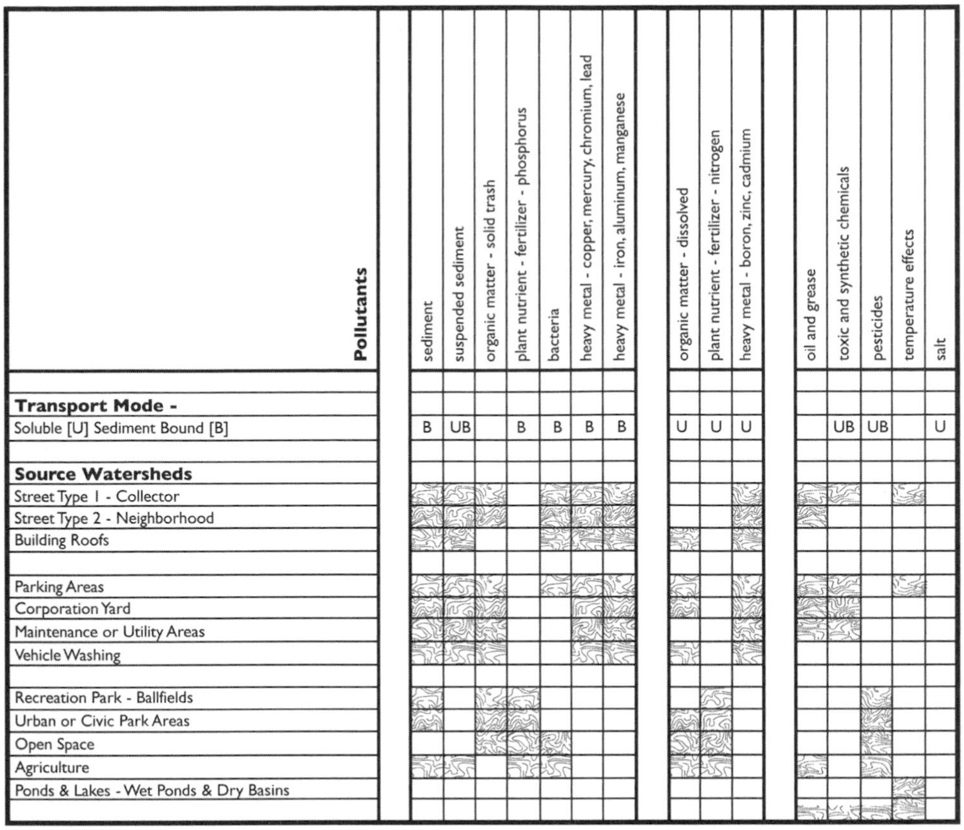

Pollutants	sediment	suspended sediment	organic matter - solid trash	plant nutrient - fertilizer - phosphorus	bacteria	heavy metal - copper, mercury, chromium, lead	heavy metal - iron, aluminum, manganese	organic matter - dissolved	plant nutrient - fertilizer - nitrogen	heavy metal - boron, zinc, cadmium	oil and grease	toxic and synthetic chemicals	pesticides	temperature effects	salt
Transport Mode -															
Soluble [U] Sediment Bound [B]	B	UB		B	B	B	B	U	U	U		UB	UB		U
Source Watersheds															
Street Type 1 - Collector															
Street Type 2 - Neighborhood															
Building Roofs															
Parking Areas															
Corporation Yard															
Maintenance or Utility Areas															
Vehicle Washing															
Recreation Park - Ballfields															
Urban or Civic Park Areas															
Open Space															
Agriculture															
Ponds & Lakes - Wet Ponds & Dry Basins															

Figure 15-3 A chart showing pollutants and their sources.

enter natural systems. The following section describes common pollutants found in storm water from urban and developed areas.

Flowing runoff dislodges pollutants or dissolves certain pollutants and carries them in its flow. Once pollutants are exposed to runoff, they are transported in two ways: the dissolved or soluble phase and the sediment bound or solid phase (Figure 15-3).

Soluble pollutants, those that are dissolved in water, are carried within the runoff water by a weak attraction to water molecules. These pollutants are very mobile, because they essentially become part of the runoff water and flow where the water flows. Generally, soluble pollutants can be removed only by chemical treatment or through biological uptake by plants or soil organisms. Biological uptake occurs when there is extended contact between storm water and vegetation or soil microorganisms.

Pollutants transported in the sediment-bound—or solid phase—are either attached to or are part of soil or dust particles, organic matter, or are solids themselves. For example, a metal such as iron can be transported while attached to soil particles or it can be transported as individual granular particles. The mobility of sediment-bound pollutants depends on the transport of the sediment particles.

Sediment particles themselves have two methods of transport. Smaller sediment particles are held up or "suspended" in water and seen as cloudy or muddy water. Larger sediment particles roll or hop along the land surfaces or stream bottoms from the force of the moving water. Thus, sediment-bound pollutants may be either up in the water with the small, suspended particles or in the bottom sediment with the larger particles.

Sediment

Sediment may come from soil erosion on bare areas or unstabilized construction sites, or it may come from impervious surfaces in developed areas where soil particles are deposited by traffic and wind. All land areas will contribute some sediment, but unprotected or disturbed areas can contribute huge amounts of sediment from relatively small areas. Any particles of dirt and dust on the ground—or lying on a road, roof, or parking lot—will wash off during a storm and become sediment in storm water. Industrial air emissions of dust, particulates, and even smoke become sediment in storm water. Sediment poses a double threat to water quality. It is a pollutant, and it also carries other pollutants with it. Often, the sediment-bound pollutants are more harmful to water quality than the sediment itself.

Organic Matter

Organic matter refers to natural materials such as leaves, sticks, grass clippings, and animal wastes and to human-made materials such as paper, garbage, and other trash that finds its way into storm-water runoff. Organic matter also includes dissolved substances from tree leaves, paper, or plastic wastes. Most organic matter occurs in the form of large solid pieces that quickly settle out of the runoff, but the dissolved substances present a more serious problem. These dissolved substances serve as food for bacteria and other organisms, which not only multiply but also consume oxygen, harming local wildlife. If this consumption reduces the oxygen to very low levels, the water may become foul, producing strong odors, and the number and mixture of aquatic species will change.

Bacteria

Urban areas have large populations of pets, generate much garbage and other wastes, and have significant numbers of native animals such as pigeons, sea gulls, squirrels, and mice, all of which contribute bacteria to storm-water runoff. Leaking sewers and sewer overflows, which occur more frequently in older urban areas, are especially strong sources of bacteria. Tending to attach to soil particles and settle out of the water, bacteria accumulates in deposited sediments, presenting a threat to health and safety if the sediments are stirred up.

Heavy Metals

Some of the metals found in storm-water runoff include the following:

- Copper, mercury, chromium, and lead
- Iron, aluminum, and manganese
- Boron, zinc, and cadmium

Metals in storm water come from automobile emissions, weathering paints, wood preservatives, motor oils, and industrial and commercial spills and releases. Other sources include natural minerals in rocks, soil, road salt, and vegetation. Zinc found in runoff comes from metal roofs and gutters. Metals in storm water are toxic to many forms of life and, in extreme situations, can contaminate public water supplies. Since metals can accumulate in aquatic animals, toxic amounts can move up the food chain, eventually affecting humans who consume fish or shellfish with high levels of accumulated metals. The metals of most concern in storm water are lead, copper, cadmium, chromium, and zinc. However, many other metals have been identified in storm water.

Toxic and Synthetic Chemicals: Pesticides

A wide range of toxic and synthetic chemicals can be found in storm water, mainly from manufactured products that have had chemicals leached from them, from industrial processes, and from fossil-fuel combustion and lubricating oils. Heavily used highways have shown high concentrations of synthetic chemicals, mainly combustion products. Pesticides used for controlling nuisance vegetation and animal pests may be picked up by storm-water runoff. Many of the synthetic chemicals exhibit toxic effects on various aquatic plants and animals. As with the metals, some synthetic and toxic chemicals bind with sediment and will settle out of the water. Although these chemicals may be tied up in the sediment for long periods, they can be redissolved in the water if the chemical and biological conditions change. Many of the chemicals can accumulate in the food chain, possibly threatening aquatic life, fish, and food for humans.

Oil and Grease

Oil and grease in runoff show up as rainbow-colored slicks or sheens on puddles and streams. Oil and other lubricating agents leak from vehicles and are washed during rainstorms from roads, parking lots, and any areas of intense automobile use. Fuel spills and improper storage of fuel contribute to storm-water pollution. Most of the oil and grease binds to sediment, eventually settling to the bottom of water bodies. There, the oil and grease concentrate and can adversely affect the organisms that live in the bottom sediments.

Plant Nutrients: Fertilizer and Phosphorous

Common plant nutrients include nitrogen and phosphorus compounds, which are chemicals found in commercial fertilizers and animal manures that promote and sustain desirable plant growth. However, when these same nutrients reach water bodies, they can cause undesirable growth of algae, bacteria, and plants, creating nuisance algae blooms and overgrowth of bacteria and plants in the water. Since only small amounts of nutrients are required for accelerated growth of algae and plants, controlling the amount of nutrients entering storm water is very important to protect receiving waters. Nutrients enter storm water from a variety of sources, including runoff from fertilized lawns and gardens, agricultural fields, leaks from sanitary sewers, and wastewater from septic tank systems. Intensely landscaped areas, such as golf courses and industrial and commercial parks, can contribute large amounts of nutrients to storm water. Excess plant nutrients in water cause a process called eutrophication, which occurs as plant nutrients accumulate in a water body, causing increasingly heavier growths of plants and algae and reducing the amount of oxygen in the water available to fish and other animals. As eutrophication progresses, water bodies can experience algal scums and blooms, cloudy and discolored water, strong odors, and fish kills, and disagreeable tastes and odors can arise in drinking water. Although eutrophication occurs naturally at a slow rate, it is greatly accelerated by storm-water pollutants.

Urban Storm-Water Management: Low-Impact Design

Ecologically and natural-based systems can be integrated with infrastructure, architecture, and landscape architectural design to lessen the impacts of urbanization on water quality and to remove pollutants from storm water. Water quality protection measures are combined with efforts to improve public space, create and enhance wildlife habitat, articulate natural systems in urban environments, and create planted and tree-lined streets. This multipurpose design concept is called low-impact design (LID); LID emphasizes integration of storm-water management with urban planning and design and promotes a comprehensive, watershed-based approach to storm-water management. Low-impact design can be integrated into any development type, from public open spaces and recreational areas to high-density housing and industrial areas. It aims to mimic predevelopment drainage patterns and hydrologic processes. The most effective application of LID is a comprehensive approach that includes site design, source controls, and treatment controls (described below).

Site Design: Primary Goals

Careful site design can minimize the impacts of storm-water runoff from the outset. The more that storm-water management is integrated into each step of the design process, the easier it is to create a successful and multipurpose storm-water management strategy for a given site. Integrating storm-water management into the design process from the outset minimizes the impact of storm-water runoff. Integrating the management of storm water into site design for a given site maximizes the potential for successful storm-water control.

Preservation and Protection of Creeks, Wetlands, and Existing Vegetation

In addition to enhancing the natural beauty of an area, creeks, wetlands, and existing vegetation provide natural drainage features, collect storm water, filter runoff, and recharge groundwater. These features define and enhance the quality of a site and inherently convey and treat storm water. Vegetation naturally manages storm water, because foliage captures rainwater, thereby slowing its progress and facilitating its infiltration into the soil.

Preservation of Natural Drainage Patterns and Topography to Inform Site Design

Through careful analysis of a site's drainage patterns and topography, existing drainage networks can be used as a framework around which to organize development. Changing the topography of a site through grading significantly increases the chances of diminishing water quality by delivering sediment to receiving waters.

Minimize and Disconnect Impervious Surfaces

Land hardened by such structures as houses, patios, driveways, and transportation infrastructure are referred to as impervious surfaces. To control the volume of storm water, it is best to minimize such surfaces and to disconnect them. This allows designers to treat smaller quantities of runoff from multiple areas on a site, rather than treating larger and more polluted amounts of storm water from an entire area. Concentrations of pollutants are decreased when impervious surfaces are disconnected. Furthermore, disconnection facilitates strategic treatment of storm water and reduces its flow.

Strategically Channel the Storm-Water-Flow Path from First Contact to Discharge Point

Storm-water conveyance systems define the travel of storm water from initial surface contact, where the transition from rain to storm water takes place, to the final destination or discharge point, after decontamination treatments have occurred.

Consideration of Storm Water as a Resource, Not a Waste Product

Traditional storm-water management viewed storm water as a nuisance, as something to be eliminated as quickly as possible. Today, we realize that it is actually an underutilized resource that can reduce the demand on the potable water supply. Storm water provides a valuable supply of water for nonpotable purposes, including irrigation, toilet flushing, and cooling towers.

Treat Storm Water at Its Source

Storm-water treatments are most effective when the various physical, biological, and chemical processes that remove pollutants are aimed at removing one pollutant at a time. The principles that underlie storm-water treatment technologies suggest that treating storm-water pollutants at their source through the use wet ponds, swales, porous pavements, and filters reduces not only the cost of treatment but also the potential that multiple pollutants will have to be addressed later on.

Treatment Trains Used to Remedy a Wider Scope of Pollutants

Treatment train, a term coined by Horner and Skupien in 1994, refers to a series of separate storm-water treatment techniques or devices.[1] Because complete storm-water treatment cannot always be attained through the use of a single best management practice, it is often necessary to

---

[1]Horner, R.R., J.J. Skupien, E.H. Livingston and H.E. Shaver. August 1994. *Fundamentals of Urban Runoff Management: Technical and Institutional Issues*. Terrene Institute, Washington, DC, in cooperation with U.S. Environmental Protection Agency.

devise a series of treatments to remove pollutants. Each unit in a treatment train is designed to remove specific pollutants, and generally the train is designed to remove larger pollutants, like big pieces of trash, first and finer pollutants, such as suspended solids and chemicals, further down the train.

Source Controls

Management measures that deter pollutants from contaminating rainwater are called source controls. In addition to implementing LID practices during the site design process, designers should identify the places when storm-water pollution starts and use source controls to prevent or minimize the impact. Using nonchemical pesticides and green roofs are examples of source controls that prevent runoff from picking up chemicals or pollutants from roof contact. Source controls may further reduce runoff from impervious surfaces on rooftops, driveways, parking lots, and roads. Management of water balance through the reduction of runoff volume is the chief purpose of source control.

Site-design strategies and source-control measures minimize the quantity and improve the quality of storm-water runoff from a site. However, it is impossible to eliminate all surfaces that will contribute runoff. Treatment controls must therefore be implemented to accommodate the remaining runoff from the site. Treatment controls are permanent storm-water BMPs, such as vegetated swales or flow-through planters designed to receive and treat runoff from the site. Treatment-control best management practices are typically designed to accomplish one or more of the following six storm-water treatment strategies: infiltration, detention, biofiltration, harvesting or retention, bioretention, or conveyance. Each of these treatment strategies is described below (Figure 15-4).

Treatment Control BMPs

Infiltration

Taking storm water to a holding place and then allowing it to slowly infiltrate through the soil removes pollutants. Soil collects pollutant particles from water in much the same way an air filter collects dust particles from the air. Some pollutants chemically attach to soil particles. Other pollutants are changed by biological uptake of soil microorganisms. In order to use the infiltration treatment types, it is necessary to have site soil with moderate permeability rates. Soils with very high infiltration rates will release the storm water directly into groundwater without having time to filter pollutants, and soil with very low infiltration rates will not filter the water at all.

- *Infiltration basin:* An infiltration basin is a shallow holding area that is designed to infiltrate storm water and to use the natural filtering ability of the soil to remove pollutants in storm-water runoff. Infiltration facilities store runoff until it gradually filters through the soil and eventually into the water table. This

Sediment Bound Pollutants	sediment	suspended sediment	organic matter - solid trash	plant nutrient - fertilizer - phosphorus	bacteria	heavy metal - copper, mercury, chromium, lead	heavy metal - iron, aluminum, manganese	Soluble Pollutants	organic matter - dissolved	plant nutrient - fertilizer - nitrogen	heavy metal - boron, zinc, cadmium	Complex pollutant treatments	oil and grease	toxic and synthetic chemicals	pesticides	temperature effects	salt	Pollutants
																		Transport Mode -
																		Soluble [U] or Sediment Bound [B]
	B	UB		B	B	B	B		U	U	U			UB	UB		U	
																		Treatment types
	■	■	■	■	■	■	■		■	■	■		■	■	■		■	Good Housekeeping at Source
	■	■		■	■	■	■		■	■	■			■	■			Infiltration Trench
	■	■		■	■	■	■		■	■	■			■	■			Infiltration Basin
						■	■				■							Pervious/Porous Pavements
	■	■		■	■	■	■		■	■	■		■	■	■			Biofilter
	■	■		■	■					■				■	■			Vegetated Swale
	■	■		■	■	■	■		■	■	■		■	■	■			Bioretention
	■	■		■	■	■	■		■		■			■	■			Wet Pond
	■	■		■	■	■	■		■	■	■		■	■	■			Constructed Wetlands
	■	■		■	■	■	■		■					■	■			Extended Detention Basin
																■		Shade Ponds

Figure 15-4 Similar to Figure 15-3, this chart describes pollutants and treatment methods to remove them from storm water before they enter natural systems.

practice has high pollutant removal efficiency and also recharges groundwater.

- *Infiltration trench:* An infiltration trench is a long, narrow, rock-filled trench with no outlet that receives storm-water runoff. Runoff is stored temporarily in the void space between the stones and infiltrates through the bottom, into the native soil.
- *Subgrade direct infiltration areas:* Subgrade direct infiltration areas are the same as infiltration trenches, but they are placed below grade, underneath plazas, streets, or sidewalks. Storm water can be piped to the subgrade infiltration areas or allowed to infiltrate directly through permeable paving sections.
- *Permeable paving:* Permeable paving systems allow a portion of rainwater to infiltrate through the paving rather than running across it and being picked up further down the line.

Depending on site and design considerations, it is useful to implement these infiltration techniques in conjunction with one another—for example, permeable modular paving over subgrade direct infiltration areas (Figures 15-5 and 15-6).

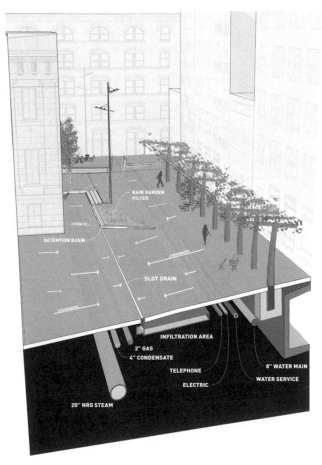

Figure 15-5 Storm-water is filtered through soil and vegetative uptake. This diagram illustrates the biofilter used at San Francisco's Mint Plaza, an outdoor public space and arts venue.

Biofiltration

Similar to soil-infiltration techniques, with biofiltration storm water is filtered through plants to remove pollutants. Adding biomass or living plants to the filtration equation increases the ability to remove pollutants from water by creating complexity and increasing the quantity of microorganisms present in soil and plants to act as filters.

Vegetated swale and flow-through planters. Vegetated swales are open, shallow channels, with plants covering the side slopes and bottom, that collect and slowly convey runoff flow to downstream discharge points. They are designed to treat runoff through filtering by the vegetation in the channel, filtering through a designed subsoil matrix, and/or infiltration into the underlying existing soils. They trap particulate pollutants, promote infiltration, and reduce the flow velocity of storm-water runoff. Vegetated swales are part of a storm-water drainage system and can replace curbs, gutters, and storm-sewer systems (Figure 15-7).

Flow-through planters operate in the same way as vegetated swales, but they tend to be built in space-constricted urban environments. The sides may have built curbs or walls to integrate with the site design, but the filtering process occurs the same way.

Rain gardens. Rain gardens are depressed landscape areas designed to capture and infiltrate storm-water runoff. Rain gardens include wet-tolerant plants in permeable soils with high organic content that absorb storm water and transpire it back into the atmosphere. Rain gardens are similar to bioretention except that they do not typically include engineered soils or an underdrain connection, and they are more appropriate for residential landscaping or low impervious areas with well-draining soils. The shallow depression fills with a few inches of water during a rain event. Vegetation assists with the uptake of pollutants and the absorption.

Bioretention. The bioretention treatment type functions as a soil- and plant-based filtration device that removes pollutants through a variety of physical, biological,

Figure 15-6

and chemical treatment processes. These facilities normally consist of several techniques layered together, including a vegetated swale, sand bed, pond area, organic or mulch layer, planting soil, and plants. The storm-water runoff's velocity is reduced by passing the vegetated swale and subsequently distributed evenly along a ponding area. Filtration of the stored water in the bioretention area's soil and into the underlying soils occurs over a period of days. It is important to provide adequate contact time between the plant and soil surfaces and the pollutant for the removal process to occur. Because of the layered complexity of the bioretention system, it is considered very effective in storm-water pollutant removal.

Figure 15-7 Vegetated swale and flow-through planters filter storm water through vegetation and subsoil.

Detention and Settling

A high level of sediment can be reduced by allowing it to settle in dry detention basins or wet retention ponds with extended holding times. Longer holding times are especially important, because a longer holding time means more sediment and finer sediment particles will be removed.

Wet ponds. Wet ponds—also known as storm-water ponds, retention ponds, and wet extended-detention ponds—are constructed basins that have a permanent pool of water throughout the year and an average depth of 4 to 6 feet. Ponds treat incoming storm-water runoff by settling and biological uptake. The primary removal mechanism is settling as storm-water runoff resides in this pool, but pollutant uptake also occurs through biological activity in the pond. Wet ponds are among the most widely used storm-water practices. While there are several different versions of the wet pond design, the most common being the extended-detention wet pond, where storage is provided above the permanent pool in order to detain storm-water runoff and promote settling (Figure 15-8).

Constructed wetlands. These constructed wetlands are constructed basins that have a permanent pool of water that is wide and shallow, with an average depth of 18 inches, a high degree of vegetation coverage, and some areas of open water. Wetlands are among the most effective storm-water practices in terms of pollutant removal. As storm-water runoff flows through the wetland, pollutant removal is achieved through settling and biological uptake within the wetland. Flow through the root systems allows the vegetation to remove dissolved pollutants from the storm water (Figure 15-9).

Dry extended-detention ponds. Dry extended-detention ponds—also known as dry ponds, extended-detention basins, detention ponds, and extended-detention

Figure 15-8 Wet ponds, also known as storm-water ponds, retention ponds, and wet extended detention ponds, are constructed basins that have a permanent pool of water throughout the year. Ponds treat incoming storm-water runoff by settling and biological uptake.

Figure 15-9 Constructed wetlands: Wetlands provide the highest habitat value of all of the best management practices, providing the highest level of storm-water polishing.

(a)

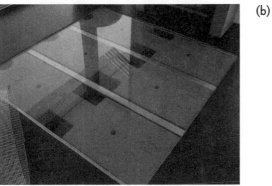

(b)

Figure 15-10 a, b An ingenious water catchment-and-storage modular system from Australia, Rainwater HOG.

ponds—are basins whose outlets have been designed to detain storm-water runoff for some minimum time (e.g., 48 hours) to allow particles and associated pollutants to settle. Unlike wet ponds, these facilities do not have a large permanent pool.

Rainwater Harvesting

The counterpart to water quality is water quantity. If we conserve water in our daily habits, there is that much less water to clean and treat before it reenters our natural systems (Figures 15-10 a and b).

An effective way to conserve water for nonpotable purposes is through the use of a cistern or constellation of cisterns. Cisterns—or containers usually used to catch and hold water—may be small, a gallon or two, or much larger. Some underground cisterns hold tens of thousands of gallons of water. While underground cisterns are common, they may also be found at or above ground level, where the force of gravity may be employed for water reuse. Used since Greek and Roman times, cisterns are especially effective in the management of storm water. Small cisterns may be used for single homes, and larger cisterns may be utilized for service to an entire community or residential area. Cisterns may be equipped with pumps for nonpotable uses such as irrigation or toilet flushing, and all must be outfitted with screens to prevent clogging and to prevent them from becoming an insect breeding ground. Additionally, they need access to light to inhibit algae growth. Cisterns of today are much more sophisticated than those used during ancient times. While most commonly used for irrigation, cisterns can also be constructed with filters and water purification systems when the water is to be consumed.

Another way to improve water quality is through the use of green roofs. Also referred to as eco-roofs, vegetated roofs, and living roofs, green roofs incorporate vegetation and soil over part or all of a roof's surface.

Compared with solid surface or traditional rooftop materials, green roofs have numerous environmental benefits, including a cooler temperature and the filtration of contaminants through the vegetation from runoff water, which improves water quality. Green roofs are especially beneficial as a means of reducing concentrations of copper, zinc, and polycyclic aromatic hydrocarbons (PAHs). Additionally, green roofs reduce the volume of runoff from storm water through engineered soil absorption. Numerous studies show that green roofs absorb 75 percent of water from rain events of one-half inch or less. Through root uptake and soil absorption, many pollutants from rainwater are filtered out. The benefits of green roofs increase as the vegetation matures over time (Figure 15-11).

A combination of BMPs, constructed in a series to target specific pollutants, is called a treatment train. Treatment trains not only improve water quality, they also improve the long-term efficiency and reduce the maintenance requirements for each treatment BMP involved in the train. In the same way that prerinsing dirty dishes increases the efficiency of a dishwasher, removing sediment prior to infiltration of storm water will improve the long-term capacity of the underlying soils to infiltrate water by preventing sediment from clogging pore spaces

Figure 15-11 Green roofs filter contaminants through the vegetation from runoff water therefore improving water quality.

that allow the movement of water through the soil. Common treatment train configurations include:

- Silt trap—swale—wetland
- Cistern—rain garden
- Flow-through planter—infiltration trench
- Eco Roof—vegetated swale

Water Conservation in the Landscape

Designing the water-efficient, sustainable landscape planting design is extremely important. Planting design is particular to its region. Local climate, local soil conditions. and local amounts of rainwater all inform planting design. A planting design is generally sustainable if it is related to the given conditions of its place. Water efficiency depends both on the amount of rainfall in a given year and the types of plant communities desired in a project's design. Typically, it is best to use plant species either native to or adapted to your local climate and wildlife habitats. Using nonnative species that may grow in your region, but that behave in an aggressive manner and outcompete plants native to your local ecosystem, has proven to be detrimental to native wildlife habitats. For example, certain species of honeybees have adapted to gathering nectar from certain types of native plants; if those are outcompeted by nonnative plants, then the honeybee may move to another region, or it may become extinct. Vegetation is the backbone of wildlife habitat, creating consequences far up the species chain.

In California, with its multiple local microclimates, low yearly rainfall, and specifically adapted plant and animals species, planting design hinges around the local context of the site and water use. (Native systems could enhance or possibly be harmed by planting invasive species.) If you choose plants in response to the site conditions, the new plantings will probably become established easily. There will be no need for the special fertilizing, pest control, and heavy irrigation that have become common practice. The plants grow easily

because they are adapted to the place. This practice may reduce the amount of water used for irrigation.

At a large scale, many cities have created reclaimed water systems for irrigation. Reclaimed water is water from the wastewater treatment plant that has been treated to levels appropriate for nonpotable reuse. Using reclaimed water is part of a large-scale balancing act. The energy used to clean and transport the reclaimed water should be balanced against the amount of water needed for irrigation at all. For small-scale irrigation, cisterns can be used to trap water from the building's roof and reuse it for local irrigation.

With all the natural treatment types used to treat storm water through biological processes, planting the correct plant species is very important to their success. As in any planting design, understanding the goals of the development program and the long-term maintenance regime informs the design. The planting design will relate to the local soil and infiltration rates, the amount of time the water will be held near the plants, and the local climate and planting zone.

Plants that grow very quickly are very effective for pollutant removal, because as they grow they uptake pollutants into their biomass, and the faster they grow, the more pollutants will be removed. This is called phytoremediation. Many typical wetland plant species grow very quickly and are very effective in pollutant removal. Wetland plants are often used in biofiltration planting design. This is appropriate if the infiltration soils drain slowly and moderately; however, depending on the amount of local rainfall, it is easy to get caught between irrigating the high water use wetland plants in high infiltrating soils. Therefore, planting design for biofiltration areas is very specific to locale.

Integral to localized and native planting design, drought tolerance, and local water usage is appropriate species pest control. Common practice involves chemical pesticides to kill pests. These chemicals make their way into storm water and must be removed before the storm water reenters natural systems. The chemicals found in pesticides are both sediment-bound chemicals and water-soluble chemicals requiring multiple treatment types to remove them from water. For this reason, integrated pest management (IPM) is being researched and implemented. An ecological approach to suppressing pests, IPM utilizes information on the life cycle of pests, along with low-risk pest control techniques, to keep pests at acceptable levels in an environmentally safe way. Because pest problems are often symptomatic of ecological imbalances, the goal is to plan and manage ecosystems to prevent organisms from becoming pests in the first place. This means developing landscape plans that focus on the use of native or plant species suited to a particular climate and local soil conditions. Integrated pest management guidelines help to reduce or eliminate the use of chemical pesticides, thereby reducing the risk that storm-water runoff will mobilize pesticides and carry them to natural water systems.

16 Sustainable Neighborhoods and Communities

Matt Raimi, Aaron Welch, and Sarah Pulleyblank Patrick, Raimi + Associates

What Are Sustainable Communities?

Much of this book has focused on aspects of sustainability centered on building design and construction. What has not been discussed in detail is how characteristics external to a building—streets, land-use patterns, transportation systems, and regional settlement patterns—affect sustainability. These topics are the subject of this chapter. While these topics are typically the purview of city planners, transportation planners, or urban designers, they provide the context for building-level design. Integrating buildings within a larger neighborhood, citywide, and regional sustainability framework is crucial to comprehensive sustainable development and the successful practice of sustainable architecture.

A sustainable community can be defined as a city, town, or neighborhood that is built in such a way (and uses its resources so) that it meets the needs of the present without compromising the ability of future generations to meet their own needs.[1] As mentioned elsewhere in this book, sustainable development has been described as the integration of "the three Es"—*environment*, *economy*, and *equity*. A sustainable community adopts and pursues policies to address all three of these pillars of sustainability.

Evidence of the need for sustainable communities abounds. According to the Global Footprint Network, humans surpassed the world's ecological carrying capacity sometime in the late 1980s. Humanity's current ecological footprint is higher than it has ever been. This means that humans currently require the resource-equivalent of about 1.2 planets to provide their food, timber, and fiber and to absorb their waste and emissions.

By exceeding global ecological carrying capacity,[2] humans are depleting the planet's ecological capital, as evidenced by various forms of ecological degradation, including climate change.[3] In this context, local policies for conservation of energy and resource use are of global importance and will be increasingly relevant and valuable in the long-term planning horizon.

In an increasingly interconnected and globalized world, local environmental challenges—such as air and water quality, waste management, and weather-related emergencies—are often affected by forces beyond the reach of local government, such as global weather systems and national or international consumption patterns. At the same time, local decisions about land use, transportation, or building design can have regional or even global impacts, such as through climate change, decreased regional air quality, or global resource depletion.

Further evidence on the need for sustainable communities is presented by the Intergovernmental Panel on Climate Change (IPCC) in its report titled *Climate Change 2007: Synthesis Report*. The report states that the warming of the climate system is unequivocal and most of the observed increase in global average temperatures since the mid-twentieth century is very likely due to the observed increase in greenhouse gas concentrations generated by humans. The report links these increases in global temperature to a host of impacts from species extinction to an increasing burden from malnutrition and cardiorespiratory and infectious diseases. The IPCC—which received the Nobel Peace Prize in 2007 for its work—asserts that making development patterns (more specifically, land-use

---

[1] Paraphrased from the Brundtland Commission definition of sustainability. United Nations, "Report of the World Commission on Environment and Development," General Assembly Resolution 42/187, December 11, 1987.

[2] Global Footprint Network: http://www.footprintnetwork.org/gfn_sub.php?content=global_footprint.

[3] Intergovernmental Panel on Climate Change (IPCC), *Climate Change 2007: Synthesis Report. Contribution of Working Groups I, II and III to the Fourth Assessment Report of the Intergovernmental Panel on Climate Change,* eds. R. K. Pachauri and A. Reisinger (Geneva, Switzerland: IPCC, 2007).

and transportation decisions) more sustainable can help to mitigate and reduce the vulnerability of communities to the consequences of climate change.[4]

Cities can address environmental challenges by implementing sustainable development policies specifically focused on the three Es of sustainability. Environmental degradation can be mitigated by creating land-use and transportation patterns that minimize the need to use the automobile, reduce energy and resource consumption, and incorporate practices to protect local ecological resources such as waterways, plants, and animal life.

Cities can also help to create sustainable economies that conserve the earth's resource base indefinitely, while providing an adequate standard of living for all. A community with a sustainable economy provides jobs, housing, education, and other services for its entire population while limiting consumption of the natural resources. Economic sustainability is also achieved by creating a dynamic, diverse, and resilient commercial and industrial sector that can provide jobs and income for the residents and government. Sustainable communities also promote equity between generations and among different groups in society. They recognize the necessity of equality and fairness and reduce disparities in risks and access to benefits between groups.[5]

As noted throughout this book, integrated design creates a *whole* that is greater than the sum of its parts. While sustainable component parts, such as green buildings, may be positive in themselves, creating a sustainable community requires planning and design at the city and regional level, not just the building level. City policies should address issues including building location, urban design, transportation, regional settlement patterns, community health, and even social sustainability. Supporting sustainable architecture with smart planning and urban design is essential to a fully sustainable built environment.

This chapter presents an overview of planning as it relates to sustainable communities and discusses the characteristics of sustainable communities, including the location of development, urban design, environmental siting, and green technology. It also provides an overview of the common land-use tools used by local governments that can be modified to implement sustainability principles.

■ A Brief History of Planning as It Relates to Sustainability

Interest in developing sustainable communities has arisen in the last couple of decades in response to growing concerns about environmental degradation and a growing

awareness among policy makers and citizen groups that communities built with a single purpose—such as a bedroom community or office park—are not economically, socially, or environmentally viable over the long term. In recent years, research has provided strong evidence to support these concerns.

Consequences of Sprawling Development Patterns

There are significant environmental consequences of the conventional development pattern. Global climate change is a serious threat to our nation's security and prosperity. Chemicals in the environment—from, most notably, the chemical industry, with its origins in modern

THE SEPARATION OF LAND USES

According to planning convention, land is usually said to have a residential, commercial, or industrial "use," depending on the type of activity it supports. For instance, a factory would be an industrial land use, while a suburban housing development or an urban apartment complex would be a residential use. The suburban land-use pattern that dominated development in the United States during the latter half of the twentieth century was characterized by a rigid separation of land uses. This approach to planning developed for a number of reasons. One cause was the change in American cities in the early twentieth century. They were rapidly industrializing, which led to increased air pollution and its health impacts. As factory workers, many of them new immigrants, crowded into cities, the real and perceived danger of infectious disease epidemics rose, and some city dwellers became fearful of the increasing ethnic diversity. After World War II, the optimistic desire for a peaceful life free of the cares of the city was coupled with an intense need to house the booming population. Eventually, a rigid separation of residential, commercial, and industrial land uses developed as a solution to all of these issues, and this became the basis of suburbia—low-density homes far from commercial or industrial districts, primarily accessible by car. This strict separation of uses is different from the form taken by most cities and villages throughout history and across diverse cultures.

[4]IPCC, *Climate Change 2007: Synthesis Report*, 143.
[5]The President's Council on Sustainable Development, *"Towards a Sustainable America:* Advancing Prosperity, Opportunity, and a Healthy Environment for the 21st Century," May 1999.

warfare, and the development of plastics and pesticides—have contributed to overall environmental degradation. Land is being converted to suburban development patterns at an alarming rate. Critical habitats are lost daily and thousands of species face extinction or are imperiled.

There are also economic and social costs as well. According to the U.S. Census Bureau, as of 2005, Americans spend more than 100 hours commuting to work each year, exceeding the two weeks of vacation time frequently taken by workers over the course of a year.[6] The rising cost of oil, and consequently of gasoline, has made long commutes extremely costly. Urban sprawl is also a burden on local government, because it forces limited resources to be spent on building new infrastructure rather than on maintaining existing infrastructure. As sprawl encourages populations to move outside of older established communities, the tax base of these communities is diminished, requiring a reduction of services to the remaining population.[7]

Planning and the Automobile

The dominant development pattern of the second half of the twentieth century is often referred to as *conventional* development or *sprawl*. This pattern—which enforces a strict separation of land uses, low-density development patterns, and a reliance almost exclusively on the automobile for transportation—arose only recently in human history as the combined result of the popularization of the automobile, significant subsidies provided by government, cheap energy, and the unprecedented prosperity experienced in the United States since the end of World War II.

The Model T car, first sold in 1908, began an era of widespread access to the automobile. This access allowed the masses to buy automobiles and thus provided an alternative to public transportation and walking. It also enabled buildings and uses to be more separated and allowed people to live further from their jobs, thus creating cities that were more spread out. But the dream of personal freedom was not fully realized until the creation of the national roadway network made automobile travel realistic. The federal government has been subsidizing road construction since 1916 when President Wilson signed the Federal Aid Road Act, which dedicated $5 million to help states build new roads. As of 2006, government spending on highways alone totaled almost $94 billion.[8] To a great degree, funding for roadways has come at the expense of transit investments. Thus, the federal government promoted automobile use through its direct funding actions (Figure 16-1).

The federal government also subsidized housing construction that supported sprawling residential development patterns. The subsidies began with the creation of the Federal Housing Administration (FHA) in 1934.[9] This system created the opportunity for a large majority of the U.S. population to buy homes. Unfortunately, the FHA program was structured in such a way that it encouraged the construction of single-family homes on the outskirts of urban areas and discouraged the construction of multi-family homes and other denser housing products.[10] The four Levittown planned communities in New York, New Jersey, Pennsylvania, and Puerto Rico are perhaps the most iconic of the postwar push for suburbia. These communities were built with mass-produced assembly line houses; often as many as thirty houses were constructed in a day. These communities and other developments, such as Garden City, came out of a vision of utopia that separated the home with the wife and children from the work place where husbands spent their days. This utopia was segregated in terms of land use, income, gender, and race and depended on the automobile and other modern technology run by cheap energy and funded by the constant expansion of the U.S. economy. Such communities would not have been possible without the automobile.

Figure 16-1 The road to suburbia.

---

[6]U.S. Census Bureau, "Americans Spend More than 100 Hours Commuting to Work Each Year," news release, *Census Bureau Reports*, March 30, 2005.

[7]SprawlGuide, "Problems with Sprawl; Costs to local governments," http://www.plannersweb.com/sprawl/prob_tax.html.

[8]U.S. Department of Transportation (DOT), "Funding for Highways and Disposition of Highway-User Revenues, All Units of Government" (Washington, DC: U.S. Department of Transportation, 2006), http://www.fhwa.dot.gov/policy/ohim/hs06/pdf/hf10.pdf.

[9]U.S. Department of Housing and Urban Development, Federal Housing Administration, http://www.hud.gov/offices/hsg/fhahistory.cfm.

[10]Sprawl Guide, "Roots of Sprawl," http://www.plannersweb.com/sprawl/roots_housing.html.

Figures 16-2 a, b One of the four planned Levittown communities, the result of the postwar push for suburbia.

This vision of utopia continues to have a strong hold on the American imagination. However, in recent decades, changing economic, environmental, and social realities have challenged the viability of these development patterns. Downtown centers with their lively, thriving businesses and ample sidewalks became empty and dangerous at night. The suburban enclaves lost their sense of place and charm, becoming generic, dull, and disconnected, and walkable retail centers morphed into strip centers and shopping malls. Because mass transit and modes of travel shifted from rail to automobiles, proximities to other communities and larger transportation hubs were loosened and in some cases abandoned altogether (Figures 16-2 a, b).

Smart Growth and New Urbanism

Over the past few decades, as policy makers, urban planners, and architects have discovered the high costs associated with the current pattern of development, a series of movements have formed to promote more sustainable development patterns. While the U.S. Green Building Council (USGBC) and other organizations have successfully promoted green building techniques, other agencies and organizations have focused on promoting development patterns that create more sustainable communities. Two of the most prominent movements in the promotion of sustainable communities are Smart Growth and New Urbanism.

Smart Growth

Smart Growth is a planning strategy to help communities develop and grow in a way that supports economic prosperity, environmental conservation, and a strong and fair society. The Smart Growth movement materialized in the late 1990s as a reaction to suburban sprawl. State-level and local land-use legislation—particularly in Oregon, Colorado, and Maryland—was formalized in 1996 in a set of guiding principles created by the U.S. Environmental Protection Agency (EPA) through its Smart Growth Program, which is supported by the Smart Growth Network, a coalition of more than thirty-five national and regional organizations. According to the Smart Growth Network, there are ten principles of smart growth that should guide development and conservation in communities. The following are the ten principles of smart growth:

- *Create a range of housing opportunities and choices.* Providing quality housing for people of all income levels is an integral component in any smart growth strategy.
- *Create walkable neighborhoods.* Walkable communities are desirable places to live, work, learn, worship, and play, and therefore they are a key component of smart growth.
- *Encourage community and stakeholder collaboration.* Growth can create great places to live, work and play—if it responds to a community's own sense of how and where it wants to grow.
- *Foster distinctive, attractive communities with a strong sense of place.* Smart growth encourages communities to craft a vision and set standards for development and construction, which respond to community values of architectural beauty and distinctiveness, as well as expanded choices in housing and transportation.
- *Make development decisions predictable, fair, and cost-effective.* For a community to be successful in implementing smart growth, it must be embraced by the private sector.
- *Mix land uses.* Smart growth supports the integration of mixed land uses into communities as a critical component of achieving better places to live.
- *Preserve open space, farmland, natural beauty, and critical environmental areas.* Open-space preservation supports smart-growth goals by bolstering local economies, preserving critical environmental areas, improving our communities quality of life, and guiding new growth into existing communities.
- *Provide a variety of transportation choices.* Providing people with more choices in housing, shopping, communities, and transportation is a key aim of smart growth.
- *Strengthen and direct development toward existing communities.* Smart growth directs development toward existing communities already served by infrastructure, seeking to utilize the resources that existing neighborhoods offer, and conserve open space and irreplaceable natural resources on the urban fringe.
- *Take advantage of compact building design.* Smart growth provides a means for communities to incorporate more compact building design as an alternative to conventional, land-consumptive development.

New Urbanism

The Congress for the New Urbanism (CNU) was founded in 1993 by a group of architects, including Peter Calthorpe, Andrés Duany, Elizabeth Moule, Elizabeth Plater-Zyberk, Stephanos Polyzoides, and Daniel Solomon. The CNU was reacting to many of the same issues as smart-growth proponents: sprawl and its negative environmental and social impacts, including extreme auto orientation, careless infrastructure demands, and the isolation of economically disadvantaged populations. The movement views the loss of open space, the continuing degradation of our built heritage, the development of communities designed for the automobile, and increasing social and economic divisions as interrelated issues that can be addressed through sound urban development. More specifically, New Urbanism is about the design of communities for people, rather than cars.

The Charter of the New Urbanism, which is the guiding document of the movement, identifies three basic scales of development: the *region*, the *neighborhood*, and the *building*. At each scale are a series of principles that define the quality and character of the built environment and help to form working definitions of sustainable communities. The components of the CNU charter are summarized below.

The Region and the City

A region is comprised of a number of cities, towns, and communities. New Urbanism views individual cities as part of a larger region and emphasizes that, when planning for future development of a city, one must understand its place within the larger region and in relation to adjacent cities. The specific principles are as follows:

- The metropolis has an important environmental, economic, and cultural relationship to surrounding farmland and natural landscapes.
- Infill development conserves environmental resources, economic investment, and social fabric.
- New development should be organized around existing neighborhoods and districts; where this is not possible, it should be organized as viable towns and villages with a jobs and housing balance.
- Cities and towns should benefit people of all incomes and avoid concentrations of poverty.
- The region should be supported by a framework of multimodal transportation options.

- Revenues and resources should be shared more cooperatively among municipalities and regional centers.

Neighborhood, District, and Corridor

The primary building blocks of cities are neighborhoods, districts, and corridors that mix uses, rather than traditional land-use districts that separate uses one from another. Neighborhoods are primarily residential areas that are pedestrian friendly, have a unique character or identity, and are developed around one or more common focal points such as parks, schools, or shopping areas. Districts are predominantly single-use areas that are physically distinct from other parts of the city. Districts are the primary job and retail centers in cities, though in fast-growing areas, single-use, physically separate subdivisions could also be defined as districts. Corridors are linear, often mixed-use development areas that are located on major transportation corridors such as arterial streets. Transit-supportive development is focused along corridors. The specific principles are as follows:

- Neighborhoods should be compact, pedestrian friendly, and mixed use.
- Street networks should be interconnected to encourage walking, shorter automobile trips, and energy conservation.
- A broad range of housing types and price levels strengthens a community's civic bonds.
- Transit corridors can help revitalize urban centers, while highway corridors can detract from existing centers.
- Appropriate densities near transit stops permitting public transit to become a viable alternative to the automobile.
- Concentrations of civic, institutional, and commercial activity should be embedded in neighborhoods and districts, not isolated in remote, single-use complexes.
- A range of parks and open space should connect and be distributed within neighborhoods and districts.

Block, Street, and Building

At this scale, the details of the built environment—defined both by architectural and landscaping details—are proportioned to the pedestrian. Block dimensions and building designs place equal emphasis on pedestrian and vehicular uses. The specific principles area as follows:

- A primary task of all urban architecture and landscape design is the physical definition of streets and public spaces as places of shared use.
- Individual architectural projects should be seamlessly linked to their surroundings. This issue transcends style.
- The revitalization of urban places depends on safety and security. The design of streets and buildings should

reinforce safe environments, but this should not come at the expense of accessibility and openness.

- In the contemporary metropolis, development must adequately accommodate automobiles. It should do so in ways that respect the pedestrian and the form of public space.
- Streets and squares should be safe, comfortable, and interesting to the pedestrian. Properly configured, they encourage walking and enable neighbors to know each other and to protect their communities.
- Architecture and landscape design should grow from local climate, topography, history, and building practice.
- Civic buildings and public gathering places require important sites to reinforce community identity and the culture of democracy. They deserve distinctive form, because their role is different from that of other buildings and places that constitute the fabric of the city.
- All buildings should provide their inhabitants with a clear sense of location, weather, and time. Natural methods of heating and cooling can be more resource efficient than mechanical systems.
- Preservation and renewal of historic buildings, districts, and landscapes affirm the continuity and evolution of urban society.

THIRTEEN PRINCIPLES OF NEW URBANIST NEIGHBORHOODS, DEVELOPED BY ANDRÉS DUANY AND ELIZABETH PLATER-ZYBERK

1. The neighborhood has a discernible center. This is often a square or a green and sometimes a busy or memorable street corner. A transit stop would be located at this center.

2. Most of the dwellings are within a five-minute walk of the center, an average of roughly 1/4 mile or 1,320 feet (0.4 km).

3. There are a variety of dwelling type—usually houses, row houses, and apartments—so that younger and older people, singles and families, the poor, and the wealthy may find places to live.

4. At the edge of the neighborhood, there are shops and offices of sufficiently varied types to supply the weekly needs of a household.

5. A small ancillary building or garage apartment is permitted within the backyard of each house. It may be used as a rental unit or place to work (for example, an office or craft workshop).

6. An elementary school is close enough so that most children can walk from their home.

7. There are small playgrounds accessible to every dwelling—not more than a tenth of a mile away.

8. Streets within the neighborhood form a connected network, which disperses traffic by providing a variety of pedestrian and vehicular routes to any destination.

9. The streets are relatively narrow and shaded by rows of trees. This slows traffic, creating an environment suitable for pedestrians and bicycles.

10. Buildings in the neighborhood center are placed close to the street, creating a well-defined outdoor room.

11. Parking lots and garage doors rarely front the street. Parking is relegated to the rear of buildings, usually accessed by alleys.

12. Certain prominent sites at the termination of street vistas or in the neighborhood center are reserved for civic buildings. These provide sites for community meetings, education, and religious or cultural activities.

13. The neighborhood is organized to be self-governing. A formal association debates and decides matters of maintenance, security, and physical change. Taxation is the responsibility of the larger community.

Source: The Thirteen Points of Traditional Neighborhood Development, New Urbanist Design, available for download at http://newurbanist.com/principles.asp.

LEED for Neighborhood Development

As discussed in Chapter 18 and elsewhere in this book, the U.S. Green Building Council is the leading third-party certifier of green building projects in the country. The USGBC's line of green building rating systems, called Leadership in Energy and Environmental Design (LEED) was launched in 1998. Within the LEED program, there are six different rating systems, each focused on a different type of building development. What these rating systems all have in common is a focus on green construction technologies implemented at the building level, primarily internal to the building.

The USGBC's latest rating system product, called LEED for Neighborhood Development (LEED-ND),

addresses smart locations and neighborhood pattern and design in addition to building-level green construction techniques. LEED-ND is completing pilot testing and will be launched nationwide in 2009. It has been jointly developed by the USGBC, the Congress for the New Urbanism, and the Natural Resources Defense Council, one of the United States' leading advocates for smart growth. As such, LEED-ND is a fusion of best practices from each of these movements, and it is a best practices checklist for sustainable communities. A new development, or even an existing neighborhood, that adheres to a major rating system will exhibit many of the best practices for land use, transportation, design with nature, urban design—green technology implemented at both the building and neighborhood level.

Characteristics of Sustainable City Planning

A smart location, good urban design, environmentally appropriate siting, green technology, and social sustainability are the major components of creating sustainable communities. They should set the stage for sustainable architecture and should be integrated fully with all sustainable projects. Each of these topics is discussed below.

Smart Locations

Selecting and planning for the location of development is fundamental to sustainability. Transitioning developed land back to a naturalized state is extremely difficult and often impossible, so selecting where development will be located is often a permanent decision. Smart locations use land efficiently and support both transit use and walkability. On the other hand, development on undeveloped land far from transit and population centers makes walking and transit use difficult and consumes large amounts of land. Even if a building uses green construction techniques, a poor location is likely to neutralize or overshadow any resulting sustainability benefits.

Location within the City and Region

Building on previously developed sites is a key element of sustainable land use. A *greenfield* site is one that is not previously developed and usually consists of ecologically productive land such as forests or farmland. Conventional suburban development involves subdividing greenfield land for building and relies on the unlimited supply of inexpensive undeveloped land. However, one of the key principles of sustainability is that natural resources, including greenfield lands, are limited. Previously developed land, on the other hand, can be used and reused indefinitely. As the supply of cheap greenfield land diminishes, and as open space, agricultural land, and habitat for wildlife become increasingly valuable commodities, previously developed sites will become an increasingly important requirement for sustainable development.

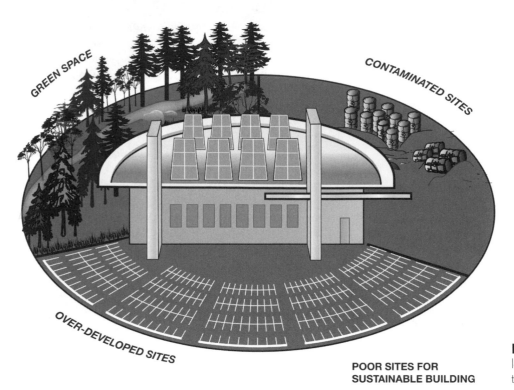

GREEN SPACE

CONTAMINATED SITES

OVER-DEVELOPED SITES

POOR SITES FOR
SUSTAINABLE BUILDING

Figure 16-3 A green building located with little regard to proximity to greenfields or parking lots.

"Leapfrog" development—which sprawls further and further away from a city center and leaves large tracts of vacant land within the city's limits—consumes and fractures greenfield land rapidly. On the other hand, an infill site is surrounded or mostly surrounded by previously developed land. Infill development on previously developed sites uses land efficiently and preserves coherent *greenbelts* of accessible open space around cities. As described below, it also supports transit and walking far more effectively than leapfrog development.

ENVIRONMENTAL BENEFITS OF LOCATION

A study prepared by the U.S. Environmental Protection Agency compared the transportation and environmental impacts of greenfield development versus infill development in three metropolitan areas—San Diego, California; Montgomery County, Maryland; and West Palm Beach, Florida.[11] The study located the same amount of development in each of the two

different sites within the region. Infill sites were chosen based on their central city location, the availability of infrastructure, and the availability of land while the greenfield sites were located based on the potential to develop in the near future. The study found that in all three metropolitan areas, the infill site had lower vehicle miles traveled (VMT) and reduced emissions of air pollutants. For example, in San Diego, the infill site had 52 percent lower VMT than the greenfield site, 88 percent lower carbon monoxide (CO) emissions, 55 percent lower carbon dioxide (CO_2) emissions, and 58 percent lower nitrogen oxide (NOx) emissions. Thus, the study found that the location of a development within the region produced significant transportation and environmental benefits.

Brownfield Redevelopment

Brownfield sites are previously developed (and usually infill) sites that have been contaminated through industrial use, storage or disposal of toxics, or other uses. Old gas stations, industrial facilities, or military bases are common examples of brownfield sites. Because these sites usually require cleaning up of existing contamination before they can be built on, they can be complicated

[11]E. Allen, G. Anderson, and W. Schroeer, *The Impacts of Infill vs Greenfield Development: A Comparative Case Study Analysis*, #231-R-99-005 (Washington, DC: U.S. Environmental Protection Agency, Office of Policy, 1999).

and expensive to redevelop and often sit vacant. However, from a sustainability perspective, brownfield sites are particularly desirable locations for development. Successful brownfield redevelopment achieves the benefits of an infill and previously developed location, restores a site's ecological quality, and removes the health threats posed by contamination. While it is obviously preferable to avoid creating brownfield sites in the first place, redevelopment of existing ones is a key priority for sustainable land use.

Transit-Oriented Development

Locating development near existing transit services increases the chance that people will use public transit. Because successful public transit requires a certain level of population density to support it, public transit in most low-density suburban areas is impractical, expensive, and infrequent. However, locating near existing transit service (usually in urban areas or near town centers) both supports transit systems and offers building inhabitants an alternative to automobile use (Figure 16-4).

Shifting mode share from automobiles to transit can have a number of air quality, quality of life, and public health benefits. Numerous studies have found that a major determinant of transit use is the proximity to high-frequency and high-quality transit service. Data from the National Personal Transportation Survey of Americans found that for normal daily trips, 70 percent of people will walk 500 feet (one-tenth of a mile), 40 percent of people will walk 1,000 feet (one-fifth of a mile), and 10 of people will walk one-half a mile.[12] A study prepared by University of California, Berkeley professor Robert Cervero found that people living near the Bay Area Rapid Transit (BART) commuter-rail stations in the San Francisco Bay Area were about five times more likely to travel to work by rail than the average resident of the same city. Cervero also found that the mode share for rail trips drops by about 0.85 percent for every additional 100 feet from the BART stop.[13] Thus, locating residential and nonresidential development within safe and attractive walking distance of transit can increase overall transit use, reduce rates of driving, and improve overall environmental quality and quality of life for a community.

Development located near transit—widely referred to as "transit-oriented development"—has become an approach to development that is increasingly accepted and promoted by cities, neighborhoods, and transportation agencies. There are developers, architects, and economic feasibility consultants that specialize in it, and to some degree it has become a building type with

Figure 16-4 Transit-oriented development.

[12]Richard K. Untermann, "Accommodating the Pedestrian: Adapting Towns and Neighborhoods for Walking and Bicycling," in *Personal Travel in the U.S., Vol. II, A Report of the Findings from 1983–1984*, NPTS, Source Control Programs New York: Van Nostrand Reinhold, 1984).

[13]Robert Cervero, "Ridership Impacts of Transit-Focused Development in California," Working Paper No. 176, University of California Transportation Center, 1993.

its own unique design requirements. Transit-oriented development can often include much less parking than is usually required by city ordinances.

Mix of Uses

Though it is still considered best practice to separate polluting or heavy industrial uses from residential and commercial uses, there is an increasing preference for allowing residential, commercial, and live-work land uses to mix and reinforce each other. Locating development near a mix of residential and commercial uses decreases the need to travel long distances for goods and services. Living and working in the same building, or in close proximity, reduces the environmental impacts of a long commute. A mix of uses encourages walking and cycling to meet daily needs, and when a car trip is necessary, it is often shorter than in conventional suburban locations. Historical city centers and urban areas often contain a diverse mix of uses, because many were built before suburban development—with its rigid separation of uses—was popular. City centers and urban areas also have a higher population density, which can more easily support a diverse mix of uses.

Uses can be mixed horizontally—for instance, where residential buildings are located next to a corner store—or can be mixed vertically, where a single building contains multiple uses. Examples of mixed-use buildings include storefronts with workshops in the rear of the building, ground-level retail stores with housing on upper floors, or home businesses. Most historic cities or towns throughout the world contain mixed-use buildings. While mixed-use buildings are discouraged or often illegal in conventional suburban development, they are once again becoming accepted in American cities, advocated by proponents of smart growth, new urbanism, and sustainability.

Design with Nature

Locating development in a way that is sensitive to its natural setting is an important aspect of protecting local environmental quality. This is particularly important for development sites on or near farmland, floodplains, plant and wildlife habitat areas, steep slopes, and wetlands. From a sustainability perspective, building on infill and previously developed sites is preferable to building on greenfield sites, because previously developed sites are less likely to contain valuable biological resources like farmland, wetlands, and plant and wildlife habitat. Floodplains and steep slopes—which can lead to increased erosion, safety risks, destruction of habitat, and increased water pollution—are also less likely to occur on previously developed land, though this is not always the case, as evidenced by hilly cities like San Francisco or flood-prone cities like New Orleans or the towns along the Mississippi River floodplain. Wherever development takes place, the environmentally appropriate treatment of the site is crucial to achieving truly sustainable development.

Farmland

Avoiding development on agriculturally productive land is a key element of sustainable site selection, as well as of new urbanism and smart growth. The American Farmland Trust estimates that over the five-year period between 1992–1997, 6 million acres of agricultural land—an area the size of Maryland—was irreversibly converted to developed uses. This rate of conversion was 51 percent faster than the ten-year period from 1982 to 1992. The reason for this increasing pace of agricultural-land conversion is low-density sprawl. For instance, the American Farmland Trust also estimates that during the period from 1982 to 1997, the amount of urbanized land in the United States increased by 47 percent, while the U.S. population only grew by 17 percent. Similarly, since 1994, development of housing lots larger than 10 acres has resulted in 55 percent of land developed in the United States.[14]

Building compact buildings on infill or previously developed sites near city centers is a reliable way to avoid building on farmland. The practice of preserving greenbelts of contiguous, undeveloped land around urban areas also contributes to farmland preservation. Though farmland is important as aesthetically pleasant open space, its existence is also crucial to "food security," as it is a reliable supply source of food for a city or country.

Habitat and Wetlands

Sustainable site development should conserve or restore native wildlife habitat and wetlands. The World Wildlife Fund's Living Planet Index, which measures global trends in terrestrial, marine, and freshwater vertebrate species, estimates a 27 percent decline in these species from 1970 to 2005. Along with pollution, the spread of invasive species, overexploitation of species (as overfishing or poaching), and climate change, habitat loss is one of the major human causes of global species decline.[15] Habitat loss can result from urbanization as well (Figure 16-5).

The primary components of sustainable species and habitat management are preserving existing resources, restoring degraded resources, and sustainably managing these resources into the future. Like farmland, pristine habitat areas are extremely difficult and sometimes impossible to restore once they have been compromised. This means that preserving existing ecological resources is a priority for sustainable site selection, and new development should not locate in habitat or wetland areas. If an area's native habitat has been degraded by previous building, invasive species, or human activity,

---

[14]All data in this paragraph comes from the American Farmland Trust, "Farming on the Edge" project data, http://www.farmland.org (accessed September 2008).

[15]World Wildlife Fund, Global Footprint Network, and the Zoological Society of London, "2010 and Beyond: Rising to the Biodiversity Challenge," published by The World Wildlife Fund, Gland, Switzerland, April 2008.

redevelopment of the area can be a good opportunity to restore habitat. This can include such techniques as native planting, removing invasive species, refilling wetlands that have been drained, restoring natural hydrology in creeks and rivers, and establishing wildlife rehabilitation programs. Habitat can also be preserved or restored elsewhere in the community as part of a development project. Once development has occurred, it is equally important to ensure that any programs or restoration projects that have been instituted are continued into the future and integrated with human activity on a site.

Steep Slopes

Urban development on steep slopes can cause increased soil erosion, which both degrades species habitat and puts stress on natural water systems. On the other hand, steep slopes that are preserved in a natural, vegetated state maintain topsoil and wildlife habitat and naturally filter and slow storm water and other runoff. Steep slopes that have been stripped of native vegetation can be made more sustainable by replanting native vegetation. Vegetated steep slopes are also less likely to pose such safety dangers as landslides and flooding. To the extent possible, new buildings should avoid areas with slopes of greater than 25 percent. If development on slopes greater than 25 percent does occur, steps should be taken to avoid the negative impacts described above.

Floodplains

Avoiding new development on known floodplains is an important aspect of choosing a sustainable site. Many rivers and creeks in urban areas have been channelized, piped, or covered, both to protect existing development from flooding and to open up new areas (formerly floodplains) for development. However, intact floodplains provide open space and often contain important plant and wildlife habitat or agricultural land. Avoiding development in floodplains in the first place protects rivers and streams, which are often flood controlled or channelized only after people building in floodplains realize the risk of flooding. Finally, functioning floodplains play an important role in cleaning and filtering storm water, and when they are intact they can often create a natural hydrological system that contains flooding to a large degree.

RIVER … OR STORM DRAIN?

The Los Angeles River, famous as the site of the drag-racing scene in the movie *Grease*, is essentially a concrete storm channel. The river was paved over in the early twentieth century so it would drain rapidly in case of heavy rainfall and prevent flooding of development that had occurred in the river's floodplain. As a result, the river has little ecological function and is dry for most of the year, except when seasonal floods rush through it, washing large amounts of debris and pollution into the Pacific Ocean. The river also now fails to percolate surface water into underground water tables, contributing to the Los Angeles area's increasingly common drought conditions. Before being "channelized," the river was the Los Angeles area's primary year-round source of freshwater and was the central location for fishing and agriculture by Native tribes and early settlers (Figure 16-6).

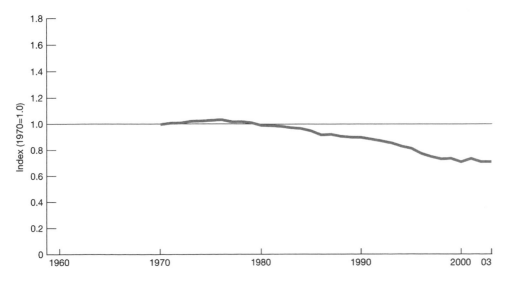

Figure 16-5 World Wildlife Fund's Living Planet Index.

Figure 16-6 The Los Angeles River, an example of a natural water body that functioned to support the regional ecosystem, converted to a storm-water management system.

Sustainable Urban Design

High-quality urban design is a fundamental element of sustainable communities. However, for the latter half of the twentieth century, most conventional suburban development took a mass-produced, cookie-cutter approach to urban design. Typically, conventional suburban development is also poorly connected to nearby uses and is extremely auto oriented. A key component of sustainable city planning—as well as of New Urbanism and Smart Growth—is that cities and towns be walkable and designed for more than just the faster and faster flow of automobile traffic. The key components in achieving this—compact development, connectivity, street design, facilities that cater to pedestrians, cyclists, and public transit, a diversity of building and housing types, and access to parks and other public space—are discussed below.

Compact Development

Compact urban form is a fundamental requirement for walkability, reduced transportation demand, a diverse mix of uses, and the prevention of sprawl. The degree of compactness is typically measured in terms of density or intensity. Density typically refers to the number of dwelling units (houses, apartments, town houses, duplexes, etc.), or buildings per unit of land. Intensity, as measured by floor area ratio, typically refers to commercial or mixed-use buildings and measures the total amount of building area per unit of land.

The relative compactness of development is important, because how close buildings are to each other impacts how far people have to travel between destinations. When densities are low, as in most suburban neighborhoods, driving is the most effective mode of

DENSITY AND DRIVING RATES

Empirical evidence has found a strong relationship between the density of development and the amount that people drive. A 1994 study by researcher John Holtzclaw compared twenty-eight neighborhoods across northern California and found that a doubling of density, accompanied by high-frequency transit service, a mix of land uses, and pedestrian amenities, resulted in up to a 30 percent reduction in the average vehicle miles traveled (VMT) per person.[16] In a follow-up study in 2002, Holtzclaw and others studied neighborhoods in San Francisco, Chicago, and Los Angeles.[17] This study reaffirmed the results of the earlier study and found that a doubling of density resulted in a VMT reduction of 32 percent in Chicago, 35 percent in Los Angeles, and 43 percent in San Francisco. Interestingly, the study also found that higher densities, a mix of uses, high-frequency transit service, and pedestrian amenities enabled residents to own fewer cars.

transportation because homes are far from each other and from destinations like schools, shops, and workplaces. In cities, where buildings are closer together, homes may be within walking distance of shops or other destinations. Higher concentrations of people, which are found in more compact environments, also make public transit economically feasible, whereas low-density areas cannot afford or support such infrastructure. Compact development is also more sustainable, because it uses less land to provide housing or jobs for the same number of people and uses infrastructure—such as water, sewer, and electricity facilities—more efficiently.

Buildings and the Urban Fabric

The fundamental idea that sustainable urban design should enhance public space underlies many of the concepts included in this chapter. A high-quality urban fabric is essential to creating sustainable cities where people want

[16]John Holtzclaw, *Using Residential Patterns and Transit to Decrease Auto Dependence and Costs* (San Francisco: Natural Resources Defense Council; Costa Mesa, CA: California Home Energy Efficiency Rating Systems, 1994).
[17]John Holtzclaw, et al., "Location Efficiency: Neighborhood and Socio Economic Characteristics Determine Auto Ownership and Use—Studies in Chicago, Los Angeles, and San Francisco," *Transportation Planning and Technology* 25 (March 2002): 1–27.

to live, walk, gather, and stay. Buildings interact with and contribute to the urban fabric, but because architectural design is often done one building at a time, it can be easy to treat a building as a self-contained entity. However, buildings designed without attention to their external integration within the community miss a crucial component of creating sustainable communities. A common analogy for city streets and other public spaces is that they are "public rooms." Buildings are the walls, streets, and sidewalks are the public room's interior. Sustainable communities have comfortable, well-designed, and well-apportioned public rooms. The buildings that meld well with their surroundings are often the most successful in creating a high-quality urban fabric.

Buildings have an important role in creating "walkable streets," comfortable pedestrian environments that encourage walking and thus enhance public health and decrease environmental impacts. The proportions of the "public room"—that is, its building heights compared to its street widths—should feel comfortable to people on the street. Buildings that are too low in comparison to the street lack a sense of place, enclosure, and pedestrian scale. Buildings set far back from the street and separated from the sidewalk by large parking lots will provide even less of a sense of a "public room" at a pedestrian scale. Excessive blank walls, infrequent building entrances, shuttered windows, and unattractive building facades also deteriorate the pedestrian environment.

Many of these negative elements conspire in one of the most well-known modern examples of a poor pedestrian environment—the suburban commercial strip mall. In areas with strip mall development, it is common to find a wide street, a narrow sidewalk (or no sidewalk at all), and large parking lots separating architecturally unimaginative buildings on either side of the street. Such a location lacks any sense of pedestrian scale and actively works against any form of mobility besides the car. Ironically, many of the features of the commercial strip mall—low-density buildings, large parking lots, and deep building setbacks—are required by law in many municipalities. However, if buildings can provide appropriate building-height-to-street-width ratios, pleasant and inviting building facades, and a sense of place, they can enhance sustainability. They can encourage connection with the community, increase the quality of the urban environment, and encourage walking, which improves public health and decreases environmental impacts from transportation (Figure 16-7).

Housing Diversity

Housing diversity is achieved when a variety of housing types are provided within a community. Providing quality housing for people of all income levels and at all stages of life is an integral component of a sustainable community strategy. No single type of housing can serve the varied needs of today's diverse households. By providing a wide range of housing types—e.g., single-family homes, town houses, apartment buildings, and special needs housing—a community can provide housing options for a wide variety of people, such as students, young

Figure 16-7 A walkable street in San José, California.

PARKING REQUIREMENTS

In most cities in the United States, city laws require new development to include a minimum amount of parking. These minimum parking requirements are often set according to suburban standards or to accommodate peak parking demand, which occurs infrequently and leaves the large parking lot unused at most times. In a suburban environment, with single-family housing or big-box retail stores, these parking minimums can be easy to meet. However, for complex infill development projects, they can be the nail in the coffin and make a project financially infeasible. These minimums are sometimes impossible to meet due to space limitations and cost concerns. For instance, one study observed that providing just one structured parking space per unit in an urban apartment building increased the cost of each unit by up to 20 percent.[18] Many cities have recognized some of these issues and reduced or eliminated parking minimums for infill projects, projects located near transit, or projects that seek to reduce building users' transportation demand through various mechanisms.

families, and seniors. This mix enables people to stay in the same community even as their needs change. For instance, when two young professionals get married and have children, their housing needs will change; they will require more space, parking, and access to play space. Conversely, when children grow up and leave home, older couples need less space and may want to spend less time maintaining a house or yard. By providing different types of houses in the same community, a city makes it possible for these families to stay there, even as their needs change.

Allowing for multiple types of housing in each neighborhood also allows a community to support a more diverse population and more equitable distribution of households of all income levels across the region. This means that people who earn less but are vital parts of any community—such as teachers or public servants—are able to live and work in the same community. This adds to sustainability by bringing people's homes closer to where they work and thus reducing the need for driving

and other forms of transportation. It also adds to the sense of community when people can live, work, watch their children grow up, and retire all in the same place.

Historic Buildings and Adaptive Reuse

Reusing as much of a building as possible—whether it be the entire building, just the building shell, or just salvageable components of the building—is a key principle of sustainable architecture discussed elsewhere in this book. Building preservation and restoration, particularly of an historical or architecturally significant buildings, is also an important element of sustainable urban design and city planning. It not only saves materials, it can create a "sense of place" that is crucial to sustainable, human-friendly communities. Refurbished historical buildings or neighborhood landmarks can become important public gathering places, can generate interest in and connection to a city, and can be a public demonstration of a city's priority of regenerating and investing in itself. An attractive and interesting urban environment encourages a diverse mix of uses, walkability, public gathering, and social cohesion and encourages further investment in existing communities (Figure 16-8).

Connectivity

Connectivity is a measurement of the directness, or number, of safe route choices available between different origins and destinations. Neighborhoods and communities with high connectivity improve people's ability to walk to work, to stores, and for recreation; decrease the length of car trips when they do drive; and enhance social connection. High physical connectivity

Figure 16-8 Interesting, high-quality architecture and urban design create a sense of place.

[18]Donald S. Shoup, *The High Cost of Free Parking* (Chicago: Planners Press, American Planners Association, 2005), 143–144.

UNIVERSAL ACCESSIBILITY

Universal accessibility is design for equal access by all people, regardless of physical disabilities, social class, ethnicity, or background. For architecture and urban design, universal accessibility means designing buildings, parks, street crossing, and other public space for equal enjoyment and ease of use by all. Universal access is not just about providing access, but about providing *equal* access. For instance, a wheelchair ramp that leads to a building's side entrance rather than its front entrance provides access, but it is not equal access. Specific techniques of universal design include designing residential units to be compliant with the Americans with Disabilities Act, designing "stepless" entrances to residential housing, building sidewalks on all streets and making them wide enough for a wheelchair, and constructing ramps at traffic intersections.

within a city can enhance biking networks and residents' access to parks, schools, businesses, neighbors, and other community resources, and levels of connectivity have been shown to be a major factor in people's willingness to walk.[19] The classic example of an area with low connectivity is the suburban cul-de-sac. For a resident living on a cul-de-sac, it might be impossible to walk to a nearby house or business simply because there is no through connection. Driving or walking to the same destination might require a long, circuitous route. Sustainable communities, by contrast, have high physical connectivity, especially for pedestrians, cyclists, and public transit users. This typically means that streets are laid out on a grid or modified grid with relatively short block lengths (of 600 feet or less) (Figure 16-9).

Transportation Choice and Facilities

In 1980 total annual roadway vehicle miles traveled (VMT) in the United States was around 1.5 trillion. By 2006 it had doubled to 3.0 trillion, far outpacing population growth over the same period and indicating a monumental shift in transportation behavior.[20] The U.S. Energy Commission reports that transportation activities now account for around 30 percent of greenhouse

Figure 16-9 Residents of this suburban cul-de-sac have low connectivity to much of their community and neighborhood.

[19]S. Handy, "Understanding the Link Between Urban Form and Nonwork Travel Behavior," *Journal of Planning Education and Research* 15 (1996): 183–98.

[20]U.S. Department of Transportation, Bureau of Transportation Statistics, Table 1-33, from *National Transportation Statistics 2008*, http://www.bts.gov/publications/national_transportation_statistics/pdf/entre.pdf.

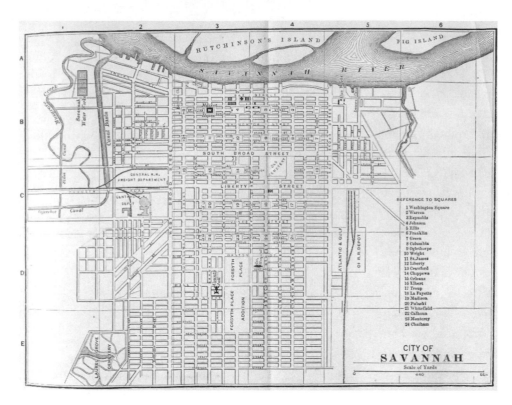

Figure 16-10 Street grids found in traditional neighborhoods create a more pedestrian-friendly environment with higher connectivity.

gas emissions in the United States.[21] Most VMT miles in the United States are from single-occupancy car travel. Per mile traveled, single-occupancy car use generates more greenhouse gas emissions than any other mode. Most other modes of transportation, however—including walking, cycling, car sharing, carpooling, and public transportation—have significant sustainability advantages. They cause less pollution and fewer greenhouse emissions per passenger (with the exception of some cases in which underused public transit moves very few people per trip), encourage physical activity and health, can be less expensive, and provide opportunities for people who are not able (or choose not) to own a car.

Compact development, as described above, makes non-automobile transportation—including walking, cycling, car sharing, and public transportation—much more likely to be successful. Providing a higher number of attractive facilities for these transportation options also encourages their use.

Pedestrian Facilities

The best practice for providing pedestrian facilities is to include sidewalks on both sides of all streets or to provide equivalent provisions, such as designated walking paths or trails. Streets or public areas entirely or partially closed

to automobile traffic can also serve as important pedestrian facilities. These pedestrian facilities should provide safe access across barriers, such as busy streets and railroad tracks, to a variety of interesting destinations, such as businesses, community facilities, parks, plazas, and other public spaces. Crosswalks, raised crosswalks, pedestrian islands, and *curb bulb outs* are all common techniques for easing pedestrian crossings of busy streets and marking public space as pedestrian rather than car oriented. *Traffic calming* on busy streets, through the use of decreased speed limits, street planting, traffic diverters, meanders, curb bulb outs, medians, or other techniques, can increase pedestrian comfort and safety. *Streetscaping*—street trees, landscaping, and street furniture—provides pedestrians with shade, beauty, and comfort. As mentioned in this chapter, buildings that provide a pleasant street wall with points of interest are optimal for high-quality pedestrian facilities. Real and perceived safety from crime is also an important factor in enabling people to use pedestrian facilities freely (Figure 16-10).

Bicycle Facilities

Like pedestrian facilities, bike facilities should be arranged in a connected network, providing safe and pleasant access to a wide variety of interesting destinations. Unlike pedestrians, bicycles often function as, and share the road with, other vehicles, and the goal of a successful bicycle network is to decrease conflicts with other vehicles while protecting cyclists and making their ride

[21]U.S. Department of Energy, Energy Information Administration (EIA), "Distribution of Total U.S. Greenhouse Gas Emissions by End-Use Sector," *Emissions of Greenhouse Gases Report*, November 28, 2007 (Washington, DC: U.S. Department of Energy, EIA, 2007), http://www.eia.doe.gov/oiaf/1605/ggrpt.

Figure 16-11 The space required to move the same number of passengers using different modes of transportation.

Figure 16-12 The public spaces in Paris, France, offer quintessential examples of *streetscaping*.

more comfortable. Typically, on-road bike facilities are categorized as Class I, Class II, or Class III. A *Class I* bikeway is a completely separated bicycle right-of-way for the exclusive use of bicyclists or bicyclists and pedestrians. A *Class II* bikeway is a striped lane of a certain minimum width (a "bike lane") designated for the exclusive use of bicyclists on a shared roadway. A *Class III* bikeway is shared between cars and bikes and does not provide a Class II bikeway but connects sections of the bike network or is preferable in some way to other streets. The *bicycle boulevard* is a type of bike facility that is being used by an increasing number of American cities. Bicycle boulevards are shared between cars and bicycles, but

they run along low-traffic streets that include bike-friendly installations like traffic diverters, bike-only street crossings, street plantings and meanders, car-only speed bumps, and other facilities that can make biking on the street easier than driving on the street. Most efforts to improve on-street bike facilities in cities involve expanding and improving the bike network from this palette of facilities.

Sufficient and well-placed bicycle parking also encourages cycling. Compared to car parking, bike parking takes up very little space. It can often be widely distributed near building entrances without the need for major site or building redesigns, and a single converted car parking space can provide multiple bike parking spaces. Including secure, long-term parking within multifamily residential or office buildings is also considered a best practice, as is providing showers for bicycle commuters. Some cities have begun to create standards for the amount and location of bike parking to be included in building projects. For instance, the City of Emeryville, California, has begun requiring a certain level of bike parking as a condition of approval for most building projects, and recently drafted a bike-parking ordinance that requires all short-term bike parking to be closer to building entrances than car parking.

Transit Facilities

Public transit includes such services as buses, bus rapid transit, light rail such as streetcars or subways, regional or intercity rail, flexible-route services, taxis, and ferries.

Figure 16-13 This multistoried *bike parking facility* at the train station in Amsterdam, Netherlands, holds around 7,000 bikes and is full on most days.

Figure 16-14 The City of Berkeley, California, developed a series of *bicycle boulevards* to provide a safe transportation network for cyclists.

The sustainability advantages of locating sufficiently dense development near existing public transit have been discussed in this chapter's section on transit-oriented development. However, providing and improving transit facilities as part of building and planning projects is also an important part of creating sustainable communities. Many people do not use public transit, because it is less comfortable, convenient, or affordable than using a car. However, providing enhanced transit service encourages ridership and reduces driving rates.

Often, improving transit facilities is accomplished through a combination of efforts. Many of these can seem insignificant or minor in isolation, but taken together they can create an overall sense of comfort and quality and enhance users' experience. When transit service already exists, new development should provide illuminated and covered (or at least partially enclosed) shelters at all transit stops within or near the project. This protects transit riders from wind and rain and provides a sense of safety and belonging. Loading and unloading platforms for bus or rail service increases safety and comfort. Transit stops should also have schedule and route information posted, and cities and neighborhoods should have centralized kiosks and web-based resources that provide publicity and information about transit service available in the community. As with bicycle and pedestrian facilities, the provision of high-quality public transit can often have implications for street design. Bus or light-rail service can profit from dedicated street lanes, separate rights-of-way, or the ability to control traffic signals, allowing transit vehicle to bypass the ebb and flow of traffic and maintain on-time service.

Car-Sharing Facilities

Car-sharing systems provide convenient, affordable access to shared cars for short periods of time and can reduce demand for individual car ownership. A 2006 study found twenty-eight car-sharing programs operating in thirty-six cities in North America.[22] Another study in 2007 found around 600 car-sharing operations worldwide, with approximately 348,000 individuals sharing 11,700 vehicles. Each car-sharing vehicle put into service in North America was estimated to reduce the need for between six and twenty-three private vehicles (the averages are slightly different in Europe and Australia), and the demand for car sharing—as a result of increased fuel costs, better understanding of car sharing, and limited or expensive parking—is estimated to be growing.[23] Sustainable cities or developments can provide car-share parking spaces in prime locations near transit and activity centers, install signage advertising, car sharing, and promote its availability.

Community Facilities

A complete, sustainable city offers facilities and services—schools, libraries, civic buildings, community centers, places of worship, recreation facilities, community gardens,

[22]Susan A. Shaheen, Adam P. Cohen, and J. Darius Roberts, "Carsharing in North America: Market Growth, Current Developments, and Future Potential," *Transportation Research Record: Journal of the Transportation Research Board* 1986 (2006): 116–124. 10.3141/1986-17.
[23]Susan A. Shaheen and Adam P. Cohen, "Worldwide Carsharing Growth: An International Comparison," Institute of Transportation Studies, University of California, Davis, Research Report UCD-ITS-RR-07-34 (2007).

parks, and other public places—to serve the diverse needs of residents in different stages of life. These public amenities are critical to meeting a community's cultural, social, spiritual, and physical needs, and they can be a key reason that people decide to stay and invest in a city or neighborhood. Parks and open spaces are particularly important for urban environments where green space and places of refuge and solitude are in short supply. High-quality community facilities can reinforce and be reinforced by other sustainable community concepts discussed in this chapter—including connectivity, walkable streets, compact development with a mix of uses, building design that contributes to the urban fabric, adaptive building reuse, and designing with nature. Public facilities can serve as important sites for building community, improving social cohesion and integration, and fostering citizen involvement. Public facilities should be in a central location in a neighborhood or city, and should be easily accessible by public transit, walking, and cycling.

Green Technology

Many green building technologies and infrastructure can be implemented between multiple buildings or even across whole neighborhoods or cities, and they have broad, positive environmental impacts. Focusing only on single buildings can miss some of these potential synergies and broad design approaches. Examples of such techniques include solar orientation of blocks and buildings, on-site renewable energy sources, the reduction of heat island effect, xeriscaping, district heating and cooling, green infrastructure, and green streets.

Solar Orientation
The way buildings are oriented affects their ability to use solar energy both actively (such as for photovoltaic cells) and passively (such as for natural lighting or direct solar heating through windows and walls). Correct solar orientation is a well-known requirement for designing individual green buildings. However, the ability of individual buildings to effectively use solar heat and light is constrained by their interaction with surrounding buildings and the layout of streets and blocks, and an awareness of these underlying factors is an important element of sustainable city design and planning.

The ultimate goal of correct solar orientation is to ensure that passive or active solar collectors get sufficient and regular direct sunlight. In the northern hemisphere, sunlight from the south is stronger and more consistent year-round than sunlight from other directions. By contrast, north-facing vertical building faces are almost always shaded, and east- or west-facing vertical building faces receive inconsistent levels of sunlight, depending on if the sun is rising or setting. For this reason, the preferable solar orientation for city blocks that contain compact

(higher-density) building development is along or near an east-west axis, with the east-west axis of the block significantly longer than the north-south axis. This lengthier east-west orientation opens up the greatest number of south-facing vertical building surfaces to sunlight and thus provides the greatest opportunity to harvest solar energy. It also decreases east- and west-facing vertical surfaces and allows sunlight to shine on the building block more consistently throughout the day. Narrower north-south block depths also decrease the amount of building space that is far from sunny south-facing windows.

It should be noted that the above guidance is specifically for dense building blocks. For sites with low density or with buildings that are far apart, it may be preferable to orient the buildings themselves so their length is along an east-west axis, which could make a north-south block layout preferable. The underlying goal of solar orientation, whatever the site, is to maximize southern exposure and a building's ability to use solar energy.

Heat Islands
Heat islands are isolated areas within cities where the ambient temperature is much higher than surrounding areas. Heat islands result from unshaded pavement, rooftops, and other hardscapes that absorb heat from the sun and then radiate it, and they can make the human experience of a city very unpleasant. Studies by the Local Government Commission of California have shown that wide streets without a tree canopy can be 10 degrees warmer on hot days than narrow, shaded streets close by.[24] Neighborhoodwide or citywide techniques to counteract heat island effect include comprehensive tree planting and maintenance programs and building streets and projects with less pavement. Regularly using roofing or paving materials that reflect instead of absorb solar energy can reduce heat island effect. Vegetated roofs or other landscaped areas, open-grid paving, and covering parking with reflective roofs can also reduce heat island effect by replacing or shading hardscapes that would otherwise absorb and emit heat. A coordinated, citywide approach to reducing heat island effect will have a far greater impact than individual efforts by single buildings.

Regionally Appropriate Planting
Planting species that are appropriate to the climate where they will grow is a sustainability priority that can lead to reduced water use, improved plant-survival rates, decreases in maintenance requirements, consistent wildlife habitat, and the ability of plants to withstand climatic conditions. However, many cities, developers, and architects select street trees and landscaping based on their aesthetic appeal or, at least, with limited thought to the

---

[24]Local Government Commission, "Local Government Commission Report," Newsletter 30, no. 8 (August 2008): 2.

resources that will be required to maintain them. Native plants, which evolved to be particularly suited to the specific biological conditions of different regions, are often the best choice for planting. They tend to be drought tolerant in more arid climates and suited to their region's unique climatic conditions, such as fog, high amounts of rainfall, wind, or the presence of certain pests. Though the benefits of native planting have been suggested elsewhere in this book, its widespread positive effects can only be achieved if implemented on a citywide level.

Shared On-Site Renewables

Producing energy from renewable sources is a widely recognized necessity for a sustainable energy economy. It avoids many of the negative environmental effects—such as greenhouse gas emissions, polluting emissions, and the impacts of petroleum exploration—associated with fossil-fueled energy production. Installing renewable energy sources to service multiple buildings or homes is often more cost and energy efficient than renewable energy sources that serve only a single building, similar to the district heating and cooling systems described below. Examples of renewable energy sources for which this is the case include geothermal wells and electrical systems such as wind turbines, photovoltaic (solar) systems, combined heat and power plants using biofuels, hydroelectric power, and wave or tidal power. Installing shared renewable energy sources requires coordination between multiple buildings or landowners and is, therefore, most successful for buildings that have the same owner, are developed at the same time, or are part of a coordinated effort by a city, developer, or other organization.

District Heating and Cooling

In conventional development, individual buildings have self-contained heating and cooling systems. These systems must be designed to a high enough standard to meet a building's *peak load*—the times of the day when a high number of users or weather conditions put high demand on the system. *District heating and cooling*—direct heating and cooling of multiple buildings through a centralized thermal system—is an alternative to this. District heating and cooling can distribute peak heating and cooling loads across a much larger system, requiring less infrastructure and capacity per individual building, increasing efficiency per building, and lowering energy-distribution costs.

District heating or cooling sources can be both conventional and renewable. Common renewable sources include steam from geothermal wells, chilled water from natural water bodies, passive solar heat, or combined heat and power plants that utilize biofuels. Nonrenewable thermal sources for district heating and cooling—such as steam harnessed from industrial processes, "waste" heat harnessed from electricity generation or industrial processes, or centralized conventional boilers or air-conditioning systems—can also achieve systemwide efficiencies.

As with the various shared on-site renewable energy sources, installing district heating and cooling usually requires coordination between multiple buildings. Groups of buildings or dwelling units that are in close proximity to each other—such as hospitals, schools, other institutional complexes, or high-density residential and mixed-use buildings—are often the most feasible locations for district heating and cooling, since they require less extensive shared infrastructure than district heating and cooling in dispersed low-density development.

Energy-Efficient Infrastructure

Citywide infrastructure, such as streetlights, traffic lights, park lights, water pumps, and sewer treatment, make up a significant portion of a city's municipal energy consumption. Therefore, installing energy-efficient infrastructure, either as part of property development or as old infrastructure is retired, is an important opportunity for increased environmental sustainability. Examples of energy-efficient infrastructure include light-emitting diode (LED) technology for traffic and other lights, adjustable-power water pumps, and renewable microgeneration-powered lights, such as small photovoltaic panels.

Healthy Planning

The legal and historical link between city planning and public health is strong. In fact, a city's legal ability to enact planning regulations comes explicitly from its capacity to exercise police power, defined in most state and federal law as the protection of health, safety, and general welfare. Modern American city planning and zoning grew explicitly in response to the public health crises that arose from the rapid industrialization and urbanization of the late nineteenth and early twentieth centuries. Early planners required sanitary sewers to prevent cholera epidemics and zoned city blocks to buffer residential neighborhoods from polluting industries, often resulting in a strict separation of all uses that is still common today.

However, despite its historical connection and legal standing, addressing public health through city planning became less common. One reason is that early planning practices successfully resolved many of the public health issues plaguing urban areas during the early twentieth century, such as overcrowding and the close proximity of housing to heavy industry. Health professionals began to focus on disease treatment, education, and discouraging unhealthy behaviors, while planning professionals shifted their attention to such issues as economic development and transportation. In particular, planners focused on how to accommodate rapid population growth and the desire for unlimited personal mobility through driving. Zoning increasingly became a means to protect property values, and infrastructure projects more often served to bolster the tax base.

Recently, however, the planning and public health professions are rediscovering the impact of planning on public health. Planning decisions underlie people's daily and habitual decisions, which largely dictate levels of public health—where to live, work, and travel, what to eat and where, and when to play, socialize, and be physically active. Evidence suggests that many conventional planning practices (that encourage a separation of uses and high rates of automobile use) are bad for public health. It is already well recognized that chronic disease rates in the United States are rapidly on the rise. Since 1980, the number of obese Americans has doubled to more than one-third of the population[25] and the prevalence of type 2 diabetes has doubled.[26] The asthma rate among children has more than doubled.[27] Based on current obesity trends, for the first time in American history, children are not predicted to live as long as their parents.[28]

While it is undoubtedly just one cause among many, there is increasing documentation that a strictly automobile-oriented built environment—with strictly separated uses accessible only by car—contributes to most of the leading, chronic public health problems in the United States. The primary impact on public health of what might be called an auto orientation is its complicity in suppressing physical activity. Limited physical activity is a primary risk factor for heart disease, cancer, stroke, diabetes, and Alzheimer's disease—five of the top ten causes of death in California. It is also a primary risk factor for obesity (fastest-growing disease in the United States, along with diabetes),[29] and obesity in turn increases the risk of myriad chronic diseases. Higher density, walkable urban form, transportation choices, and access to recreation all increase physical activity, which can have positive health impacts.[30]

Empirical studies have proven this point. A study by Lawrence Frank and his colleagues compared highly walkable neighborhoods (with higher-density development, a mix of uses, and an interconnected street network) to less walkable neighborhoods. Frank et al. found that 37 percent of residents of the highly walkable neighborhoods met the recommended weekly levels of physical activity, compared to only 18 percent of individuals in the less walkable areas.[31] Another study by Frank and his colleagues found that a 5 percent increase in walkability is associated with a 32 percent increase in minutes of walking and biking, a 6.5 percent reduction in per capita vehicle kilometers traveled, and a one-quarter-point reduction in an individual's body mass index, which is a measure of overweight and obesity.[32]

Planning has other impacts too. Emissions from transportation sources are strongly linked with respiratory diseases, and automobile accidents consistently kill over 40,000 Americans each year. Land-use decisions impact people's access to nutritious foods, health care, and safe as well as to active public spaces and their exposure to air pollution and toxic releases. Poor mental health is associated with a number of factors related to planning, including long commute times, exposure to crime, lack of transportation choice, and lack of access to public spaces. More and more, planners, urban designers, and architects will need to understand how the decisions they make on a daily basis will impact the overall health and well-being of the citizens of the community.

Environmental Justice

Environmental justice is the concept that people should be protected from environmental toxins regardless of race, income, or social status. Advocates have pointed out that poor or minority neighborhoods are often subject to toxic releases from both mobile pollution sources, like freeways, and stationary pollution sources, like factories and ports, at a higher rate than other communities. For example, a 2001 UCLA study found that although Latinos represent 40 percent of the total population in Los Angeles

(Continued)

[25]Centers for Disease Control and Prevention, "Behavioral Risk Factor Surveillance System, Physical Activity Prevalence Data: California 2003," http://apps.nccd.cdc.gov/brfss.

[26]California Center for Health Statistics, Office of Health Information and Research, Death Data Tables, Cause of Death, http://www.dhs.ca.gov/hisp/chs/OHIR/tables/death/causes.htm.

[27]L. Frank et al., "Linking Objectively Measured Physical Activity with Objectively Measured Urban Form: Findings from SMARTRAQ," *American Journal of Preventative Medicine*, 28, no. 2 (February 2005): 117–125.

[28]L. Besser and A. Dannenberg, "Walking to Public Transit: Steps to Help Meet Physical Activity Recommendations," *American Journal of Preventative Medicine* 32, no. 4 (November 2005): 273–280.

[29]California Center for Health Statistics, Office of Health Information and Research, Death Data Tables, Cause of Death, http://www.dhs.ca.gov/hisp/chs/OHIR/tables/death/causes.htm.

[30]L. D. Frank, S. Kavage, and T. Litman, "Promoting Public Health through Smart Growth: Building healthier communities through transportation and land use policies and practices" prepared for Smart Growth BC, Vancouver, British Columbia, Canada, 2006, 6.

[31]L. D. Frank, et al., "Linking Objectively Measured Physical Activity with Objectively Measured Urban Form: Findings from SMARTRAQ," *American Journal of Preventive Medicine* 28, no. 2S2 (2005): 117–125.

[32]L. D. Frank, J. F. Sallis, T. Conway, J. Chapman, B. Saelens, and W. Bachman, "Many Pathways from Land Use to Health: Walkability Associations with Active Transportation, Body Mass Index, and Air Quality," *Journal of the American Planning Association* (Winter 2006): 77.

County, they represent 60 percent of residents who live adjacent highly polluting industrial facilities.[33] Another 2007 study identified multiple California cities where poorer residents were exposed to higher concentrations of toxic releases and heavy industrial uses.[34] Stationary and mobile pollutions sources cause higher rates of cancer, respiratory illness, asthma, and other negative health impacts.[35] These disparities may be partly because undesirable neighborhoods near toxic sites are all poor residents can afford and partly because poorer neighborhoods have fewer financial and political resources to oppose polluting uses that do seek to locate nearby. Contrary to the situation in many cities throughout the world, sustainable communities practice environmental justice by equal protection for all residents from toxic pollutants and their negative effects.

Planning Implementation Tools: An Overview

There are a number of tools that local governments use to guide the type, density, and pattern of development and that architects, urban designers, and planners will use on a daily basis. Each community is different, but the following are the common tools used by local governments across the country.

- *Comprehensive plans*. These plans define a long-term vision for the development and conservation of a community. The comprehensive plan, which is also called a "general plan" in some states, is typically created for a single municipality (such as a city or county). Comprehensive plans are adopted by a legislative body and set forth in words, maps, illustrations, and tables the goals, policies, and guidelines that will direct the present and future physical, social, and economic development that will occur within the jurisdiction. Common topics covered by comprehensive plans include land use, transportation, housing, environmental conservation, and public facilities and services. Requirements for comprehensive planning at the local level are defined by the state government and, thus, requirements vary from state to state. States with the strongest comprehensive planning laws include California, Florida, Oregon, and Washington.

- *Zoning ordinance*. The zoning ordinance is enacted by the legislative body of a jurisdiction that sets forth the regulations and standards for the allowable uses for real property and size restrictions for buildings within an area. More specifically, zoning identifies the detailed, allowable land uses on every parcel of land in a jurisdiction as well as the specific dimensional requirements for buildings, such as the height, setback, parcel coverage, landscaping, and parking requirements. Every parcel of land within a jurisdiction has zoning, and all structures built on that land must comply with the existing zoning regulations.

- *Design guidelines*. Some jurisdictions adopt design guidelines or standards for specific types of uses or subareas of a city. Design guidelines regulate the architectural appearance of a building or improvement to land. The overall purpose of design guidelines is to convey a sense of the preferred quality of a place. While written guidelines are an essential component of the documents, they typically also use sketches, photographs, and diagrams to covey information. Typical subjects of design guidelines include the following: building location, parking and loading, access, landscape requirements, signage, architectural style, and color palettes. In recent years, some municipalities have begun creating green building design guidelines that are more focused on achieving a desired environmental outcome, such as reduced water or energy use.

- *Functional plans or master plans*. Many jurisdictions typically adopt functional plans or master plans to provide detailed policy and design guidance on specific topics. These plans typically implement the more general vision found in the jurisdiction's comprehensive plan. Topics that are commonly covered by functional plans and master plans include parks and recreation, roadway design and street standards, bicycle facilities, and master plans for infrastructure such as water, wastewater, and storm water.

Overall, the planning tools found in jurisdictions are just that—tools. Some are used effectively by jurisdictions to promote sustainable development patterns, while others continue the business-as-usual pattern of development that has led to environmental degradation. In order to create truly sustainable community, these tools must be reformed and reshaped to ensure that the needs of people are balanced with the constraints of the natural environment.

[33]A. Carlson and J. Zasloff, "Southern California Environmental Report Card: Environmental Justice," UCLA Institute of the Environment, Los Angeles, 2001, available for download at http://www.ioe.ucla.edu/reportcard/.

[34]Environmental Health Coalition, "Building Healthy Communities from the Ground Up: Environmental Justice in California," Inkworks Press (September 2003), available for download at http://www.environmentalhealth.org/EHC_Misc_Archive/BuildingHealthyCommunities.htm.

[35]M. Pastor, Jr., J. L. Sadd, and R. Morello-Frosch, "Reading, Writing, and Toxics: Children's Health, Academic Performance, and Environmental Justice in Los Angeles" *Environment and Planning C: Government and Policy* 22, no. 2 (2004): 271–290.

▨ Resources

Jacobs, Jane Jacobs. 1961. *The Death and Life of Great American Cities*. New York: Random House.

Benfield, F. Kaid, Matthew D. Raimi, and Donald D. T. Chen. 1999. *Once There Were Greenfields*. Washington, DC: Natural Resources Defense Council and Surface Transportation Policy Project.

Leinberger, Christopher B. 2008. *The Option of Urbanism: Investing in a New American Dream*. Washington, DC: Island Press.

Farr, Douglas. 2008. *Sustainable Urbanism: Urban Design with Nature*. Hoboken, NJ: John Wiley & Sons.

Stair, Peter, Heather Wooten, and Matt Raimi. 2008. *How to Create and Implement Healthy General Plans: A Toolkit for Building Healthy, Vibrant Communities through Land Use Policy Change*. Berkeley and Oakland, CA: Public Health Law & Policy and Raimi + Associates.

Roberts, Paul. 2004. *The End of Oil: On the Edge of a Perilous New World, Boston, MA:* Houghton Mifflin.

Frumkin, Howard, Lawrence Frank, and Richard Jackson. 2004. *Urban Sprawl and Public Health: Designing, Planning, and Building for Healthy Communities*. Washington, DC: Island Press.

U.S. Green Building Council (USGBC). 2006. *LEED-ND Public Health Criteria Study*. Washington, DC: U.S. Green Building Council.

Beatley, Timothy. 2000. *Green Urbanism: Learning From European Cities*. Washington, DC: Island Press.

Shoup, Donald. 2004. *The High Cost of Free Parking*. Chicago: American Planners Association Press.

McHarg, Ian L. 1969. *Design with Nature*. Garden City, NY: Natural History Press.

Duany, Andres, Elizabeth Plater-Zyberk, and Jeff Speck. 2000. *Suburban Nation: The Rise of Sprawl and the Decline of the American Dream*. New York: North Point Press

Kunstler, James Howard. 1994. *The Geography of Nowhere: The Rise and Decline of America's Man-Made Landscape*. New York: Free Press.

Calthorpe, Peter. 1995. *The Next American Metropolis: Ecology, Community, and the American Dream*. 3rd ed. New York: Princeton Architectural Press.

Kelbaugh, Doug. 1996. *Pedestrian Pocket Book*. New York: Princeton Architectural Press.

Soleri, Paolo. 1969; 2006. *Arcology: The City in the Image of Man*. 4th ed. Cambridge, MA: The MIT Press; Mayer, AZ: Cosanti Press.

Katz, Peter. 1993. *The New Urbanism: Toward an Architecture of Community*. New York: McGraw-Hill Professional.

Alexander, Christopher, Sara Ishikawa, and Murray Silverstein. 1977. *A Pattern Language: Towns, Buildings, Construction*. Center for Environmental Structure Series. New York: Oxford University Press, 1977.

17 Case Studies

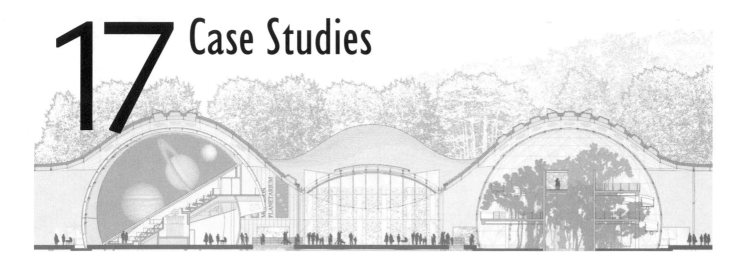

The world of green building is populated by a wealth of case study databases and top-ten lists. The case studies presented here offer a geographic range and reflect honest intention and the triple-bottom-line balance of environment, economy, and social justice (addressing issues of literacy, disease, poverty, hunger, and joblessness). This series of projects also demonstrates an extremely crucial aspect of sustainable design: how humans will need to inhabit the planet in a future of climate change and passive survivability.

Among the many strategies critical to our future patterns of life and socioeconomic conditions are vertical farming, tsunami-safe housing, repurposing of industrial waste, shelters for at-risk populations, on-site generation of clean and renewable energy, economically self-sufficient societies, transit-oriented communities, concern for regionalism in terms of cultural identity and history, and the availability of local materials. Other global challenges include dependence on fossil fuels, availability of fresh potable water, and areas with little ability to produce food.

■ I. City of Melbourne Council House Two (CH2) Office Building

Melbourne, Australia

Australia has long been on the forefront of the green building movement, a trend born of necessity in a water-starved and generally harsh climate. Council House Two (CH2), a 135,000 square foot project of the City of Melbourne, which houses several of its agencies, was completed in August 2006. It is an extremely successful building from the point of view of the building users and the owner builders. Its architect, Mick Pearce of

DesignInc, describes it as harvesting wind, rain, daylight, and night air much like a living organism, embodying biomimicry principles. It is truly an integrative building and quite possibly the single building that expresses the character of the ideal green building we have attempted to capture throughout this book.

The salient features of CH2 involve every building system and nearly every facet of high-performance integrated building design.

Water Conservation

Melbourne has permanent water-use restrictions and rationing and is confronted with the prospect, as is much of Australia, of permanent drought conditions. Council House Two has on-site black water and gray water capture and treatment systems, a strategy known as sewer mining: "This unique sewer mining system treats up to 100,000 litres of wastewater per day, and provides Class-A water that supplies 100 per cent of CH2's non-drinking water for toilet flushing, cooling and irrigation. In addition, surplus water is transported off-site for use in other buildings, fountains, street cleaning and irrigation."[1] In addition, when the fire sprinkler system is tested, the water is captured, recirculated, and reused. Rainwater is harvested for use in irrigation, toilet flushing, and cooling towers. Planters have a soil medium that stores water until the soil needs more moisture.

Daylight Harvesting

Light shelves on north-facing windows help harvest light and control glare. Glare is also controlled using planters

[1] "CH2, Setting a World Standard in Green Building Design," City of Melbourne, Australia, Web site: http://www.melbourne.vic.gov.au/info.cfm?top=171&pg=1933; see Architecture Australia for further information: http://www.architectureaustralia.com/aa/aaissue.php?article=14&issueid=200701&typeon=2.

on balconies (which also act as sun shades) and internal blinds. Angled vertical louvers (really functioning as shutters—a tropical climate-control strategy), made from recycled timber, respond to sun angles with preprogrammed seasonally appropriate set times. The louvers are powered by photovoltaics (PVs) and hydraulically operated with biobased oil.

Indoor Environment Systems

Much of CH2's indoor environment control system is expressed on the exterior of the building. The vertical timber louvers, water-shower towers, and wind turbines are highly visible. Supply-air ducts are located in the south facade and exhaust shafts on the north facade. Displacement-air ventilation replaces used air regularly. Indoor planting is healthy and abundant, averaging one plant per worker. Interior finishes were selected for their low-emitting properties. Regular air quality testing is conducted to monitor indoor pollutants.

Cooling

Exposed concrete ceilings absorb heat through their thermal mass during the day. Chilled ceilings containing circulated chilled water transfer heat at night and transport it to a phase-change material stored in a series of basement tanks (in this case, frozen stainless steel balls containing a salt solution make the entire system a giant thermal-storage battery). Heat is then removed at night through evaporative-cooling towers and via a night purge, where windows beneath concrete ceilings open, absorb the stored heat in the ceilings, and send it up through towers. Five fabric shower towers on south facade provide a space where water is misted, causing air-current cooling, another evaporative cooling process that cools both air and water.

Heating

Heating is accomplished through an underfloor hydronic system (radiant floor), and the building also uses radiators and perimeter floor vents and a raised access floor on a basement level.

Energy Generation

A gas-fired microturbine cogeneration plant meets 30 per cent of the building's needs. Waste heat from the plant heats water for the building's occupants. Twenty-three solar panels on the roof produce about 3.5 kilowatts of electricity, which is enough to power the vertical timber shutters. Six roof-mounted wind turbines generate power and also create an exhaust-air system. The elevators have regenerative braking. Domestic hot water is heated via solar hot-water panels that address 60 per cent of the building's needs, supplemented by a boiler.

Design Team

Architect and interior designer: Mick Pearce, DesignInc, Melbourne, and the City of Melbourne

Services engineer: Lincolne Scott

Environmental engineer: AEC

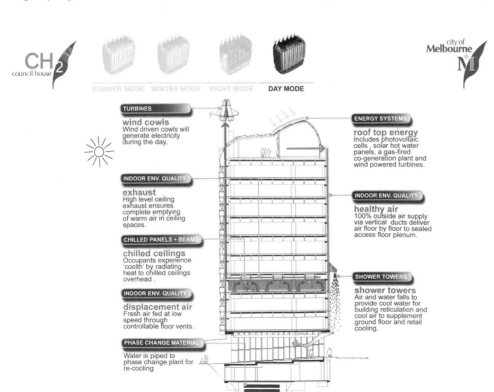

Figure 17-1 a–j The City of Melbourne Council House Two (CH2) Office Building. The section drawings show the seasonal and daily operational modes of the building's systems.

(b)

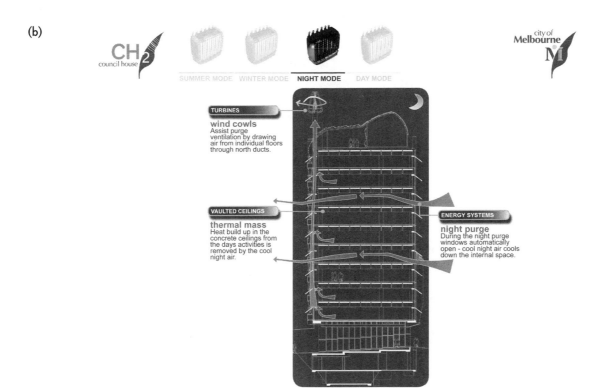

(c)

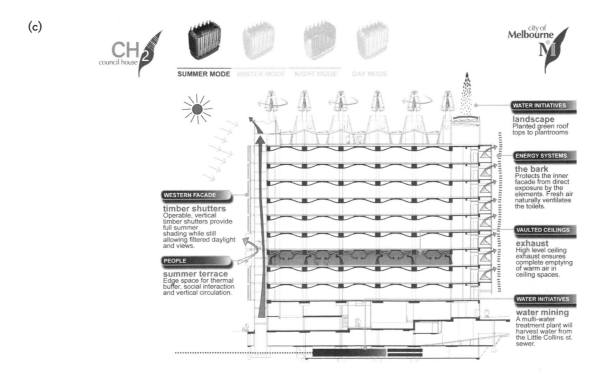

(d)

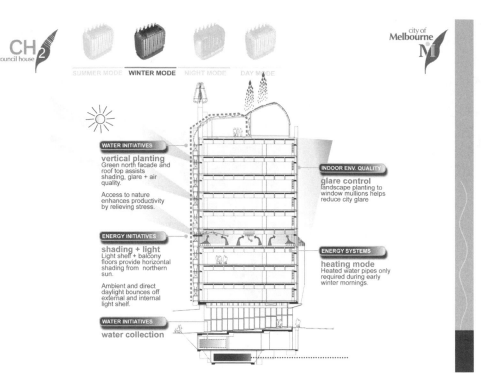

WINTER MODE

WATER INITIATIVES

vertical planting
Green north facade and
roof top assists
shading, glare + air
quality.

Access to nature
enhances productivity
by relieving stress.

ENERGY INITIATIVES

shading + light
Light shelf + balcony
floors provide horizontal
shading from northern
sun.

Ambient and direct
daylight bounces off
external and internal
light shelf.

WATER INITIATIVES

water collection

INDOOR ENV. QUALITY

glare control
landscape planting to
window mullions helps
reduce city glare

ENERGY SYSTEMS

heating mode
Heated water pipes only
required during early
winter mornings.

(e)

(f)

(g)

(i)

(h)

(j)

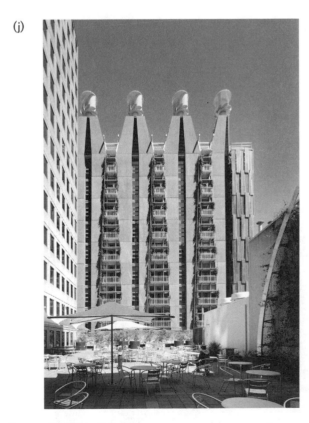

Figure 17-1 a-j *Cont'd*

Builder: Hansen Yuncken.

Cost: Approximately $41 million (US) which includes the base building and sustainability features. The return on the City's environmental investment is expected to be six years.

2. The Gish Apartments[2]

San José, California

The Gish Apartments provides affordable housing rentals to low-income tenants, and thirteen of the 35 units are set aside for residents with developmental disabilities. Developmentally disabled individuals require various levels

of care—from live-in caregivers to support staff; this range of care is provided through the local agency, Housing Choices Coalition. Gish Apartments is the first multifamily housing development in California to earn both Leadership in Energy and Environmental Design (LEED) for Homes Gold and LEED for New Construction Gold certifications from the U.S. Green Building Council (USGBC).

(a)

Site Plan

1. Light Rail Platforms
2. Restaurant
3. Hotel
4. Residential
5. Courtyard/Play Area
6. Solar Panels
7. Parking Garage Entry
8. Convenience Store Entry

(b)

[2] Source: First Community Housing.

(c)

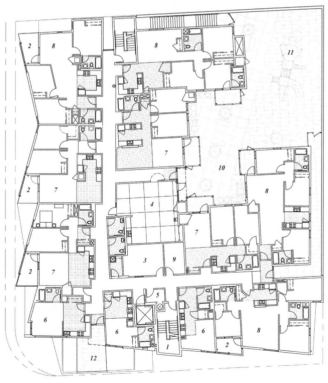

(d)

Second Floor Plan

1. Main Stair
2. Suite Balconies
3. Office
4. Community Room
5. Trash Room
6. SRO/Studio
7. Two Bedroom Suite
8. Three Bedroom Suite
9. Meeting Room
10. Courtyard
11. Play Area
12. Exterior Terrace

0   5   10   20

Figure 17-2 a–d The Gish Apartments, San José, California.

Developed by local not-for-profit First Community Housing in partnership with the City of San José's Housing Department, the Gish Apartments provides 35 units of affordable housing and 3,775 square feet of ground-floor retail space on an infill site immediately adjacent to a light-rail station and near retail and other medium-density residential areas.

Green Building Features

- A transit program for the residents, giving them annual *Eco Passes* to use on the County's light-rail and bus system, which has stops located directly across the street, thereby reducing private vehicle use and the need for parking by 25 percent.
- The Gish Apartments construction process was hampered by the necessity to clean up a contaminated site, which was formerly a gas station with underground storage tanks.
- Development density of more than 80 units per acre.
- Small unit sizes create a small footprint.
- Advanced framing techniques.
- Reduction of construction waste by more than 75 percent.
- Locally sourced materials.
- Water-efficient toilets, showers, faucets, and irrigation.
- Energy-efficient lighting, appliances, and windows.
- Rooftop photovoltaic system provides over 30 percent of common-area electrical needs.
- Low-VOC adhesives, paints, and sealants to promote good indoor air quality for building occupants, especially important for the inhabitants with sensitive immune systems.
- Green building education for the building's residents and maintenance staff.

Design Team

Architecture and design: Office of Jerome King, Architecture and Planning

Owner and developer: First Community Housing

Contractor: Branagh Construction

Commissioning: Guttman & Blaevoet

Mechanical: John Allen, VAO

Green building consultants: Simon & Associates

■ 3. The Aldo Leopold Legacy Center

Baraboo, Wisconsin

The Aldo Leopold Legacy Center (ALLC) was developed on the site of the environmentalist pioneer's family hunting shack by the foundation established by his children. It functions as a learning center and the location of the Aldo Leopold literary archives. The project scheme is a cluster of structures around a courtyard that provides necessary program functions. The buildings house offices, conference spaces, archives, interpretive exhibits, library, workshop, and a "three-season hall." The shack and farm revitalized an area that had been abandoned during the Dust Bowl, the perfect embodiment of Leopold's concept of land ethic—that land should be respected and loved rather than used and spent.

The Legacy Center is the first carbon-neutral building rated by the USGBC, and it complies with the metrics prescribed by the 2030 Challenge. It achieved a Platinum LEED certification, earning 61 of 69 possible points, the highest point tally so far earned under LEED.

(a)

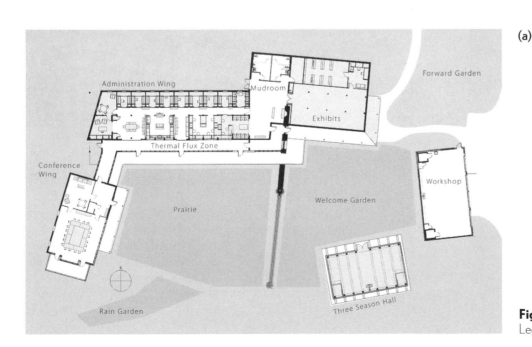

Figure 17-3 a–f The Aldo Leopold Legacy Center, Baraboo, Wisconsin.

(b)

(c)

(d)

(e)

(f)

Figure 17-3 a–f *Cont'd*

Carbon Neutrality and Energy Conservation

One of the exceptional achievements of the Legacy Center is that it is a zero-net-energy building, generating 100 percent of its energy on-site, through a solar array on the roof. The building uses as much as 70 percent less energy than a similar building type built to code. Concrete "earth tubes," buried 10 feet under the building, precondition (or moderate) the air supply for the ventilation system by using the surrounding temperature of the soil, thereby eluding the extreme temperature fluctuations of the Wisconsin seasons. Daylighting, radiant flooring, natural ventilation, high-performance insulation, envelope design that maximizes radiant heat from the sun in winter while offering protection from heat gain in summer, and appropriately sized mechanical systems yielded this impressive efficiency.

Its carbon footprint was assessed by establishing an audit of all combustion-using systems, including vehicles and fixed systems, organizational carbon expenditures such as employee air travel and energy expended for water supply, sanitation, and waste removal. Carbon offsetting was accomplished through renewable energies and sequestration of carbon via 35 acres of forest, certified through the Forest Stewardship Council (FSC). This acreage is expected to store 8.75 tons of carbon per year.

Design Team

Architecture and design: Kubala-Washatko Architects

Contractors: Boldt Construction

Environmental building consultant: Mike Utzinger, University of Wisconsin-Milwaukee School of Architecture

LEED consultant: Boldt Construction

Commissioning agent: Supersymmetry USA, Inc.

■ 4. Genzyme Center

Cambridge, Massachusetts

The Genzyme Center, completed in 2003, is a twelve-story building of 350,000 square feet that houses the headquarters for the biomedical research and innovation

(a)

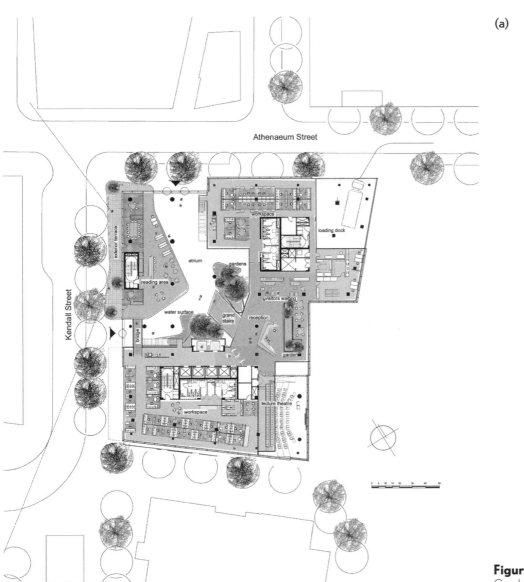

Figure 17-4 a–d Genzyme Center, Cambridge, Massachusetts.

(b)

(c)

(d)

Figure 17-4 a-d *Cont'd*

company, Genzyme Corporation, and is an excellent example of what kind of project emerges from collaborative and integrated design processes. Aside from having achieved a LEED Platinum rating for its significant brace of sustainable strategies, it demonstrates that integrated team delivery and design can ultimately contribute to measurable benefits—in this case, improved worker productivity, well-being, connection to colleagues, and exposure to nature; ultimately, this collaboratively designed building encourages a collaborative working environment.

As we have seen in earlier chapters, productivity, well-being, and reduced absenteeism are related to the quality of the indoor environment. In the Genzyme Center, the indoor environment, the central atrium in particular, tells the central story in terms of productivity but also touches on a key component of the energy systems.

Key Sustainable Design Features

- The central atrium provides light, connection with indoor gardens, communication with colleagues. Heliostats, high-tech mirrors mounted on the roof, track the sun's position and enhance the penetration of light by directing light deeper into the spaces. Reflective surfaces, including a reflecting pool, also help bounce daylight to work areas. Automatic light-dimming technology responds to the levels of light entering through the glazing and adjusts the electric lighting accordingly; the reduction in lighting energy use is expected to be 45 percent.
- Louvers on the exterior glass facade are designed to control the entry of daylight and glare through sensors, which like the heliostats follow the sun's path.
- Workers can control temperature, lighting, and entry of outside air through the use of operable windows.
- One-hundred percent of the project load is achieved through renewable sources: photovoltaics, recovered steam, and purchases of clean energy through Green-e certified sources.
- The heating, ventilating, and air-conditioning (HVAC) system design and energy: Steam recovery for heating and cooling, zoning, natural ventilation, operable windows with sensors to fan-coil units; the double facade has a ventilated void to the outside, as well as automatic shades to modulate summer heat gain reduction and allow optimal solar access in the window.
- A vegetated roof and double curtain wall provide higher levels of envelope insulation than a standard building.
- For the building as a whole, energy savings from highly efficient motors, fans, and other equipment is expected to reduce energy costs by 41 percent.
- The social dynamic of the Center's workplace is focused on the ease of creative communication among colleagues, collaborative exchanges, and the building of relationships using a less rigid structure rather than the standard corporate model. The architecture provides areas for team interaction, informal conversation, and formal presentations. The indoor gardens contribute to a healthful interior.
- Water use is 34 percent lower than for a conventional building of the same size and type. This was accomplished in part by using low-flow and low-flush plumbing fixtures.
- Fully 75 percent of the materials used in the construction of the Genzyme Center have recycled content, probably one of the only LEED buildings to attain this rate.
- The building is situated on a former brownfield site, labeled as such because of its previous incarnation as a coal gasification plant.

Design Team

Owner: Genzyme Corp. & Lyme Properties

Architect and engineer: Behnisch Architekten (formerly Behnisch, Behnisch & Partner)

Base building architecture: House & Robertson Architects

Tenant improvements: Next Phase Studios

Engineers: Bruro Happold/Laszlo Bodak Engineer

Contractor: Turner Construction

Interior gardens consultant: LOG ID Solararchitectur

■ 5. Green Building in China

Green building case studies from China have a place in this book, because the country has enormous potential both for constructing unparalleled amounts of buildings and because it has the extraordinary opportunity to address its impact—that is, if the barriers to implementing energy efficiency in buildings and obtaining access to green building materials are surmounted. If funding and the technology to support sustainable construction are available, the barriers will erode.

China is experiencing a surge of urbanization, the scale of which seems almost unreal. In 2007 more building square footage was constructed in Shanghai than presently exists in New York City's office buildings. Two billion square meters are being built out annually, but the overwhelming majority of new projects do not have energy-efficiency or high-performance building technology in the program briefing.[3] Of 43 billion square meters of office building space, only 4 percent of them have energy-efficiency strategies.

[3] "Briefing: Policies for Energy Efficient Buildings in China," UN Environmental Programme (UNEP) Sustainable Buildings & Construction Initiative, March 26, 2008, http://www.unepsbci.org/SBCINews/latestNews/showNews.asp?what=Briefing__Policies_for_Energy_Efficient_Buildings_in_China (accessed January 14, 2009).

Nevertheless, there is vital interest in making green buildings and planning ecocities, and many government and industry leaders, developers, and designers are making progress toward sustainability. The challenges faced in China are very similar to those that the green building movement in the West confronted several years ago in attempting to change the way buildings are designed and constructed. As was the case with the growing stages of the U.S. green movement in the 1970s, building energy efficiency is a primary focus. Ling Li noted that "China's five-year plan for 2006–10 calls for energy savings of 50 percent for new buildings nationwide and up to 65 percent for buildings in four large municipalities (Beijing, Shanghai, Tianjin, and Chongqing). In early 2006, the government issued a design standard for energy conservation to encourage contractors to use energy-efficient materials and adopt energy-saving technologies for heating, cooling, ventilating, and lighting public buildings."[4]

While in the West we concern ourselves with green buildings living in isolation without the goal of effecting green communities, the opposite happens in China: ecocities such as Dontang are being built, while the existing urbanized infrastructure is not receiving the benefits of sustainably designed programs. Ecocities have gotten more press in China, while individual green buildings have not. In part, as a response, the goal of the March 2008 documentary *Green Dragon*, on green building in China, was to provide the Chinese government, developers, architects, and other building professionals working in China with real and actionable opportunities for

change in construction methodology. The two buildings below outline some of the integrated building technologies currently being used in China. Each project is unique: one is a single office building, while the other is a monumentally scaled urban high-rise community.

Linked Hybrid, MOMA Development, Beijing, China[5]

The Linked Hybrid building is a series of eight high-rise towers, each with four vegetated roofs linked by a pedestrian sky bridge. It is a mixed-use project consisting of apartments (what architect Steven Holl refers to as "twenty-first century. domestic spaces"), offices, shops, school, public park, movie theater, and a high-rise pedestrian zone. Architect Steven Holl describes the project as a "city within a city," with a sky ring on one of the highest floors, creating a "utopian new world." At the base of the linked buildings is a thriving mixed-use neighborhood that is expected to provide the residents with a 24-hour urban life. Gardens at the ground level are irrigated with treated gray water collected from the wastewater generated on-site.

Key Sustainable Design Features

- Energy source: 600 geothermal wells 100 meters under the project site; ground-source heat pumps.
- The project residents' activities will produce 283 tons of cooking and bathing water, which will be treated in an on-site wastewater-treatment system and then used to irrigate the landscape.

(a)

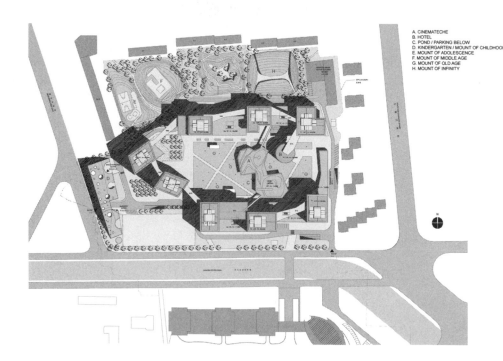

A. CINEMATECHE
B. HOTEL
C. POND / PARKING BELOW
D. KINDERGARTEN / MOUNT OF CHILDHOOD
E. MOUNT OF ADOLESCENCE
F. MOUNT OF MIDDLE AGE
G. MOUNT OF OLD AGE
H. MOUNT OF INFINITY

Figure 17-5 a–c Linked Hybrid, MOMA Development, Beijing (site plan, elevation, and view of sky bridge).

[4] Ling Li, "China Pushing for Energy-Efficient Buildings," January 25, 2007, Worldwatch Institute, http://www.worldwatch.org/node/4874.

[5] Alex Pasternack, "Beijing's Eco-Friendly Architecture," *China Dialogue*, December 20, 2006.

- Radiant slabs for floors and ceiling for both heating and cooling.
- Ventilation system: Outside air is introduced at floor level, where it pools in "lakes" and then rises as the temperature increases, to be exhausted near the ceiling, relying on the stack effect instead of the cross-polluting effects of forced air.

Design Team

Developer: Beijing Modern Hong Yun Real Estate Development Co. Ltd.

Size: 280,000 square meters (3,013,849 square feet)

Design architect: Steven Holl

Design engineer: TranSolar

(b)

(c)
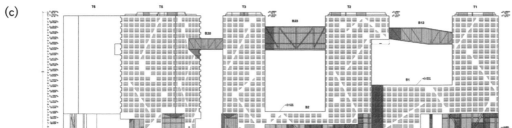

Figure 17-5 a–c *Cont'd*

Sustainability consultant: EMSI + Farr Associates

LEED-ND pilot program

Projected completion date: 2009

ACCORD[6] 21 Office Building, Beijing, China

Key Statistics

- Water use is reduced by 60 percent.
- Sixty-five percent of storm water is retained on-site.
- Energy efficiency: 70 percent savings (uses 6.8 kilowatt hours per square foot, whereas typical, comparable office buildings in China consume about 28 kilowatt hours).

Key Sustainable Design Features

- High-performance envelope and windows
- Lighting-load reduction: techniques used include daylighting, ultra-low-energy lighting

Figure 17-6 Accord Office Building (interior and exterior)

[6]The building is so named because it was developed by the Chinese Ministry of Science and Technology and the U.S. Department of Energy and is managed by the Natural Resources Defense Council (NRDC), under the auspices of ACCORD 21 (American-Chinese Coalition Organized for Responsible Development in the 21st Century).

- High-efficiency, combined chiller-thermal storage system
- Dual-cistern storm-water retention to capture water for irrigation and toilet flushing
- Pervious paving
- Vegetated roof
- Urban location connected to transit lines
- Green building education: The building houses a "green building and community design and technology demonstration training center."

Design Team

Developer: Ministry of Science & Technology, State Government building

Date completed: 2004

Area: 13,000 square meters (139,930 square feet)

Architecture and design: Gao Lin-Beijing Urban Planning & Design Institute

Sustainability consultant: NRDC/Rob Watson

LEED Gold: First LEED building in China

Additional Green Building Projects in China

- Three completed LEED-certified projects: Plantronics factory, Suzhou; the Le Sang Shopping Mall, Harbin; and the Taige Apartments, Shenzhen.
- Four LEED projects under construction: the Xingfu Ercun (XF2C) commercial building, the Silo City mixed-use complex, the Carrefour supermarket, and the Century Prosper Commercial Center.
- Chinese ecocities: Dongtan, Shanghai, Rizhao, and Chongming Island.

▓ 6. BedZED and other ZED Projects

The Bill Dunster Architects ZEDfactory, United Kingdom

The impetus behind Bill Dunster's work was to make renewable energy technologies accessible. As we have seen in previous chapters, zero energy can mean that a project draws energy only from an on-site renewable source. All ZEDFactory projects have building- or site-integrated renewable energy technology incorporated in their design.

The Beddington Zero Energy Development (BedZED) outside London, the first of Bill Dunster's projects to gain publicity because of its approach to energy, was completed in 2002 and continues to be an oft-cited case study. It is also billed as a carbon-neutral ecocommunity.

(a)

Figure 17-7 a BedZED village green.

(b)

Figure 17-7 b BedZED skylights, terraces, and roofs.

(c)

Figure 17-7 c BedZED wind scoop.

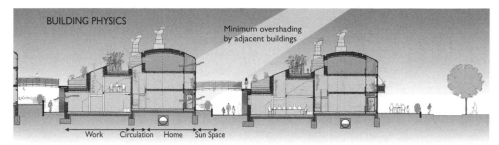

(d)

EXPOSED THERMAL MASS	In summer - produces cooling In winter - stores passive heat gains until needed

- North facing windows
- Good daylight
- Minimum solar heat gain

- Extensive South facing windows giving good, passive solar heat gain
- Glazed buffer sun space
- Minimum North glazing for daylight

Figure 17-7 d BedZED passive heating and cooling.

Figure 17-7 e BedZED, an arcade.

It is a mixed-use project that offers 82 apartment units for diverse occupants (both renters and owners) on a reclaimed brownfield site.

Key Sustainable Design Features

- Energy source: 8,363 square feet, 109 kilowatts of PVs.
- Passive ventilation by means of colorful roof-mounted wind cowls.
- Cogeneration plant powered by tree-trimming waste provides district heating.
- Passive solar design, buildings oriented toward the south, with insulated, high-performance glazing.
- Thermal mass from envelope design.
- Use of FSC-certified sustainably harvested wood (and other certified wood sources).
- Energy-use metering and monitors for each resident
- Rainwater harvesting and reuse.
- Regionally sourced local construction materials.

- Occupant waste management through recycling.
- Transportation: Because BedZED is a low-car development community, one of the first of its kind, there is a car-share program, called "ZEDcars," to reduce car ownership and driving time. Instead of being car-centric, BedZED is pedestrian oriented and in an urban, walkable location with connection to diverse forms of transportation, including public transit.
- Roof gardens provide habitat and storm-water retention.
- Salvaged and reused building materials.
- Used only low-formaldehyde products.

Efficiencies over Baseline-Comparable Buildings

- Energy source: 88,000 kilowatt hours is produced by the PVs, meeting 88 percent of heating demands. Three kilowatt hours of electrical power per person is used, 25 percent below the average in the United Kingdom.
- Fifty percent water-use reduction is achieved through rainwater harvesting and dual-flush toilets.

ZED Factory has developed several ZED housing types and kits, which are offered in conjunction with the firm's development services. All the housing types embody the same integrated building design strategies of building-integrated, renewable energy systems such as microwind turbines, PVs and solar hot water, natural ventilation, green roofs, super insulation, and high thermal-mass characteristics.

Other ZED Projects

RurualZED: Uses timber-frame construction and efficient construction methods to minimize materials waste and uses a thermal mass concrete liner.

ZED-in-a-Box: A high-density block of terraced homes using brick and block construction and individual green space; solar gain is encouraged through double-height sun spaces.

Figure 17-7 f A rural ZED carbon-neutral kit home.

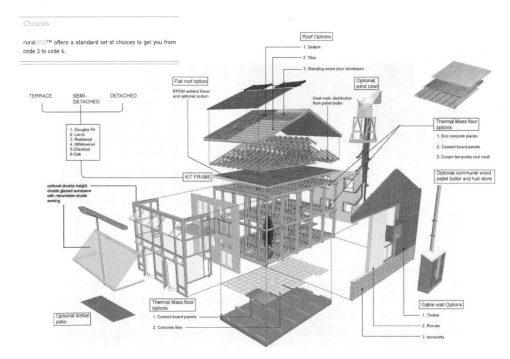

Figure 17-7 g Exploded isometric of rural Zed components.

ZED-in-a-Box Town House: Detached, semidetached, or terraced block type town houses.

Mini Solar Block: Four stories. An efficient plan meant for tight urban sites, solar gain through sloping, terraced south facade, integrated PVs, super insulated with thermal mass, outdoor space on every floor.

Urban Solar Block: Five stories. High-density, urban block housing type with apartments and duplexes with brick and block construction; and integrated PVs. Seven-bay module can be combined into several unit types. Accessible for older people and includes shared public spaces and amenities.

Figure 17-7 h Solar bow ZED.

Figure 17-7 i Solar bow ZED view through the building integrated PVs.

Figure 17-7 j A cluster of solar bow ZED structures woven into active community green space and the street grid.

■ 7. Water + Life Museums

Western Center for Archeology and Paleontology + Center for Water Education, Hemet, California

> The museum's exhibits are about local resources, so the building itself is a living example of sustainability and conservation.
>
> *–Michael Lehrer, design architect*

The twin museums in the California desert near Los Angeles represent the first museums in the United States to attain a LEED Platinum certification. The museums came to fruition because the Metropolitan Water District (MWD) of Southern California had developed one of the largest earthwork projects in the country, the Diamond Valley Lake reservoir, in Hemet. In exchange for the upheaval the project had caused the community, the MDW offered the nearly one million fossils unearthed during excavation of the reservoir a museum to call home.

Each museum has flexible program space for classrooms and meetings, exhibit and interactive space,

(a)

(b)

(c)

Figure 17-8 a-d Water + Life Museum: A building about water in the desert.

(d)

Figure 17-8 a–d *Cont'd*

laboratories, classrooms, offices, gift shop, and a café. A large outdoor terrace connects the two museums. Ten 46-foot-high towers line the facades of the project, a Stonehenge-like tribute to the exhibits inside.

Key Sustainable Design Features

- 3,000 photovoltaic panels (540 kilowatts) on a 50,000-square-foot rooftop. The PV array supplies almost 70 percent of the project's total energy demands, saving about $13 million in energy expenses over the life span of the panels.
- Energy efficiency was enhanced to 40 percent above California's Title 24 Building Energy Standards.
- Real-time energy-use monitoring.
- Heat-blocking glass on windows.
- Native desert planting irrigated with reclaimed water.
- Heating: radiant flooring and forced air.
- Daylight harvesting and daylight sensors on lighting controls.
- Though not considered green, the solution to adequately shade the structure in the desert climate resulted in 10,000 square feet of PVC-coated polyester banners—disposable after five years.

Design Team

Architecture and design: Lehrer + Gangi Design + Build

Mechanical and plumbing engineers: IBE Consulting Engineers V

Electrical and solar consultant: Vector Delta Design Group

Landscape architect: Mia Lehrer & Associates?

LEED consultants: Zinner Consultants

Cost: $36,819,064

Completion date: November 2006

Building area: 70,000 square feet on 17 acres

■ Resources

Green Building Case Study Databases

Architecture 2030: http://www.architecture2030.org.

Architecture for Humanity: http://www.architectureforhumanity.org/projects/all.

EERE High Performance Building Database: http://eere.buildinggreen.com/.

CABE: http://www.cabe.org.uk/casestudies.aspx.

Green Building Challenge archived case studies:

1998: http://greenbuilding.ca/gbc98cnf.

2000: http://greenbuilding.ca/gbc2k/gbc-start.htm.

2002: http://iisbe.org/iisbe/gbc2k5/gbc2k5-start.htm.

U.S. Green Building Council (USGBC) and World Green Building Council (World GBC): http://www.usgbc.org/LEED/Project/CertifiedProjectList.aspx and http://www.worldgbc.org/featured-projects.

American Institute of Architects, Committee on the Environment (COTE) Top Ten Lists: http://www.aiatopten.org/.

Top Ten Green Hospitals: http://www.thegreenguide.com/doc/113/top10hospitals.

18 Rating Systems and Practice Tools

Buildings are among the most long-lived physical artifacts society produces. They are typically used for 50–100 years, so their inertia has a major impact on future energy use and emissions patterns. Today's architecture will be with us for a long time.[1]

–*Edward Mazria*

Introduction

The advent of integrated building design amplifies the spectrum of possible career options for design school graduates with this new skill set. Recent integrated building regulations, codes, and guidelines impose an added layer to traditional design-firm practice. Along with standard design-firm practice, an integrated building education opens up a whole new range of career opportunities. Accreditation as a green building professional currently takes place during professional practice, but increasingly design schools are beginning to incorporate the accreditation preparation process into the professional degree curriculum. With a green building background, graduates may choose to design and construct green buildings, to consult with project teams to green their projects, or to specialize as a consultant in carbon-neutral building design or become affiliated with a green building think tank.

Whatever the career choice, green building rating systems and other practice tools are necessary as part of a building project's integrated design process.

The recent years have seen the globalization of all things green, including green buildings. Now, virtually every industrialized nation has a green building rating system.

Even smaller, less developed nations have sustainability guidelines, often based on protecting ecosystems and making efficient use of local resources. Rating systems set guidelines and target efficiencies for sustainable buildings. They may address site considerations and smart-development strategies, such as public transit access and use of materials that avoid the use of environmental and human health toxins in favor of certified and preferable materials. A complaint about many such systems is that they do not plumb the depths of sustainability; rather, they reach only to the level of least resistance. While this is true of any system in its infancy, the long-term goal is to gradually increase the intensity of the requirements after green strategies become mainstream. Eventually, the rating system becomes more robust.

What Is a Rating System?

A rating system is not the same beast as an life-cycle assessment or environmental impact and performance assessment tool, although the system's score and ultimate performance of a building can provide valuable impact evaluations and other data to stakeholders. Rating, labeling, and certification systems provide a scale for measuring a building's incorporation of green building strategies as compared with more conventional, mainstream buildings.

INTENSIFYING GREEN BUILDINGS

Climate-responsive indigenous building→Energy-efficient / rustic buildings → Green buildings → High LEED level → Living building → Restorative building.

---

[1]Edward Mazria, "It's the Architecture, Stupid! " *Solar Today* May/June (2003): 48–51; http://www.mazria.com/publications.

Naturally, these strategies have a beneficial impact on a building's performance. Building performance is not only an indicator of "whole building" sustainability but also a motivating force for other project teams. Given human nature our society's competitive economy and business models, it is not surprising that efforts toward sustainability would be propelled by the concept of a comparatively scored scale. This structure adds a competitive edge and promotes leadership in the design and construction industries. In sum, green building systems lead to "market change" in industry and manufacturing.

In order for a system to compare buildings, one against another, and produce results that allow for accurate assessment, the system must use consistent metrics. The system must be verifiable, measurable, quantifiable, and technically robust. It must also be sufficiently developed, with enough rated buildings in its portfolio relevant to a broad spectrum of building types. Finally, it must be transparent about its development and funding.

Transparency of funding is important in order to understand the agenda of the groups that develop the systems. It often comes down to whether the goal is to "self-certify" a building or to participate on an equal plane using a rating system that is unbiased, fair, and results in deep green rather than greenwash.[2]

Scoring high on a rating system is likely to provide increased eligibility for fundraising goals, high public relations value, incentive for buyers or investors, preferential as well as priority building permits in some municipalities, along with other less tangible benefits. Such systems also create market change on the materials side and increased knowledge and skill on the practice side.

The value of a voluntary rating system lies also in its cachet, branding, and name recognition. Building owners can compare performance against other buildings, with the goal of competing for high levels of sustainable certification. But most significantly, the increasing demand for green buildings and the use of rating systems is transforming the way we design, construct, and sell buildings. A green-certified building invigorates best practices.

Critics view such systems as unweighted checklists that do not really measure a project's holistic success as a green building. They argue that such systems encourage only minimal performance and benchmarking in the quest to receive a green label. In addition, many systems fall short, because they are regionally biased. Although regionally relevant benchmarks are important, applying a universal value to differing regions ends up being prejudicial.

For example, calling for humidity-level monitoring in every building is an irrelevant strategy in climates where humidity is not a problem. Critics also argue that deep green strategies can be achieved, even documented and proven, but that some types of measures will not slot into the existing framework of the rating system.

Others argue that rating systems are unnecessary and that current environmental conditions should be enough of a motivator to spur change in the way we build. Some critics think that there is no leeway in building rating systems to acknowledge deep green restorative buildings. Some rating systems are designed around one type of building. The USGBC Leadership in Energy and Environmental Design (LEED) for New Construction (NC) rating system was originally designed to apply to commercial office buildings and not hospitality projects, for example. In fact, this is why many subsets of mainstream rating systems, such as LEED, were developed, as witnessed by the emergence of LEED for Retail, Homes, Schools, and Neighborhood Development, to name a few.

The Range of Ratings

Rating systems are not new. Some have been around for almost two decades. Differences among them range from region-specific applications to impact versus performance assessment or the consideration of operations and maintenance as part of the system.

Some countries have attempted to incorporate life-cycle assessment (LCA) into their systems, as is the case with Japan's Comprehensive Assessment System for Building Environmental Efficiency (CASBEE, Figure 18-1). Industry groups like the Building Owners and Managers Association (BOMA) have instituted incentives to their members that serve as competitive motivators but are not actual ratings resulting in certification. Academic institutions and government agencies are truly on the forefront of rating system development because of their ostensible commitment to unbiased research. Municipalities have adopted rating systems or written mandatory green building guidelines as part of new legislation, offering incentives to builders. Among the directives of the Living Building Challenge, developed by the Cascadia Chapter of the USGBC, is the pursuit of "beauty" in green buildings. Other systems, like the Building Research Establishment Environmental Assessment Method (BREEAM), are grounded in quantifiable weighted strategies.

International Rating Systems

In contrast to countries of the European Union (EU) and Asia, the United States was slow to come to the

[2]K. M. Fowler and E. M. Rauch, "Sustainable Building Rating System Summary," Pacific Northwest National Laboratory, General Services Administration, July 2006.

CASBEE®

Figure 18-1 Japan's rating system is known as CASBEE, for Comprehensive Assessment System for Building Environmental Efficiency.

realization that building green is critical to energy independence and the freedom from the rising costs of energy. Concern about the impact of environmental pollutants is also widespread, as witnessed by the resolutions resulting from the Stockholm UN Environmental Programme (UNEP) convention.[3]

Many European countries, including the Netherlands, Germany, and some Scandinavian countries, have blended green construction and performance into their standard building methodology. It is beneficial to become acquainted with some of these international systems and their salient features. Refer to the accompanying table for a partial listing of international rating systems.

BREEAM

Among the oldest and most extensively used rating systems is the Building Research Establishment Environmental Assessment Method (BREEAM; Figure 18-2), which was developed in the United Kingdom in 1990 by the Building Research Establishment Ltd (BRE).[4]

BREEAM addresses the issues of management, energy use, health and well-being, pollution, transport, land use, ecology, materials, and water.[5] The multitude of systems developed by BREEAM include systems for courts, existing buildings, industrial buildings, prisons, offices, retail buildings, and schools, as well as an officially adopted "Code for Sustainable Homes," built on the BREEAM ecohomes system. The Building Research Establishment is also able to develop specific systems for international application and publishes a green guide to specifications and a software tool for "whole life costs and environmental impact" assessment.[6]

Green strategy of note: Assessment of carbon dioxide (CO_2) emissions arising from transportation effects to and from the project. A rural location would score less than an urban location with a connection to a transportation node.

green building council australia

Figure 18-3 Australia's Green Building Council implements the Green Star rating system.

In Australia

Developed in 2002 by the Green Building Council of Australia, Green Star Australia[7] (Figure 18-3) is one of the most robust rating systems globally. For commercial office buildings, it addresses issues ranging from reduction of ambient noise levels, eliminating fluorescent lighting "flicker," design for disassembly, as well as separating and protecting topsoil during construction.

Green Star is based on a combination of influences, including LEED and BREEAM, and it is unique, because it offers a tool for each phase of a building's life cycle: design, construction, occupancy, and ownership. In addition, once the rating tool delivers a result—in this case, a score based on the percentage of points earned out of the total—Green Star applies weighting factors. These are based on the environmental priorities that are represented in Australia's varied regions. Levels of certification are four, five, or six stars, depending on the degree of best practices achieved. Tools include rating systems for offices, as-built offices, and office interiors, with pilot systems for existing office buildings, health care, education, retail centers, multiunit residential projects, industrial buildings, and public buildings. Categories of green strategies are: management, indoor environment quality, energy, transport, water, materials, land use and ecology, emissions, and innovation. Green Star Australia is affiliated with the World Green Building Council.

Credit of note: Green Star encourages specifying alternatives to polyvinyl chloride–containing materials, measured at the 30 percent level (one point) or the 60 percent level (two points).

Another Australian rating system is the National Australian Built Environment Rating System (NABERS), which is managed by the New South Wales Department of Environment and Climate Change. This is a rating system for commercial or residential existing buildings meant to provide a gauge as to how well a building performs based on its "measured operational impacts on the environment."[8]

The World Green Building Council[9]

David Gottfried, one of the founders of the U.S. Green Building Council, established the World

breeam

Figure 18-2 The United Kingdom's rating system is the Building Research Establishment Environmental Assessment Method (BREEAM).

[3]"Declaration of the United Nations Conference on the Human Environment," 21st Plenary Meeting, Stockholm, Sweden, 16 June 1972 (Nairobi, Kenya: United Nations Environmental Programme, 1972), http://www.unep.org/Documents.multilingual/Default.asp?DocumentID=97&ArticleID=1503.
[4]Building Research Establishment Environmental Assessment Method (BREEAM), http://www.breeam.org.
[5]Refer to the BREEAM Fact File at http://www.breeam.org.
[6]Envest, http://envestv2.bre.co.uk.

[7]Green Building Council of Australia Web site, http://www.gbca.org.au.
[8]National Australian Built Environment Rating System (NABERS), http://www.nabers.com.au.
[9]World Green Building Council (WGBC) Web site, http://www.worldgbc.org.

WORLD GREEN BUILDING COUNCIL

Figure 18-4 The World Green Building Council.

Green Building Council (WGBC; Figure 18-4) in 1998. Today, along with the USGBC, it has partnered with the Clinton Climate Initiative and supports many international efforts toward sustainable building policies, including UNEP.[10]

The WGBC is run by business leaders, but the individual national rating systems are typically run by nonprofits embracing many types of industry. As of spring of 2008, Australia, Brazil, Canada, Germany, India, Japan, Mexico, United Arab Emirates, Great Britain, United States, New Zealand, and Taiwan were all members of the WGBC. In addition, several countries with no existing rating system are interested in joining the WGBC. These include Argentina, Chile, Colombia, Egypt, Greece, Guatemala, Hong Kong, Israel, Jordan, Korea, Nigeria, Panama, Philippines, South Africa, Spain, Switzerland, Turkey, and Vietnam.[11]

Of note: For rating systems to have universal applicability is an impossibility, so regional accommodations are considered under WGBC. For example, carpet is not typically used in India, therefore, the Indian Green Building Council suggests editing the low-VOC-emitting carpet credit to allow a point for using no carpet.

INTERNATIONAL MOVEMENTS TOWARD SUSTAINABLE BUILDING[12]

- Hong Kong: HK-BEAM (Hong Kong Building Environmental Assessment Method) was established in 2002 "for the industry and by the industry as a means to measure, improve and label the environmental performance of buildings" (http://www.hk-beam.org.hk).

- France: HQE (Haute Qualité Environnementale, or High Environmental Quality) was developed by the Association pour la Haute Qualité Environnementale. It provides certification based on an evaluation of building performance and management strategies (http://www.assohqe.org).

- Netherlands: GreenCalc—founded by the Dutch Institute for Building Biology and Ecology (NIBE) and the Dutch consulting engineering firm DGMR—measures materials, energy, and water mobility (http://www.greencalc.com).

- Singapore: The Green Mark Scheme, developed in 2005 by the Building and Construction Authority (BCA), is based on energy, site, water, project development and management, indoor environmental quality, and environmental protection and innovation (http://www.bca.gov.sg/GreenMark).

- South Africa: Green Building Council of South Africa (GBCSA), founded in 2007 in concert with the WGBC, is building a system based on Australia's Green Star, with categories focusing on management, indoor environment quality, energy, transport, water, materials, land use and ecology, emissions, and innovation (http://www.greensure.co.za/category/green-building-council-sa/).

- Portugal: LiderA (Liderar pelo Ambiente), developed in 2005 by Manuel Duarte Pinheiro, measures site, integration, resource efficiency, environmental-load impacts, indoor environmental quality, durability, accessibility, environmental management, and innovation (http://www.lidera.info).[13]

- Japan: CASBEE (Comprehensive Assessment System for Building Environmental Efficiency) was developed in 2001 by the nongovernmental organization Japan Sustainable Building Consortium; it is an assessment system and a "labeling tool." It measures "building performance against environmental 'loads,'" and also offers

[10]The goals of the WGBC as noted in its mission statement are to: "Establish common principals for Green Building Councils; serve as a global voice on behalf of Green Building Councils; support and promote individual Green Building Councils; establish a clearing for 'knowledge' transfer between Green Building Councils; encourage development of market based environmental rating systems; recognize global green building leadership" (http://www.worldgbc.org).

[11]Therese Tepe, "Monthly Update: International Growth in the Green Building Industry," August 2007, http://earthtrends.wri.org/updates/node/232.

[12]Kimberly R. Bunz, Gregor P. Henze, PE, and Dale K. Tiller, "Survey of Sustainable Building Design Practices in North America, Europe, and Asia," *Journal of Architectural Engineering* 12, no. 1 (March 2006): 33–62.

[13]Manuel Duarte Pinheiro, "The Portuguese LiderA System—From Assessment to Sustainable Management," Portugal Sustainable Building Conference (SB07 Lisbon), Lisbon, Portugal, 2007.

several tools for building phases and results in ratings of Satisfactory, A, B, or C class (http://www.ibec.or.jp/CASBEE/english/index.htm).

- Germany: Guideline for Sustainable Building, developed by the German Federal Office for Building and Regional Planning, measures energy, reusability and renewability, life span, recyclability, and nature protection and results in a scaled rating of adequate, ranging from Good through Inadequate.[14] Germany's Passiv Haus standard and Planning Package is a design guideline for low-energy buildings whose heating energy can be reduced by 80 percent.
- Italy: Casa Clima carbon-neutral and climate-friendly building rating.

The Green Building Challenge[15]

As evolution is the undercurrent of the entire green building movement, not to mention its overarching focus, it is helpful to trace the evolution of rating systems themselves. One of the progenitors of the modern rating system is the Green Building Challenge (GBC, not to be confused with Green Building Council). What started in 1996 as an international competition to select the most sustainable or most "green" building evolved into a collective effort to design a building performance and environmental impact assessment tool known as the Green Building Assessment Tool (GBTool).

The GBTool was intended to have international application in a variety of settings, with regional and cultural priorities and considerations. It was also envisioned as a basis from which countries could "selectively draw ideas to either incorporate into or modify their own tools."[16] The areas of weighted performance for the GBTool were resource consumption, loadings, indoor environmental quality, quality of service, economics, preoperations management with a commuting transportation plan, and still in development. Selected GBC buildings whose

teams took up the challenge were included in a database developed by National Renewable Energy Laboratory and the U.S. Department of Energy, the High Performance Building Database.[17]

The GBC was associated with a series of "World Sustainable Building Conferences," including Tokyo's Sustainable Building Conference, Action for Sustainability, in 2005.[18] At that time, GBC's research and development mission was redefined and the GBC was "repositioned" under the International Initiative for a Sustainable Built Environment (iiSBE).[19] The iiSBE continues to organize and convene the World Sustainable Building Conferences every three years, in partnership with the UNEP and the International Council for Research and Innovation in Building and Construction (CIB). The most recent conference was SB08 in Melbourne, Australia.

Of note: The GBTool formed a solid basis for national rating systems and motivated many countries to adopt their own green building programs, initiatives, and guidelines.

The Living Building Challenge

The Living Building Challenge (Figure 18-5) was authored and conceived by Jason McLennan prior to his joining the Cascadia chapter of the USGBC, where he now serves as the principal investigator overseeing the development of the standard and associated tools. The "Challenge" is meant to be just that: a challenge. Instead of a guideline or directive to employ best practices, the system is comprised of sixteen mandatory prerequisites that all need to be fulfilled to obtain certification. Project teams may not apply for a rating until operations are in effect for one year after occupancy.

Figure 18-5 Version 1.3 of the Living Building Challenge—"no credits, just prerequisites"—was launched in August, 2008.

---

[14]Bundesamt für Bauwesen und Raumordnung (Germany's Federal Office for Building and Regional Planning), English translation of the Web site: http://www.bbr.bund.de/cln_005/nn_25998/EN/Home/homepage__node.html?__nnn=true (accessed May 21, 2008).

[15]Energy Efficiency and Renewable Energy (EERE), http://www.eere.energy.gov/buildings/highperformance/gbc.html.

[16]Raymond J. Cole, "Report: Review of GBTool and Analysis of GBC 2002 Case-Study Projects," School of Architecture and Landscape Architecture, University of British Columbia, December 12, 2002.

[17]EERE, http://www.eere.energy.gov/buildings/database/.

[18]The SB05 Tokyo Declaration, "Action for Sustainability," at the 2005 World Sustainable Building Conference in Tokyo (SB05Tokyo) brought together more than 1,700 participants from over 80 countries and regions to discuss global cooperation, mutual understanding, innovation of technology and social systems, and other important topics. They recognized the "significant impacts current building practices and human settlement patterns have on resource use, global environmental degradation and climate change" and resolved to support the Kyoto Protocol by implementing sustainable building strategies. Source: Declaration of the participants of SB05 Tokyo, September 29, 2005.

[19]International Initiative for a Sustainable Built Environment, http://www.iisbe.org.

The Living Building Standard goes beyond the USGBC's LEED requirements in that it pushes teams to use sustainable design strategies that, while not in common practice, are well within the reach of current green building practice. An example of one of these noteworthy strategies to supply a building's annual energy consumption through on-site renewable energy, essentially a "net zero energy" building.

Also noteworthy are the "red listed" chemicals that are prohibited from use in a Living Building.[20]

Another two credits call for "net zero water," which requires harvesting of rainwater and management of storm water on-site. Prerequisite Thirteen demands a high level of indoor air quality by calling for emissions testing of VOC-containing materials, rather than the LEED-mandated VOC content limits.

Systems Developed by Government and Academia

Nearly all North American rating systems have had the participation of government and academia in the early stages of their development. Government agencies in the United States have leaned toward the environmental assessment and life-cycle analysis aspects of green building. Often they are hybrids of guidelines, best practices, and ratings. Still others are focused on a single attribute of sustainability, most typically, energy.

The U.S. EPA, for example, has developed a rating system to gauge energy efficiency of comparable building types. Buildings that are eligible by virtue of high performance may earn an Energy Star rating from the U.S. EPA. Increasingly, governments on the municipal, state, and federal levels have adopted green building practices, and guidelines, and mandated LEED-level certification for various project types.[21]

Niche Systems with Application to Other Building Types

Specialized systems for targeted building types have arisen from the precedents just described. Other indus-

Figure 18-6 *Green Guide for Health Care.*

try groups, such as hospitality, justice systems, and retail operators, have adopted green guidelines. A good example of a target building type is the *Green Guide for Health Care* (GGHC)[22] (Figure 18-6). Developed by the health-care sector, it is self-certifying.

Though not granting any specific award, GGHC provides the health-care industry and health-care building designers with a set of comparative metrics. The guide's thematic structure is based on LEED, and it is currently being balloted by the USGBC membership for eventual use as the LEED for Healthcare Rating System.

The guide is best described not so much as a rating system but as a tool kit for a "best practices guide for healthy and sustainable building design, construction, and operations for the healthcare industry." (Green Guide for Health Care web site home page) Critical to the health-care industry is how hospitals are managed sustainably, promoting the health of staff and patients alike. For this reason, the guide is divided into construction and operations guidelines.

Of note: The GGHC underscores the importance of minimizing hospital waste, as well as the management of chemicals, including pharmaceuticals, and chemicals used in radiology and sterilization methods. It mandates removal of polychlorinated biphenyls (PCBs) and the application of asbestos management.

Collaborative for High Performance Schools[23]

The Collaborative for High Performance Schools (CHPS) was developed in 1999 by the California Energy Commission and the utility companies Pacific Gas & Electric, Southern California Edison, and San Diego Gas & Electric together with Charles Eley, and later with nonprofit organizations (Figure 18-7). Their mission was to improve the energy efficacy of California school buildings and to define the term "high performance." CHPS is an excellent framework for understanding the broad range of issues related to high-performance buildings, with specific emphasis on schools.

Using eighty-five possible points in six categories of strategies, including sustainable sites, water, energy, materials, indoor environmental quality, and policy and operations, CHPS sets forth planning and design goals that apply to both modernization of existing school buildings and new construction.

---

[20]"Materials Red List, Prerequisite Five, Living Building Challenge: In Pursuit of True Sustainability in the Built Environment, Cascadia Region Green Building Council, version 1.3, August, 2008. The red-listed chemicals are: added formaldehyde, halogenated flame retardants, PVC (except for code-required PVC wiring), mercury (except for low-mercury fluorescent lighting), CFC/HCFC, neoprene, cadmium, chlorinated polyethylene and chlorosulfonated polyethylene (except for HDPE and LDPE), wood treated with creosote, arsenic or pentachlorophenol, polyurethane, lead (except for solder and off-grid solar battery systems), and phthalates, http://www.cascadiagbc.org. The exceptions to these prohibited chemicals are viewed as temporary until more benign alternatives are on the market. http://www.cascadiagbc.org.

[21]Because the adoption of LEED rating system requirements in legislation changes almost monthly, it is wise to consult the USGBC Web site for additions to the roster: http://www.usgbc.org.

[22]Green Guide for Health Care, http://www.gghc.org (accessed on March 22, 2008).

[23]The Collaborative for High Performance Schools, http://www.chps.net.

Figure 18-7 Collaborative for High Performance Schools.

There are two ways to achieve recognition that a building has incorporated the CHPS criteria: through CHPS verification by a third party ("CHPS Verified" or recognized system) or through free self-certification under "CHPS Designed." A minimum of 32 points must be achieved. The sustainable building and operations strategies of CHPS embody many goals that have applicability to other systems and building types.

Enterprise Foundation's Green Communities

Green Communities is unique among the systems developed by agencies, applying exclusively to affordable housing projects. If a project team is able to meet a minimum number of points in the criteria outlined by Green Communities, it is eligible for grants, loans, and trainings. The criteria are partitioned into eight categories of integrated design: site, location and neighborhood fabric, site improvements, water conservation, energy efficiency, materials use beneficial to the environment, healthy living environment, and operations and maintenance.

Of note: Recognizing that low-income populations should benefit from green building attributes and that social justice is a large component of sustainability, the Green Communities criteria captures twenty-three strategies pertaining to indoor environmental quality in areas such as mold prevention, adequate exhaust and ventilation, separation of combustion sources, PVC-flooring avoidance, and pesticide avoidance.

Systems Developed by Trade or Industry

Green Globes is a Web-based rating system operated in the United States by the Green Building Initiative, originally a consortium of "interests from such sectors as financial services, retailers, wholesalers, appliance manufacturers and other building material providers."[24] Developed in Canada, it was based on the BREEAM system. In Canada, Green Globes is known as Go Green/Go Green Plus ("Visez Vert") and is operated by BOMA. Green Globes addresses seven sustainable design categories: project management, site, energy, water, resources, emissions and effluents, and indoor environment.

Of note: Green Globes delivers immediate feedback by asking a team member to complete an online questionnaire, thereby assisting in measuring a project's efforts to incorporate green strategies. It is basically a self-confirming, rather than a certifying, process.

Regional Systems

Minnesota Sustainable Design Guide 1997[25]

The *Minnesota Sustainable Design Guide* (Figure 18-8) is probably the most tenured rating system in the United States. The guide assists designers with all the phases of a building project: concept design, construction, post-occupancy, operational and performance, evaluation, and remedial measures. Using fifty strategies, the guide focuses on six major issues, echoing many other rating systems: site, water, energy, indoor environment, materials, and waste.

The strategies addressed by the guide are ranked according to team priorities and goal-setting exercises. To amplify these strategies, the guide does something that many other rating systems do not: it evaluates performance by setting minimum goals for each strategy the team employs.

Austin Energy Green Building Rating Systems[26]

In addition to a very successful renewable-energy and energy-efficiency program, the community-owned power company, Austin Energy (Figure 18-8), has returned its profits annually to fund city services. It also has the distinction of being the first city in the United States to develop a green building program. This work formed the foundation for many U.S. rating systems, including LEED.

Austin Energy's rating systems for residential and commercial buildings are remarkably robust, offering

Figure 18-8 Green Building Austin.

[24]Green Building Initiative, http://www.thegbi.org.

[25]The State of Minnesota Sustainable Building Guidelines, *Minnesota Sustainable Design Guide* (1997), http://www.msdg.umn.edu.
[26]Austin Energy, http://www.austinenergy.com.

Figure 18-9 GreenPoint Rated is a residential rating system for California.

Figure 18-10 U.S. Green Building Council (USGBC) and Leadership in Energy and Environmental Design (LEED).

extensive green building strategies after the basic requirements are met. The city requires meeting the standards for its municipal buildings and most of its private sector commercial buildings.

In the 150-point residential system, the basic requirements focus on adequate ventilation, water reduction through fixture selection, low-VOC paint, ceiling fans, fluorescent lighting, insulation and filtration, duct leakage prevention, and heating- and cooling-equipment efficiency.

Once the basic strategies are attained, "Choice Measures for Points" can be pursued in the categories of site selection, home design, construction waste management, building structure and enclosure, thermal and moisture control, plumbing and appliances, mechanical, performance testing, electrical, interior construction and finishes, site work and landscaping, and additions and innovations.[27]

For the 77-point commercial building rating system, the format is similar, with eight categories of basic requirements: e.g., systems commissioning, storm-water runoff and water-quality control, roofing to reduce heat islands, energy-use efficiency, water-use reduction, low-VOC interior paints and coatings, recycling collection and storage, and construction waste management. For points, projects pursue strategies in eight categories: integrated team structure, site, energy, water, indoor environmental quality, materials and resources, education, and innovation.[28]

Austin Energy Green Building also provides a Multi-Family Rating system, with 74 points available, a similarly themed two-tiered system.

Using weighted analysis, the rating system awards up to five stars (one star equals entry level and five stars indicate a very high level of green), with the fourth and fifth stars achievable only if systems commissioning is done by a third-party verifier.

Of note: One of the hallmarks of Austin Energy's program is that it emphasizes siting and envelope design, mandating efficiently designed and installed heat-

ing, ventilating, and air-conditioning (HVAC) systems (e.g., encouraging design for stack and cross-ventilation), lighting, low-VOC paints, and many water conservation measures, such as rainwater harvesting and limits on landscaping with turf grass.

California's GreenPoint Rating

Alameda County in California's San Francisco Bay Area developed a series of green building guidelines in 2000 meant to steer green home design. The guidelines were crafted by a broad spectrum of government, nonprofits, private industry, and design and building professionals, and are a product of a self-described, community-based program. From this basis emerged the GreenPoint rating system (Figure 18-9), and it was intended to be compatible with LEED for Homes, National Association of Home Builders (NAHB) guidelines, and Energy Star for Homes ratings. The nonprofit organization Build It Green guides and manages the process. Currently, there is a dual-branding collaboration between LEED and GreenPoint. GreenPoint offers points in the categories of energy, indoor air quality and health, resources, and water; 50 points or more are needed for a rating.

Of note: GreenPoint has several sustainable strategies of note, among them are radon-resistant construction, deconstruction instead of demolition, fire-safe landscaping, dematerialization, and reduced-formaldehyde content for cabinetry, countertops, trim, subfloors, treads, and shelving.

The U.S. Green Building Council Leading Market Transformation

Leadership in Energy and Environmental Design (LEED) is the suite of rating systems developed in 1998 by the USGBC (Figure 18-10). The LEED system was developed to produce a market-driven, consensus-based national rating system for high-performance buildings. Through the collection of rating systems, LEED is designed to address the life cycle of many scopes: new construction, major reno-

[27]Austin Energy Green Building Guide to the Single-Family Home Rating, vol. 8.0 and 8.1, available for download at http://www.austin-energy.com/energy%20efficiency/Programs/Green%20Building/Participation/aegbResidentialRating.pdf.

[28]Austin Energy Green Building Commercial Guidebook, vol. 1, 2008, published by Austin Energy, 2008, available for download at http://www.austinenergy.com/Energy%20Efficiency/Programs/Green%20Building/Participation/participationFormsAndGuides.htm.

Figure 18-11 The mission of Architecture 2030 is "to rapidly transform the US and global Building Sector from the major contributor of greenhouse gas emissions to a central part of the solution to the global-warming crisis." Imperative 2010 refers to the challenge posed by the founders of Architecture 2030 to help "ecological literacy become a central tenet of design education."

vations, core and shell, and existing buildings and building types—office interiors, schools, retail, health care, homes, and neighborhood developments—across the phases of design, construction, operation, and maintenance.

The USGBC awards certification on four levels—certified, silver, gold, and platinum, depending on the number of points accrued in five sustainable design umbrella categories and innovation credits. Over the years, LEED has grown more robust, setting the standard of achievement gradually higher to motivate participants to aspire to construct restorative buildings that contribute to, rather than burden, global health.

Since the inception of LEED through June 2008, 55,391 individuals have become LEED Accredited Professionals (AP), a recognition awarded to those who have demonstrated knowledge of green building techniques, the rating system, and its process. By the end of 2008, 7,400 projects are projected to be certified. As of May 2008, over 13,000 projects are registered to pursue LEED certification. Still, in spite of, or perhaps owing to, its significant advances, LEED's development has been accompanied by its share of controversy.[29]

As with many such innovations, LEED has experienced the turbulence of the integral, structured growth process for which it was designed. In 2005, although trade association members had been allowed membership to USGBC as individuals and had contributed input toward LEED's development, the USGBC voted to admit industry trade organizations, albeit without voting status.

Other major controversies dominated discussions in the first years of LEED, including decisions about the appropriateness of allowing a LEED credit or innovation point for PVC avoidance; whether to add language to the certified-wood credit that would allow industry-based certifications, in addition to those of the Forest Stewardship Council, to be used as a standard for sustainably harvested wood; by what means life-cycle analysis should be incorporated into LEED; and how to approach HVAC refrigerants' ozone-depleting potential and global warming potential.[30, 31]

Where industry has pushed back hard against LEED efforts to improve the environmental impact of materials, the USGBC has had difficulty bringing its process to conclusion. Spurred by a 2001 proposal to provide credit in LEED for PVC avoidance, a Technical and Scientific Advisory Committee (TSAC) was convened by the USGBC to study the issue of the health effects and negative environmental impacts of PVC. After six years of deliberation, including an interim draft report, the TSAC issued a final report in 2007 that left the issue open, finding that "when we add end of life with accidental landfill fires and backyard burning, the additional risk of dioxin emissions puts PVC consistently among the worst materials for human health impacts,"[32] but stopping short of recommending a PVC-avoidance credit.

In the meantime, the *Green Guide for Health Care* in the United States and programs in other countries, such as Australia, have incorporated such strategies in their green building guidelines and rating systems; they have encouraged the avoidance of PVC, other persistent organic pollutants, and additional chemicals of concern.

Developments as of 2006 were groundbreaking for LEED. After learning that the American Institute of Architects (AIA) and other organizations had considered carbon-reduction proposals, the USGBC decided to adopt carbon-reduction goals based on the 2030 Challenge, the concept of Architecture 2030, a nonprofit organization developed by architect Ed Mazria with the support of many international design professional organizations[33] (Figure 18-11). Mazria's unstinting efforts produced the following targets and conclusions:

---

[29]Over the years, many suggestions on how to make LEED a more robust system have been made, including: Randy Udall and Auden Schendler, "LEED is Broken—Let's Fix It," 2005, http://www.igreen-build.com/cd_1706.aspx.

[30]"The Treatment by LEED of the Environmental Impact of HVAC Refrigerants," approved by LEED Steering Committee, October 25, 2004, approved by USGBC Board, November 8, 2004.

[31]USGBC Technical and Scientific Advisory Committee (TSAC), "Summary of Findings," in *Assessment of the Technical Basis for a PVC Related Materials Credit for LEED,* 88, line 24, February 2007 (Washington, DC: U.S. Green Building Council, 2007). This document can be found on the USGBC's Web site: http://www.usgbc.org/DisplayPage.aspx?CMSPageID=1633.

[32]Ibid.

[33]The Architecture 2030 Mission Statement: "Architecture 2030, a nonprofit, non-partisan and independent organization, was established in response to the global-warming crisis by architect Edward Mazria in 2002. 2030's mission is to rapidly transform the U.S. and global Building Sector from the major contributor of greenhouse gas emissions to a central part of the solution to the global-warming crisis. Our goal is straightforward: to achieve a dramatic reduction in the global-warming-causing greenhouse gas (GHG) emissions of the Building Sector by changing the way buildings and developments are planned, designed and constructed." Architecture 2030, http://www.architecture2030.org.

INTEGRATED PROJECT/TEAM DELIVERY

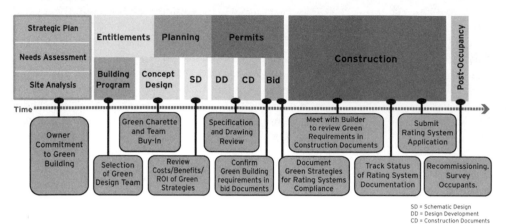

SD = Schematic Design
DD = Design Development
CD = Construction Documents

Figure 18-12 The Integrated Project Team Delivery Model.

• A reduction of fossil fuel use for new buildings by 60 percent in 2010, 70 percent in 2015, 80 percent in 2020, and 90 percent in 2025, leading to carbon neutrality in 2030 (using no fossil-fueled greenhouse gases emitting energy to operate).[34]

• The incorporation of sustainability into architecture school curricula by the year 2010, as described in Mazria's 2010 Imperative, which calls for all studio projects to incorporate sustainable design considerations in their projects, as well as achieving "ecological design literacy in education" and carbon-neutral school campuses.

The 2030 Challenge recommends two approaches to these necessary reductions:

• Increase building energy efficiency.
• Rely on energy from renewable sources instead of from coal-fired power plants.

As Mazria's philosophy validates, energy efficiency in buildings can be implemented today, and the techniques end up costing less while simultaneously benefiting the economy and environment.[35]

The USGBC, in concert with the Clinton Climate Initiative, teamed with American Society of Heating, Refrigerating and Air-Conditioning Engineers (ASHRAE), the Alliance to Save Energy, the International Council for Local Environmental Initiatives, and the WGBC to "mobilize leading green building experts from around the globe with the goal of increasing the inventory of green buildings around the world." For the USGBC membership and its LEED projects, this partnership created a mandatory goal to increase energy efficiency in buildings by 14 percent for new construction and by 9 percent for renovations.[36] In addition, building as projects that attain a platinum rating will receive a rebate of their certification review fees.

Released for ballot in May 2008 and intended to be in use by March 2009, LEED 2009 represents a major effort to overhaul the LEED rating system by incorporating weighting[37] and regionally appropriate strategies for varying building types and climates. In recognition of the impending pressure on the global supply of fresh drinking water, LEED will now demand enforced water-conservation goals in every building. One of its goals is to become compliant with International Organization for Standardization (ISO) with a third-party-verified certification process. The new LEED 2009 will lend flexibility to specific building types as well as unusual site or climatic conditions not naturally slotting into an existing LEED suite.

LEED Categories of Sustainable Design Strategies

There are six thematic categories of LEED issues:

• Site development (*Sustainable Sites*).
• Water consumption and conservation (*Water Efficiency*).

---

[34]According to the Architecture 2030 target discussion: "These targets may be accomplished by implementing innovative sustainable design strategies, generating on-site renewable power and/or purchasing (20% maximum) renewable energy and/or certified renewable energy credits," http://www.architecture2030.org.

[35]Edward Mazria and Kristina Kershner, "The 2030 Blueprint: Solving Climate Change Saves Billions," 2030, Inc., Architecture 2030, April 7, 2008, http://www.architecture2030.org/pdfs/2030Blueprint.pdf.

[36]LEED for Homes and Neighborhood Development are exempted from this goal at the time of this writing.

[37]According to a May 1, 2008, "LEED 2009 Introduction Memo" from the LEED Steering Committee and Staff to the USGBC Board of Directors, "The term 'weightings,' as it is used herein, refers to the process of redistributing the available points in LEED so that a given credit's point value more accurately reflects its potential to either mitigate the negative or promote positive environmental impacts of a building."

- Energy strategies and atmosphere impacts (*Energy and Atmosphere*, all intertwined in today's focus on carbon reduction and atmospheric depletion).
- Efficient use of resources and waste management (*Materials and Resources*).
- Indoor environment (*Indoor Environmental Quality*, related to the quality of indoor air as well as temperature, humidity, cooling, heating, daylighting, access to the outdoors, and ventilation).
- Innovation in environmental strategies (*Innovation in Design*).

These categories arch over most building types and are consistently present in most LEED products. The future of LEED is a single system, LEED 2009 (mentioned above), from which teams may draw a number of credits suited to a project. Ideally, this will address differences in site, building type, and regional specificity.

A Synopsis of Systems to Standards[38]

In the United States, public policy, codes, and ordinances are frequently found at the municipal level, as are incentive programs, such as expedited or priority-permitting structures like those in Chicago and San Francisco. State and federal codes and standards are not as widespread, though a few forward-thinking states and federal agencies, such as the General Services Administration, have adopted LEED or equivalent guidelines. California has crafted a green building code, which is described in Chapter 4.

At least three sustainable building design standards are in the process of development and balloting:

- The ASHRAE / USGBC / IESNA Standard 189 on High-Performance Green Buildings.
- The National Green Building Standard for home building construction practices, developed by the National Association of Home Builders and the International Codes Council (ICC).
- The GBI-proposed American National Standard 01-2008P: Green Building Assessment Protocol for Commercial Buildings, developed by the Green Building Initiative (an ANSI-accredited standards developer), using the Green Globes rating criteria.

◼ Practice Tools that Drive the Rating System

In green building practice, you will encounter the same team-based, integrated approach that has formed the

[38]*Environmental Building News*, "Homebuilders and Code Officials Partner to Create Green Standard," March 1, 2007, http://www.buildinggreen.com/auth/article.cfm/2007/3/6/Homebuilders-and-Code-Officials-Partner-to-Create-Green-Standard/.

center of this book. In implementing the rating systems described in this chapter, it is especially important for professionals to employ this new, multidisciplinary, collaborative model in green design (Figure 18-12).

Several key planning tools are involved in implementing rating systems during a design and construction project, many of which have been identified in Chapter 1 on integrated building design. In the case of strict implementation of rating systems, the steps are necessarily prescribed and heavily detailed for several reasons, one being that clients (developers, building owners, and other stakeholders) often base their funding on attaining a rating system benchmark. For this reason, the consultant must be meticulous and thorough when guiding the rating process.

The requirements for certain rating systems are increasingly dense and open to interpretation, and this obliges the consultant to be considerably adept and familiar with the latest developments in the system being used. A system such as LEED, for example, is based on the structure of the legal profession, where continued knowledge and project-specific challenges seek an alternative path to credit compliance. In LEED, these communications are called credit interpretation rulings (or CIRs). As in law, these "precedents" guide the development of the system and are intended to encourage consistency and form a solid basis on which raters can assess the performance of a green building. In some cases, owing to the openness of law to interpretation, persuasive argument and logical thinking become requisite skills for the green building consultant.

Key Planning Tools

- *Charrettes.* In the discussion of integrated building design (Chapter 1), one of the initial steps described was to hold a charrette, to convene similar minds in order to prioritize goals for green strategies. Much has been written of the charming origins of this word: It has been a staple of architectural training since nineteenth-century Paris at the École des Beaux Arts. A charrette was a wooden-wheeled cart circulated among Beaux Arts students when it was time to collect their drawings for review. The term is still used today in design schools and in professional design practice to describe the collaborative and spontaneous creative process of design. Analyzing and critiquing the design in a workshop is an essential step in the process of green design, because—unlike an imagined ivory tower design process—design cannot succeed in a void. A successful green building is the result of a continued collaborative charrette.
- *Tracking.* This tool takes shape in devising continuous and regularly scheduled check-in contact with both client and design team members. The documentation

tools can be almost any type of spreadsheet or software program, which will be progressively updated at these check-in periods to reflect changes in design decisions, the progress of costing and value engineering the building design, the inevitable dropped ball, or construction phase changes. The idea of this tool is to make sure goals and rating system credit points do not drop off due to these variables. The consultant should look out for any weak lines of communication.

• *Specifications and drawings.* In professional practice, the drawings and specifications are part of the contract documents and are therefore critical to the success of the building's construction quality and function. To that end, it is equally as critical for the green design to become embedded in these legal documents. Unless the consultant is a professional specifications writer, it is best not to suggest actual language for green strategies. Many design and green building consulting firms choose to incorporate a standard environmental specification into the contract documents and tailor it to the project's green design goals and to the specific rating system credits being sought. Most often this language is conducted through a review of the specifications in early drafts (completion of 50 percent design documents and 50 percent construction documents). The same holds true with a drawing review process. Green consultants also review drawings for the same reasons, and at similar project phase milestones, for issues such as rating system compliant materials and finishes, but also to ensure that certain strategy goals are met. To avoid last-minute surprises, when the project is submitted for a rating system evaluation by a third party, a consultant can review the drawings to verify the design of any strategy, ranging from deck-to-deck partitions in chemical mixing areas to adequate storage space for bicycles and recycling containers.

• *Construction observation.* Weekly construction meetings are part of all building projects once ground is broken on the site. While it is not always necessary for the green consultant to be present at each meeting, it is important for her/him to walk through the site at various key phases, as dictated by the particular rating system–mandated milestones.

• *The rating system application process.* The assembly of the project's rating system application is often time-consuming, depending on the robustness and authoritativeness of the system. Clearly, the systems that carry clout are those that are more independent of bias. It pays to be wary of systems that allow a team to self-certify its green building and forego third-party verification. Such a choice may be based on financial considerations, but it may not pay off in terms of marketing, visibility, credibility, and occupant satisfaction. This level of discernment by the general public may not be sophisticated at this point, but it will be in the

future, as nondesign professionals become savvy and conversant with the differences in the systems we have reviewed in this chapter.

By now, it should be apparent that most of these tasks belong under the banner of project management. Project managers are able to apply their skills to a number of professions where long-term projects and detailed documentation are important to track. Project management in green building design is necessarily a holistic practice, and there are continuous "feedback loops" to create, review, and vet design decisions. Throughout the phases of a building project, a project manager must use these and other tools to ensure the project's success. It is no wonder that green building consultants refer to their jobs as part law and part accounting.

EXERCISES

1. Using the "sustainable sites" and "water efficiency" series of credits of the U.S. Green Building Council rating system (either LEED 2009 or one of the older rating systems), assess the environmental performance of two identical buildings, one located in a desert climate such as Tucson, Arizona, the other in a wet climate such as Portland, Oregon. Which credits are irrelevant to the building located in Tucson? Which credits address a particularly relevant environmental issue peculiar to the region? Do the strategies suggested by these credits make economic sense?

2. Compare the Australian Green Star water-reduction benchmarks to the USGBC's benchmarks. Which system's strategies are more rigorous, mandating higher efficiency percentages? What is the major difference between Australia's water-reduction strategies and those of the USGBC? What are the barriers to instituting such strategies in the United States?

3. What green building technologies should be implemented by a developing nation with the following profile? What categories of environmental strategies would be considered a priority or would offer opportunities for technological innovation? What sorts of green building technologies would be irrelevant in a rating system for this country?

Population: 147,000,000

Area: 56,000 square miles

Energy fact: Ranked among the top ten most energy-efficient countries based on gross domestic product per unit of energy.

Literacy: 41 percent

Per capita average yearly income: $350

Geography: hot, tropical climate; 60 percent arable land; and an average of 50 inches of rainfall per year.

■ Resources

Gowri, Krishnan. 2004."Green Building Rating Systems: An Overview," *ASHRAE Journal* 46, no. 11 (November): 56–60.

Whole Building Design Guide, http://www.wbdg.org.

Better Bricks, http://www.betterbricks.com.

Green Built Home, http://www.greenbuilthome.org.

High-Performance Building Guidelines (New York), http://www.nyc.gov/html/ddc/html/ddcgreen/documents/guidelines/greeng01.pdf.

High-Performance Green Building Guidelines (Pennsylvania), http://www.gggc.state.pa.us/gggc/cwp/view.asp?a=3&q=151854.

Greening Federal Facilities, http://www.eere.energy.gov/femp/technologies/sustainable_greening.cfm.

Green Building Codes and Ordinances, http://www.smartcommunities.ncat.org/buildings/gbcodtoc.shtml.

Collaborative for High Performance Schools (CHPS) Best Practices Manual 2006, available for download at http://www.chps.net/manual/index.htm#BPM

Simon, Donald. 2005. "Industry Trade Associations: Why USGBC Invited Them As Members," *Green Building Quarterly* December, 2005.

National Charrette Institute, an educational nonprofit that teaches the "transformative process of dynamic planning," http://www.charretteinstitute.org/charrette.html.

Better Bricks. 2008. "What is an Eco-Charrette?" http://betterbricks.com/DetailPage.aspx?ID=275 (accessed May 4, 2008).

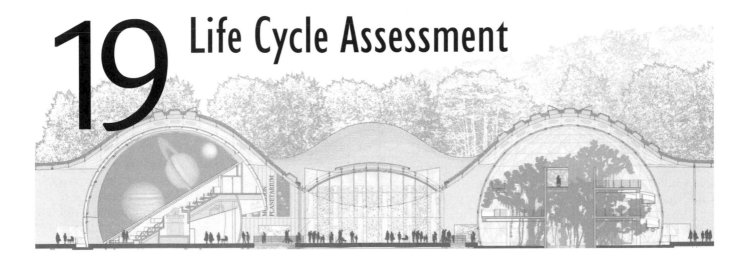

19 Life Cycle Assessment

Introduction

The challenge to humanity is to adopt new ways of thinking, new ways of acting, new ways of organizing itself in society, in short, new ways of living.[1]

In the preceding chapters we have seen how sustainable building technology responds to the environmental imbalance and degradation caused by human development. We learned that this imbalance is produced when human activity—such as manufacturing or transportation—uses fossil fuels, contributes to climate change, depletes natural resources, produces waste that does not return to the manufacturing stream or does not have downcycled uses, causes overfertilization or acidification, and damages the ozone. In addition, the concept of environmental management was introduced.

In this chapter we will discuss a type of building evaluation tool that—when used in combination with other types of building performance evaluation tools, such as energy modeling or daylight simulation—can be used to select building materials, assemblies, systems, and strategies in the most optimal manner, and with the least impact on the environment. In short, this evaluation tool can assist with environmental management.

This process is known as life cycle assessment (or LCA) (Figure 19-1). Many types of evaluation tools can be brought into play only after occupancy, such as those used to test effectiveness of installation and those that require a reporting period in order to gather data (such as energy

When we are talking about LCAs of buildings and building materials, it helps to think about the whole building effects. Everything from the skin to the HVAC to the flooring can have an effect on a building's "ecoprofile," its overall environmental impact. But the issues are pretty much the same. What can we do to decrease the use of energy? Does a certain type of window help with energy conservation over the entire life of the building? How many times will the window be replaced during the lifetime of the building? Which materials are less toxic? How important is the end of life of the building? Does it make sense to design the building for "deconstruction" when it's useful life is over? Only careful LCAs can answer these questions by measuring the environmental impacts over the entire life cycle of the building.

Figure 19-1 Life cycle assessment defined. From Rita Schenck, "Why LCA?: Building Design and Construction, Life Cycle Assessment, and Sustainability," *Reed Business Information*, Nov. 2005.

use) or to examine human perceptions and reactions to environmental strategies.

In contrast, LCA tools provide the benefit of early planning by attempting to deliver quantifiable predictions of sustainable strategy performance, economics, or operation of an integrated building.

As we have seen, one of the biggest barriers to the adoption of green building practices is the difficulty of understanding and quantifying both the environmental and financial costs associated with green buildings. Life cycle assessment offers a distinct means of quantifying and communicating the benefits of green building practices. The tools of LCA should be used in the early stages of the design process, because employing building evaluation tools early is an effective way to implement integrated building design and reduce design and construction costs.

---

[1]"Our Creative Diversity," *Report of the World Commission on Culture and Development*, Paris, UNESCO, 1995, 11.

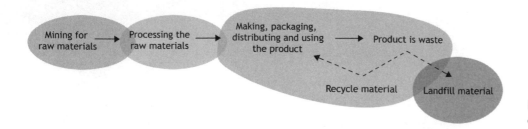

Figure 19-2 The life-cycle factors of product manufacture.

Definitions

Life cycle assessment is conceptually different than life-cycle *financial* costs, life-cycle costing (LCC). The practice of LCA is a holistic and comprehensive way to evaluate the full *environmental* burden of a material, building assembly, system, or service over its full life cycle, from extraction of raw materials, through manufacture, packaging, transport, operation, cleaning, repair, and maintenance, to disposal, recycling, or disassembly and reuse. In other words, its goal is to produce an "ecoprofile" of a building material, product, assembly, system, or whole building.

A good LCA should have *boundaries* that determine the scope of the study, and it should be robust, returning multiple *indicators*, predictions of impact potential.[2] This tool can be used to assess the environmental impacts of a full spectrum of human activities, from the embodied energy of shipping activities to the production of aluminum (Figure 19-2). For the purposes of our discussion of green building, we will focus on LCA as it applies to the construction components of buildings.

The challenge in LCA lies in determining how to characterize, quantify, and analyze these impacts and present the results in a manner useful for builders and designers. This has been a topic of much debate among scientists and engineers and is the subject of white papers, studies, and conferences. Because of uncertainties, ambiguities, and stakeholder disagreements, not to mention political reluctance to alter policy, LCA is a tool in need of refinement and the realization of its full promise is still years away.[3]

Even in its developing stages, though, where the findings are far from comprehensive, LCA can be useful in assessing or comparing the environmental impacts of different products, assemblies, or systems.[4] It does a good job of assessing energy flows if executed in a detailed, site-specific manner.

In fact, designers begin to think in terms of life cycle when they ask manufacturers about the expected durability of one carpet compared to another, for example. As Jane Bare notes, "Because LCA compares 2 or more products to each other, and these products must be comparable in all aspects of service, the durability or lifetime of the product is an important consideration when determining the functional unit within an LCA."[5]

Product manufacturers have also used LCA in the development of environmentally preferable products (Figure 19-3). For example, Interface Flooring employs the GaBi LCA tool to determine the life-cycle emissions of its carpet. The company's goal is to offset their emissions with the purchase of emissions reduction credits (ERCs), from renewable energy, energy efficiency, and carbon dioxide reduction sources.[6] Similarly, industry associations have used independent LCA research to bolster marketing claims.

Two groundbreaking studies used both LCA and LCC to illustrate the ecological and economic implications of polyvinyl chloride (PVC) and linoleum, cork, and rubber. Bosch reported that PVC was the least sustainable resilient flooring choice, compared to cork and linoleum.[7] Referring to Bosch's results, Moussatche proved through a fifty-year service LCC model that although linoleum has a higher capital cost, its operation, maintenance, and use cost is lower than PVC, resulting in a lower total-system cost.[8]

Standards and Methodology

The standard on which LCA is based is that of the International Organization for Standardization (ISO), the world's largest and most comprehensive producer of standards governing everything from climate change to cosmetics. Among its more than 3,000 technical bodies and 153 technical committees is the venerated ISO 14000 standard and certification. This covers environmental labeling and sets strategic planning for LCA. According

[2] Tom Lent, personal communication, March 8, 2007.
[3] Nadav Malin, "Life-Cycle Assessment for Buildings: Seeking the Holy Grail,". "*Environmental Building News* 11, no. 3, March 2002.
[4] R. Heijungs, et al., "Environmental Life Cycle Assessment of Products; Guide and Backgrounds," I+II, Ministry of Housing, Spatial Planning and the Environment, and the Centre of Environmental Science, Leiden University, 1992.

[5] Jane Bare, personal communication, June 7, 2007.
[6] For more information on Interface Flooring and sustainability, http://www.interfacesustainability.com/cc_soln.html.
[7] Sheila L. Jones (Bosch), "Resilient Flooring: A Comparison of Vinyl, Linoleum and Cork," Study conducted at the Georgia Tech Research Institute Fall (1999).
[8] Helena Moussatche and Jennifer Languell, "Flooring Materials—Life-Cycle Costing for Educational Facilities," *Facilities* 19, no. 10 (October 2001): 333–343.

ENVIRONMENTAL IMPACT OF EXTERIOR SURFACE PAVING MATERIALS
(Data source: The BRE Green Guide to Specifications Online: www.thegreenguide.org.uk)

LEVEL OF NEGATIVE ENVIRONMENTAL IMPACT high (3) - medium (2) - low (1)	Granite Pavers	Gravel	Concrete Pavers	Fired Clay Pavers	Asphalt
Climate change potential	1	1	1	2	3
Embodied energy: petroleum	1	1	1	2	3
Human health impact potential	1	1	1	1	3
Waste impact	2	3	2	2	3
Embodied water	1	2	1	1	1
Environmental health impact	1	1	1	1	3
Mineral resource depletion potential	2	3	1	1	1
Recycled content level	3	3	1	3	3
Recyclability/salvage/reuse	1	2	1	1	2
Frequency of Replacement	1	3	2	2	3
TOTALS:	14	20	12	16	25

Firgure 19-3 Example of BREEAM's Green Guide showing evaluations of pavement types. 1 means low environmental impact, 2 moderate, and 3 high. Source: Interlocking Concrete Pavement Institute (ICPI).

to ISO standardization guidelines (ISO, 1997a, b, 1998 a, b), LCA methodology is comprised of four steps: *goal and scope definition, inventory analysis, impact assessment,* and *interpretation.*[9]

- *Goal and scope of the study period:* Building type, along with the direction and mandate of the building stakeholders or designers, will govern the goals of the LCA exercise. If stakeholders wish to pursue the environmental impacts of a cotton-based insulation, for example, researchers will look at the harvesting of cotton, how energy intensive it is, what pesticides are used, where it is grown, as well as numerous other aspects. They will then compare these results to an alternative insulation or insulating structure.

  There are many ways to slice the analytical pie; for example, some LCA scopes focus on well to wheel (the period from oil extraction to use in vehicles), cradle to grave (the period from extraction to disposal), cradle to gate (the period from extraction to delivery), and, most appropriate to integrated buildings, cradle to cradle, the period of study between extraction and return to a second useful life, comprising a closed-loop system.[10]

  - *A goal or scope may state:* "To compare the impacts from extraction to end of life of installing

fiberglass insulation containing urea formaldehyde vs. the alternative cotton based insulation."

- *Inventory analysis:* Gathering data about materials that cause environmental effects is the second step in the LCA methodology. Data about materials and their environmental effects, tangible and intangible, directly and indirectly attributable to the life cycle of the product, is collected. Total flows—either inputs (resource consumption) or outputs (emissions)—are examined. Among the many impacts on the environment attributable to human activity are: acidification (acid rain), eutrophication (excess nutrients in water), rain forest depletion, ozone generation, ozone-depleting potential, global warming potential, natural resource depletion, and desertification. Many databases collect this data. Some are embedded in LCA tools, and others are separate systems.

  - *Inventory data may state:* "The following list and quantities of chemical emissions are the result of cotton-growing activities."

- *Impact assessment:* According to many researchers, probably the most important ISO level in the LCA process is that of life-cycle impact assessment. A life cycle assessment must quantify a material's potential impact to the environment (Figure 19-4). Impact assessment is the connective tissue between inventory and interpretation, because it is the step that assigns metrics to the inventory based on various underlying models.[11] After assembling the data from inventory

---

[9] M. A. J. Huijbregts, U. Thissen, J. B. Guinée, T. Jager, D. van de Meent, A. M. J. Ragas, et al., "Priority Assessment of Toxic Substances in Life Cycle Assessment, I: Calculation of Toxicity Potentials for 181 Substances with the Nested Multi-Media Fate, Exposure and Effects Model USES-LCA," *Chemosphere* 41 (2000): 541–573.

[10] "Trqansforming Industry: Cradle to Cradle Design," http://www.mbdc.com/c2c_home.htm. See also McDonough and Braungart, *Cradle to Cradle*.

[11] Jane Bare and Thomas Gloria, "Life Cycle Impact Assessment for the Building Design and Construction Industry," *Life Cycle Assessment and Sustainability, A Supplement to Building Design & Construction* 3: 22–24, November 2005.

databases, the user can produce materials, assembly, and whole-building assessments ranging in sophistication from a simple listing of environmental impacts to a complex software analysis.[12] While inventory represents the total flows, impact assessment "scales" the flows. Without impact assessment, "releasing a pound of mercury to the environment would look just like releasing a pound of sand."[13]

- The following steps are in the impact assessment process: *classification, characterization, normalization* (optional), *grouping and weighting* (optional), and *interpretation*. The goal of impact assessment is to quantify impacts and present them in a balanced way so builders and designers can use them efficiently.

  - *An impact assessment may state:* "When comparing the potential for environmental impacts on ozone depletion, Option A was determined to be less

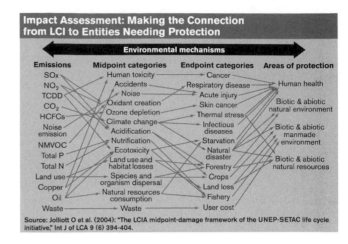

Source: Jolliott O et al. (2004): "The LCIA midpoint-damage framework of the UNEP-SETAC life cycle initiative." Int J of LCA 9 (6) 394-404.

Figure 19-5 An example of an impact assessment that studies chemical emissions from various human activities and their impacts, or endpoints.

(a)

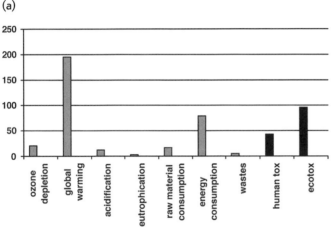

Impact profile of a chemical product.

(b)

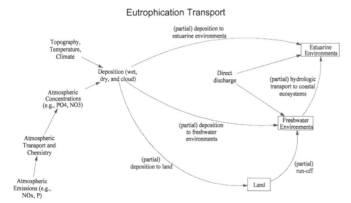

Figure 19-4 a, b The impact and transport of a chemical.

likely to cause environmental impacts on the ozone layer than Option B."

- *Interpretation:* As described, each study is populated by inventory databases and informed by impact assessment. The LCA cannot be interpreted without understanding environmental impacts. But the reality is that interpretation of an LCA is only as robust as the data that populate the inventory and impact-assessment steps.

In inventory analysis, a study may have several problems. The data gathered may not be specific to the facilities that are being studied, the data may be old, allocation may not be straightforward, or other problems may exist with the data.

In impact assessment, we are faced with the potential for data uncertainty and variability (e.g., the toxicity and half-life values may not be well known for all of the chemicals of concern) (Figure 19-5). The interpretation step needs to consider all of the strengths and weaknesses of the data and results that lead up to this step.

■ Components

The methodology of LCA is straightforward, but fairly complex at its granular levels. When we separate the components of LCA and examine their interrelationships and hierarchies, we can begin to appreciate the intricacy of the subject. Life cycle assessment can assess many things in the world, and for green building, it can assess materials and products, systems and assemblies, or whole buildings.[14]

---

[12] Monika Herrchen and Werner Klein, "Use of the Life-Cycle Assessment (LCA) Toolbox for an Environmental Evaluation of Production Processes," *Pure Applied Chemistry* 72, no. 7 (2000): 1247–1252.

[13] Bare and Gloria, "Life Cycle Assessment." 23.

[14] Shannon Lloyd, Anne Landfield, and Brian Glazebrook, "Integrating LCA into Green Building Design," *Building Design & Construction*, November 2005.

Tools

Europe has led the way for many years in the development of LCA and its tools. In North America, where researchers are often less comfortable with quantifying impact, the development has been slower. In 1969, Coca Cola commissioned William Franklin to conduct a study investigating the implications of bottling the product in plastic containers, a project considered to be the launching point for LCA development in the United States.[15]

However, it was not until 1990, when the Society of Environmental Toxicology and Chemistry (SETAC), hosted a global session, the end result of which was the development of a framework and a common terminology for LCA.[16]

A partnership with the United Nations Environmental Programme (UNEP) yielded the development of practical product evaluation tools for the LCA process under the Life-Cycle Initiative.[17] At a specialized conference on LCA and green buildings, the partnership predicted the eventual incorporation of life-cycle information for building components and ready availability of methodology and tools to support LCA in green building practice. The group adopted ISO 14040 standards to act as a further framework for these LCA advances.[18]

As one would expect, LCA tools trace the stages of ISO methodology. There are inventory database tools; software programs that use inventory to assess impacts; and overall whole building assessment tools that use both. Some overall tools yield a single score, others list a range of several scores based on impacts. In general, the lines between the steps of the LCA are often blurred, in many cases overlapping inventory and impact databases.

Examples of Life-Cycle Inventory Databases

- National Renewable Energy Laboratory (NREL), Life-Cycle Inventory Database,[19] based on ISO 14048, Oct. 12, 2006 V 1.3.1, and Athena Institute databases.
- Athena Institute's inventory databases were produced by the Athena Sustainable Materials Institute and Athena Institute International in Canada and the United States. These databases are regionally sensitive and analyze both structural and envelope materials.[20]

- Eco-Invent,[21] produced by a consortium of Swiss agencies, surveys energy, resource extraction, materials, chemicals, metals, agriculture, waste management, and transport issues. It is incorporated in overall LCA software tools such as SimaPro,[22] as well as specialized design and construction LCA tools. An associated database, the Australian LCA Database, is produced by the Centre for Design and the Cooperative Research Center for Waste Management and Pollution Control. Its data includes fuels, electricity, transport, building and packaging materials, waste management, and some data on agricultural production.[23]
- EcoQuantum and IVAM Data 4 are produced by the Dutch research agency IVAM, which is affiliated with the Environmental Science Department at the University of Amsterdam. These databases focus on energy chemical emissions and building materials data.[24]

Examples of Impact Assessment Tools

Life cycle assessment tools are used around the globe as the list in Figure 19-8 shows.

- The Tool for the Reduction and Assessment of Chemical and Other Environmental Impacts (TRACI) was developed by the U.S. EPA to study life-cycle impacts and produce sustainability metrics. This tool was designed to be consistent with U.S. regulations, guidelines, and handbooks, as well as U.S. conditions.[25]
- The *Handbook on Life Cycle Assessment* is a recent ISO publication known as the "Dutch Guidelines."[26] This is an updated version of the earlier environmental LCA guide published by the Centre of Environmental Science (CML) at Leiden University in the Netherlands.[27]
- Envest is produced by the United Kingdom's Building Research Establishment's (or BRE) Centre for Sustainable Construction. This software is used in BREEAM, the green building rating system for the United Kingdom. It produces a single score, referred to as an ecopoint, and studies climate change, fossil fuel

---

[15] Robert G. Hunt and William E. Franklin, "Personal Reflections on the Origin and the Development of LCA in the USA," *The International Journal of Life Cycle Assessment* 1, no. 1 (1996): 4–7.

[16] J. Fava, R. Denison, B. Jones, M. Curran, B. Vigon, S. Selke, and J. Barnum, eds., "A Technical Framework for Life-Cycle Assessment," Society of Environmnental Toxicology and Chemistry (SETAC), LCA Symposium Case Study, Pensacola, Florida, 1991.

[17] Ibid.

[18] Ibid.

[19] National Renewable Energy Laboratory (NREL), Life-Cycle Inventory Database, http://www.nrel.gov/lci.

[20] Athena Institute's regionally sensitive inventory databases, http://www.athenasmi.ca/tools/database/index.html.

[21] The Ecoinvent Centre, or the Swiss Centre for Life-Cycle Inventories, is a joint initiative of institutes and departments of the Swiss Federal Institutes of Technology Zürich (ETH Zurich) and Lausanne (EPFL), the Paul Scherrer Institute (PSI), the Swiss Federal Laboratories for Materials Testing and Research (Empa), and the Swiss Federal Research Station Agroscope Reckenholz-Tänikon (ART). For more information, http://www.ecoinvent.org.

[22] SimaPro 7.1 LCA Software, http://www.pre.nl/simapro.

[23] Centre for Design, http://www.cfd.rmit.edu.au.

[24] Interfaculty Environmental Science Department (IVAM) of the Universiteit van Amsterdam, Research and Consultancy on sustainability, http://www.ivam.uva.nl.

[25] U.S. EPA's Tool for the Reduction and Assessment of Chemical and Other Environmental Impacts (TRACI), http://www.epa.gov/nrmrl/std/sab/traci/. (Figure 19-7a.)

[26] Guinee, *Handbook on Life Cycle Assessment*.

[27] International Organization for Standardization (ISO), http://www.iso.org.

depletion, ozone depletion, freight transport, human toxicity to air, human toxicity to water, waste disposal, water extraction, acid deposition, ecotoxicity, eutrophication, summer smog, and minerals extraction.[28]

- Athena Institute Environmental Impact Estimator (EIE) (Figure 19-6), produced by the Athena Sustainable Materials Institute and Athena Institute International in Canada and the United States, incorporates the Athena Institute database, and it should be thought of as modeling a proposed building design in simple conceptual design terms.[29]

(a)

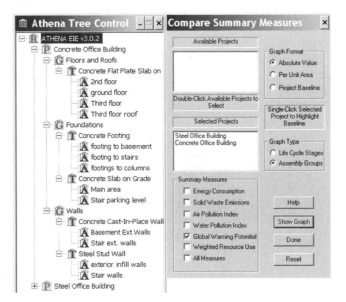

- eLCie, developed by the International Design Center for the Environment, is a suite of Web tools currently being populated with data for manufacturers and those in the building industry, and it is ultimately intended to coordinate with a comprehensive whole building design software such as Revit.[30]

Comprehensive LCA Tools

- Building for Environmental and Economic Sustainability (BEES) is a software tool developed by the National Institute of Standards and Technology (NIST) via its Building Fire and Research Laboratory. This software tool uses inventory and impact analysis to normalize and weigh data and sum them into a single score.[31] There are ten categories of impacts in the BEES system: acid rain, ecological toxicity, eutrophication, global warming, human toxicity, indoor air quality, ozone depletion, resource depletion, smog, and solid waste (Figure 19-7a).
- SimaPro 7 (System for Integrated Environmental Assessment of Products) is one of the leading comprehensive LCA tools, produced by PRé Consultants B.V.[32]

Limitations of LCA

Life cycle assessment, in its current form, has consistently cited limitations; some of the limitations found by researchers follow.

(b)

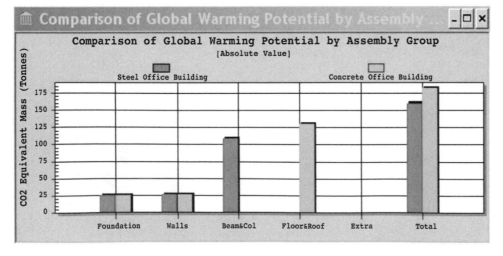

Figure 19-6 a, b Athena Institute's Environmental Impact Estimator (EIE) allows users to enter values and impacts in selected categories.

---

[28]BRE, Envest, http://www.bre.co.uk/service.jsp?id=52.
[29]Athena Institute, http://www.athenasmi.ca/tools/software/index.html.

[30]eLCie, International Design Center for the Environment, http://www.idce.org/elcie.html.
[31]National Institute of Standards and Technology, BEES http://www.bfrl.nist.gov/oae/software/bees.html and http://www.bfrl.nist.gov.
[32]Producers of other leading LCA tools are: ifu Hamburg/ifeu Heidelberg, (Umberto); PE Europe/IKP Stuttgart, (GaBi); Sinum AG, (Regis), Carbotech AG, (EMIS).

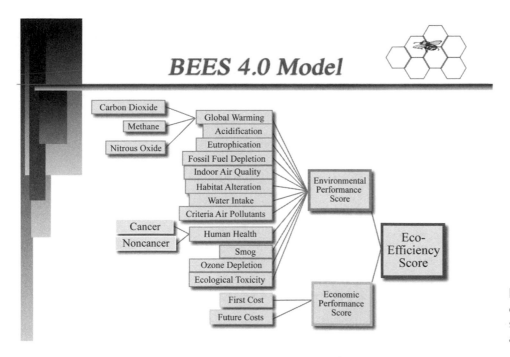

Figure 19-7a The National Institute of Standards and Technology's software tool, BEES, uses inventory and impact analysis.

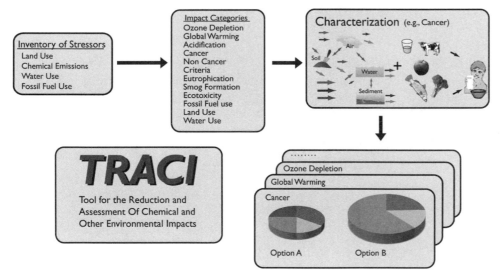

Figure 19-7b TRACI was developed by the U.S. EPA to study life-cycle impacts and produce sustainability metrics.

Because of the range of uncertainties and the variability and incompatibility of data, LCA is a time-consuming and complex evaluation tool.

We have seen that LCA data are hard to standardize and quantify. Many researchers are urging the development of a single protocol, such as NREL's Life-Cycle Inventory Database, which "provides a cradle-to-grave accounting of the energy and material flows into and out of the environment that are associated with producing a material, component, or assembly."[33]

Life cycle assessment does not consider sociological implications, such as the issues of social justice that are encountered when resources are extracted from developing countries, altering patterns of living and habitat. Leading researcher Gregory A. Norris believes this controversy can be addressed by focusing on reducing poverty, thus reducing public health impacts in the developing world (Figure 19-9). He proposes launching a social inventory database that would categorize issues such as child labor minutes, wages paid, and job-related injuries.[34]

[33]National Renewable Energy Laboratory (NREL), Life-Cycle Inventory (LCI) Database Project, http://www.nrel.gov/lci.

[34]Gregory A. Norris, "Social Impacts in Product Life Cycles: Toward Life Cycle Attribute Assessment," *International Journal of LCA* 11, special issue (2006): 97–104.

LCA Tools and What They Do

	Country	Comments
Level 1A Tools		
SimaPro	Netherlands	While the countries of origin vary, these tools
GaBi	Germany	can be used in different regions by selecting
Umberto	Germany	or incorporating the appropriate data. But
TEAM	France	the task is best done by LCA practitioners for whom the tools are intended.
Level 1B Tools		
BEES	USA	Combines LCA and life cycle costing. Includes both brand-specific and generic data.
LCAiT	Sweden	Streamlined LCA tool for product designers and manufacturers.
TAKE-LCA	Finland	LCA tool for comparison of HVAC products, including energy content of the product and energy consumption.
Level 2 Tools		
Athena Environmental Impact Estimator (EIE)	Canada/USA	All of these tools use data and incorporate building systems that are specific to the country or regions for which they were designed.
BRI LCA (energy and CO2)	Japan	
EcoQuantum	Netherlands	
Envest	United Kingdom	
Green Guide to Specifications	United Kingdom	
LISA	Australia	
LCADesign (under development)	Australia	
Level 3 Tools		
BREEAM	United Kingdom	Uses LCA results from the Level 2 Green Guide.
GBTool	International	Experimental platform that accepts LCA results or performs a rudimentary LCA calculation using built-in calculators.
Green Globes	Canada/USA	Assigns a high percentage of resource use credits based on evidence that a design team has conducted LCA using a recognized Level 1 or 2 tool.

Figure 19-8 International Life Cycle Assessment tools.

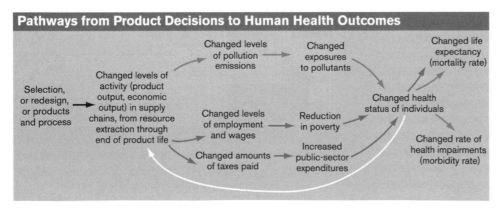

Figure 19-9 Researchers have studied how issues of social inequity fold into an LCA inventory database.

Of particular controversy is the belief among many researchers that LCA does not adequately calculate human-health impacts.[35] This is largely owing to the uncertainty about calculating human toxicity impacts, since these impacts are dependent on many factors. Even the list of which chemicals to include in the impact assessment may be dependent upon what inventory data is available.

Additionally, different impact models may or may not take into account various human exposure pathways and/or total body burden. The pursuit of the health legacy

[35]Tom Lent, "Toxic Data Bias and the Challenges of Using LCA in the Design Community," presented at GreenBuild 2003, Pittsburgh, PA.

of chemical emissions is its own field of study, one that continues to be a source of controversy among manufacturers, health professionals, and LCA scientists.

The U.S. Green Building Council's PVC report, cited in an earlier chapter, used Ecoinvent, among other LCA databases, along with the SimaPro modeling tool, to compare both the environmental- and human-health impacts of siding, flooring, and window frames manufactured with PVC, wood, and aluminum, among other materials. Its final report was issued in February 2007.[36]

Responses

Some suggested responses to the limitations of LCA science are offered by researchers at the Institute of Environmental Sciences (CML) at Leiden University, Netherlands.

They propose three approaches to overcoming LCA's limitations: "(1) LCA Extension, the development of one consistent model; (2) Toolbox, using separate models in combination; and (3) hybrid analysis, combining models with data flows between them."[37]

For students and practitioners of green building design, this last suggestion seems most accessible. Regardless of the approach the student wishes to take, however, he or she should always approach an LCA report with a healthy dose of skepticism and ask questions about what assumptions and limitations are embedded in the report. In other words, test the assumptions that form the underlying basis of the study and investigate whether the assumptions made are consistent with the goals of the study.[38]

Another response to limitations of LCA, green building programs, product certification, and standards is the Pharos Project, a collaborative project of the Healthy Building Network, Cascadia Green Building Council, and the University of Tennessee Center for Clean Products.[39] The Pharos Project, named after the lighthouse of Alexandria, was developed to provide a comprehensive view of the impact of the life cycle of materials. Indicators are collected in an online database on products and their manufacturers for sixteen impact categories in three sectors: Health and Pollution (examining such issues as toxic releases and climate impacts); Environment and Resources (looking at habitat impact and embodied water usage); and Social and Community

(dealing with living wage and socially responsible corporate practices). A Pharos rating will carry a 0–10 score in each indicator category, designed to provide guidance to designers in a manner similar to a nutritional food label (Figure 19-10).

Pharos covers issues LCA cannot and goes beyond material certification to address many needs in the green materials industry. It is designed to encourage transparency in product content, arm the designer and specifier with knowledge, allow dynamic setting of goals to reflect progress in the building materials manufacturing industries, and reward manufacturers who pursue continuous improvement toward environmental ideals, instead of limiting research and development to the lowest minimum green labels or standards.

LCA into LEED Process

One of the difficulties of LCA is trying to decide what to do about the systems' inherent trade-offs (e.g., one option is better for global warming, whereas another option is better in terms of human toxicity).

To resolve issues such as these requires a consistent valuation (or weighting) process. The LEED building rating system, which considers materials flows, would be an optimal place to do weighting, because users are already comfortable with a level of subjectivity.

For example, rating system points are given to practices that are considered to be better for the environment, even though no quantification exists to show that two items, both worth 1 point each, are "better" to the same extent. In one case, designing locations for bike racks are given a single LEED Sustainable Sites credit, as is the specification of a range of low VOC-emitting materials.

In September 2004, the USGBC's Life Cycle Assessment working group began an "LCA into LEED" project commissioned by the LEED Steering Committee. Advisory working groups comprising over sixty volunteers representing LCA experts, manufacturers, trade associations, academia, federal government, nonprofits, and USGBC LEED committees released a report in December 2006 containing recommendations on how best to incorporate LCA into LEED.

Developing building materials from a preapproved list of building materials or assemblies or an LCA tool for use by design teams were among the recommended options for integrating LCA into LEED.[40] The updated LEED 2009, the result of the rating system's first major shift, is intended to provide LCA weighting.

[36]TSAC, PVC Task Group, "Assessment of the Technical Basis for a PVC-Related Materials Credit for LEED," February 2007. For database, refer to http://www.usgbc.org/News/PressReleaseDetails.aspx?ID=2957.
[37]Helias A. Udo de Haes, Reinout Heijungs, Sangwon Suh, and Gjalt Huppes, "Three Strategies to Overcome the Limitations of Life-Cycle Assessment," *The Journal of Industrial Ecology* 8, no. 3 (Summer 2004): 19–32.
[38]Jane Bare, personal communication, March 6, 2007.
[39]Pharos Project Web site, http://www.pharosproject.net (accessed July 14, 2008).
[40]U.S. Green Building Council (USGBC), "Integrating LCA into LEED," Working Group A (Goal and Scope), Interim Report #1 (Washington, DC: USGBC, 2006), http://www.usgbc.org/ShowFile.aspx?DocumentID=2241January 14, 2009).

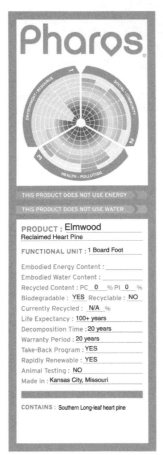

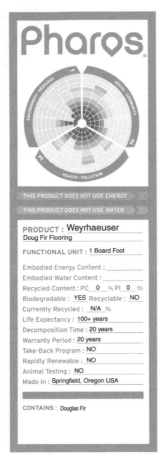

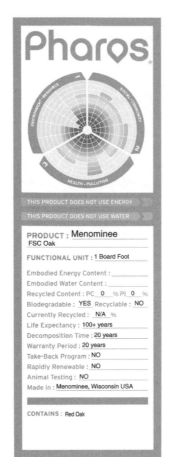

Figure 19-10 Much like a nutritional food label, the Pharos ecolabel is intended to help consumers understand the life-cycle components of the materials they select.

LCA Checklist for Designers

Nadav Malin

- Don't attempt to perform your own LCA studies unless you want to devote significant resources to making that endeavor a specialty.
- Encourage product manufacturers to perform LCAs on their products and make the results available by asking product reps for LCA data. Refer to ISO-standard Type III Environmental Product Declarations (third-party reviewed LCA results), the work of the Sustainable Products Purchasers Coalition, and/or the BEES software from NIST as mechanisms for making that data available.
- Ask key questions about any LCA data provided to assess its reliability and applicability to your decision. Examples of such questions include:
  - *What are the sources of the data?* How much is based on primary information directly from the operations, as opposed to databases of industry-average data? Of the industry-average data, is it regionally specific (U.S. as opposed to Europe) and fully transparent to users or peer reviewers?
  - *What assumptions are included* about the functional unit and the service life of the product(s) in question; do these correspond to your situation?
  - *What are the uncertainty factors in the information?* No commonly used databases currently include this information, but "uncertainties of 20% or more are likely," according to Norris. If users ask, there will be pressure to provide an answer.
  - *What is assumed about the products' maintenance requirements* and/or impact on building operations?
  - *Do the impact categories included in the results capture the important information*, or might the results by skewed by leaving out key categories?

- Resist the temptation to reduce LCA results to a single score for each product. The weighting required to do this introduces assumptions that may not be appropriate, and too much information is lost. Look instead at the results across all available impact categories and make your own assessment based on those results.

- Whether or not reliable LCA results are available, always apply life-cycle thinking and critically review any product information to support your choices. Resources based on life-cycle thinking include *EBN* articles and GreenSpec product listings from BuildingGreen, as well as GreenSeal product labeling standards.

- Look at the whole building from a life-cycle perspective and aim to minimize overall environmental impacts while optimizing performance. In general, such an approach suggests that addressing the ongoing impacts of building operation, including energy use, water use, and maintenance impacts should be a higher priority than choosing materials with lower upstream environmental burdens.

Source: *Environmental Building News* 11, no. 3 (March 2002).

The assembly of appropriate data to inform design decisions is an overwhelming and daunting prospect. Those reading LCA reports should exercise skepticism and ask questions about any underlying uncertainties, because such reports often look more accurate than they may be.[41]

Caution should be exercised to avoid making LCA the entire raison d'être of building design. We have seen the limitations of LCA and its layers of complexity, but for our purposes, until the practice of LCA reaches common usage by architects and designers, we can make use of general techniques such as collecting and understanding environmental inputs and outputs[42] and using a personal ranking system based on our own environmental priorities. This presents an opportunity to put more global issues, such as climate change and carbon neutrality, as well as human health impacts, into higher focus, depending on the interests of the student.

Finally, it must be understood that LCA is a new paradigm that teaches users to think critically while facilitating the decision-making process. This way of thinking is LCA in its essence; it is life-cycle thinking.

As designers, we are accustomed to solving problems and striving for the most optimal solution in terms of function and esthetics. Following from that, designers of green buildings typically think in terms of life cycle. Because of the frequent inaccessibility of data and methodology and expensive LCA tools, life-cycle thinking is a skill that should become ingrained, a very necessary first step toward understanding LCA.

To go a step further, the student may wish to explore different software tools and imagine how to employ them in tandem with the other themes of this book. The LCA field is evolving rapidly such that we are seeing the introduction of even newer tools with even more relevance to sustainable design. As with other techniques, LCA supports and gives weight and value to green building knowledge. The process will assist one in moving from student to practitioner.

EXERCISES

1. Illustrate the life cycle of cork, linoleum, or polyvinyl chloride (PVC) and provide a listing of environmental impacts of the material you select.

2. Select a global environmental issue you view as particularly relevant or cogent and develop a list of potential impacts of specific building products to this impact. Give examples of specific types of materials that impact it positively and negatively. Propose future technologies that would respond to these impacts (e.g., CO2-eating algae).

3. Explore one of the LCA tools mentioned in the chapter and give five reasons why the tool would be useful for green building analysis. List what you believe are the limitations of that tool.

Resources

Cole, Raymond J., Nigel Howard, Toshiharu Ikaga, and Sylviane Nibel. 2005. "Building Environmental Assessment Tools: Current and Future Roles." Issue Paper, Action for Sustainability, The 2005 World Sustainable Building Conference in Tokyo, Japan, September 27–29.

Malin, Nadav. 2002. "Life-Cycle Assessment for Buildings: Seeking the Holy Grail," *Environmental Building News* 11, no. 3 (March).

McDonough, William, and Michael Braungart. 2002. *Cradle to Cradle: Remaking the Way We Make Things*. New York: North Point Press.

Guinee, Jeroen B., ed. 2002. *Handbook on Life Cycle Assessment: Operational Guide to the ISO Standards: Eco-Efficiency in Industry and Science,* 1st ed. Norwell, Maine: Kluwer Academic Publishers, 2002.

---

[41] Tom Lent, personal communication, March 8, 2007.

[42] There is a comfortable synergy here between life-cycle impact investigations and the ecological-global footprint theories developed by Dr. Mathis Wackernagel, Footprintnetwork, http://www.footprintnetwork.org.

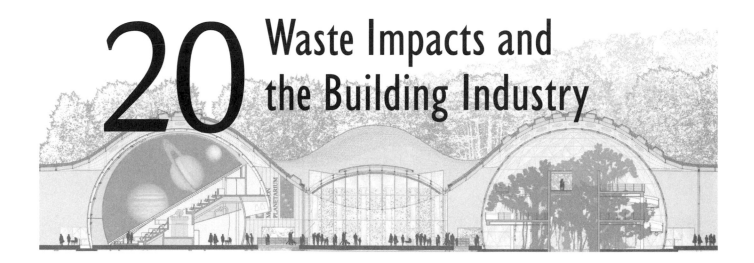

20 Waste Impacts and the Building Industry

The U.S. municipal solid waste stream has more than doubled since 1960, partly owing to increased population and partly because the average U.S. resident produces 4.3 pounds of garbage per day—1.6 more pounds than 30 years ago.

—*Germany, Garbage, and the Green Dot: Challenging the Throwaway Society,*
Bette K. Fishbein[1]

Waste and resources are closely linked, as the discussion of resource efficiency in Chapter 13 showed. Because of its presence in our daily lives and its sheer volume, waste has an impact. Consequently, waste disposal presents a dilemma because of the amount of land it takes (its footprint) to store or to degrade it. Landfill itself can almost be considered a resource, inasmuch as the area it consumes has the potential for being biologically productive land otherwise. There are many types of waste, from virtually every industry, from solid waste to medical waste to hazardous waste (Figure 20-1). In this and the chapter that follows, we will focus on construction and demolition (C&D) waste.

Waste has significant impacts on the environment, as we notice daily. Waste generation and disposal has an impact on natural resources. When waste goes to landfill, it occupies productive land and soil. We need to manage waste as wisely as we manage productive resources. Landfill fires are a hazard affecting the air quality of local communities and the larger atmosphere as a whole due to transmigration. Chemical transmigration can be defined as the property of passing from one medium to another, or chemicals' ability to travel beyond human-defined geographical borders. This characteristic

Figure 20-1 An accumulation of waste.

can cause chemical deposits in the environment far from their origins. In this way, waste generation and disposal can be a contributing factor to the climate change crisis.

Landfills can leach harmful and toxic substances into groundwater, soils, and nearby agricultural land on which local communities depend. In many cases, the contamination by landfill can have more far-reaching effects as contaminants travel through the food web and end up in our bodies.

Examples of pervasive landfill pollutants in waste disposal sites are the prevalence of heavy metals, organic carbon, nitrogen, and heavy metals. Organochlorines are also of concern. They are organic chemicals with a least one chlorine atom; they are typically found in pesticides. Organochlorines are used in a variety of industries, including paper, solvent, and plastic, and they are a landfill byproduct as well. As detailed in Chapter 5, many chemicals, such as organochlorines, are resistant to the process of decomposition, making their presence

---

[1]Bette K. Fishbein, *Germany, Garbage, and the Green Dot: Challenging the Throwaway Society* (New York: Inform, 1994), http://informinc.org.

Figure 20-2 Electronic waste, or *e-waste*, is banned from landfills in parts of the European Union. Lack of product stewardship on the part of the manufacturer means that much e-waste ends up in parts of the world with fewer environmental regulations.

in disposal areas a source of pollution that will last for centuries, a condition known as bioaccumulation.

Another reason waste has an impact on the environment is because landfill disposal sites encroach on greenfields and open space that could be biologically productive areas for sustaining life or active outdoor spaces for nearby communities. In fact, to read data on disposal options is to encounter a litany of ways to subject the natural environment to the demands of human activity: we use deep injection and surface impoundment, release waste into bodies of water and onto sea beds, store waste in permanent "mines," deposit waste for treatment through evaporation or drying or incineration on land or sea. Industrialized nations even export waste to developing countries, because disposal is inexpensive and regulations more relaxed[2] (Figure 20-2).

The Life Cycle of Waste

Waste has a life cycle, a subset of a traditional life cycle, represented in the "end of life" phase. But waste is shed at every phase of the traditional life cycle. If waste is considered in the process cycle, for example, that of building materials manufacturing, it has the following characteristics or phases (Figure 20-3):

- Resources are used to extract or harvest raw feedstock and waste is generated through inefficient harvesting of materials.
- Byproducts of industrial harvest or extraction methods are shed, such as process water, air emissions, noise, odors, with the potential for toxic chemical releases.

- During the manufacturing phase, the same byproducts are shed. During the transportation of goods to distribution centers, and to and from project sites, waste byproducts occur in the form of carbon emissions of combustion engines and impacts from shipping.

By specifying regionally harvested and manufactured recycled-content, salvaged, and rapidly renewable materials, architects and designers can have a beneficial impact on this waste source. These attributes are addressed in the chapters on resource efficiency.

In the use and maintenance phase, waste is shed:

- During *janitorial activities:* No matter how small the scale, janitorial activities shed waste in the form of spent cleaning products, solutions, and tools used for maintenance. As we have seen, these chemicals end up in the environment at some point or another. Selecting low-maintenance materials, establishing green housekeeping procedures, and using environmentally benign cleaners can reduce this form of waste.
- *At the end of life cycle:* At the end of the useful life of a material, product, or system, they can be sent to the following streams: recycling, landfill, incineration, or agricultural uses. By incorporating a concept known as extended manufacturing responsibility, waste can be limited during this cycle.

The definition of waste may seem obvious, but defining it will add understanding to how waste is measured and managed internationally. Loaded with pejorative meaning, the term "waste" has many connotations: lack of value ("that meeting was a waste"), meaninglessness ("a waste of time"), squandering ("a wasted opportunity"), and so on.

In this chapter, we will try to transform the notion of waste and think of it as a commodity, as we would

---

[2]Nathaniel C. Nash, "Latin Nations Getting Others' Waste," *New York Times,* December 16, 1991.

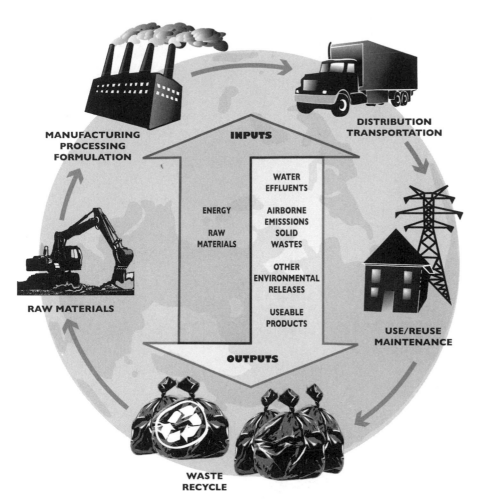

INPUTS

ENERGY
RAW
MATERIALS

WATER
EFFLUENTS
AIRBORNE
EMISSSIONS
SOLID
WASTES
OTHER
ENVIRONMENTAL
RELEASES
USEABLE
PRODUCTS

OUTPUTS

MANUFACTURING
PROCESSING
FORMULATION

DISTRIBUTION
TRANSPORTATION

RAW MATERIALS

USE/REUSE
MAINTENANCE

WASTE
RECYCLE

Figure 20-3 The life cycle of waste.

an actual natural resource. Waste actually provides a resource in that it can be gathered, salvaged, reused, recycled, or downcycled. It is only waste when it goes to a landfill, or "grave," and has no more purpose, hence the term "cradle to grave."

The Australian government has defined "waste" in legislation titled Environmental Protection Act 1994. Waste includes "any thing that is (a) left over, or an unwanted byproduct, from industrial, commercial, domestic or other activity; or (b) surplus to the industrial, commercial, domestic or other activity generating the waste. A thing can be a waste whether or not it is of value."

The European Union's "Directive 2006/12/EC of the European Parliament and of the Council of 5 April 2006 on Waste" divides waste into sixteen categories, including waste types such as residues of industrial processes, contaminated material, and unusable products.

The supporting document "Directive on the Landfill of Waste (1999/31/EC)" sets ambitious goals to reduce landfill waste by 75 percent of 1995 rates by 2010, to 50 percent by 2013, and to 35 percent by 2020. It also sets deadlines for banning from landfills corrosive, oxidizing, flammable, and explosive waste, liquid hazardous waste, infectious hospital and other clinical wastes, and tires.

In China, picking up on policies from Japan and Germany, a "circular economy" model is under development, one that relies on the concepts of industrial ecology—"one facility's waste, in order to achieve highly efficient use and recycling of its resources (including energy, water, and materials), is another facility's inputs." This policy builds on the 3Rs (reduce, reuse, and recycle) concept of materials management.[3]

International recommendations for waste management were set in the *United Nations Conference on Environment and Development's Agenda 21,* "Waste Hierarchy," now recognized by a number of countries[4]:

[3]According to the U.S. Environmental Protection Agency, "The 3Rs Initiative was introduced by Japan at the 2004 G8 Summit held at Sea Island, Georgia, and endorsed by world leaders at the Summit. Japan formally launched the 3R Initiative in April 2005. In March 2006, representatives from around the world shared knowledge of 3Rs activities, communicated future plans, and considered transboundary movement of 3Rs-related goods, materials, and products" (http://www.epa.gov/swerrims/international/factsheets/ndpm-3rs-initiative-and-materials-management.htm).

[4]Agenda 21, the Rio Declaration on Environment and Development, was adopted by more than 178 governments at the United Nations Conference on Environment and Development (UNCED) held in Rio de Janerio, Brazil, 3–14 June 1992.

- Prevent or minimize.
- Reuse or recycle.
- Incinerate with heat recovery.
- Use alternatives to incineration and make safer material selections, such as composting or biological reprocessing.
- Landfill the residue.

The U.S. Environmental Protection Agency (EPA) regulation pertaining to waste is called the Resource Conservation and Recovery Act (RCRA), which governs the disposal of solid and hazardous waste. The U.S. Congress passed RCRA on October 21, 1976, to address the increasing problems the nation faced from our growing volume of municipal and industrial waste. RCRA, which amended the Solid Waste Disposal Act of 1965, set national goals to:

- "Protect human health and the environment from the potential hazards of waste disposal.
- Conserve energy and natural resources.
- Reduce the amount of waste generated.
- Ensure that wastes are managed in an environmentally-sound manner."[5]

Hospital Waste

Before we consider construction and demolition (C&D) waste), it would be helpful to introduce the subject of health-care waste. Though distinct from C&D waste, issues surrounding hospital waste are closely associated with the health-care industry's efforts to green not only their operations but their buildings as well (Figure 20-4). An introduction to these issues will form an excellent example of how integrated building design can best achieve its goal of whole building. It is beneficial for green building designers to understand these functions, safety mechanisms, and accommodations in order to design thoughtfully.

Hospitals in the United States generate 7 to 10 kilograms (kg) per bed per day of health-care waste (HCW), while in contrast, the Middle East produces 1.3–3 kg per bed per day.[6] Add to the sheer volume this represents the advent of super bugs and a variety of new immune-system and antibiotic-resistant illnesses, along with the difficulty of their diagnosis, treatment, and prevention, and you have conditions demanding disposal scrutiny.

Hospital waste and its particular disposal complexities were regulated beginning in the twentieth century. Because of special disposal regulations, the industry has

Figure 20-4 Hospital waste.

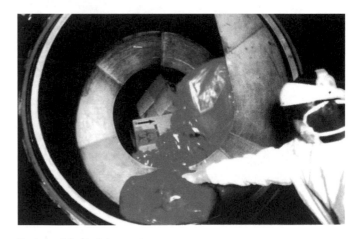

Figure 20-5 A hospital-waste incinerator.

been called upon to practice responsible waste management. Among the many types of hospital waste are several that are pertinent to the building industry in that HCW sometimes contains endocrine-disrupting chemicals and heavy metals, as do certain building materials.

Much medical waste is disposed of in landfills, but incineration is the typical disposal method. Neither disposal method prevents chemical intrusion into the environment and life (Figure 20-5).

In recent years, the largest health-maintenance organization (HMO) in the United States, Kaiser Permanente, has set a goal to eliminate persistent organic pollutants from their operations; mercury from their fluorescent fixtures;

---

[5]Resource Conservation and Recovery Act (RCRA), http://www.epa.gov/epaoswer/osw/laws-reg.htm.
[6]WHO, Definition of HCW, hazards and public health impact.

polyvinyl chloride (PVC) from their indoor flooring materials and intravenous (IV) bags; and other new strategies.

Clearly, the future of green building lies in the health-focused, preventative sustainability of green hospital buildings. Students should look to the design of health-care facilities to anticipate innovations in green building.

Integrated Waste Management

The concept of integrated waste management refers to the combined practice of several waste management techniques, including source reduction (also called waste prevention), composting, incineration, recycling (reuse, salvage, and downcycling), and landfills.

The construction industry has developed best practices for C&D waste that include such techniques as on-site sorting, streamlined materials delivery, and storage, as well as designating haulers to convey waste to relevant separate facilities.

Many of these techniques save the contractor money by avoiding tipping fees, but they also increase paperwork, especially for tracking and weighing. In some communities with such salvage and recycling infrastructure in place, the rate of C&D waste diversion from the landfill is as high as 90 percent.

Through the phases of construction, renovation, and demolition, there are several opportunities to design waste management plans and develop best practices. The key to responsible and successful C&D management is to think "buildings of today are the forests of tomorrow—a

Figure 20-7 Construction debris box, one of the indispensable pieces of the builder's rented equipment.

potentially huge resource for materials that can be reused and recycled in future construction. . . ."[7]

Hand in hand with the concept of waste diversion from landfill is the practice known as "green demolition," which, in addition to encompassing best practices of waste management, also considers the social and economic benefits to the community. (The concept will be explored in more depth in Chapter 21.) In 2003, the University of Florida Powell Center for Construction and Environment developed a green demolition certification,[8] much like a green building rating system. Its goals were to:

- Divert demolition debris from landfills
- Recover materials for reuse and recycling
- Contribute to the environmental and economic health of the community
- Provide a safe and healthful work environment
- Regard necessary building removals as a community development opportunity
- Retain historic building character in a community

The spectrum of waste management includes preventing waste from being generated in the first place, while at the same time exploring efficient ways to deal with the waste that has been generated. Figure 20-8 demonstrates some of the spirit of the first principle—preventing the generation of waste at the actual construction site.

According to the EPA, "136 million tons of building-related C&D waste was generated in the United States in

Figure 20-6 A truckload of wood being hauled away for sorting and possible reuse.

[7]Bette K. Fishbein, *Building for the Future: Strategies to Reduce Construction and Demolition Waste in Municipal Projects,* INFORM 5, no. 1 (1998): 1–102, New York.
[8]Brad Guy, "Green Demolition Certification," University of Florida Powell Center for Construction and Environment, partners in the Deconstruction Institute, founded with a grant from the Florida Department of Environmental Protection, August, 2003.

Figure 20-8 Michelle Kaufmann Designs' Smart House being unloaded at the building's site with a crane. Modular prefabricated housing is making a resurgence as an efficient and factory-controlled construction process.

1997.[9] In contrast, 209.7 million tons of municipal solid waste was generated that same year."[10]

There are three types of C&D waste:

- Inert or nonhazardous
- Hazardous (per the EPA's Resource Conservation and Recovery Act)
- Hazardous components regulated by some states

Most C&D waste is nonhazardous[11] and can be recycled through local infrastructure; some of the nonhazardous waste that can be locally recycled includes: wood-based materials, pallets, metal, glass, paper, and plastic.

Other sources of C&D waste include concrete and concrete-containing products, as well as steel and aluminum.

Still other materials are recyclable through manufacturer take-back or reclamation programs (carpet and gypsum board, for example). Land-clearing and excavation debris can be channeled to transfer stations, to sand and gravel companies, municipal composting facilities, and other end uses. Strategies for C&D diversion can be found in Chapter 13 on resource efficiency as well as in the chapter that follows.

Benefits of Construction Waste Management

According to the USGBC, construction waste management is the diversion and/or redirection of construction,

PLASTIC RECYCLING STATISTICS

Polyethylene terephthalate (PET) and high-density polyethylene (HDPE) are the two major types of plastics recycled in the united States. Statistics from 2006 reveal that PET containers available for recycling grew by 7 percent over the production of 2005. PET container collection increased by 9 percent from 2005. The increased collection produced a higher PET recycling rate of 23.5 percent for the third year. The HDPE recycling rate went up to 27.1 percent in 2005. Still, there is room for more robust recycling. In 2004, U.S. consumers threw out three times as many billion pounds of plastic than they recycled.[12]

renovation, demolition, and deconstruction materials and their redirection to the manufacturing loop or to donation, refurbishment, or reuse activities.[13] This is often referred to as "closing the manufacturing loop" (Figures 20-9–20-11).

Construction waste management practices are powerful tools in the effort to move to a cradle-to-cradle production model, but the process is not complete unless the resultant products with recycled content (recovered material) are in turn purchased and reintroduced into

[9]U.S. Environmental Protection Agency (EPA), *Characterization of Construction and Demolition Debris in the United States, 1997 Update* (Washington, DC: U.S. EPA, 1997).

[10]U.S. EPA, *Characterization of Municipal Solid Waste in the United States, 1997 Update,* Report No. EPA530-R-98-007 (Washington, DC: U.S. EPA, 1997).

[11]Resource Conservation and Recovery Act, *Code of Federal Regulations (CFR),* title 40, secs. 260–279, (1976).

[12]2006 Final Report on Post Consumer PET Container Recycling Activity, National Association for PET Container Resources (NAPCOR) and The Association of Post Consumer Plastic Recyclers (APR), Sonoma, California (2006).

[13]U.S. Green Building Council, http://www.usgbc.org.

Figure 20-9 Glass and concrete being recycled.

Figure 20-10 Wood from a disassembled barn.

the cycle. It pays to recycle rather than dump, because tipping fees are high, and there is money to be made and saved from recycling efforts (Figure 20–12).

Recycling pays from micro to macro scale: from soda cans to concrete. Recyclable materials have value today, although markets had to be created in order for waste to become valuable. There is an active market in recycling nationwide. According to the California Integrated Waste Management Board, "[w]ithin California, recycling and reuse activities make up a major industry. This provides direct employment comparable to the manufacturing of machinery and the motion picture/video industry."[14]

The most frequently recycled C&D materials are metal, glass, concrete, asphalt, and paper products, such as cardboard packaging. Commonly salvageable and reusable materials are brick, rock, soil, lumber, and fixtures, all of which can be diverted from landfill. Other C&D recyclable materials that may not yet provide an economic return—because of distant infrastructure—are gypsum, carpet, ceramic tile, and plastic pipe.

The combined activities of construction, renovation, and demolition account for more than half of the solid waste produced in the United States. There are many options for C&D waste disposal, but, inevitably, landfill is one of the destinations for this waste, especially waste that is contaminated by coatings or adhesives or bonded with these to otherwise recyclable materials. By managing landfills as a resource, using them only for specified materials and waste types, we can extend their lifespan, avoiding the need for new landfills.

Figure 20-11 Brick is a commonly reused building material.

---

[14]California Integrated Waste Management Board (CIWMB), *Diversion Is Good for the Economy: Highlights from Two Independent Studies on the Economic Impacts of Diversion in California, March 2003* (Sacramento: CIWMB, 2003), report.

DIVERSION IS GOOD FOR THE ECONOMY: HIGHLIGHTS FROM TWO INDEPENDENT STUDIES ON THE ECONOMIC IMPACT OF DIVERSION IN CALIFORNIA, MARCH 2003, CALIFORNIA INTEGRATED WASTE MANAGEMENT BOARD

Recycling and reuse is a significant segment of the economy.

The California Recycling Economic Information Study, based on 1999 data, quantified the recycling and

(continued)

reuse industry in California and found it to be a highly diverse industry that is well-established and organized. The study found that California's recycling and reuse industry consists of:

- 5,300 establishments
- 84,000 direct employees
- $2.2 billion annual payroll
- $14.2 billion annual revenues

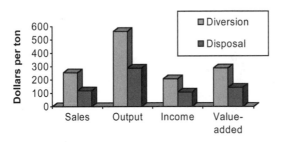

Figure 20-12 Waste diversion creates dollars.

EMISSIONS FROM INCINERATION

The incineration of municipal waste involves the generation of climate-relevant emissions. These are mainly emissions of CO_2 (carbon dioxide) as well as N_2O (nitrous oxide), NOx (oxides of nitrogen), NH_3 (ammonia), and organic C, measured as total carbon.... CO_2 constitutes the chief climate-relevant emission of waste incineration. The incineration of 1 mg of municipal waste in municipal solid waste (MSW) incinerators is associated with the production or release of about 0.7 to 1.2 mg of carbon dioxide (CO_2 output).[15]

Incineration

Because incineration is so prevalent, best practices for this type of disposal include segregating waste types and incineration of appropriate ones. Materials containing PVC and mercury should not be incinerated. In order to

protect the environment and, consequently, health, incinerators should be located away from agricultural areas, schools, and water supplies. Correct design, operation, and maintenance, as well as training for facilities workers, should all be considered in developing incineration practices.[16]

Unfortunately, incineration is a very typical disposal method that generates significant carbon dioxide emissions, as the statistic in the sidebar illustrates. Germany, although one of the highest European Union generators of emissions from incineration, has incinerator plants that are typically equipped with heat-energy recovery systems, thus compensating for the carbon dioxide emissions to a measurable degree.[17]

Waste to Fuel

Pyrolysis is a technology that converts waste into a solid, liquid, or gas. The solids can be used to make other products, like charcoal. Resultant liquids such as oil or gas, can be further refined or used as part of the combustion process.

Gasification, which is a process of burning carbon-based waste or biomass into hydrogen or methane, results in "syngas," a fuel that can be used for a variety of applications. Some gasification plants can convert coal into hydrogen and electricity and store carbon dioxide underground, where fewer greenhouse gases will escape. Gasification is considered a clean form of waste disposal and has the added benefit of converting waste to fuel. Gasification of biomass, or biologically based materials, is considered carbon neutral because the carbon dioxide emitted during burning is compensated for when biomass crops are grown. Crops, wood, solid waste, and alcohol fuels are other examples of biomass. The biomass gasification technology embodies the principle of converting waste to energy, which may be creatively classified as renewable. Waste energy is the second-largest source of biomass energy. In 2005, 3,298 trillion Btu of biomass energy were consumed in the United States.[18]

Digester processing can be used for organic materials waste disposal through anaerobic or mechanical digestion. The resultant biogas becomes a fuel and is used in developing countries as a low-cost form of waste disposal and energy production. This waste-to-energy model has the dual benefit of handling waste and producing fuel.

[15]Bernt Johnke, "Emissions from Waste Incineration," *Good Practice Guidance and Uncertainty Management in National Greenhouse Gas Inventories, Conference Paper 455*, 455–468 (Kanagawa, Japan: Institute for Global Environmental Strategies for the Intergovernmental Panel on Climate Change, 2002), http://www.ipcc-nggip.iges.or.jp/public/gp/gpg-bgp.html (accessed January 15, 2009).

[16]World Health Organization, WHO Fact sheet No. 281, October 2004, "Health-care waste management: To reduce the burden of disease, health-care waste needs sound management, including alternatives to incineration" (http://www.who.int/mediacentre/factsheets/fs281/en/index.html).

[17]Johnke, "Emissions from Waste Incineration," pages 455–468.

[18]Energy Information Administration, Official Energy Statistics from the U.S. Government, http://www.eia.doe.gov/cneaf/solar.renewables/page/trends/table6.html.

Figure 20-13 The changing role of waste is exemplified in source reduction on a large scale, where separation of disposed materials creates market opportunities for materials otherwise destined for landfill. Again, waste is a resource. Pictured is a demonstrator of an automated waste sorting device, developed by U.K. science and technology company QinetiQ, that uses defense industry sensing and target tracking technologies to autonomously separate various types of waste materials for recycling.

Best Practices

In addition to waste diversion of demolition debris, it is also critical to adopt best practices at the top of the stream. Source prevention of waste is the name given to limiting the amount of waste generated at the beginning of demolition and construction activities. Source prevention can occur during all phases of construction and during building operations and maintenance.

Beginning in the early phases, it is important to design with disassembly, durability, and minimal use of materials in mind.

During operations and maintenance, it is important to keep a building well maintained, because its increased life span, as well as its continued functionality and durability, will postpone the need for demolition.

For example, educating occupants about reducing the waste they generate in the lunchroom or copy room can also go a long way toward reducing waste in terms of building operation. Although not a heartening thought for future designers and builders, the essence of successful waste

Figures 20-14 Salvaged and reused waste materials are repurposed as art.

Figures 20-15 A statement on waste using waste materials.

prevention with minimal impact on the environment is not to build at all, and instead reuse existing building stock. The next chapter will delve into the management of C&D waste.

EXERCISES

1. Brainstorm with your colleagues about a possible new technology for waste disposal. Select a particular waste stream, e.g., biological materials or wood scraps from a construction site, used rubber tires, etc. What technology could push the envelope with regard to carbon dioxide emissions and health impacts to humans near the waste-processing site? How could your new technology be used to harness heat energy for another use?

2. One of the most imposing barriers to the movement toward zero waste is that we are consumer society. The other barrier is a burgeoning population expected to reach over 9 billion by the year 2050. How can green builders and city planners balance the two?

3. What is meant by a "materials economy"? The term is defined in the video *The Story of Stuff*, by Annie Leonard, available for download at http://www.storyofstuff.com.

4. Comment on the messages in Figures 20-14 and 20-15.

Resources

The Story of Stuff, by Annie Leonard, a short animated film sponsored by the Tides Foundation and the Funders Workgroup for Sustainable Consumption and Production, 2007. http://www.storyofstuff.com.

U.S. Environmental Protection Agency (EPA): The Resource Conservation and Recovery Act (RCRA), Wastes Information Resources: RCRA Online, http://www.epa.gov/epawaste/inforesources/online/index.htm.

Whole Building Design Guide, http://www.wbdg.org.

U.S. Green Building Council, http://www.usgbc.org.

Waste Management Series, Volume 1, *Waste Materials in Construction: Science and Engineering of Recycling for Environmental Protection*. G. R. Woolley, J. J. J. M. Goumans, and P. J. Wainwright, editors. New York: Pergamon Press.

Fundamentals of Building Construction: Materials and Methods. 2003. Edward Allen and Joseph Iano. Hoboken, NJ: John Wiley & Sons.

Ferguson, J., N. Kermode, C. L. Nash, and W. A. J. Sketch. 1995. *Managing and Minimizing Construction Waste: A Practical Guide*. London: Institution of Civil Engineers.

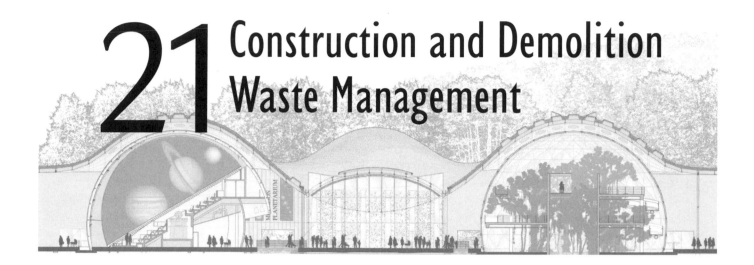

21 Construction and Demolition Waste Management

Between the years 2000 and 2030, projections indicate that 27 percent of existing buildings will be replaced, and 50 percent of the total building stock will be constructed. Consequently, it is critical to focus on conserving building materials and energy by integrating lifecycle building practices into standard building practices and policies.
—*LifeCycle Building Challenge,*
U.S. Environmental Protection Agency and
American Institute of Architects, December 17, 2008

Builders have become increasingly focused on resource recovery as an alternative to placing materials in landfill, the proverbial "grave" of a life cycle scenario. According to the U.S. Environmental Protection Agency (EPA), "[b]uilding demolitions account for 48 percent of the waste stream, or 65 million tons per year; renovations account for 44 percent, or 60 million tons per year; and 8 percent, or 11 million tons per year, is generated at construction sites."[1] Resource recovery is a term frequently used in the waste industry, where waste is viewed as a potential source of usable materials through thermal or biological processing. End products include fuel, soil-enrichment materials, and compost energy and chemicals that can be used in manufacturing new products, as we have seen.

This concept is also known as "secondary resource recovery."[2] For the builder, however, there are many activities on site that can creatively divert materials from even the cleaner disposal methods. In chapters 20 and 13, on resource efficiency, we reviewed types of demolition and construction materials and techniques for their salvage, recycling, and reuse.

Diversion

Among the diversion techniques for salvaged materials are the "take-back" programs for certain types of clean goods: shipping materials, packaging, pallets, building furnishings, and computers. Increasingly, we are seeing manufacturer take-back programs for carpet and gypsum board and other materials considered difficult to recycle.

These materials will end up as part of the manufacturing materials "loop," and the programs are structured such that manufacturers see the economic benefit to their production. This concept is often referred to as "extended producer (or manufacturer) responsibility" (EPR) or "product stewardship." It requires manufacturers to be responsible for their products until the end of the products' complete life cycle.

This concept only works if the consumer of the materials, in this case, those who design and construct buildings, connects the two ends of the loop by linking used materials with the product distribution chain. Extended producer responsibility regulations have been adopted in many states and in over thirty countries.[3]

Materials-donation and materials-exchange boards[4] are another way to draw maximum efficiency from a material or product and divert it from the waste stream. Reuse of materials and donations of clean materials can benefit organizations like Habitat for Humanity, as well as aid and relief organizations for victims of natural disasters.

---

[1]U.S. Environmental Protection Agency (EPA), *Characterization of Building-Related Construction and Demolition Debris in the United States,* Report No. EPA530-R-98-010 (Prairie Village, KS: Prepared for the U.S. Environmental Protection Agency Municipal and Industrial Solid Waste Division Office of Solid Waste by Franklin Associates, 1998).
[2]Government of New South Wales, Department of Environment and Climate Change, http://www.emrc.org.au/glossary.asp?pg=137 (accessed March 30, 2008).

[3]San Francisco Department of the Environment (SF Environment), http://www.sfenvironment.org/our_programs/interests.html?ssi=3&ti=4&ii=95 (accessed March 29, 2008).
[4]Green Goat is a Web site that connects builders with sources for waste and recycling: http://greengoat.org/index.html.

Design for Disassembly

Strategies that will make future demolition of buildings less wasteful and more efficient include the concept of "disassembly," that is, "designing for deconstruction and disassembly" (DfD) (Figure 21-1). The Chartwell School in Seaside, California, designed by EHDD, makes use of DfD, a process that the architectural firm researched and pioneered. Many consumer products, such as Steelcase's "Think" chair, are designed for disassembly, the motivation being waste reduction and resource-use reduction by a factor of ten.[5]

Unfortunately, several barriers to mainstream adoption of DfD exist, including the increased reliance on coatings and finishes for many building materials, the use of mechanical fasteners that are difficult to remove, and increasingly engineered and composite materials that are "difficult to remove because of their chemical complexity."[6]

The *Whole Building Design Guide* defines deconstruction of buildings as the "systematic disassembly of a building, generally in the reverse order of construction, in an economical and safe fashion, for the purposes of preserving materials for their reuse."[7]

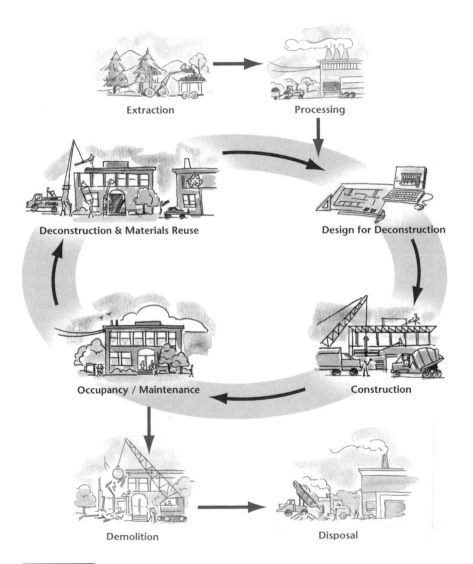

Extraction

Processing

Deconstruction & Materials Reuse

Design for Deconstruction

Occupancy / Maintenance

Construction

Demolition

Disposal

Figure 21-1 Design for disassembly techniques are part of a closed-loop system.

---

[5]"Factor 10 is the goal of being ten times as productive with half the resources (materials and energy), leading to a factor 10 improvement in efficiency" (*The Dictionary of Sustainable Management*, Presidio School of Management, http://www.sustainabilitydictionary.com/f/factor_10.php). Concepts originated from the book *Factor 4* by Ernst von Weizsäcker, founder of the Wuppertal Institute for Climate, Environment and Energy, with L. Hunter Lovins and Amory Lovins of the Rocky Mountain Institute, and subsequently elaborated on with the concept of factor 10, developed by the United Nations Environment Programme, Factor 10 Institute, http://www.factor10-institute.org/seitenges/Factor10.htm.

[6]Brad Guy and Nicholas Ciarimboli, "Design for Disassembly in the Built Environment: A Guide to Closed-Loop Design and Building," prepared on behalf of the City of Seattle, King County, WA, and Resource Venture, Inc. by the Hamer Center for Community Design, The Pennsylvania State University, 2006, 3.

[7]Tom Napier, "Construction Waste Management," *The Whole Building Design Guide*, http://www.wbdg.org/resources/cwmgmt.php (accessed March 29, 2008).

Strategies for DfD are the subject of entire professional conferences, and the practice of DfD itself has affected agency and municipal regulations and guidelines for construction and demolition. To provide for efficient deconstruction, however, the design of buildings needs to be restructured in every design and construction phase, from conceptual design to construction with materials and products that are optimally dismantled.

Charles Kibert cites twenty-seven detailed "Principles of Design for Disassembly," first published as a doctoral dissertation by Philip Crowther in 2002.[8]

Among Crowther's DfD principles with an impact on sound construction practices are the following:

- Do not apply secondary finishes to materials.
- Materials that are "inseparable" should be made from the same material.
- Provide consistent and permanent identification of materials.
- When constructing, use a minimum number of components.
- Avoid chemical connections such as adhesives and use mechanical fasteners instead.
- Use interchangeable parts for the building system.
- Use modular and prefabricated components.
- Make sure there is a separation of structure and cladding.
- Provide access to building components for ease of disassembly.
- Make sure there is enough room (adequate tolerances) to allow space for disassembly tasks.
- Identify each component in a permanent way.
- Keep spare component parts in storage.
- Record information on the disassembly process and data on the building.[9]

The builder will cover some of these principles to a certain degree in the normal course of practice, but many of these concepts require shifts in standard methods. Information on warranties, for example, is typically turned over to the building owner upon completion of construction. With DfD, the contractor should include additional information on maintenance, repair, and future disassembly.

Construction Waste Management Plans

As mentioned previously, there are financial benefits for the contractor who manages demolition and construction waste wisely.

In practice, large construction companies track their materials costs and waste-hauling expenses. But to achieve meaningful and measurable landfill diversion and increased recovery rates, the contractor may need to more closely track collection bins, waste-hauler details, donations and material exchanges, weight tags, and the costs involved in each activity. The U.S. Green Building Council (USGBC) Leadership in Energy and Environmental Design (LEED) Rating System describes a protocol for documenting and calculating diversion rates under its construction waste management credit.

As part of sound construction practices, contractors are frequently required to produce a written construction waste management plan. Such a plan describes in advance of construction how the contractor intends to proceed with handling the waste generated by the job.

The builder should describe the types of materials the crew intends to remove and salvage from any existing structures, along with vegetation and dirt or soil on the site. During construction, the building crew will place collection bins for separate waste types and for storage of mixed wastes.

On-site sorting of wastes is more labor intensive but creates efficiencies down the line. The plan should also describe the frequency of collection and where the waste is to be hauled, whether a recycling facility, nonprofit collection agency, city landscaping department, a materials exchange, or landfill. Documentation is required as proof of waste diversion, and so the contractor is charged with creating a paper trail, very similar to the chain of custody documentation required for wood that is certified as sustainably harvested.

Green Demolition

Waste also impacts local communities and the builders themselves. As we have seen throughout this book, sustainable and integrated design entails thinking about social issues as well as those relating to design and construction of buildings. The concept of green demolition heavily weights this component of demolition in three major ways: to encourage thinking about maximizing economic benefit of correct demolition, to provide a safe work environment for construction crews, and to preserve culturally and historically significant buildings and neighborhoods. The Deconstruction Institute issues green demolition certificates to provide incentives and give building owners marketing visibility. Of 52 credits, teams are asked to comply with all prerequisites and at least 25 credits.

The credits fall under three major categories, including opportunities to propose innovative demolition strategies. Under the building category, credits are awarded for site issues such as leaving vegetation in place and providing

[8]Philip Crowther, "Design for Disassembly: An Architectural Strategy for Sustainability," doctoral dissertation, Queensland University of Technology, 2002, and cited in Charles J. Kibert, *Sustainable Construction: Green Building Design and Delivery* (Hoboken, NJ: John Wiley & Sons, 2005), 300.
[9]Kibert, *Sustainable Construction*, 300.

an erosion and sedimentation control plan. Materials recovery credits are based on actual materials recovered as well as embodied-energy recovery. Waste reduction practices are calculated using the ratio of total building volume to recovered materials.

Under planning and land-use categories, infill of blighted areas is encouraged. Validation of green demolition practices and infrastructure is promoted using the concept of industry building. The same applies to community building, which would offer apprenticeships and donations to nonprofits. Under materials management, the certification requirements fold logically into the potential for the construction of a new building on the same site using the recovered materials.

Under environmental health and safety, worker health is promoted through green demolition training and the offer of incentives and training for job-site safety. To properly manage unanticipated discovery of hazardous materials, specific practices are encouraged, such as surveys for existing sources of asbestos and lead and a plan for notification and disposal. Applications for green demolition certification are independently verified.

Other Job-Site Waste Strategies

Construction and demolition (C&D) waste management falls to the builder, but often city and state agencies will get involved, as will the rest of the design team. There are several basic strategies that a good plan will fold in:

- Lay out recycling and debris bins in a major "path of travel" on- and off-site so that trades are forced to use them. Some schools of thought encourage the use of debris piles surrounded by a containment method to avoid wash off from storms. Piles are more easily viewed and monitored for appropriate disposal than bins or dumpsters.
- Engage and educate crew and subcontractors as to mandatory waste management techniques.
- Purchase materials in bulk to avoid overpackaging.
- Reuse or return packaging and containers to suppliers or manufacturers, a concept known as "product stewardship."
- Use scrap wood instead of full-length new wood stock.
- Combine partially full containers of wet-applied products such as paint to avoid wasting them. This will cut down on the cost of ordering more supplies than are actually used.
- For materials that require heating or mixing, mix the materials in smaller batches to avoid waste, particularly if the cure time is especially fast.
- During the architectural and engineering design phases, use value engineering to make efficient use of building products, by using one product for multiple purposes, for example.

- Many municipal recycling facilities are now accepting commingled waste and sorting it at their site. This method requires less effort and less preplanning by the builder. For larger jobs, this method can often yield higher rates of waste diversion.

Laws governing responsible practices for C&D waste disposal have been enacted in Seattle, San Francisco, and many other cities. Many of these U.S. cities specify benchmarks for percentage of waste diversion. Several have made waste management goals a prerequisite for demolition and construction permits. Ultimately, successful C&D waste diversion relies on organized on-site project supervision, a knowledge of local recycling and diversion infrastructure, and a well-written waste management plan.

Clearly, the opportunities for development of waste management best practices are numerous. These opportunities are very broadly distributed and involve cities, recycling facilities, design teams, construction crews, regulatory agencies, and building occupants who continue the effort toward waste reduction during building occupancy (Figure 21-2).

Successful construction and demolition waste management involves large-scale practices that must divert high volumes of building materials waste, but it also involves community-level participation, in the same way that small-scale recycling efforts did in the early 1970s. (Figures 21-3, 21-4, and 21-5) In this way, the loop of waste diversion is completed by means of judiciously used materials, as well as through heightened awareness and conscientious building operations. With a robust combination of practices and partner participation, business as usual is experiencing a necessary shift.

C&D WASTE COMPRISES:

- 40%–50% concrete and mixed rubble
- 20%–30% wood
- 5%–15% drywall
- 1%–10% asphalt roofing
- 1%–5% metals
- 1%–5% bricks
- 1%–5% plastics

Source: U.S. EPA[10]

---

[10]U.S. EPA, "Construction and Demolition (C&D) Materials," http://www.epa.gov/epawaste/conserve/rrr/imr/cdm/index.htm.

(a)

DEMOLITION DEBRIS RECOVERY PLAN
WORKSHEET
Construction and Demolition Debris Recovery Program
City and County of San Francisco
Environment Code Chapter 14; Ordinance No. 27-06; SFE Regulations 06-05-CDO

PLAN TYPE: ☐ **NEW PERMIT APPLICATION** ☐ **FINAL REPORT**

General Instructions:

- Demolition Debris Recovery Plan (DDRP) WORKSHEET must be completed and submitted to San Francisco's Department of Environment (SFE) for all Department of Building Inspection (DBI) Full Demolition Permit applications (Form #6). Submit to SFE at address at bottom of this page.
- The DDRP must demonstrate that the demolition project will achieve a minimum of 65% diversion from landfill.
- After SFE approves the DDRP, it will be returned to you to submit to DBI before issuance of the Demolition Permit.
- Demolition permits will not be issued by DBI without an approved DDRP.

Demolition Permit Application No. _____ Permit Application Date _____

Project Address _____ Project Block/Lot# _____

Permit Applicant Name _____ Phone (___) _____

Permit Applicant Address _____

Contact Name _____ Phone (___) _____

Contact Address _____ Fax (___) _____
(if different from above)

_____ E-Mail _____

Describe building being demolished: Type _____ Square Footage _____

Complete the Diversion Rate Table on the reverse side of this worksheet indicating the disposition by material type of all project materials. See www.sfenvironment.org/c&d for possible facilities or markets to take materials. **For new permit applications**, provide ESTIMATED tons. **For final reports**, provide ACTUAL tons based on receipts you have received from facilities. Information included in the final report is subject to verification by SFE.

Instructions for completing the table on the reverse side of this worksheet.

Column 1 – This is the **total** tons of materials generated from this project listed by material type.
Column 2 – Materials that will be separated on site in usable condition taken to a salvage facility for reuse. Also includes materials reused on site such as wood forms, and inerts used as backfill, etc.
Column 3 – Materials separated on site that will be taken to a facility to be reprocessed into a new product. This includes source separated materials such as wood, metal, cardboard, drywall, landscape debris, etc.
Column 4 – Materials that are not source separated on site and are taken to a facility that will process mixed construction & demolition debris for recovery. Materials taken to a SF-Registered Mixed Debris Facility will be credited with 65% diversion. For non-registered facilities, the diversion credit may be lower.
Column 5 – Unrecoverable material (trash) that is directly hauled to a disposal facility or landfill.
Column 6 – Name of facility(s) you intend to use for reuse, recycling or disposal of each material generated from the project.

Submittal Instructions
Submit this completed and signed form to: Department of the Environment, 11 Grove St., San Francisco, CA 94102. Attention: C&D Demolition Debris Recovery Plan.

For any questions regarding this worksheet, the Ordinance or regulations, please call the Department of the Environment at (415) 355-3700 or see www.sfenvironment.org/c&d

03.17.08   Page 1 of 2

Figure 21-2 An example of a debris-recovery plan that assists builders in calculating their diversion rates.

Diversion Rate Table (*See Instructions on the front side of this form for column descriptions*).   (b)

Material Type (Tons)	1 Total Tons Generated	2 Salvage or Reuse	3 Recycling (source-separated)	4 Mixed Processing Facility	5 Disposal (Trash)	6 Facility or Destination
Example: Wood	*50*	*5*		*45*		**Building Resources/SFR&D**
Wood, Pallets & Lumber (clean & unpainted, no pressure-treated wood)						
Cabinets, Fixtures, Doors, Windows, Equipment						
Metal						
Carpet						
Carpet Padding						
Cardboard						
Ceiling Tile						
Drywall (used and painted)						
Green Waste						
Concrete						
Asphalt						
Brick, Masonry, Tile						
Rock/Dirt/Soil						
Mixed Debris						
Other (please specify)						
Sorted, Non-Recyclable, Non-Compostable Debris (please describe)						
TOTAL	A	B	C	D		

Calculate **Your Diversion Rate** using the following formula:

$$\boxed{\underline{B}} + \boxed{\underline{C}} + \boxed{\underline{D} \text{ X \_\_\_(DR)}^*} = \boxed{} \text{ Divide by } \boxed{\underline{A}} = \boxed{} \text{ X } 100 = \boxed{\text{Your Diversion Rate}} \%$$

[* If you are taking materials to a SF-Registered Mixed Debris Facility (pursuant to Ordinance No. 27-06) calculate D x .65 (65% minimum diversion rate (DR) requirement for registered facilities). If material is processed by a non-registered facility, the facility diversion rate (DR) may be lower; please check with the facility for their diversion rate (DR).]

If **Your Diversion Rate** is less that 65%, provide justification why the project cannot meet the 65% diversion requirement

_____

List all transporters that will be removing material off site (*provide additional page if necessary*)

1)_____ 2)_____ 3)_____

I AGREE TO SUBMIT A FINAL REPORT for this Demolition Permit WITHIN 30 DAYS AFTER COMPLETION OF THE DEMOLITION PROJECT; FINAL REPORT MUST VERIFY THE ACTUAL DIVERSION ACHIEVED & **INCLUDE ALL RECEIPTS FROM FACILITIES.**   ***ESTIMATED DATE OF COMPLETION***: _____

Submitted by (signature):_____**Date**_____

Print Name_____ **Title**_____

FOR OFFICIAL CITY USE ONLY
DATE PLAN/REPORT RECEIVED BY SFE _____
APPROVED _____ NOT APPROVED _____ DATE _____
COMMENTS _____   _____
APPROVED BY _____ NAME & TITLE _____

Figure 21-2 Cont'd

Figure 21-3 Recycling bins, in Budapest, Hungary.

Figure 21-4 Waste collection on a small scale.

Figure 21-5 A street-side cardboard compactor in Budapest, Hungary.

EXERCISES

1. Develop a waste management plan for a small residential project: a wood-frame house with grading for a hardscape terrace. Assume there is a derelict wood structure on-site that needs to be demolished.

2. Collect statistics on construction waste from the United States and compare it to rates in another country.

3. The images in Figures 21-3, 21-4, and 21-5 are examples of waste management practices outside the United States. In Budapest, Hungary, for example, recycling opportunities exist at the neighborhood level. Discuss possible strategies for incorporating neighborhood infrastructure waste-diversion technologies for the region you live in. Discuss the possible pitfalls, level of community awareness, and both the positive and negative ramifications of installing and incentivizing technology that addesses a broader scope of waste materials.

4. Conduct a hypothetical waste audit for a building, household, or school using a waste audit tool. Refer to the "Resources" section of this chapter.

■ Resources

Energy Information Administration, Official Energy Statistics from the U.S. Government: http://www.eia.doe.gov.

Waste Audit Tools:

Kansas Green Teams, "How to Conduct a Waste Audit," http://www.kansasgreenteams.org/how-conduct-waste-audit.

Race Against Waste, "Waste Audit Tool," (applies to Irish infrastructure, but nevertheless addresses themes common to the U.S.), http://www.wasteaudittool.com/.

Oregon Green Schools, "What's in Your Waste?" http://www.oregongreenschools.org/pdf/Whats-in-your-waste.pdf.

Pennsylvania, Department of Environmental Protection, "Conducting a Waste Audit," http://www.dep.state.pa.us/dep/deputate/airwaste/wm/recycle/FACTS/ComRec.htm.

Waste Management Organizations

California Integrated Waste Management Board (CIWMB) Web site: http://www.ciwmb.ca.gov/ConDemo.

International Solid Waste Association (international body).

Solid Waste Association of North America (North America).

Saint Lucia Solid Waste Management Authority.

U.S. EPA C&D Debris Web page: http://www.epa.gov/epa-oswer/non-hw/debris.

Waste Management Association of Australia (Australia peak industry body).

Whole Building Design Guide, Construction Waste Management (CWM) database: http://www.wbdg.org/tools/cwm.php?s=NY.

Extended Producer Responsibility (EPP)

British Columbia's Product Stewardship Programs: http://www .env.gov.bc.ca/epd/epdpa/ips/index.html.

Product Policy Institute: http://www.productpolicy.org/resources/ index.html.

Product Stewardship Institute: http://www.productstewardship.us/.

Deconstruction

The Deconstruction Institute, http://www.deconstructioninsti-tute.com.

"Design for Disassembly in the Built Environment: A Guide to Closed-Loop Design and Building," Brad Guy and Nicholas Ciarimboli, prepared on behalf of the City of Seattle, King County, WA, and Resource Venture, Inc. by the Hamer Center for Community Design, The Pennsylvania State University,2006.

Materials Exchanges

U.S. EPA Materials and Waste Exchange, http://www.epa.gov/ epawaste/conserve/tools/exchange.htm.

Minnesota Materials Exchange, http://mnexchange.org/index.htm.

California Materials Exchange (CalMAX), http://www.ciwmb. ca.gov/calMAX/

Materials Exchange Information (MIXInfo), http://mxinfo.org/.

Zero Waste Network, Resource Exchange Network for Eliminating Waste (RENEW), http://www.zerowastenetwork. org/RENEWDEV/index.cfm.

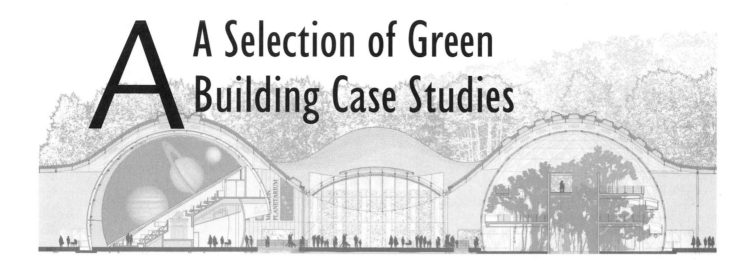

A A Selection of Green Building Case Studies

The following listing of integrated buildings is not meant to be comprehensive. It will provide a spectrum of buildings, from buildings with a salient sustainable feature to those with integrated sustainability goals. Buildings are arranged by building type and range from new construction from the late 1990s to current green building, as well as conceptual and unbuilt projects.

For further listings of green building case studies, refer to the "Resources" section of Chapter 17, where green building databases are listed.

▣ Museums

California Academy of Sciences, Golden Gate Park, San Francisco, California

Owner: California Academy of Sciences

Architecture and design: Renzo Piano Building Workshop and Chong Partners Architecture

General contractor: Webcor Builders

Green and engineering consultants: Arup

Completion date: 2008

Building area: 409,000 sq. ft.

Green building goals of note: 2.5-acre vegetated roof with six species of native California plants; natural ventilation through operable windows, and louvers and skylights that operate automatically with the assistance of sensors.

LEED Platinum

▣ Schools and Higher Education

Waldorf High School, San Francisco, California

Architecture and design: 450 Architects, San Francisco

General contractor: Oliver & Company

Green consultant: KEMA

Completion date: September 2007

Building area: 23,410 sq. ft.

LEED Gold

Green building goals of note: Recycling, repurposing of demolished materials; heating, ventilating, and air-conditioning (HVAC) system operable on 100 percent outside air with economizer; monitors for building management system as part of the green building in the curriculum program.

Figure A-1a
A section through the building shows the vegetated roof, ventilation areas, and skylit spaces.

Figure A-1b An aerial rendering shows how the building's green roof meets the photovoltaic-integrated overhang. Coconut husk planting trays were used to accommodate the steep slopes of the roof.

Figure A-2a Exterior view of the LEED Gold rated Waldorf High School, San Francisco, designed by 450 Architects.

Figure A-1c The building canopy with integrated photovoltaics.

Figure A-1d Planting for the vegetated roof is comprised of eight native species, including four wildflower varieties, forming a habitat for the threatened Bay Checkerspot butterfly.

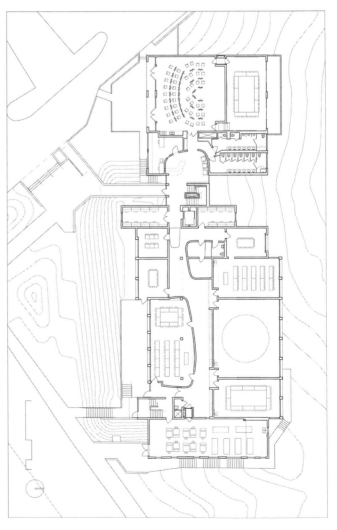

Figure A-2b San Francisco Waldorf High School, main floor plan.

Figure A-2c The Waldorf High School's science classroom provides daylit interior spaces and Forest Stewardship Council-certified wood casework.

Figure A-3a The Minnaert Building's outsize lettering elements also provide entry to a covered bicycle parking area.

Minnaert Building, University Centre De Uithof, Utrecht, Netherlands

Owner: Utrecht University

Architecture and design: Neutelings Riedijk Architecten

Completion date: 1997

Building area: 96,875 sq. ft.

Green building goals of note: Roof openings allow rainwater to spill into a collecting pool in the central space, where it then circulates throughout the building, serving as both a rainwater harvesting system and a source of coolth for the building, assisted by night air water cooling.

The University of Nottingham, Jubilee Campus, Nottingham, England

Architecture, design, and master plan: Michael Hopkins and Partners

Completion date: 1999

Project area: 20 acres

Green building goals of note: Site water collection in small artificial lake provides cooling for buildings; project was built on a multilayered brownfield site, formerly a coal mine, bicycle factory, and chemical processing site. Wind cowls assist in air exhaust from buildings. Energy use is half that of a typical energy-efficient building, yielding an estimated 75 percent less carbon dioxide (CO_2) emissions than best practices. Materials containing polyvinyl chloride (PVC) were largely avoided in the project.[1]

Figure A-3b The Minnaert's interior spaces are cooled by stored rainwater circulating through the building, after which the water is deposited into an indoor pool.

Figure A-3c Exterior view of the Minnaert Building, designed by Neutelings Riedijk Architecten.

[1] "The Jubilee Campus, University of Nottingham," Jim McCarthy Robin Riddall Christian Topp, *Arup Journal,* February 2001. http://www.arup.com/_assets/_download/download27.pdf

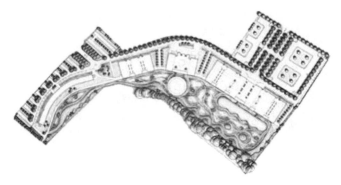

Figure A-4a The University of Nottingham Jubilee campus site plan, Hopkins Architects.

Figure A-4c Wind cowls exhaust air to the outside.

Figure A-4b The centrally planned library consists of a single floor plane that provides circulation through the building.

Mont-Cenis Academy, Herne-Sodingen, Germany

Owner: Akademie Mont-Cenis, Entwicklungsgesellschaft Mont-Cenis, Herne

Project architects: Jourda Architects, Paris and HHS Planer + Architekten BDA, Kassel Completion

Date: 1999

Green building goals of note: One of the first buildings to utilize building-integrated photovoltaics (BIPVs), this project incorporated solar cells into the facade as structural glazing, to the roof as overhead glazing and as shading devices, thus combining architectural elements with power generation of 600,000 to 650,000 kilowatt hours per year.

(a)

Figure A-5 a–c Exterior views of the Mont Cenis Academy. The project was one of the first to incorporate building-integrated photovoltaic panels.

(b)

(c)

Figure A-5 a–c *Cont'd.*

Adam Joseph Lewis Center for Environmental Studies, Oberlin College, Oberlin, Ohio

The Adam Joseph Lewis Center's design team is a who's who of green building luminaries.

Architecture and design: William McDonough & Partners

Energy analysis: Steven Winter Associates

Indoor air quality consultant: Hal Levin & Associates

Daylighting: Loisos/Ubbelohde

Lighting: Clanton & Associates

Green development services: Rocky Mountain Institute

Green building goals of note: An integrated building-landscape system, the project has a "living machine" that treats wastewater and recycles it for use in irrigation and toilet flushing. Because the landscape is a reconstruction of a historic wetlands, and because together with the building it functions as a biological ecosystem, the project is considered an example of a restorative building.

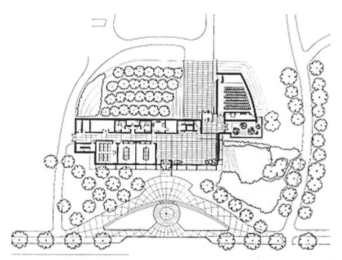

Figure A-6a Oberlin Environmental Studies Building site plan.

Figure A-6b The exterior of the Oberlin Environmental Studies Building, with wetlands in the foreground.

Sidwell Friends Middle School, Washington, D.C.

Owner: Sidwell Friends School

Architecture and design: Kieran Timberlake Associates

Environmental building consultant: GreenShape

General contractor: HITT Contracting

Building area: 72,500 sq. ft.

Completion date: September 2006

LEED Platinum

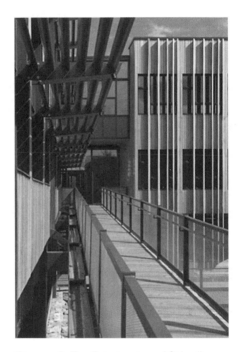

Figure A-7a Exterior view of Sidwell Friends School with the shading devices, fins, and louvers.

Green building goal of note: The school's central courtyard sits atop a constructed wetland that provides on-site wastewater treatment to direct water for reuse in irrigation, toilet flushing, and in cooling towers.

Chartwell School, Seaside, California

Architecture and design: EHDD

General contractor: Ausonio, Inc.

Completion date: 2006

Building area: 21,000 sq. ft.

LEED Platinum

Green building goal of note: Optimized daylighting strategies and heightened acoustical design to support student performance; achieved a Collaborative for High Performance Schools (CHPS) rating.

Figure A-8a A large amount of glass surface area and proper building orientation were keys to the success of the Chartwell School's daylighting strategy.

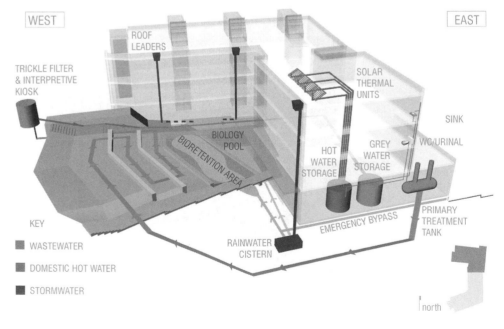

WEST

EAST

TRICKLE FILTER & INTERPRETIVE KIOSK

ROOF LEADERS

SOLAR THERMAL UNITS

SINK

BIORETENTION AREA

BIOLOGY POOL

HOT WATER STORAGE

GREY WATER STORAGE

WC/URINAL

KEY

■ WASTEWATER

■ DOMESTIC HOT WATER

■ STORMWATER

RAINWATER CISTERN

EMERGENCY BYPASS

PRIMARY TREATMENT TANK

north

Figure A-7b The water system's three streams: wastewater, storm water, and domestic hot water.

■ Commercial Office

Ken Yeang

Without question, the most visionary and prolific designer of green buildings is Malaysian architect Ken Yeang of T. R. Hamzah & Yeang International. His aesthetic and green philosophy is based on designing bioclimatic skyscrapers that respond to, rather than repel, regional climatic conditions. Some of Yeang's goals in building green skyscrapers relate to indoor environmental comfort and energy efficiency, incorporating ecological design in a vertical environment.

EDITT Tower (Ecological Design in The Tropics), Singapore

> Client: URA (Urban Redevelopment Authority), Singapore (Sponsor), NUS (National University of Singapore) (Sponsor)
>
> Under construction: Tower structure containing retail, exhibition spaces, and auditorium uses

Figure A-8b The Chartwell School's multipurpose room has abundant daylight access.

Figure A-9 Gardens on every level of the EDITT Tower are an effort to reintroduce greenscape to the existing "zero-culture" site.

1. Low ventilation intake
2. High ventilation exhaust
3. Spectrally selective glazing in thermally broken frame
4. Daylighting in internal hallway
5. Operable skylight
6. Peel-n-stick photovoltaics
7. 30 kw PV transformer connected to electrical grid
8. Radiant slab heating
9. Low emitting materials
10. Certified wood framing with modular design-walls at 24" o.c., roof joints at 48" o.c.
11. Rain catchment system used for toilet flushing
12. Native landscaping
13. Utility raceway

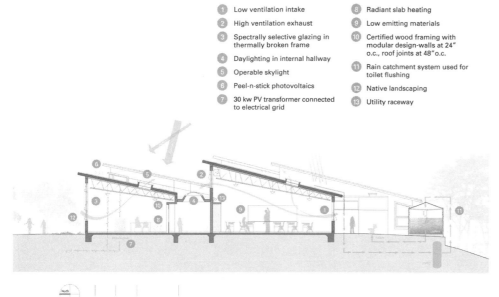

Figure A-8c A sectional drawing through the building illustrates envelope design and other green building strategies.

Gross area: 26 stories, 64,938 sq. ft.

Green building goals of note: To restore the ecosystem and bring organic matter back to the "zero-culture" site; continuous vertical planted terraces, a form of vertical farming; 55 percent water, self-sufficient through gray-water reuse, black-water treatment, and rainwater capture and storage; photovoltaics provide almost 40 percent of the building's energy needs; wind walls direct air to the interior for thermal comfort.

Menara Mesiniaga, IBM Tower, Subang Jaya, Selangor, Malaysia

Owner: IBM

Completion date: 1992

Building area: 14 stories, 132,887 sq. ft.

(a)

(b)

Green building goal of note: This signature building represents the sum of the firm's studies into bioclimatic design through such strategies as vertical landscaping, passive energy-efficient features such as exterior sun shades, and ventilated elevator and stair shafts.

(c)

Figure A-10 a–c Also known as the IBM Building, the Menara Mesiniaga building's core is naturally ventilated, and its exterior is clad in a curtain wall that provides shading and prevents heat gain.

David L. Lawrence Convention Center, Pittsburgh, Pennsylvania

Owner: Sports and Exhibition Authority of Pittsburgh and Allegheny County

Architecture and design: Rafael Viñoly Architects

General contractor: Turner Construction Company

Completion date: 2003

Figure A-11a Pittsburgh's David L. Lawrence Convention Center is sited on the banks of the Allegheny River, taking advantage of views and daylight.

Figure A-11b Seventy-five percent of the Convention Center's spaces are daylit.

Building area: 1,500,000 sq. ft.

LEED Gold

Green building goal of note: Potable water reduction by 50 percent through the use of in-building water treatment; 75 percent of the spaces are daylit, which leads to a large lighting-load reduction.

Condé Nast Building, Four Times Square, New York

Owner: Durst Corporation

Architecture and design: Fox & Fowle,

General contractor: Tishman Construction Corporation

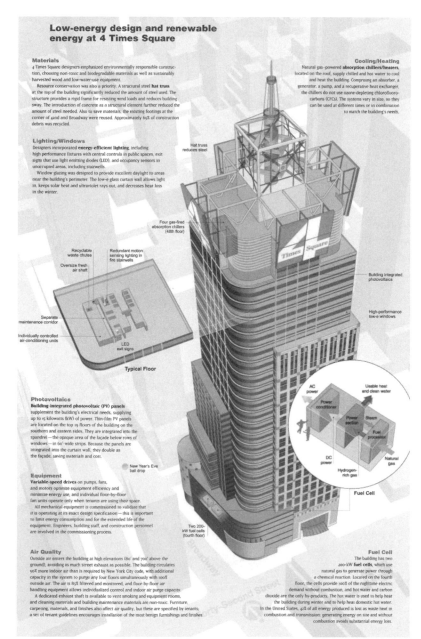

Figure A-12a The sustainable design features of the Condé Nast building at Four Times Square.

Figure A-12b An exterior rendering of the Condé Nast building at Four Times Square, New York.

Energy advisor: Rocky Mountain Institute, Snowmass, CO; Natural Resources Defense Council; and Steven Winter Associates

Completion date: 1999

Building area: 48 stories and 1.6 million sq. ft.

Green building goals of note: Using floor-by-floor control of ventilation, airflow at 50 percent more than standard building ventilation; the Condé Nast building is the first green skyscraper in North America.

Hearst Tower, New York

Owner: Hearst Corporation

Architecture and design: Foster + Partners

General contractor: Turner Construction Company

Completion date: 2006

Building area: 46 stories, 856,000 sq. ft.

LEED Gold

Green building goals of note: Diagrid construction (no vertical steel elements) reduced steel material use by 20 percent relative to a comparable conventional structure. Rainwater harvested and stored for irrigation; water will also be used for an "icefall" water feature that humidifies and cools the building. In 2008, Hearst Corporation began a zero-waste policy at the building. Hearst Tower was the first building in the United States to receive a green building tax credit.

Figure A-13a An exterior view of Hearst Tower designed by Foster + Partners.

Figure A-13b The building's diagonal structure reduces material usage by 20 percent.

Figure A-13c The café atrium space in the Hearst Tower.

Commerzbank Headquarters, Frankfurt, Germany

Owner: Commerzbank AG

Architecture and design: Foster + Partners

General contractor: Hochtief (UK) Ltd

Mechanical: J. Roger Preston with P&A Petterson Ahrens

Completion date: 1997

Building area: 53 stories 1.3 million sq. ft.

Green building goal of note: The office building was "conceived as a soaring high-tech glass-and-steel tower punctuated by open-air gardens."[2] Winter

Figure A-14a The Commerzbank Tower's garden-filled atrium.

Figure A-14b Exterior view of the Commerzbank.

[2]Nicolai Ouroussoff, "Why Are They Greener than We Are?" *New York Times*, May 20, 2007.

gardens allow for natural lighting, interstitial space between the exterior skin and the occupied spaces, superior ventilation, and connection with nature.

Edificio Malecón, Buenos Aires, Argentina

Owner: Newside SA

Architecture and design: HOK

Completion date: 1999

Building area: 12 stories, 125,000 sq. ft.

AIA COTE Top Ten Green Building 2002

Green building goals of note: Narrow floor plate to reduce solar heat gain; exterior sun shades; individual controls for airflow and cooling; located on a former brownfield site.

Figure A-15 Edificio Malecón in Buenos Aires, designed by HOK.

▓ Residential/Housing

The Solaire, 20 River Terrace, New York

Owner: Albanese Organization, Inc. and Northwestern Mutual Life, Corporation

Architecture and design: Cesar Pelli & Associates

Environmental building consultant: Green October

Energy consultant: Steven Winter Associates

General Contractor: Turner Construction Company

Completion date: 2003

Building area: 27 stories, 357,000 sq. feet

LEED Gold

Green building goal of note: First in-building black water treatment system in which 100 percent of the wastewater is treated then used for toilet flushing and cooling tower. In addition, the building has a rainwater harvesting system and a green roof.

Margarido House, Oakland, California

Owners: Mike McDonald and Jill Martenson

Architecture and design: David Wilson and Chris Parlette, Tim McDonald

Contractor: McDonald Construction & Development

Completion date: 2008

Building area: 4,600 sq. ft.

(a)

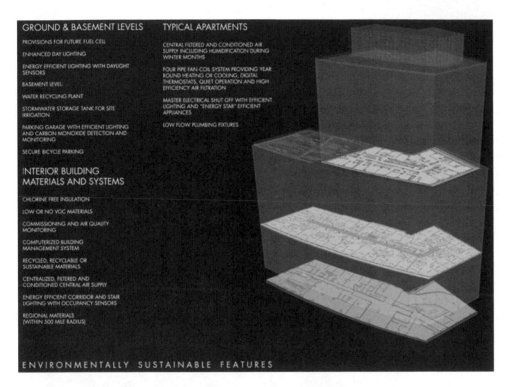

GROUND & BASEMENT LEVELS

PROVISIONS FOR FUTURE FUEL CELL

ENHANCED DAY LIGHTING

ENERGY EFFICIENT LIGHTING WITH DAYLIGHT SENSORS

BASEMENT LEVEL:

WATER RECYCLING PLANT

STORMWATER STORAGE TANK FOR SITE IRRIGATION

PARKING GARAGE WITH EFFICIENT LIGHTING AND CARBON MONOXIDE DETECTION AND MONITORING

SECURE BICYCLE PARKING

INTERIOR BUILDING MATERIALS AND SYSTEMS

CHLORINE FREE INSULATION

LOW OR NO VOC MATERIALS

COMMISSIONING AND AIR QUALITY MONITORING

COMPUTERIZED BUILDING MANAGEMENT SYSTEM

RECYCLED, RECYCLABLE OR SUSTAINABLE MATERIALS

CENTRALIZED, FILTERED AND CONDITIONED CENTRAL AIR SUPPLY

ENERGY EFFICIENT CORRIDOR AND STAIR LIGHTING WITH OCCUPANCY SENSORS

REGIONAL MATERIALS (WITHIN 500 MILE RADIUS)

TYPICAL APARTMENTS

CENTRAL FILTERED AND CONDITIONED AIR SUPPLY INCLUDING HUMIDIFICATION DURING WINTER MONTHS

FOUR PIPE FAN COIL SYSTEM PROVIDING YEAR ROUND HEATING OR COOLING, DIGITAL THERMOSTATS, QUIET OPERATION AND HIGH EFFICIENCY AIR FILTRATION

MASTER ELECTRICAL SHUT OFF WITH EFFICIENT LIGHTING AND "ENERGY STAR" EFFICIENT APPLIANCES

LOW FLOW PLUMBING FIXTURES

ENVIRONMENTALLY SUSTAINABLE FEATURES

(b)

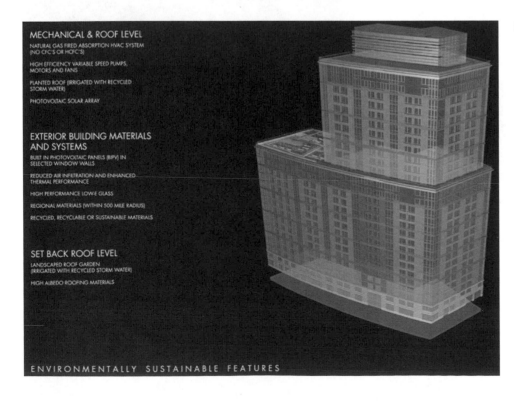

MECHANICAL & ROOF LEVEL

NATURAL GAS FIRED ABSORPTION HVAC SYSTEM (NO CFC'S OR HCFC'S)

HIGH EFFICIENCY VARIABLE SPEED PUMPS, MOTORS AND FANS

PLANTED ROOF (IRRIGATED WITH RECYCLED STORM WATER)

PHOTOVOLTAIC SOLAR ARRAY

EXTERIOR BUILDING MATERIALS AND SYSTEMS

BUILT IN PHOTOVOLTAIC PANELS (BIPV) IN SELECTED WINDOW WALLS

REDUCED AIR INFILTRATION AND ENHANCED THERMAL PERFORMANCE

HIGH PERFORMANCE LOW-E GLASS

REGIONAL MATERIALS (WITHIN 500 MILE RADIUS)

RECYCLED, RECYCLABLE OR SUSTAINABLE MATERIALS

SET BACK ROOF LEVEL

LANDSCAPED ROOF GARDEN (IRRIGATED WITH RECYCLED STORM WATER)

HIGH ALBEDO ROOFING MATERIALS

ENVIRONMENTALLY SUSTAINABLE FEATURES

Figure A-16 a, b Two diagrams illustrate the solaire's sustainable design features.

Figure A-16c The Solaire's building-integrated photovoltaics.

LEED for Homes Platinum for a custom home, Greenpoint rated

Green building goal of note: Radiant flooring and geothermal heating and cooling, siding made from recycled kiln trays, vegetated roof, rainwater and groundwater catchment, and rainscreen wall construction.

Figure A-17b Deep overhangs help shelter homes from direct solar access.

Figure A-16d Exterior view of the Solaire.

Figure A-17c Exterior view of the Margarido House.

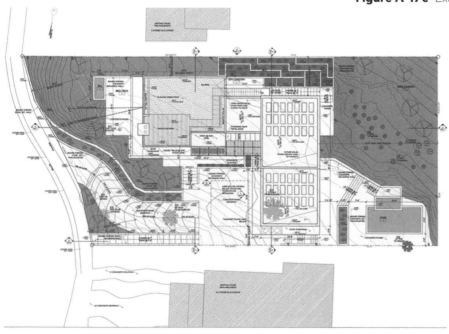

Figure A-17a Site plan for the Margarido House.

Water Structures, Netherlands

Fourteen floating and thirty-two amphibious homes in Maasbommel, along the Meuse River.

Architecture and design: Factor Architecten

Engineer and general contractor: Dura Vermeer

Completion date: 2007

Building area: 37 homes

Green building goals of note: Responds to the climate change crisis, and flexible construction can help the buildings withstand a 13-foot rise in sea level. Though moored to steel piers, floating homes have concrete tubes to provide flotation and buoyancy.

The Dutch firm Waterstudio designs structures, "watervillas," for living near or in the water. The homes' decidedly modern aesthetic sets them apart from water settlements of London and other parts of the Netherlands.

Shipping Container Structures

These are current all over the world—Spain, South Africa, the United States, Canada, and New Zealand—by architects and designers as diverse as LOT-EK and Foxe & Fowle. As is typical of alternative forms of construction, these dwellings or living clusters are made from available materials, the ubiquitous shipping container, symbolic above all, of the concept of embodied energy. Ironically, these containers, having traveled many nautical miles before their final sustainable and repurposed use, represent a significant amount of energy and carbon emissions.

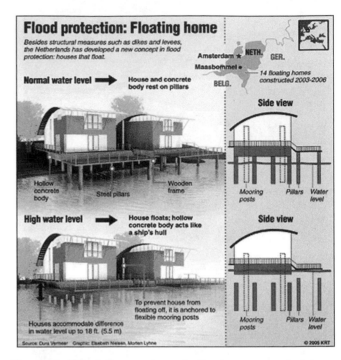

Figure A-18b A diagram shows the flood protection capabilities of the homes.

Figure A-19a Watervilla, Lubeek Family, Amsterdam.

Figure A-18a Amphibious homes in Maasbommel, designed by Factor Architecten.

Figure A-19b Pole houses, also designed by Waterstudio.

Figure A-20 SeaTrain House, constructed from shipping containers, designed by Office of Mobile Design, Los Angeles.

Figure A-21 Project 7Ten, designed by Melinda Gray, GRAYmatter, a LEED NC Platinum home.

Figure A-22 Strohhaus, designed for a private client by Felix Jerusalem, uses a resource-efficient construction technique—panelized, prefabricated elements—pressed straw panels clad in translucent plastic, for a modern interpretation of an alternative construction technique.

Project 7Ten, 710 Millwood Avenue, Venice, California

Developer: Tom Schey, Minimal Productions, environmentalist Kelly Meyer

Architecture and design: Melinda Gray, GRAYmatter

Completion date: 2007

LEED Platinum

Green building goals of note: In addition to proven strategies, such as rainwater harvesting and low-emitting interior finishes and furnishings, the developers of 7Ten salvaged usable wood from the site's existing structure to provide building materials for low-income families in Mexico. The majority of 7Ten's proceeds will be donated to Healthy Child Healthy World, a nonprofit that educates the public on chemicals in the environment, especially those that affect children's heath. First LEED for New Construction Platinum Home in the U.S.

Strohhaus, a Modern Straw-Bale Structure, Eschenz, Switzerland

Architecture and design: Felix Jerusalem

Completion date: 2005

Green building goal of note: Prefabricated formaldehyde-free compressed straw panels, both structural and

acoustical, clad in translucent plastic—almost a "truth wall" that reveals its materiality.

■ Health Care

Oregon Heath and Science University Center for Health and Healing (OHSU CHH), Portland, Oregon

Architecture and design: GBD Architects

General contractor: Hoffman Construction Co.

Completion date: 2007

Building area: 16-stories, 412,000 sq. ft.

Figure A-23 The LEED Platinum Oregon Heath and Science University Center for Health and Healing in Portland.

Figure A-24 The Boulder Community Hospital, noteworthy as a "first" health-care project to receive LEED Silver certification.

(a)

LEED Platinum

Green building goals of note: Sixty percent energy-cost reduction compared to base case conventional building according to Oregon's Energy Code. Other features include on-site wastewater treatment, on-site cogeneration plant (combined heat and power), photovoltaics, and naturally ventilated stair shafts.

Boulder Community Hospital Foothills Campus, Boulder, Colorado

Architecture and design: Boulder Associates and OZ Architecture

Completion date: 2004

Building area: 154,000 sq. ft.

LEED Silver

Green building goal of note: This is the first U.S. hospital to receive a LEED certification (Silver). The site design preserves 32 acres of open space for public use and increased the size of an existing native wetlands area. As a result of sustainable landscape design and drought-resistant native plant species, the project anticipates a 53 percent reduction in potable water use compared to a conventional building of the same size and type.

The Patrick H. Dollard Discovery Health Center, Harris, New York

A residential school and outpatient facility for neurologically disabled patients

(b)

Figure A-25 a, b The Patrick Dollard Discovery Health Center designed by Guenther 5 Architects.

Architecture and design: Guenther 5 Architects

Completion date: 2003

Building area: 2 stories, 28,300 sq. ft.

Green building goal of note: Building is on an abandoned agricultural site, and the vision was to restore habitat and open space. Low-emitting materials including PVC reduction were also a health priority. Ground-source heat pumps assisted in the 48-percent energy savings.

■ Research

Smithsonian Tropical Research Institute Research Station (STRI Research Station), Bocas del Toro, Panama[3]

Architecture and design: Kiss + Cathcart

Completion date: 2003

Building area: 7,530 sq. ft. on raised concrete piers

(c)

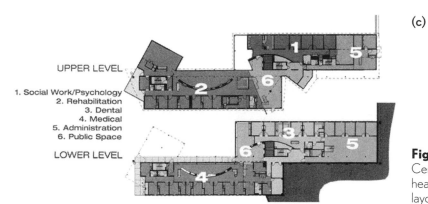

UPPER LEVEL

1. Social Work/Psychology
2. Rehabilitation
3. Dental
4. Medical
5. Administration
6. Public Space

LOWER LEVEL

Figure A-25c Narrow floor plans at the Dollard Health Center increase opportunities for daylight access, passive heating and cooling, but also lead to efficient program layout and a less-intrusive building footprint.

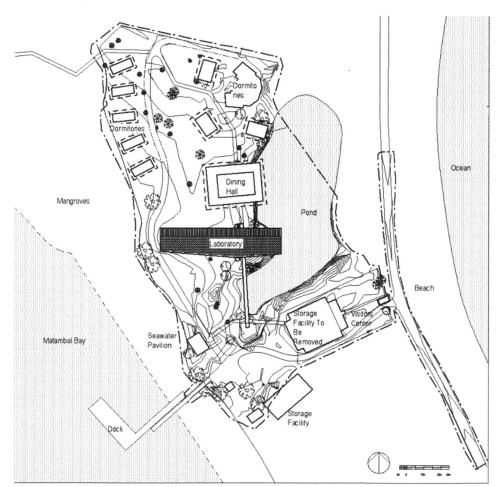

Figure A-26a STRI Research Station site plan, revealing a low-impact building footprint.

[3]Source: http://www.eere.energy.gov/buildings/database/mtxview.cfm?C FID=21415328&CFTOKEN=77072700.

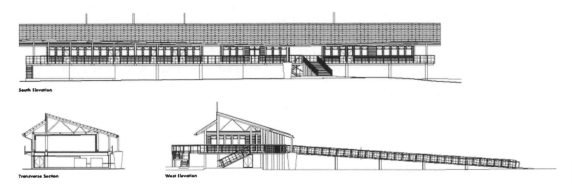

South Elevation

Transverse Section   West Elevation

Figure A-26b Building elevations: a long, low profile means low impact in the vertical plane.

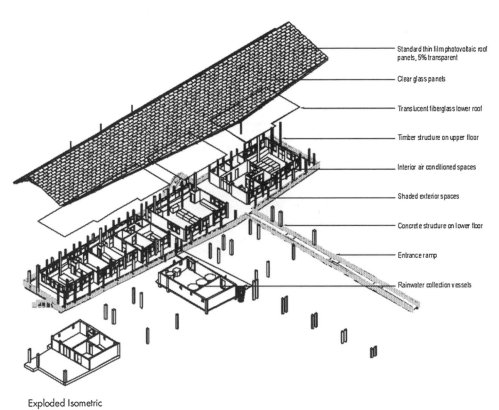

Standard thin film photovoltaic roof panels, 5% transparent

Clear glass panels

Translucent fiberglass lower roof

Timber structure on upper floor

Interior air conditioned spaces

Shaded exterior spaces

Concrete structure on lower floor

Entrance ramp

Rainwater collection vessels

Exploded Isometric

Figure A-26c An exploded isometric drawing.

Figure A-26d Exterior view of the STRI Research Station.

Green building goals of note: This research station contains a lobby, classrooms, conference spaces, and laboratories. The focus was to design the building, the site of a former sawmill, to have a "net zero impact." Although not quite all the building's energy needs are produced from the roof-mounted PVs, the system also functions to collect rainwater. In addition, the conditioned rooms can be operated separately, cutting down on power usage. The wide roof overhangs and slender floor plan allow for passive cooling strategies and natural ventilation.

Figure A-26e A view upwards of the translucent photovoltaic roof of the STRI.

Recreation Center

Steinhude Sea Recreation Facility, Steinhude, Germany

Owner: City of Steinhude

Architecture and design: Archimedes GmbH, Randall Stout Architects

General contractor: IHV Objektbau

Completion date: 2000

Building area: 3,190 sq. ft.

Green building goals of note: Completely energy independent, powered by on-site PVs and a seed-oil cogeneration microturbine. The recreation facility also has eight solar-powered boats, and it incorporates both gray-water reuse and rainwater harvesting technology.

Places of Worship

The Jewish Reconstructionist Congregation, Evanston, Illinois

Architecture and design: Ross Barney Architects

Completion date: 2008

Building area: 32,000 sq. ft.

LEED Platinum

Green building goals of note: Fulfills the Jewish spirit of stewardship and "healing the world," using responsible environmental-building strategies such as gabion-rubble foundations and attention to daylight harvesting.

(a)

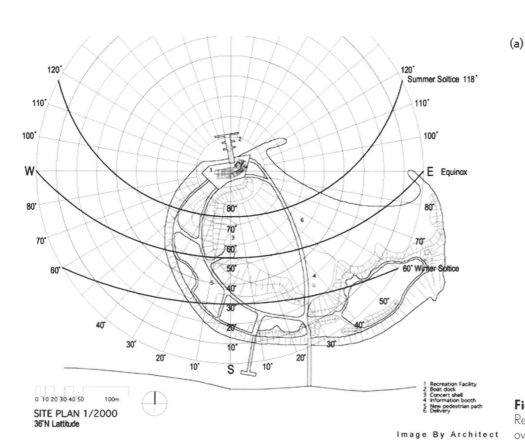

SITE PLAN 1/2000
36°N Lattitude

1 Recreation Facility
2 Boat dock
3 Concert shell
4 Information booth
5 New pedestrian path
6 Delivery

Image By Architect

Figure A-27a The Steinhude Sea Recreation Facility site with sun path overlay.

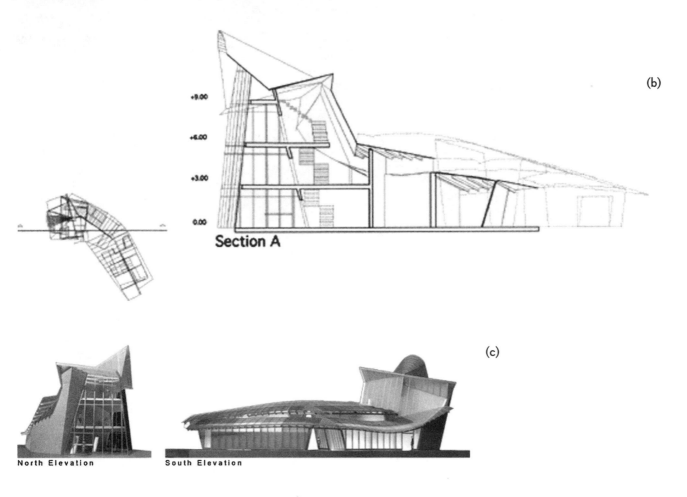

(b)

+9.00
+6.00
+3.00
0.00

Section A

(c)

North Elevation

South Elevation

East Elevation

West Elevation

Figures A-27 b, c Sections and elevations reveal how the building's form responds to climate and site.

Figure A-27d Exterior view of Steinhude facility.

Figure A-27e Interior view showing abundant daylight access.

Figure A-28a The Jewish Reconstructionist Congregation designed by Ross Barney Architects.

Figure A-28b Worship space with daylight and view access.

Figure A-28c The gabion wall with Jerusalem stone is symbolic of, as well as a practical cover for, the building's mechanical equipment.

St. Gabriel of the Sorrowful Virgin Parish, North Ontario, Canada

Owner: Passionist Community Canada

Architecture and design: Larkin Architects Ltd.

General contractor: Martin-Stewart Contracting Ltd.

Landscape architect: Ian Gray & Associates

Completion date: 2006

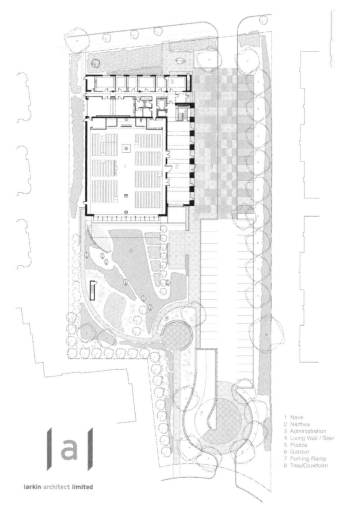

1 Nave
2 Narthex
3 Administration
4 Living Wall / Stair
5 Piazza
6 Garden
7 Parking Ramp
8 Tree/Cruxiform

larkin architect limited

Figure A-29a Designed by Larkin Architects, St. Gabriel of the Sorrowful Virgin site plan.

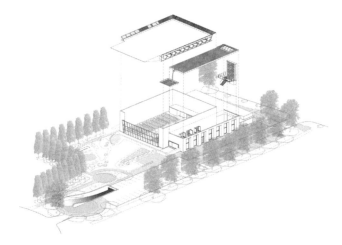

Figure A-29b Exploded floor plan.

Figure A-29c A place of spiritual practice provides daylight and views in St. Grabriel.

Green building goals of note: Employing principles of "ecotheology," this building uses 40 percent less energy than code requires. Provides a connection with the exterior landscape through an indoor living wall.

Nonprofit Organizations

Heifer International Headquarters, Little Rock, Arkansas

Architecture and design: Polk Stanley Rowland Curzon Porter Architects, Ltd.

Environmental building consultant: Elements, a division of BNIM

General contractor: CDI Contractors, LLC

Completion date: 2006

Building area: 5 stories, 94,000 sq. ft.

LEED Platinum, AIA COTE Top Ten Building 2007

Green building goal of note: To "nurture the environment while combating hunger," according to Jo Luck, president and CEO of Heifer.[4] To that end, it was built on the site of an industrial switching yard, thus restoring a brownfield site to a wetlands area. The building is designed to be durable, with a 100-year anticipated lifespan.

St. Anthony Foundation Headquarters Building, San Francisco, California

Owner: St. Anthony Foundation (completely funded with private donations)

Architecture and design: HKIT Architects

(a)

Figure A-30a Heifer International Headquarters, exterior view, designed by Polk Stanley Rowland Curzon Porter Architects.

(b)

(c)

Figure A-30 b, c Open offices create flexible circulation space and shared daylight.

[4]Jill Bayles, "Heifer: Building Toward a Green Future," Heifer International, http://www.heifer.org/site/c.edJRKQNiFiG/b.201577/.

General contractor: Nibbi Brothers

Commissioning: Taylor Engineering

Green consultants: Simon & Associates, Inc.

Completion date: 2008

Building area: 5 stories, 46,200 sq. ft.

Green building goals of note: St. Anthony's Foundation provides clothing, food, medical help, employment programs, residential treatment, and shelter to the homeless and poor population of San Francisco, California. Its mission of "restoring health, hope and human dignity" is embodied in this green building with a compact footprint and green operations. In addition, as part of their mission to educate, St. Anthony's has pledged to educate the public and its visitors on green buildings and their benefits.

Figure A-31a Exterior view of St. Anthony Foundation Headquarters, designed by HKIT architects.

Figure A-31b A view to the exterior from one of the classrooms.

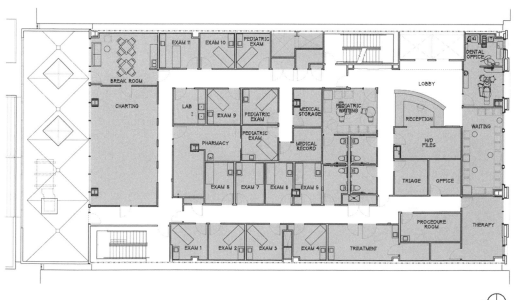

St. Anthony Foundation Office Building

San Francisco, California

FLOOR 2 - CLINIC

HKIT ARCHITECTS

Figure A-31c Floor plan of the free medical clinic on the second floor.

▪ Concepts that Push the Limits

BRE Innovation Park, Watford, Hertfordshire, England

Net Zero Carbon Demonstration House:

Kingspan Lighthouse

Architecture and design: Shephard Robson

Concept: These prototype houses are designed to respond to "accelerated climate change."

Awarded Level 6 in the Code for Sustainable Homes in the United Kingdom.

Green building goals of note: Structural insulated panel (SIPs) construction with high insulating value; 40-degree-canted roof accommodates PVs at optimal inclination; PVs supply the structure's entire electricity needs; whole-house mechanical ventilation with heat-recovery system; gray-water and rainwater recycling; wind catchers to supply passive cooling and ventilation.

Woven House, Bamboo

Design: Søren Korsgaard

Concept: Uses a regionally associated and low-tech building material (bamboo) with a modern interpretation, using traditional weaving as a foundation for construction method.

Figure A-32 The Kingspan Lighthouse demonstration house designed by Shephard Robson.

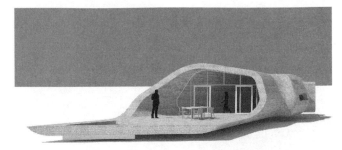

Figure A-33 The Bamboo Woven House concept design by Danish architect Søren Korsgaard.

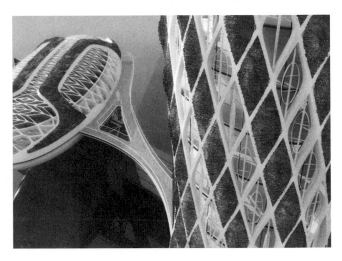

Figure A-34 The Anti Smog Concept Building, designed by Vincent Callebaut Architectures.

Anti Smog: An Innovation Centre in Sustainable Development, Paris

Design: Vincent Callebaut Architectures

Concept: To "disasphyxiate" the 19th Arrondissement, through its goal of cleaner air. Two building components—the "solar drop" with PVs and the "wind tower" with building-integrated wind turbines—are coated with a titanium dioxide finish, which in theory will interact with ultraviolet rays to reduce air pollution, in essence, making the building self-cleaning.

MVRDV's Pig City, An Imaginary Project

Concept: Liberate the footprint of the Dutch countryside by creating an urban, high-density space for farming practices, in this case, a high-rise tower for raising pigs, with outdoor vegetated areas of projecting balconies. The building would be powered by the manure produced by the pigs and incorporate humane slaughtering methods.

Figure A-35 MVRDV's imaginary Pig City.

(a)

▦ Communities

PRISMA, Nuremberg, Germany

Mixed-used and socially balanced building complex.

Owner: Karlsruher Insurance Company

Architecture and design: Joachim Eble Architektur

Energy design: SUNNA

Completion date: 1997

Scope: Four buildings and an atrium

Green building goals of note: Energy use is 46 percent below German energy code; naturally ventilated atrium space, heat exchanger; naturally supplied evaporative cooling, 80 percent of glass roof is operable. A rainwater-collection system uses water for interior "bioclimatic walls" and irrigation. Electromagnetic fields in electrical systems were isolated. The project team used the Green Building Challenge Assessment Framework and Green Building Tool (GBTool) environmental assessment software.

Berea College, Eco Village, Berea, Kentucky

Scope: Fifty apartments, a state-of-the-art child development laboratory, a commons house, and a sustainability and environmental studies (SENS) demonstration house. The "ecological machine," wetlands, permaculture food forest, and individual gardens are other community features.

Green building goals of note: Seventy-five percent energy-use reduction; 75 percent water use reduction per capita; composting toilets; on-site treatment of black water to "swimmable" quality through the

(b)

Figure A-36 a, b PRISMA's glass roof over the atrium space acts as the building's lungs. Eighty percent of the roof is operable, allowing for naturally conditioned ventilation.

Figure A-36c Exterior view.

(d)

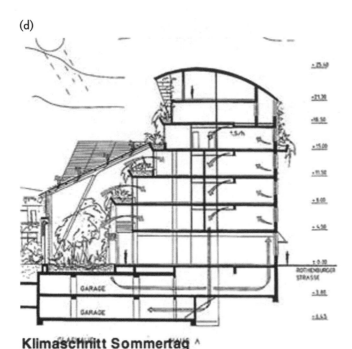

Klimaschnitt Sommertag ∧

(e)

Klimaschnitt Sommernacht

Figure A-36 d,e Section diagrams showing day and night summer cooling and ventilation of the PRISMA building.

"ecological machine," a biologically based water-treatment system in the same vein as the Adam Joseph Lewis Center for Environmental Studies at Oberlin College, Oberlin, Ohio.

Centro Las Gaviotas, Sustainable Community, Vichada Province, Colombia

Date: 1971

Developers: Paolo Lugari and Gunter Pauli

Figure A-37 Brea College.

The United Nations has recognized Las Gaviotas as a model of sustainability.

While Gaviotas is not technically an ecovillage, it deserves mention here, if for no other reason than its status as an influencing factor in Colombia's placement among the top ten most sustainable countries in the world. But its crowning value lies in the process of its founding and the pattern of its social structure. It is a green community, in essence.

Gaviotas was initiated by inventor and engineer Paolo Lugari in 1971 as a sustainable community. It was planned, organized, and constructed by engineers and scientists from many regions. More than thirty years later, it is a completely self-sufficient community in many ways:

- The community reforested 8,000 hectares of Caribbean pines in an area that was once a fertile rainforest but had become dry grassland, the llanos of Colombia. The result was a beneficial change in the soil chemistry, improved availability of water, and—despite what one would assume—flourishing of the monoculture and creation of a diverse community of wildlife and plant species.
- Appropriate technology and renewable energy was used to design easily constructed machinery, from solar thermal water purifiers to a simple water pump powered by a children's seesaw—a Gaviotas windmill.
- Renewable and self-sufficient, Gaviotans tap the pines for resin, process it on-site, and sell it to other enterprises. Animal waste is used for compost and methane, which is in turn used to power the former hospital. Renewable energy is generated through on-site solar, wind, and biodiesel generators, a microhydroelectric plant, and wood-powered steam generators. Gaviotans grow their own food, using organic and hydroponic technology, and raise animals.

- Las Gaviotas has a self-sufficient economy through sales of resin from its pine forest and the manufacture and sale of its technological innovations for tropical climes—e.g., the solar collectors, wind turbines, and the innovative water pumps powered by seesaws.
- A social experiment, Gaviotas has no mayor or police force. It is located in a region notorious for violence among three warring factions: the right-wing paramilitaries, the leftist guerillas, and the Colombian military.

Las Gaviotas II, to be named Marandua, is being developed by Gunter Pauli, former chief executive officer of the Ecover, the ecohome product manufacturer. It will be located in the same province as Gaviotas but sited on part of a military reserve donated to the project by the Colombian Air Force. A *World Watch* article noted that this "commitment by the military to sustainable development as a path to peace is unprecedented in the history of any Latin American military."[5]

Figure A-38a The hydro-electric turbine: even a short water-level drop can provide power, contrary to expectations.

Figure A-38b Solar thermal hot-water panels for the hospital roof at Las Gaviotas.

Vertical Farming: A Primer

Graham Grilli

What is a vertical farm?

- Vertical farm's are basically agricultural skyscrapers. They combine greenhouse (often soil-free) gardening methods, reuse natural resources, and use far less land than traditional farms. They provide a low-resource, extremely localized food source for sustainable urban food production.

First appearance of vertical farms:

- Vertical farming can be (with some degree of license) traced back as far as 600 BC, when the Hanging Gardens of Babylon were constructed by Nebuchadnezzer II. Apparently created to please his wife's yearning for her homeland and not entirely focused on food production, as are modern vertical farms, it was the first documented structure of this type in an urban setting. The gardens reached heights of 75 feet and employed complicated technology to support the heavy weight of plants and soil, as well as to protect the structure from degrading due to moisture.

The reasons:

- Almost 41 percent of the earth's land is currently used for agriculture.
- Population is growing at exponential rates (from 6.7 billion today to an estimated 9.2 billion by 2050), meaning food needs will be ever greater.

(*Continued*)

[5]Richard E. White and Gloria Eugenia Gonzalez Marino, "Las Gaviotas: Sustainability in the Tropics." *World Watch,* May 1, 2007, volume 20, number 3, 18–23.

- Food sources are being pushed further and further from population centers, driving up economic and environmental impacts of food transportation.

The precursors:

- Hothouses and greenhouses: Indoor growing environments provide farmers much greater control over plant growth and success, often allowing plants that would otherwise flounder in a given climate to flourish.

- Hydroponics and aeroponics: Experimentation with soil-free agriculture has been prevalent for some time. Many of the proposed methods result in greatly reduced contaminant runoff, and the controlled environments required by these methods often reduce the need for chemical fertilizers and pesticides in the first place.

- Skyscrapers: While not considered revolutionary today, the skyscraper addressed many of the challenges faced in early urban environments. Skyscrapers allowed tenants or businesses to occupy a very small "footprint" within an urban landscape, effectively addressing the prohibitive costs of available urban land and also dramatically cutting down the need for transport into urban centers, as vast numbers of residences and businesses could be contained within a small area.

The vertical farm:

- Vertical farms can incorporate all of these principles and more, creating concentrated centers of food production in urban environments.

- Closed-system vertical farm environments can be engineered to cycle water and nutrients, greatly reducing resource use.

- In some proposed designs, vertical farms would also be used as a filtration system, effectively transforming gray or blackwater into productive agricultural materials and, in some cases, returning pure, drinkable water.

- According to National Aeronautics and Space Administration research, over 100 kinds of produce can be effectively grown in indoor, soil-free environments—in some cases, more effectively than when using land!

- Vertical farms can dramatically increase viable food production in and around urban centers and allow the ever-shrinking available land on the planet to nourish the ever-growing population of hungry citizens while simultaneously eliminating the need to store and transport these many types of produce.

Figure A-39 Mithun's vertical farm diagram.

■ Resources

Skyscrapers: The New Millennium. 2000. Edited by John Zukowsky and Martha Thorne. Chicago: Prestel/The Art Institute of Chicago.

Sustaining: Tower Blocks, Present Context, an interactive web site to assist in high rise building remodels, http://www.sustainingtowers.org

Bioclimatic Skyscrapers, rev. ed. 2000. T. R. Hamzah, Kenneth Yeang. London: Ellipsis

Weisman, Alan. 1999. *Gaviotas: A Village to Reinvent the World.* White River Junction, Vermont: Chelsea Green Publishing Company.

B Alternative Construction Technologies

Modern architecture typically expresses its construction method, but at times the technique is hidden. With alternative architecture, it is more often the case that the structure reveals the process with which it is built. Less frequently, it is expressed within conventional, familiar building types.

Some of the construction techniques listed below yield curvilinear plans, stacked elements or sculpted materials and organic shapes found in nature, or modular pieces that result in vaulted shells or curved roof elements. They can be used in the construction of load-bearing elements or as fill between standard post and beam framing.

Alternative construction techniques speak of the hands that shape them, and for that reason are often thought of as rudimentary structures built from need with available materials. Indeed, this is often the case, but modern interpretation of these tested techniques has bestowed increasing credibility to them, especially when it comes to human need—disaster relief and refugee housing, for example. Without question, many of the pioneers of alternative construction lean toward these ethically based themes, a vital current of all architecture and one that must be expressed to achieve sustainability.

Insulation values of alternative construction techniques are often quite variable, depending on whether wood or clay is the predominant "ingredient." Even if the insulating value per inch is low, it is important to remember that many alternative building techniques involve thick walls, so the insulating value can be increased. Many of these techniques yield wall elements with thermal mass properties, which can aid in insulating efficiency.

Various alternative construction techniques lend themselves to decorative embellishment, spontaneous and otherwise, while others require the more rigid formulas of construction using regular modules. In all cases, alternative construction techniques make use of readily available, abundant materials—jute, flax (and other biofibers), animal dung, mud, agricultural waste products—that define a particular region or climate.

Clay, Adobe, or Mud Brick

Buildings using this technique are found all over the globe. Adobe is a mixture of clay, water, sand, and a binder that can include fibrous agricultural waste materials or even dung (Figure B-1.) Mud can also be used with materials such as glass bottles or metal food cans, as well as a myriad of other additives, described in the listings that follow. Adobe construction is the muse to other earthen techniques, also, described below.

Cob

Cob is another earthen technique often used interchangeably with rammed earth, but without the cement binder;

Figure B-1 Mud construction is used all over the world.

303

it is a mixture of clay, straw, and sand and is considered a historical building technique easily recognized in its Welsh, Irish, and English incarnations—a plastered mud house with a thatched roof (Figure B-2.) Cob technique is also found in the Middle East and Africa. The technique appeals to alternative builders because of its ability to be sculpted, its use of waste materials, and its pest-resistant properties. Each course is tamped down, or "cobbed," to impart strength and to aid in curing. Tamping down was originally carried out with the aid of animals.

Rammed Earth, Pisé, and PISE

As in other mud techniques, rammed earth, its French cousin *pisé de terre*, and its modern interpretation,

"pneumatically compacted stabilized earth" (PISE), involve earth, sand, clay, and a binder, usually cement (Figure B-3). The earth is compressed or compacted into a single-sided form through tamping or, in the case of PISE, using a spray technique, after which the formwork is removed. When cured, a rammed earth wall can have the appearance of a stone wall.

"Earthbag" Construction, Ceramic Houses

The late Nader Khalili was an architect and pioneer in alternative construction techniques that have application to particular housing needs. Earthbag architecture has its precedent in sandbagging techniques used in military shelters and flood control. Khalili invented

Figure B-2 Cob is a tamped-earth technique.

Figure B-3 Lou Kimball's rammed earth house, completed in 2003, earned a five-star Austin Energy Green Building Rating, an award that recognizes deeper green strategies than most conventional rating systems.

Superadobe – earthbag, a process of filling regular sand-bags or long tube-like fabric bags, which are coiled compressively to create shell structures. The coils are reinforced with barbed wire and plastered, resulting in an earthbag dwelling (Figure B4). Other materials, such as wood chips, agricultural waste (such as rice hulls), or sand and cement, can be used for filler. Khalili worked with the United Nations to devise plans for refugee shelters and with the National Aeronautics and Space Administration on lunar and planetary habitat designs.

Khalili's Geltaftan technique, a Persian term that means baked or fired woven clay, was the basis for his ceramic houses. An adobe-earth mixture is shaped into blocks and stacked to create a room, then a heat source is introduced to the space and the structure is fired at high temperatures to fuse the materials and produce a ceramic finish (Figure B5). The idea behind Geltaftan technology was to produce durable structures that can more success-fully resist seismic forces than structures that use other masonry techniques and rudimentary materials.

Paper-Based Cinder Blocks

Another unit in the masonry arsenal are "masonry" mod-ules made from recycled paper, which yields surprisingly durable structural elements. Quite conventional-looking structures can be the result of paper block construction, as it is installed like other masonry units.

Figure B-4 Earthbag construction is both utilitarian and expedient. This image shows a prototype Eco-Dome under construction at Cal-Earth institute in 2001 (design by Nader Khalili, constructed by Cal-Earth).

Figure B-5 The Rumi Dome ceramic structure developed by architect Nader Khalili.

Cordwood Masonry or Stacked Timber and Stack Wall

Cordwood construction uses the ends of felled trees in a stacked design joined with an insulating mortar that sometimes uses sawdust as an additive (Figure B-6). Cordwood can be used with cob or bale techniques as well as with wood framing as an infill. Its basic element, wood, is most practically sourced as a residual product from forestry and lumber mills and other wood-processing industries.

Straw Bale

This technology has the most visibility of all the alternative construction technologies described here. (See Appendix A for a modern interpretation of straw-bale construction; see Figure B-7.) Many are the hands-on, barn-raising workshops offered in Northern California's countryside. Straw bales are made from residual agricultural straw or grass formed into large blocks, often machine-compressed

to increase their density and their load-bearing ability. Bales are bound together with pins of various types and can be used as structural walls, often strengthened by reinforced steel bars (rebar), or as framing infill. Straw bale is typically clad in layers of stucco or plaster.

Bamboo

From Colombia to India, there is a thriving community of bamboo builders and experts in bamboo joinery, preservative treatment, foundation design, and the like. Bamboo is desirable in many respects: it is considered rapidly renewable, which means it regenerates quickly, often within five to six years; it is extremely durable and rates well on the wood hardness scale; and it is thus suitable for many applications, including flooring and as structural members. Because bamboo timbers are hollow, they present a challenge in designing modern joinery and foundations. Concrete and reinforcing steel can be used to create connections that are more rigid (Figure B-8).

Earth-Bermed and Earth-Sheltered Structures

Earth-bermed or earth-sheltered structures are either fully or partially covered by built-up areas of earth (Figure B-9). Earth-sheltered structures have covered roofs and walls, while earth-bermed structures have covered walls and a conventional roof. Berms have precedent in military and site-management practices to control storm water or erosion. Like sandbagging, berms were used in trench-warfare barriers. In the construction of houses, berms function as insulation, thermal mass, and acoustic control and provide a comparatively even indoor temperature. "Elevational" earth-bermed houses are covered on all

Figure B-6 Cordwood construction can incorporate other elements, such as glass and stone.

Figure B-7 Straw-bale construction in progress.

Figure B-8 Engineer Jeorg Stamm has developed ingenious methods for bamboo joinery, such as this hangar joint.

Figure B-9 Earth-bermed structure concept in the United Kingdom.

sides by earth, preventing an even exposure to daylight and limiting air circulation. "Penetrational" earth-bermed houses are entirely covered with earth but allow for window and door openings, thus promoting better ventilation and airflow. Earth-bermed structures have superior energy efficiency owing to the dense insulating properties of earth. Unquestionably Tolkienesque, earth-bermed and earth-sheltered structures have an enchanting yet survivalist aesthetic.

Ferro-Cement

Ferro-cement is a material mix made of water, sand, and cement, which sandwiches construction-weight metal mesh (Figure B-10). It is essentially the historical precursor to modern reinforced concrete technology, having its roots in the fresco process. The result is a thin shell system that performs well in seismic zones and is often cited as a construction technology for passive survivability.

Figure B-10 The Mexican interpretation of ferro-cement lends itself to fanciful and colorful sculptural forms, in this case the Nido De Quetzalcóatl project in Naucalpan, Mexico, designed by Javier Senosiain of Arquitectura Orgánica in 2008.

Figure B-11 An Earthship in the snow, Taos, New Mexico.

Figure B-12 Gabion basket-wall construction is used for both structural and retaining walls and as a cladding wall design element at the ZED Earth Centre in Doncaster, United Kingdom, by Bill Dunster. The cages are filled with crushed concrete from local construction sites. Refer also to case study A-28.

Earthships

Earthships are constructed from salvaged tires rammed with earth (Figure B-11). They are the off the grid, autonomous houses developed in the 1970s by Mike Reynolds, founder of Earthship Biotecture. They were called earthships because they were envisioned as self-sufficient housing types, capturing and reusing rainwater, generating electricity on-site, and providing an economical construction method using a ubiquitous waste material. Interior nonstructural walls in the Earthship houses are sometimes made with glass bottles or cans (tin-can building) embedded in concrete. The Greater World Community is an Earthship village in Taos, New Mexico.

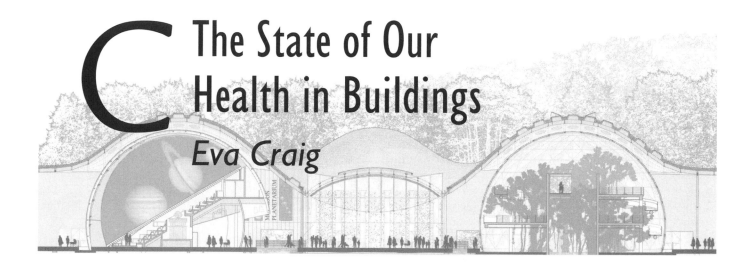

C The State of Our Health in Buildings
Eva Craig

A Harmful Home?

Many people do not know that their homes can be detrimental to their health. Standard building practices and products in our homes contain chemicals that not only pollute our environment but also our bodies. Many chemicals have been linked to specific diseases whose incidence is on the rise (see the table on "Sources of Chemicals and Their Health Risks," below).

The idea that a home could cause harm is not only antithetical to our ideas of home but fundamentally disturbing. Consequently, it is not surprising that some people, despite the clear evidence to the contrary, prefer to believe that the chemicals to which we are exposed in our everyday environments are either benign or well regulated. In order to prevent harm, however, we must have the courage to understand the unpleasant reality of pollution inside our homes. Fortunately, today more so than ever, we have the scientific knowledge required to evaluate potential threats and to design environments that are safe for humans.

Maxims of the Past

In your effort to design more healthful spaces, you will encounter people who will try to downplay the need to change current practices. They may use familiar sayings to maintain hope in the belief that there is no cause for concern. Many familiar sayings, however, originated a long time ago, in preindustrial times, when current threats were either nonexistent or scientifically undocumented. So, to help elucidate a few key concepts of

Figure C-1 Protestors near the site of a chemical plant in their community.

309

environmental pollution and its effect on our health, the following discussion will be structured around three well-known sayings.

That which does not kill you makes you stronger.

This saying is true for certain natural substances, such as certain bacteria that can help strengthen the immune system. Exposure to synthetic substances, however, is rarely beneficial. Bacteria and natural toxins have been part of our evolutionary past for millions of years—long enough for our bodies to evolve defenses against some of them. Most synthetic substances in our homes were introduced around World War II or later, not long enough ago for our bodies to adapt physiologically.

Substances for which we do not have defenses include synthetic chemicals that mimic hormones, also called endocrine disruptors. Hormones are chemical messengers that travel through our bloodstream delivering messages that trigger specific changes in our cells (i.e., cell division or cell decay). A hormone is a string of molecules that exerts its effect by binding to molecular receptors in our cells. Think of the hormone as a key, and the receptor as a keyhole. When the right hormone locks into the right receptor, it triggers a cascade of biochemical events at the level of our DNA. Our genes then produce their programmed chemicals, which in turn transform the cell's physical characteristic or behavior.

Many synthetic chemicals happen to resemble natural hormones so closely that they can lock into hormone receptors. They can thus trigger, just like a hormone, a chain of reactions involving our genes.[1] However, instead of being introduced into the bloodstream at precise times (as are hormones produced by the body), they come at entirely random times, bringing about transformations that are not meant to happen. For example, cancerous tumors often occur as a result of a hormone-mimicking substance directing some cells to divide but failing to direct others to die. Rather than making us stronger, stress on the fundamental level of our DNA undeniably weakens us.

The dose makes the poison.

This saying implies that while a substance may be poisonous in a large dose, it is likely to be harmless in a small dose or a trace amount. The saying supports the comforting belief that even though some substances are undeniably toxic, they are not harmful to us in small amounts. This saying is inappropriate in the context of environmental pollution for several reasons.

Frequency of Exposure

A certain dose size can have minimal effect after a single exposure but a disastrous effect if exposure recurs over a period of time. Rather than appearing suddenly, health problems develop gradually through long-term, low-level exposures. For example, small doses of lead or mercury add up to severely toxic concentrations over time.[2] The frequency of a small dose can make a poison.

Chemical Reaction with Other Substances

The saying fails to acknowledge the fact that a small dose of one substance can activate or magnify the effect of another substance. For example, workers in polyvinyl chloride (PVC) factories who suffered noncancerous lesions in the liver caused by vinyl chloride exposure unknowingly escalated their liver damage into full-blown liver cancer simply by drinking alcoholic beverages.[3] The risks of many building industry chemicals have not been evaluated, let alone their combinations. A combination of small doses of various substances can make an unexpected poison.

Biomagnification

The saying above also implies that dilution, or making the relative size of a dose smaller by dispersing it over a large area, could be a way to mitigate pollution. Dilution, however, is not effective when food chains in the ecosystem reconcentrate the pollutant. In the food chain, plants are eaten by herbivores, which are in turn eaten by carnivores. However, to consume enough energy to sustain life, herbivores must eat a large volume of plants and carnivores must eat a large volume of herbivores.[4] Consequently, a trace amount of a contaminant present in a plant will become more concentrated in a herbivore and even more concentrated in a carnivore. Even if the finished product is benign, the toxic substances released into the environment during the manufacturing, recycling, and disposal processes must be carefully considered. A small dose can be biomagnified into an environmentally persistent poison.

---

[1] Ted Schettler, Gina Solomon, Maria Valenti, and Annette Huddle, *Generations at Risk: Reproductive Health and the Environment* (Cambridge, MA: The MIT Press, 2000), 5.

[2] "ToxFAQs: CABS/Chemical Agent Briefing Sheet, Lead," Agency for Toxic Substances and Disease Registry (ATSDR)/Division of Toxicology and Environmental Medicine, p. 4, Department of Health and Human Services, Atlanta, Georgia, January 2006, available for download at http://www.atsdr.cdc.gov/cabs/.

[3] Sandra Steingraber, *Living Downstream* (New York: Vintage Books, 1998), 68.

[4] U.S. Geological Survey, Department of the Interior, Toxic Substances Hydrology Program, "Biomagnification," http://toxics.usgs.gov/definitions/biomagnification.html.

Timing

For synthetic chemicals, the timing of exposure can be even more impactful than the dose size. The substance that illustrates this concept dramatically is thalidomide, a drug prescribed during the late 1950s and early 1960s to pregnant women to ease morning sickness. Babies in the womb exposed to minute doses of the drug during the fifth to eighth week of gestation suffered severe limb deformations, while babies exposed to larger doses in later weeks had either entirely different health problems or no problems at all.[5] Thalidomide is not a substance that would clandestinely enter our system from something in our environment, but because it is a drug, the scientific data on its effects is far more exhaustive than those of synthetic substances used in the building industry. Were there sufficient resources devoted to the study of all synthetic chemicals used in building products, consistent conclusive evidence would be found. The timing of a small dose can make a poison, especially in young people.

Trace Amount

How small is a trace amount, and is its minute size truly insignificant? Very low concentrations of a substance in a product are typically measured in parts per million (ppm, e.g., $1 in $1,000,000) or parts per billion (ppb, e.g., $1 in $1,000,000,000). Such ratios seem so minute that one would, at first, discount the importance of trace amounts. However, let us consider the ratios of active ingredients in some popular drugs. It takes a concentration of only 30 ppb ($30 in $1 billion) to make Cialis, the erectile dysfunction drug effective. Even more staggering is the small amount of contraceptive that makes low-hormone birth controls effective in preventing pregnancy—only 0.035 ppb (3.5 cents in $1 billion).[6]

In 2005, the Centers for Disease Control and Prevention released data on 148 substances measured in the blood and urine of several thousand people; the list included pesticides, toxic metals, polychlorinated biphenyls (PCBs), and plastic ingredients. The study found that the blood of many people today contains levels of toxic chemicals like PFCs (stain repellents) and Badge-40H (a plastics ingredient) at 45 ppb and greater. Lead causes brain damage at only 21 ppb.[7] So, when someone says that a product contains only a trace amount of a certain chemical, remind them that it only takes an equivalent of

$21 in $1 billion to damage a baby's brain for life. Many synthetic chemicals are effective and/or harmful in surprisingly minute doses.

Safe Levels

For many chemicals, there are no safe levels prescribed by law simply because conclusive scientific studies have not been commissioned or turned into legislation. For other chemicals, allegedly safe levels have been set by agencies such as the U.S. Environmental Protection Agency (EPA) or U.S. Occupational Safety and Health Administration (OSHA). However, these regulatory standards have been most often designed for average adult males rather than for more vulnerable individuals such as children, females, or the elderly. In addition, safe-level thresholds are not established solely with the goal of protecting human health[8] but, rather, to balance many factors, including economic impacts.

> My exposure to (*fill in blank*) did not make me sick.

There are many variations of this one, including: "your grandfather smoked like a chimney and lived to be a hundred." Such statements are often offered as if they were proof of universal human resilience.

We Are Not All the Same

Some people are more susceptible than others to developing disease. In the case of cancer, this is due primarily to three inherited or acquired conditions: altered genes in the body's cells, abnormal hormone levels, or a weakened immune system. People differ widely in their ability to eliminate cancer-causing agents to which they have been exposed, or to repair DNA damage that was caused by such agents.[9] One person may weather exposure that would be fatal to another.

Our Own Resilience Changes Over Time

The same individual may respond differently to harm at different points in his or her life. A child's developing brain can be damaged by a trace amount of lead, while an adult's

[5]Sandra Steingraber, *Having Faith* (New York: The Berkley Publishing Group, 2001), 42.
[6]Ken Cook, President, Environmental Working Group, "Ten Americans," lecture, July 21, 2008, Tides Foundation, http://www.tides.org/index.php?id=980.
[7]National Center for Environmental Health Division of Laboratory Services, *Third National Report on Human Exposure to Environmental Chemicals,* Department of Health and Human Services, NCEH Pub. No. 05-0570 (Washington, DC: Centers for Disease Control and Prevention, 2005), 1.
[8]U.S. Environmental Protection Agency, Ground Water and Drinking Water, "Setting Standards for Safe Drinking Water," http://www.epa.gov/OGWDW/standard/setting.html.
[9]U.S. Department of Health and Human Services (DHHS), National Institutes of Health (NIH), National Cancer Institute (NCI), National Institute of Environmental Health Sciences (NIEHS), *Cancer and the Environment: What You Need to Know, What You Can Do,* NIH Publication No. 03-2039 (Washington, DC: DHHS, NIH, NIC, and NIEHS, 2003), 2; http://www.niehs.nih.gov/health/docs/cancer-enviro.pdf,

brain may be fine at that level of exposure. An older person, whose body has been compromised by environmental stresses over a lifetime, may not be able to resist harm with as much resilience as a young adult. The time of life at which the exposure occurs sets the magnitude of its effect.[10]

Delayed Symptoms of Harm

Symptoms of very few serious diseases appear as acute reactions to exposure. Most cancers, for instance, take ten to fifteen years to manifest, up to forty-five years in the case of brain cancer.[11] Someone who has been severely exposed to a carcinogen may not experience symptoms for many years. It is this delay in the appearance of symptoms that makes it possible for manufacturers to market severely toxic products. The more time that elapses between the exposure and the symptom, the more difficult it is to link them as cause and effect.

The Cocktail of Chemicals

Severe environmental pollution is a phenomenon of the last fifty years. A hundred-year-old grandfather may have lived at least fifty years in an environment relatively free of hormone-mimicking substances, for example. The Environmental Working Group (EWG) found a disturbing fact during the study of pollutants present in umbilical cords: even people living in remote pristine regions of the world have environmental contaminants in their blood. The only pure blood they found was archived in a blood bank and belonged to soldiers before they were sent to fight in Southeast Asia in the early 1950s.[12] Our world today undeniably contains a more complex cocktail of chemicals than the world of previous generations, so our bodies may not have a chance to manifest the same resilience as the bodies of previous generations.

HEALTH STATISTICS[13]

- Autism, tenfold increase from early 1980s to 1996.
- Male birth defects, doubled from 1970 to 1993.
- Childhood asthma, doubled from 1982 to 1993.
- Childhood leukemia, 62 percent increase from 1973 to 1999.
- Sperm counts, 1 percent yearly decline from 1934 to 1996.

SOURCES OF CHEMICALS AND THEIR HEALTH RISKS[14]

Chemical	Source products	Health risks
PBDEs (polybrominated diphenylethers)	Flame retardants in furniture foam, upholstery fabrics	Brain development, thyroid function, suspected carcinogen
PCBs (polychlorinated biphenyls)	Insulation, lubricants (banned in the United States)	Cancer, nervous system damage
PCNs (polychlorinated naphthalenes)	Wood preservative, varnishes, fabric dyes	Liver and kidney damage
PFCs (perfluorinated chemicals)	Fabric and carpet stain repellents	Cancer, birth defects
Alkylphenols	Plastics, maintenance products	Endocrine disruption
DEHP (Di(2-ethylhexyl) phthalate)	Carpet, upholstery fabrics, shower curtains	Endocrine disruption, sperm damage

---

[10]Ibid, 4.

[11]Devra Davis, *The Secret History of the War on Cancer* (New York: Basic Books, 2007), 258.

[12]"PFCs: Global Contaminants, PFOA is a pervasive pollutant in human blood, as are other PFCs," Environmental Working Group, April 3, 2003, http://www.ewg.org/reports/pfcworld.

[13]Jane Houlihan, Jane, Timothy Kropp, Richard Wiles, Sean Gray, and Chris Campbell, *Body Burden: The Pollution in Newborns* (Washington, DC: Environmental Working Group, 2005), 25.

[14]Rudel, Ruthann A., David E Camann, John D Spengler, Leo R Korn, and Julia G Brody, "Phthalates, Alkylphenols, Pesticides, Polybrominated Diphenyl Ethers, and other Endocrine-Disrupting Compounds in Indoor Air and Dust," *Environmental Science & Technology* 37, part 20: 4543–4553.

■ Summary

As comforting as they may be, the sayings about our health have, in the last century, become inaccurate in the context of synthetic chemicals (including endocrine disruptors and carcinogens) that have become ingredients of many building materials and products. These substances can enter our bodies through the air we breathe, the water we drink, and through direct skin contact, without being detected by our senses. Public health statistics suggest that we have become participants in an entirely unmonitored dangerous and large-scale chemistry experiment. Which chemicals (or which combinations) will prove to be the trigger of the most dramatic side effects remains to be seen. As future building industry professionals, you are in a unique position to change the status quo by making sure that each building is designed for human health and wellness.

Please refer to the chapters on chemicals in the environment for more information on some of these substances and their building-industry sources, and use this knowledge to avoid them in your practice. Luckily, there are many alternative products available today. Through your commitment to designing places that do not harm the people, you will effect change in the standards of the building industry. What good is a beautiful building if it harms its inhabitants?

Glossary

ANSI. American National Standards Institute

ASHRAE. American Society of Heating, Refrigerating and Air-Conditioning Engineers

ASTM. American Society for Testing and Materials

BIFMA. Business and Institutional Furniture Manufacturer's Association

Biofiltration. A water treatment strategy where storm water passes through plants to remove pollutants. Two examples of biofiltration techniques are vegetated swales and flow-through planters.

Biomimicry. The study of nature's systems and design lessons to create technologies that address the challenges of modern civilization. Biomimicry's main proponent is Janine M. Benyus, in her book, *Biomimicry: Innovation Inspired by Nature* (New York: Morrow, 1997).

Biophilia. Edward O. Wilson's concept that humans have a bond with other living systems. Translated literally, *biophilia* means "love of life."

Bioretention. A plant-based filtration device that removes pollutants through a variety of physical, biological, and chemical treatment processes.

Black water. Waste water from toilets. Building integrated or natural systems can be used to treat black water for certain types of reuse. Sewer mining is a term given to the reuse of black water.

BRI (building-related illness). Often used synonymously with sick building syndrome (SBS), BRI differs in that the illness can be more confidently ascribed to a building's indoor environment. Building-related illnesses can have immediate or latent effects, such as effects related to lung cancer and indoor radon exposure.

Brownfield. A property with actual or perceived environmental contamination resulting from the previous use of the site, e.g., a gas station or leather-processing facility. Land with higher concentrations of hazardous contaminants are known as Superfund sites.

Chain of custody. Originating in forensic science, the documentation or paper trail that proves the custody, control, transfer, and disposition of evidence. In the case of green building design, chain of custody refers to the sourcing process of certified wood. The Forest Stewardship Council accredits certification agencies, who in turn perform third-party audits of forests, then issue certificates as tracking documentation that terminates with the vendor, supplier, or consumer.

Commissioning. Originating in the ship-building industry, the quality control process of ensuring that the mechanical systems of a building—heating, ventilating, and air-conditioning (HVAC), plumbing, electrical, fire-life safety, and building security—operate as designed (owner's performance requirements) and intended (basis of design document). This is a green strategy, because it reduces the risk of ongoing, undetected systems failures and accompanying wasted resources.

Composite wood. An engineered wood product such as particle board and medium-density fiberboard, made from wood-based materials, usually preconsumer, and bound with adhesives. Wherever possible, it is important to select formaldehyde-free composite wood. Composite-wood panels are used as substrate for countertops, cabinetry, and casework.

Constructed wetlands. Constructed basins having a wide and shallow permanent pool of water with an average depth of 18 inches, a high degree of vegetation coverage, and some areas of open water. As storm-water runoff flows through the wetland, pollutant removal is achieved through settling and biological uptake within the wetland.

Cradle to cradle. The opposite of the cradle-to-grave construct. Cradle to cradle means that a product never leaves the manufacturing, use, and disposal loop. Every component of a product or material can be used as a technical (synthetic but nontoxic) or biological nutrient (organic), using nature's processes as a model. A book by the same name was written by Bill McDonough and Michael Braungart (see Bibliography).

Cradle to grave. A life-cycle analysis that considers the manufacture, use, and disposal of a material, product, or system; the nonsustainable opposite of cradle to cradle model.

CRI (Carpet and Rug Institute). According to its mission statement, CRI is "the science-based source for the facts about carpet and rugs." CRI issues emissions-based testing ratings for carpet products known as Green Label and Green Label Plus.

Dematerialization. A term from the economics profession and the manufacturing industry, meaning doing more with less. In the context of green building, it means to use less material when constructing a building in order to conserve embodied energy and resources. The term is sometimes used to refer to the substitution of a high-carbon activity for a low-carbon activity.

Embodied energy. Sometimes referred to as embedded energy, embodied energy accounts for the energy expended during the harvest, mining, manufacture, transportation, installation, use, maintenance, and disposal of a material, product, or system. The same concept can be applied to embodied water.

Environmental tobacco smoke (ETS). Second-hand smoke, a known carcinogen, responsible for more than 3,000 deaths per year in the United States, according to the U.S. Environmental Protection Agency; referring to tobacco smoke that enters the environment and is inhaled by the occupants of that environment, also called "passive smoking."

Formaldehyde. A semivolatile organic compound (SVOC) found naturally in the outdoor air, wood products, and forest fires but also occurring in tobacco smoke and automobile exhaust. Formaldehyde is used as an adhesive binder in pressed materials such as composite woods, ceiling tiles made from paper pulp and fiberglass insulation, and often found in consumer goods such as cosmetics; a probable human carcinogen.

Gray water. Waste water from the activities of washing clothes, cleaning, cooking, and bathing. Many municipalities provide infrastructure for treated gray water.

Green roof. Also ecoroof, vegetated roof, and living roof; the incorporation of vegetation and soil over part or all of a roof's surface, resulting in numerous benefits, including: cooler ambient temperature, reduction of storm-water runoff through engineered soil absorption, provision of habitat, insulating qualities, and filtration of contaminants through the vegetation, thus improving water quality. Green roofs are especially beneficial as a means of reducing concentrations of copper, zinc, and polycyclic aromatic hydrocarbons (PAHs).

Impact assessment. One of the levels of life cycle assessment (LCA); the analysis of positive or negative environmental impacts posed by a building, material, product, or system.

Impervious paving (surfaces). Hard-surface materials such as landscape pavement, parking lots, and sidewalks that do not allow storm-water infiltration or groundwater recharge and, instead, cause runoff, erosion, sedimentation, flooding, and the transport of pollutants to wildlife habitats, wetlands, and agricultural land.

HVAC (heating, ventilation, and air conditioning systems. Sometimes referred to as HVAC&R (refrigeration).

ISO (International Organization for Standardization). Acronym adapted from the Greek *isos*, meaning "equal"; the ISO creates standards and many have been incorporated into international treaties. The ISO's 14000 series, environmental management, relates to green building practices.

Life cycle assessment (LCA). The environmental impact analysis of a product, material, or system, throughout its cycle of harvest, mining, manufacture, transportation, installation, use, maintenance, and disposal. Classic LCA categories of environmental damage include: greenhouse gas generation, acidification and eutrophication, smog production, ozone depletion, ecotoxicity, human toxicity, pollution generation, desertification, land use, and resource depletion.

Life cycle cost (LCC). Often confused with LCA, LCC refers to the financial costs associated with the harvest, mining, manufacture, transportation, installation, use, maintenance, and disposal of a material, product, or system.

Low-impact design (LID). A comprehensive, watershed-based multipurpose design approach to storm-water management and urban planning that considers site design, source controls, and treatment controls.

MCS (multiple chemical sensitivity). Individuals with MCS are highly sensitive to organic chemicals, including environmental tobacco smoke, pesticides, formaldehyde, plastics, liquid volatile organic compound–containing products, and fragrances (see *VOCs*).

MSDS (materials safety data sheet). An international reporting document that describes the nonproprietary components of products containing volatile organic compounds. Standard categories within the MSDS include: physical data, toxicity, health effects, first aid, reactivity, storage, disposal, protective equipment, and spill-handling procedures.

New Urbanism. A movement founded in 1993 as a reaction to sprawl, loss of open space, extreme auto orientation, the degradation of our built heritage, careless infrastructure demands, the isolation of economically disadvantaged populations, and the development of communities designed for the automobile. New Urbanism is about the design of communities for people, rather than cars.

PBT (persistent bioaccumulative toxins). These chemical pollutants are toxic, persist in the environment, and bioaccumulate in food chains and thus pose risks to human health and ecosystems. The biggest concerns about PBTs are that they transfer rather easily among air, water, and land, spanning program, geographic, and generational boundaries. Source definition: U.S. Environmental Protection Agency, http://www.epa.gov/pbt/pubs/aboutpbt.htm.

Pervious paving (surfaces). Often confused with permeable paving, where water moves around the paving material, pervious (or porous) paving allows water movement through the paving material. Both systems allow for groundwater recharge and reduce the potential for runoff, erosion, sedimentation, flooding, and the transport of pollutants to wildlife habitats, wetlands, and agricultural land; the opposite of impervious paving.

Phthalates. Plasticizers, or softening esters, used in a variety of applications, from cosmetics to other personal care products. Phthalates are used to soften plastics such as polyvinyl chloride (PVC), paint, detergents, adhesives, ink. An endocrine disruptor with suspected association with diabetes and asthma and impacts to liver health.

Rain gardens. Depressed landscape areas designed to capture and infiltrate storm-water runoff.

Rainwater harvesting. The capture, storage, and reuse of rainwater, accomplished through mechanical roof systems or natural runoff, which is stored in cisterns or tanks. Rainwater can be treated and reused on-site for industrial purposes, irrigation, or drinking water.

Recycled content. First used with regard to the paper recycling industry; recycled materials are considered in terms of their first use, either preconsumer (postindustrial) waste resulting from manufacturing or postconsumer waste, a preferable level, because the material components have passed through a previous use and thus are kept out of the landfill or incineration waste stream.

SBS (sick-building syndrome). An unhealthy indoor environment caused by poor indoor air quality, lack of proper ventilation and air movement, along with volatile organic compound emissions from building products and mold (see *VOCs*).

Smart growth. A planning strategy developed in the late 1990s as a reaction to urban sprawl, smart growth helps communities develop and grow in ways that support economic prosperity, environmental conservation, and a strong and fair society.

Stakeholder. A person, entity, or agency that has some investment, either as an owner, funder, occupant, or designer, in the design and construction and ultimate outcome of the building project.

Synthetic chemical. An artificially made anthropogenic chemical, often used to manufacture fertilizers and pesticides.

Thermal comfort. As defined by AHSRAE, "the state of mind that expresses satisfaction with the surrounding environment" in terms of temperature, humidity, air movement, and ventilation.

TOD (transit-oriented development). A land-use design concept used to describe mixed-use communities located within easy proximity to various forms of public transportation.

VMT (vehicle miles traveled). As defined by the U.S. Bureau of Transportation Statistics, "one vehicle traveling the distance of one mile. Total vehicle miles, thus, is the total mileage traveled by all vehicles" (http://www.bts.gov).

VOCs (volatile organic compounds). Sometimes more frequently known as hazardous airborne pollutants (HAPs); chemicals that have low water solubility and high vapor pressure, which means they emit vapors rapidly at room temperature. Volatile organic compounds can emit ground-level smog, and they are components of many wet-applied building products and materials such as paint, adhesives, coatings, sealers, and sealants. Often the first signal of the presence of a VOC is the odor, which lingers in porous material sinks for weeks to months after application. Many VOCs are known or suspected human carcinogens.

Watershed. The physical barrier between two aquatic systems and the area that drains into other water bodies.

Wet ponds. Also known as storm-water ponds, retention ponds, and wet extended-detention ponds, wet ponds are constructed basins that have a permanent pool of water throughout the year and have an average depth of 4–6 feet. Ponds treat incoming storm-water runoff by settlement and biological uptake.

Wetlands. An area of land that in some seasons remains saturated with rain or groundwater; intermediate environment connecting terrestrial and aquatic systems.

Bibliography

Print Resources

Alexander, Christopher. *A Pattern Language: Towns, Buildings, Construction*. Oxford: Oxford University Press, 1977.

Allen, Edward. *How Buildings Work: The Natural Order of Architecture*. 3rd ed. Oxford: Oxford University Press, 2005.

Allen, Edward, and Joseph Lano. *Fundamentals of Building Construction: Materials and Methods*. Hoboken, NJ: John Wiley & Sons, 2003.

American Society of Heating, Refrigerating and Air-Conditioning Engineers (ASHRAE). *ANSI/ASHRAE, IESNA Standard 90.1-2007, Energy Standard for Buildings Except Low-Rise Residential Buildings*. Atlanta, GA: ASHRAE Press, 2007.

———. *The ASHRAE Green Guide*. 2nd ed. The ASHRAE Green Guide Series. Atlanta, GA: ASHRAE Press, 2006.

———. *ASHRAE Indoor Air Quality Guide, Best Practices for Design, Construction, And Commissioning*. Produced by AHSRAE in partnership with AIA (American Institute of Architects), USGBC (U.S. Green Building Council), BOMA (Building Owners and Managers Association), SMACNA (Sheet Metal and Air Conditioning Contractors of North America), and the EPA (Environmental Protection AgencyRelease expected in Fall 2009.

Anastas, Paul T., and John C. Warner. *Green Chemistry: Theory and Practice*. Oxford and New York: Oxford University Press, 1998.

Baechler, Michael C., and Pat Love. *Building America Best Practices Series: Volume 1, Builders and Buyers Handbook for Improving New Home Efficiency, Comfort, and Durability in the Hot and Humid Climate*. NREL/TP-550-36960. Golden, CO: U.S. Department of Energy (DOE) by the National Renewable Energy Laboratory, 2004. Downloadable from: http://www.eere.energy.gov/buildings/publications/pdfs/building_america/36960.pdf.

Baechler, Michael C., Z. Todd Taylor, Rosemarie Bartlett, Theresa Gilbride, Marye Hefty, and Pat M. Love. *Building America Best Practices Series: Vol. 2, Builders and Buyers Handbook for Improving New Home Efficiency, Comfort, and Durability in the Hot-Dry and Mixed-Dry Climates*. Washington, DC: U.S. Department of Energy, Building America Program, 2005. Downloadable from: http://www1.eere.energy.gov/buildings/building_america/.

Baechler, Michael C., Z. Todd Taylor, Rosemarie Bartlett, Theresa Gilbride, Marye Hefty, Heidi Steward, and Pat M. Love. *Building America Best Practices Series: Volume 3, Builders and Buyers Handbook for Improving New Home Efficiency, Comfort, and Durability in the Cold and Very Cold Climates*. Washington, DC: U.S. Department of Energy, Building America Program, 2005. Downloadable from: http://www1.eere.energy.gov/buildings/building_america/.

Baechler, Michael C., Z. Todd Taylor, Rosemarie Bartlett, Theresa Gilbride, Marye Hefty, Heidi Steward, Pat M. Love, and Jennifer A. Palmer. *Building America Best Practices Series: Vol. 4, Builders and Buyers Handbook for Improving New Home Efficiency, Comfort, and Durability in the Mixed-Humid Climate*. Washington, DC: U.S. Department of Energy, Building America Program, 2005. Downloadable from: http://www1.eere.energy.gov/buildings/building_america/.

Baechler, Michael C., Z. Todd Taylor, Rosemarie Bartlett, Theresa Gilbride, Marye Hefty, Heidi Steward, Pat M. Love and Jennifer A. Palmer. *Building America Best Practices Series: Volume 5, Builders and Buyers Handbook for Improving New Home Efficiency, Comfort, and Durability in the Marine Climate*. Washington, DC: U.S. Department of Energy, Building America Program, 2005. Downloadable from: http://www1.eere.energy.gov/buildings/building_america/.

Baechler, Michael C., Theresa Gilbride, Kathi Ruiz, Heidi Steward, and Pat M. Love. *Building America Best Practices Series: Volume 6, High-Performance Home Technologies: Solar Thermal and Photovoltaic Systems*. Washington, DC: U.S.

Department of Energy, Building America Program, 2007. Downloadable from: http://www1.eere.energy.gov/buildings/building_america/.

Baird, Stephen. "Sustainable Design: The Next Industrial Revolution," *Technology Teacher* 67, no. 4 (2008): 11–15.

Banham, Reyner. *The Architecture of the Well-Tempered Environment*. 2nd ed. Chicago: University of Chicago Press, 1984.

Beatley, Timothy. *Green Urbanism: Learning from European Cities*. Washington, DC: Island Press, 2000.

Benfield, F. Kaid, Matthew D. Raimi, and Donald D.T. Chen. *Once There Were Greenfields*. New York: Natural Resources Defense Council and Surface Transportation Policy Project, 1999.

Berry, Thomas. *The Great Work: Our Way into the Future*. New York: Random House/Crown Publishing Group/Three Rivers Press, 2000.

Berry, Wendell. *The Unsettling of America: Culture and Agriculture*. Rev. ed. San Francisco, CA, and Washington, DC: Sierra Club Books, 2004.

Berry, Wendell, with Wes Jackson and Bruce Colman, eds. *Meeting the Expectations of the Land: Essays in Sustainable Agriculture and Stewardship*. New York: North Point Press, 1984.

Blanc, Paul D. *How Everyday Products Make People Sick: Toxins at Home and in the Workplace*. Berkeley and Los Angeles: University of California Press, 2007.

Bonda, Penny, and Katie Sosnowchik. *Sustainable Commercial Interiors*. Hoboken, NJ: John Wiley & Sons, 2006.

Brand, Stewart. *Clock of the Long Now: Time and Responsibility, the Ideas Behind the World's Slowest Computer*. New York: Basic Books, 2005.

Brown, G. Z., and Mark DeKay. *Sun, Wind and Light: Architectural Design Strategies*. 2nd ed. New York: John Wiley & Sons, 2000.

California Energy Commission. *2008 Building Energy Efficiency Standards for Residential and Nonresidential Buildings*, CEC-400-2008-001-CMF. Sacramento, CA: California Energy Commission, 2008.

Calthorpe, Peter. *The Next American Metropolis: Ecology, Community, and the American Dream*. 3rd ed. New York: Princeton Architectural Press, 1995.

Carmody, John, Stephen Selkowitz, Dariush Arasteh, and Lisa Heschong. *Residential Windows: A Guide to New Technology and Energy Performance*. 3rd ed. New York: Norton, 2007.

Carmody, John, Stephen Selkowitz, Eleanor S. Lee, Dariush Arasteh, and Todd Willmert. *Window Systems for High-Performance Buildings*. New York: Norton, 2004.

Carson, Rachel. *Silent Spring*. Boston and Cambridge, MA: Houghton Mifflin and Riverside Press, 1962.

Colborn, Theo, Dianne Dumanoski, and John Peterson Myers. *Our Stolen Future: Are We Threatening Our Fertility, Intelligence, and Survival?—A Scientific Detective Story*. New York: Plume, 1997.

Diamond, Jared M. *Collapse: How Societies Choose to Fail or Succeed*. New York: Viking Penguin, 2005.

Duany, Andrés, Elizabeth Plater-Zyberk, and Jeff Speck. *Suburban Nation: The Rise of Sprawl and the Decline of the American Dream*. New York: North Point Press, 2000.

Elizabeth, Lynne, and Cassandra Adams, eds. *Alternative Construction: Contemporary Natural Building Methods*. Hoboken, NJ: John Wiley & Sons, 2005.

Earley, Sandra Leibowitz. *Ecological Design and Building Schools: Green Guide to Educational Opportunities in the United States and Canada*. Oakland, CA: New Village Press, 2005.

Emerson, Ralph Waldo. *Nature and Selected Essays*. New York: Penguin Classics, 2003.

Ewing, Reid, and Richard Kreutzer. *Understanding the Relationship between Public Health and the Built Environment: A Report Prepared for the LEED-ND Core Committee*. Washington, DC: U.S. Green Building Council and Congress for the New Urbanism, 2006.

Farr, Douglas. *Sustainable Urbanism: Urban Design with Nature*. Hoboken, NJ: John Wiley & Sons, 2008.

Flannery, Tim. *The Weather Makers: How Man Is Changing the Climate and What It Means for Life on Earth*. New York: Grove Press, 2001.

Freed, Eric Corey. Green Building & Remodeling For Dummies. Hoboken, NJ: John Wiley & Sons, 2008.

Frumkin, Howard, Lawrence Frank, and Richard Jackson. *Urban Sprawl and Public Health: Designing, Planning, and Building for Healthy Communities*. Washington DC: Island Press, 2004.

Gissen, David, ed. *Big & Green: Toward Sustainable Architecture in the 21st Century*. New York and Washington, DC: Princeton Architectural Press and National Building Museum, 2003.

Golding, William, *Lord of the Flies*. New York: Penguin, 1999.

Graham, Peter. *Building Ecology: First Principles for a Sustainable Built Environment*. Hoboken, NJ: John Wiley & Sons, 2002.

Guenther, Robin, and Gail Vittori. *Sustainable Healthcare Architecture*. Hoboken, NJ: John Wiley & Sons, 2007.

Guha, Ramachandra. *Environmentalism: A Global History*. New York: Longman, 2000.

Hawken, Paul. *Blessed Unrest: How the Largest Movement in the World Came into Being and Why No One Saw It Coming*. New York: Viking Press, 2007.

Hawken, Paul, Amory Lovins, and L. Hunter Lovins. *Natural Capitalism: Creating the Next Industrial Revolution*. Snowmass, CO: Rocky Mountain Institute, 2008.

Jacobs, Jane. *The Death and Life of Great American Cities*. New York: Random House, 1961.

Katz, Peter. *The New Urbanism: Toward an Architecture of Community*. New York: McGraw-Hill Professional, 1993.

Kelbaugh, Doug. *Pedestrian Pocket Book*. New York: Princeton Architectural Press, 1996.

Kellert, Stephen R., Judith H. Heerwagen, and Martin L. Malor, eds. *Biophilic Design*. Hoboken: John Wiley & Sons, 2008.

Kibert, Charles J. *Sustainable Construction: Green Building Design and Delivery*. 2nd ed. Hoboken, NJ: John Wiley & Sons, 2008.

Kline, Benjamin. *First Along the River: A Brief History of the U.S. Environmental Movement*. Oxford: Rowan & Littlefield, 2000.

Kunstler, James Howard, *The Geography of Nowhere: The Rise and Decline of America's Man-Made Landscape*. New York: Free Press, 1994.

Kwok, Alison G., and Walter T. Grondzik. *The Green Studio Handbook, Environmental Strategies for Schematic Design*. Oxford, UK, and Burlington, MA: Architectural Press, 2007.

Lam, William. *Sunlighting as Formgiver for Architecture*. New York: Van Nostrand Reinhold Company, 1986.

Lechner, Norbert. *Heating, Cooling, Lighting: Design Methods for Architects*. 2nd ed. New York: John Wiley & Sons, 2001.

Leinberger, Christopher. *The Option of Urbanism: Investing in a New American Dream*. Washington DC: Island Press, 2008.

Leopold, Aldo. *Sand County Almanac and Sketches from Here and There*. New York: Oxford University Press, 1949.

Lovelock, James. *Gaia, A New Look at Life on Earth*. Oxford: Oxford University Press,1982; orig. 1979.

Maiellaro, Nicola. *Towards Sustainable Building*. New York: Springer, 2001.

Marsh, George Perkins. *Man And Nature: Or Physical Geography As Modified By Human Action*. Whitefish, MT: Kessinger Publishing, 2008.

Mazria, Edward. *The Passive Solar Energy Book*. Emmaus, PA: Rodale Press, 1980.

McCormick, John. *Reclaiming Paradise: The Global Environment Movement*. Bloomington: Indiana University Press, 1989.

McDonough, William, and Michael Braungart. *Cradle to Cradle: Remaking the Way We Make Things*. New York: North Point Press, 2002.

———. *The Hannover Principles, Design for Sustainability*. 10th ed. Charlottesville, VA: William McDonough & Partners, McDonough Braungart Design Chemistry, 2003.

McHarg, Ian. *Design with Nature*. New York: John Wiley & Sons, 1992.

Mendler, Sandra, and William Odell. *The HOK Guidebook to Sustainable Design*. New York: John Wiley & Sons, 2000.

Mollison, Bill. *Permaculture: A Designer's Manual*. Edited by Reny Mia Slay. Illustrated by Andrew Jeeves. Tyalgum, Australia: Tagari Publications, 1997; orig. 1988.

Moore, Fuller. *Environmental Control Systems*. New York: McGraw Hill, 1993.

Muir, John. *My First Summer in the Sierra*. Whitefish, MT: Kessinger Publishing, 2008.

Newbold, Heather, ed. *Life Stories: World-Renowned Scientists Reflect on Their Lives and the Future of Life on Earth*. Berkeley and Los Angeles: University of California Press, 2000.

Orwell, George. *Animal Farm*. Fairfield, IA: 1st World Library Literary Society, 2004.

Preiser, Wolfgang, and Jacqueline C. Vischer, eds. *Assessing Building Performance*. Burlington, MA: Butterworth-Heinemann, 2004.

Roberts, Jennifer. *Good Green Homes*. Salt Lake City, UT: Gibbs Smith, 2003.

———. *Good Green Kitchens: The Ultimate Resource for Creating a Beautiful, Healthy, Eco-Friendly Kitchen*. Layton, UT: Gibbs Smith, 2006.

———. *Redux: Designs that Reuse, Recycle, and Reveal*. Layton, UT: Gibbs Smith, 2005.

Roberts, Paul, *The End of Oil: On the Edge of a Perilous New World*. Boston: Houghton Mifflin, 2004.

Schettler, Ted, Gina Solomon, Maria Valenti, and Annette Huddle. *Generations at Risk: Reproductive Health and the Environment*. Cambridge, MA: The MIT Press, 2000.

Schumaker, E. F. *Small Is Beautiful: Economics as if People Mattered*. New York: Harper Perennial, 1989.

Shoup, Donald C. *The High Cost of Free Parking*. Chicago: American Planners Association Press, 2005.

Soleri, Paolo, *Arcology: The City in the Image of Man*. 4th ed. Mayer, AZ: Cosanti Press, 2006; Cambridge, MA: The MIT Press, 1969.

Soleri, Paolo, and John Cobb, Jr. *Arcosanti: An Urban Laboratory?* Santa Monica, CA: VTI Press, 1987.

Stair, Peter, Heather Wooten, and Matt Raimi. "How to Create and Implement Healthy General Plans: A Toolkit for Building Healthy, Vibrant Communities through Land Use Policy Change," Public Health Law & Policy. Oakland, CA: Raimi+Associates and Public Health Law and Policy, 2008, http://www.healthyplanning.org/toolkit_healthygp.html.

Stein, Benjamin, John S. Reynolds, Walter T. Grondzik, and Alison G. Kwok. *Mechanical and Electrical Equipment for Buildings,* 10th ed. Hoboken, NJ: John Wiley & Sons, 2005.

Steingraber, Sandra. *Living Downstream: A Scientist's Personal Investigation of Cancer and the Environment*. New York: Vintage Press, 1998.

Thoreau, Henry David. *Walden, or, Life in the Woods*. New York: T. Y. Crowell & Company,1899.

Thornton, Joe. *Pandora's Poison: Chlorine, Health, and a New Environmental Strategy*. Cambridge, MA: The MIT Press, 2001.

Van der Ryn, Sim. *Design for Life: The Architecture of Sim van der Ryn*. Salt Lake City, UT: Gibbs Smith, 2005.

Van der Ryn, Sim, and Stuart Cowan. *Ecological Design*. Washington, DC: Island Press, 2007.

Williams, Daniel E. *Sustainable Design: Ecology, Architecture, and Planning?*. Hoboken, NJ: John Wiley & Sons, 2007.

Wilson, Edward O. *Biophilia*.

Yeang, Ken. *The Green Skyscraper: The Basis for Designing Sustainable Intensive Buildings*. Munich: Prestel, 2000.

Yudelson, Jerry. *Green Building A to Z: Understanding the Language of Green Building*. Gabriola Island, BC, Canada: New Society Publishers, 2007.

Yudelson, Jerry, and S. Richard Fedrizzi. *The Green Building Revolution*. Washington, DC: Island Press, 2007.

Zackman, W., and N. Carlisle. *Low-Energy Building Design Guidelines: Energy-Efficient Design for New Federal Facilities*. Golden, CO: National Renewable Energy Laboratory, 2001.

Internet Resources

California Energy Commission. *California's Energy Efficiency Standards for Residential and Nonresidential Buildings* (2008). http://www.energy.ca.gov/title24/

California Energy Commission. *Integrated Energy Policy Report* (2007). http://www.energy.ca.gov/2007_energypolicy/index.html

Energy Information Administration. *Official U.S. Energy Statistics.* http://www.eia.doe.gov/cneaf/solar.renewables/page/trends/table6.html

Heschong Mahone Group. *Skylighting Guidelines: Energy Design Resources* (1998). http://www.energydesignre-sources.com

International Code Council (ICC). *2006 International Energy Conservation Code* (2006). Available at http://www.iccsafe.org/e/prodshow.html?prodid=3800S06

Millennium Ecosystem Assessment. "Millennium Ecosystem Assessment General Synthesis Report: Ecosystems and Human Well-Being" (2005). http://www.maweb.org.

WEB-SITE RESOURCES

American Council for an Energy-Efficient Economy: http://www.aceee.org

American Institute of Architects' Committee on the Environment: http://www.aia.org/cote/

ANSI (American National Standards Institute): http://www.ansi.org

Apollo Alliance: http://www.apolloalliance.org

Architecture 2030, The 2030 Challenge, and The 2010 Imperative: http://www.architecture2030.org

ASTM (American Society for Testing and Materials): http://www.astm.org

Athena Sustainable Materials Institute: http://www.athenasmi.org

Austin Energy Green Building: http://www.austinenergy.com/go/greenbuilding

Better Bricks: http://www.betterbricks.com

British Columbia Ministry of Environment: http://www.env.gov.bc.ca

Build It Green: http://www.builditgreen.org

Build It Green, *Access Green Directory*: http://accessgreen.builditgreen.org

Building Materials Reuse Association: http://ubma.org

California Integrated Waste Management Board, Recycled Content Product Database: http://www.ciwmb.ca.gov/rcp

California, State of, DSA's EPP Database: http://www.eppbuild-ingproducts.org

Canada Green Building Council: http://www.cagbc.org

CAS (Chemical Abstracts Services): http://www.cas.org/exper-tise/cascontent

Cascadia Region Green Building Council, Living Building Challenge: http://www.cascadiagbc.org

Center for Maximum Potential Building Systems: http://www.cmpbs.org

Clean Production Action: http://www.cleanproduction.org

Clinton, William J., Foundation: http://www.clintonfoundation.org

Clinton, William J., Foundation Climate Initiative: http://www.clintonfoundation.org/what-we-do/clinton-climate-initiative/

Collaborative for High Performance Schools (CHPS): http://www.chps.net

Davis Energy Group, Inc: http://www.davisenergy.com

Deconstruction Institute: http://www.deconstructioninstitute.com

Ecolect Online Material Community: http://www.ecolect.net

Ecological Footprint Quiz: http://www.myfootprint.org/en/

Energy Design Resources: http://www.energydesignresources.com

Environmental Building News, Building Green: http://www.buildinggreen.com

Environmental Design and Construction: http://www.edcmag.com

Environmental Working Group: http://www.ewg.org

Environmental Working Group Chemical Index: http://www.ewg.org/chemindex/

European Environment Agency Environment Themes: http://www.eea.europa.eu/themes/

Forest Stewardship Council: http://www.fsc.org

Forest Stewardship Council U.S.: http://www.fscus.org

Global Eco-Labeling Network (GEN): http://www.globalecola-belling.net

Global Footprint Network: http://www.ecofoot.net

Global Green USA: http://www.globalgreen.org

Global Reporting Initiative's (GRI): http://www.globalreporting.org

Green Building Alliance: http://www.gbapgh.org

Green Building Council Australia: http://www.gbca.org.au

Green Building Pages: http://www.greenbuildingpages.com

Green Built Home: http://www.greenbuilthome.org

Green Home Guide: http://www.greenhomeguide.com

Green Progress, Green Building, and Sustainable Development: http://www.greenprogress.com

Green Seal: http://www.greenseal.org

Greener Buildings: http://www.greenerbuildings.com

Greenfacts: http://www.greenfacts.org

GreenGuard Environmental Institute, http://www.greenguard.org

Healthy Building Network: http://www.healthybuilding.net

Hong Kong BEAM (Building Environmental Assessment Method) Society: http://www.hk-beam.org.hk

Indian Green Building Council: http://www.igbc.in

Institute for Market Transformation to Sustainability: http://www.mts.sustainableproducts.com

International Organization for Standardization (ISO): http://www.iso.org

Japan Green Building Council, CASBEE (Comprehensive Assessment System for Building Environmental Efficiency: http://www.ibec.or.jp/CASBEE/english/index.htm

Leonardo Academy: http://www.leonardoacademy.org

Mexico Green Building Council (Consejo Mejicano de Edificación Sustentable): http://www.mexicogbc.org

Minnesota Building Materials Database: http://www.building-materials.umn.edu

Natural Step: http://www.naturalstep.org

New Buildings Institute: http://www.newbuildings.org

New Zealand Green Building Council : http://www.nzgbc.org.nz

Oikos: http://www.oikos.com

Organisation for Economic Co-Operation and Development (OECD) Environmental Directorate, Environmental Data and Indicators: http://www.oecd.org/department/0,2688,en_2649_34441_1_1_1_1_1,00.html

Partnership for Advancing Technology in Housing, *The PATH Guide to Green Building*: http://www.pathnet.org

Pharos Project: http://www.pharosproject.net

Post Carbon Institute: http://www.postcarbon.org

Product Stewardship Institute: http://www.productstewardship.us

Redefining Progress: http://www.rprogress.org

ReGreen, ASID, and USGBC: http://www.regreenprogram.org

Rocky Mountain Institute: http://www.rmi.org

Scientific Certification Systems (SCS): http://www.scscertified.com

Scorecard, The Pollution Information Site: http://www.scorecard.org

SFEnvironment: http://www.sfenvironment.org

Smart Growth Network Online: http://www.smartgrowth.org

South Coast Air Quality Management District: http://www.aqmd.gov

Stop Waste, Green Building Home: http://www.stopwaste.org/home/index.asp?page=7

Sustain Lane Government: http://www.sustainlane.us

Sustainable Design Resource Guide of Colorado, Denver Committee on the Environment (COTE): http://www.aiasdrg.org

United Kingdom Green Building Council : http://www.ukgbc.org

United Nations Department of Economic and Social Affairs, Division for Sustainable Development, Indicators of Sustainable Development: http://www.un.org/esa/sustdev/natlinfo/indicators/isd.htm

United Nations Environment Programme: http://www.unep.org

United Nations Environment Programme / Sustainable Buildings and Construction Initiative (UNEP / SBCI): http://www.unepsbci.org

U.S. Department of Energy, Energy Efficiency and Renewable Energy: http://www.eere.energy.gov/buildings/

U.S. Environmental Protection Agency, Comprehensive Procurement Guidelines: http://www.epa.gov/cpg/

U.S. Environmental Protection Agency, Source Ranking Database, Exposure Assessment Tools, and Models: http://www.epa.gov/oppt/exposure/pubs/srd.htm

U.S. Green Building Council (USGBC): http://www.usgbc.org

U.S. Green Building Council, Green Home Guide: http://www.greenhomeguide.org

U.S. National Library of Medicine, Toxicology Data Network, TOXNET: http://toxnet.nlm.nih.gov

Whole Building Design Guide: http://www.wbdg.org

World Resources Institute, Earth Trends Environmental Information: http://ww.earthtrends.wri.org

Worldwatch Institute: http://www.worldwatch.org

▦ FILMS

The Story of Stuff, Annie Leonard. Sponsored by the Tides Foundation and the Funders Workgroup for Sustainable Consumption and Production. http://www.storyofstuff.com

Blue Vinyl, A Toxic Odyssey. Judith Helfand and Daniel B. Gold. 2002.

Trade Secrets: A Bill Moyers Report. Bill Moyers and Sherry Jones. Produced by Sherry Jones. New York: A Production of Public Affairs Television, Inc., in association with Washington Media Associates, Inc., A Presentation of Thirteen / WNET New York, 2001. http://www.pbs.org/tradesecrets

Illustration Credits

Chapter 1

1-1 Image courtesy of PHA Consult

1-2 Illustration by Killer Banshee Studios

1-3 Illustration by Killer Banshee Studios

1-4 Image courtesy of the Water Environment Research Foundation

1-5 Source: British Sustainability Plan, a strategy for sustainable development, Securing The Future, in conjunction with Strategic Framework, One future - different paths, 7 March 2005, DEFRA (Department of Environment and Rural Affairs) http://www.defra.gov.uk/sustainable/government/publications/uk-strategy/index.htm

1-6 Source: Ted Kesik, University of Toronto; illustration by Killer Banshee Studios

1-7 Image courtesy of Battle McCarthy

1-8 A, B, C eQUEST® 3-D Display Example. eQUEST is a registered trademark of James J. Hirsch.

1-9 Reforestation: Growing Tomorrow's Forests Today®, ©1998, 2000. American Forest & Paper Association, Inc.

1-10 Echaine: Energy Wood Production Chains in Europe.

1-11 Image courtesy of Landco Land Developments

1-12 Image courtesy of Tanked Australia, Rainwater Storage Solutions

1-13 The Pharos Project™ is a project of the Healthy Building Network

1-14 Courtesy of DTR Corporation. Illustration by Killer Banshee Studios

Chapter 2

2-1 Image from the Army Corps of Engineers, photographer: Timothy H. O'Sullivan

2-2 Image from FSA/OWI Collection, photographer: Andrea Feininger

2-3 Working Class Movement Library, Salford, UK

2-4 Image from Right Livelihood

2-5 Photographer: Martin Rowe

2-6 The Harvard Theatre Collection, Houghton Library

2-7 Image from US National Oceanic & Atmospheric Administration

2-8 Photo courtesy of the Exxon Valdez Oil Spill Trustee Council

2-9 "Pouring Milk, 1957," Ivor Nicholas

2-10 Image © Metropolitan Museum of Art, painting by Thomas Cole

2-11 Image courtesy Library of Congress, photographers: Underwood & Underwood

Chapter 3

3-1 Image courtesy FSA/OWI

3-2 Image courtesy Edmonston Studio

3-3 Image courtesy San Francisco Green Party

3-4 Image courtesy of the United Nations Department of Public Information.

3-5 Image courtesy of the United Nations Department of Public Information.

3-6A Image courtesy of IISD/Earth Negotiations Bulletin

3-6B Image courtesy Alinor, E Pluribus Anthony (GNU Free Doc License V 1.2)

3-7 ©2008, 2030, Inc./Architecture 2030. All rights reserved. Used with permission. Data source: U.S. Energy Information Administration.

3-8 Image courtesy of the United Nations Department of Public Information, Photo Library.

Chapter 4

4-1 © Kirsten Jacobsen

4-2 MK Lotus™ Home by Michelle Kaufmann/Photo by John Swain Photography

4-3 Photo: ©Huib Blom/www.dogon_lobi.ch

4-4 Image courtesy U.S. News & World Report Magazine Photograph Collection; photographer: Warren K. Leffler

4-5 B and C Image courtesy of Energy Information Administration, U.S. Department of Energy

4-6 Design by Shane Kohatsu and Emi Fujita, 2007

4-7 Arcosanti image from the book *Arcology: City in the Image of Man,* 1969.

4-8 Image courtesy of Cameron Johnstone, ESRU

4-9 Data source: USGBC; illustration: Killer Banshee Studios

4-10 Technische Universität Darmstadt, 2007

4-11 Source: US Department of Energy

4-12 Data source: USGBC; illustration: Killer Banshee Studios

4-13 Data source: USGBC; illustration: Killer Banshee Studios

4-14 CADE Windery/Pechara Studio Inc.

4-15 This table was developed by the National Renewable Energy Laboratory for the U.S. Department of Energy

4-16 Image courtesy of KMD Architects.

Chapter 5

5-1 Image courtesy FSA/OWI, photographer: Alfred T Palmer

5-2 Image courtesy US EPA Office of Air Quality Planning & Standards

5-3 Image from Bureau of Entomology & Plant Quarantine, Agricultural Research Administration, US Department of Agriculture, and the US Public Health Service, Federal Security Agency, 1947

5-4 Photographer: Pfc. Mary Rose Xenikakis, 22nd Mobile Public Affairs Detachment, US Army

5-5 "Playground and Chemical Plant, Texas City, Texas," © Sam Kittner/kittner.com

5-6 Image and Data Source: Mark Rossi and Tom Lent, "Creating Safe and Healthy Spaces: Selecting Materials the Support Healing," in *Designing the 21st Century Hospital* (Center for Health Design & Health Care Without Harm, 2006), page 66. (hhttp://www.healthy-building.net/healthcare/HCWH-CHD-Designing_the_21st_Century_Hospital.pdf).

5-7 Image courtesy of Playmakers Recreation

5-8 Photographer: Brian K Grigsby, SPC5, US Army

5-9 Image courtesy of Nature's Control, www.naturescontrol.com

5-10 Alison Curtis, Castlereagh Borough Council Technical & Environmental Services Department

5-11 "Summertime Blues," photo by Jay Black.

Chapter 6

6-1 Data originally compiled by Dr. John Pollack, Sydney University. Illustration: Killer Banshee Studios

6-2 Image courtesy office of US Representative Maurice Hinchey

6-3 Image courtesy WA Toxics Coalition, photographer: Jim Dawson

6-4 With courtesy of the Environmental Protection Department of the HKSAR Government. Non-exclusive rights.

6-5 Image courtesy National Waterproofing Systems

6-6 © Killer Banshee Studios/killerbanshee.com, 2008

6-7 Image courtesy U.S. Geological Survey and the U.S. Environmental Protection Agency

6-8 EMF Frequency chart from Cutnell Phys v7—Wiley

Chapter 7

7-1 "Breeze" © Philip Holker 2008

7-2 Image courtesy photographer: Galiel

7-3 "In the Shadow of the Power Plant" © Bill Mattocks

7-4 Image courtesy FSA/OWI, photographer: Alfred T. Palmer

7-5 Image © Marian Keeler

7-6 Image courtesy Air Advice

7-7 Image courtesy photographer: Berserkerus

7-8 Data gathered by Leon Alevantis

Chapter 8

8-1 Personal Environments®, Image courtesy of Johnson Controls, Inc., Milwaukee, WI

8-2 Image courtesy of Tate Access Floors, Inc.

8-3 Council House 2 drawing courtesy of the City of Melbourne

8-4 Council House 2 drawing courtesy of the City of Melbourne

8-5 Diagram courtesy of Watt Stopper/Legrand.

8-6 "Ronchamp Interior" © Diego Samper

8-7 Image courtesy of Austin Energy Green Building.

8-8 Manufacturer: Architectural Grilles & Sunshades, Inc., Mokena, IL

8-9 "Bel-Air Mini Mobile Greenhouse." Design: Mathieu Lehanneur in collaboration with David Edwards; Harvard, Best Invention Award, 2008.

8-10 Image courtesy of Patrick Blanc.

8-11 Center for Building Performance and Diagnostics, Carnegie Mellon University/ABSIC BIDS™ 2007 and Stephen R. Kellert, Judith H. Heerwagen, Martin L. Malor, eds., *Biophilic Design* (Hoboken, NJ: John Wiley & Sons), 2008, figure 8-3.

8-12 Center for Building Performance and Diagnostics, Carnegie Mellon University/ABSIC BIDS™ 2007 and Stephen R. Kellert, Judith H. Heerwagen, Martin L. Malor, eds., *Biophilic Design* (Hoboken, NJ: John Wiley & Sons, 2008), figure 8-4.

Chapter 9

9-1 Source: Sun, Wind & Light, illustration: Killer Banshee Studios

9-2 Photograph by Bill Burke

9-3 Illustration: Killer Banshee Studios

9-4 Image courtesy California Energy Commision, Commissioner Arthur Rosenfeld

Chapter 10

10-1 © Killer Banshee Studios/killerbanshee.com, 2008

10-2 Illustration by Bill Burke

10-3 Image courtesy Philip Ronan (under Creative Commons v2.5)

10-4 Bill Burke

10-5 Image courtesy Building Energy Codes Program Resource Center, ASHRAE 90.1

10-6 Illustration: Killer Banshee Studios

10-7 Image courtesy Historic American Buildings Survey, Everett H Keeler

10-8 Photograph © Alison Kwok, 2008

10-9 Photograph by Bill Burke

Chapter II

11-1 Source: Sun, Wind & Light, illustration: Killer Banshee Studios

11-2 Bob Theis, Architect

11-3 Illustration by Karen Buse

11-4 Illustration by Karen Buse

11-5 Image courtesy National Fenestration Rating Council

11-6 Illustration: Killer Banshee Studios

11-7 Bill Burke/Killer Banshee Studios

11-8 Illustration by Bill Burke

11-9 Illustration by Bill Burke/Killer Banshee Studios

11-10 Illustration by Bill Burke/Killer Banshee Studios

11-11 Illustration by Bill Burke

11-12 Photograph courtesy of Sun Light & Power, Berkeley, CA

11-13 © Energy Efficiency Solar/Marc Geller, 2008.

Chapter 12

12-1 Photograph by Bill Burke

12-2 Image courtesy Sunoptics Prismatic Skylights

12-3 Image courtesy Sunoptics Prismatic Skylights

12-4 Illustration by Karen Buse

12-5 Image courtesy of Robert A. Marcial.

12-6 Photograph by Bill Burke

12-7 Photograph by Christopher Meek/UW-IDL

12-8 Image courtesy of Robert A. Marcial.

12-9 Image courtesy Dan Varvais

12-10 Illustrations by Karen Buse

12-11 Photograph by Bill Burke

12-12 Bill Burke

12-13 Photograph by Bill Burke

12-14 Illustration by Bill Burke

12-15 Bill Burke

12-16 Illustration by Killer Banshee Studios

12-17 Illustrations by Karen Buse

12-18 Images courtesy of Taylor Engineering

12-19 Photograph courtesy of Sun Light & Power, Berkeley, CA

12-20 Photograph by Bill Burke

Chapter 13

13-1 Photograph courtesy of Paul Hawken

13-2 Image courtesy of Global Footprint Network.

13-3 A, B Images courtesy of Global Footprint Network.

13-4 A, B Images courtesy of Global Footprint Network.

13-5 Image courtesy California Academy of Sciences

13-6 Image courtesy of EHDD Architecture

13-7 Image courtesy of HP/hp.com

13-8 Image courtesy Remarkable Ltd.

13-9 © Killer Banshee Studios/killerbanshee.com, 2008

13-10A Courtesy of Practical Farmers of Iowa.

13-10B Photograph: Jennifer Nicholson

13-10C Image courtesy of Mississippi Genome Exploration Laboratory

13-10D Image courtesy of Kirei USA

13-10E Image courtesy of Chris 73 under Creative Commons 2.5 License

13-10F Image courtesy of Bonded Logic, Inc.

13-11A © Killer Banshee Studios/killerbanshee.com, 2008

13-11B Image courtesy of Citilog, Stubby and Maria Warmbold.

Chapter 14

14-1 Image courtesy Network for Climate Action, creator, Greenwash Guerrillas

14-2 © Killer Banshee Studios/killerbanshee.com, 2008

14-3A Photograph by John Swanlund

14-3B Image courtesy of Imoeba/Lawrence Leung

14-4 Photograph by Taneli Rajala [under cc2.5]

14-5 Courtesy of the Office of Environmental Health Hazard Assessment (OEHHA) under the umbrella of the California Environmental Protection Agency

14-6 Specification Section 1350 was originally written as the basis for California's Modular Office Furniture Specification, then developed as the environmental specification for the Capitol Area East End Complex Building 225 (the Department of Education building), Sacramento, California, completed in 2001. Authors included Leon Alevantis of the California Department of Health Services. 1350 has been incorporated in the Collaborative for High Performance Schools as well as the California Department of General Services (DGS) standard agreement for engineering and architectural services.

14-7 Image courtesy of Greenguard Environmental Institute.

14-8 Cradle to Cradle™ is a service mark of MBDC.

14-9 Image courtesy of the australian government's Water Efficiency Labeling and Standards Act 2005 (The WELS Act).

14-10 Greenhouse Friendly, Offsets and Verification, Department of Climate, Australia

14-11 Image courtesy of the Directorate of the General Environment of the European Commission, European Union Eco-label Programme.

14-12 Photograph by Killer Banshee Studios/killerbanshee.com, 2008.

14-13A © 2008 Scientific Certification Systems

14-13B © 1996 Forest Stewardship Council A.C., The Mark of Responsible Forestry

14-13C Cradle to Cradle™ is a service mark of MBDC.

Chapter 15

15-1 Image courtesy California Department of Water Resources

15-2 Illustration: Killer Banshee Studios

15-3 Pollutant source chart, Jamie Phillips, CMG Landscape Architecture

15-4 Pollutant treatment chart, Jamie Phillips, CMG Landscape Architecture

15-5 Mint Plaza infiltration diagram, Brennan Cox, CMG Landscape Architecture

15-6 Mint Plaza rain garden, Elizabeth Lamb, CMG Landscape Architecture

15-7 Vegetated swale, Jamie Phillips, CMG Landscape Architecture

15-8 Ohlone detention pond, Jamie Phillips, CMG Landscape Architecture

15-9 Crissy Field constructed wetland, Jamie Phillips, CMG Landscape Architecture

15-10A Image courtesy of Rainwater HOG

15-10B Image courtesy of Rainwater HOG

15-11 Lick School green roof, Kevin Conger, CMG Landscape Architecture

Chapter 16

16-1 Image from advertisement in *Look* magazine, 1947. GE® is a registered trademark of General Electric Company.

16-2 Image courtesy of the Jeffery J. Auchter Library of Residential Design, © Levitt Homes, Levitt & Sons.

16-3 Illustration: Killer Banshee Studios

16-4 Image courtesy California Metropolitan Transit Commission

16-5 Image courtesy of Global Footprint Network.

16-6 Image courtesy Library of Congress Historic American Engineering Record Collection

Chapter 17

Chapter 18

Chapter 19

Chapter 20

20-6   Image courtesy of Houston Advanced Research Center

20-7   Image courtesy of Steve Carlton

20-8   © 2008 J. B. Spector/Museum of Science and Industry

20-9   Image courtesy of Frank G. Lane, Gabbert Cullet Co. Inc., Williamstown, WV.

20-10   Image courtesy of E. K. Lowry.

20-11   Photograph by Brian Stevens

20-12   Image courtesy of the California Integrated Waste Management Board (CIWMB)

20-13   © QinetiQ

20-14   © Antony Gormley. Waste Man, 2006. Household waste and furniture. Photo: Antony Gormley. Courtesy of Jay Jopling/White Cube (London)

20-15   Image courtesy of Enzo De Martino, artwork of H.A. Schult

▉ Chapter 21

21-1   Image courtesy of the Environmental Protection Agency Pollution Prevention Office Region 4

21-2   Images courtesy SF Environment, a department of the City and County of San Francisco

21-3   © 2008 Kathryn Hyde

21-4   © 2008 Kathryn Hyde

21-5   © 2008 Kathryn Hyde

▉ APPENDIX A

A1   A, B Images courtesy of the California Academy of Sciences

A1   C,D Images courtesy of Jennifer Nicholson, © 2008 D.J. Nicholson

A2A   © Mark Darley

A2B   Image courtesy of 450 Architects

A2C   © Mark Darley

A3A   © 2007 Ed Vliestra, The Netherlands

A3B   Image courtesy of Marco Amoroso

A4A   Image courtesy of Hopkins Architects Ltd.

A4B   Photograph by Martine Hamilton Knight/Builtvision

A5   A, B Photographer: Arnold Paul

A6A   Courtesy of William McDonough + Partners

A6B   © 2008 Barney Taxel, courtesy of William McDonough + Partners

A7A   Courtesy of Sidwell Friends School

A7B   © Kieran Timberlake

A8 A,B Image courtesy of EHDD Architecture. Photographs by Michael David Rose

A8C   Image courtesy of EHDD Architecture

A9   © 2008 T.R.Hamzah & Yeang Sdn. Bhd.

A10   A, B, C © K. L. Ng/Aga Khan Trust for Culture

A11A   Image courtesy of Grant Lindsay

A11B   © 2007 Douglas T. Muth

A12A   Image courtesy of Kiss + Cathcart Architects. Photograph by Janna Johannsen

A12B   Image courtesy of FXFOWLE Architects

A13A   Photographer: Alsandro

A13B   Image courtesy of Foster + Partners. Photograph by Nigel Young

A13C   © Foster + Partners

A14A   Image courtesy of Foster + Partners. Photograph © Nigel Young

A14B   © Ian Lambot

A15   Photograph by Daniela MacAdden, courtesy of HOK

A16   A, B Images courtesy of Pelli Clarke Pelli Architects

A16   C, D Photographs: Fly/Killer Banshee Studios

A17A   © Plumbob, LLC

A17   B, C © Mariko Reed

A18   A, B © Factor Architecten BV/IR Ger Kengen. Illustration by Killer Banshee Studios

A19A   De Hoef. Waterstudio, NL. Photograph: Pieter Kers

A19B   Stillthouses Polder. Waterstudio, NL

A20   Image courtesy of Jennifer Siegal, Office of Mobile Design

A21   Image courtesy of Melinda Gray, AIA, Architect, Graymatter Architecture. Photograph by Keith Gaynes.

A22   Image courtesy of Felix Jerusalem

A23   Image courtesy Oregon Health & Science University Center for Health and Healing

A24   Architect: Perkins + Will; photograph: David Allee

A25 A, B, C, D, E Images courtesy of Kiss + Cathcart, Architects

A26 A, B, C © Randall Stout Architects, Inc.

A26 D, E Photographs © Peter Hübbe

A27 A, B, C Images courtesy of Ross Barney Architects/ Photographs by Hedrich Blessing Photographers

A28 A, B Images courtesy of Larkin Architects, Limited

A28 C Photograph by Steven Evans

A29 A, B, C Images courtesy of Heifer International. Photographs by Ray White.

A30 A, B, C Images courtesy of Saint Anthony Foundation and HKIT Architects. Photographs by Misha Bruk.

A31   Image courtesy of Ieuan Compton

A32   Image courtesy of Søren Korsgaard, Architect, Denmark

A33   Image courtesy of Vincent Callebaut Architectures/ www.vincent.callebaut.org

A34   © MVRDV

A35 A,   B, C, D, E   Images courtesy of Joachim Eble Architektur

A36   Courtesy of Berea College

A37A   Image courtesy of Hollister Knowlton

A37B   Photograph by Diego Samper

A38A   © Mithun

APPENDIX B

B1   Photographer: Vmenkov

B2   Designed and built by Ken Neal, Ken Neal & Associates, Newbury, UK. Photograph by Jason Cole.

B3   Image courtesy of Lou Kimball, AIA, Architect

B4   Image courtesy of Khalili/The California Institute of Earth Art & Architecture (Cal-Earth)

B5   Image courtesy of Khalili/The California Institute of Earth Art & Architecture (Cal-Earth)

B6   Photograph by Graham Strouts/zone5.org

B7   Photograph by Carolyn Roberts

B8   Bamboo spherical joint developed by Christophe Porges and Jorg Stamm. Photograph courtesy of Jorg Stamm.

B9   Image courtesy of ZED Factory

B10   El Nido de Quetzalcóatl image courtesy of Javier Senosiain, Senosiain Arquitectos

B11   © Kirsten Jacobsen

B12   Image courtesy of ZED Factory

APPENDIX C

C-1 "Tired of Smelling My Air," © Sam Kittner/kittner.com

Index